PIROUETTE

PIROUETTE

Pierre Trudeau and Canadian Foreign Policy

J.L.GRANATSTEIN

ROBERT BOTHWELL

University of Toronto Press
Toronto   Buffalo   London

© J.L. Granatstein and Robert Bothwell 1990
University of Toronto Press
Toronto   Buffalo   London
Printed in Canada

ISBN 0-8020-5780-2
ISSN 0068-7685

∞

Printed on acid-free paper

F
1034.3
T7
G72
1990

Canadian Cataloguing in Publication Data

Granatstein, J. L., 1939-
  Pirouette : Pierre Trudeau and Canadian foreign policy

(Canada in world affairs)
Includes bibliographical references.
ISBN 0-8020-5780-2

1. Canada – Foreign relations – 1945-
2. Trudeau, Pierre Elliott, 1919-
3. Canada – Politics and government – 1963-1984.*
I. Bothwell, Robert, 1944-   II. Title.   III. Series.

FC625.G73 1990   327.71   C90-093480-8
F1034.2.G73 1990

Publication of this work has been assisted by the Canada Council and the Ontario Arts Council under their block grant programs.

This is the concluding volume in the Canada in World Affairs series of the Canadian Institute of International Affairs.

The mission of the Canadian Institute of International Affairs is to promote an understanding of international affairs by providing interested Canadians with a non-partisan, nation-wide forum for informed discussion, analysis, and debate. The Institute as such is precluded by its constitution from expressing an official opinion on any aspect of world affairs. The views expressed are therefore those of the authors alone.

Contents

Acknowledgments

This book was suggested to us by the Canadian Institute of International Affairs with the intention that the whole of the Trudeau period be covered as the final volume in the CIIA's Canada in World Affairs series. The Institute has been a benign master, assisting us when needed and never interfering. We are most grateful to David Stafford.

Once commissioned, this book could not have been written without the cooperation of the Department of External Affairs and its officers. The department allocated funds to pay for the screening of its records so that we could examine them. This 'sanitization,' required under the terms of the Access to Information legislation, removed cabinet documents and material from foreign governments from the files; it did not prevent us from piecing together the story. Even so, the department files are very rich, a treasure trove for the historian. Regrettably, the department also required that interviews with serving officials be off-record.

Such restrictions obviously create concerns for scholars, and not least for us. In our view, however, it was better to see the files and talk to the policy makers than not to be permitted to do so. The only negative result has been a profuse use of 'confidential interview' or 'confidential source' in our notes. We recognize that readers trying to track down the source of statements may be frustrated, and we apologize for this.

Happily, we were also able to secure access to a variety of hitherto closed non-governmental records and personal papers, and these collections contained material of substantial use. We also conducted interviews in Canada, the United States, Europe, and Asia, most of which were on the record.

The research on which this book is based has been funded by the Social

Sciences and Humanities Research Council of Canada and the Canadian Institute for International Peace and Security. The Department of National Defence awarded Granatstein a post-doctoral fellowship, the Department of External Affairs assisted, and the Canadian Institute of International Affairs and York University's Centre for International and Strategic Studies gave us small start-up grants at a time when they were most necessary. Some of the research on Canadian-American relations that we have relied on here was previously undertaken by Bothwell with John Kirton; we are grateful to him for allowing us to make use of this material.

We have been greatly assisted by many people: at External Affairs, Dacre Cole and John Hilliker; at the Directorate of History, Department of National Defence, Norman Hillmer; at the Bank of Canada, Jane Witty and her able staff; at the National Archives, Ian McClymont and his helpful staff; at the Privy Council Office, Commodore Lawrie Farrington and Thelma Nicholson. Ivan Head was most cooperative in giving us his time and in arranging a conversation with Pierre Trudeau for us.

In Japan, Toru Takemoto helped greatly by arranging interviews. In Beijing, Diana Lary went out of her way to arrange interviews and generally ease matters, and Bernie Frolic and Paul Evans of the Political Science Department of York University, who actually know something about Canada's China policy, were unfailingly generous and cooperative. In Germany, Gustav Schmidt arranged interviews for us and even created a conference at the Ruhr Universität Bochum around our visit. Brian Long of the Department of External Affairs included Granatstein in a conference in Moscow that allowed research to be undertaken there, and once in the USSR, Ambassador Vernon Turner facilitated matters. In Bonn, the embassy staff could not have been more helpful. In London, Ian Drummond gave us shelter – and even conducted one interview on our behalf. William Rodney helped by arranging interviews in Victoria for us. Douglas Bland read the defence sections and saved us from many errors of interpretation; Willis Armstrong read much of the Canadian-American material with a similar result; others who cannot be named also read chapters.

On our repeated visits to Ottawa, our friends William Young, Paul Marsden and Linda Goldthorp, William Kaplan and Susan Krever, and Chris and Anne Waddell attended to our comfort with assiduity and care.

We benefited greatly from the extraordinarily able research assistance of Alan Bass, Chad Reimer, and Barbara Treviranus.

To all of these, to all who put up with our questions and our importunings for access and information, and to many others we cannot name, our sincere thanks.

JLG and RB

Preface

While accepting the foibles and feebleness of their national leaders at home, Canadians paradoxically wish to believe that their prime ministers have recognition abroad. Mackenzie King, a figure of derision to many of his countrymen, for example, was transformed into an international statesman the moment he landed in London, Washington, or Paris. Without King, Canadians were told in 1945, Canada's prestige would wane. To judge from the election results that year, the people believed this story.

Essentially, Canadians then – and now – wanted their country to transcend itself. Afflicted by geography, Canadians have converted size into grandeur without ever succeeding in carrying grandeur one step further – into national advantage. Lester Pearson, as secretary of state for external affairs from 1948 to 1957, probably did as much as any Canadian leader to make the best use of the country's positive attributes while minimizing the weaknesses. The Suez crisis of 1956, to cite the example that won him his Nobel Peace Prize, showed Pearson and his country at their best. But as prime minister from 1963 to 1968, Pearson's sure touch seemed to fade. At home, his governments stumbled and staggered; abroad, the international environment of the Cold War and the Vietnam War did not readily lend itself to dazzling breakthroughs, brokered by selfless Canadian diplomats. Indeed, to many Canadians, Pearson's foreign policy seemed to have turned into a dreary and predictable refrain of always supporting the Americans, boosting NATO, and condemning the Soviets.

Thus, the critics who had been calling for change in Canadian policy had great expectations when Pearson announced his decision to step down as prime minister in December 1967. The campaign for the Liberal succession that resulted was long and contentious, but when the party's delegates made their choice on 6 April 1968, the new leader was Pierre Trudeau, a Montreal law professor who had been in parliament only since 1965 and in the cabinet for just one year. Trudeau formed his cabinet and almost instantly dissolved parliament. In the general election of 25 June 1968 he swept to victory, a triumph that seemed to be a direct result of his buoyancy and sexy image.

The critics had wanted change, and nothing the new prime minister did for his first two years in power gave them grounds for pessimism. The sweeping foreign policy review, the recognition of China and the opening of friendlier relations with the Soviet Union, the cut in the armed forces stationed in Europe with NATO – all combined to make those critics of the Pearsonian policy that had dominated Canada's relations with the world since the end of the Second World War feel that the millennium had finally arrived and that the new leader was setting out to attack the very structures of the Cold War. George Faludy, the emigré Hungarian-Canadian poet, put it neatly: Trudeau was 'so intelligent and persuasive that one was very often tempted to believe him even if he *was* a politician.'

As time passed, however, the foreign and defence policy of the Trudeau government began to look and sound more like that of the Liberal government that had preceded it in power. The armed forces acquired new tanks and aircraft, contracts were let for anti-submarine warfare frigates, and the prime minister actually began to speak as if he understood the utility of NATO. France's meddling in Canada, begun in the mid-1960s, continued and became a matter of great importance to the nation after President de Gaulle's abortive 1967 visit, the October Crisis of 1970, and the rise to power of the Parti Québécois in 1976. The subsequent efforts to patriate the constitution pitted the Trudeau government against most of the provinces, and, in London, the British government showed little interest in assisting the dominion. If the historic links with Britain and France were increasingly difficult to maintain in the complex new world of the 1970s, the heralded new ties to Beijing and Moscow produced almost nothing of substance.

Checked in the east, Trudeau's foreign policy began to place a Pearson-like emphasis on international do-goodism, to stress peacekeeping (though much less fervently), to offer foreign aid (though with only a little more money), to sing the praises of the Commonwealth (with less emphasis on Great Britain and more on the non-white states) and francophonie, and to wrestle with relations with the United States.

The difficult Canadian-American relationship inevitably occupied most of the prime minister's and the government's foreign-policy time. Trudeau had to deal with Presidents Nixon, Ford, Carter, and Reagan, and relations with the first and the last especially were difficult. Nixon's August 1971 economic measures seemed to threaten Canada's cherished special relationship with Washington, and the search for a 'third option' – interpreted as a link to Europe and the Far East – and for contractual relations with the European Community and Japan began soon after. Those links, though negotiated with impressive skill, ultimately produced little result as Canada's trade and investment continued on their unswerving continental course. But Trudeau's government had the capacity to produce surprises for Canadian-American relations, as the National Energy Policy amply demonstrated, and relations with Reagan's America were testy, something demonstrated as well by Trudeau's 1983–4 peace initiative. That initiative also had a resonance much like that of the policies Trudeau had adopted in 1968–70: the leader once again was setting out to attack the very structure of the institutionalized Cold-War world. In the end, the effort proved quixotic, as the prime minister and his advisers must have known it would.

Pierre Trudeau, we argue, had little long-term, consistent interest in foreign policy. When he came to power in 1968 he knew the world better than most leaders, but as a traveller, not as a student of policy. His interests in defence matters in 1968, as in 1984, were non-existent; his concerns with foreign policy were eclectic, if not flighty. Some issues, such as the Third World and disarmament, held his interest throughout his sixteen years in power, but even here the concentrated attention he gave to them was strictly limited. Domestic matters, and especially the place of Quebec within Canada, always stood highest on his agenda, and properly so. That was the primary challenge to Canada's survival as a nation.

In such circumstances, it was probably inevitable that Canadian foreign policy seemed to come full circle between 1968 and 1984. First, at both the beginning and the end of his long tenure, Trudeau tried to tackle the rigidities of the world system. Second, the rejection of the Pearsonian helpful-fixer role, proclaimed at the outset of his term in office, was followed by Trudeau's effort at the end of his administration to play global peacemaker. The only difference was that Lester Pearson, a professional diplomat who understood the importance of timing and preparation and appreciated the limited capacity of smaller countries to shape the agenda of great powers, did it better.

No one could argue that Trudeau's foreign-policy pirouette was handled flawlessly. Nonetheless, the prime minister was always worth watching. His style and grace, his intelligence and fearsome concentration, his capacity to shock and titillate the country and the world always made his activities the focus of attention. Which other Canadian would slide down a banister or twirl behind the Queen's back? Who else, more seriously, would have fought the French and threatened the British, gone toe-to-toe with the United States, and won the affection and genuine regard of the Third World? On balance, the fundamentals of Canadian foreign and defence policy altered scarcely at all in his time in power, but never once in his long tenure did Pierre Trudeau fail to captivate the country with the illusion of change.

Trudeau demonstrates his diplomatic form

Gérard Pelletier on safari to Niger, 1970

Canada enforces its northern sovereignty

Diplomatic recognition

Frankly yes: Prime Minister Edward Heath addresses his Commonwealth
colleagues

Trudeau visits Nixon, December 1971

'We're not anti-Arab or anti-Israel, but we are anti-American': Mitchell Sharp searches for fuel

Energy minister Donald Macdonald sorting out Canadian energy policy

Between friends: Trudeau with Gerry Ford in Washington

Prime Minister Harold Wilson explains the special nature of the Common Market to Pierre Trudeau

Fireside chat: Trudeau meets Carter, 1977

Allan MacEachen

Claude Morin takes a puff

WIN, PLACE OR SHOW?

Clark, Trudeau, and Broadbent, 1979

Joe Clark attends the 1979 Commonwealth conference

Canadian embassy staff rescue six American diplomats from Iran

By 1980 détente had fallen on evil days. Here Leonid Brezhnev checks his arsenal

'So what's the fuss? Even if one crashes in a populated area, the chances of hitting a Liberal voter are nil!': Trudeau reflects on the relation between diplomacy and politics

The peace initiative: Trudeau's peace mission, 1983

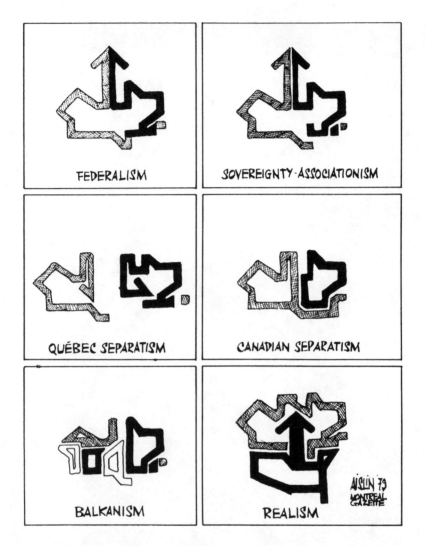

Canada's political options, 1968–84

Part One

Genesis

1

Trudeau Takes Over:
The Defence and Foreign Policy Reviews

The East Block, Friday, 28 March 1969: Secretary of State for External Affairs Mitchell Sharp, National Defence Minister Léo Cadieux, and a gaggle of senior officials from their departments met in Sharp's office to coordinate their plans for the critical weekend cabinet meeting that would decide the Trudeau government's policy for its military participation in NATO.

The conferees met in a mandarin's stage-set, behind green baize doors (then the sign that an office-holder had arrived) in Sharp's office at the southwest corner of 'the Eastern Departmental Building' or, as it was commonly known, the East Block. First used by Sir John A. Macdonald, the office had passed to External Affairs in 1914 and then to its minister, Lester B. Pearson, in 1948. That was when Canada was present at the creation of NATO, when the alliance with the Americans was confirmed, and when Canada embarked on the liberal (and Liberal) promotion of peace, security, and good international relations. Mike Pearson was gone, shuffled off to teach international relations at Carleton University and to do good works around the world, but everyone in the room had known him, liked him, and worked for him. They had no desire either to change or to challenge the Pearson legacy.

As the ministers and public servants settled onto the leather chesterfields and spread out their heavy briefing books, they knew they faced a problem. It was located ten offices down the hall, in the prime minister's suite – not far for even the most leaden-footed messenger but, in Trudeau's opinion, light years removed in time and thought. That was why defence policy was being re-examined; that was why the cabinet was being summoned, on a Saturday, to run through the justification for spending the taxpayer's money on such items as an infantry brigade and an air division in Europe instead of on medicare or old-age pensions. That was why External Affairs was involved: on such fundamental issues it was the diplomats, not the generals, who did the thinking and the talking for both departments. The arrangement had always worked well in the past and, despite the inscrutability of the present prime minister and his habit of asking irritating questions, it would work again, or so they believed.

The ministers present worked well together. Senior in rank and experience in Ottawa was Mitchell Sharp, who was also deputy prime minister. He enjoyed a considerable public reputation. An able parliamentarian, he expressed his character in what a journalist called 'a strong, decent face, tough as the rubber in a handball, its effect enhanced by red hair and piercingly honest eyes.'[1] Sharp had spent twenty-four of his fifty-seven years in Ottawa. In the 1950s he had been deputy to C.D. Howe, the 'minister of everything'; in the 1960s he had perpetuated Howe's business contacts with the Liberal party. Under Pearson, Sharp had managed economic policy, latterly as finance minister, and, as the government's chief economic thinker, he had beaten off the nationalistic assaults of Walter Gordon, his chief rival for Pearson's often wavering support. But then, as Sharp looked down the cabinet table at Pearson, he could reflect that Pearson *had* to listen – he was there because his ministers were there.

Trudeau was different. He had never known Howe, and he would never have enjoyed the company of CD's business friends. He did not necessarily differ from Sharp on economic matters or on the follies of economic nationalism, and he obviously valued his minister's palpable honesty and integrity. But he had promised the Finance Department to Edgar Benson, one of his earliest political supporters, and though Sharp played a critical role in making Trudeau Liberal leader, he had initially been a competing candidate for the post; thus he had to give way. Offered his choice of the other senior portfolios, Sharp chose External Affairs, displacing Paul Martin, another defeated rival for the leadership. Martin went to the Senate, and Trudeau went on to triumph in the general election of June 1968 which produced the first majority government since 1962.

Others had wanted External Affairs; nobody much had sought National Defence. So Trudeau kept the incumbent, Léo Cadieux, both when he took office in April 1968 and when he shuffled his cabinet into more permanent assignments after the election.

Unlike Sharp, Cadieux was not a power in national Liberal politics, not even in the busy affairs and intrigues of the Quebec wing. Balding, dapper with his pencil-thin mustache, he looked his sixty years. A journalist by profession, and a war correspondent from 1942 to 1945, he had held minor political positions before winning election to parliament in 1962. He was the kind of honest and upright foot soldier the Liberals needed to fight off the Créditiste menace in Quebec and, later, to lend solidity to the party's ministerial team. But no one expected Cadieux to innovate or surprise, and he fulfilled expectations. Those well informed in Ottawa matters considered that he matched his department in this respect.[2] Unlike Sharp, Cadieux had few political claims on Trudeau – he had supported Minister of Transport Paul Hellyer at the leadership convention – beyond his ability to administer his department and keep out of trouble.

The bureaucrats watched quietly as the ministers picked up their briefing books for the next day's cabinet. (Every cabinet meeting was preceded by a briefing book outlining the rationale for the policy decisions the ministers were expected to take; after 1968, ministers were expected to read them.) Inside it, they knew, was their own cabinet memorandum, a justification of Canada's existing NATO policy. As the document on the table, it would set the terms of the debate.

Expectation turned quickly to consternation. There was another document, No. 310/69, in the binder. Entitled 'A Study of Defence Policy,' it delivered nothing less than a complete alternative to the existing policy. Now there would be two documents on the table, and there could be no doubt which one would have priority, for the new document came directly from the Prime Minister's Office. Red faced, the ministers asked the officials to leave. Passing through Sharp's outer office, one of them picked up the telephone to tell his wife he would be home early, only to hear a torrent of emotional French. It was Cadieux talking to the prime minister. The receiver was replaced before Sharp took his turn on the line; in later years Sharp remembered clearly what he had said.

'Have you lost confidence in your Minister of National Defence?' Certainly not, Trudeau replied. Then why had Trudeau had his own office prepare and circulate a paper that attacked his minister's position? Trudeau said that he had already attacked other papers presented to cabinet, so why not this one? That was different, Sharp retorted. He had never before issued a paper that directly confronted a departmental position. 'I will withdraw it,' Trudeau promised. 'I didn't mean this.' 'I hope so,' Sharp rejoined, 'as I've asked Léo not to resign immediately.'[3]

The paper was withdrawn, and formality and propriety were observed. The study of 'Canadian defence policy' remained, officially, unstudied. Its points, both explicit and implicit, had nevertheless been made, for the briefing books had already been circulated. It was clear that Canada's NATO policy faced a fight for survival the next morning, with the outcome depending on the moods and preferences of a prime minister whom few of his ministers understood.

When Pierre Trudeau won the leadership of the governing Liberal party on 6 April 1968 and, indeed, even after he swept to victory in the general election of 25 June 1968, he was almost an unknown quantity to the public, to politicians, and to the Canadian public service. In parliament only since 1965, a cabinet minister only since 4 April 1967, he had a political record as sparse as that of any leader elected in any democracy in this century. That, of course, was much to his advantage in a Canadian political situation that had been marred by mudslinging and scandals, and dominated by party leaders like Lester Pearson and John Diefenbaker who seemed to have been around forever. Trudeau was new and fresh, completely unhampered by the political baggage that weighed down his competitors for the leadership.

But if Trudeau had a limited political record, his views on many subjects were known. He had written a substantial number of academic articles on Quebec politics and thought, extraordinary for their tough language and rigorous logic, and his polemical pieces in *Cité Libre,* the small journal he had helped found in the early 1950s, were well known to those who followed the Quebec scene. He had long opposed the *nationalistes* in his province, denouncing them in philosophical and personal terms, and he was suspicious of all forms of nationalism as a result of his experiences in Quebec – and his understanding of the wretched excesses that had shaped the twentieth century's record of war and genocide. On the positive side, Trudeau had a public record of vigorous support for federalism, pluralism, and the participation of citizens in the life of their country.

His interests, his primary reasons for entering public life, unquestionably related to domestic policy, to securing a proper place for French Canadians as citizens of Canada. As a corollary, Trudeau viewed national unity as all important. Far from taking Canada's internal balance for granted, he was willing to commit every resource his government possessed to shore up the position of the federal government and with it, he believed, the possibility that Canada could continue to exist as a single, coherent country. That conviction would dominate Trudeau's approach to foreign policy as much as it did to atomic energy, textiles, or air transport.

Within these limits, Trudeau had a long and public position on foreign-policy subjects. He had always been a traveller, venturing to countries off the beaten track. He had been in China during the civil war that preceded Mao's victory, in the Soviet Union in the early 1950s, and in Africa. He had returned to China in 1960 and, with his friend Jacques Hébert, had written a book the following year on his experiences.[4] His interest in the Third World and his concern for the process of development were genuine and longstanding.

So was his horror of nuclear weapons. In January 1963, on the verge of entering federal politics in the election that all could see coming, Trudeau had been appalled by Pearson's reversal of his party's policy of refusing nuclear weapons. Pearson had been supported by the opinion polls, and his action helped to precipitate the breakup of the Diefenbaker government. Trudeau angrily declined a Liberal nomination and used the editorial pages of *Cité Libre* to excoriate Pearson and his party in extreme terms, citing 'brutal cynicism,' 'selfish docility,' and those who 'tremble with anticipation because they have seen the rouged face of power ... What idiots they all are!'[5] The ferocity of the language was different from that found in comparable English-language journals, and it stung the Pearson Liberals. Other Trudeau articles dissented on the Vietnam War and on United States policy, at a time when most Liberals, and most Canadians, assumed that the Americans must be correct.

The new leader was no diplomat, that was evident. If one believed his press clippings, he thought that diplomacy itself was outmoded. In 'the early days of the telegraph,' he told one reporter, 'you needed a dispatch to know what was happening in country A, whereas now most of the time you can read it in a good newspaper.'[6] This criticism was not far off the mark, and its accuracy may have helped to account for some of the fury that Trudeau's comments aroused among Canada's foreign-service officers as they toiled on the thousand-and-one tedious tasks not covered in 'state of the nation' dispatches. They consoled themselves as best they could with the hope that this storm too would pass, given the limited amount of time the prime minister could afford to devote to their affairs.

The new prime minister was even less informed about the Department of National Defence. He had never served in the armed forces, and during the war he had managed to make a lark out of his rudimentary cadet training. To him, the military was completely foreign, a world populated by men who trained to kill. One revealing sign came in the middle of the 1968 election when Trudeau asked Bill Lee, formerly a wing commander in the Royal Canadian Air Force but then the Liberal campaign tour organizer, 'Why would a guy as smart as you waste his time in the military?'[7] The incomprehension was total.

Trudeau was no typical Canadian. He was fluently bilingual, still a rarity in the parochial Canada of the 1960s. Though forty-nine years old in 1968, he remained a bachelor and was often found in the company of attractive women. His mind was unquestionably first class, precise, clear, and rigorous. Canadian policy, to his mind, must serve Canadian interests. The trouble was it no longer did, so obsessed was it with the Soviet-American struggle and the alliance system created at the end of the 1940s. He could not see the Soviet Union or the People's Republic of China in demonological terms, he had become bored with the unthinking rhetoric of the Cold War, and his rational mind rejected the idea of a balance of terror founded on nuclear weapons and the expenditure of billions of dollars on weaponry. For two decades, Trudeau told a British television interviewer, 'Canada's foreign policy was largely its policy in NATO, through NATO.'[8] Trudeau simply believed that Canadian foreign policy had to serve Canada's national interests, especially its need to keep French- and English-speaking Canadians together, and recognize the new problems, such as the split between the North and the South, that threatened the future stability of the globe.[9] In some ways, curiously enough for such a sophisticate, Trudeau sounded like a classical Québécois, suspicious of European entanglements and far more concerned with Quebec, Canada, and North America than anything else.

Trudeau's views of the world were expressed with rare clarity, but in one form or another they were not uncommon in the 1960s. The questioning of Canada's place in the Western alliance had begun in earnest after the Cuban missile crisis of October 1962. The world had seemingly come close to nuclear armageddon and, while many Canadians were upset that the prime minister of the day, John Diefenbaker, had not rallied decisively to President John F. Kennedy's side, many others were horrified at the holocaust that had nearly been loosed on the world. A few even looked at the implications of the crisis in a different way.

At issue for them was not why the United States had failed to consult Canada as the North American Air Defence Agreement of 1958 apparently required. The true point was the sudden realization that whatever Canada had to contribute to a military confrontation between East and West was now fundamentally unimportant and would always be so in the future. 'Our fate,' one senior defence planner in Ottawa later put it, 'would be determined by the United States' strategic arsenal, and not by our own efforts.' Once the politicians grasped that fact, he reasoned, the

Canadian armed forces became just 'diplomatic baggage that had to be carried around but for that reason had to be kept as light as possible.'[10] No one quite said it, but in and out of government many clearly understood the situation just the same, and as a result defence budgets began to drop in real terms and the strength of the armed forces to fall. In the circumstances, radical restructuring of the armed forces could be undertaken. Under the Pearson government, the three Canadian services were unified into one armed force wearing a single uniform. Militia colonels and naval reserve commodores complained, but the public largely accepted the destruction of honoured traditions.[11] Very simply, the Canadian military were now perceived as relatively unimportant in the modern world.

At the same time, the Department of External Affairs, Canada's foreign service, was beginning a generation-long period of unrest. The service's founders were still around, and Lester Pearson was in fact the prime minister. Promotion, however, was beginning to slow in a department with relatively young men at the top,[12] where the pay was insufficient, and the policies were increasingly hoary with age. Support for NATO, for example, seemed to be policy only because NATO had always been there, not necessarily because NATO was essential to Canada. Lord Ismay, NATO's first secretary-general, had said that the object of the alliance was 'to keep the Americans in, the Soviets out, and the Germans down.'[13] If so, those goals no longer seemed urgent to some younger officers in the foreign service.

If there were stirrings within External Affairs, there was far more open complaint in academe. Younger academics, trained to be critical in American graduate schools, had begun to denounce Canada's 'slavish' obeisance to the United States, then just beginning to be trapped in the quicksands of Vietnam. Their learned articles attacked Canadian policy, denounced Ottawa's 'quiet diplomacy' with Washington, and questioned the necessity of NATO, Canadian membership in it, and a Canadian military commitment to the defence of Western Europe.[14]

Worse still from the government's point of view, there were a number of cabinet ministers who had begun to question Canadian foreign policy and to resent the way Paul Martin shut out other ministers from serious discussion of external affairs.[15] Leading the group was Walter Gordon, minister of finance from 1963 until November 1965 and minister without portfolio in 1967–8. Gordon was a powerful nationalist force in the party, even though in 1967–8 his economic views were overshadowed by those of the more pragmatic Mitchell Sharp. Pearson had not completely discounted Gordon even if, in a pinch, he no longer trusted completely the views of a man who, to younger Liberals, represented their party's conscience. In July 1967 Gordon and two other ministers, Pierre Trudeau and Jean Marchand, had met with Marcel Cadieux and Basil Robinson, the two senior officials in the Department of External Affairs, to discuss NATO and NORAD.[16] Gordon found the official case for the continuation of joint air defence arrangements with the United States compelling, but he was far from persuaded by the argument advanced for NATO. 'I believe we should continue as members,' he wrote in a private note, 'and that we should continue to make a contribution to NATO forces. However, we should plan to reduce these forces (preferably at a faster rate than is presently contemplated),[17] and should think very carefully before we agree to the replacement of existing equipment, etc., when it becomes obsolete.' His reasoning, one that was shared to some extent by cost-conscious officials in the Finance Department, was clear: Canada was relatively less important now that Europe had recovered, and as a result the Western Europeans could 'contribute more to their own defence.'[18] He expressed the same views in the Cabinet Committee on External Affairs and Defence in September where he won little support in the face of opposition from Martin.[19]

In the circumstances, Pearson (who as a NATO founder recalled that Canada's European garrison was not originally intended to be permanent)[20] and Martin did what they might have been expected to do. They sponsored two senior diplomats, one Canadian and one American, to prepare a paper on the nature of the Canada-U.S. relationship. The report held no surprises: the diplomats argued that Canada's influence with Washington was served best by keeping disputes within channels and by practising 'quiet diplomacy.'[21] But 'quiet diplomacy' was the last thing the department's critics wanted. In the terms of the day, they wanted to 'shout it out,' to let Canada's views be known regardless of the consequences. In the first years of the Vietnam War, they argued, both duty and morality demanded no less.

Later, to evaluate Canada's place in the world, and especially 'areas of policy which had been under criticism mainly in academic circles,'[22] the Department of External Affairs called on one of its founders and saints, Norman Robertson, to write what was intended to be a critical and questioning report. Robertson certainly had the necessary background. Twice undersecretary, twice high commissioner in London, and once ambassador in Washington, Robertson had made the policies he was now to review. To assist him Martin named two of the department's coming men, Geoffrey Murray and Geoffrey Pearson, the latter the prime minister's son but already known as a sceptic where some of Canada's mainstream policies were concerned.[23]

The result was intellectually respectable but politically disappointing.[24] Robertson took advantage of the Harmel Report (drafted by the Belgian foreign minister, Pierre Harmel) on 'The Future Tasks of the Alliance,' which were defined as détente and deterrence. These were useful points to counter those critics who had always argued that NATO was frozen in immobility. Canada's nearness to the United States prohibited neutrality; that being so, Canada's standing and influence were best served by staying in NATO, even if the withdrawal of troops from Europe was unlikely. Canada needed Europe, Robertson wrote, for an 'extra margin of confidence and security' in dealing with the United States. He did not argue, as perhaps he might have, that to weaken the Canadian role in NATO would not enhance Ottawa's place in the eyes of European governments. Robertson's report is interesting both because of the support it attracted within the department and the ease with which it was dismissed without. Before the ink was dry in April 1968, the department was busy with yet another study of the case for and against keeping troops in Europe.[25]

There was good reason for External Affairs to worry. Trudeau had made no secret during the leadership campaign of his view that Canadian foreign and defence policy and its makers were frozen in the past. In the cabinet after April 1967 he had begun to turn his formidable mind to foreign-policy questions. Moreover, as justice minister, he had responsibility for constitutional questions and had become an expert on the constitutional implications of foreign policy. He convened his own think tank for informal, sandwich lunches.* They concentrated on the constitution, but since they were dealing with fundamental questions, discussion flowed into other areas of foreign policy as well as Canada's national and international interests. Relations between Trudeau and the able men around him developed quickly. In particular, the relationship with Allan Gotlieb served as a way for Trudeau to become better briefed and informed on foreign policy generally, a subject on which Gotlieb had strong – and revisionist – views.[26]

---

* Its members included Allan Gotlieb, the head of Legal Division in the Department of External Affairs; Max Yalden, Marcel Cadieux's adviser on federal-provincial matters; Michael Pitfield, an assistant secretary to the cabinet; Carl Goldenberg, one of Montreal's most prominent lawyers and a perennial royal commissioner; Jean Beetz, another Montreal lawyer; Marc Lalonde, from the Prime Minister's Office; and Ivan Head, from the justice department.

However unhappy Trudeau may have been with External Affairs and Canadian foreign policy, he clearly thought something could be done with the department and its officials. While he was considering whether to run for the Liberal crown, he told one friend that he doubted he could do anything to secure change as prime minister, whereas as secretary of state for external affairs he thought he could accomplish something.[27] That belief was presumably contingent on being able to shake up the External Affairs bureaucracy to make it more responsive to its political masters and more reflective of modern – and possibly different – Canadian national interests. He expressed this view best in a year-end television interview, broadcast on New Year's Day, 1969: 'part of my job as Prime Minister is meeting from time to time with the Ministers and their officials ... and shaking them up as best I can and sometimes I do it publicly ... Often I do it privately around the council table and saying – look, go back to first questions – we don't want to know first if aircraft A is better than aircraft B, we want to know if we should have aircraft, and if neutrality isn't better than engagement in a defence alliance and so on.'[28] This was the man who was at the helm in Ottawa, faced with the necessity of doing things that would distinguish his government from that of Lester Pearson.

Trudeau's first comments on the need to re-examine Canadian foreign policy after he became prime minister were made in conversation with President Bourguiba of Tunisia, in Ottawa for a visit on 10 May 1968. Trudeau stressed his pragmatism and realism and the necessity for Canada to use its limited resources in the most efficient way possible. He also pointed to his desire to recognize China and to strengthen relations with Asia generally and with francophonie. In this conversation, however, it was the defence of North America that most concerned Trudeau. It seemed possible that the requirements of continental air defence – and the enormous pressure building in the United States for an anti-ballistic missile defence system that might well require Canadian participation – could oblige Canada to shift resources, at present devoted to the defence of Europe, to North America. He did not want Canada to withdraw precipitately from Europe, or to do anything that might provoke a chain reaction.[29]

Those moderately reassuring remarks were followed on 15 May by a cabinet decision to carry out 'a comprehensive review ... [of] Canada's armed forces policy, including alternative forces' structures and costing.' This review, to be completed by 15 July by the departments concerned in consultation with the Privy Council Office (the first time that the PCO had been given a place in shaping defence policy),[30] was to be explicitly designed 'to permit the government to consider possible alternative modifications in future policy.'[31] When Léo Cadieux protested that he had difficulty reviewing defence policy without knowing the future shape of Canadian foreign policy, the secretary of state for external affairs indicated that a review was already under way in his department. Reflecting his own views and those of his department, Sharp added that, as of now, it looked as if the result would be a continuation of present policy.[32] But Trudeau was not prepared to let the opportunity pass. 'It was intended that the forthcoming review of Canadian foreign policy,' he said, 'should take into account possible changes more basic than those contained in a review which had already been made' by Norman Robertson.[33]

As a result, Sharp on 27 May sent the prime minister a long memorandum detailing the review he proposed his department should undertake. He set out Category One areas, where there had been controversy, such as membership in NATO and the recognition of China, and Category Two areas, where policy, such as relations with francophonie or with Western Europe generally, might be re-evaluated. The first category was to receive urgent examination, the second to be examined in depth. Other subjects, such as the Commonwealth, Canada-U.S. relations, and the United Nations, Sharp defined as Category Three, and said that they would be reviewed in line with a schedule of forthcoming international meetings.[34]

Trudeau's demand for a review had upset the External Affairs establishment, as did his election-campaign statement of 29 May 1968 on foreign policy, even though it was largely drafted by Geoffrey Murray of the department.[35] The prime minister announced 'a thorough and comprehensive review of our foreign policy which embraces defence, economic and aid policies ... Our approach,' he said, reiterating the line he had taken with Bourguiba, 'will be pragmatic and realistic,' but he then pointed out that 'the defence strategies of our time are neither static nor restricted in scope. NATO and NORAD ... are complementary in their strategic importance and implication.' Trudeau committed his government to 'take a hard look, in consultation with our allies, at our military role in NATO and [to] determine whether our present military commitment is still appropriate to the present situation in Europe.' Most ominously, perhaps, he spoke of Canada's need 'not so much to go crusading abroad as to mobilize at home our aspirations, energies and resources ... Our paramount interest is to ensure the political survival of Canada as a federal and bilingual sovereign state. This means strengthening Canadian unity as a basically North American country.'[36] Canada's internal problems were genuine and serious enough, but the hint that Canada was going to turn inwards must have chilled many in External Affairs and National Defence. In any case, after Trudeau's smashing electoral victory on 25 June, both the prime minister and those around him might be forgiven for believing that the new direction had received the public's approbation. Unfortunately, as a Privy Council Office official later noted, it seemed that the Department of External Affairs did not accept the election results.[37]

Nevertheless, responsibility for the foreign-policy review fell to the Department of External Affairs assisted by Treasury Board, the Privy Council Office, and the Department of Finance. In charge was Geoffrey Murray, ironically the draftsman of the Robertson review that had drawn scorn for its perceived rejection of change. For the defence review, responsibility rested with the Departments of National Defence and Defence Production, the Treasury Board, the Privy Council Office, and the Department of External Affairs.[38] This last department, thanks to its deeply ingrained feeling that defence was too important to be left to the military, was quick to offer suggestions.[39] To Trudeau too, National Defence was not a strongly led department. It was afflicted with the belief that Canada had to be involved in everything and with a policy that, in consequence, seemed to be based on incrementalism – each year something new was added on without ever questioning what it was all for.[40] Within the department, Léo Cadieux gave the responsibility for the review to the branch headed by the vice-chief of the Defence Staff. The work of preparation was done by J.F. Anderson, DND's director of finance (international), Michael Shenstone of the Defence Relations Division of External Affairs, and Charles Marshall of DEA's Defence Liaison (1) Division. Their first outline, dated 30 May, was essentially a justification of policy, not a review.[41]

At External Affairs, Sharp had already authorized the creation of an interdepartmental Special Task Force on Europe, known as STAFEUR, directed by Robert Ford, ambassador to the Soviet Union, and Paul Tremblay, ambassador to Belgium and a senior officer with service in Ottawa in defence-related areas and at the United Nations. Effectively in charge of this major examination of Canadian relations with Europe was John Halstead, the head of the European Division in the department. Since NATO was the most contentious issue and since the prime minister had asked for the review on this subject to be complete by mid-July, a special study of this question received top priority. By June 1968 its working paper was already in its fourth draft[42] and it moved ahead in coordination with the defence-policy review underway at National Defence.[43] The rest of the foreign-policy review effectively stalled for almost ten months.

Despite Trudeau's repeated comments on the need for change in foreign policy made during the election campaign (or perhaps because they were campaign remarks), few in the bureaucracy seemed to take the prime minister's resolve seriously, although officers who knew Trudeau personally warned that he was determined. The Cabinet Committee on External Affairs and National Defence had spent substantial time in July looking at the first version of the defence review and the ministers had summarily rejected it on the grounds that it merely defended the status quo. That was a shock, even though the cabinet had been explicitly told that the reviews could not produce a restatement of existing views.[44] It was also unexpected that some ministers, led by Donald Macdonald, who had been named only a few days before to the presidency of the Privy Council, were taking a decidedly pacific line. Macdonald was thirty-six years old, forceful and intelligent, and his views on foreign policy and defence had been shaped by the ferment of the 1960s and by parliamentary trips he had made to NATO.[45] On 11 July he expressed outrage that the drafters of the review had not considered the possibility of neutrality for Canada, and he urged his colleagues to withdraw all Canadian forces from Europe. How, he asked, could Canada improve its relations with Czechoslovakia if we had aircraft in Germany ready to bomb Prague? Canada should play the same role as Iceland in the alliance.[46]

Nor did Trudeau do much to ease the concerns of National Defence and External Affairs. He had told the cabinet on 19 July when it considered the report of the committee that there should be no public statements 'which could be interpreted as supporting a continuing commitment to NATO by Canada. It should be made very clear that the continuing thing is the reassessment of foreign and defence policy.'[47] Curiously, Trudeau had told Mitchell Sharp that, after reading the defence-review papers, he now understood why Canada had to continue its contribution to NATO. He had also expressed himself as 'scandalisé' by Macdonald.[48]

Perhaps that contributed to the uneasy complacency in the bureaucracy which continued almost unaltered. In August, General F.R. Sharp, the vice-chief of the Defence Staff, prepared a justification for DND's estimates for 1969–70. His assumption, stated in a memorandum to the chief of the Defence Staff and based on a cabinet decision of 19 July, was that the military would be provided with the resources necessary to carry out its commitments.[49] But the cabinet also ordered a full-scale review of defence and foreign policy, with all alternatives to be plumbed. The review paper, the cabinet agreed, was to set out 'the pros and cons of each policy option.'[50] Exasperated, Marcel Cadieux, the undersecretary of state for external affairs, wrote in a private memorandum on 29 October that the department had already been forced to restart the review twice. It was extraordinary, he noted, that with this young, vigorous, and supposedly articulate leader, 'c'est que nous n'arrivons jamais à savoir ce qu'il veut.'[51]

Like his minister Mitchell Sharp, Marcel Cadieux seemed to outsiders to embody the status quo he had done so much to create. The son of a Montreal postman, Cadieux had made his way through classical college and law school by dint of his extraordinary drive and tough intelligence. Then, at the age of twenty-five, he joined the Department of External Affairs in 1941 at a time when few French Canadians had any interest in working in the public service. He was sceptical of those who came from easier circumstances than he. A privileged background and a private income were disqualifications in his view, a conviction that had been bolstered into a principle by his service in London under Vincent Massey, Canada's wartime high commissioner to Great Britain. To Cadieux, the Canadian diplomat (the title of his book on the subject) should be one 'selected on a merit system, graded according to his abilities and his energies,' and giving the 'impression of earnestness, of industry, of some self-consciousness, perhaps, but also of genuine and strong devotion to the public service.'[52]

If Massey and London helped shape the young Cadieux, service in Indochina in 1955 with Canada's team on the International Control Commission scarred him. Always a devout Catholic, Cadieux spent every moment he could assisting his co-religionists to flee from communist persecution. Thereafter, his religion acted as a multiplier to his anti-communism.[53]

Cadieux tried to live up to his own conception of the diplomat's role by emulating Norman Robertson and Hume Wrong, men he deeply admired. But he was increasingly distant, even disconnected, from the generations of Foreign Service officers that followed his own. His service at NATO and in Indochina had made him a convinced opponent of communism and Soviet expansion, a 'conservative' influence on the Department of External Affairs.[54] He had what one subordinate described as a 'fulminating personality,'[55] for although he was as much a Cartesian as Pierre Trudeau, Cadieux tended to reinforce his logic by pounding the table. The effect was not always conducive to the free flow of ideas from the junior ranks. Cadieux, as Allan Gotlieb said in his eulogy, 'was a man who cared. Often he more than cared. He was passionate ... Faced with a committed Marcel, what colleague was not moved by the enormous sense of personal involvement, by the out-pouring of his concern, by the passion that could arouse people, change things and events.'[56] By temperament, by origin, and by attitude, it was unlikely Cadieux and Trudeau would get on well. On *nationalisme* in Quebec they agreed; on the nexus of relations between Canada, Quebec, and France they took much the same view; but on the NATO question, Trudeau and Cadieux began from different points and reached different conclusions. In any case, agreement did not mean sympathy.

That Trudeau was not a prime minister like the others slowly began to sink in. On 30 September, with Cadieux in attendance, he had talked with French Prime Minister Couve de Murville in Quebec City and asked him, the leader of a country that had withdrawn its troops from NATO, what the consequences for the alliance would be if Canada did the same. Undoubtedly affected by the Russians' crushing of the 'Prague spring,' which Ottawa had duly protested but not to the point of agreeing to a NATO statement that 'there would be no immediate reduction in member commitments to the Alliance,' Couve advised caution.[57] But after Basil Robinson of External Affairs saw the prime minister privately on 7 November, External Affairs and National Defence finally began to realize that it might not be possible to persuade Trudeau of the error of his intentions. He told Robinson that his intent was to force the department into a truly fundamental reappraisal of policy. He was not at all sure, he went on, that 'it was right for us to be thinking so much about the European threat. Perhaps we should be worried much more about civil war in North America,' an idea that was much in the air as blacks rioted in the cities of the United States and college students protested with increasing vehemence against the Vietnam War. 'He did not want in ten years time to look back on the present and have to say, "Why in God's name did we not realize what was happening on our own door step?" '[58]

If any still doubted Trudeau's intention to force the defence- and foreign-policy reviews to return to first principles, they were finally disabused in what Marcel Cadieux described as a 'quasi-catastrophique' meeting on 9 December between the prime minister, the defence and external affairs ministers, and their senior officials.[59] Trudeau had posed a long series of questions about NATO:

Will the US sacrifice Europe and NATO before blowing up the world? ... What is the point of having large conventional forces if they are going to lose the conventional battle anyway[?] ... Is NATO the best way to secure peace at the moment? ... When are we going to arrive at a plan to achieve peace by not getting stronger militarily? ... Can we assume that Russia wants war because it invaded Czechoslovakia? We do not want war but we [ie, the United States] landed troops in Lebanon, we sent troops to the Dominican Republic. Are these situations not similar? ... In what way is NATO of value to Canada? ... Is the purpose of NATO going to be reviewed with the idea of restraining Germany?

Such questions, Trudeau told his audience, 'must be considered' in the defence- and foreign-policy reviews.[60]

Fundamental questions, while not extraordinary in a university seminar, were certainly unusual for a Canadian prime minister to pose to his bureaucracy. And they led Marcel Cadieux to worry that Trudeau 'ne semble pas croire du tout au danger soviétique,'[61] something especially worrisome in the aftermath of the Czechoslovakian repression. Another of those attending, General Sharp, was also struck by the same concern. He wrote a paper for himself and his minister to try to answer 'the most fundamental' of the questions Trudeau had posed – 'Is there a Russian threat?' He concluded that there was no certain answer, at least not one that could hold for the future. To him, predictably, the best course for the West to follow was to continue to maintain 'nuclear and conventional deterrent forces.'[62] Mitchell Sharp, also deeply troubled, wondered if he should not resign to alert the public.[63]

Yet another shock to the departments, and not least to their ministers, came on 25 January 1969 when Eric Kierans, the postmaster general, spoke in a by-election campaign before a Nanaimo, BC, Liberal audience on the defence review. Kierans went well beyond the usual practice of ministerial statements on contentious issues:

Given the limitations imposed upon us by membership in NATO, and also the scope for initiative that still remains, is that membership worthwhile, is it the best choice that we can make?

I believe it is not worthwhile.

I believe we can do better. More than that, I believe we *must* do better ... Canada's withdrawal from its military commitments [to NATO] would hasten this day of reckoning – the realization by people on both sides of the Berlin wall that these billions are being spent each year, not as a deterrent against the other side, but to impose order on themselves.[64]

Kierans was someone who said what he wished without much concern for the political fallout,[65] but, in this instance, he had cleared his speech with Trudeau.[66]

By this date, as the defence review continued within the Departments of External Affairs and National Defence, time constraints were at last beginning to impinge on the process. On 10 April 1969 a NATO ministerial meeting was scheduled to take place in Washington to celebrate the alliance's twentieth anniversary, and in May the defence planning committee was to meet in Brussels. Sharp was determined that any decisions on Canadian membership in and military commitments to NATO be announced before that April gathering.[67] The STAFEUR report, called by Sharp the most 'thorough study of any aspect of Canadian foreign policy by a wide group of government officials equipped to calculate the various factors that serve Canadian interests,' was sent to cabinet ministers on 28 February.[68] Sharp told the prime minister that his officials had conducted a seminar early in the new year with a large group of selected academics, including many who had opposed the trend of the Pearson government's policy; that public discussion had been deliberately encouraged; and that the hearings on defence and foreign policy conducted by the Standing Committee on External Affairs and National Defence of the House of Commons were taken fully into account in the STAFEUR process.[69] The consultation did not stop there. As late as mid-March at least one group of ministers, most favouring an end to the NATO commitment, met with like-minded academics in Toronto.[70] And, of course, the External Affairs drafters had talked extensively with officials in the Prime Minister's Office as they struggled to understand Trudeau's intentions.[71]

Taken together, the STAFEUR report and the defence-policy review, similarly completed by the end of February and submitted to the Cabinet Committee on External Affairs and Defence, covered all the options from unarmed neutrality for Canada to the status quo.[72] There was, however, no doubt whatsoever that the weight of the argument in both papers, and especially the STAFEUR report which was shaped by its being written in the aftermath of the Soviet Union's invasion of Czechoslovakia,[73] argued strongly for Canadian membership in the North Atlantic alliance and for a continuing, if perhaps smaller, military contribution to NATO as an earnest of Canada's stake in the defence of Europe.[74] The maintenance of peace in Europe, the STAFEUR team had suggested strongly, was a vital interest for Canada, the most important area after the United States.[75]

Whether that was true or not, the cabinet committee was sharply divided in its reaction to the STAFEUR and National Defence papers, and one meeting on 7 March turned into a 'real confrontation.' As Paul Hellyer noted, a substantial number of his colleagues were in favour of 'abandoning NATO for moral, or national, or some other grounds.' They were, in his view, 'pretty naive in their appreciation of the totalitarian mentality. Just negotiate – be nice – and everyone will see reason. What a wonderful world we would have if they were right.' Hellyer added that it 'looks like a knock-em-down drag-em-out fight, however, and it will be interesting ... as to whether the Prime Minister gets his way (out of NATO).'[76] The full cabinet was to determine its course at a special weekend meeting on Saturday and Sunday, 29 and 30 March, and Trudeau was scheduled to announce the new Canadian policy on 3 April.

At this point, Trudeau decided to play another card. He possessed some foreign-policy expertise on his own staff in the person of Ivan Head. Head had been hired to help out on the constitution, but he was also a former diplomat and law professor and inevitably he assisted with speeches and advice on foreign policy when required. Several times during the winter of 1968–9 Trudeau turned to Head for help when he considered that External Affairs had not done enough for him; in March 1969 he turned to Head again.[77]

Head had no objections. Only thirty-eight years old, vigorous, and with abundant confidence in his own abilities, he seized the opportunity. It was a heaven-sent opportunity for one who had always been something of an iconoclast on NATO, at least in his own view. Others thought differently. Head was 'very pro-Soviet at this time,' in the memory of Ambassador Ford, always tending to downplay the Soviet threat or 'anything negative about the Soviets.' He was also 'pretty woolly' about disarmament.[78]

Head assembled a team from the Treasury Board and the Privy Council Office to handle the assigned task.* It was styled the 'Non-Group' to underline its secret status.[79] The Non-Group's paper, 'A Study of Defence Policy' (Cabinet Document 310-69), projected armed forces of 50,000 after ten years, forces to be limited to domestic duties, except for 1800 Canada-based soldiers assigned to NATO's Allied Command Europe mobile force. The nuclear-strike role of the air force's CF-104s in Europe, weapons that, Head cautioned, might be perceived by the Soviets as intended for a first strike, would be abandoned, along with the NATO

---

* The group included Head, Henri de Puyjalon from Treasury Board, Hume Wright and Marshall Crowe from the PCO, and Colonel Robin Bourne, then on attachment to the PCO from DND.

brigade's Honest John surface-to-surface missiles with their nuclear war-heads.[80] As that suggested, the PMO paper did not advocate a unilateral withdrawal from NATO, but it calculated that Canada, by remaining a member, could exercise its influence from within to try to change the alliance. The paper, unlike those prepared by officials in Defence and External Affairs, reflected the thinking of the new group of ministers, and especially Prime Minister Trudeau.[81]

Room 340-S in the Centre Block on Parliament Hill was less imposing but more functional than the old cabinet chamber in the East Block. On Saturday morning, 29 March 1969, it was a large cabinet of twenty-eight ministers who were eligible to sit down around the table. Trudeau had brought some of the new generation into office and into the cabinet, but not, as yet, very many. In fact, Trudeau's cabinet was not significantly different from Lester Pearson's. Sitting at the table was a minister senior even to Pearson, Paul Martin, who had graced every Liberal cabinet since Mackenzie King's. Martin might have reflected that he was just sixty-five, only sixteen years older than the prime minister. In the 1968 convention, however, he went down to defeat, adjudged old before his time, and was shuffled off to be government leader in the Senate. Martin accepted the situation: the Liberal party was his life, and loyalty to party and leader was second nature. But if the Liberal party stood for something in foreign policy, it was the policies of Pearson and his predecessors: the alliance of liberal democracies in the face of a powerful communist adversary. NATO was the centrepiece of that policy, and Martin was not the man to see it lightly changed.

Sharp and Léo Cadieux agreed with him, and there were others who could be counted on to take the same side. Paul Hellyer, Pearson's defence minister, represented the right wing within the cabinet. Big, awkward, uncomfortable in public, he seemed to embody the past when, in fact, he was four years younger than Trudeau. He believed in active interventionist government, and, in foreign policy, he was deeply sceptical of those who would break Canada's established policies and rupture its alliances.

John Turner, the minister of justice, was anything but yesterday's man. Still under forty, a Rhodes Scholar, bilingual, strikingly handsome, with an attractive wife and young family, outgoing and hearty where his leader was shy and introverted, he was often taken to be Trudeau's logical successor. Unlike Trudeau, Turner's connections went back to earlier generations of Liberals, and he took their ideas more seriously, and perhaps more reverentially, than the prime minister did.

One minister who definitely did not accept the wisdom of the establishment was Donald Macdonald, the president of the Privy Council. Macdonald might have been taken to be an establishment type himself: cousin of a general, graduate of Toronto, Harvard, and Cambridge universities, and member of parliament for Toronto-Rosedale, which included some of Canada's most privileged turf. But 'Thumper' – a reference to his arguing style – was also iconoclastic and outspoken. The youngest man (and with Hellyer, the tallest) at the cabinet table, he had not the slightest intention of being overawed or overborne by his seniors. With Eric Kierans, who had already broadcast his conclusions on foreign policy, Macdonald would lead the charge against NATO, and support would not be lacking.

Other ministers were less forward. Don Jamieson, Newfoundland's representative in the cabinet, was strongly pro-American. His political instincts were acute, honed by a life of mixing broadcasting with politics. The one had made him a millionaire, or so it was rumoured; the other had made him a minister. Allan J. MacEachen, Nova Scotia's cabinet member, was less flamboyant than Jamieson but far more knowledgeable about Ottawa, where he had first come as a junior member of parliament in 1953. A defeated candidate for the Liberal leadership in 1968, MacEachen was known to bide his time and to keep his own counsel, if not always his temper. Politically canny, he nevertheless harboured a surprisingly idealistic streak.

The minister of trade and commerce was Jean-Luc Pepin, a University of Ottawa political science professor best known for his engaging television lectures on the Canadian constitution. Pepin may have thought that if he could explain that dreary topic he could explain anything, and so he did – sometimes on several sides of an issue as his agile mind debated with itself. Pepin would find NATO a challenging topic for his expository and analytical talents.

Gérard Pelletier and Jean Marchand were Trudeau's closest friends and longest associates in the cabinet. Neither had been in politics before 1965, but both were in the ascendant in 1969. Marchand had handled a tough assignment as the first minister of manpower in the Pearson government, and he was about to try another, as first minister of regional economic expansion, with a large staff and a creative mandate. Pelletier in 1969 was mostly concerned with bilingualism and securing a statutory protection for the rights of French Canadians inside the government of their country; but he was not inclined by experience or temperament to side with the establishment and its unimaginative policies.

In general, things looked grim for both the Department of External

Affairs and the Department of National Defence. Sharp and Cadieux had both realized for some time that the status quo could not be defended in its entirety; for them, the operative word was reduction, not withdrawal. In particular, Sharp, as a former finance minister, understood the financial costs that could be involved in trying to re-equip the 10,000-man contingent in Europe at a time when the cabinet as a whole was desperately seeking money for more politically attractive programs.[82] Still, the battle had to be fought in the meeting, where the pro-NATO ministers made up a majority.[83]

Trudeau himself, some still believe, preferred to see Canada remain in NATO and even keep some troops there. Hellyer, however, had discussed that question with the prime minister earlier in the month and had no doubt that his desire was to get all the forces out of Europe.[84] The cabinet minutes and Hellyer's diary, in fact, show the prime minister playing a major role at the two-day meeting. 'He is a most tenacious as well as a clever fellow – and really doctrinaire,' Hellyer wrote. 'He said "If we can reach a position honestly – OK. If we can't or if we are split down the middle we will bloody well start over again. We may be laughed at – but we will eventually reach an acceptable position," ' by which, Hellyer added, Trudeau meant 'acceptable to him.'

The prime minister began the discussion of the defence-policy review by asking if the cabinet rejected neutralism and non-alignment and if there was unanimity that Canada needed 'some form of arms.' In fact, there was no unanimity, several ministers calling for neutrality. Trudeau himself observed that 'Canada's present military establishment was determined not to impress our enemies but rather to impress our friends' – in that case, he argued, it was logical 'to think in terms of other domestic or international contributions that could be made which would carry with them the same degree of political persuasion.' That having been said, however, Trudeau declared that the consensus was for some form of alignment for Canada.

But what kind of alignment? Did ministers want Canada to participate in collective-security arrangements with other states? To begin this segment of the discussion, Trudeau called on Donald Macdonald to read his paper which advocated withdrawal from NATO. Sharp and Hellyer spoke forcefully against Macdonald's recommendation, but Trudeau then intervened to suggest that 'the protection of European territory could be left to Europeans' and that Canada's first priority should be 'on this Continent to protect the second strike capability of the United States.' He added that Canada had an 'inverted' policy: 'We should be protecting our internal security, defending our three seas, and then considering other possible international commitments. It was not logical or rational to not protect that which was ours.' For Pierre Trudeau, the proper policy was Canada first. The discussion carried over into Sunday morning, Trudeau concluding this phase by turning the meeting to the proposition, 'Yes we will remain a member of NATO *but* on different terms and with increased control over our own contribution.'

Again the discussion ranged widely. Agriculture Minister Bud Olson wanted the troops out of Europe within a two- or three-year period. Macdonald and Health and Welfare Minister John Munro agreed. Finance Minister Benson was dubious about the financial benefits of withdrawal and feared that 'an abrupt withdrawal would tear the Canadian military structure to pieces.' Again Trudeau summed up his seminar's conclusions: NATO was a useful institution; still to be decided was the role of Canada's forces in the alliance.

To lead the discussion, Trudeau put a series of propositions to his ministers, the most important being the last one: 'It is the object of the Canadian Government to reduce and at the earliest possible date, end, the stationing of forces in Europe.' Several ministers batted the propositions around, but there was no conclusion, the meeting ending with the prime minister's decision to have prepared, in consultation with Sharp and Cadieux, a document to put before the cabinet on 1 April.[85]

This had been an extraordinary cabinet session, possibly an unprecedented one. For two days, the battle had raged with the anti-NATO ministers growing 'more militant and unbending' on the Sunday. 'It is interesting to see some of the chaps getting off the fence and lining up with the Prime Minister,' Hellyer noted, adding that 'there was a perceptible change notwithstanding the argument which has favoured remaining in N.A.T.O. if Canada is to make any contribution to collective defence at all.' Hellyer was certain that Trudeau finally was 'showing his hand more and more' in the second day of debate. 'The [PMO] paper he circulated is really "advice." He is trying desperately to get his way and may well succeed in the end.'[86]

The Privy Council Office prepared the NATO position paper and sent it to the Department of External Affairs on Monday, 31 March. There, Basil Robinson and some of his officers worked well into the night trying to adapt the paper to the department's way of thinking, even going so far as to include the so-called Pepin formula, presented in cabinet by Jean-Luc Pepin. Pepin's formula called for Canada to stay in NATO, to phase out its nuclear role, and to discuss the form of Canada's conventional-force contribution. Sharp was to present this revised draft to cabinet on 1 April; apparently he failed to do so.[87]

In any case, the PCO draft prepared for the prime minister restarted the debate. As Hellyer noted, Cadieux 'threatened to resign. The PM said cabinet had [once, in the Diefenbaker era] broken up over defence policy but it was a bit soon in the life of this administration for that.' Trudeau agreed to have the document redrafted.[88] The cabinet discussions over the weekend had left matters unresolved and confused. The ministers and their officials agreed that Canada was to stay in NATO, but there was no common understanding on the form of the troop commitment to the alliance. A working party to implement the decision found the Privy Council Office and Treasury Board representatives insistent that reduction equalled withdrawal, a position that astounded Sharp when he learned of it.[89]

Defence Minister Cadieux and the prime minister duly met on 2 April to consider whether a compromise was still possible between them. Trudeau began by saying that he understood his minister's position. If Cadieux felt he had to resign, then he should do so, but was there no common ground? Cadieux wrote out a phrase that, he insisted, must be in the prime minister's statement: 'a planned and phased reduction,' not a withdrawal. Trudeau agreed and the crisis was over,[90] though not before Sharp told the cabinet on 3 April that Ross Campbell, the ambassador to NATO, had said that the force cuts would break Canada's treaty commitments. Macdonald asked which commitments, and Sharp proved unable to cite chapter and verse.[91] As a result, the prime minister's redrafted memorandum won cabinet consent on 3 April.

Trudeau was briefed before his announcement by Jim Nutt, the director-general of political-military affairs in DEA. Cannily, the official urged the prime minister to be cautious on all questions about timing, about the size of force cuts, and about the Canadian air role in NATO. Those suggestions, accepted by Trudeau, became the basis of DEA's struggle in the coming months for a 'balanced' approach.[92] In any case, Trudeau's public statement on 3 April defined Canada's priorities in defence as sovereignty, North American defence, NATO, and peacekeeping, and he rejected 'a non-aligned or neutral role' for Canada and paid due tribute to NATO's contribution to peace. Then Trudeau turned to the nub of the matter: 'Canadian forces now are committed to NATO until the end of the present year. The Canadian force commitment for deployment with NATO in Europe beyond this period will be discussed with our allies at the meeting of the defence planning committee of NATO in May. The Canadian Government intends, in consultation with Canada's allies, to take early steps to bring about a planned and phased reduction of the size of the Canadian forces in Europe.'[93]

The reaction at home and abroad to this shift in policy was relatively restrained. American officials indicated their 'disappointment,' and Progressive Conservative leader Robert Stanfield said that after a nine-month review of Canadian foreign policy, the only proper diagnosis of the result was a false pregnancy. In Paris there was no criticism, and Pierre Siraud, French ambassador in Ottawa at the time, considered the Canadian decision 'tout à fait normale.'[94] In Bonn, spokesmen called the decision 'not opportune,' and Foreign Minister Willy Brandt, coincidentally in Ottawa on a scheduled visit, added his protests on 7 and 8 April, but not strongly enough to force any change.[95] Sharp, however, did receive a rough ride from his colleagues at the NATO ministerial meeting in Washington, British Defence Minister Denis Healey being particularly vituperative.[96] 'I did not enjoy the 20th anniversary meeting in Washington,' Sharp recollected.[97]

The prime minister was unmoved by the criticism. In a speech to the Alberta Liberal Association in Calgary on 12 April, he argued that 'we have to remain free to decide our own foreign policy. And when we are told that we shouldn't be taking a free ride to peace in the world, when we are told that if we withdraw from NATO even in any degree this will lead other countries to withdraw from NATO, I don't admit this ... And in our case, where our contribution to Europe ... is marginal, but where we still believe that NATO is an important force in the world, we are entitled ... to ask questions about our participation in NATO.' Canada had no foreign policy except that flowing from NATO, Trudeau said, and it was simply wrong to have a military alliance determine foreign policy. 'It should be your foreign policy which determines your military policy.'[98]

False pregnancy the announcement may have been, but the size of the cutback remained a major issue. Indeed, one infantry battalion commander preparing to take his unit to Europe was briefed at Canadian Forces Headquarters early in April and told that his battalion and the entire Canadian NATO force were to return to Canada in January 1970.[99] But if that was the initial DND view, it did not last long. The first figure to emerge, as the working group pored over the entrails of the cabinet decision, was for a total commitment of 3200–3500 for the NATO contingent. It might have made sense for the Canadian NATO force to be either air or land, but to avoid an interservice fight the chief of the Defence Staff decided that 'bits and pieces' of both would remain.[100] Then when External Affairs received a draft of a House of Commons speech prepared by Ivan Head for Trudeau, the undersecretary told his minister that most of it was 're-edited extracts' of the PMO paper on defence policy. He added furiously that 'Passages in that paper leading to the conclusion that Canada might leave a small force in Europe have, however, been removed.'[101] As a result of the malice and confusion, Trudeau could only tell parliament that it might be August before final decisions could be made on the NATO force. Although the Liberal caucus strongly favoured keeping troops in NATO, Trudeau had carried his party with him after a strongly emotional pitch in caucus on 23 April.[102] The Liberal majority in the House of Commons then dutifully supported the government's new policy.

Nonetheless, within the bureaucracy the infighting over the size of the force continued unchecked. The 3500-man force survived a meeting of defence- and foreign-policy officials with the prime minister on 28 April when the case for it was advanced by General Jean Allard, the chief of the Defence Staff. Trudeau, who ordinarily did not react well to Allard's bull-in-the-china-shop approach,[103] had been at his Socratic worst, asking why 3500 and why not some other figure and questioning National Defence's desire to continue to keep civilian dependents in Europe. One observer concluded that Trudeau had still not determined his own position on complete withdrawal but was probably leaning that way, if he could keep his cabinet together in the face of such a decision.[104] On 30 April the minister of national defence recommended to his colleagues that the Canadian force in Europe be reduced to approximately 3500, the final figure to be determined after discussions on the configuration of the Canadian force with the NATO allies. This was duly agreed to on 20 May. At a later meeting of the full cabinet, the prime minister, as always concerned to free Canada from nuclear commitments, told Cadieux that if NATO wanted Canada to continue the nuclear-strike role of the CF-104 squadrons, that proposal would have to return to cabinet for decision.[105]

Léo Cadieux had to present this attenuated force to his NATO colleagues in Brussels on 25 May. He decided the best way to give the defence ministers the bad news was at a luncheon at the residence of the Canadian ambassador to NATO before the formal session. 'We had a gentleman's agreement that in the afternoon at the general meeting that matter would not be raised but I willingly gave them a description of what we were planning to do for their private information. And everybody,' he remembered a decade later, 'really jumped on me.'[106] One American later described it as 'the toughest talk I have ever heard in an international meeting.'[107] The Americans themselves, sensitive to European fears that Canada's cuts might be a stalking horse for American withdrawal, were very harsh with Cadieux (though President Nixon was willing to entertain the idea as an eventual possibility).[108] The Belgians and Dutch especially were deeply shaken, the Belgian defence minister actually bursting into tears at the news. Healey was again brutally frank, telling the press after the formal meeting that 'if someone passes the buck, somebody else has to fill the gap.'[109]

No one was more aware of that than Cadieux, and on the aircraft taking him home from Brussels he again seriously considered resignation. Only the argument of his deputy minister, Elgin Armstrong, that if he resigned the cuts would be much worse than if he stayed, persuaded him to hang on. Hellyer, who had resigned from the cabinet in late April because of Trudeau's cold reception of the report of the task force on housing he had led, was on the aircraft with Cadieux. He argued that Cadieux's position was strengthened because of his own resignation – if Trudeau lost two senior ministers in the space of a few weeks he would face major difficulties.[110]

So Cadieux stayed. On 23 June he told parliament that the overall strength of the forces was to be reduced by some 20 per cent to 80,000–85,000 men, and the defence budget would be fixed for the next three years at $1.8 billion.

Over the summer, the struggle in Ottawa went on to determine the size and form of the NATO force. Exercises were run to see if a small mechanized battle group could play a useful wartime role, and the conclusions were generally reassuring.[111] There were consultations with NATO to determine the shape of the force, and the supreme allied commander (SACEUR), General A.J. Goodpaster, recommended that the 'current military posture' be maintained 'as nearly as possible'; if that was impossible, he asked for a total force of 6359. The chair of DND's Force Structure Working Group, however, recommended a total force of 4000.[112] In fact, thanks in part to the continuing struggle by Cadieux and External Affairs, and to the insistence of the chief of the Defence Staff that a Canadian NATO contingent have some capacity to defend itself,[113] the final force strength, approved by cabinet on 13 August,[114] was 25 per cent greater than the recommended figure.

Léo Cadieux's statement in parliament on 19 September, finally announcing the structure of the NATO force for the next three years, noted that Canada would 'phase out our brigade group and our [air] division in Germany by the fall of 1970, when we will establish co-located land and air elements under one Canadian headquarters ... They will use present equipment and will have a combined total strength of approximately 5,000 personnel.' That force, the minister said, will be able to play a 'meaningful though reduced role.' The land element of

2800 would be a mechanized battle group with its 'operational role' still undefined, although one without nuclear weapons. Eventually, the Combat Group, as it came to be called, was given a counter-attack role in support of American or German units. General W.C. Leonard, its first commander, later estimated that his men were good 'for about one and a half counterattacks.' Leonard added that even though the Combat Group had no nuclear weapons under its control, he continued to have access to such tactical weapons, provided only that they were fired by American or other NATO forces. The country's nuclear virginity, in other words, was completely spurious.[115] The air component was to consist of three squadrons of CF-104 aircraft, one in reconnaissance and two in a nuclear-strike role to be concluded by January 1972. For the post-1972 period, Cadieux said, the government's intention was to equip the land force for a light air-mobile role and to convert the air element to conventionally armed reconnaissance or ground-support tasks. The minister also announced other changes in the forces and fixed their total strength at 82,000.[116] The defence review was finally over, more than sixteen months after it had begun.

The final word on the NATO review probably belonged to Ivan Head. In a triumphant letter to a friend in External Affairs, Trudeau's aide pointed to a recent Gallup Poll that showed 51 per cent 'in favour of what we had done. This, I think, is a clear indication of the willingness of Canadians to accept policies which are carefully formulated, clearly enunciated and firmly implemented.'[117] That was Head's opinion, and possibly even the prime minister's. It was not that of the Departments of External Affairs or National Defence.

The foreign-policy review process meanwhile lumbered on. STAFEUR's Report on Canada and Europe, a full study of Canada's European policy, had already been completed. In the fall of 1969 a ministerial mission had made an extended trip to nine Latin American countries, and its report was tabled in parliament on 24 January 1969.[118] In addition, the Department of External Affairs had organized a seminar with the cooperation of the Canadian Institute of International Affairs on Latin America in March 1969. Academics, businessmen, journalists, and government officials participated, providing grist for a Latin American Task Force within External Affairs.[119] At much the same time, George Ignatieff, former ambassador to the United Nations and then the permanent representative to the Disarmament Commission in Geneva, was placed in charge of another task force reviewing possible courses of action at the United Nations, including arms control and disarmament policy.[120]

In addition, as Mitchell Sharp told the prime minister on 25 March, there were plans afoot for seminars, meetings, and studies on the Pacific and on aid.[121]

This was impressive progress – of a sort. But it was leading only to a series of papers on specific subjects with no direction or overall theme. The first attempt to impose a direction on the process came in May, when Geoffrey Pearson prepared a memorandum, 'Canadian Foreign Policy: Looking Ahead and Looking Back,' that set down an outline for the review and called on External Affairs to improve its planning procedures.[122] That attempt failed, the prime minister deciding (after a fight between the Prime Minister's Office, the Privy Council Office, and the Department of External Affairs) that individual papers should be published as they were completed, with a white paper following in the spring of 1970.[123] But the task of 'sanitizing' classified papers troubled the minister and officials in External Affairs. They were seriously concerned with the time taken up by reviews that, as Marcel Cadieux noted, 'restrain our ability to be creative on current problems. The sooner the review phase is over, the more resources we will have for initiatives & operations.'[124] The answer was to place one officer in charge of the review, and the choice was Geoffrey Murray, head of a newly created Policy Analysis Group. Ironically, the chief draftsman of the Robertson report that Trudeau had scorned as a defence of the status quo was now to prepare the blueprint for the new regime's foreign policy.

By September, Murray was well under way. Cabinet had received reports on policy towards Europe, Latin America, and the United Nations, and on international development or aid; although each had contained recommendations, no action had been taken, ministers apparently preferring to defer decisions until the proposals on each area could be fitted into the overall picture.[125] The white paper, Murray said, was expected to deal with policy and operations 'in broad philosophical terms ... with such matters as Canada's interests, objectives and goals in the field of foreign policy, with the international environments, probably in the form of "alternative worlds," in which Canadian policy will have to be shaped and executed; with other constraints on that policy, in particular the Canadian resources available either actual or potential. One could reasonably expect that the conclusions ... could at best be expressed in the form of options.' Murray was convinced, quite properly, that his first priority had to be the drafting of a general paper. His intention was to set out a 'line of questioning' so that this paper and the area papers would deal with five elements: interests, objectives, international environment, other constraints, and options.[126]

While Murray was continuing his work, other aspects of foreign policy were considered elsewhere. A Foreign Operations Task Force, headed by Sydney Pierce who had served in senior economic posts in External Affairs and as associate deputy minister in the Department of Trade and Commerce, had been created. The whole government was in the throes of reorganization, responding to the lash being wielded by Michael Pitfield, the deputy secretary to the cabinet, and Canada's external-relations bureaucracy was not to be spared. Pierce's mandate was to look at all Canadian operations abroad and to propose a more efficient organization. To this end, his group drew up an outline for the consolidation of operations abroad and set it within the context of a management process. The assumption of the task force, expressed like so much of the Trudeau government's papers and reports in the buzzwords of the day, was that 'the maximum degree of integration consistent with the most effective achievement of governmental objectives and efficiency in the use of resources for these purposes' called for the consolidation of personnel and support services into a unified foreign service.[127] The detailed proposals of the task force will be considered in chapter 8; all that needs be said now is that its recommendations for consolidation abroad, together with cuts in budget and personnel – 314 establishment positions lost, department strength cut by 170, and the firing of sixty-three officers – announced on 24 March, added another element of uncertainty for a department that was already reeling under the impact of change forced upon it by the Trudeau government.[128]

Meanwhile, on 18 November, the Priorities and Planning Committee of cabinet, the key directing group of ministers in Trudeau's administration, received an External Affairs memorandum on foreign policy in the 1970s that set out 'a conceptual framework within which to consider the external policies and programmes' of the government. The cabinet committee accepted the main points of this memorandum on 4 December:

a. Foreign policies are basically an extension of internal policies, conditions and interests;

b. To establish the right priorities, to identify divergent policies and to achieve some degree of coherence it is necessary to look at foreign policy in its totality;

c. In the seventies, Canada is likely to be as active in the foreign field as in the past but in different, perhaps more modest ways;

d. Continuous coordination will be necessary within the Government to ensure optimum effectiveness.[129]

Murray, the draftsman of this and subsequent memoranda on the review, now tried to capture his conceptual framework graphically. To this end, he employed a hexagonal model, apparently suggested to him by Jim Davey of the Prime Minister's Office,[130] which virtually defies description. An inner hexagon set out the national goals of Canadian policy: sovereignty and independence, peace and security, democracy and justice, economic growth, harmonious natural environment, and quality of life. On an outer hexagon were policy or program objectives, specific to different areas of foreign policy. For Canada-U.S. relations, for example, one early listing of objectives included developing relations with the United States while ensuring through continuous vigilance Canadian independence and sovereignty; promoting contacts with 'areas of residual francophonie' in the United States; supporting efforts to control pollution; and encouraging increased awareness of Canadian culture and identity in the United States.[131] Complicating matters further were coloured bands on the sides of the hexagon. The inevitable result was acute puzzlement for most who received the draft. The chief of the Defence Staff, for example, told Marcel Cadieux that the method employed was 'exceedingly complicated. Some parts of it are not clear ... The method is open to criticism because of the extent to which it relies for its success on the degree of accuracy' of the 'Forecasts for the Seventies' that underlay the process.[132] Almost certainly, Murray was aware of the problems, but he was a prisoner of the expectations – and flow charts – of the Privy Council Office and the prime minister. Conceptual frameworks were demanded; conceptual frameworks would be provided.[133]

Murray's draft of the white paper, now becoming known as the general paper, was circulated throughout the department in November. Severe criticisms had been offered by divisions, and Murray produced a second version on 16 January 1970. This too was not universally hailed, one senior officer characterizing it as narrow, expedient, uninspiring, negative, and vulnerable to public criticism.[134] Another draft went to the undersecretary on 12 March, with Murray's comment that he had tried to fill the gap created by the absence of a specific paper on Canadian-American relations by beefing up the references to the United States in the general paper. He admitted that he might have overdone it, but no one could complain that the Americans had been left out.[135] A further draft, dated 2 April, without the hexagonal charts (one minister was said to have complained that the hexagon looked like a stop sign!),[136] failed to win the prime minister's approbation, was redrafted yet again, and the hexagon reinserted.[137]

At the same time, work on the final versions of the specialized papers continued. The European paper, drafted by John Halstead, reached Murray on 26 March. It was, Halstead said, based on the STAFEUR report, compressed, updated, and modified for publication.[138] All five papers were soon approved in cabinet committee,[139] and the review, under the general title *Foreign Policy for Canadians,* was made public on 25 June 1970. The format was unique – six multi-coloured booklets in a slipcase – with one general pamphlet and separate papers on Europe, the Pacific, the United Nations, Latin America, and international development. In the end, the stop sign was not printed (although it did later emerge for public scrutiny), wiser heads presumably prevailing.

The six pamphlets that made up the review bluntly rejected the 'help-ful-fixer' role that had been the hallmark of Pearsonian diplomacy. In its place was an inward-looking concern for the national interest, for economic growth as the focus of Canadian foreign policy, followed by social justice and the quality of life. Policies on other themes 'would merely be placed in a new pattern of emphasis. Emphasis on sovereignty and independence, in any event, primarily depends on the extent to which they are challenged ... Peace and security depend mainly on external developments.'

To a substantial extent, the past was being abandoned for the strange new god of national interest: 'Canada, like other states, must act according to how it perceives its aims and interests ... In essence, foreign policy is the product of the Government's progressive definition and pursuit of national aims and interests in the international environment. It is,' the review said, 'the extension abroad of national policies.'[140] All this implied a new devotion to 'dollar diplomacy' that disturbed many. (This 'nonsense about "real diplomats" disdaining salesmanship,' George Ignatieff snorted from Geneva: 'I sold Pigs unassisted by T&C in Belgrade, to say nothing of appalling pickles in the London Ideal Home Exhibition.')[141] It implied much less willingness to try to play a role in preserving peace, and it certainly suggested a decreased emphasis on NATO and Europe, the brave words of involvement in the 'Europe' pamphlet notwithstanding.[142]

But involvement was not abandoned: the emphasis on social justice suggested a greater effort in international development. The placing of the quality of life as a priority demonstrated a new concern for the environment. The high priority given economic growth reflected a realistic emphasis on Canada's vital necessity to trade. And the calls for coordination abroad were essential.

The white paper was seriously flawed. The United States, Canada's best friend and main foreign-policy problem, received short shrift, as did the Commonwealth, the Caribbean, and Africa, glaring omissions that drew scornful comments. There were almost no clearly stated objectives and no detailed appraisal of Canadian economic policies abroad. Few new initiatives were spelled out, though the desire to recognize China, already stated publicly, was reaffirmed,[143] and even the hoary question whether Canada should join the Organization of American States was fudged – although the Latin American Task Force had called for Canada's membership and Sharp was said to favour it.[144] Above all, *Foreign Policy for Canadians* had substituted systems analysis for idealism; it had replaced a role abroad with a conceptual framework; and it had given Canadians a jargon-laden rationale for self-interest in place of an often inspirational policy that at times in the past had seemed fit for heroes.[145]

No one felt this more sharply than the architect of Canada's postwar policy. Lester Pearson was outraged by the white paper, and he marked up his copy of the pamphlets with scathing comments. Peace and security was 'third in priority!' 'Peacekeeping is put alongside indeed *after* "light aircraft manufacture." ' Foster social justice – 'baloney!'[146] More calmly, Pearson wrote a private memorandum on *Foreign Policy for Canadians* in which he condemned the suggested direction for its 'disengagement and passivity,' for suggesting that the time had come 'to withdraw from what is considered to have been an over-extension of international activity and commitments ... to "lower our profile" and adopt a more modest posture.' For Trudeau's predecessor, the white paper was simply wrong:

We will never get a world of peace, security and good international relations by the pursuit of national self-interest as the principal objective of foreign policy ... 'national interest,' unless it includes as a first priority our interest in peace and security, is a shaky and misleading formula for policy. The promotion of national interest in the narrow, traditional sense merely evokes resistance from other nations, also in the name of national interest, and this inevitably leads to confrontation and conflict.

Surely a far better foreign policy is that which is based on a national interest which expresses itself in co-operation with others; in the building of international institutions and the development of international policies and agreements, leading to a world order which promotes freedom, well-being and security for all.[147]

Pearson may well have been correct, but no one in the Prime Minister's Office was listening. In the time between Pearson's departure from office and his death in January 1972, Pierre Trudeau never once consulted him about foreign policy.[148]

The review process was now almost complete. A paper on relations with the United States did not appear until two years later, after events had forced a reappraisal of Canada's 'special relationship' with its neighbour. What had been achieved for the two years of agonizing reappraisal?

The government's defence review had produced a cut of 50 per cent in the NATO troop commitment, a certain degree of hostility from Canada's allies, and the definite appearance of change by the Trudeau government. The white paper had cut loose Canadian policy from its past and substituted new and different priorities for those that had prevailed since 1945. The appearance of change again was to the fore.

Above all, by seizing control of the foreign-policy process, Trudeau had successfully shaken up the entrenched bureaucracies of External Affairs and National Defence. He had insisted on reviews that would begin with first principles, and he had demanded that the cabinet be presented with genuine choices so that the politicians could decide on Canada's course. That he had persisted until he succeeded in securing these goals, that he had force fed new ideas into the bureaucracy, was the most important result of the defence- and foreign-policy reviews of 1968–70. Without any doubt, Canadian foreign policy was now Pierre Trudeau's to direct.

Part Two

Errand in the Wilderness:
Canada and the United States

2

A Curious Absence:
High Policy in the Relations
of Canada and the United States

Foreign Policy for Canadians was released for sale on 25 June 1970. First reports were reassuring. There was a certain amount of press attention among 'serious' journalists. Interested citizens were buying the booklets, taking them home, and, presumably, reading and digesting them.

It was not, admittedly, an arduous task. Totalling 185 pages, the publication would not have taxed any thinking Canadian. Yet its reception was different from what had been expected. Readers found the treatment of Canadian foreign policy curiously incomplete. Despite its brevity, Foreign Policy for Canadians was not succinct. Despite its title, it was not specific enough to be 'policy.' And despite its claim to deal with matters 'foreign,' it did not attempt to prescribe a Canadian approach to the United States. The only question it raised was whether Canada had a foreign policy and, if so, whether it included an American policy. After a few weeks, except for scattered specialists, it disappeared. Unquoted, it was also unmourned. The booklets themselves became a curiosity if not a conundrum: How could so much labour, so much anticipation, generate so little heat, and such slight effect?

The answer was not hard to find. The review was self-contradictory as well as incomplete. There was no guiding principle in Canada's foreign policy because there was no overwhelming external challenge to Canada's integrity or its self-interest. The review could even be read, as one astute critic pointed out, as permitting *either* international crusading (helpful fixing) *or* economic self-interest.[1]

Since there was no well-established goal for Canadian policy, it followed that the means to pursue it were undefined. Quiet diplomacy was wounded but not slain. Open-mouth diplomacy, however, had not replaced it as the medium of choice. Yet the open-mouth technique was representative of the spirit of the age of Aquarius, of Woodstock, of Janis Joplin, and all the other prophetic signs of the 'Greening of [North] America.'[2]

The idea of the greening of society reached Canada from the United States, flowing through the airwaves, travelling with draft-age emigrants opting out of the Vietnam War, appearing in magazines and books. *Death Goes Better with Coca Cola* was the title chosen for a short-story collection in 1967: Vietnam was its leitmotif.[3] In 1968 and 1969 Canadians could stand, figuratively but sometimes literally, along the border and watch columns of smoke rising from Los Angeles, Washington, and Detroit. The year 1968 witnessed the assassinations of Martin Luther King and Robert Kennedy, the political eclipse of one president and the election of another who seemed to have been dredged from the swamps of the Cold War. The idea that Canada was an alternative society to the United States had, under the circumstances, a certain appeal. It was an appeal that Trudeau himself represented and exploited, for in 1968 the prime minister had been the candidate of youth, with a rose between his teeth, a carnation in his lapel, his athletic body on display in hotel swimming pools across the land. It was a paradox of the time that the United States, which had created the youth culture, where young people were a power in every area of life from music to design, should be seen as sclerotic or geriatric, its institutions and dominant attitudes a carapace waiting to be sloughed off by those fortunate enough, and young enough, to green.

Youth culture, and youthful assumptions, were common to both young Canadians and young Americans. Interestingly, young English Canadians assumed that they were closer in culture to Americans than to their French-speaking counterparts.[4] That may or may not have been true, although a common language was an obvious bond. Quebeckers had a harsher opinion of the United States than did citizens in other provinces. To complete the paradox, more Quebeckers – 70 per cent – wanted free trade with the United States.[5] Language, however, did not prevent the spread of American styles in music or dress to Quebec. The music that travelled to Canada, French and English, included not only rock and roll but country and western. Chicago and Chicoutimi were not so far apart.[6]

In the late 1960s the flow of Canadians to the United States abated; and in 1971, for the first time in sixty years, Americans coming to Canada outnumbered the Canadians moving to the States.[7] 'I was twenty-three when I reached Canada in April 1969,' one draft-age refugee remembered. 'I knew nobody here. I didn't know what to expect,' except one thing. 'When you came to Canada, you never expected to go home.'[8] The majority of military-age Americans moving to Canada were well-educated, charter members of the middle class. Some never adapted, and when the American government later proclaimed an amnesty, many chose to go home. Not all returned; those who stayed were absorbed into Canadian life and did not develop into a large or autonomous pressure group.[9]

Some Canadians welcomed the Americans, whether out of hospitality, fellow-feeling, or the belief that the immigrants brought valuable skills to their new nation. Others did not, arguing that the Americans would consciously or unconsciously undermine true Canadianism. But both sets of opinion could agree that the Canadian alternative to the United States was becoming credible.

Canadians seemed to think so, in increasing numbers. In 1956 Canadians were asked whether they thought that 'the Canadian way of life [was] being influenced too much by the U.S.' That year, only 27 per cent replied in the affirmative, 63 per cent in the negative. How, in 1956, could anyone be too much influenced by the styles, the attractions, the magnetism and – perhaps – the money of the United States? Ten years later, the figures had a very different balance: fully 53 per cent of Canadians thought the United States had 'too much influence' on their 'way of life,' while only 36 per cent replied in the negative. When the poll was next taken, in 1974, 'too much' had grown to 57 per cent of Canadian responses.[10]

The nature of Canadian nationalism is a much-debated subject on which few Canadians agree. Opponents of the various 'nationalist' personalities or policies in the early 1970s complained that opposition to foreign investment was a purely Canadian syndrome. Yet no country is immune to the sentiment, as the Americans have more recently discovered.[11] Most Canadians would agree that their sense of country relates to and reacts with their sense of the United States, and that they are sensitive to what Americans think about themselves. In short, Canadian reactions to the United States are an extraordinarily deep-seated and frequently contradictory cultural phenomenon – one determined at any given point by the indices of American as well as Canadian national feeling. The sense that Americans had lost confidence in themselves, in their society, in their foreign policy, and even in their system of government[12] had direct consequences inside Canada, both in the tone of public debate and, inevitably, in Canadians' expectations of what their government should do in response.[13]

Not all Canadians took an interest in foreign policy, of course. If we narrow our focus to 'political Canadians,' using those who attended Conservative and Liberal national leadership conventions in 1967 and 1968, there was no large difference on foreign policy or defence issues. Both Conservatives and Liberals agreed with the proposition that 'there should be special laws to regulate foreign (mostly US) capital.' They did not agree that 'Canada should bring its foreign policy more closely into line with the US,' and each party was split as to whether 'Soviet communism is no longer a threat to Canada.'[14] The delegates may well have been more liberal, or more left, on these issues than Canadians generally, but the fact that voting delegates of both parties were inclined to take a softer line on foreign policy and defence than would have been acceptable ten years earlier helped to set the context in which politicians and bureaucrats had to formulate Canada's American policies.

There was, of course, another dimension to Canadian opinion on foreign policy – that of the radical-socialist-Marxist left.[15] One polemical suggestion, the title of a book published in 1970, was *Close the 49th Parallel*.[16] Inside, almost all the essays bemoaned the lamentable domination of Canadian sport, political science, defence policy, media, even science by the United States. 'The Americanization of Canada is first and foremost a function of the penetration of the Canadian economy by American monopoly capitalism,' the book's editor proclaimed.[17] Students, intellectuals, and socially aware elements in general should take note and resist before it was too late.

It would have been hard to write, let alone publish, such a book in 1960 or even 1965. It was not hard in 1970, or for years thereafter. 'Close the 49th Parallel' was an attitude, not a policy, but attitudes have a habit of creeping into policy formulation. Ironically, Canadian anti-Americanism was largely a reflection of its native American source.[18] On the other side, friends of the United States, like defenders of its government and social system at home, were cast down and discouraged by events in that country, and had difficulty mustering the enthusiasm, let alone the arguments, that would have been necessary to keep Canada in balance between pro- and anti-American currents of thought.

The balance therefore shifted, just at a point when 'quiet diplomacy' was going out of fashion and confrontation was coming in. David Lewis, the NDP member of parliament for York South and later leader of the party, showed how far the trend had gone when he argued in 1970 that Canada should not be 'soft' on the Americans but should 'speak out ... without using weasel words.'[19]

Critics like Lewis recognized that there were two streams to Canadian evaluations of the Americans, one internal and the other external. The internal yardstick was directed against American cultural and economic penetration. It formed a backdrop against which the nationalism of the Trudeau government's internal programs might be measured – and by that standard the Liberals did not rank very high. Caution was the hallmark of Trudeau's domestic programs between 1968 and 1972. The government ran a surplus, foreign investment was not curbed, and the 'just society' that the Liberal party had touted in the 1968 election was left to the free flow of market forces which, admittedly, also produced a rise in living standards for Canadians during this time. Perhaps, after all, it was not a bad way of securing justice, but it was not the spectacular kind of action that would have pleased the government's critics.[20] For them, the medium had truly become the message, and neither in economic policy nor in culture did the government have any desire to shout it out.

The second stream, external evaluation, involved direct diplomatic action. The most prominent target for action was American involvement in the Vietnam War; it was also the least tractable subject for Canadian influence on the U.S. government. Pressure on the Canadian government to object to American policy grew steadily after 1965, but as the Canadian ambassador to Washington observed in the privacy of his diary, 'even when the sun of favour is shining, there are outer limits for a foreigner to exchanges of thought with the Washington higher management. For one thing, the President never listens – or at any rate never listens to foreigners.'[21] As a result, Prime Minister Pearson was trapped in an uncomfortable squeeze between the realities of Canadian relations with, and influence on, the United States and the spirit of the times.

That this was so was heavily influenced by the structure of Canadian-American relations that had grown up since formal government ties were established in the 1920s. Pearson had actually been part of the first Canadian mission to the United States, and one of his American contemporaries boasted that until the mid-1950s he had known every member of the Canadian foreign service. Americans dealing with Canada were frequently surprised by what one U.S. observer called 'the ubiquitous personal communication links [with other Americans] built up over decades by Canadians.'[22]

Pearson had lived and worked in the United States long before he became a diplomat; half the Pearson family had emigrated there. Trudeau studied at Harvard in 1944. Mitchell Sharp had worked under an ex-American, C.D. Howe, and in the 1950s and 1960s constantly dealt with high American officials. Their experience was not unique. Many

Canadian families (and not just English-Canadian families) had their American cousin with whom to compare notes and standards of living – almost always to the detriment of Canada.[23]

Canadians believed that their interests did best under Democratic administrations. Perhaps on bilateral issues that was so. The Pearson government had restored relations with the Americans on defence issues under John F. Kennedy and had gone on under his successor Lyndon Johnson to negotiate the 'automotive vehicles and parts agreement,' universally known as the Autopact, in 1965. The strength of Canadian-American ties was reflected in the negotiation and ratification of such an agreement: support from multinational business, in this case the large automobile companies; from labour, where 'international' (American-headquartered) unions were the norm; from the Washington bureaucracy, which saw the treaty as a first significant step towards freer trade; and from politicians, who perceived no threat to their constituents' interests in such a deal. This was what even David Lewis (who after all had strong links with Canadian labour, including the international unions) agreed was a 'special relationship.'[24] But would it ever be so special again?

Canada's footing was less sure on 'global' issues. There, Canadian-American relations were less special – by 1968 perhaps not special at all except in a negative sense. Those Americans with moderate knowledge of Canada looked apprehensively towards the north.[25] Anti-Americanism north of the border was nothing new, but it was getting increasingly shrill and combining with demands that the government take Canada out of NATO and NORAD. What was known about Trudeau's views on those subjects was not comforting, and the fact that he was known to be reviewing Canadian external policy did not promise well.

Americans examining their northern border warned their countrymen that Canada was not a nation to be 'taken for granted.'[26] That phrase, trite but true, aptly characterized American assumptions that Canadians were so like themselves that they could be understood merely by extrapolation. It was a view that a Maine congressman in 1967 called 'cavalier ... and infuriating,' but it was widely held and frequently expressed to Canadians on the assumption that Canadians would, of course, understand.[27] Too often Canadians felt they did, indeed, understand.

The Canadian policy review had not greatly advanced Canadian policy vis-à-vis the United States. Everyone noticed that there was no booklet that dealt with the United States, and almost no one was impressed by the excuse that the presence of the United States was so pervasive that it needed no separate treatment. As the American scholar Robert Endicott

Osgood put it in testimony to the Standing Committee on External Affairs and National Defence (SCEAND), the Canadian review was too vague and abstract to be useful. The problems it raised might be resolved in a lecture or a seminar, but hardly in real life. Osgood contrasted the Canadian review, unfavourably, with the simultaneous examination of U.S. policy by the incoming Nixon administration. It had been highly specific, and while that was no guarantee of success, it was nevertheless a better platform from which to launch a successful policy.[28] Of course, Canada had not been at the centre of the American review.

The review of American policy, like Trudeau's, took as its starting point the possibility that external commitments might no longer be proportionate to the benefits derived from them. Public disaffection with government policy had reached a far more exaggerated level than in Canada, as mass demonstrations and marches on Washington made manifest. Yet it was not clear whether the bases of popular support for American foreign policy had truly shifted, or whether the Vietnam War by itself was responsible for most of the discontent.[29] If Vietnam was the cause of the prevalent malaise, how could it be excised so as not to unnerve other American allies whose allegiance was still considered valuable to American interests?

President Nixon and his principal foreign-policy adviser, Dr Henry Kissinger of Harvard, eventually produced a strategy, summarized by a perceptive critic – the same Osgood who testified in Ottawa – as 'military retrenchment without political disengagement.'[30] American interests continued to be broadly defined, including the advantages of maintaining worldwide bases and alliances; at the same time, allies including South Vietnam were urged if not compelled to take more responsibility for their own defence. The whole package became known as the Nixon Doctrine.

Such a policy was all the more acceptable because, in 1968–72, it was widely believed that the Soviet military threat to the West was no longer as acute as it had once been. Perception and policy were happily combined – and, it should be noted, neither perception nor policy was fundamentally at variance with the Trudeau government's view of the world.

Nevertheless, what Kissinger and company believed, and what they required from their allies, were two different things. If the Americans thought the allies needed a vision of American steadfastness, they expected the allies to in turn demonstrate some constancy – constancy as interpreted by a highly partisan president and administration. Did Trudeau's Canada fit the bill?

At first glance, perhaps. Trudeau had not troubled to identify himself with the outgoing Democratic administration of Lyndon Johnson. 'We got the idea that Trudeau didn't want anything to do with us,' Johnson's secretary of state remembered. 'The attitude was hell, these guys are on the way out anyway.'[31] When Nixon and the Republicans moved into Washington in January 1969, there was no need for the Canadians to atone for any presumptive Democratic partisanship.

That said, it could not be disguised that Trudeau was a Liberal and that Nixon was not. The Canadian prime minister communed with the ex-Canadian economist and Harvard professor John Kenneth Galbraith, an admitted liberal and no friend to the Republican administration in Washington. Although Canada was seldom reported in the United States, early rumblings were felt in March 1969 when Trudeau was quoted as saying that an American anti-ballistic missile system then under consideration would endanger the peace of the world. Kissinger moved to squelch 'an over-reaction on our part' – presumably some authorized fulmination from the White House.[32] A few days later, as Trudeau's defence policy review moved towards its climax, one of his old Harvard professors approached his erstwhile colleague, Kissinger, to get him an appointment with Nixon so as to discuss 'the drift in Canadian policy toward neutralism.'[33]

Whatever the instinctive White House response to errant Canadian sentiment, negative American opinion of Trudeau was muted or mute. Canadian assessments of Nixon for their part were cautious. Formidable as Nixon might be, he was not likeable. The president was not a gifted communicator, Trudeau was told. He lacked charisma and strained to prove his sincerity. He was not inclined to give of himself, preferring to be insulated behind a praetorian guard of California cronies. He looked at problems from a long-range view and was not given to quick solutions. He was prepared to spend a year on a problem before it began to be settled.[34] He was also, as time would show, mistrustful to a fault, especially of those with connections to his many enemies. Yet he was 'confident and self-assured' on policy matters, especially foreign policy, which he used to compensate for his relatively modest domestic accomplishments. 'A complex man,' Trudeau would say in 1985, 'full of self-doubts ... very strange.' And yet, he added, 'even without Kissinger he would have had a shrewd appraisal of world politics.'[35] Trudeau adopted a professionally dispassionate approach to Nixon, treating him less as a discrete personality than as the embodiment of the American executive branch. He therefore merited 'respect,' and got it, as did the other occupants of the Oval Office, Gerry Ford and Jimmy Carter. Trudeau did draw the line at Ronald Reagan, but that is the subject of another chapter.[36]

On foreign policy, Trudeau learned, it was the national security adviser, Henry Kissinger, who counted. Kissinger dealt with great issues and grand strategy; less important matters could be left to the secretary of state, William Rogers, the titular head of the American government's foreign-policy establishment. Together, Nixon and Kissinger formulated policy on the issues that, they agreed, must concern them. Heading the list, obviously, were East-West diplomacy and Vietnam. Somewhat further down were certain European questions, followed by the rest of the world and non-security matters. Given the limited amount of presidential time available, such economy of effort made eminent sense.

In American diplomatic practice, Canada was bracketed with Western Europe. A 'Europeanist' by the Canadian embassy's definition, Kissinger did not rank Canada very high in the European constellation – perhaps on the level of Belgium.[37] He gave no sign that Canadian views, or Canadian contributions, were essential or even important in his vision of world order. 'He didn't take Canada seriously,' Dick O'Hagan, the embassy's man in charge of press and public relations, recalled. 'I could understand it ... He felt, "I'm a big league guy and I can settle big league problems." '[38] It would not be easy to get, and retain, Kissinger's attention.

The Canadians tried. In 1970 Canada sent down to Washington one of the country's most expert political diplomats, Marcel Cadieux, an experienced international lawyer. He had been undersecretary, and there were those who suspected that he considered himself undersecretary still. Cadieux loaded the files in Ottawa for the next five years with learned and perceptive analyses of events. In terms of the daily conduct of business, however, his efforts were largely wasted, for few in the American capital were interested in what he had to say on the larger questions of politics, and economic affairs, the embassy's bread and butter, rolled on without any need for, or benefit of, high-level political negotiations. It was all the worse because of Kissinger's monopoly over the high-flying, high-policy end of diplomacy.

In such a league, in Kissinger's opinion, Canada had little to offer. When the Canadian ambassador finally got to see Kissinger, according to a witness, he brought with him a thick briefing book. Kissinger raised his eyebrows. 'Well,' he said, 'I hope you didn't come here to talk to me about the sex life of the salmon.'[39] It was only one indication of how

Cadieux found Washington bitterly disappointing; that was especially so when events began to move in a direction that he was not well equipped to handle.[40]

If Cadieux found Kissinger disappointing, Trudeau did not. According to Jules Léger, governor general from 1974 to 1979, Trudeau was 'fasciné par Kissinger – par sa force physique aussi bien que par sa force intellectuelle.' He considered Kissinger's views to be attractive and found the man altogether impressive. Léger added that Trudeau 'est souvent pris par les personnalités politiques qui font montre de vigueur physique.'[41] Kissinger's charm – an attribute not generally stressed by his chroniclers – may also have played a part. 'As soon as he could divine the object of any petitioner,' an American ambassador wrote, 'he would proclaim that object to be his very own, and proceed to discover a great and possibly unanticipated commonality of purpose as well as a deeply shared mutual respect.'[42]

No doubt Kissinger also found Trudeau intriguing, but he did not find him importunate. Trudeau was not prepared to allow Vietnam to determine the pace of Canadian-American relations, nor was he engrossed by American politics or American concerns. Like other thoughtful Canadians, however, he speculated on the implications for the longer term of racial conflict and urban disorders across the border, and the State Department briefed Nixon to discuss these concerns when Trudeau paid his first call on the new president.[43] Unlike Martin or Pearson, he had few personal connections in the United States; his most spectacular American acquaintance of the period was the actress Barbra Streisand, his date on several well-publicized occasions.

Trudeau's fondness for spectacular dates seems to have been a quality Kissinger shared; perhaps it was a symptom of a broader rapport. At any rate, they had no difficulty in agreeing that they were witnessing 'la disparition de la position spéciale que le Canada possédait vis-à-vis Washington.'[44] As far as they were concerned, a special Canadian-American relationship was outside their personal experience. Neither man, in 1969, saw its utility as outweighing its liability – at a time when the Canadian political elite seemed determined to assert Canada's autonomy and distinctiveness as far as the Americans were concerned.

The demise of the special relationship was nevertheless greatly exaggerated. That was because Canadian-American relations transcended what presidents and prime ministers, and their minions, said and did. When American scholars spoke of multifarious contacts between Canadians and Americans they referred to a phenomenon that predated, and dwarfed, the formal diplomatic contacts across the forty-ninth parallel.

The private side of Canadian-American relations largely determined what the public side would discuss. The subject may not have been global, as Kissinger and Nixon defined it, but it was indubitably large. The United States supplied most of the external investment that flowed to Canadian industry ($9 billion in manufacturing in 1968);[45] and supplied, as well, many of the executives who managed the Canadian branch plants of American firms. In terms of its business culture, Canadian executives closely followed American trends and fashions; but the same was true of labour as well, as 'international' (meaning bi-national) unions sought support and representation on both sides of the border.[46] This attracted considerable criticism from those who were concerned that the Canadian government, and Canadians in general, were losing control of their own institutions. Without an autonomous Canadian economic sector, they argued, the government's ability to make decisions, and even to be properly informed of the facts it needed to make decisions, was in question. Proponents of American investment discounted such fears, pointing out that Canadian sovereignty as such was unimpaired, and that the remedy of restricting or closely regulating foreign investment might be worse than the disease in terms of lost opportunities or foregone growth. Thus, one ('nationalist') group stressed the internal perils to Canada of untrammelled foreign investment, and the other (equally 'nationalist') group the external dangers to a vulnerable economy that was obliged to compete in an interdependent world. The Autopact of 1965 demonstrated the interdependence between certain Canadian and American institutions.[47]

The Autopact was based on a number of tenuous assumptions. First, it assumed that the auto industry would continue to be dominated by the 'big three' American automakers, GM, Ford, and Chrysler, with their well-established factories on both sides of the border. Second, it presumed that the problem to be confronted was a Canadian deficit in the auto trade. It was a reasonable enough assumption, given that the imbalance in the Americans' favour in 1965 was U.S. $703 million, and it gave rise to a number of special clauses in the agreement that protected Canadian production. A reduction in the trade imbalance came as no surprise, but when the imbalance actually reversed itself, there was consternation. By 1968, Canada had a $22 million surplus, and by 1972, $527 million. With the Canadian industry powerfully stimulated, was there any longer a need for special protection for Canada? When, Simon Reisman, the Canadian negotiator of the Autopact, lunched with his American counterparts in Washington in 1970 or 1971, one of them remarked, 'you just don't have many friends down here any more.'[48]

Such reflections cast a shadow over strictly bilateral issues, as we shall see (chapter 4), but they were not crucial to overall relations between Trudeau and Nixon.

The first step was to establish communications. Most diplomatic traffic was handled through the Canadian embassy in Washington, since the American embassy in Ottawa, through most of Trudeau's time in office, was in the hands of political appointments.[49] The Canadian envoy in Washington, A.E. (Ed) Ritchie, was an old Washington hand who had served briefly as chargé at the embassy in the 1950s. His strength lay on the economic side of external policy, and he was proficient at catering to his government's economic policy abroad. But as an ambassador his links were with the State Department, and Secretary of State William Rogers and the State Department counted for little in Kissinger's Washington. 'You never kidded yourself,' Ritchie remarked, 'that Rogers was going to change the world.'[50]

When Trudeau visited Washington in March 1969 he adapted to the Washington style. On the sidelines stood Kissinger and Trudeau's own foreign-policy adviser, Ivan Head; to Head fell the duty of briefing the prime minister and preparing his speeches. This was correctly perceived in External Affairs as a reproach, for Trudeau did not like its briefings or its manner of preparing his speeches;[51] but it was not entirely so. Nixon had his own foreign-policy staff, and they expected to deal with their Canadian opposite numbers. It was a situation that Mitchell Sharp accepted with considerable external grace. If that was what Trudeau wanted, he had his reasons which, by definition, were sufficient.

The meeting accomplished little of a concrete nature. Trudeau wanted to hear Nixon's and Kissinger's view of the world, and his officials wanted to establish that the Canadian and American leaders could communicate civilly and coherently when required. Trudeau for his part wanted it established that Head could call Kissinger whenever necessary; and it was done. For the rest the Canadians had few illusions. 'It's great if you're the guest,' Head recollected, 'but you have to remember that for Nixon it's one of three or four appointments in an afternoon.'[52]

Nixon and Trudeau traded platitudes in public and compliments in private. No harsh words were exchanged, thereby masking the fact that, as Kissinger put it, 'it cannot be said that Trudeau and Nixon were ideally suited for one another.' Nixon would later say as much, referring to the Canadian prime minister on at least one later occasion as 'that asshole Trudeau.'[53] As to Trudeau's real opinion of Nixon, we can only speculate.[54]

What was important was that Nixon did not exploit the opportunity, either in March 1969 or subsequently, to lecture Trudeau on the rights and wrongs of Canadian foreign policy; nor did Trudeau read Nixon sermons on the morality of deploying an anti-ballistic missile system, even though that was much desired by Canadian commentators. As Trudeau told the cabinet, Nixon hoped Canada would not withdraw from NATO, but he did indicate 'in strict confidence' that 'he too hoped to bring troops back in time.' Within days of his return from Washington, Trudeau authorized cuts in Canada's forces in Europe; and within months Canada would recognize the Communist government of China. It was a policy that might have affronted the old Nixon; it did not greatly trouble the new.

It did irritate some of Nixon's supporters. Their reaction was conveyed by 'one of the highest officials of the State Department' to a well-connected Canadian journalist. It was that Canada had 'crawled on its belly' before the Peking regime, thereby losing 'the respect of decent Americans' and imperilling transborder relations.[55] It was, perhaps, fortunate that Nixon and Kissinger were contemplating a visit to Mao's China to chat over tea with its rulers. Despite resentment at lower levels, the administration would not use China, or NATO, as a club to beat Trudeau, partly, we must assume, because Canadian policy was not regarded as especially significant, at least in multilateral terms. Capitalizing on this insignificance, Trudeau put a value on inaction: 'We may be excused, I hope, if we fail to take too seriously the suggestion of some of our friends ... that our acts – or our failure to act – this or that way will have profound international consequences or will lead to widespread undesirable results.'

That left bilateral relations as a field of endeavour. Here, Trudeau, primed by Head, was eloquent. Addressing the National Press Club in Washington, he pointed out that Canada depended on foreign trade, especially with the United States, where Canada sold and bought more than any other country in the world. In fact, Trudeau added, Canada bought more than the next four American trading partners (Japan, Britain, Germany, and France) combined. There was, of course, an obvious disparity between the two countries; and in one of his most frequently misquoted phrases, Trudeau tried to illuminate the disparity: 'Living next to you is in some ways like sleeping with an elephant: no matter how friendly and even-tempered the beast, one is affected by every twitch and grunt.'[56] The reporters heard elephants, thought mice, and confused the two, placing a Canadian mouse in bed with an American elephant. And so it stuck in the public memory – an image, an attitude, but no single policy.[57]

The Americans did not really expect there to be any policy. Relations with Canada, to American officials, meant bilateral issues. As one senior Kennedy and Johnson administration official, McGeorge Bundy, later reflected, Canadian-American issues are inclined to be 'both complex and relatively minor so that it would be hard to treat them effectively except at disproportionate length.' Bundy was writing as a historian, but the comment reflects his experience as a White House aide. 'The real wonder,' he added, 'is not that Canadians occasionally get annoyed when Washington fails to pay fair attention to problems that are large in Ottawa, but rather that the Canadian government, more often than not, makes allowances for its large neighbor and goes on to do at least its share in resolving differences.'[58]

Despite frequent contacts between Canada and the United States, at the United Nations or at NATO, there was seldom any urgency to them. On world issues and matters of global policy, positive Canadian opinion counted for little. Negative opinion, however, mattered, though not in quite the way that advocates of open-mouth diplomacy thought. If the Americans believed themselves obstructed or thwarted by Canada, then they might take it out in bilateral policy. And bilateral policy meant maintaining the world's largest trade flow, not to mention the patterns of life and standards of living of millions of Canadians. Those same millions, however, had views and feelings about Vietnam. If for no other reason, Canadian policy had to be carefully gauged.

The Vietnam War continued. In conformity with the Nixon Doctrine, U.S. troop strength in the Southeast Asian nation declined from its peak of 542,000 in January 1969 to 45,600 in July 1972. This occurred in spite of a major North Vietnamese offensive in April 1972, to which the Americans responded by launching an air offensive, by stages extended to cover all of the north except the capital, Hanoi, its harbour, Haiphong, and a strip along the Chinese border.[59] Trudeau kept mum when the bombing started in April, and in May, when it was broadened, he argued that American bombing of North Vietnam could hardly be criticized when the North was maintaining twelve divisions in the South.

The American response halted the North Vietnamese army, but it did not prevent Hanoi from improving its strategic position or from stiffening its terms in the Paris peace talks. Nixon and Kissinger wanted the war wound up by election day, in November, but the day came and went. Nixon won anyway, by a landslide. In the excitement it was not considered significant that the new Congress was more strongly dominated by the Democrats, or that certain Republican tactics during the election had attracted police attention. Nixon got 'Four More Years!'

Simultaneously Trudeau, in the Canadian general election of 30 October 1972, lost his majority and came within a whisker of defeat, emerging with 109 seats in the House of Commons to the Progressive Conservatives' 107. The balance of power, in a House of 264, lay with 31 NDP, 15 Social Credit, and 2 Independent MPs. Neither the NDP nor the Créditistes – all from Quebec – approved of the American war in Vietnam. Nor did public opinion, though by 1972 Canadians found many other grounds for irritation with the United States.[60]

But how to conclude the war? The North Vietnamese appeared, at least to the American administration, to have unreasonably hardened their position in the negotiations. With North Vietnam stiffening its terms, American options appeared to be limited. As Kissinger later wrote, 'The North Vietnamese committed a cardinal error in dealing with Nixon: They cornered him.' Cornered, Nixon lashed out, determined to end the war at the earliest possible date, and to end it by a display of overwhelming military force.[61] Ending the war, of course, meant ending it on terms that preserved some measure of American self-esteem.

The bombing was therefore renewed on 18 December, to last for twelve days. Hanoi and Haiphong, previously exempt, were specifically targeted. The attacks did considerable damage, and presumably played a role in bringing the North Vietnamese back to the table in a more reasonable frame of mind.[62] By concentrating on the mechanisms of peace, the Americans were able to blot out the larger principles at stake; and on 13 January 1973 a draft agreement was ready.

Inside Canada, public attention for the moment focused on the bombing and its aftermath. Charges that the Americans were indulging in terror tactics, in barbarism, were not lacking, not merely from fringe radicals but in calmer political and journalistic circles. Opinion in External Affairs was considerably more varied, ranging from outright sympathy for the Americans to disapproval that such a counter-productive tactic had been chosen.[63] Trudeau was at first reticent, but pressure began to mount for a parliamentary resolution that would tell the Americans just what Canadians thought.

Trudeau and his house leader, Allan MacEachen, could do their sums just as well as the next person. Why offer a hostage to fortune by allowing the NDP to exploit the bombing? Parliament opened on 4 January and the next day the House of Commons approved a government motion condemning the prolongation of hostilities in Southeast Asia.

The American government, or at least that section then in Washington and not at the conference table in Paris, was not pleased. Canadian diplomats explained as best they could that the motion was for domestic political consumption. Nixon was not mollified. The Canadians should know better. The hapless Canadian ambassador, Marcel Cadieux, who was if anything strongly pro-American on Vietnam, was frozen out. Administration personalities boycotted the embassy and passed the word that Canada had joined Sweden and a number of other countries on 'the shit list.'[64] Unofficially, that meant that ranking Americans had to deal with their Canadian counterparts at lunch or at cocktail parties. Their offices remained off limits.[65]

There was only one exception. The United States needed Canada to help cement the peace terms. To supervise the implementation of a truce, there was to be an International Commission of Control and Supervision (ICCS). It would be divided between western and communist nations, the latter being Hungary and Poland and the former Indonesia and Canada.[66]

This was not a surprise. After the departure of Pearson and Martin, the Canadian government worried less about the consequences of the Vietnam War.[67] Canada remained a member of the old International Commission for Security and Control in the states of the former Indochina (it is properly abbreviated as ICSC, but was universally called the ICC at the time) with a mission in Saigon, the South Vietnamese capital. The control commissions – one each for Vietnam, Cambodia, and Laos – were effectively paralysed by 1968, and in 1969 the Canadian government gave serious thought to withdrawing all Canadian personnel from the region.[68]

They decided not to, but Vietnam, and Canada's role on the ICC, continued to be a domestic embarrassment. Revelations in the Pentagon Papers, published in 1971, showed extensive contacts in the 1960s between Canadians and Americans in Vietnam; the opposition inside and outside parliament used the contacts as a club to thwack the government. Canadian officials in Saigon were therefore instructed to have as little as possible to do with the Americans. This was a blow to those on the spot, most of whom sympathized with the South Vietnamese government and its American ally.[69]

A further blow was the collapse in 1972 of the old ICC. The commission members took pleasure in releasing contradictory press releases commenting on one another's conduct. It was an unhappy episode, but a lively memory, as the possibility of another peace commission became more urgent.[70]

Back in Ottawa, the Departments of External Affairs and National

Defence had been discussing how Canada might be built into the settlement in Paris. Canadian officials had few illusions as to the meaning of such a settlement. International supervision of a truce, or a subsequent election, might be part of any agreement. Yet international supervision could well be an optical illusion and, in the worst case, it might prove to be completely unworkable. If Canada pointed this out, or, worse, was forced to withdraw, it could, plausibly if unfairly, be blamed for jeopardizing peace. Sharp did not disagree with this analysis.[71] Fortunately no decision had to be reached. As if by osmosis a consensus evolved that, if called, Canada would serve, but would act without illusions and therefore without hope. Meanwhile, officials and ministers pondered international supervisory mechanisms, apprising the Americans of their conclusions.[72]

Trudeau and Nixon did not raise the matter when they met in December 1971 and April 1972; when press reports reached Ottawa that 'peace was at hand' in Paris, there had been no American pressure on Canadian policy to force Canada into a putative peacekeeping force. That did not matter very much. Canada was willing.[73]

On 26 October 1972 Rogers informed the Canadian government that the Americans wanted Canada to be a member of a new international control commission for Vietnam. The form projected (initially a tripartite commission that required unanimity for decisions) guaranteed failure, at least in Canadian eyes, but that was not the point. It would be an illusion; Canada had been assigned a large part in the masquerade as an American nominee. Canada was assured there was no urgency, since a final settlement might be weeks or even months away. But the Canadian government's political timetable was different from Kissinger's in Paris; an election was at that point only four days away.

An interdepartmental task force was established the same day, 26 October, to consider what would have to be done, and to make recommendations to cabinet.[74] The government meanwhile was publicly coy; Sharp talked of 'speculation.' Privately he balked in discussions with Rogers, resulting in minor changes in the housekeeping aspects of the protocol establishing the future International Commission of Control and Supervision; the Americans were not interested in, and probably could not secure, radical alterations to the draft statute.[75] In self-defence Ottawa developed a scenario in which Canadian participation would be withdrawn should the ICCS not work – a virtual certainty. By the middle of December a provisional term of sixty days was being considered. That in itself demonstrated that Sharp had no choice but to consent to a Canadian role in a peace he knew would be purely formal.

The cabinet, when it considered the matter, reviewed the implications that Canadian consent or refusal would have for bilateral relations with the United States.[76] In its view, and that of most Canadian diplomats, the benefits to be obtained from the scaling down of the war and the end of American involvement far outweighed the obvious deficiencies of the proposed ICCS. While bilateral relations with the United States had most weight, Ottawa was mindful of 'Canada's general position as a member of the international community,' a Pearsonian concept that had survived five years of Trudeau.[77]

By the time the Paris agreement was signed, on 27 January, the policy debate inside the government was over. Canada would join the ICCS for a sixty-day trial period. If the commission worked as desired, the sixty days could be extended. If not, then Canada would exit. When the invitation arrived from Paris, it was promptly accepted.[78]

Orders went out to find 290 suitable Canadians, civilian and military, to go to Saigon. The orders were not universally welcomed. Some of those chosen objected because the job would be futile; others objected because it would disrupt their careers and home life; still others carefully studied the mechanisms of early retirement. Nevertheless, 290 were found, and sent to join their chief in Saigon.

Their chief, Michel Gauvin, was a career foreign-service officer who had joined the department out of the army after the Second World War. He had served in Vietnam on the old ICC (like a third of the External Affairs officers) and subsequently been ambassador to Ethiopia and Greece. He was still ambassador in Athens, and was simply moved to Saigon on secondment, in case his assignment was temporary. Gauvin had a reputation for being tough and forthright, and was by nature an activist. He did not hesitate to send lengthy telegrams detailing the events of the day in Saigon to Ottawa, despite anguished protests from the Vietnam desk; nor was their tone sympathetic to the communist cause, which he had witnessed, and condemned, on his previous tour of duty in Hanoi and Saigon. As far as most Canadians were concerned, these qualities were commendable.[79]

Contrary to the Canadian tradition of 'quiet diplomacy,' Gauvin, on explicit instructions from Ottawa, indulged in 'open-mouth' diplomacy, running press briefings that were always lively and enlisting publicity as one of the tools in performing his job. As a result, he joined the small corps of Canadian diplomats with a perceptible and well-defined public reputation – assisted, it should be observed, by regular confidential briefings of the press at home in Ottawa.[80]

He joined his Indonesian, Polish, and Hungarian colleagues in Saigon on 29 January for the initial meeting of the ICCS. It did not go well. Delays, administrative problems, and disagreement characterized its early meetings, and soon it issued its first, Canadian-drafted, press release.

Its most important immediate task, as far as the Americans were concerned, was to supervise the repatriation of prisoners of war. That task was accomplished in February and March, to the accompaniment of tremendous publicity from the American media. On the surface the commission was demonstrating its effectiveness; in the background, however, there was continuing bickering and division. In the Canadian delegation's view, the Hungarians and the Poles would get away with murder if they were allowed to, but at that stage they would not obstruct if the Indonesians could devise a face-saving compromise.[81]

By early March it was clear that Sharp's sixty-day deadline would have to be extended. Too short a time had elapsed to show whether or not the ICCS would ultimately succeed. While it was paralysed in some of its actions, such as investigating complaints of North Vietnamese violations of the truce, it was doing the job the Americans expected of it by repatriating prisoners. That peace was far from universal, and that ICCS helicopters were regularly fired upon, could be ascribed to the untidiness that must occur at the end of a long war. Thus, Canadian withdrawal on 27 March, the sixtieth day, would seem premature to the Americans, the press, and the public; it was argued that the cabinet should sign on for another temporary term of duty and wait for events. The time that should elapse was left indefinite, but a suggestion of ninety days or three months began to find favour.[82]

For such a publicity-dependent enterprise, it was appropriate that Mitchell Sharp make a prominent, public gesture to show the extent of Canadian concern and the seriousness with which the question was being taken in Ottawa. The minister decided to go to Hanoi and Saigon in person and collect impressions on the spot. Meanwhile he could put off American pressures to stay by referring to his fact-finding voyage.

Sharp arrived in Saigon on 17 March. There, Gauvin gave him no specific recommendations. While the situation was not good, it was too early to think of withdrawal. 'We [were] told,' one of Sharp's entourage said, 'that if Canada pulls out the whole peace-keeping operation will collapse like a pack of cards.'[83] For different reasons, Sharp heard the same song in Hanoi.

Returning to Canada, the minister reported to the House of Commons' Standing Committee on External Affairs and National Defence. There was little positive to be said about the state of peace in Southeast

Asia, he told committee members, but the ICCS was doing some good work and thousands of prisoners of war were being released. Soon, as a result, all American forces in the South would have departed.[84] A week later, on 28 March, Sharp told the House that the government had decided to stay, for another trial period, to last ninety days. The Americans, who had been displaying every sign of extreme anxiety – offering at one stage to have Nixon speak to the leader of the opposition, Robert Stanfield, if that would help Trudeau's decision to stay – must have breathed a profound sigh of relief.[85]

Not everyone agreed, including some diplomats on the spot in Saigon. In their opinion, the commission already stood revealed as a farce, no better than its ICC predecessor; to give it another trial period defied both facts and logic.[86] Unless Canada could threaten to leave on short notice, its representatives would lose a large part of their leverage in 'persuading' their commission colleagues to take their propositions seriously.

Feelings among Canadians in Saigon were exacerbated by the death of Captain Charles Laviolette, along with two Hungarians, an Indonesian, three American crewmen, and two Viet Cong liaison officers, when their helicopter was shot down by communist forces. Gauvin protested strongly, and argued that the shooting was unprovoked because, at that time, he believed Laviolette's helicopter was where it was supposed to be. He added the unpalatable fact that the troops doing the shooting belonged to the North Vietnamese army rather than to some local guerrilla unit. To state that highly probable fact in public was practically to support the South Vietnamese demand that northern forces be withdrawn prior to any elections. The North Vietnamese had reacted predictably.[87] They wanted to renew the war, and, since Laviolette's helicopter had in fact been off course, shooting it down was not, in the conditions then obtaining, an irrational response.[88]

Quarrels over the Laviolette incident consumed much of April. A dispute over the status of an Indonesian-Canadian investigation that showed further serious North Vietnamese infiltration into the south helped take up May, and the Hungarians and Poles refused to give the Indonesian-Canadian report any official countenance. It could barely be said that the commission was functioning at all. Only reports that condemned the South Vietnamese could be accepted by the whole commission, and, by the end of July there were ten.[89]

May was also the month in which the government had again to decide whether to continue the Canadian presence in Vietnam. Pressure from the United States resumed: Canadian withdrawal, diplomats were informed, would be a blow to American hopes for a general peace.

Reminders were not lacking that Canadian-American relations seemed to have improved in recent months and that this happy state was owing to Canadian willingness to serve on the ICCS. An interdepartmental task force was examining, and disagreeing about, Canadian-American economic relations. Kissinger himself phoned Ottawa on 25 May to urge that Canada stay, but by then the government was close to a decision.

A white paper had been prepared outlining Canadian experience on the ICCS, and the cabinet had it under consideration. The paper considered what the American administration wanted, or thought it wanted. Those desires had to be set against a growing belief in American political circles that 'peace with honor' – a phrase beloved of the Nixon administration – had not been achieved and that the diplomatic manoeuvres in Saigon were nothing more than a charade. That development was associated with the deterioration of Nixon's domestic position: the Watergate hearings and consequent scandal were in the offing. Whether a particular Canadian action upset Nixon was of less concern than it might have been a few months earlier.[90]

It was Kissinger rather than Sharp who told the world that Canada proposed to withdraw its delegation to the ICCS, not on 30 June, as originally proposed, but, in response to American urgings, on 31 July. Kissinger added that he knew Canada had its reasons for its decision, and that 'we regret it but understand it.'[91]

With Canada on the way out, the last few months in Saigon should have been relatively tranquil, but tranquillity was not on the roster of Gauvin's favoured qualities. Canada was commission chairman for the month of June, and as chairman Gauvin was prepared to use his position to secure the commission's acceptance of the long-disputed Indonesian-Canadian report documenting North Vietnamese infiltration of the South. When the Poles and Hungarians refused to go along, Gauvin simply adjourned the commission, refusing to hold any meetings until the communist members agreed to treat it as a genuinely deliberative body. When they continued to refuse, Gauvin sent the disputed document on anyway to the moribund joint military commission that was supposed to receive reports from the ICCS. Though both sides presented plausible technical arguments in support of their positions, the real issue, as Douglas Ross has observed, was other: 'A competent ICCS was anathema to the communist side. Investigators might "discover" [North Vietnamese] troops.'[92]

A last flurry was caused by the detention of two Canadian captains by the communists while they were travelling in the back country. They were eventually released after considerable pressure by Gauvin, and a few weeks later they were on their way out of the country, along with the rest of the Canadian ICCS team.

A skeleton mission remained in Saigon for another twenty months. In April 1975, with the North Vietnamese on the outskirts of the city, it was evacuated, its possessions, including an official car, loaded on a Canadian transport aircraft. Its local Vietnamese employees were left behind. Ottawa later explained that this was because the Canadians could not compel the South Vietnamese authorities to let them out.[93]

Canada's service on the ICCS signified two contradictory tendencies in Trudeau's external policy. In acceding to Nixon's and Kissinger's request to join the international commission, the Canadian government apparently accepted that American global commitments were necessarily linked to the development of Canadian-American relations. But attention to the Americans was not the sole reason for Canadian cooperation; had that been so, the Canadian government might have paid more attention to American requests that Canada stay on in Vietnam in the summer of 1973. Perhaps, had the Americans been more forceful in pressing Canada to remain, the Canadian government would have conceded the point. For whatever reason, the American government did not insist. It had, by the summer of 1973, troubles enough of its own as the Watergate scandal deepened.

In terms of its own domestic priorities, the cost to Canada in money and in political disruption was not great. There was little criticism of the government's assumption of responsibility in Vietnam, and less of its decision to depart. With the lack of credibility of the international control commission abundantly established, the Canadian government took its leave and made its point: Canada would act for peace, but not in a charade.

3

The Amiable Beast

It was not an ordinary Sunday night. The three American television networks cleared their programming; across the border, Canadians took note and tuned in. The president of the United States was about to address his citizenry. At eight sharp the presidential eagle crest appeared; just after, there were the familiar jowls and the sound of the slightly quavering voice, carefully modulated to indicate firmness and competence. 'Good evening,' Richard Nixon began. 'I have addressed the nation a number of times over the past two years on the problems of ending a war. Because of the progress we have made toward addressing that goal, this Sunday evening is an appropriate time for me to turn our attention to the challenges of peace.'[1]

That day, 15 August 1971, the challenges were proclaimed formidable, but, as always in Nixon's speeches, surmountable by a people who knew how to respond to challenge. There would be a wage-price freeze to confront inflation; there would be tax credits and concessions to stimulate American industry. There would be more. Nixon had ordered Secretary of the Treasury John Connally to 'suspend temporarily the convertibility of the dollar into gold.' Effective immediately, there would be a 10 per cent surcharge on dutiable imports. All these things were necessary to keep the United States Number One in the world economy and not Number Two, or Three, or Four.[1] Privately, Nixon was more concise: 'We have too long acted as Uncle Sugar and now we've got to be Uncle Sam.'[2]

Around the world, economists and pundits blinked. For some the surprise was past, for Nixon had sent a personal message with news of his forthcoming speech to leaders in Paris, London, Tokyo, Bonn, Mexico, Rome, Madrid, and Ottawa.[3] But knowing Nixon's speech in advance did little to soothe uneasy spirits. Despite ritual assurances to American allies, it was clear that the U.S. government was unilaterally altering the terms of international trade.

In Ottawa the prime minister was unable to receive Nixon's message. He was 'afloat in the Adriatic' on vacation. The minister of finance, Edgar Benson (always called 'Ben Benson') was said to be in Breda, in the Netherlands, sampling wine vintages.[4] Holding the fort – and his head – in Ottawa was the deputy prime minister and minister for external affairs, Mitchell Sharp.

Sharp knew that something was impending. The press was full of reports of unfavourable American trade balances, the American deficit, and the weakness of the U.S. dollar. Canada had just racked up a surplus of $1.15 billion in the auto trade in 1970, so the newspapers told their readers. The Americans were said to be unhappy; perhaps they would ask that the safeguards in the 1965 agreement be modified or abolished.[5]

Perhaps not, or, at any rate, not just yet. With parliament in recess and ministers scattered across the country and around the world, there was no sense of impending crisis. When it came, on a Sunday evening usually devoted to nothing more complex than digestion, responses quickly escalated from concern to consternation, and to panic, but only for some. For Ottawa had a bromide.

In Holland, Benson packed his bags and headed for the airport, teeth clenched around his trademark pipe. Two days of vacation were definitely not enough. The unflappable finance minister had just endured two years of tax reform, which left the tax system more or less where he found it. And now this. As the aircraft cruised westward he might have reflected on the absence of warning, of any hints or nudges from Washington for America's Canadian partners.

There were plenty of intergovernmental committees between Washington and Ottawa. As minister of finance, Benson sat on two, interministerial committees on defence and economics. Defence had not met since 1964, to nobody's great sorrow. The Americans were busy in Vietnam, and the Canadians were not anxious to hear about it. That would give the opposition another stick with which to beat the government on the unpopular jungle war.

The Economics committee had lasted longer – into Benson's own time as finance minister. It might not even be properly moribund, though the Americans showed not the slightest enthusiasm for scheduling a meeting.[6] But economics too was touchy, fraught with nationalist land mines carefully planted by the Liberal party's senior economic statesman, Walter Gordon, whose disapproval of American investment was second only to his distaste for the course of the Trudeau government. In future elections, Gordon's friends suspected, he might even vote NDP, and with him an increasingly nationalistic generation of young Canadian voters.

The nationalists were uneasily aware that their views might not command majority support, either in politics or in the polls. Continentalism, the ideology of absorption and dependence, might have gone too far.[7] In 1970, Americans accounted for $26.1 billion in investment in Canada; Canadians, by contrast, owned only $3.3 billion in the United States.[8] There was already enough American capital in Canada, according to 62 per cent of Canadians (67 per cent in the west, 70 per cent in Ontario, 53 per cent in the Maritimes, and 48 per cent in Quebec).[9] In October 1970, 46 per cent of Canadians polled opted for a 'buy-back' of control of American-owned businesses in Canada, and 32 per cent opposed. Only in the cash-starved Maritimes did opinion favour keeping things as they were.[10]

A Liberal government was inclined to give ear to such talk.[11] Some members of the cabinet were known to favour steps to affirm Canadian control over the economy, in the tradition of the Watkins report of 1968, or the Gordon report of 1958. Early in 1971 talk centred around a 'Canadian Development Corporation,' a project sired by Gordon and modelled on his own firm, Canadian Corporate Management. It would be a crown company – favoured instruments of government policy – and would direct investment towards Canadian enterprise. There was every indication that it would be popular.[12] The CDC stepped onto the national stage in 1971, and the government intervened 'to prevent the sale of a Canadian-owned oil company to foreign interests.'[13]

While the government guided investment into (or away from) Canadian-led businesses, many thought it should also screen new money entering the country from abroad. A parliamentary committee chaired by Ian Wahn (with a Liberal majority) recommended a screening agency in August 1970, and, as the winter of 1970–1 drew on, there were reports that Herb Gray, the minister of national revenue and a prominent nationalist, had commissioned another study of the foreign-investment problem. The Herb Gray Report, as it was called, was much more strident and sceptical of the impact of foreign investment on the Canadian economy than its intellectual ancestors, the Watkins and the Wahn reports. It was submitted to cabinet in May 1971 and sent out again for further study. It would be leaked to the public later in the year.[14]

There was not quite as much new money to go around in the 1970s as there had been. As a Canadian briefing paper put it in June 1969, there had been 'a sharp decline in the deficit on current account, some decline in the inflow of long-term U.S. capital, and the emergence of a large offsetting flow of short-term capital to the U.S.'[15] The Canadians recognized that the Nixon administration was 'preoccupied with United States balance of payments difficulties'; they could hardly help noticing, since the American government had begun to refer to the decline in its trade surplus with Canada 'in public statements.'[16]

The United States, in the early 1970s, faced growing pressure on the dollar. It was not a new problem, but by the summer of 1971 it was acute. The search for a solution fell within the province of John Connally, a former governor of Texas and a Democratic convert to the Republican cause. Connally's political style mimicked that of his political mentor, Lyndon Johnson. To Johnson, the outside world had divided neatly into friends or fiends; the difference with Connally was that the number of fiends had grown exponentially since the 1960s. The fiends, collectively, were responsible for America's balance-of-payments problems, and America could no longer afford to ignore the situation. Canada, exempted from earlier American monetary remedies, was plainly part of the problem in Connally's view: the northern neighbour was just another freeloader at the trough of American generosity.

Connally was not alone in downplaying assurances of Canadian virtue. A growing number of American officials came to believe that Canada was adept at twisting every international rule to its own advantage. Even the Autopact, with its accompanying safeguards guaranteeing investment and production in plants north of the border, was sceptically reviewed. To the officials who sponsored it in 1964–5, it looked like a hopeful avenue that could lead to a broader free-trade area in North America; by 1970–1 it looked like a dead end. In the opinion of some American officials, it was difficult to persuade Canadians to admit that there was even a problem.

As a good Texan, the treasury secretary did not believe in sugar-coating any bad news with the niceties of diplomacy or politeness. 'As time went on,' Kissinger wrote mildly, 'I began to suspect that Connally was sufficiently Texan to relish a good scrap for its own sake.'[17] The first step in a good scrap was to occupy the strongest possible position, and so Connally recommended, and Nixon accepted, a wide range of measures ranging from emergency import surcharges to devices for the promotion of American exports. Included in Connally's list of evils to be remedied was the Autopact; its suspension would be announced on the night of 15 August 1971 while the president emitted an appropriately doom-laden television broadcast to the nation and the world.[18]

Connally's measures were prepared in the strictest secrecy, but in Washington this meant letting a largish number of people in on it. If a measure were to be implemented, it would require implementers, as, for instance, the State Department. State's economic policy makers therefore found themselves called back to work on a hot weekend in August to assist in the necessary preparations for Nixon's speech. One of them, Julius Katz, a deputy assistant secretary for economics, riffled through a pile of draft press releases and came, in due course, to the announcement that the Autopact would be ended. Katz had been a progenitor of the Autopact. Even in 1971 he believed that it was a good thing, in spite of some notable deficiencies. Terminating the Autopact would certainly cause the Canadians pain: 32 per cent of Canada's exports to the United States in 1970 consisted of automotive products (compared to 5 per cent prior to the Autopact).[19] Its cancellation would also be harmful to American interests; the method of its cancellation, unilaterally abrogating a solemn international obligation, would be worse still. Katz took his case to Secretary Rogers, and Rogers took the matter up with Connally. Perhaps because the Autopact and Canada did not bulk very large on most official agendas, permission was received to pull the Autopact announcement from the pile of press releases. To conceal its absence, a massive recopying of documents was required, to the great irritation of Nixon's White House staff.[20]

It was a narrow escape, but when Katz passed the message on to Ottawa, for judicious distribution to his Canadian counterparts, he was not generally believed.[21] The Canadians had more pressing matters to concern them, for, like the rest of the world, the Canadian government was not given much warning of what to expect. The Japanese caught the spirit best when they transliterated the English word, 'shock' into 'shokku.' Ever since, the American actions of August 1971 have been the 'Nixon shokku'; and, for once, the word accurately conveys the feelings of the day.

It was Mitchell Sharp who received notification of what was intended, in a phone call from Washington just prior to Nixon's television broadcast. 'I thought it was part of a dream,' he said later.[22] For one so schooled in the intricacies of Canadian-American relations – Sharp had been in the business for thirty years – it was a shock to find the Americans departing from customary, and approved, practice. There followed a letter from Nixon to Trudeau, inviting the Canadians to Washington to discuss the issues raised in the president's address.

The dominant figure in organizing the Canadian response was inevitably Simon Reisman, the deputy minister of finance. 'The point of the whole thing, Mr. Sharp, is confidence,' he told the acting prime minister, and confidence required that Sharp immediately go to Washington to set the Americans straight on Canada's state of innocence.[23] In public and in private, the Canadians assured themselves that Nixon must mean some other country, and not Canada.[24] It must be that the Americans did not know enough about Canada's position; they must be put right.[25] This argument, Canadians knew, had worked before; as recently as 1964 it had been tried on Johnson's secretary of the treasury, Douglas Dillon, 'an enlightened and liberal man,' and it had worked. Unfortunately, observers agreed, Connally was not Dillon; just possibly he might mean the absurdities he had been uttering.[26]

Connally, as it turned out, did mean them, and had set an hour aside to lecture the Canadians from behind his imposing desk. It would not be Sharp who would perch on the secretary's penitential chair, but Benson, Trade Minister Pepin, and a posse of officials. Their principal adviser would be Reisman. It would be, literally and figuratively, a hot day in Washington.

What followed entered legend. Benson was not one of the stars of the Trudeau cabinet, but rather the accidental beneficiary of his early support of Trudeau for the Liberal leadership. Witnesses remember a rumpled and sweating Benson slumped in a chair listening to Connally, tall and erect, uttering his version of reality; unluckily for the secretary he missed his cue, and briefed the Canadians with a position paper intended for the Japanese. When Paul Volcker, who was assisting him, pointed out the mistake, Connally grumpily turned to the subject at hand. It did not improve his temper that Reisman, who accompanied Benson, interrupted from time to time to point out errors in fact, logic, and economics.[27] The two teams parted on poor terms, though Reisman afterwards denied that he had really stubbed out his cigar on Connally's elegant desk; he had merely let some ashes fall. Subsequent meetings with slightly less senior Americans were no more fruitful: as Reisman stated after a conference on 26 August, 'the Canadian delegation had hoped for far more positive results.'[28] Meanwhile Trudeau, back from Yugoslavia, told Canadians to stay calm: Nixon's measures were a blow, but retaliation would only make matters worse.[29]

The Canadians reported back to an ad hoc crisis team hastily established in an annex to the Lord Elgin hotel, and they conferred in Paris and London with their allies in the G-10 group of finance ministers. (The Group of Ten, or G-10, was a loose association of finance ministers from the major Western industrialized states as well as Japan.) The Americans let it be known that they were interested in an appreciation of the Canadian dollar against their own; in response, the provinces let out yelps of pain.[30] Connally had at least promised he would relent on including Canada in the American measures if the Canadians could present him with an 'iron-clad' proof that they had not sinned. As a Canadian analysis pointed out, nobody then could define what 'iron clad' meant.[31] The real meaning was clear: Canada would not be exempted.

The government's crisis team was confident that it faced a real emergency in which Canada could no longer rely on its 'special relationship' with the United States. Press reports spoke of closing factories and rising unemployment – up 1 per cent in a month.[32] That the special relationship was already doddering politically no one could deny, but that paralysis should creep into its economic limbs was most surprising. The diagnosis was grave. Between 40,000 and 100,000 people would be thrown out of work in Canada, adding between 0.75 and 1 per cent to the unemployment rate. Legislation was prepared to compensate for job losses and to keep affected companies in operation. Benson carefully explained to Connally that grants and subsidies were for jobs, and not for exports to the United States; presumably Connally was to believe that the resulting production would be stockpiled or sent to the Third World.[33]

Complicated negotiations and manoeuvres followed. One American source argues that it was only in the follow-up discussions that Connally really learned to dislike the Canadians. Perhaps that was because the talks were about details, where the Canadians concentrated their expertise and their energy. Discussions focused on defence-production sharing, Canadian uranium exports (the Americans kept them out), and tourist allowances. The Canadian negotiators were prepared to make concessions on tourist allowances – the amount of duty-free goods Canadians could bring back – but with no movement on the other side, they refrained.

On television, Trudeau told the nation that he did not think the Americans 'know much or care much about Canada,' and promised he would do his best to explain matters.[34] Canadian ministers warned American audiences that Canada could not afford to buy American products if it was never allowed to run a surplus on merchandise trade; besides, Canada was still in deficit on current account, to judge by the latest figures from 1970. (As frequently happens in Canadian-American relations, the two sides had different statistics, in this case a difference of $1 billion.)[35] As with the cruise of the *Manhattan* (see chapter 4), American action was stimulating Canadian reaction: incredulity, then disappointment, and finally a determination to go it alone if necessary. The latter feeling was admittedly more prevalent among the pundits, the nationalists, and the left wing, but their opponents were beginning to wonder whether the nationalists had not been half right all along. Economic nationalism had received a fillip.[36]

Trudeau himself told a group of American intellectuals and journalists that he had an aversion to excessive nationalism; as applied to the United States that meant that he was not hostile to American investment. 'The Prime Minister is not an idiot,' explained an embassy official to a White House contact, and was unlikely to believe the 'idiotic' things often said about American investment.[37] An aversion to nationalism certainly did not blind the prime minister to the American kind. He made a pointed reference to the unfairness of the American demands when he asked, rhetorically, 'Are you saying that your economic system is leading you to buy up as much of the world as possible?' That would be the result if Canada and other countries were not allowed through trade to earn American dollars in order 'to pay the interest and dividends we have to pay you each year.'[38]

This seemed a commonplace. In fact, it derived from Ivan Head's reading of the neo-Marxist American economist Paul Sweezy. True to his inspiration, Sweezy refurbished the Leninist idea that imperialism was the last phase of capitalism. It was with that proposition in mind that Trudeau asked the questions he did.[39]

No expedient was spared to mobilize American opinion on Canada's behalf. If Connally was unmoving, then he would have to be bypassed. It was an urgent matter because, according to Peter Dobell, the government learned in November that the Americans were setting up a series of bilateral meetings with their principal trading partners; they had not bothered to set one up with Canada. Nor had it helped that Nixon had gone on record with the gaffe that Japan was the largest trading partner of the United States; though subsequent American statements recognized the facts, they had a soothing and patronizing tone, as if Canada's place in the trading statistics was an accidental anomaly. Those trading statistics, however, were showing less immediate impact from the American surcharges than had been feared. It was for two reasons, then, short-term urgency and longer-term necessity, that Head decided to use his special line to Washington to talk to Kissinger. And, to his relief, 'Mr. Kissinger, apparently surprised that no meeting was being organized with the prime minister, undertook to set one up.'[40]

There were many reasons for Kissinger's willingness to accommodate Head. The two men got on well enough and, though Canada was generally a trouble-free country, it was not insignificant. If Canada was getting upset about Connally's policies, might that not have important consequences in terms of allied support for Kissinger's other policies: détente with the USSR and an opening to China?[41] On the morning of Trudeau's visit, 6 December 1971, Nixon told his staff that it was a 'good time to go bilateral w[ith] Canada, Brazil, Mex[ico]. Could do it this week,' he continued. 'Conn[ally] agrees with this.'[42]

This time Nixon and Trudeau had something of real importance to discuss. Trudeau made it clear that it would not be the surtax. He and the president would tackle larger issues; the rest would be dealt with by a contingent of ministers and officials.[43] There were two meetings: in the Oval Office, among Nixon, Trudeau, Kissinger, and Head; down the hall among senior ministers and officials, including Benson and Pepin from Canada and Connally and commerce secretary Maurice Stans from the United States. The lesser meeting was unsuccessful: one Canadian present described it as 'knee-deep in blood.' When Trudeau and Head returned to their hotel, they met a gloomy group. But Trudeau was grinning.

Everything, it turned out, had depended on the leaders' conference. It lasted two hours, and in preparation Trudeau had himself carefully briefed. From his briefing he distilled a miniature lecture in economics which, with all deference, he served up to Nixon. He passed over Nixon's gaffe on trading figures, supposing that the president had simply been wrongly briefed. Repeating, in effect, what he had already said in public, Trudeau asked if the U.S. government had taken the conscious decision that Canada must never be in surplus with the United States?[44] But that would mean that Canada, in order to finance its deficit, must sell more of itself to the Americans. If so, then the Canadian government must draw its own conclusions and formulate policies that, Trudeau implied, might not be to the Americans' liking. 'He just seized Nixon and backed him into a corner,' a witness recalled. Nicely, one presumes, for Nixon did not take kindly to being cornered.[45]

Then Kissinger took over, while Nixon made demurring noises in Trudeau's general direction. The Canadians must be accommodated, the national security adviser argued. It would not work if Nixon simply issued orders, but it could be done. And, Head concluded, ultimately it was. In any case, he stayed behind with Kissinger to work out what had been said, and more specifically what would be done. Their conversation crowned a successful day.[46]

Dinner followed the economics seminar. There were about twelve men present; to the Canadians' surprise and pleasure, it too was organized like a seminar. Nixon asked the American guests, all with some acquaintance of Canada, to state what they thought of Canadian-American relations.

The effect was evidently inspiriting. Trudeau bubbled when he conveyed to the press the gist of what had been said. Miraculously Nixon announced, 'specifically as regards Canada, we don't want to gobble you up.' Quite the contrary: the United States did not intend to use its trade relations with Canada to accumulate a surplus with which to buy up what remained of the country. In one of his lesser inspirations, Trudeau asserted that 'This to me was a fantastically new statement in the mouth of the President of the United States, and it was said with utmost simplicity and not at all in a grudging way.'[47]

It did not take long for the press and the opposition to make sport of Trudeau's remarks. His trip to Washington had produced the assurance that the American government recognized Canada as an independent country. More impressive were the private pledges that Head and Trudeau took away with them. Specifically, Canada would not be 'penalized in any future settlement'; its exchange-rate practices (Canada had gone to a floating dollar in 1970) would not be challenged; and the emergency surcharges were about to be lifted in any case.

Why did Kissinger give those assurances? In his memoirs he claimed that he and Nixon had concluded that Connally's tough measures had run out of steam. Connally had attracted people's attention, as intended. Some benefit had accrued, though less than expected. To keep on with the treasury secretary's policies would be counterproductive and damaging to the United States' interest as the leader of the Western alliance. Global politics demanded that Nixon and Kissinger negotiate a way out of the impasse.[48] When, two weeks later, the Group of Ten met at the Smithsonian Institution in Washington, only Canada was not required to repeg its currency to the American dollar. That exemption had been arranged, carefully and discreetly; and it was, quite definitely, an exemption.[49] It might be said that the 'special relationship' was not quite dead, merely undergoing analysis in Dr Kissinger's global clinic.

Ottawa was chosen as the venue for the next meeting, mainly because Nixon had not yet officially visited Canada. He repeatedly put off the occasion, in July 1969, in January 1970, and again in 1971.[50] He came in April 1972, election year in both Canada and the United States. Ottawa had not been treated to a full-scale presidential visit for some time, and Canadians had forgotten how much was at stake when the leader of the free world touched foreign territory. There were advance men and secret-service agents. There were communications specialists who could patch the president in to the American command in Saigon or to his negotiators at the peace conference in Paris. There were his secretary of state and his national security adviser, as well as his efficient chief of staff, Bob Haldeman. Knowing that the advance team would visit their embassy, American diplomats in Ottawa hastily took regulation photographs of their president out of bottom drawers and hung them in prominent places.[51]

Preparations in Ottawa included a thorough review of Canadian policies that the guests might wish to discuss. Similarities with U.S. policies were identified and appropriately emphasized. The government's third option, then in process of formulation, was found to be similar to the Nixon Doctrine, which called for a more equal burden-sharing among America's allies. It was true that Canada's policy called for 'important but limited changes in some dimensions of our relationship with the United States,' but there would continue to be 'extensive interdependence.' As Canada had reassessed its commitments abroad during the foreign-policy review, so was the United States reviewing promises it had made in a previous generation. Canada was seeking to reduce its vulnerability to American actions, but in a context of overall co-operation.[52]

Nixon impressed his hosts and his diplomats. His speaking style was flawless, his mastery of his brief apparently complete. 'I've seldom seen anyone hold the audience in the palm of his hand like Nixon did in that speech in Ottawa,' said one American eyewitness. 'It wasn't just platitudes. It was remarkable.'[53] Nixon's speech to the Canadian parliament on 14 April specifically repudiated most of the platitudes that had encrusted orations on Canadian-American relations over the previous fifty years. Taking his theme from his discussions with Trudeau the previous December, Nixon told his audience that it was time 'to move beyond the sentimental rhetoric of the past. It is time for us to recognize that we have very separate identities; that we have significant differences; and that nobody's interests are furthered when these realities are obscured ... 'What we seek,' Nixon added later in his speech, 'is a policy which enables us to share international responsibilities in a spirit of international partnership.' It was, in other words, an application of the Nixon Doctrine that sought to offload some of America's too-heavy responsibilities on the allies. In exchange, the allies were offered a less censorious American scrutiny of their policies and foreign pursuits.

There were no surprises in Nixon's speech as far as Trudeau was concerned. He had read and approved most of it, according to Canadian sources. Nixon's own records show that the president gave close thought to the speech, and carefully guided its development. If there was direct Canadian input it was very well hidden.[54] The audience, especially those who took Canadian economic nationalism at face value, was impressed.

It was a public success, one that could not have been hoped for or predicted. In private, Canadian opinions were more reserved, perhaps because the Canadians were unimpressed by the behaviour of Nixon's entourage, especially Haldeman, who was almost frantically possessive of his master's time.[55] Only later did the Canadians discover why. While Nixon was in Ottawa it had been necessary to take further decisions about his bombing program in Cambodia, and the necessary orders were almost certainly issued from his travelling White House in Ottawa.[56]

Fortunately for the tranquillity of the visit, these circumstances were not known. For Vietnam continued to be an important, if slightly subterranean, issue, a touchstone of the acceptability of American policy and leadership. As long as the war continued, the fair words of Nixon's speech would fall on fallow ground as far as a large section of Canadian opinion was concerned.

The turmoil of the Watergate scandal, which was almost continuous from the spring of 1973 until Nixon's resignation as president in August 1974, precluded much high-level diplomacy in the years that followed. That was just as well, since Trudeau had troubles of his own, beginning with his near-defeat in the federal election of October 1972 and continuing through the perils of a minority government. These had their impact on the conduct of foreign policy. Because Trudeau was dependent on the social democratic and nationalist New Democratic Party for his parliamentary majority, his natural tendencies towards intervention in the management of the economy were enlarged. A Foreign Investment Review Agency (FIRA) was established in 1973. Nationalist tendencies were especially pronounced in the energy sphere.

The surge of nationalist opinion in Canada continued to influence the Trudeau government even after it recovered its parliamentary majority in the federal elections of July 1974. Canadian concerns could be cultural ('Too much influenced by American TV, say 59%') or economic ('Risk lower living standards but buy back Canada – 58%').[57] The government responded. On culture, it enacted a long-buried proposal from a 1962 royal commission to eliminate the tax deductibility of Canadian advertising in American magazines. The Canadian editions of *Time* and *Reader's Digest* were most affected. While the *Digest* made its own compromise and survived, *Time* refused and its Canadian edition perished in March 1976.

Television advertising was different. There was no question of 'Canadian editions' of American television programs, and Canadians certainly would not stand for any interruption in the flow of their favourite American shows. Nor did they care who put on the advertising that paid for the U.S. programs they were watching. Through the Canadian Radio and Television Commission, the government permitted the replacement of, for example, CBS commercials with their counterparts from the Global Television Network. 'Sixty Minutes' therefore arrived in Toronto on Sunday evenings in its simultaneous Global reproduction, with the relevant Canadian commercials attached. The U.S. border stations' advertising hinterland was proportionately reduced, along with their revenues.[58] The 'border broadcasting issue' was born, and it enjoyed a lusty and lengthy life thereafter as a regular item on Canadian-American agendas.

Trivial in itself, the border broadcasting issue had a certain nuisance potential. Border-city congressmen could be counted on to take an interest as part of their own media relations at home. Complaints, legal and political, were entered, and successive U.S. administrations could count on pressure from a vocal interest group with a particular claim. As John Holmes observed, 'Their politics are their priority'; he might have said the same, on this issue, of Canada.[59] Canadian national priorities, in this case, trespassed on the particular or local interest of American business, which retaliated by elevating its grievance to a national forum where it collided with other issues that the Canadian government valued more highly. Yet because of the symbolic importance of cultural autonomy, it was out of the question for Canada to negotiate a settlement.

Indeed, the demise of the special relationship might not have mattered very much for the bulk of Canada's relations with the United States. As the Canadian foreign-affairs specialist Peyton Lyon noted to a Canadian Senate committee, ' "Special" in this sense means easy, informal, extensive, responsive and in short friendly,' and on many if not most levels the relationship continued to be 'special,' bolstered by the fact that the peoples of both countries regarded one another as 'our best friend.'[60]

Nevertheless, the purported death of the special relationship on the level of Nixon and Trudeau did perturb officials who sought a political basis for Canada's relations with the U.S. government. There were obvious differences in the political actions of the two countries, with the Americans increasingly convulsed with worries over demonstrations, riots, and the intractable question of race. Visitors to Washington got a practical illustration as they passed areas of the American capital burned out in the riots that followed Martin Luther King's assassination in 1968. The Canadian embassy worried over these signs of instability in the

United States, while recognizing that the majority of Americans continued placid in the face of radical demonstrations. But could Nixon, lacking any ability to inspire his people, manage to pull Americans together?[61]

The collapse in Vietnam occurred nine months after the political demise of Richard Nixon, and well into the third term of the Trudeau government. As an issue in Canadian politics, Vietnam was defunct. The coincidence of agitation on the subject with Nixon's presidency leads to a general consideration of the management of Canadian-American relations in a period when the United States was a negative symbol in Canadian politics, and when its president was possibly the most unloved, and perhaps the least respected, American leader in Canadian history. Even when Nixon was on the verge of resigning, in the summer of 1974, Canadian diplomats worried whether he might not attempt a 'mad-dog' act to recoup his political standing by exploiting some international emergency that he had himself created.

It was a contradictory situation, because Nixon was also among the most administratively competent, and possibly among the most politically daring, American presidents in the last forty years. At the beginning of his term, Canada was estranged from the United States, in spirit if not in letters of protest, on a variety of foreign-policy issues: East-West divisions, the place of China in the world community, as well as a host of bilateral issues ranging from investment to the Autopact.

The Nixon administration dealt with these problems on two levels. Nixon and Kissinger managed the grand picture,[62] leaving the housekeeping details, including economics, to others. Kissinger once quipped that economic policy was the paradise of the second-rate; it was more important to compose grand strategy by dealing with Russia and China than it was to draft tariffs and regulate gas flows. His view was altered in office, despite the success that attended the openings to the East and the Far East.[63] The Americans were on the way to recognizing China, instead of Taiwan; they ended the Vietnam War, and in a manner that had to be accepted as generally desirable by Canada; and confrontation with the USSR was replaced by détente. When these matters were discussed with Canada, there is every reason to accept that they were pleasing to Canadian ears.

On bilateral issues, largely economic, the record is less consistent. U.S. administration policy was more likely to be influenced by domestic opportunism. Canada was important to the U.S. economy, but few at the political level of government recognized how important. In the early 1970s, Canada accounted for almost half of American foreign investment; it was the largest source of American imports, including oil, minerals, and forest products; and it was the largest market for American exports. Informed American observers considered that their country had practically formed an integrated economy with Canada, with massive interdependence as the result.[64]

After-dinner speakers of the period, including politicians and bureaucrats, made much of the ending of the special relationship. Yet, the occasion most often cited, the 'shokku' of 1971, also demonstrated that many if not most of the essential components of that relationship were still alive. That Nixon did not love Trudeau is clear,[65] yet he always behaved rationally towards Canada.

More, inevitably, remained to be done. Some Americans predicted that the combination of Canadian nationalism and a host of unsolved bilateral issues would mean trouble down the road. Some major effort on the automobile agreement, oil and gas, defence procurement, environmental questions, and the security of American investment was required. It would not be easy, since Canadians had a pronounced reputation as difficult and tenacious where their economic interests were concerned; but if the existing situation were not dealt with soon, it would surely get worse.[66]

Events were in train that would alter accepted practice. Before they had run their course, Canadian-American relations, and the balance of power in the bureaucracy, would shift, making External Affairs' comfortable superiority, and even its autonomy, things of the past. These events centred on energy.

4

Freezing in the Dark

Citizens of a northern country can ill afford to disregard fuel. Nevertheless, Canada's history, punctuated as it is with energy shortages and crises, does not display any continuous concern on the subject. In the mid-1970s, however, a variety of circumstances concentrated Canadian minds on fuel, but the changes that were afoot were far broader than simply a perceived shortage of energy.

The world Trudeau had inherited in 1968 was changing its outline by the middle years of the next decade. The Soviet Union was expanding its military, though at a cost. There was war in the Middle East, and the subsequent emergence of an oil suppliers' cartel. The United States government was weak in the aftermath of Watergate and Vietnam. Henry Kissinger became secretary of state, Richard Nixon departed, and Gerald Ford became accidental president.

Pierre Trudeau meanwhile won a third term in July 1974, demolishing the opposition parties on the way to his second majority government. Shortly afterwards, Mitchell Sharp was out as external affairs minister, though still in the cabinet,* while Herb Gray was out altogether. Paul Martin, the last holdover from the governments of the 1940s and 1950s, retired from the Senate to become high commissioner in London. Jean Marchand and Gérard Pelletier were in political decline, though not entirely eclipsed. Gordon Robertson, clerk of the Privy Council, moved off in 1975 to become the government's adviser on the constitution.

Not that the faces that replaced them were altogether new. Allan J. MacEachen, whose parliamentary career stretched back to 1953, became

---

* Sharp left the cabinet in 1976 and was later appointed northern pipelines commissioner.

external affairs minister. His standing in the government would hence-forth be second only to Trudeau's; some commentators argued, however, that it was easier to stand out in *this* government.[1] In his other significant appointment, Trudeau made thirty-seven-year-old Michael Pitfield clerk of the Privy Council – a controversial appointment among the greying mandarinate in Ottawa.[2] They interpreted Pitfield's appointment as a threat to the old system of autonomous departments, and they were not wrong.

The prime minister had decided to bring order and system to govern-ment. Problems were to be examined thoroughly before solutions could be devised. It was the age of the task force, but also a period when political considerations weighed more heavily than they once had done.

Some things went unchanged for the moment. Ivan Head held on in Trudeau's office, until pressure from MacEachen forced him out. His job remained communication with Trudeau's counterparts abroad, and with his own: Brent Scowcroft, Kissinger's successor as national security adviser, for example. 'We were able to communicate heads of govern-ment views back and forth,' Scowcroft recalled, 'with no bureaucratic interference at all.'[3]

To judge from the evidence, the subject most frequently disputed was energy. It was a topic little understood, but until 1972 there was no obvious need, since it was usually wrapped in a cocoon of statistics of a more or less cheerful kind. They confirmed that in some broad sense everything was as it should be. Though the government dealt with energy, it handled it at arm's length through specialized agencies. Even the appointment of a minister of energy, mines and resources (a depart-ment cobbled out of several older offices) in 1968 did little to change this state of affairs. What, after all, was the need if things were going well?

Oil and gas were one area where Canada was obviously flourishing. From practically nothing in 1947, Canadian production had soared, thanks to the abundant hydrocarbons under the western plains. The oil and gas lay mainly in Alberta, which licensed its export to the rest of Canada and the United States; and that export was encouraged by the federal government. In the 1950s Ottawa had promoted oil and gas pipelines from Alberta to Ontario; one of them, on government insis-tence, was built entirely inside Canada – a gesture that illustrated the predominance of politics over economics and, incidentally, the existence of a lingering distrust of the United States.[4] Economic security demanded political control; political control expressed physical possession.

Political control was defined in the National Oil Policy of 1961 which, in the interest of Alberta's ongoing prosperity, required that Canadians west of a line just outside Ottawa (the Borden line) fuel themselves with the domestic product, at a premium of between 25 and 35 cents per barrel (on a price of roughly $2.70 per barrel). Ontario grumbled, but it paid.[5] The Atlantic provinces and Quebec got cheaper petroleum; the Venezuelans, who supplied the oil, griped that they had the worst of the deal.[6]

To advise and regulate the international as well as domestic trans-boundary flows, there was a National Energy Board (NEB); its American equivalent was the Federal Power Commission (FPC). In that relationship, Canada responded in a natural way to American demand, exporting, or hoping to export, large quantities of natural gas. That was possible because both sides considered themselves, and treated each other, as reliable partners.

Canadian oil and gas profited the Canadian balance of payments, pre-empting imports and serving as a valuable export. The Americans, with their own very large oil and gas industry, responded variably. The main variable was called 'national security.'[7] National security meant a rich and functioning American oil and gas industry, instead of unreliable imported oil. (There was some embarrassment over cheaper Canadian oil and gas in the Maritime provinces, over the border from New England.)[8] American multinationals dominated the international oil business, con-tributing lavishly to the success of statesmen from Texas, Louisiana, and other petroleum-producing states.[9]

The same multinationals ran the oil business in Canada. Every year they told the public, and Ottawa, how much more oil there was than the year before, since discoveries consistently outran production.[10] The NEB, which relied on their data, was pleased. The system was obviously work-ing, and so was the NEB and its export-oriented policies.[11] There was grumbling on the left that Canadian resources ought not to be confided to foreigners to run and to profit from, but most people accepted the situation.

The cabinet took practically no interest in the NEB's activities; as long as there was 'an exportable surplus' of Canadian oil and gas, the NEB perfectly fulfilled its function by exporting. According to one of Tru-deau's ministers, Don Jamieson, the cabinet felt itself at a disadvantage with the NEB. It had the ultimate authority to overrule its expert regula-tors, but could not alter their published reports in any way. Jamieson felt the board was 'contemptuous' of ministers who questioned its judgment, which, in the minister's view, took on 'some of the colourations of [the] industry' they regulated.[12]

The government would have had difficulty making up its mind in terms of competing pressures at opposite ends of the country. The west wanted to export its oil and gas and opposed restrictions. The east wanted its cheap Venezuelan crude. The east included Quebec, the government's political mainstay.[13] Higher prices might undermine Quebeckers' appreciation of the economic benefits of remaining within Canada. The existing two-price system was just the ticket. Let the surplus continue to be exported, especially since there was a surplus.[14]

There were some disturbing signs to the contrary. In 1956, exploratory drilling peaked in the United States; four years later, the ratio of reserves to production also peaked. After 1960, more oil was produced than found in the United States.[15] The 'national security' oil quotas had ensured that American oil would be depleted before anyone else's.

The solution, according to Canadian spokesmen, lay north of the border. Through the 1960s, missions to Washington sang the same cheerful song: buy Canadian and buy security. When Trudeau met Nixon in March 1969, the two men comfortably discussed the possibility of a continental energy policy. The pressure for such a policy, however, was on Trudeau's side; the reluctance, if not resistance, was on Nixon's. If Trudeau was offering a solution to a problem, Nixon had first to be convinced that there was one.

Some Americans took the matter more seriously. The figures surely did not lie; because they did not lie, it would soon be necessary to supplement oil production from the 'lower forty-eight' by a bonanza from the north – the far north, in fact: the American Arctic.

When the Northwest Passage was finally found in the 1850s, it was also discovered that it was easier to walk across it than to sail through it: for most of the time, ice made it impassable. A few ships did sail along the passage in the twentieth century, but they demonstrated that it took years, not months, to traverse. Yet the passage was there, and, in theory, it was similar to other straits around the world that connected one ocean with another. This logic also connected the Northwest Passage to international politics.

So matters stood until the late 1960s. No other country challenged Canada's right to exercise sovereignty over its own Arctic land, but there was considerable debate over Arctic waters, whether in their solid or liquid form. The Americans were interested in those waters that connected Alaska with the Atlantic because, with the discovery of oil on Alaska's north slope, it occurred to them that there might be a commercial use for the Northwest Passage. To prove it, a specially reinforced oil tanker, the ss *Manhattan,* was dispatched across the Canadian Arctic in September 1969.[16]

The Humble Oil Company's ship *Manhattan* set a number of records. It was the largest ship ever to go through the passage. It took the shortest time, fifteen days, going from east to west. It also had to be assisted by Canadian icebreakers. Finally, for a tanker, it attracted a record amount of attention, much of it centred on the implications for Canadian sovereignty.[17] Another consideration was what might happen if the ice crushed a fully loaded tanker in the Arctic archipelago. Environmentalists were alive to the disastrous consequences of such an oil spill both for the ecology and for the fragile economy of the native population in the region; a disaster in the English Channel in 1967 had shown what might happen. That disaster was repeated, on a lesser scale, when the tanker *Arrow* ran aground in Chedabucto Bay, Nova Scotia, in 1970.[18]

For the time being the Canadian government declined to speculate on what it might do. It knew well enough that the American government considered all important straits to be international waters, where the u.s. navy would sail without requiring permission from coastal states. Canada by itself was not the problem; rather, it was the precedent Canada would set.[19] But were not the Americans themselves setting a precedent with the voyage of the *Manhattan?* And, having sailed once, would it not sail again? As astute observers pointed out, Canadian nationalist nerves were tetchy. Canadians felt their resources were on the verge of another American 'steal,' and the government must step in.[20] These doubts were widely shared. Frequently repeated, they helped define a new attitude in Canadian public opinion, against pollution and for national action. The voyage of the *Manhattan* helped to bring about the very reaction the American government least wanted: a disposition to assert some form of Canadian jurisdiction over the frozen seas of the Arctic.[21]

Canada had already been diverging from what the Americans considered acceptable practice in the law of the sea.[22] In the spring of 1970 it diverged further, after a stiff debate among ministers. External Affairs' Legal Division managed the issue and made the necessary presentation to cabinet. There it ran into difficulties, but these were not confined to the cabinet level, as international lawyers elsewhere in the civil service took up the issue and worried over it, advising their ministers on what was right and wrong in Canada's proposed approach to the law of the sea.

After hinting for several months that it would decide that the waters of the Arctic were in an obvious way 'special,' and that their icebound solidity demanded different treatment, the government finally introduced an Arctic Waters Pollution Prevention bill on 8 April 1970. The prevention of pollution in the Arctic, the government asserted, required Canadian control over all commercial shipping in the north, control that would be enforced by fines and other penalties against polluters. In case there was any doubt as to the international law on this matter, Canada declined to accept the adjudication of the International Court of Justice.[23]

The Americans were annoyed – some said very annoyed. Nixon is reported to have refused to speak to Trudeau when the Canadian prime minister phoned to announce his government's policy.[24] Some Canadian officials, and Senator Paul Martin, a firm supporter of international jurisdiction, bemoaned what had been done; but they did their complaining in private.

The Americans had not quite given up. They attempted to put together an international conference to establish a multilateral Arctic regime that would pre-empt strictly national jurisdiction. The Canadians responded with delay, and by rounding up support from other polar states. By the summer of 1970 they had Sweden, Norway, and Iceland on side and also – after a June visit by Ivan Head – the Soviet Union, the country with the longest Arctic seacoast. Italy told the Americans that if they held a conference without Canada, it could only be viewed as a hostile act towards the Canadians; Italy would not support such action.[25]

The *Manhattan* sailed through the Northwest Passage again, but only after its owners agreed to Canadian conditions on safety and responsibility for pollution. That was the end of the matter: a technical triumph, the *Manhattan*'s voyages were economic nonsense.[26]

The economic failure of the *Manhattan* left the field open to an alternative form of energy transport: pipelines. The United States still needed Alaskan natural gas, if the price was right. But after that, what about Canada? The same geological forces that shaped Alaska persisted on the other side of the Canadian-American border. If the presumed wealth of the Canadian north could be linked to an American pipeline, could not both countries benefit? Canadian studies of a possible northern pipeline got underway in 1968, not long after Alaskan oil was discovered.[27] If the connection from the Arctic to the lower forty-eight ran through Canada, Canadians stood to benefit not only from the opening of their own oil and gas fields, but from the lucrative spin-offs from pipeline construction. The logic of cooperation was very strong – to Canadians.

But it was not necessarily so in Washington. There, a cabinet task force, called the Shultz Committee after its chairman, Labor Secretary George Shultz, recommended a comprehensive energy deal with Canada but pointed out that eastern Canada's dependence on offshore supply was a window of vulnerability. Existing American oil quotas on Canada should remain until the Canadians themselves took steps to safeguard supplies to their eastern provinces.[28]

Nixon did not agree. Instead of instituting talks looking to a continental energy policy, he moved in the opposite direction. He announced that the existing system of quotas would be extended, pending further studies.[29] Shultz, however, would not be part of those studies; the strongest advocate of a continental energy policy was the only one of the cabinet task force who was not asked to carry on his work.[30]

Energy was the domain of the Canadian Department of Energy, Mines and Resources (always abbreviated to EM&R). Even its name at the time seemed somewhat faddish; it was like having a department of water or trees. Energy, after all, was something one took for granted, except as an export commodity. It was precisely as a potential export that the minister of EM&R, Joe Greene, understood it. It was his job to sell Canadian energy, whether oil, gas, or uranium, at the best possible price. Greene, an Ottawa Valley lawyer, prized his oratorical ability, his folksy manner, and his supposed resemblance to Abraham Lincoln. Though known as a mild nationalist, he well understood that nationalism would get him into trouble. That was demonstrated by the sulphurous reaction the Alberta oil patch gave to an early speech Greene made in Denver; thereafter his fires were banked, if not altogether quenched.[31] His job was to sell oil and gas.[32]

A continental energy policy? 'Extremely interesting,' Greene opined in December 1969, after hearing the first American proposals.[33] The NEB forecast 'a five-fold increase in Canada's oil production by 1990 and' – good news – 'a long-term shortage in the United States.' Even the discovery of vast quantities of oil on the north slope of Alaska could not compensate, in the long run. Admittedly, short-term prospects were uncertain.[34] The best way to improve those prospects was to link American demand for natural gas with the Canadian desire to supply oil, or so Greene proposed in May 1970.[35] The American government continued to believe, at the highest level, that it retained a margin for error – a margin that could be expressed in terms of reserves and time; it continued to dawdle.[36]

Negotiators worked steadily through 1970 and 1971 to produce an agreement, with the undersecretary of state for external affairs, Edgar Ritchie, heading the Canadian team. (Among the Canadians power was shifting from the NEB to EM&R, with the appointment of an active deputy minister, Jack Austin, to the energy department.)[37] What the Americans sought was what the White House termed 'a common oil policy ... connecting current and future Canadian reserves to our market.'[38] The Canadians resisted what the Americans described as 'adequate national security precautions,' explaining that complicated 'trade-offs between Eastern and Western Canada' made the proposal difficult to manage or even to analyse.[39]

But the Canadians wanted too many things from the United States to shy away completely. The principal desideratum was the location of a pipeline to carry Alaskan natural gas. It should, the Canadians asserted, run through Canada. According to Austin, 'the Canadian alternative ... would go a long way toward making production of oil from the Athabasca Tar Sands economical ... an almost limitless supply of oil. In addition ... it would stimulate considerable exploration in northern Canada.' All this should be highly desirable from the standpoint of national security.[40]

In the meantime, the Canadians made do with remarkably generous American oil-import quotas which had been put in place in 1969. With oil under quota, oil shortages appeared and prices rose. American government policy responded inappropriately, lunging towards price controls whose effect was to keep higher-priced supplies off the market. The Canadian government for its part continued to resist an oil pact with the Americans.

The Middle East, where the United States was Israel's firmest supporter, now entered the picture. Israel occupied large Arab territories. Arab states, even distant ones such as Kuwait, pondered the situation, and what they could do to reverse it. Contemplating their assets, they discovered oil. Arab oil abundance was linked with American oil shortage. To this a third ingredient was added: political confidence among Arab states that the U.S. government would not intervene to protect the interests of the 'Big Seven' oil companies:[41] the price of oil rose, and the multinationals could not prevent it. Unfortunately for the multinationals, most Americans and Canadians continued to believe that the big oil companies controlled both market and price.[42]

When Trudeau and Nixon met again, in April 1972, energy as such was relegated to the background,[43] but the Alaska pipeline was not omitted. The month before, the U.S. Department of the Interior had released an environmental impact statement, 3500 pages long, for such a pipeline (called Alyeska). Responses were invited and, despite the short time allowed, some were received. Donald Macdonald, Greene's successor as minister of EM&R, wrote from Ottawa, pointing out the impending construction of a Mackenzie valley highway and urging that the oil pipeline be directed through Canada. He offered security of supply and, pending construction, 'extra Canadian crude.'[44]

The U.S. government did not agree. There would be a pipeline across Alaska to the sea, and then tankers to American Pacific ports.[45] It cannot be said that Nixon's decision surprised Canadians; Trudeau was briefed in December 1971 that the U.S. government was 'committed to the construction of the Alyeska line.'[46]

Washington's decision did not please all Americans. The American mid-west, for example, could not see how it would be advantaged by consigning more fuel to the energy-rich west coast. Hoping to rescue the situation, Donald Macdonald now proposed a creative compromise. It contemplated merging the American project with a Canadian pipeline; the availability of American funds would be a godsend, if not a necessity, to a Canadian pipeline that would bring Arctic oil south from the Beaufort Sea to market. Indeed, the Canadian government was in the process of spending $43 million to see what could be done.[47] The Nixon administration, however, was not impressed.

Nevertheless, it continued its contradictory policy of importing all the Canadian oil it could absorb. Demand rose throughout 1972 and, at the end of the year, the Interprovincial Pipeline had reached capacity. If, after January 1973, it met American demand, it would not have enough oil left to service its Canadian customers.[48]

A hasty set of ad hoc, voluntary controls was put in place for February; it ensured Canadian supply only, as an NEB official put it, 'by the skin of our teeth.' Next, on 15 February 1973, the NEB assumed the power to license oil exports. These powers met the existing crisis, but they might also be serviceable for a doubtful future. Canadian reserves, an NEB study showed, were not rising; it followed that the exportable surplus must fall, at least until various forms of miracle products or technologies came on stream – tar sands or Arctic petroleum.[49]

That summer, gasoline shortages developed in the United States. Controls on Canadian gas imports followed in June. International oil prices were rising, and the rises were posted at Canadian as well as American gas pumps. Trudeau's minority government (which had inflation to worry about) contemplated the problem with an active, interventionist glint in its eye.[50] Besides political pressures, especially from the left,[51] the strongest advocates of a national oil company were within the federal bureaucracy and cabinet.[52]

Trudeau produced new policies. In September he announced the oil pipeline to Montreal. There would be a voluntary freeze on petroleum prices and a 'control mechanism' to break the lock step between Canadian petroleum prices and those in the United States.[53]

The real blow fell in October 1973. Israel and its Arab neighbours were at war, and the U.S. government announced it would resupply the embattled Israelis. The Arabs responded by invoking the oil weapon, cutting off supplies to 'enemy' states, principally the United States, and cutting production, while guaranteeing supplies to 'friendly' countries whose actions had not displeased them. Simultaneously, the governments of oil-producing states – united in a cartel whose name, OPEC, the Organization of Petroleum Exporting Countries, would soon become a household word – drastically raised the price of oil. A crisis had been widely predicted; when it occurred, it affected both Canada and the United States. Though endless discussions had concentrated on just such a contingency, no one had agreed on what to do.

The Canadian government had resisted American pressure to build storage capacity in the Maritime provinces, even as part of a deal to remove the irritation of American quotas.[54] Now it did not know where it stood; naturally it hoped for the best.[55] In Ottawa the hiatus in policy was duly noticed, and was the occasion for some blame-trading among the various bureaucracies of the capital; it was taken as a sign by some that the government's highly touted rationality had yet to produce a reasoned policy or appropriate conclusions.[56]

Canada could not escape the repercussions of the 1973 oil boycott. Not only was eastern Canada dependent on offshore oil, but much of it flowed through the United States and was necessarily affected by the Arab boycott. Those shipments were arranged through the multinational oil companies; would those companies respect their Canadian commitments when the United States was in need? Of course, Canada would not escape the price rise.[57] As Peter Dobell observed, the government was caught flat-footed, with minimal representation in the Middle East and none at all in the most important oil-producing country, Saudi Arabia. It had, as he put it, 'failed to anticipate events.'[58]

The consequences were not long in manifesting themselves. Atlantic Canada, the poorest part of the country, was simultaneously the most exposed. Quebec, the most politically doubtful province, suddenly saw its economy threatened by ferocious rises in the price of fuels. Indeed, from Manitoba east, Canada's provinces took an immediate and pessimistic interest in the trend of world oil prices. The Maritime provinces, already pensioners of the federal government, saw their fuel costs double, and faced the possibility that not all their needs could actually be met; the shortfall was predicted to be roughly 20 per cent.[59] To assist, the government ordered the Canadian Commercial Corporation to buy any oil it could find, at apparently any price; it was guarding against shortages, but it was also indicating mistrust for the oil multinationals.[60] By taking a strong hand, the government hoped it was pre-empting self-centered provincial initiatives.[61]

Opinion in the three oil and gas-producing provinces – Saskatchewan, British Columbia, and, especially, Alberta – took a different turn. When Trudeau announced in December 1973 that there would be a nationally owned oil company, eyebrows rose further, at least in the oil patch. Though the future Petro-Canada would be established without nationalizing any of the existing oil companies, its creation could hardly be taken as a vote of confidence in their performance, present and future. When the oil companies announced their very large profits for 1973, Petro-Canada's political future was assured.[62]

Already, in September 1973, the federal government had frozen the price of domestically produced oil at the existing level of $3.80 a barrel. Subsidies would bring the cost of imported oil down to a single national price, lower than the world price. To pay for imported oil for eastern Canada, an export tax was levied on oil. The tax rate was defined as the difference between the Chicago price and the new Canadian standard of $3.80. An oil pipeline would immediately be built to connect Montreal with western Canadian supplies.

The Americans would pay the world price for Canadian crude oil; Canadians, however, would not. It was a neat solution; in the Macdonald royal commission's retrospective opinion, 'as a rent-collection device, the package was superb.' The Americans, of course, were paying the rents, and the rents were not insubstantial. They rose from 40 cents a barrel in September 1973 to $6.40 a barrel a year later.[63]

There was one last sting, from the American point of view, in the new Canadian oil policy. The oil for Montreal and points east had to come from somewhere. But western oil wells were already operating at capacity.[64] The solution, therefore, was gradually to divert Canadian exports from the United States; over ten years, oil exports to that country would fall to zero.[65]

This news was not at all well received south of the border. Some parts of the northern United States had no practical alternative to Canadian fuels. Indignation ensued. One Harvard economist demanded that the U.S. government immediately retaliate by imposing a tax on Canadian oil piped through the United States. The Canadian argument that the United States should rely on its northern neighbour for assured supply had borne strange and distant fruit.[66]

Despite its logical problems, the position of the American government was accepted in press coverage in Washington. Canadian ministers bitterly reflected that their own newspapers were doing a fine job of repeating arguments that originated in the economic division of the State Department. That should not have occasioned any particular surprise: the same people who were pained by Canada's refusal to share American burdens (and costs) tended to believe that the North American economy must ultimately become (and to some extent already was) a cooperative whole.[67]

The Canadian response was directed by Donald Macdonald and his officials in EM&R. It was pointedly not managed by External Affairs, even though External Affairs made a valiant effort to persuade cabinet to let it coordinate this most important aspect of Canadian foreign policy.[68] There was a problem here which transcended the question of energy. External Affairs had never been especially strong in its economic divisions, even though individual economists had from time to time given the department some insight into matters of external trade.[69]

As was natural when important multifaceted questions of policy were rehearsed, an interdepartmental committee was appointed, in this case the Interdepartmental Committee on Oil.[70] The Canadian government was at pains to make short-term adjustments where and when required. Speeches emphasized the gradualism and reasonableness of the Canadian approach. It was known that the Canadian government was encouraging, and would soon be considering, a project to build a natural-gas pipeline from Alaska, via Alberta, to the U.S. market. Trudeau had said so in December; so had the minister of northern affairs, Jean Chrétien, in Yellowknife in January.[71] Macdonald went to Washington in February for a well-publicized meeting with William Simon, the American energy 'czar.'[72]

The Canadian case turned on a broader concept of reciprocity than the Americans used. They had frozen prices in the recent past and had not thought to pass on the saving to their Canadian customers. Now the Canadians could argue the American position, and Simon at least seems to have experienced déjà vu. He reversed the American position, blaming the State Department for concocting a grossly self-serving argument.[73]

Macdonald did not prevail on points alone. Except to border cities, all the oil pumped in Canada was not enough to make a substantial difference to the United States as a whole. And for the border cities it was important to reach an orderly arrangement.[74] The Americans would not retaliate, under the circumstances, though Simon did hope that Canada could lower its tax.[75]

Macdonald was aware that not all American policies are shaped by the executive branch, and he tried to keep key senators and congressmen informed.[76] Nevertheless, in January 1974 Senator Lawton Chiles of Florida introduced a resolution in the Senate denouncing Canada's 'high-jacking $6 million a day out of our pockets.' Senators Jackson and Magnuson sounded off in September, while the U.S. ambassador to Canada, William Porter, told a Winnipeg audience that same month that the Canadian tax 'looks discriminatory in nature.' That every govern-ment, including the American, discriminates in favour of its own citizens, and rejects criticism of its actions, was not stressed.[77]

These events reflected the internal agendas of only two countries, Canada and the United States. Henry Kissinger, however, was exerting himself during 1974 to establish an international front of consuming countries. He managed to organize an international body, the Interna-tional Energy Agency. It was founded in September, and attached to the common economic organ of the first world, the OECD in Paris. But despite its French location, it did not command the allegiance of the French government, which refused to join; and its cooperative functions were cast at the level of advice rather than command. Canada, naturally, joined, but Canada, like the IEA's other members, continued to pursue its own autonomous energy policies.[78]

The Trudeau government faced a second front in its energy battles: Alberta. The Progressive Conservative government of Alberta and its friends among the oil companies disliked Ottawa's interventionist poli-cies. Premier Peter Lougheed complained frequently and vehemently, though to little effect as far as Ottawa was concerned.

If Trudeau or Macdonald would not speak for oil and Calgary, Lougheed certainly would. Though his arguments often seemed exagger-ated to other Canadians, in his own milieu he was a moderate; and he was driven by a sense that the economic boom that had made Alberta's economy since the 1940s would drain away with the province's proved reserves. From Lougheed's point of view – and he was not alone – the government of Alberta must exploit the opportunity so fortuitously offered by OPEC. But unlike OPEC, Lougheed thought in a continental context.[79] Since Trudeau did not, there were the makings of a clash.

It was against this background that Trudeau prepared for his first meeting with Nixon's successor Gerald Ford in December 1974.[80] The prime minister appreciated the importance of getting off on a good footing but was puzzled how to prepare. What did the Americans want to talk about?

The agenda drafted in Washington had nothing on it but generalities. What then should he say?

A lack of specifics meant a dearth of complaints, at least from the American point of view; and perhaps it was not such a bad time. The Great Lakes Water Quality Agreement, signed in 1972, had been stymied by Nixon's reluctance to release the necessary funds to implement it. In October, two months into Ford's administration, the Americans promised there would be no further difficulty in finding money.[81] *Time* and *Reader's Digest* would be problems, but they would not be insurmountable.[82]

Still, they were an irritant; so was the NEB's attitude to energy supplies, and a 'beef stabilization' program which, by keeping out American beef, stabilized the Canadian price at a new, high level. At what point, Trudeau mused, would the Americans say that they had had enough. Perhaps they would want cooperation on other things, his staff suggested: using food, which North America produced in abundance, to offset OPEC's oil weapon, for example. It was continentalism but from a different, and quite novel, angle. Perhaps the Americans had discovered that they needed Canada after all.[83]

Perhaps, another adviser suggested, Kissinger had a Grand Design? It would not be out of character. Or would they be obsessed with dark thoughts of Trudeau's Canada as a communist beachhead? And what of Ford? Surely one should play to his strength as a simple politician. Perhaps, too, the president was worried about the Canadian policy of diversification – the third option, in plainer language.

In the end, however, it boiled down to energy. Trudeau was advised that he could hardly offer the Americans oil that Canada did not have; as for natural gas, 40 per cent of it was already pledged to the Americans on long-term contracts, which Canada would be foolish to abrogate. A program to constrict exports to the United States was announced in November 1974; there were special arrangements for states in the northern tier, where refineries depended on Canadian supplies. In 1976 there would be a direct swap: Canadian oil went south, matched by an equal amount of American oil going north.[84]

As to the pipeline, some Americans wanted one; those who did represented some of the biggest oil firms in the business, as well as strong political forces.[85] The favoured route was the Mackenzie Valley, connecting with both the Alaska fields and Canadian reserves in and around the Mackenzie Delta. Imitating the Americans' own environmental review procedures, the Canadian government in March 1974 appointed Mr

Justice Thomas Berger of the BC Supreme Court to assess how best to build a pipeline across the tundra.[86]

Berger was early into the field, but once there he decided to be thorough. His investigation was just hitting its stride in December and no one could exactly say when it would be finished. That was no great concern, Trudeau knew: while there might be a pipeline project, there was no assured finance. For a pipeline that might cost in the billions, that was no small matter. For the moment, at least, the prime minister refused to mortgage the negotiations, or to prejudge Berger, by promising a pipeline.[87]

The context of Trudeau's briefing is almost as interesting as the subjects discussed. The only other politician present was Allan MacEachen.[88] For Canadian-American issues as a whole, it was MacEachen who would do the necessary coordination.[89] And so the Canadians set out for Washington.

The discussion unrolled more or less as planned. Trudeau and MacEachen met with Ford and Kissinger on 2 December, and later attended a state banquet with appropriate ceremony and speech. Ford, who came from a Michigan district not far from the border, who had belonged to a Canadian-American parliamentary group, and who believed that Canadians were, after all, not unlike Americans, held Canada in friendly if not entirely familiar regard. He knew that border-state Americans worried about Canadian energy supplies: twenty-two congressmen had just told him so.[90] But he was resolved, even if he disagreed, never to be disagreeable with such a close ally. Trudeau responded appropriately.[91]

Ford and Kissinger touted a united consumers' group to resist OPEC, and Trudeau agreed enthusiastically. The Americans accepted the inevitable phasing out of Canadian oil exports to the United States, with modifications on the timing and rate of the phase-out. Trudeau reminded his listeners, in case they had forgotten, that bilateral trade between Canada and the United States was the largest in the world; beef, meanwhile, was relegated to a joint committee of officials for discussion.

Trudeau enjoyed another of Kissinger's global surveys and, in return, the Canadians stressed that Canadian perceptions and goals were similar to the Americans' own, on NATO, détente, and disarmament. Even in defence Canada hoped to impress by purchasing American long-range patrol aircraft.[92]

Not surprisingly, the conferees concluded that both countries ought to try genuine consultation and not just advance notice on any move that might adversely affect relations. It was a hoary solution to a real

problem; like previous resolutions of this kind, it would be better honoured in the breach than the observance.[93] Nevertheless, MacEachen got
a promise that he would have access to Kissinger on demand. Sparingly
used, it was a serviceable privilege.[94] Knowledge that the minister had
this key was useful in beating off challenges to External Affairs' predominance back in Ottawa. As a special departmental study concluded in the
fall of 1975, 'the increasing impact of bilateral and multilateral subjects
bearing implications for Canada's relations with the USA emphasizes the
need for a coordinated government approach to dealing with the USA,
characterized whenever possible by careful forward planning.'[95]

Energy remained the main item, MacEachen reported on his return.
The Americans recognized that Canadian oil and gas by themselves could
not solve their energy problems. Because the Canadian government
had given attention to specific difficulties caused by the cutbacks, 'USA
irritation with our export policies' was reduced. It helped that Canada's
energy plan closely resembled the Ford administration's own rationale
for energy self-sufficiency. A pipeline deal was always possible because
of perceived shortages of natural gas; the danger was that the American
government would commit to a rigid solution before Canada's own
regulatory studies – Berger's foremost – were complete. Besides, was
Canada a reliable supplier in the aftermath of the oil cutbacks?

Finally, there were environmental and broadly 'cultural' concerns: the
Garrison Dam in North Dakota, which threatened water quality north
of the border,[96] and the border television problem.[97] They did not make
the task of Canada's diplomatic apologists in the United States any easier.

MacEachen's unexceptionable report stirred up quite a storm in
Ottawa. Industry, Trade and Commerce was indignant. There were large
issues at stake, and IT&C's mandate – its 'recognized prerogatives' – was
being trampled upon. If External Affairs had a primary responsibility, so
did IT&C, and the answer was coordination, not subordination. IT&C's
deputy minister, Gerry Stoner, lamented that 'so much time is wasted
on jurisdictional bickering'; he promised to sort it out with External's
deputy, Basil Robinson.[98] If External suggested that only on 'vital' issues
there were difficulties, then in IT&C's experience, Stoner pointed out,
every American interest was classified as 'vital.'[99]

For all MacEachen's political cunning and high standing in the Trudeau ministry, his department's management of Canadian-American
relations was under attack – just as Kissinger paid an infrequent visit to
Ottawa. Its public aspect was less than desired, because of some
unguarded words by Kissinger about his former chief, Nixon, in front
of a live microphone; in private things seem to have gone well. Kissinger

was pleased with Canada's role in the complicated energy and New International Economic Order negotiations then under way; so much so that he was prepared to override opposition from within the State and Treasury departments and to give the Canadians what they most wanted: a seat at the economic summit.[100]

Canada had been excluded, at French insistence, from the first meetings of the western economic summits; but since then things had changed. Italy was to get a summit invitation, though its economy was smaller than Canada's. The Americans concluded that under the circumstances, Canada should come too, and the next summit would be held on American territory.[101] Gerald Ford would issue the invitations, and Canada would get one. 'Canada,' he told Canadians, 'is no longer a minor partner but a country which rightfully takes its place in the economic and political councils of the world.'[102] He did not add publicly that, in the view of the U.S. government, it was doing a favour to a friendly government in political trouble by 'giving Canada recognition as a key economic power.'

The reason the Trudeau government needed help from its friends was internal. The government in 1975–6 turned its attention largely inward. At Thanksgiving, 1975, the prime minister announced a federal program of wage and price controls; with living costs rising by almost 11 per cent in 1974–5, and with extraordinary pressure on wages and salaries, there was serious disquiet across the country.[103] But the wage-and-price-control program flew in the face of the government's 1974 election promises, and the effect was to damage its credibility. Though Trudeau controlled a majority in parliament, his political wings were clipped: the government had lost its freedom to manoeuvre.

That was especially true in energy policy. With wage and price controls the government's key concern, the two-price system for Canadian oil and gas was reinforced; the export tax remained in place, and, as Canada again became a net importer of petroleum in 1976, an excise tax on gas was added to subsidize further the domestic price.[104] Surveys nevertheless found Canadians to be at least 'fairly satisfied' with their lot, a perception that was reinforced by a notable dip in the number of Canadians migrating south and by a rise in the number of Americans going north; the two curves intersected at the beginning of the 1970s, with more Americans moving than Canadians; the Canadian edge was still being maintained in 1976.[105]

The Canadian edge was also reflected in public-opinion surveys of the period. When Canadians were asked in 1975 whether they should 'stay as [they] are' in foreign policy, as opposed to moving closer to the United

States or to Europe and Asia, the largest number plumped for the status quo. In no region was moving closer to the United States particularly favoured; nor did the third option, which involved closer ties to Asia and Europe, command as much support as its proponents would have liked.[106]

Fortunately, the U.S. government was not about to challenge its Canadian counterpart over the third option or anything else. Many of Canada's policies were irritating, but not important enough to quarrel over. According to Ford's national-security adviser, it was 'well, there go the Canadians again.' The Canadians had to be indulged, 'a patting on the head kind of thing.'[107]

Though Trudeau's personal relations with the president remained good, even cordial – the two men shared a liking for skiing – he did not have to contend with Ford's prestige as a factor in Canadian public opinion. In the Canadian media, as in the United States, Ford was regarded as slightly comic, a clumsy, if decent, figurehead.[108] Ford, meanwhile, was busy trying to get re-elected; if any foreign-policy issues came to his attention, they were, with one exception, not Canadian.[109]

The exception, Taiwan and the Olympics of 1976, did not do Canada any particular good with the American public (see chapter 7). The storm passed, leaving a residue of distrust in U.S. public opinion, but without direct policy consequences. Relations resumed between Trudeau and Ford. The Americans were celebrating their bicentennial and Canada obliged with the gift of a picture book, *Between Friends*, that highlighted pleasing similarities between the two neighbouring countries. It was appropriate that Ford, who had represented a border district, was the man to receive it. There was still room for Ford to play a final useful role; he had, indeed, already played it as the Olympic crisis brewed by issuing an invitation to the economic summit. Italy joined at the same time and, together, from the American perspective, the two countries represented the smaller powers.[110]

Kissinger's attention to Canada's global significance, as a weight in his larger machinations, ironically meant that he continued to devalue specifically bilateral issues in the relationship. These issues were, however, meat and drink to Ambassador William Porter. A former undersecretary and a very senior diplomat, Porter was said to have been sent to Ottawa for rest and relaxation after strenuous service in the Paris peace talks that ended the Vietnam war. Instead of grand strategy, bombers, and mines, he now dealt in tax credits, Saskatchewan's provincialization of its potash mines, and Canada's foreign investment controls, FIRA.

Energy was in a state of suspended animation. At the beginning of 1976 Canada and the United States signed an agreement that promised to keep international pipelines secure; at the same time, hearings were in progress on several fronts to assess the meaning, if not the desirability, of gas supply from the north. Some claimed that the whole issue had been blown out of proportion, and that southern reserves were sufficient to go on into the 1990s.[111] The time for decision there had not yet come.

Not even on energy was there any bilateral accord. The Trudeau government paid little attention to Porter's protests or, apparently, to Porter; and so, in December 1975, he served up drinks and on-the-record criticism of Canadian policies in a Saturday-night party for selected reporters at his residence in Ottawa. (The criticism was of the variety usually termed 'unofficial,' so as to give it a more candid aspect.)[112] Porter wanted, he later said, to 'clear the air' for his successor.[113]

The occasion got the desired headlines; and the headlines, as Porter must or should have anticipated, were critical. Kissinger was travelling in Europe, but the incident caught up with him even there. What was the real state of Canadian-American relations, the secretary was asked. 'Excellent,' Kissinger replied. Porter, already out on a limb, felt it crack under him. 'My friend Kissinger noted which way the wind was blowing,' he subsequently commented, 'and said I had spoken without State Department clearance which of course was not true. I am not a fool.'[114]

Unluckily, Porter had chosen a tactic that made him appear so. The government did not tremble or convulse, and the opposition did not take up Porter's cause. Neither did other Americans, except for the special-interest groups most directly affected. The storm in the Canadian teacup passed; and so did Porter, who went on to become ambassador to Saudi Arabia.

Kissinger already had his eye on his successor. Thomas Enders, assistant secretary for economic affairs in the State Department, was regarded as a coming man. Talented and abrasive, he was characterized by one admirer as 'the most impressive man in his forties in the Foreign Service'; 'absolutely brilliant,' according to others.[115] (He was impressive in another way: he stood six foot eight, and was certainly the tallest man in the Foreign Service.) He already had considerable background in Canadian issues, of both the bilateral and the multilateral kind, which occupied a certain amount of the time of his bureau in the State Department. Unluckily for him, his background did not stop there; he had also served in the U.S. embassy in Cambodia during the American bombing of that unhappy country, and the opposition in Congress was becoming interested in the subject. A youngish man, he was believed to have ' "peaked" too soon, making influential enemies in Congress' and even in the State Department.[116] Kissinger had sent Porter to Canada to get him out of Washington; for a different reason he did the same for Enders, whom he admired. It was in a sense a promotion (an embassy, and not a minor one) and recognition for a man his age; and for Canadians a vigorous American diplomat was quite a change from the valetudinarian Porter.[117]

Although Enders came to Ottawa before the Ford administration expired, his appointment, and the departure in September 1976 of MacEachen to concentrate on the Trudeau government's political battles, marked the end of an era. The Ford interim had continued but not resolved the existing irritations in Canadian-American relations; but the state of the relationship was not much the worse for it. It was, perhaps, better than before, because American defeat in Vietnam, and the confusion and division that followed at home, had the effect of concentrating the U.S. official mind elsewhere. In general, Canada and the United States were friendly, Trudeau and his government tended to agree with Kissinger on larger questions, and Trudeau and Ford got on well. All these developments made the relationship a happier one than it had been for some time. Trudeau and Ford met twice during 1976, once in Washington and once in Puerto Rico; nothing seems to have disturbed their happy confabulations.

Much talk was devoted at the time to whether the Canadian-American relationship was particularly special. Many, in the wake of 1971, believed that it was not. Perhaps its 'special' characteristics had been transposed. In the past, in the August 1971 'shokku,' for instance, the friends of Canada in the administration (or, rather, in the government, among the civil servants in the State Department or the Treasury) had tried to protect Canada's bilateral concerns against the consequences of the global policies subscribed to by Secretary Connally. This was less true in the mid-1970s. The friends were less apparent in the Treasury or in the State Department, though they were still present; and they were more apparent on the political level and in the office of the president. Bilateral issues had as often as not become irritants: in energy, in measures to fight pollution, in cultural policy, there were special American interests that had been offended. Porter found an echo when, in April 1976, some Republican congressmen complained in a published report about 'deteriorating relations between the United States and Canada.' External Affairs Minister MacEachen promptly rejected the characterization,[118] but he could not entirely expunge it from the agenda.

Kissinger and MacEachen held a farewell meeting in the summer, with a trip by the minister to Washington. As usual, their conversation leaned heavily towards the geopolitical: Korea, South Africa, and relations between the developed world and developing countries, in which MacEachen had taken a special interest. The prospects there were none too promising, the two men agreed; from the American point of view, a confrontation between developed and undeveloped nations was not unthinkable, although certainly undesirable.[119] When conversation turned to bilateral issues, Enders did most of the running; and Kissinger proved not averse to turning matters ranging from maritime boundaries to energy to pipelines over to committees of officials.[120]

Overall, Canada's position remained secure, largely because the guiding minds of the administration refused to promote such petty concerns to the top of their agenda. But changes were in train. Economics, and especially energy, remained important. Political diplomacy and strategic thought were in the decline. The American economy had proved vulnerable once, in the oil crisis, and the memory lingered at home and abroad. Congress was asserting itself. Canadian-American relations were coming to mean more than the occasional interactions of two national executives, a change ill-suited to the guiding minds at the State Department and their counterparts in Ottawa. It was high time for Dr Kissinger to be leaving, and leave he did, with the Democrats' arrival in January 1977. A new face, a new party, and a new administration would be taking his place.

Trudeau was not, in the circumstances, an absolute asset. His attitudes towards Americans had not changed. His indifference to the currents of American life was legendary. 'The only American media he bothered following was American movies,' Keith Davey, the Liberal election strategist, told an interviewer.[121]

American views of Trudeau were similarly distant. 'Some people considered him a bit too imperial for a politician,' according to the *New York Times* correspondent in Ottawa.[122] Others wondered that someone from so small and relatively insignificant a country should give himself the air of a world statesman.[123] But most saw him in the context of his well-publicized separation from his wife in 1976: that at least was good 'news.'

Jimmy Carter was also news in Canada. He was unexpected, to say the least. His interviews with the press – admitting to various human foibles, such as lust – his denunciations of Washington in the wake of Watergate, his folksy manners, his brother Billy and his peanut farm, all served up the proper mix of human interest and politics that are the daily fare of television news and front pages. It was almost, but not quite, like Harry Truman, whose memory was enjoying something of a revival in the mid-1970s as a contrast to what had come afterward.

Carter was a Democrat, like Truman, and he was by most standards a liberal. In many respects, his views were compatible with those in fashion in Ottawa. He was an environmentalist on such issues as the Garrison diversion in North Dakota and pollution in the Great Lakes. He believed in consultation between America and its allies, and he was greatly concerned for human rights. The Cold-War consensus, he believed, had broken down, and he was interested in replacing it with a concept of 'world order.' Trudeau, who had argued much the same line for nearly ten years, generally concurred. He was 'immensely in harmony with Carter's general world outlook,' a close observer later argued.[124]

A nuclear engineer, Carter had spent time in Canada as a junior naval officer: had the experience rubbed off? Polite, deferential, and conciliatory by nature, Carter hoped for much from Trudeau, his senior in acquaintance with the affairs of the great world; and Trudeau had much to gain from Carter. Carter's association with the Trilateral Commission, an elite think-tank, indicated a disposition to treat international problems in concert and in common with American allies, including Canada.[125] It may have seemed odd to some that Carter closely associated his country's foreign policy with a basic morality of conduct, but it was still difficult to sort out rhetoric from reality.[126]

It went without saying that Carter knew little or nothing about Canadian-American issues, nor was his secretary of state, Cyrus Vance, any better grounded. Vance was a Wall Street lawyer with extensive Washington connections and experience. According to the Canadian embassy, he had a strong general background in foreign relations and valued ties to the allies. Though unaware of the specifics of bilateral issues, 'in conversations with the Embassy ... he appeared to be well-disposed towards Canada.' Well-disposed, but also worried. 'He expressed concern over what he termed the erosion of ties binding the Canada/USA relationship. He seemed to have a sense that things are not what they used to be and said that perhaps new efforts should be made to improve the relationship.'[127]

Less, apparently, was known of Zbigniew Brzezinski, the national security adviser. Brzezinski was the son of the prewar Polish consul-general in Montreal, and had graduated from McGill in economics and political science in 1949. After taking a master's degree, he moved on to Harvard for a doctorate, then a job, and finally a transfer to Columbia, where he became a Russian specialist. Brzezinski's views on the subject of the Soviet Union were well enough understood: he was sceptical of détente. He also believed that Kissinger had unduly depreciated the economic side of foreign policy. This led the Canadian embassy to conclude that Brzezinski would 'assign highest importance to relations with Europe, Japan and Canada rather than the Soviet Union and China.'[128] They did not go on to speculate what perspective his Montreal upbringing or his Polish background had given him on the question of Canadian nationalities; would he assume a similarity between French-Canadian nationalism and the Polish variety?

Neither Brzezinski nor Vance had much experience in the leading bilateral question in Canadian-American relations: energy. That was where the vice-president, Walter Mondale, came in. Mondale was a senator from Minnesota when Carter chose him to balance the Democratic ticket in the north. Since he came from a border state, Canadians often assumed that Mondale knew something about their country – and he did – in part because Canadian energy policy had a very real impact on Minnesota. He had first met Trudeau over breakfast in Washington in December 1974, followed by a visit to Ottawa in February 1975 to discuss energy. To Canadian officials, Mondale, 'unlike other senators ... consistently took a moderate view of Canadian actions and concentrated on seeking cooperative and concentrated solutions to the problems affecting his state.'[129] Because Carter assigned his vice-president at least some useful tasks, Canadian diplomats hoped that he would be directed their way. They were not disappointed: after less than a month in office Mondale was on the line to Ottawa, transmitting Carter's position on the next world economic summit.[130]

A state visit by Trudeau to Washington had been in the offing for some time. In November 1976 Ivan Head raised the possibility with Carter's advisers while on a trip to Georgia; he emphasized that the visit should be early, a symbol of the importance to be assigned relations with Canada and the closeness of the two countries. An agenda, mostly economic, was agreed by mid-January and, by 25 January, five days into Carter's term, the date was set.

Despite the official concentration on an economic agenda, Trudeau's visit was important because it occurred in the aftermath of René Lévesque's success in the Quebec election and the projection of separatism as a real political possibility. Economics and energy, whether continental or worldwide, had therefore to take second place to an issue on which the American media overwhelmingly favoured the position of the Canadian government.[131] As political theatre, as well as political substance, the visit was opportune.

There was one wrinkle. The Canadian embassy believed it had been bypassed by Head and the Prime Minister's Office; and the ambassador nursed a grievance. Jake Warren had already been bumped from London, which he liked, to accommodate Trudeau's appointment of Paul Martin. Some believed that when he left the public service, which he shortly did, it was because he felt slighted in his profession. Accurate or not, the story got about and caused harm.[132] Head, rightly or wrongly, got some of the blame, but without Head, could the visit have been arranged as expeditiously or successfully?

What Trudeau gained in promptness and symbolism was paid for in content. It would be impossible, the Americans warned, for them to handle a heavy bilateral agenda, but the visit went ahead because they were interested in Quebec, Ottawa wanted to bring the Carter administration 'on side,' and because it had become traditional for Canadian and American leaders to assign each other pride of place in foreign visits.[133]

How Trudeau and Carter dealt with the problem of Quebec we have mentioned elsewhere (see chapter 5), and we shall consider other points on their agenda here. Their discussions were wide-ranging, from Cuba and its influence in the Caribbean to multilateral trade negotiations, the Autopact, and the impact of American extraterritoriality on Canada. Carter's tone throughout was respectful, even deferential; Trudeau, who knew very well what was at stake, reciprocated.[134]

The two men were basically compatible, according to the American note-taker at their early meetings. Both were autodidacts, and both liked to come to meetings fully briefed. Whether Canada entered Carter's mind after Trudeau left his presence was irrelevant, because when together each man knew, and understood, the music they were supposed to play.[135]

Perhaps Carter compared Trudeau's cool competence to what he already considered to be Helmut Schmidt's windy arrogance. Trudeau may even have given the American leader too favourable an impression of what to expect in foreign statesmen; while the president and Trudeau may have disagreed in their assessments of Schmidt, on certain other personalities their views were very similar.[136] As a result, the American administration's attitude to Trudeau and to Canada was possibly excessively favourable, as sharing their own admirable values and exemplary among nations.[137]

Carter's primary interest in Canada was political, yet most bilateral issues were economic. As under Ford and Kissinger, so under Carter and Vance: politics overshadowed economics but could not entirely compensate for it. Nor did Carter's global preoccupations leave time to worry over the connection that Canadians made between politics and economics. That was left to be handled by officials; fortunately they handled it, on the whole, rather well. Carter did not get what he hoped for from Trudeau, in terms of global support and understanding, but it remained a matter of degree. Certainly, Tom Enders later remarked, Carter became disappointed in Trudeau; but then Carter wanted more of everybody than he could possibly get.[138]

Relations between Trudeau and Carter were never less than cordial. In Enders's recollection, that was because the dominating issue in Canada from 1977 to 1980 was national unity and the question of Quebec. It did not leave much room for other policy initiatives, especially of the nationalist kind.[139] The nationalist initiatives of the 1972–6 period continued – FIRA, Petro-Canada, and the Canada Development Corporation – but they were not added to. And in Don Jamieson, Canada had its most pro-American minister of external affairs in history.[140]

Jamieson was a Newfoundlander, twenty-eight years old when the island joined Canada in 1949. Confederation had not been his preference: he had argued for an economic union between Newfoundland and the United States instead of political absorption into Canada. Once the decision had been made, Jamieson accepted it and was elected as a Liberal to the House of Commons in 1966. Trudeau gave him a succession of ministerial jobs, culminating in Industry, Trade and Commerce in 1975–6 and finally External Affairs. In political terms, Jamieson was able, respected, and senior: he sat on the Priorities and Planning Committee of cabinet, and he was political (patronage) minister for Newfoundland. Jamieson was the kind of man who had strewn his favours carefully; he expected, in the course of his life, to recall most of them.[141] External Affairs was a good reward, though it occasionally entailed the burden of the prime minister's company: he preferred to keep his admiration of the prime minister at a distance. Trudeau, for his part, liked Jamieson and respected his political judgment. There would be no second-guessing here. Less intellectual than MacEachen, he was at least initially less congenial to his officials. Sensing that Jamieson might require someone both well organized and tough, his department assigned him Derek Burney as his executive assistant; it would be Burney's first difficult assignment, but not his last.[142] Jamieson, in any case, remained minister until the Trudeau government's defeat in May 1979.

Jamieson could afford to be pro-American. He came from the least prosperous province, where economic nationalism did not play as well as it did in Ontario. The United States in Newfoundland terms meant bases and dollars, the more the better. So it would not be for Jamieson to try out new theories on the Americans; at the same time, he may not have been the man to appeal to the streak of idealism in the president or to the realpolitik in Brzezinski. In taking a softer line towards the Americans, however, Jamieson was not alone: Jack Horner, an Alberta member of parliament who moved across the floor to join the Liberals in 1977, to be rewarded with Industry, Trade and Commerce, and Jean Chrétien as minister of finance were also regarded as favouring the southern neighbour. 'Reluctantly,' Richard Gwyn wrote in 1980, 'Trudeau's critics gave up calling him anti-American.'[143]

Certainly they would have had difficulty extending the label to Canadian energy policy between 1976 and 1979. The government badly wanted access to Arctic natural gas, to be used in what the NEB predicted would be a petroleum shortage in the 1980s. It worried about American pipelines crossing Canadian territory, and Canadian pipelines crossing American territory. It preferred tapping into a pipeline for which the Americans would pay. And though it was open-minded on what route such a pipeline should take – there were two alternatives by 1976, the Mackenzie Valley and the Alaska Highway – it was clear that a pipeline should be built. Given the make-up of the cabinet in the late 1970s, there were no surprises in the offing.

There were, however, what the political scientists like to call exogenous variables, which we for the sake of convenience will call wild cards. The first was, perhaps, predictable, sooner or later. Unluckily for Carter, it happened sooner. The Americans were facing a natural-gas supply crisis in the winter of 1976–7. It was a cold winter; American policies for ensuring the best use of natural-gas supplies were improvident; and U.S. oil companies withheld gas from the market in the hope that better interstate pricing policies would eventuate. The shortage had a spectacular public impact: schools and factories closed, and more than a million workers were laid off.[144] Before he had been a month in office, a large part of Carter's political agenda had been set.

Another variable was the security of international pipelines from national interference; that was wrapped up in a treaty negotiated between 1974 and 1977, and signed on 28 January 1977: it secured uninterrupted supply, and national treatment, for pipelines crossing either Canadian or American territory.[145] But this was only one issue among many. Chief among them was Mr Justice Berger, still beavering away on his northern pipeline report. It took over three years, in the event: three years of hearings up and down the Mackenzie Valley, of studies, and finally of careful writing. On 9 May 1977 Berger was ready.

His report was a body-blow to the syndicate that hoped to build a Mackenzie Valley pipeline. There should be no pipeline for at least ten years, Berger reported. His objections were environmental and sociological: damage to the environment and to the society of the northern native peoples would be irreversible, while economic benefits would be insufficient. Better to prepare the political and social ground first, to settle native land claims, and put in place a stable and acceptable regime in the north. Meanwhile, exploratory work could go forward in the hope of identifying the actual oil and gas potential of the Arctic littoral. If the government were really set on a pipeline, Berger added, then it might choose the Alaska Highway route (presumably because that was where the environmental damage had already been done). Even the Alaska Highway option required research, consultation, and action on native land claims; but that was somebody else's study.[146]

The recommendation for delay came as no shock to those who already believed that there was no immediate necessity for a pipeline from the northern frontier. Their reasoning might be different, but the conclusion was the same. There was plenty of gas in Alberta, actual and potential, to last into the mid-1980s.[147]

An NEB report in July wrapped up the Mackenzie Valley pipeline and officially interred it. Instead, it endorsed the Alaska Highway proposition, subject to route changes, linking Fairbanks with Dawson City and adding a spur along the existing Dempster Highway from Dawson to the Mackenzie Delta. At the same time, the Americans resolved that on balance – a very nice balance – the Alaska Highway route was to be preferred over both the Mackenzie Valley and an all-American pipeline-and-tanker route involving liquefied natural gas. The Americans, however, had their doubts as to whether any pipeline at all was really needed.[148]

The next move was up to the Canadian cabinet. The cabinet had already polled Canadians to discover how much latitude it had in making a decision; perhaps to their surprise, Goldfarb, their pollster, reported that 'Canadians are really looking to the government for objective leadership in the northern pipeline issue.' It was leadership in the right direction, of course, because Goldfarb also found that people would support a joint Canadian-American pipeline; at the same time, where the environment and native rights were concerned, 'at least on an emotional level, people will tend to support the findings of Berger.'[149]

Happily, Berger's investigation applied only to the Mackenzie Valley.

The opposition parties, Progressive Conservatives, Créditistes, and the NDP, were divided or favourable, with little to do but chime in when the government presented its policy: the Alaska Highway or Alcan route. On 5 August parliament endorsed the government's choice, Ed Broadbent of the NDP going so far as to plump for 'an unequivocal commitment in principle to the Alcan route.'[150]

The government now had a green light to negotiate with the United States, and it lost no time in doing it. Basil Robinson, who had retired as undersecretary of state for external affairs, was appointed Canadian pipeline commissioner, under the overall authority of Allan MacEachen who, though president of the Privy Council, was given responsibility for pipeline affairs. From 1970 to 1974 Robinson had been deputy minister of northern affairs, and he had been MacEachen's deputy at External Affairs for two years. His mandate was to negotiate a pipeline; given the expectations the cabinet and public opinion in general entertained of the importance of a pipeline, success was more than usually a desideratum.[151] To safeguard its agreed object, the cabinet generated an ad hoc committee to supervise negotiations. The Americans, in contrast, let it be known that they were not so sure: that there were circumstances in which the pipeline would not be desirable.

Carter assigned Dr James Schlesinger, his energy adviser, to head the American team. Schlesinger, who had actually served in Ford's cabinet as defence secretary and who would soon emerge as secretary of energy in Carter's, was a heavyweight in the administration. Negotiations began in Ottawa on 17 August 1977, continued in Washington, and returned to Ottawa at the end of the month. The routing of the pipeline (through Dawson or not), who was to pay the cost of the Dempster spur, and the stability of property taxes were among the issues discussed. At one point Trudeau found it useful to intervene directly with Carter over the phone; Carter repaid his call by instructing his negotiators to be less intransigent.[152]

On 2 September 1977, after a seven-hour negotiating session, agreement was reached between MacEachen and Schlesinger. The Canadians had got the mega-project they sought, or so it appeared. That meant jobs: jobs for Canadian industry that would supply the pipeline, and jobs for the many construction workers and their camp followers who would build the line. As much as $4 billion would accrue, or so the government claimed. (Total costs were estimated at $10.3 billion – a figure which, like all construction estimates, must be treated with due caution.)[153] The prospects of bringing Mackenzie Delta gas south were much brighter, and the Americans would share the costs of the Dempster Highway spur.

The Americans would get a pipeline crossing Canadian territory, and they had secured a cap on property taxes. As Schlesinger pointed out, bringing Canadian gas on stream was no bad thing for the American economy or the American consumer.[154]

Students of government-energy relations in Canada have contended that the Americans got the better of the negotiation. It was the Canadians who wanted the pipeline, the Americans who had the alternatives – a different pipeline, or none at all.[155] For the Canadians it was the fact of the construction that mattered; for the Americans, it was the price of the gas at the other end.[156] These respective positions gave the Americans a further advantage in the months and years that followed the pipeline agreement.

The Canadian government set up a Northern Pipeline Agency, appointed a commissioner – Mitchell Sharp, who left politics for the occasion – and waited. As they waited, conditions changed. A natural-gas surplus reappeared, and pressure to export it resumed. As pressure increased in the southern gas fields, it decreased in the Arctic.[157]

Both the American and Canadian governments tried to take advantage of the situation. A Quebec and Maritimes pipeline was in contemplation – why not finance it by using it to export natural gas to New England? The Americans saw it differently. Natural gas exports to the United States should be used to support the construction of the Alaska Highway route. At the time of writing, the Quebec and Maritime pipeline had reached eastern Quebec; its extension to the Maritimes has been, as the saying goes, 'indefinitely delayed.'[158]

Trudeau and Carter met in March 1979 to resolve the impasse. It was, in fact, their last meeting, and it was appropriate that it should deal with a question that was so remote (though increasingly familiar) from their respective fields of interest and expertise. The Americans wanted gas exports via the existing ('prebuilt') natural-gas pipelines. They got it: Trudeau and Carter agreed that gas exports now would actually help to bring Mackenzie Delta gas south, later.[159]

The argument was wearing thin even as an election was called in Canada. After Trudeau was defeated, prospects for an Arctic pipeline receded even further. This was for two reasons: Alaskan gas was considered by now to be too expensive, and it was becoming apparent that the Alaska natural-gas pipeline would cost even more than the $12–14 billion originally projected. Puffs of support and publicity from Carter's White House were not enough to keep the project's spirits up or its investors interested. By the end of the year the project was on its last legs, just as Joe Clark's brief Conservative government was defeated in the House of Commons and another election called in Canada.

Finally, it was agreed to go ahead with the so-called 'pre-build' gas lines from the existing Alberta fields to American markets in California and the mid-west. The pre-build was originally conditional on the eventual 'build'; but after the pre-build was built, and gas flowing, little more was heard of the northern links to Alaska and the Mackenzie Delta. In early 1990, world oil and gas prices are such that the Alaska Highway natural-gas pipeline remains unconsummated.

The Northern Pipeline Agency lingered on. Sharp went regularly to the office to preside over its files and archives, and it would only be wound up in the spring of 1988 as another election approached. Except by historians, its passing was unnoticed and unmourned.

The pipeline had absorbed time and energy in Ottawa and Washington without adding anything to the energy supply of North America. The Alaska Highway pipeline remained, in effect, a pipe dream. The economics of energy, especially the abundance of natural gas, postponed the Alaska Highway gas pipeline, a year here, two years there. Although it remained a factor in Canadian governments' calculations into the mid-1980s, it has never been revived.

It hardly mattered. New oil and gas reserves continued to be discovered, and the export trade did not disappear. Exports of natural gas in 1974 were more than 27 billion cubic metres; in 1984 they were 21 billion. As of the mid-1980s, Canada was a net exporter of oil.[160]

The pipeline had been a major item on Enders's agenda, but it was not the only one. There was also the ancient question of the fisheries. Attention to the fisheries was one way the federal government could express its affection for Maritimers; neglect of, or decline in, the fisheries meant that the government of the day received a black mark. The mid-1970s were a period of decline and concern. There were decreasing fish stocks on the Atlantic coast, fuel was rising in price, and existing companies had problems marketing their product. $200 million in aid was tendered, but that was not all.

Canada wished to extend its maritime boundaries; to do so, it was using multilateral negotiations on the law of the sea. International opinion had tended for some time towards a 200-mile economic zone in addition to the generally (though not universally) conceded 12-mile territorial limit. In terms of jurisdiction, the United States gained the most because of its overseas dependencies; Canada's harvest of underwater territory was less than 30 per cent of the Americans'.[161]

The simple proclamation of an economic zone did nothing to alter existing arrangements along the coasts. Canada and the United States had been generally cooperative, forming what External Affairs' legal adviser called 'a sort of coastal coalition against the depredations of distant-water fishing states.'[162] The adverse conditions that afflicted Canadian seamen tended to occur south of the border as well; it followed that American politicians from seaboard states were just as attentive to the interests of their constituents as Canadian politicians were to theirs. As lines of jurisdiction fluctuated off the coasts, Canada and the United States resorted to bilateral agreements that protected the historic rights of each country to fish off the other's coastline. A 1970 agreement codified the reciprocal privileges; after extensions it was replaced by another, interim, agreement in February 1977.[163]

The fisheries question was rolled into a general negotiation between Canada and the United States to cover maritime boundaries, the management of offshore hydrocarbon (oil and gas) resources, and the curation of fish stocks. Marcel Cadieux was appointed Canadian negotiator; Lloyd Cutler was his American counterpart.

The negotiations were long and complex. On the Canadian side, there was considerable interchange with affected interests but, interestingly, not a great deal with the Canadian embassy in Washington. As a perceptive observer has suggested, this may have been because Cadieux as a former ambassador believed he already understood the Washington context. On the American side, the negotiators seemed to neglect the fishing interests involved, a neglect that did not enhance the American industry's support for whatever deal was eventually produced.[164] Considered as an intellectual exercise, it is conceded even by Canadian sources that Cadieux had much the better of the deal. Approached as a political proposition, it is evident that Cadieux's negotiation was too successful. He had to succeed, for relations in the fishery touched a new and complicated low in 1978 as the two countries and their fishermen traded injunctions, threats, and bans. (Jamieson's officials joked at the time that the only item in his daily dispatches sure to catch and retain the minister's attention was fish; at the time, such items were frequent.)[165]

In March 1979 four interconnected agreements were announced. One sent the maritime boundary (the Georges Bank dispute) to arbitration in the International Court of Justice. Two more dealt with the Pacific fishery. Finally, there was an agreement regulating the Atlantic fishery, in terms of shares and access. It was generally believed in the northeastern United States to favour Canada; and, probably, it did.[166]

The Carter administration recommended the treaty to the Senate, and there it languished for the next two years. In part this was because the Senate had other, more important, matters on its agenda, such as the strategic arms limitation treaty (SALT II) negotiated with the Soviets. In part it was because of the complexity of the reciprocal regime established by the treaty, which created real problems of access and jurisdiction.[167] New England senators were senior in the relevant committees, and though New England was not unanimous on this issue, it became clear that opponents had the advantage over proponents. Concluding that the nays had it at home, New England's senators plumped for the contrary. On this issue they called in their political chits. The Atlantic fisheries became another casualty of the Carter administration's political naïveté; when the treaty was withdrawn from the Senate by the Reagan administration, its action was little more than a recognition of the inevitable.

The other item, arbitration of the maritime boundary through the Gulf of Maine, was detached from the fisheries agreements and sent to the International Court of Justice at The Hague. The court's decision was not rendered until October 1984; it divided the rich fishing ground of Georges Bank between the two countries. Some American fishermen regretted the decision, which gave Canada a guaranteed place in the Gulf of Maine fishery, and political rumblings followed; but that was a question for the Mulroney government to deal with.[168]

Few of the great issues that loomed in January 1977 had been satisfied by the time Carter left office. Quebec, of course, remained unresolved. As long as it did, the federal government was not likely to prove adventurous in assuming new commitments abroad. Oil and gas negotiations seemed to have produced the foundations of a cooperative policy, but the foundations were laid for only half a structure. The rest of the structure stretched over a policy void. Though some American commentators urged that 'the onus is on the United States to honor its commitment to Canada,' nothing was done to forward a project that might have shored up common interests.[169]

By 1981 relations between the Canadian and American governments had reached such a historical low that another blow was not unexpected. Despite the surface tranquillity of the interchanges between Carter and Trudeau, and the competence of their diplomatic staffs, no common understanding had been reached that could have anticipated the next round of quarrels.

Part Three

Defining the Country

5

One Country or Two?

The 24th of July 1967 was brilliantly sunny in the St Lawrence Valley. The day promised well – the perfect weather for a motorcade, as yet another of Canada's centennial visitors prepared to journey from Quebec City to the world exposition, 'Expo,' in Montreal, along provincial highway number 2. Most motorists preferred the modern autoroute south of the river, so as to halve the driving time between the capital and the metropolis; but the rural population was still concentrated north of the river, and especially along the old highway, renamed for this occasion the 'Chemin du Roy.'

The name was opportune, some observers mused. Canada's state visitor was not called king of France but president of the French republic. That did not prevent his keeping a court, or from ruling France in a style that at least some of his royal predecessors would have found appropriate. Not that those kings had established a perfect record. The last French king to rule Canada, Louis XV, allowed his great North American colony to slip away in a diplomatic blunder; and his imperial and republican successors in France accepted as a fact that the French of Canada were no longer part of the life or destiny of France. But after 207 years Charles de Gaulle had come to redress the balance, to pay, as he put it, 'la dette de Louis XV.' Eighteenth-century France had wrongfully abandoned its North American subjects, and that day, travelling along a road laid out under that same Louis XV, de Gaulle intended to restore the links that bound old France to the new.

The crowds that surged along the side of the Chemin du Roy confirmed what de Gaulle believed: what he saw were Frenchmen; and what he was doing, in July 1967, was liberating them. By nightfall, the presidential cavalcade was passing through Montreal's outer suburbs, heading for the city's ornate hôtel de ville, where dignitaries awaited.

The official host, Mayor Jean Drapeau, was slightly nervous, not because he was to receive one of the twentieth-century's living monuments, but because he had noticed a trend in the monument's Canadian utterances. The day before, arriving in Quebec City, de Gaulle had intoned to his audience, 'vive le Canada.' But since then, and especially at a formal dinner tendered by Premier Daniel Johnson, the word 'Canada' had been notably missing from the president's vocabulary. There were many in Quebec who found that a pleasing omission. Few of them, however, were friends of the mayor of Montreal.

It was almost 7:30 PM when de Gaulle pulled up. The president thanked the mayor for the 'indescribable' scenes of welcome in Montreal. It was evident that he wished them to continue. Drapeau, bearing in mind that he was mayor of a multiracial city as well as host of a universal exposition, drily replied that the delirious reception was what a 'great cosmopolitan city' would do for a great man.

'Cosmopolitan' was not precisely the word de Gaulle wished to hear. He had heard what the old French-Canadian nationalist historian Abbé Groulx had termed 'l'appel de la race,' and he wished to respond. Brushing aside Drapeau's suggestion that he come and meet the official guests, he asked for a microphone to address the 5,000 who had managed to crowd into the narrow square in front of city hall. Alas, Drapeau replied, there was no microphone on the balcony. He believed he had made sure there was none. 'Pas de micro?' exclaimed de Gaulle. But there was. His bodyguard had spotted it, his technicians had arranged it, and, tested, it worked. And so de Gaulle began to speak.

It was not, perhaps, a masterpiece of oratory, but it struck the right pitch. In the manner of bedtime stories, de Gaulle lowered his voice. 'I'm going to tell you a secret,' he told the crowd, and the television cameras. 'Tonight, all along my route, I found myself in an atmosphere just like the Liberation.'

In front of his television set in Ottawa, Prime Minister Pearson sat up with a jolt. The liberation that de Gaulle referred to was the liberation of France from the Nazis in 1944. It did not strike Pearson as the happiest simile that the old general could have chosen.

De Gaulle was just warming up, and, as he warmed, his voice rose. 'Vive Montréal!' A roar from the crowd. 'Vive le Québec!' Another roar. 'Vive le Québec ... libre!' This time the roar continued, almost drowning out the last words: 'Vive le Canada français et vive la France!'[1]

De Gaulle went happily to bed that night; the next day he would tour

Expo. Quebec separatists celebrated far into the night. 'Vive le Québec libre,' after all, was one of their favourite slogans. It sounded better than 'cent ans d'injustice,' their celebration of Canada's centennial; and what had up until then been a year of negation and denial suddenly became a time of affirmation – of liberation, just as de Gaulle said.

The reaction in Ottawa was decidedly more negative. As de Gaulle visited the world's fair, on 25 July, the cabinet met, twice. There was no mistaking what de Gaulle had said or what he meant. Pearson knew: de Gaulle had predicted the demise of Canada in a private conversation in 1964. Paul Martin, the secretary of state for external affairs, told his colleagues, 'the Government should entertain no illusion about the possibility that de Gaulle would retract; he believed every word he said and did not even care whether the Government agreed with him or not.' As Lionel Chevrier, the government's commissioner for state visits, would confirm, de Gaulle was persuaded by 'the people's reaction to his speeches,' and was convinced of 'the strength of the separatist movement.' Worse, in Martin's view, was the fact that 'there was no mistaking the enthusiasm for de Gaulle in Montreal and at Expo.'

The cabinet decided that they must respond or be thought weak, both in Canada and in France. A mid-day adjournment allowed Pearson and Martin, along with Jean Marchand, the minister of manpower and immigration, Allan MacEachen, the minister of national health and welfare, and C.M. Drury, the minister of industry, to draft a public statement. When the statement was ready, however, the cabinet was not. Hesitations were expressed by Robert Winters, minister of trade and commerce and a Toronto MP; by Mitchell Sharp, minister of finance; and by Marchand, who now warned his colleagues that if de Gaulle were forced to depart, the people of Quebec 'would not understand the reasons of his departure' because they, unlike de Gaulle, 'failed to see a relationship between General de Gaulle's speeches and separatism. People applauded him,' Marchand continued, 'because he was a great man and a French-speaking great man at that.'

Despite these misgivings, the cabinet concluded that a statement rebuking de Gaulle's city-hall oration must be issued, and issued forthwith. When Pearson read out the statement to the television cameras, it told de Gaulle that 'certain [of his] statements ... are unacceptable to the Canadian people and its Government,' and rebuked the comparison between the liberation of France and his country cavalcade through Quebec. In authorizing the statement, the cabinet realized that de Gaulle would probably seize the occasion to leave Canada without visiting Ottawa; and so he did.[2]

Pearson had told his colleagues that public opinion outside Quebec would accept nothing less; and the evidence, from newspapers, documents, and polls, suggests that he was right. What the cabinet also understood was that English and French Canadians were sharply divided on the issue. As Marchand said, to French-speaking Canadians, de Gaulle was a great man who also happened to be French. His presence and his obvious sentiments were a tonic; but they might not be, after all, a magic elixir that would banish those annoying 207 years after the British conquest, or restore French Canadians to a majority in North America. No words, not even de Gaulle's, could accomplish these feats.

But de Gaulle's words were hardly without effect. Canada, on its hundredth birthday, was revealed to be a nation divided; as the British governor general, Lord Durham, had opined in 1838, 'two nations warring in the bosom of a single state.' Pearson had hoped to avert the conflict, but by 1967 he had exhausted the expedients at his command. He would not detract from the remaining centennial celebrations, but in December, after all the visitors had gone home, he announced his retirement from politics, to take effect after a Liberal party convention had chosen a new leader. It was obvious to all that the new leader would have to concentrate on Quebec.

Pierre Trudeau's ascendancy over the minds of Canadians began on a February day in 1968. Daniel Johnson, the premier of Quebec, had just finished telling the constitutional conference that Quebec needed, desired, and had to have a renewed Canadian federation. In such a federation there would still be a federal government, with powers over currency, banking, foreign trade, and defence, to be 'exercised in consultation, not only with Quebec, but with all the provinces.' It was, in Quebec terms, a moderate speech. It accepted that Canada should continue as well as survive; as Johnson liked to say in speeches around the province, it did not make sense for a man to divorce his wife one day only to remarry her the next.

It did not escape notice that he had not put foreign policy on his list of federal powers. Presumably foreign policy was *discutable*; perhaps Johnson hoped, when the dust settled, that it would be divided into a Quebec jurisdiction and a Canadian sphere. Matters could, of course, go further, so that foreign relations would be exercised, not by the federal government, but by Canada's ten provinces or, failing total devolution, by Johnson's favorite nostrum, the 'two nations' of northern North America, Canada and Quebec.[3]

Inside the Parliament Buildings the assembled premiers and functionaries were pondering the question, 'What does Quebec want?' There were two answers, liberal and nationalist, but only the nationalist one was generally familiar in the late 1960s.[4] If Johnson were to be believed, Quebec wanted virtual sovereignty. Quebec, he said, was already sovereign in respect of its existing constitutional responsibilities. The argument was not peculiar to Johnson or his Union Nationale government. The previous Liberal government of Jean Lesage had proclaimed in 1965 that Quebec did and should possess the right to represent itself abroad when provincial matters came under discussion, and to do so without interference from Ottawa. Johnson's position on representation abroad was no different; but here it is useful to recapitulate the events that had led to Quebec's assertion of its right to a provincial foreign policy.[5]

By 'abroad,' Quebec officials generally meant France. France had taken little notice of Quebec in two centuries since 1760; and, though Quebec was necessarily more attentive to its former mother country, it was not always impressed. The French consulate-general in Montreal did the necessary commercial business, but seldom strayed outside its function, while the consulate in Quebec City was a sleepy post with a minimal staff. Only in the 1960s, with the advent of Jean Lesage and the Liberals in Quebec City, and the simultaneous reign of Charles de Gaulle in France, did business pick up.

Lesage visited Paris, met de Gaulle, and opened a 'délégation générale' in 1961.[6] De Gaulle was sympathetic; as he told his entourage, there was a new wind blowing in Quebec. Quebec was becoming nervous about its culture and French heritage, just as the French were recognizing that there were relatively few predominantly French-speaking states around the world. As the French empire passed into limbo between 1958 and 1962, France and Frenchmen looked for company and found Quebec, also modernizing. With 5.1 million Canadians reporting French as their mother tongue, according to the 1961 census, and with most of these in 'la belle province,' Quebec became the second largest concentration of francophones in the world.[7]

French-speakers or francophones in Canada were aware that their language needed reinforcement, in terms both of quality and of quantity; for even in Quebec, immigrants, the fastest-growing segment of the population, were passing to the anglophone side. A rapprochement with Paris was, from the point of view of language, defensive in nature, an essential component in a longer-term strategy to keep French alive in North America. And so, to a degree, it seemed in France. Given the prevailing ignorance in France of conditions in North America, it was even possible to exaggerate the disabilities under which the French in

Canada laboured;[8] not many paused to credit a system that permitted Lesage and, after 1966, Daniel Johnson to travel to Paris to share their troubles with their distant metropolitan cousins.[9]

As relations warmed between the French of France and the French-speakers of Quebec,[10] the Canadian government first took notice, and then took fright. The Pearson government was not anxious for a confrontation with the Lesage regime, and Pearson himself was convinced that he could find a middle way that would permit Quebec its necessary self-expression while preserving Ottawa's essential powers to direct Canadian foreign policy. Sometimes, his colleagues thought, he went too far.

When Paul Gérin-Lajoie, Lesage's minister of education and a constitutional expert, told the world that he thought that Canada's external sovereignty was divisible into federal and provincial packets, Pearson shrugged. 'Paul doesn't mean it,' he would say. Few of his colleagues concurred. Pearson would even consider devolving functions on the provinces, and particularly on Lesage's Quebec. When the prime minister returned from one meeting with Lesage with the bases for such a devolution worked out, the horrified External Affairs lawyers and their allies moved heaven and earth, and their minister, to oppose him.[11]

Increasingly, as the 1960s wore on and Quebec's demands for new powers and more room failed to abate, nerves in Ottawa frayed. There was increasing doubt that the government of Quebec was in control of its policies or that its functionaries were to be trusted. Suspicion centred on Claude Morin, the deputy minister of federal-provincial relations. He was an able, even brilliant, expositor of a strong nationalist line; professionally, he could hold his own with the various officials that the federal government fielded for federal-provincial conferences. Morin's interest, by 1965, was turning more and more to the field of international relations where, some believed, it was possible for Quebec to assert its interests and therefore its jurisdiction. In the 1930s the courts had held that the government of Canada could not exercise full power over the external aspects of provincial jurisdiction. But if the federal government could not, who could?

The Lesage government, stimulated by its advisers, proposed to fill the gap. When it asserted an independent role in international relations in 1965, both through the negotiation of a cultural accord with France and through its claim to manage its own foreign relations in its own jurisdiction, Ottawa turned its attention to damage control.[12]

Paul Martin, the minister of external affairs, issued a statement asserting that federal control over foreign relations was unique and intact. To prove that it was, a sleight-of-hand, an 'umbrella agreement' or *accord cadre*, was negotiated to cover France's cultural agreement with Quebec. The government of Canada gave its consent to cultural relations between the governments of France and Quebec – in other words, gave those relations an autonomous dimension that would permit direct visits and consultations between Quebec City and Paris. The formality seemed pointless to many observers, but to the Department of External Affairs it meant that no precedent, either in domestic constitutional law or in international practice, had been established that could be used to justify further adventures in independence on the part of Quebec. A triumph of form over substance could reflect as well as mask a deeper reality. In the 1910s and 1920s the British empire conceded the substance of international relations to Canada while retaining the forms intact, but in the end Canada had got rid of the forms as well.

'I remember being told by Claude Morin,' Jean Chrétien later said, ' "We'll separate from Canada the same way that Canada separated from England: we'll cut the links one at a time, a concession here and a concession there, and eventually there'll be nothing left." '[13] It seemed so simple: an incident, once repeated, became a precedent; repeated often enough, precedents broadened into convention, leaving only the hollow shell of legality to mask the federal position.

When the Quebec Ministry of Federal-Provincial Relations changed its name to the Ministry of Intergovernmental Affairs, heads turned. And when it was noticed, even before the change of name, that the ministry had turned its attention from domestic Canadian problems such as the distribution of pension funds to larger questions of the transfer of powers from the federal to the provincial level, Ottawa's unease grew.

De Gaulle's intervention in July 1967, repeated several times that same year, gave substance to federal worries and complaints over Quebec's plans. Discussing the events of the past year with a high federal civil servant in January 1968, Johnson placed the blame for de Gaulle's irruption on the view advanced by some of the general's 'own experts and ... by some Quebec technocrats who were in secret communication with de Gaulle, that Quebec would secede.' Johnson himself was, he said, 'against separatism in any way, shape, or form.' But negotiations over the points that divided Quebec and Ottawa would nevertheless be left to those same technocrats who were already regarded as crypto-separatists by their counterparts in the federal capital. It was, as so often with Johnson, a case of two steps forward, two steps back.[14]

As the 1968 constitutional conference approached, the federal government prepared its position. *Federalism and International Relations,* a booklet prepared by a team of federal lawyers, was passed out to conference participants on 7 February. Its conclusions were uncompromising. It was true that Canada was founded on difference and diversity, but this did not prevent the federal government from dealing with the world outside; indeed, it framed the identity that Canada existed to defend. Because Canada was diverse, its several parts need not become divergent; only the federal government could see Canada as a whole and therefore properly represent it or any of its components.

What did that imply for external affairs? Law and custom were clear on that. First, 'in official dealings with other countries, that is to say in the conduct of foreign relations in the strict sense of that term, only the Federal Government is empowered to act on behalf of Canada. The statement applies to the negotiation and conclusion of treaties and other international agreements, to membership in international organizations, and to the right to accredit and receive diplomatic representatives.' Problems there might be in the management of the external expression of a diverse country, but no true solution could be found that devolved Canadian sovereignty into the hands of 'provincial, linguistic and cultural interests.' That, the report's authors argued, 'would lead to the disintegration of the Canadian federation.'[15]

It was clear that in this area, at least, the federal position was fixed. But what about the provincial contention – the emotional foundation of Quebec's case – that only a majority francophone government could properly represent the 'nation' of Quebec?

The minister of justice, Pierre Trudeau, had served notice that he did not consider that the future of French Canada depended on two nations, special status, or even devolution of powers. His was the liberal version of the French-Canadian past, and the liberal prescription for its future. Trudeau favoured individual rights over collective demands; one of his particular bug-bears was nationalism in all its forms, including and especially the French-Canadian version. 'We must not,' he told Quebec Liberals on 28 January 1968, 'confuse the rights of French-Canadians with the legitimate or illegitimate desire of a provincial government to build itself a little empire.'

Trudeau took the same line in addressing the constitutional conference on the morning of 6 February. Johnson had referred, sneeringly, to the 'député de Mont-Royal.' The member for Mount Royal retorted that Quebec's premier was, after all, merely the 'député de Bagot'; he was not an oracle, merely a politician. Prime Minister Pearson hastily called a coffee break. Perhaps Trudeau had been impolitic; perhaps it was not the time to take a firm line with the government of Quebec. The risks were great: if Trudeau's hard line did not succeed, what then?[16]

When the conference broke up without agreement on a new constitution, some English-Canadian nerves were fraying. The Toronto political economist and Canadian nationalist Abraham Rotstein denounced 'the forthright and intemperate exercise of Trudeau's ideological convictions on the evils of nationalism.' Quoting with approval the editorialist Claude Ryan – he was, after all, writing in Ryan's own newspaper – he predicted that Trudeau would succeed only in 'poison[ing] the climate of reconciliation' unless he mended his ways.[17]

Trudeau would have replied that there was no 'climate of reconciliation,' at least none that Johnson could define; nor was he about to help the Quebec premier out of a box where his own theories, added to some of the inescapable certainties of Canadian life, had placed him. For Johnson knew, and had known since the previous fall, that Quebec independence was neither in his grasp nor in his power.

De Gaulle's visit had given a noticeable fillip to the cause of Quebec separatism. He had 'heard' the Quebec people, the French president told his entourage, and soon his ministers and diplomats were hearing them too.[18] But what exactly had the general said when he shouted out, 'Vive le Québec libre'?

When offered a choice of interpretations, in a poll in August 1967, just over half of the Quebeckers interviewed plumped for the following: 'The general meant that Quebec is actually free and that he was glad that this is so.' Only 17 per cent maintained that de Gaulle meant to urge Quebec to separate from Canada. Had the general's visit been a good thing? Certainly, according to the majority of respondents, and Ottawa had been 'too hard' on him when it said his words were 'unacceptable.' But regardless of Pearson's reproaches, in the opinion of 40 per cent of Quebeckers de Gaulle should have gone to see Pearson anyway. The earth, apparently, had not suddenly moved when de Gaulle opened his mouth to speak.[19]

Without any significant popular resonance behind it, the demand for 'égalité où indépendance' that was the stock in trade of nationalist intellectuals in the 1960s remained windy rhetoric. And when Johnson, already suffering from the coronary deficiency that was later to kill him, retreated to Hawaii to recuperate in the fall of 1967, bad news pursued him. A group of financiers headed by Paul Desmarais arrived from Montreal to confer with the premier. Quebec's economic situation was unhealthy, Johnson was told; proof of instability, of the kind that a lunge for independence would afford, would be highly undesirable. Under pressure, Johnson revised his priorities.[20]

The economy was one area where France could not help.[21] De Gaulle, some time after Johnson's painful interview with the businessmen, told one of his diplomats that he 'regret[ted] that French business remain[ed] timorous and that little [had] been done in the economic sphere.' Nevertheless, the president loftily added, Johnson had not been forward in the fight for sovereignty, despite his (and France's) encouragement; he was 'a politician and not a statesman.'[22] But it was Johnson, not de Gaulle, who would have to pay the bills – economic and political.

While de Gaulle announced his vision of Quebec as a sovereign state in a press conference in November, Johnson engaged in constitutional revisionism, not the pursuit of Quebec's sovereignty, at a conference in Toronto. Officially, Johnson made no comment on de Gaulle's remarks; unofficially, as one of the Quebec delegation exclaimed in front of the press, 'Save us from our friends!'[23] But only up to a point.

The friends had in mind the establishment of a firm international precedent where Canada would not be allowed to save face and where, if all went well, Canada would not be allowed to save itself. The friends were powerful, and included some of de Gaulle's entourage, some officials in the Quai d'Orsay, and some dreamers, moved by the idea of a French Family Robinson cast adrift on the shores of Kebeca Incognita. Most important, de Gaulle himself was Quebec's chief friend in Paris.[24]

Whether or not the French president's oration of 24 July 1967 had been an unanticipated accident, by the end of that year de Gaulle was openly anticipating the collapse of the artificial Canadian federation and the erection on its ruins of a sovereign French-speaking Quebec. In August it was announced that French aid to Quebec would be considerably increased. In November, de Gaulle himself pronounced that Quebec would find its sovereign future; privately he had already minuted that Lester Pearson's feelings on the subject were of no account. His ambassador in Ottawa, François Leduc, had consistently emphasized the positive in his dispatches from the Canadian capital after July 1967. There was no disposition on the part of the Canadian government to break relations, de Gaulle was told; on the contrary, the Canadians preferred to pass off the July incident as if it had never happened.[25]

De Gaulle took this to be a sign of weakness. The Canadians did not dare retaliate; yet at the same time they ignored his prophecies. It was an unsatisfactory combination. Within his own government, he acted to promote the standing of the French consulate in Quebec City. Unlike other consulates, it would no longer report to Paris through the French embassy in the national capital; of course, de Gaulle did not believe that Canada had a national capital in the strict sense.[26]

Trudeau had chosen to place himself athwart de Gaulle's wishes by the simple fact of publicly opposing and ridiculing Daniel Johnson's nationalist and autonomist version of Quebec. Johnson, curiously, had no effective response: his biographer describes him in 1968 as caught in Trudeau's talons ('entre les griffes de Trudeau'). Since de Gaulle, regardless of his personal opinion of the Quebec premier, had chosen sides in Quebec's political battle, he was bound to refuse to cooperate with any Canadian attempt at reconciliation.

Trudeau secured the Liberal leadership on 6 April 1968 by a slim margin at a party convention. Shortly afterwards the Canadian correspondent for the French state-broadcasting system phoned Trudeau's headquarters in order, as he wrote, 'to convey my congratulations to the new chief of the federal Liberal party and the future prime minister of Canada.' He spoke to one of Trudeau's associates, an anglophone who spoke 'reasonable French' and who had one pressing question to ask: 'Do you believe that General de Gaulle will agree to see M. Trudeau?'

The answer to that could come only from the general, and it was not long in coming. On 10 April the French embassy wrote to Paris to suggest various ways of reducing Franco-Canadian tensions by taking advantage of Pearson's departure and Trudeau's succession. Trudeau, Leduc pointed out, was 'a pragmatist and an intelligent realist, with whom this embassy has personal relations and with whom it is possible to have it out, in a direct and friendly way, even on such a delicate subject.' The embassy had done its best, but it would not suffice. De Gaulle wrote on the margins of the dispatch, in words whose flavour is best conveyed in the original French: 'Nous n'avons aucune concession ni même aucune amabilité à faire à M. Trudeau qui est l'adversaire de la chose française au Canada.'[27]

De Gaulle's dictum would have come as no surprise in some circles in Ottawa. In Leduc's opinion, an arrangement with Trudeau personally was the best, and possibly the only, way of bypassing what he called 'l'hostilité irréductible des hauts fonctionnaires actuels des Affaires extérieures.' He did not add that it would also short-circuit the ultras in the French bureaucracy: in de Gaulle's circle at the Elysée, in some sections of the Quai d'Orsay, and in the office of the minister of education, Peyrefitte. But with de Gaulle's own enmity towards what we might call the 'chose canadienne' confirmed if not amplified by the advent of Trudeau as prime minister, the ball was in the court of the 'hauts fonctionnaires.'[28]

There were not many high-ranking French Canadians in the Canadian civil service in the late 1960s. Ottawa was an ethnically divided city, with a French quarter, Lowertown, a French suburb, Vanier, and a French twin, Hull, on the Quebec side of the Ottawa River. But although French Canadians and English Canadians rode the same buses, paid more or less the same taxes, and worked in the same offices, their private lives were usually very different.

As well they might be. Although promotion was not barred to French Canadians in the public service, the rules of the game dictated that they must succeed in another language. French-Canadian civil servants had to be bilingual, above the most menial level; but English Canadians were not required, or even expected, to reciprocate.[29] When L.B. Pearson, as external affairs minister in the 1950s, discussed the benefits of language training with his senior officials, he meant learning Russian or Chinese; he had to be reminded that there was another language, and another problem, closer to home.[30]

By 1966 Pearson had adjusted his priorities. He announced that bilingual requirements were being extended to civil servants in Ottawa; and the next year, 1967, the Public Service Commission announced the appropriate regulations. A hundred years after Confederation, French had 'arrived' as a language of work in the national capital.[31]

French Canadians, however, were already there. In the Department of External Affairs there were already French-speaking officers: forty-three out of 158, in 1949. Of that number, thirteen were considered 'senior,' nine 'intermediate,' and twenty-one 'junior.' These numbers slowly increased over the intervening years, but not as fast as the total number of officers in the department; the proportion of French, therefore, tended to shrink. When the department's bilingual character was surveyed for a federal royal commission, French Canadians were held to be in a state of 'permanent under-representation.' That representation accounted for 21 per cent of the department's officer class in 1965 – about 7 per cent less than the proportion of French Canadians in the general population. By 1972 recruitment, along with the reconstruction of the department in 1969–70, had raised the proportion of francophones to 24.8 per cent; because the concurrent reorganization had dealt severely with some of the existing employees, the feeling persisted that the francophone intake had climbed into the department over the bodies of their anglophone predecessors.[32]

It was not a comfortable situation. In the view of some French-Canadian officers, it was even less comfortable because of the paradoxical fact that the department's top civil servant, Undersecretary Marcel Cadieux, was himself French Canadian. Observers recalled that Cadieux ran a lively ship, where the life of the mind was respected and cultivated, but where niceties and details were sometimes neglected.[33]

One very large detail was probably beyond Cadieux's control. External Affairs was no longer the nice little ship it had been in the days of Norman Robertson. Promotion was slower than in the 1950s or early 1960s. The department had expanded, and not many had retired; the great postwar intake of officers had become senior, and opportunities for responsibility were limited; perhaps they were already contracting. Some promising officers had already left: Ivan Head on Trudeau's staff was one; Marshall Crowe in the Privy Council Office was another.

Younger foreign-service officers took a less altruistic view of the meaning of their careers than their predecessors had ostensibly done: it was an interesting life, many agreed, but just as many thought that that was because it gave them an 'opportunity to travel' and 'experience new cultures.' The 'opportunity to promote Canadian interests, [and] in general to serve Canada' was ranked considerably lower. Somewhere between 1945 and 1975 the focus had shifted. Moreover, French Canadians in the 1970s were more likely to stress personal satisfaction than altruism as benefits accruing from the job. It may be that Cadieux's severity with his own language group derived from his grasp of their attitude. In 1964, at the suggestion of Norman Robertson and Gordon Robertson, the cabinet secretary, he had become undersecretary of state for external affairs. Paul Martin, the minister, later wrote that he and Gordon Robertson 'both felt that Cadieux was the right man, given the government's aim of creating closer relations with France and francophone countries.' If that was the aim, it backfired.[34]

Cadieux was a man of ideas and principle. It did not matter to him that he was often alone in his passion. One thing he cared about was being Canadian: the emergence of Quebec nationalism in the 1960s he considered a blind alley, while the pretensions of the Quebec government to independent jurisdiction in international affairs he considered abhorrent, if not treasonable. The true course of Quebec's interests lay in exploiting opportunity in Ottawa. 'He said,' his colleague Paul Tremblay remarked in 1981, 'that those among us who represented Quebec in the federal government remained faithful to the motto of their province – they remembered.' The nationalists, while recognizing Cadieux's abilities and regretting his attitudes, repaid the compliment: Cadieux and other francophone federal civil servants were 'objectively allies of the English establishment' ['alliés objectifs de l'establishment anglophone'] in the view of Claude Morin.[35]

That would have been news to Cadieux. Believing that his promotion affirmed the place of the French fact in Canada, and that meritorious French Canadians could hold their own with their English-speaking counterparts, Cadieux considered that Morin and his friends were undermining a position laboriously and painfully achieved. As far as Morin was concerned, Cadieux might even be right, but neither he nor his nationalist colleagues cared. And as Morin knew, there were those among Cadieux's francophone subordinates who sympathized more than a little with the assertion of a Quebec role in international relations. Even among those who did not, there were some who were uneasy at his insistence on carrying a dispute in the family, among French Canadians, to the point of involving the English. 'They won't thank you for it, Marcel,' one of his contemporaries told him. Just wait: if the English found it expedient, they would abandon Cadieux, and where would he be then?[36]

Morin was the master of his own foreign policy, and carrying it out did not require Ottawa's permission. French ministers and officials paraded through Quebec City; Cadieux's vehement protests to the French embassy were heard but not heeded, nor did a trip to Paris in November 1967 produce any better results. Whether or not the French ambassador or even the undersecretary at the Quai d'Orsay sympathized with Cadieux and Canada did not, by this stage, matter very much; the main effect of Cadieux's interventions was to make Leduc's final months in Ottawa less pleasant than they might otherwise have been. Since no serious business was being transacted, they could hardly have made them less productive.

As far as Cadieux was concerned, French hostility to Canada – to the existence of Canada in its current form – must be taken for granted. The evidence supported him, and his personal experience confirmed it. As long as de Gaulle directed France's Canadian policy, it did not matter that individual French diplomats sympathized with the Canadian cause. It followed that Canada must act to confound and frustrate French collusion with Quebec.[37]

Cadieux saw External's Legal Division as the first line of defence for Canadian unity. It was an unusual choice, enforced to a degree because more usual means had been bypassed or neutered. The embassy in France was ineffective. The ambassador, Jules Léger, was virtually persona non grata with de Gaulle. Though Léger was an eminently sane and moderate personality, his prescriptions for Franco-Canadian harmony were perennially ineffective: they depended on a miraculous intervention that might calm de Gaulle's francophone ardour; but de Gaulle was in full control of the French government. On an issue of symbols, especially, no one dared contradict him, and even after his July 1967 escapade in Montreal, criticism of him within government circles was muted and ineffective. There was, however, another problem. Canada's relations with France, be they economic or political, were not of such significance that they could affect any substantial French interest. The ties of interest that might otherwise have bound French allies to Canada were in this case sadly lacking.[38]

Legal Division was not itself a large group, because its lawyers took regular rotation through 'line' jobs in embassies and in other divisions; and not all lawyers in External Affairs remained enamoured of the law. Traditionally, 'Legal' operated on two fronts: abroad, it represented Canadian interests in international negotiations; at home it advised the undersecretary and fought off jurisdictional raids by the Department of Justice.[39]

To head the division, Cadieux appointed Allan Gotlieb. Gotlieb was a Winnipeger who had arrived in External Affairs by way of Oxford and the *Harvard Law Review;* seven years later, at the age of thirty-seven, he was made head of Legal Division and two years further on, in 1967, he assumed the title of legal adviser and assistant undersecretary – just where Cadieux had been three years earlier. The rapid promotion, and the parallels with Cadieux's own career, did not pass unnoticed.

Cadieux then added to Gotlieb's standing. All papers and dispatches with a constitutional or federal-provincial bearing were to be routed through Gotlieb's office. Its mandate was to deny and combat the legitimacy of provincial intrusions into foreign policy. Cadieux realized that where federal policy was in fact in deficit – as on relations with francophone Africa – it would have to respond. And, as France's colonies achieved formal independence in the early 1960s, Cadieux pushed Canadian missions into them and hired French-speaking officers as staff.[40]

The choice of Legal Division as the focus for the struggle with France and Quebec should not have puzzled some of Gotlieb's colleagues as much as it apparently did. Obviously there were personal reasons for Cadieux's decision, but there were other points in its favour. In Cadieux's view, and in that of some at least of his legal staff, Quebec was embarking on a struggle that had been defined in legal terms. Gérin-Lajoie, who led off in 1965, was a considerable legal scholar, an expert in the evolution of Canadian sovereignty from British dependency, precedent by precedent, earlier in the century. It became Legal Division's task to block the creation of precedents, using whatever arguments came to hand, bit by bit, point by point.

In February 1968, for example, Quebec and France signed an agreement creating the 'Office franco-québécois de la Jeunesse.' It had been negotiated without reference to Ottawa and, learning of its existence and of its approaching signature, Ottawa asked for a copy. This the Quai d'Orsay supplied. The next day the Canadian embassy announced that the agreement conformed to the 1965 umbrella agreement between Canada and France, and that Canada accordingly had no objection to make; but it complained that tardy notification had forced it to make an unduly hasty study of the matter. Further notes to the Quai argued that advance notice would be useful for the future.[41]

The effect was sometimes to blur what might have been a clear-cut confrontation, what one non-lawyer called 'a smokescreen approach.' But that, according to an External lawyer, was just the point. The government of Canada's tactic was to blur a clear-cut situation that might not, perhaps could not, have been advantageous to its own side. Thus, when news was received of a Quebec initiative, External Affairs cranked out permission by return mail, even though, and perhaps especially because, permission had not been sought.[42]

Gotlieb's appointment brought him into contact with all the senior officials directly concerned with the 'Quebec problem': of these the most senior was Marc Lalonde, policy adviser in Pearson's office. The policy Lalonde was most concerned with was the government's response to France, and to Quebec. Lalonde now became close to Trudeau.

Trudeau himself was frequently seen in parties around town between 1965 and 1968, nursing his single drink, often standing by himself in a corner, observing what transpired. One of his friends worked for the French embassy – and the embassy would report, in April 1968, that it enjoyed 'personal connections' with Trudeau. After de Gaulle's speech, Trudeau's diplomatic friend returned wearily home after the normal round of abuse that the French were then reaping in Ottawa to discover a personal note from Trudeau. The note assured him that he retained his confidence and friendship. As for 'Vive le Québec libre,' Trudeau preferred to treat it as low comedy. 'Vive le St Pierre et Miquelon libre,' he would shout in August 1967, while driving his Mercedes convertible down Ottawa's Wellington Street.[43]

Cadieux was not a member of Trudeau's immediate circle. He knew Trudeau, of course, for they met in Ottawa in the early 1950s when Trudeau served briefly in the Privy Council Office. But unlike Cadieux, Trudeau left. Unlike the diligent diplomat, Trudeau had the luxury of a private income and the reputation of a wealthy young man about town. He could afford his independence, his opposition to received opinions, and his contrariness; partly because of this, on subjects other than Quebec and the constitution, his views were not Cadieux's.[44]

But they agreed on the constitution. Until 1965 Cadieux had been fighting a lonely battle in Ottawa. The Quebec government was scrambling further and further out on a dangerous limb, leading in his view to sovereignty and independence. Pearson, however, would not take it seriously. Then Trudeau became Pearson's parliamentary secretary in 1966 (he was first elected in the general election of 8 November 1965), and brought a different attitude to the Prime Minister's Office. He had been fighting separatists for four years in the columns of his magazine, *Cité Libre,* and he took them very seriously indeed. Finally Cadieux had a soul-mate, or so it must have seemed from the outside. But it was at this point that the differences in character came into play. To Cadieux, Trudeau was a dilettante. True, the dilettante had been projected into the highest offices of state, but to a driven, serious-minded man like Cadieux, there was something illegitimate about a process, or an accident, that could produce such an incredible result. Though he had to live with Trudeau and make the most of his new situation, he did not approve. There were, in any case, ideological differences too.

Trudeau was the man who had travelled to Moscow at the height – or depth – of the Cold War. Perhaps he had learned something from the experience; but the senior generation of foreign-service officers could not be entirely sure. Trudeau had spoken out against nuclear weapons, and especially against nuclear weapons on Canadian soil; to a generation of diplomats who had struggled to put together a Western alliance and a nuclear strategy, this was folly at best, heresy at worst. For Cadieux, with his Vietnam ICC experience behind him, the evils of communism were self-evident; but Trudeau was just as impressed by the dangers in the Western strategy of confronting communism, and among those dangers he numbered the possibility of nuclear war.[45]

Cadieux did not know that Trudeau's entourage was developing ideas and programs for external affairs over the winter of 1967–8 (see 11 above); Trudeau had not announced that he would run for the Liberal leadership, and would not do so until after the constitutional conference in February. During the winter it was generally believed that Jean Marchand, Trudeau's friend and the minister of manpower and immigration, would run. Only in February did it suddenly become very important what Trudeau thought about Canada's foreign policy. And by then Canada was engaged in another imbroglio with France.

Most Canadians have never heard of Gabon. It nestles on the equator, on the west coast of Africa, just above Congo and just below Cameroun. In 1990 the population was roughly 1.2 million, though the area is greater than the Federal Republic of Germany. Until 1960, Gabon was a colony of France; the national capital, a French colonial foundation, was appropriately named Libreville. Indeed, among the former French colonies in Africa it was particularly dependent on aid and experts from Paris; as recently as 1964 France had intervened to save the Gabonese government from a coup d'état. Some observers thought that Gabon had subsequently been inclined to take policy advice from Paris very seriously indeed.[46]

Gabon's sole official language was (and is) French; that fact places it among the twenty-six countries where French (or a variant of French) is officially recognized. In de Gaulle's circle, the French language counted among France's international assets. To Alain Peyrefitte, de Gaulle's minister for research and later minister of education, 'the heart of the nebula of public and secret friendships lies in the community of French-speaking nations. Even if France has ceased to be the world's diplomatic and juridical language, it is still the second language of the elite.'[47]

Expanding the francophone nebula was on de Gaulle's agenda, but the idea was no stranger in Quebec. Federalists like Gérard Pelletier, a journalist and, since 1965, a Liberal MP, and nationalists like Jean-Marc Léger of Le Devoir, championed closer ties between French-speaking nations. For Pelletier, of course, Canada was the nation in question; for Léger, priority went to Quebec.[48] And if French-speakers were franco-phones, it followed that their world-wide language community was francophonie, even if, as Léger has written, francophonie implies quite different things to its several beholders.[49]

During the 1950s and early 1960s a number of international franco-phone organizations sprang up, for universities, journalists, and culture generally. The idea, and its several organized expressions, attracted the interest and support of prominent African politicians such as Léopold Senghor, president of Senegal; and it was well calculated to appeal to the francophile elites that the French left behind them.

One organization the French promoted was a group of education ministers, drawn from France and its former African colonies. It was this organization that Peyrefitte mentioned to his Quebec hosts while on a visit to the province in September 1967. The education ministers would be meeting in February 1968 in Libreville. Peyrefitte did not need to add that, except for Quebec, all the participants would represent sovereign states. Quebec, its delegates, and its flag, would be treated as equals. Perhaps Quebec would like to come?

Quebec would, and the provincial cabinet gave its approval on 20 September. Education was an indubitable provincial power, and it was in the throes of change. How better to guide that change than by referring to the experience of other francophone countries? In Quebec City, Daniel Johnson commissioned Claude Morin to take charge of the project, as deputy minister of intergovernmental affairs; and in Paris Peyrefitte transmitted the word that Quebec would attend.[50]

It did not take long for Ottawa to learn what was up. Ottawa and Quebec had, in any case, few secrets from each other: leaks from sympathizers, not to mention ordinary and frequent interchanges at the level of the bureaucracy, took care of that. Soon External Affairs was on the line to Quebec, to ask what Ottawa could do to help, in the context of safeguarding Canada's interests as a whole. Canada was, for example, in diplomatic touch with Gabon (having recognized it in 1960) through non-resident missions. There was a modest aid program that applied to formerly French Africa, but, as Jules Léger, Canada's ambassador in Paris, had pointed out in May 1966, 'in these countries the nature of France's role as the former colonial power makes us prudent. We don't want to take the risk of identifying ourselves too closely with France so as not to run the risk of an anti-colonial backlash.' It was a sensible observation; but like other larger prudences, it would soon be overtaken by events.[51]

Morin canvassed the relevant ministers in Quebec, and, to no one's great surprise, discovered that the province's attitude was firm and clear. An international conference on the subject of education was merely the extension of Quebec's undoubted provincial jurisdiction; conversely, a federal delegation to an education conference constituted interference. Quebec would not play second fiddle to Ottawa on such an occasion. Although Quebec defended its participation in international activities on functional grounds, it was clear that symbols played a most important role.[52]

Ottawa suspected that a negative reply would be forthcoming. Fortuitously, it had already had an opportunity to advance its own symbolic case, and to define its own future actions. At the end of 1966 an invitation had arrived from Togo, addressed to the Canadian minister of justice, inviting his attendance at a francophone law conference. The minister, Lucien Cardin, could not be spared; but in his stead the government appointed another francophone jurist, the prime minister's parliamentary secretary, Pierre Elliott Trudeau. Trudeau promptly accepted and quickly departed, despite indications from Africa that the invitation had in fact gone to Ottawa by mistake.[53]

Trudeau visited Cameroun, Niger, Ivory Coast, Togo, Senegal, and Tunisia. It was a time to gather impressions – what was Quebec doing in the way of aid to Africa – and to make impressions. In Cameroun, for example, Trudeau pointed out that Canada was also a federal state, subject to divisive pressures just as in his host country. The point was taken. Similarly, Trudeau made a favourable impression on President Bourguiba of Tunisia; and Bourguiba thereafter took a friendly attitude towards the Canadian federal government. On returning home, Trudeau made the point that federal authority in external affairs was not as yet threatened by Quebec's own activities in Africa, but that it could be, unless the federal government filled the void that presently stood for a Canadian 'policy' in francophone Africa. Thus, more time and money must be spent on Africa. Perhaps a Maison de la Culture in Paris, separate from the embassy, would serve as a base for future efforts among French-speaking peoples. Finally, and immediately, the cabinet must define and promulgate its policy on federalism and international affairs.[54]

That would be done in time for the constitutional conference in February 1968. In the meantime, diplomacy of both the federal-provincial and the external kind would have to do. Quebec was warned that its participation in an international conference without a Canadian presence would be unfortunate; as for Gabon, its putative sponsor, it was not easy to deliver the message. The Gabonese government, in a note dated 30 January 1968, had pretended that the Quebec education minister was being invited strictly in his personal capacity; this was, of course, untrue.[55]

Canada drafted a response, which was wired to the nearest Canadian embassy. The Canadian ambassador to Cameroun would, ordinarily, have had the responsibility of delivering Canada's views to the Gabonese government, but he had not yet presented his credentials to Gabon. When he tried to travel to Libreville, he was turned away. He persisted, and was eventually seen by a junior official in Gabon's office of protocol. This occurred on 1 February, four days before the conference was to open and with the Quebec minister of education, Jean-Guy Cardinal, already en route. The impoliteness of the Gabonese officials, and their insistence on minor points of protocol, suggested that their tactics had been dictated from Paris, or at any rate by Parisian officials on the spot.[56]

Consideration of the details of Gabon's behaviour took some time to filter through to Ottawa. There were problems of communications, for France controlled the telephone circuits in its former African colonies, and the Yaoundé embassy was obliged to ask the Americans to send the details by their more secure 'flash' network.

On 4 March 1968 Canada announced that its ambassador designate to Gabon would not present his letters of credence to that country's government. The action terminated such diplomatic relations as existed between the two countries, though it fell short of a formal break. Pearson accompanied the announcement with a promise that the federal government would do its utmost to secure proper provincial and francophone representation on delegations abroad.[57]

Gabon responded to Pearson's criticism of its insincerity with a sarcastic reference to the amount of Canadian aid it was receiving: two teachers and two scholarships. If Pearson wished to push matters even further, it announced, he could remove this Canadian assistance. The Gabonese did not suggest that if the Canadian aid had been more imposing, their attitude would have been more forthcoming, but the conclusion is tempting. Implicitly, the Canadian government was drawing such a conclusion, for as the governments squabbled, a Canadian mission headed by the former federal minister of transport, Lionel Chevrier, was visiting francophone Africa, laden with promises of aid.[58]

The connection between aid and attitude was almost shamelessly explicit in the Canadian expedition; Chevrier had in fact offered to go to Gabon in early February, just as the education conference was taking place. But Chevrier's mission was also addressing an internal as well as an external constituency: in the aftermath of the constitutional conference, Chevrier would symbolize both the effectiveness and the commitment of Ottawa's policy towards other francophone countries.[59]

Though Gabon was a blow, it was mitigated by the fact that that country was distant and, ultimately, insignificant. Worse, however, was in prospect. The Libreville conference of francophone education ministers was scheduled to continue in Paris in April; Quebec would of course attend. Pearson protested in a letter to Johnson; and New Brunswick, whose premier, Louis Robichaud, was himself francophone, attempted to enlist Quebec as a partner in a combined federal-provincial delegation. In Quebec City it was suspected that Robichaud's motive was to embarrass Johnson, showing that Quebec cared not at all for francophones living outside the province – a perception that in terms of Quebec's stand for provincial autonomy would have been more or less exact. As if to confirm a further suspicion that Ottawa had put Robichaud up to it, Pearson repeated the argument that francophones outside Quebec could only be represented by a larger, Canadian delegation. On 11 April Canada also directed a request to the French, asking to be represented at the forthcoming conference.[60]

In a statement released on 12 April, Jean-Guy Cardinal announced that he would again head the Quebec delegation, adding that the federal government could have nothing to do with education in any of its aspects. That same day, Jules Léger was recalled for consultations; he would return to Paris only after the Cardinal visit was over, on 30 April.

Cardinal was favourably and prominently received in France. Peyrefitte gave him three separate interviews, even while stressing in public the technical, non-political, nature of the discussions on education. Canada was not, of course, invited, a fact that was regretted in the protest note that Léger brought back to Paris and presented to the French government on 3 May.

Claude Morin gives the gist of the note in his *L'art de l'impossible* (1987), but it is possible to improve on his account. Canada protested that France had taken upon itself the interpretation of the Canadian constitution. To this Louis Joxe, a French cabinet minister, gave two replies. First, France would accept any interpretation of the constitution that Canada and Quebec could agree on, since France had no interest in making its own interpretations. Second, the correctness of the Canadian government's analysis of its constitution would have to be studied closely before the French government could respond. Both Léger and Joxe understood just whose opinion would count in such a study: the French government would continue to accept the Quebec government's interpretation of the propriety and constitutionality of its actions. Although Léger pointed out that the advent of the Trudeau government made a new beginning possible, and that a continuation of the existing 'atmosphere' implied 'an unfavourable turn' in Franco-Canadian relations, de Gaulle's government did not especially care.[61]

The French government for the moment had other matters to occupy its attention. In May 1968 a student insurrection in Paris shook de Gaulle's regime to its foundations. Just as Pierre Trudeau was dissolving the Canadian parliament and starting his triumphal election tour, de Gaulle was scrambling to stay in power and, more seriously, to keep his fifth republic in being. The year 1968 was, of course, one of civil disturbance around the world, and Canada had not been exempt. Trudeau was helped in capturing a parliamentary majority on 25 June by a public confrontation with a bottle-throwing separatist mob in Montreal. The prime minister stood his ground while Premier Johnson and other notables scuttled for cover. Because this occurred on the eve of the election, voters retained a vivid, impromptu image of the man they were to confirm in the first of his sixteen years in power. Nor, as it turned out, was the image of Trudeau, standing his ground before threats and taunts, not to mention a barrage of bottles and other garbage, inappropriate.[62]

On the day of the Canadian election de Gaulle replaced François Leduc as ambassador to Ottawa. His successor would be France's chief of protocol, Pierre Siraud. Siraud was personally instructed by the general in his mission: there would be no change in France's attitude to Canada.

That would not necessarily make Siraud's mission unpleasant. He would have to endure periodic reproaches from Marcel Cadieux, but there were areas, atomic energy for example, where the two countries were actively cooperating and where the Canadians hoped that progress would begin to counter-balance the lure of a sovereign francophone Quebec. In respect of such subjects, Siraud could behave like a normal ambassador; but on political topics his hands were tied. There, he could offer little or nothing to the Canadian government. Though he met Trudeau several times, and admired his evident qualities, he could do nothing for him. Trudeau, for his part, shrugged: 'Mais je ne comprends pas la France,' he told the ambassador.[63]

Much of France's policy was difficult to understand; but it was equally difficult to say just where the control of policy lay. Discussions with senior French diplomats, including Jean-Daniel Jurgensen, Marcel Cadieux's opposite number at the Quai d'Orsay, produced promises of correct behaviour: notification of visits, assurances that France would not stray outside the umbrella agreement of 1965, and the like. Despite Jurgensen's evident sympathy for the Quebec nationalist cause, there is no special reason to suppose that these assurances were insincere.[64]

Yet the previous fall, and again in the summer of 1968, certain French personalities made appearances in New Brunswick and Manitoba, not to mention Quebec itself. The most notorious of them was Philippe Rossillon, an individual who enjoyed a quasi-official standing on some of de Gaulle's committees for the promotion and defence of the French language. These expeditions created a problem of definition, for the French emissaries were neither civil servants nor, exactly, ministers; their true significance and authority were unknown and perhaps unknowable. Daniel Johnson, in an apt phrase, called them 'francs-tireurs.'[65]

The significance of Rossillon, and of other Gaullist travellers in Canada, is that they contributed to the continued low state of Franco-Canadian relations. This did not displease de Gaulle, who happily revealed to a press conference on 9 September that the world had already experienced the dissolution of a number of federations. He was pleased to identify several, all former British colonies: Canada, Rhodesia, Malaysia (which had seen the secession of Singapore), Cyprus, and Nigeria, currently in a state of civil war.

Trudeau was bound to reply and, on 11 September, he did. Federalism, he predicted, was the way of the future, not a relic of an unhappy past. France, a unitary state, was not an exemplar of political stability, as its many constitutions showed. Perhaps French brains had been so addled by the recent disruptions in their own country that they had 'not ... recovered all their logical faculties.'

The prime minister did not stop there. France had sent a 'secret agent,' one Rossillon, into Manitoba to stir up trouble. His activities had been reported to Ottawa by the Manitoba government; Trudeau denounced 'this underhanded and surreptitious way' of doing business by an 'agent of a foreign state.' The cabinet considered a break in relations, and so informed the French. Rossillon's cloudy status assisted the French government in denying Trudeau's assertions; and perhaps, after all, his activities were only an example of Peyrefitte's 'public and secret friendships' based on the French language – the secret handshake that sealed allegiance to a francophone fraternal order. It was no accident that Peyrefitte characterized these relationships, private and public, as 'a nebula.' Certainly they were nebulous.[66]

Although France tried to increase the proportion of solids and decrease the content of gases in its Quebec policy – announcing a 50 per cent increase in aid for the province – it continued to rely primarily on symbols in Canada and Quebec. Where Quebec was concerned, the ambassador was empowered to offer all aid short of help: plenty of cultural and diplomatic support, but little in the way of investment. Investment could, after all, be got anywhere, as he would tell a later premier of Quebec; but only France could supply culture. Nothing could have better summed up the 'guerre des illusions,' the battle of symbols, that had characterized relations among the governments of France, Quebec, and Canada; and symbols were not immediately realizable as firm political assets, either in Quebec or in Canada as a whole.

Cultural diplomacy could do little to alter the real balance of forces in Quebec or Canada; indeed, as the lack of large-scale alternative investment from France became apparent, politics in the province took a more openly pro-federalist direction. But before they could be fixed, there were further changes among the personalities at the top.

Daniel Johnson's health continued to deteriorate through the summer of 1968. When he returned to work in September, it was largely in defiance of his doctor's orders. Having set himself against medical advice, he aggravated the situation by undertaking a strenuous trip to the Manicouagan damsite, and then enjoying a late but convivial evening. The next morning, 25 September, he was dead.

In Ottawa, Marcel Cadieux recorded his sadness at the death of an old friend from university days. Johnson had built his life around success in politics, and success had crowned his efforts – at least until the appearance of Trudeau in politics. That had been 'a very hard blow' for Johnson, and, the undersecretary added, 'I truly believe that it hastened his end.'

As things stood, Cadieux believed that Johnson's death was advantageous for the federal cause. The Quebec premier had been due to visit Paris (the visit had been repeatedly put off for health reasons), and it was certain that de Gaulle would have used the occasion for more mischief. Moreover, Johnson's political party, the Union Nationale, had been 'decapitated.' With Johnson gone, could the party sustain its position on the constitution?[67]

That remained to be seen. Jean-Jacques Bertrand, Quebec's minister of justice and of education and a Union Nationale veteran, succeeded to the premiership on 2 October. Bertrand was more solid, more reliable than the elusive Johnson; and, as events proved, he was by far the more secure federalist. He was less interested in international affairs than Johnson had been, and he did not appreciate the recent 'acrobatics' of the Quebec-Ottawa-Paris triangle.[68] When Bertrand and Trudeau met at the end of October, they happily discovered solidarity on key points. Bilingualism, which Trudeau held out as the alternative to separatism, was a policy that Bertrand favoured.

They agreed as well to avoid useless confrontations between provincial and federal officials. Did the premier know, Trudeau asked, that his officials ('les technocrates du Québec') wanted to involve officials from France in technical discussions over the expansion of Dorval airport? Bertrand was taken aback. No, he said, it was news to him.

The federal prime minister and the Quebec premier did not agree on all things: that would have been too much to expect. But where Johnson at the beginning of the year had referred the federal government back to Claude Morin, Bertrand hesitated. 'M. Bertrand doesn't seem to harbour too many illusions about M. Morin,' Cadieux wrote. 'He told the prime minister that, if he wanted to get in touch with him confidentially, he ought to use [Julien] Chouinard,' his cabinet secretary. Chouinard was well known, and favourably regarded, in Ottawa; he too was considered to be a federalist.[69]

Johnson's death attracted considerable attention in France. De Gaulle sent his prime minister, Maurice Couve de Murville, to attend the funeral; Trudeau took advantage of the occasion to meet his French counterpart while he was changing planes at Dorval airport. To Couve, Trudeau argued that France's activities in Canada had had the effect of weakening the French-Canadian presence or influence in the country as a whole. And while Couve replied that of course Quebec was in a special position as the home of the French fact in Canada ('le foyer du fait français au Canada'), to which France must give 'une attention particulière,' he also added that France did not believe in separatism ('la France ne croyait pas au séparatisme') and even considered that policy to be madness ('une folie'). Separatism, once achieved, would throw French Canadians into the American melting pot. That said, there was little to separate the views of the two men, even when Trudeau asked what France would do as regards equal treatment for other Canadian provinces with French-speaking minorities, or when he asked about a forthcoming francophone educational conference in Kinshasa, Zaire.[70]

Trudeau's interview with Couve should have promised well, yet, in the event, it had little issue: where Canada was concerned it was de Gaulle, and not his prime minister, who called the shots. Nor was de Gaulle isolated in throwing support to Quebec's most extreme pretensions in the international sphere. Quebec had its 'amis français,' as Claude Morin dubbed them: enthusiastic, imaginative, and influential friends as they proved to be. They included Jean-Daniel Jurgensen, Bernard Dorin, a counsellor in the French diplomatic service, and, on the political side, Philippe Rossillon and Xavier Deniau. It would be rash to impute careerism as a motive for their activities; as Morin says, Jurgensen's 'sympathies for Quebec were known.' It is equally true that in the atmosphere of 1968–70 their careers would not be harmed by a display of zeal on behalf of Quebec's national and international identity. Because the war with Ottawa would be fought on the terrain of international law, it was inevitably a war of symbols; and symbols, however potent, need not be costly. The fiscal limits of policy were not therefore immediately in evidence in this 'war of conferences' or, as some called it at the time, 'la guerre des drapeaux.' At the same time, some inside the French foreign service perceived that their careers might suffer a slowdown if they tried too obviously to plead a contrary case. Thus, for the moment, the ultras had the initiative in the formulation and expression of France's Canadian policy.[71]

It was a puzzling policy, since its objectives were expressed either as ideals ('self-determination,' 'national liberation,' the grandeur of the

French language, or the French way of doing things) or as means to an unclear end. The immediate cause at issue in the late 1960s was that of francophonie, which was given a variety of interpretations. That francophonie might have political uses was seldom denied; that it was a political end in itself was not generally admitted. Jean de Broglie, a former minister in de Gaulle's government, published an article in *Le Monde* in which he criticized the ephemeral nature of the various projects for francophonie then current. De Broglie did not mince words. Instead, he wrote, 'Il faut le dire ouvertement. La francophonie sera finalement politique, ou elle ne sera pas' [It has to be said in the open. Francophonie must be, in the end, political, or it will not be at all].[71]

Gabon had been the first incident in the conference war. Two new conferences were in the offing in the fall of 1968, and lines had been drawn long before the death of Daniel Johnson. One, deriving from the association of French-speaking African countries, looked to embodying francophonie in a permanent structure. The other, to be held in the Congolese capital of Kinshasa, would bring together ministers of education from the francophone world. Preparations for both conferences went forward simultaneously in the fall and winter of 1968–9.

The Kinshasa conference, held in January 1969, would become a first test of relations between Ottawa and the new government in Quebec City. Bertrand spoke fair and promised well; but could he, in fact, deliver on his promises? His government has been described as classically ministerial, leaving each minister in charge of his individual department; perhaps that is why certain departmental policies continued unchecked during his premiership, from September 1968 to April 1970. Among these may be counted the pursuit of educational and cultural autonomy from federal government interference, in conjunction with the French government. Bertrand himself did not exacerbate the problem; during his mandate he did not undertake any trips to France. His health gave cause for genuine concern, though it did not prevent him from seeking, and winning, the permanent leadership of the Union Nationale at a convention in June 1969. Lacking Bertrand, the French had no objection to receiving the ultra-nationalist minister of education, Jean-Guy Cardinal, in his place; and so it was Cardinal who enjoyed the inexpressible pleasures of a state visit to General de Gaulle.[73]

It was true that Cardinal was not Bertrand, and that any minister, however powerful, senior, or fervently nationalist, did not have quite the same cachet as the premier. The French government put the best face on matters and toasted Cardinal and Quebec at a dinner at the presidential palace, celebrating, as de Gaulle put it, 'the establishment of direct relations between New France and France, between Quebec and Paris.'[74]

While Cardinal supped in Paris, his associate minister, a Union Nationale member named Jean-Marie Morin, was on his way home from an educational conference in Kinshasa, capital of the Congo. Congo (later renamed Zaire) was a former Belgian colony that had recently come through a bitter civil war to overcome the separatist aspirations of several of its richest provinces. Though French-speaking, it was not dependent on French aid, whether civil or military; nor were its leaders bound by happy memories of Paris and French culture. The Gabonese incident itself may have given pause to some francophone leaders – even those more closely bound to Paris than Congo's – and in any case the Chevrier mission had swept through in the last months of the Pearson government, making tangible Canada's regard for Africa and shortening the distance between African needs and the Canadian treasury. President Mobutu of Congo (K) – so called to distinguish it from Congo (B) across the Congo River – had also held discussions with Paul Martin, Trudeau's leader in the Senate; in their conversations his country's recent experience with separatism did not pass unmentioned.[75]

Mobutu made it his personal business to invite Ottawa to attend the Kinshasa conference; his summons arrived in December 1968. Quebec's invitation, which Claude Morin hoped to obtain from a more reliably francophile source, had not yet arrived. Constrained by this circumstance, the Quebec government accepted a compromise that would permit it to attend as part of a Canadian delegation. The details were still being laboriously worked out when, early in January, Quebec's own separate invitation finally arrived. The Quebec position, as outlined by Cardinal and Morin, promptly hardened. Two distinct delegations, one from Quebec and the other from Ottawa, were in prospect.

At this juncture, a third message arrived. This one told the Quebec government that Mobutu expected only one delegation from Canada: Quebec was disinvited. By coincidence, Mobutu's message arrived just as Quebec (Claude Morin) and Ottawa (Marc Lalonde) reached agreement. Quebec would be formally designated in plaques on the table as 'Canada-Québec'; the other provinces to be represented, New Brunswick and Ontario, would sport similar designations. Jean-Marie Morin would act, with Louis Robichaud of New Brunswick, as co-chairman of the Canadian delegation. Rules were laid down for the display of flags and for Robichaud's precedence as the senior politician on the spot. The Quebec delegation, while maintaining a distinctive identity, were told to avoid creating untoward incidents.[76] This, on the whole, they did.

A subsequent report from two senior federal officials, Lalonde and Max Yalden of External Affairs, concluded that the pan-Canadian delegation had operated well enough, and that its 'Canadian' and 'Quebec' sections had actually drawn closer together as a result of shared experiences. That this was so owed nothing to the good offices of the French delegation, which went out of its way to treat non-Quebeckers as non-existent. The Quebeckers, as a result, bore the brunt of the French delegation's paternal attentions and, by the end of the conference, some, at least, had begun to wonder whether France's rediscovery of 'New France' did not mean that the French wanted to restore their old colonial predominance.[77]

Kinshasa was, therefore, a setback for Claude Morin and a distinct improvement in Ottawa's position. A Canadian delegation had been invited to an international educational conference, and a Quebec delegation had not been. This affirmed that Canada possessed only one sovereign authority, and that even on education it was expressed through Ottawa. The Canadian delegation that was sent included representatives of two other provinces with large francophone minorities, indicating that Quebec was not unique, even in Canada, in advancing the rights or interests of French Canadians; more bluntly, French Canada was larger than Quebec. Finally, the Canadian invitation signified that, all things being equal, even distant countries would oppose separatism and uphold the principle that diverse cultures could and should find harmony in a single state. With the Nigerian civil war raging, African states did not have to look far afield for the consequences of separatism; that Charles de Gaulle had expressed his sympathy for the Biafran rebels (and had drawn a pointed comparison with Quebec) did not advance Quebec's cause in Africa ... nor, as it happened, did it help the rebels' cause in Ottawa. When Trudeau ironically asked a reporter, 'Where's Biafra?' the answer, as far as many in official Ottawa were concerned, was obvious: it was alive and well and living across the river in Quebec.[78]

Kinshasa was only the second battle. As the conference wound down, the next event was gearing up: a conference of French-speaking states to take place in Niamey, the capital of Niger.

Niger stretches across west Africa, straddling Nigeria to the east, north, and west. Most of the country is desert, or practically so. It would be peculiar if the government of Niger were not aid-conscious, and it would be almost equally strange if the amount of aid it received was enough to satisfy the country's needs. As host government, Niger's perception of its world had an obvious importance; and Niger's world view might well have been affected by Chevrier's visit to Africa in the winter of 1968.

Other Canadians who met President Diori found him frank, friendly, and explicit. The francophonie conference, for which Niger would be host and would therefore issue invitations, was overdue. The French government was pressing him to act, and to include Quebec in the list of invitees. His own foreign ministry, with the help of French advisers, took the same point of view. (On one occasion a Canadian diplomat arrived to see the foreign minister; as he entered the room a French adviser, who had just briefed the minister on what to say, was leaving.)

Caught between his sense that Canada's position was the right one – in light of the Nigerian civil war just across the border – and his dependence on France, Diori waffled. Could Canada help him out by coming to an agreement with Quebec on a common delegation, and thereby sparing him a painful dilemma? In hopes of such a solution, Diori would willingly put off the francophone conference into the new year; but he made it clear that a solution there must be. For though he did not say so, Diori must have had little doubt that he would be forced to follow France's advice on such a matter.[81]

The Chevrier mission struck a sensitive, but not necessarily vulnerable, point in France's relations with its former colonies. France had made them independent, but expected that it would continue to occupy most of their international horizons, in large part because of their francophone background. There were exceptions, to be sure, like Guinea, which had rejected de Gaulle and which had in turn been rejected by France; but the rest were bound to France by ties of sentiment as well as self-interest. As to sentiment, their elites dreamed of a world in which the French language would enjoy a status at least remotely comparable to that of its rival, English.[80] To fulfil that dream, francophonie, it was all-important to secure the cooperation of the French government – as long as France remained a unique source of succour. The emergence of Canada on the scene altered the picture somewhat.

Even before de Gaulle's mission to Quebec in 1967, some personalities from Africa had made their way to Ottawa. Their appearance sparked increasing interest. French-language Canadians had long complained that Africa meant only English-speaking countries as far as the government of Canada was concerned. The perception was not inaccurate, though prejudice or preference for the familiar may be only part of the explanation. The French, already established, regarded Canadian (even French-Canadian) aid-givers as intruders. The External Aid Office did not have enough French-speaking staff to put forward a proper effort. Local governments, according to a 1966 study, were not thought to be 'reliable enough to exploit, or even formulate realistic requests for straightforward technical assistance.'[81]

Prominent individuals in Quebec, such as Jean-Marc Léger, had struggled against the phenomenon and had, by 1967, largely bypassed the agencies of the Canadian government in favour of a France-centred, francophone association.[82] Gérard Pelletier, Trudeau's friend, fellow-MP, and, since April, secretary of state in Ottawa, had made it his personal business to shake up official attitudes.[83]

So it is not surprising that in July 1968 Maurice Strong, the director of Canada's External Aid Office (later rebaptized CIDA), could reflect on substantial progress in the provision of funds to French-speaking Africa. As a result of Chevrier's mission, he told his employees, $30 million had been committed to French-speaking African countries, and $40 million over five years.[84] It was a substantial sum, at least as compared to the $19.3 million budgeted for francophone Africa in 1961–6. In rendering the aid, Canadian officials argued that their country had two principal interests. The first was Africa's peaceful and orderly evolution; the second was to influence African states to recognize Canadian interests and to encourage them to act with those interests in mind. President Diori, who was slated to receive Canadian wheat and a total aid package of $2.8 million, was doing just that.[85]

French interests, however, were in a better position to make themselves felt. There were an estimated 3000 French personnel, civil and military, in and around Niamey. Even to hold a conference Diori needed French help, and to that end the Quai d'Orsay dispatched a middle-ranking diplomat and a retired general. They would handle details, but they would necessarily offer advice. There was little doubt in the Canadian embassy in Paris as to what that advice would be, even though senior officials at the Quai d'Orsay had assured Canadian diplomats that France had absolutely no intention of interfering in the organization of the conference. Taken as a whole, the Quai was not enthusiastic about holding a francophone conference, perhaps because it held the possibility of opening up the whole question of France's relations with its African ex-colonies; but the opportunity for further mischief-making in Canada was, for some, irresistible. For though opinion among the professionals in the French foreign office was distinctly divided on the rights and wrongs of de Gaulle's intervention in Quebec, there was no hesitation in the office of the foreign minister. There should be a direct invitation to Quebec, with a copy to Ottawa.[86]

It was no coincidence that Yvon Bourges, a junior minister in the Quai d'Orsay, visited Niamey in mid-November, in order to discuss French aid. The day after his arrival, 17 November, Diori issued an invitation directly to Jean-Jacques Bertrand, to send a 'delegation' of his own choosing, one that might include Quebec's minister of education. His own minister of education would be asking Cardinal, 'personnellement.' This applied, Diori added, no matter what the outcome of discussions between Quebec and Ottawa might be, but he nevertheless hoped that negotiations between the two Canadian capitals would have a happy result.

Diori gave no reasons for his change of attitude, but they are now sufficiently clear. Bourges had brought with him both a carrot and a stick. The carrot was a French promise to compensate Niamey for any loss of Canadian aid in the aftermath of an invitation to Quebec. If, however, Niger preferred to shore up the $2.8 million of Canadian assistance by persisting in respecting the Canadian government's definition of its own constitution, then France would boycott the forthcoming conference. The French in fact went further, and told Diori that he should invite Quebec by itself, without Canada. Ottawa might, if it wished, be represented by Quebec.[87]

Diori, much embarrassed, sent a special envoy to Ottawa to explain what had happened. There is no better indication of the significance that the Canadian government attached to the issue of Quebec's separate attendance at Niamey than the fact that Trudeau himself left a cabinet meeting to receive Diori's representative. What he learned was certainly not to his liking, although the news could have been worse. Diori had indeed invited Quebec, but he had refused the French demand to exclude Ottawa. He begged Trudeau, under the existing difficult circumstances, to be understanding.[88]

The French position, as expressed by Bourges to Diori, went further than Claude Morin and his associates in Quebec City had expected, though Morin conceded the possibility in his memoir that some ' "francs-tireurs" québécois' had given the province's 'amis français,' who seem to have abounded at the Quai d'Orsay and who were almost certainly represented in Niamey as 'advisers,' a shove. At the same time, Diori's letter to Bertrand was not quite everything that Morin might have wished, since it stopped short of recognizing Quebec's sovereign interest in the approaching proceedings. Nevertheless, Bertrand tried out the idea that the Canadian government should simply appoint the Quebec delegation as its own; he did not, however, pursue the matter when Ottawa refused.[89]

According to information reaching the Canadian government, the

French envisaged a francophone agency that would deal with multilateral cultural and technical cooperation; bilateral exchanges, as well as political and military topics, were excluded from its mandate. Canada would not be a member of the agency, but Quebec would enjoy full status and would contribute 20 per cent of its relatively modest budget. (France's own contribution would be 45 per cent, Belgium's 10 per cent, and the other states would make up the rest.) Quebec, the French made clear, would be a 'country' ('pays') just like the rest.[90]

The Canadian government faced a number of urgent decisions. Should Canada be represented at Niamey? Yes, because a failure to appear would leave the field to Quebec alone. A quick visit by Paul Martin, government leader in the Senate, in December confirmed Diori's personal views, as well as Ottawa's own invitation to the Niamey conference.[91] Should Canada accept the agency proposed by the French? No, both because the agency was obnoxious in conception and design, and because creative diplomacy among France's erstwhile African clients might still alter the shape of the future francophone body. Should Canada retaliate against Niger? No, presumably because Niger had made it abundantly clear that it was acting under compulsion. The most important question was whether Quebec would agree to cooperate in forming a Canadian delegation; the answer to that would be forthcoming on 26 November when Marc Lalonde and Allan Gotlieb met with Claude Morin and Julien Chouinard.[92]

The two sides proved to be less at odds than might have been expected. Quebec faced a financial crisis and needed Ottawa's help. Bertrand was better disposed to compromise than Johnson had been. Chouinard may well have been a moderating presence on his colleague; certainly the federal side had more confidence in the cabinet secretary than they did in their old adversary Morin. And they sensed, no doubt correctly, that Bertrand wished a reasonable agreement. There was some discussion, but no immediate conclusion about the placing of Canadian and Quebec flags. There was also a hesitant exploration of personalities to be sent, Chouinard letting it be known that Bertrand would prefer not to send Cardinal. On the crucial point, a single delegation, there was agreement. Although the French were known to be insisting on an immediate conference, in mid-December, both Quebec and Ottawa were disposed to postponement into the new year, if for no other reason than the convenience of the Christmas season.[93]

Negotiations dragged on between the two governments. In January a date for the Niamey conference was finally set: 17 February. No agreement with Quebec had yet been reached. Even though the basic composition of a single delegation had been agreed, there were differences as to wording; and Quebec let it be known that it was concerting its position on the substantive issues of the conference with France, rather than with Ottawa. Bertrand at the beginning of February authorized an agreement on forms to be followed – much like those at Kinshasa – and restricted Quebec's participation to subjects that lay strictly within its constitutional bounds. In case of disagreement among the various components of the Canadian delegation, which would include Ontario and New Brunswick as well as Quebec, the Canadians would abstain from voting. Since Quebec and Ottawa also managed to concur on the outline of a future francophone organization, the scope for public disagreement seemed to be limited.[94]

That did not prevent eruptions at the conference. Marcel Masse, who headed the Quebec group, was closer to Daniel Johnson in temperament and attitudes than he was to the circumspect Bertrand. He would act to insure the maximum of publicity to his province and, by extension, to himself as its battling champion. French officials had made sure that a number of honoured, non-governmental, guests were present, and these included Pauline Julien, a noted Quebec chanteuse and a fervent separatist. Julien added her own counterpoint to a speech by Gérard Pelletier when she shouted out, 'Vive le Québec libre!' Pelletier, however, had the last word. Meeting Julien later at a reception, he gently remarked, 'Pauline, tu chantes mieux que tu cries.'[95]

Masse let it be known that he was not content with the Trudeau-Bertrand agreement that was the foundation for the Canadian delegation's participation at Niamey. The sheer size of the combined Canadian delegations was cause for comment. And comment abounded, since in addition to the governmental delegates a sizeable contingent of reporters descended on Niamey, making it a three days' wonder on front pages from St John's to Victoria.[96] The French, Rossillon and Dorin, did their bit, and appeared to get on the nerves of the Africans as much as of the Canadians.

Though the spectacle was somewhat embarrassing for Niger, it was not without its beneficial side-effects. Pelletier and Masse offered competing donations: a thousand books from Quebec, as well as television consultants to come; this could be offset by Pelletier's promise that Niger would soon see the total of its aid from Canada increase.

The real action centred on the shaping of the future francophonie. That, the various delegations decided, would take time – and a second conference. This conference should stick to agreement in principle, with some kind of provisional organization of modest size tacked on to the principle. The principle of cultural and technical assistance, and a cooperative organization to embody them, was therefore approved. Also approved was the sentiment that countries, not governments, should be members of the future organization, now dubbed the 'Agence de cooperation culturelle et technique' – ACCT.

It remained to establish a provisional committee that would set about preparing the next, definitive, conference. The French had a nominee ready, a Canadian as it happened. Jean-Marc Léger had been, since the 1950s, an enthusiast for francophone unity. As a political writer for Le Devoir, he was also a well-known separatist.

Pelletier knew Léger, personally and politically; he was, as Léger later wrote, 'un camarade de longue date.' He met the French candidate for a 'brief but very frank interview,' in which he asked whether Léger could set aside his political enthusiasms to become, in effect, a neutral international civil servant. Léger assured him that he could. Though some members of the Canadian team had their doubts, Pelletier acceded to Léger's nomination; he knew, in any case, that his old friend had substantial support among the Africans and that rejecting him would be difficult.[97]

So Léger it was, and with him the acceptance of a francophone organization that counted Canada, and Canada-Quebec, among its founding members. At least it was not Quebec alone.

Canada's ability to follow through on promises made in – or to – Niamey was less in question than Quebec's or even France's. The disturbances of 1968 had not been good for the French economy, and France ended the year with less in the way of foreign-exchange reserves than its government found desirable. Retrenchment was also the order of the day in Quebec, where the provincial government had urgent matters before it – some of them costly. France was engaged in its own constitutional debate, concentrated on a referendum at the end of April 1969. De Gaulle took the referendum very seriously, so much so that when his side failed to carry the day, he promptly resigned.

De Gaulle's departure did not solve the Franco-Canadian imbroglio in one fell swoop. Quebec had become a cause among Gaullists of a certain stripe, and it remained a preoccupation for some officials in the Quai d'Orsay. De Gaulle's successor as president, Georges Pompidou, owed his position to Gaullist support, and, to keep his majority in the legislature, he cultivated the good opinion of some of the wilder extremes of Gaullist thought. The attraction of the idea of an independent Quebec was not felt only on the right, or among those who, like de Broglie, dreamed of a revived French empire. The left was beginning to get 'le goût du Québec,' as was perhaps inevitable in an age where the call of national liberation was strongly felt in liberal circles, however ill-informed or distant from the territory in question.[98]

Pompidou's personal views on Quebec are unknown, but in the early stages of his presidency he seems to have felt he would not suffer politically if he demonstrated a lively sympathy for the special relation-ship with Quebec; or if he let it be known, not very obliquely, that he was not inclined to invite Trudeau to visit him in Paris. When the French consul-general in Quebec City asked for instructions, he was told that they remained the same as before; the French ambassador received an identical message.[99] Later, after the election of a Liberal, federalist government in Quebec, there are indications that the Elysée modified its attitude; whether these modifications in the direction of Canadian unity were merely opportunistic cannot as yet be known.[100]

Certainly more information was available on Quebec in France than ever before, due in part to the indefatigable efforts of Jean-Louis Mallen, the Quebec correspondent of French radio and television. Mallen had become a fervent supporter of nationalism and separatism in Quebec, and did his best to bring his compatriots to regard Quebec independence as a serious and favourable possibility.[101]

It was, admittedly, a long way from the snows of Quebec to the sands of Africa, but it was a leap that certain elements in the government of Quebec had already made in their imagination. Jean-Guy Cardinal did not hide his belief that, if necessary, Quebec's international standing would be assured by the instant recognition the new country would receive from twenty African states. Trudeau's government had taken note, and, as we have seen, had taken measures.

So had Bertrand. As the Niamey conference was going forward, another constitutional conference was convened in Ottawa, where Que-bec presented a white paper on provincial powers in external affairs. It held no surprises. Quebec had the right, constitutionally, to enter agreements in areas of its own jurisdiction with foreign countries. Although that was so, the province conceded that Ottawa's jurisdiction over foreign policy conferred a kind of negative paramountcy on the federal authority, a right of veto over provincial initiatives that infringed on broader considerations of Canadian external policy. Practically, the Quebec paper suggested that the provinces assume most of the functions of cultural diplomacy, leaving the federal government in an advisory if not custodial position at international conferences where the 'Canadian' delegation would be comprised mostly of provincial delegates. On the essential question of francophonie, Quebec would supply delegation chairmen, while federal representatives kept watch to ensure that Canada's foreign policy was respected.[102]

This functional division of the external-affairs power did not appeal to the federal government. Its vision of its external responsibilities was broader than Quebec's, and it declined to confide, as a matter of routine, real power to the province. Though Ottawa should be ready to listen to provincial representations, it could not concede the substance of its power without risking its eventual loss.

Following the February 1969 conference at Niamey, officials in External Affairs and the Prime Minister's Office were pleased. They had outstripped Quebec's modest aid program and had made Canada's presence felt alongside the French – though French aid to Africa still dwarfed Canada's, both in amount and in variety. They hoped that their French antagonists were suitably downcast, but they did not discount the power of illusion in controlling their actions.

Quebec had attended Niamey as part of a larger Canadian delegation, but that was no guarantee that Quebec would continue as part of a larger Canadian whole. Jean-Marc Léger had no qualms about contacting Quebec and, as a fledgling international civil servant, about calling directly on the Quebec government, as if that government were the sovereign equal of every other participant in the future francophone agency. Ottawa was annoyed about the symbolism of Léger's visits to Quebec, but it was their results that mattered in the end. While Léger's travels to Quebec engendered considerable heart-burn in Ottawa, conversations with him in Ottawa were not unfruitful.[103]

Léger also sought advice from his counterpart in London, Arnold Smith, the Canadian secretary-general of the Commonwealth. His task was difficult, Léger admitted, and different from the Commonwealth's in its inception. The Commonwealth had a well-established sense of identity, while the future Agence had to rely on a legal statute. His job was to create, within that statute, the sense of shared purpose that distinguished the English-speaking organization. The spokesmen for the Commonwealth, for their part, warned Léger that too close an identification with the former metropolitan power would prove counter-productive; it seemed to Smith's staff that Léger had taken the point.[104]

It remained formally to define what the scope of the future agency would be; to draft its statutes; to endow it with funds; and, most important from the Canadian point of view, to regulate the criteria for membership. How best could Canada's single sovereignty be safeguarded? The actual substance of the conference was secondary, not merely in Ottawa but in Quebec City and also in Paris. As to substance, Canada preferred it uncomplicated: annual meetings at the ministerial level, an administrative council charged with overseeing the implementation of the ministerial decisions, and a secretariat.[105]

The principal Canadian position was plain. The government of Canada alone represented Canada and all its parts abroad; thus, Quebec could not by itself be a member of an international agency. The draft statutes of the ACCT, compiled by Léger's provisional secretariat under Diori's direction, reflected this position. Moreover, only Ottawa was directly invited to a second conference at Niamey; Quebec would have to content itself with being part of a Canadian delegation. Taking these circumstances into account, the federal position seemed to be strong, and its perceived strength was reflected in the attitude that Ottawa took in negotiations with Quebec in the winter of 1970. Since the circumstances were favourable, it was time to secure Quebec's recognition of the primacy, if not the exclusivity, of Ottawa's power in external affairs.[106]

Quebec's posture, publicly expounded, was the opposite, although privately there were doubts and hesitations. Marcel Masse, as intergovernmental affairs minister, toured France in January 1970. There, he publicly repeated Quebec's demand for control over the external aspects of its constitutional powers. He obviously had an attentive audience, not only in the media, but in the Quai d'Orsay, where Quebec's 'friends' were moving heaven and earth to secure a separate invitation for the province to attend the conference. Unfortunately for their efforts, they were not sufficiently influential, even in Paris, to secure a French threat of boycott should Quebec not be able to attend in its own right. Though Morin tried out the idea that Quebec might refrain from attending Niamey II on his friends in Paris, he was told that would be going too far. France would attend regardless, and Quebec's interests would be damaged.[107]

The Quebec view was still what one might expect. Not only should Quebec be represented in ACCT, though as a 'government' not as a 'country,' but a Quebec representative should act as chairman of the Canadian delegation. The federal government refused. Trudeau expressed its arguments for an undivided sovereignty, without positive effect, in a conversation with Bertrand in mid-February. By that point the organization of the Canadian delegation was bulking larger, and it was still undecided whether Quebec, or even France, would attend the feast. At the end of the month, with the conference only weeks away, the two governments were deadlocked. Though Quebec was prepared to go to Niamey as part of a Canadian delegation this time, it wanted to rein in the federal delegates; if a question falling within Quebec's provincial competence arose, and the federal and provincial representatives failed to agree, Bertrand asked that the delegation as a whole abstain. Trudeau reluctantly agreed, and in his reply to Bertrand (received on 12 March) he met most of Quebec's requirements for distinctive identification of its delegates. Similarly, he conceded that the minister representing Quebec could speak 'in the name of Quebec' when he dealt with provincial subjects and viewpoints. When international matters were under consideration, however, the Quebec representative should speak as a member of the Canadian delegation. With that understanding, the Quebec delegates set out for Niamey.[108]

The two groups of Canadians sat uneasily together. The representatives of Ottawa had one set of objectives; those from Quebec had quite different desiderata. The Quebeckers wanted the draft statutes amended so as to permit their province to become a member in its own right. For all their reliance on Bertrand, and on Chouinard as a known federalist, Ottawa's representatives had not been able to negotiate a final accord on the structure of ACCT with Quebec. Without such an accord, the Canadian position at Niamey was weakened, and possibly undermined, in advance. It was still possible for the French to play their 'Quebec card,' knowing that the federal government would shy away from publicly revealing the division that underlay the façade of diplomatic unity.[109]

When the Canadians arrived in Niamey, they were nevertheless a single delegation, with Pelletier at the head and Julien Chouinard as vice-chairman. (The choice of a senior civil servant may seem odd; but Bertrand had chosen this moment to call a provincial election, which necessarily concentrated all his ministers' attention at home.) The conference agenda seemed to be satisfactory, and Diori and his advisers had done everything possible to accommodate the Canadian contention that 'countries' and not 'governments' were the sole invitees. The draft statute prepared by the provisional secretariat promised well, and it appeared that after prolonged disputation Canada and Quebec would find a happy joint home inside the ACCT. We cannot be entirely certain what the Quebec delegates thought, but, according to Claude Morin, they worked quietly and apparently effectively at communicating their government's viewpoint. Under Chouinard's guidance, they refused to supply the verbal fireworks that had characterized the previous Niamey conference. Chouinard himself continued to enjoy excellent relations with his Ottawa counterparts, who were doubtless relieved that their particular bête noire, Claude Morin, had decided not to go to Africa.[110] It was a circumstance from which the Ottawa delegates could draw some comfort, but, as time would show, they were excessively optimistic.

The French government had exerted itself. It produced a draft statute all its own, since Léger's secretariat had patently failed in its task of securing separate status for Quebec. It pressed various African countries to support a separate invitation for Quebec. Aspects of the Quai d'Orsay's thinking had been revealed over the weeks preceding the conference, to the dismay of the Canadians. Jurgensen presented the final French draft to Pelletier on 16 March.

It contained several unpleasant surprises. It spoke of governments and not countries. Any government with competence in the cultural and technical fields belonging to ACCT could join; and instead of the unanimous consent required under the previous, non-French draft, it would require only a two-thirds vote to admit them. Besides governments, governmental agencies and non-governmental associations could also become members. Anticipating Canadian objections, the French were prepared to allow a right of veto over the actions of their constituents to governments having authority over international relations. Further than that, the French told the Canadians, they would not go.

If Canada would not accept the French draft, then the French would see to it that the conference failed and that no francophone organization was established. (There was some talk of doing without Canada altogether, but that would have crippled the budget of the francophone organization.) Then, as a next step, they would found an organization even more to France's liking, from which Canada would be excluded. Pelletier recognized this as blackmail; he rejected the details of the French plan as soon as he heard them, but it was a real question whether he could do anything about it.[111]

The French initiative, which the Canadians were convinced had been coordinated with the 'amis' in Quebec, became the focus of discussion in the conference. Within the French draft, it was the status of Quebec, and the role of associations, that attracted most attention. As discussion proceeded, it became obvious that the Canadian position was by no means as strong as it had been the year before, with only three delegations (Belgium, Cameroun, and Burundi) overtly supporting Pelletier.[112] The bulk of the other African delegations believed that the reservation of a right of veto was a sufficient recognition of Canada's concerns over Quebec. Only on the less important issue of membership for associations of various kinds did the Canadians win much support; but it would appear that the French were from the beginning prepared to sacrifice that point, considering it a useful lever in prying governmental membership from the reluctant Canadians.[113]

'I thought we had more friends in Africa,' one of the Canadian delegation mournfully remarked to Jean-Marc Léger. But they did not – at least not on an issue where Ottawa's objections were considered by most participants to be insignificant at best, and stridently self-serving at worst. Canada's standing was not improved by putting forward a draft amendment that a member of the Quebec delegation properly described as resembling a slice of the income-tax act.

The histrionics that accompanied the dispute between the French and the Canadians dwarfed the consideration of more routine matters; for three days it seemed that the conference was headed towards failure. The failure, however, would be blamed on Ottawa's intransigence, and there was no probability that Ottawa would do better in any future encounter. That this was so was clearer, initially, to the delegates on the spot than it was to Trudeau and his advisers in Ottawa. After prolonged consultation, Trudeau accepted Pelletier's advice. Pelletier therefore switched positions, and conceded that participating governments could indeed become members of ACCT. Pelletier announced the result at a presidential reception on 19 March, the day before the conference was scheduled to wrap up. He carefully explained that Canada's concession did not mean that Quebec had acquired any kind of sovereignty; ultimate authority still rested in Ottawa.

Strangely, the announcement did little to lighten the atmosphere in Niamey. Hastily, the conference wound itself up. There would be an Agence de cooperation culturelle et technique. It would be headquartered in Paris, as was natural. It would have a modest budget, equivalent to $300,000. The budget was a particular French goal, since France's representatives believed that Léger and his secretariat planned to be entirely too free with their money.[114] He might even be planning to create something along the lines of the Commonwealth, with consequent autonomy from French government pressures.[115] Léger's future therefore appeared, at least until the last day of the conference, to be most uncertain.[116]

Instead of a single executive officer, ACCT would have two associate secretaries-general, a dilution of the power of the office. At the last moment Diori persuaded Jean-Marc Léger to replace his name in nomination, and then manoeuvred his acceptance by the conference. The Canadian delegation had concluded, under Pelletier's direction, that Léger, though a separatist, was also, as one of them put it, 'a straight shooter.' Canada would, therefore, support him.[117]

The result was not what might have been hoped. Léger became the senior partner in a triumvirate, condemned for the next four years to spend a third of his time negotiating a common front with his two peers, a Togolese and a Frenchman. If the French delegation had, as was rumoured, any fears about the capacity of ACCT to make trouble, or to take any important initiatives, they were quelled. According to one well-informed observer, the French had demonstrated that the Agence could not be formed without them. Despite misgivings by African states, and the financial charms of Canadian diplomacy, the Agence emerged restricted and narrow in scope and function. 'There was an underlying fear,' Arnold Smith wrote in his diary, that 'French culture and language were under attack by an aggressive anglo-saxon culture and that the main battleground was Canada.'[118]

The budget did rise over time: $2 million in 1971, and more thereafter. But even in 1971 dollars ACCT was scantily funded, a funding that was reflected in the very modest stipends of its secretaries-general, who competed for the car and driver that was tardily placed at their joint disposal. One might be pardoned for concluding that the French had decided that if Léger wanted to live in Paris, he should share the experiences of ordinary Parisians. President Diori was overthrown in a coup not long afterwards,[119] a not-so-subtle reminder that in Africa it was more useful to have a friend with guns as well as money; in a coup, after all, Canada could not help.

Quebec therefore, became for the first time, a participant in an international organization. Granted, it did not do so as a sovereign state, but merely as a competent government; and its participation remained subject to a sovereign veto from the government of Canada. What all this might mean was left, once again, to Ottawa and Quebec City to work out between them. They had eighteen months to do it, for the next meeting of ACCT was scheduled to take place in Canada in the fall of 1971.

On 29 April 1970 Quebeckers went to the polls. The main contenders were expected to be the Union Nationale, the party in government, and the official opposition, the Liberals, under a new leader, Robert Bourassa. Bourassa was young, thirty-six at the time of the election; he had contended against far more senior Liberals to become leader. An economist by training, he was nevertheless considerably junior to some of the figures his political opponents could mobilize on their behalf. But Bourassa did not consider that a tremendous handicap: in the country of the blind, he would say, the one-eyed man was king.[120]

He may have been right. What Quebeckers were looking for, a polling consultant had told Quebec Liberals, was 'a young businessman with a very detailed knowledge of the economy.' He should have other characteristics too: someone who could 'bridge the gap between the generations,' someone strong enough to deal with Ottawa and 'the titans of finance.' Bourassa was not a perfect match, but he was close enough. What was certain was that none of the alternatives among the Liberals, or in the other parties, was any closer.[121]

The Liberals finished first, both in popular vote and in seats, and easily formed a majority government. The Union Nationale became the new official opposition, with the second largest group of seats. In terms of popular vote, however, the Union Nationale had been surpassed by a third party, the newly founded Parti Québécois, usually abbreviated as PQ. Unlike the two older parties, the PQ under its leader René Lévesque stood for the independence of Quebec: for the first time separatism had become an alternative, and conceivable, course of action.

The effect of the election campaign was to polarize opinion into two camps. Federalists of all stripes gravitated to the Liberals. Separatists, whether of the right or left, tended to the PQ. Nationalist opinion, however, was divided. The pre-1966 Liberal government had had a strong nationalist wing, and not all of its members had followed Lévesque out of the party when he departed in 1967. The stronger nationalists remaining among the Liberals may be described as conditional federalists during Bourassa's first government, 1970–6; and the centre of political gravity therefore was located somewhere between pure federalism and strong nationalism.[122]

Bourassa's campaign slogan in the election, 'fédéralisme rentable' ('profitable federalism') suggested a doctrine of the pocket book rather than the heart; it was not easily reconcilable with Pierre Trudeau's brand of anti-nationalist, pro-federal, politics. Looking at Bourassa, some Liberals in Ottawa remembered that he had once been close to Lévesque's faction inside the Liberal party; they might even know – it was no secret – that Lévesque's manifesto for 'sovereignty-association' had been composed in Bourassa's basement.

Bourassa's approach to government was not entirely novel. He knew that many of his senior civil servants had taken an advanced, not to say dogmatic, line in their confrontations with Ottawa, so much so that the usefulness of one of the most senior, Claude Morin, was virtually at an end. Bourassa was even less inclined than Bertrand to confront Ottawa; unlike Bertrand, he had political affinities there, and some political debts, even though the Quebec Liberals' provincial and federal wings had formally separated in 1964. When Bourassa became Quebec leader, the federal Liberal machine had supported him, even though Trudeau personally maintained his neutrality. In the 1960s, Lesage had been the strong Liberal in Quebec, and Pearson relatively weak; in the 1970s it was Pierre Trudeau who was predominant.[123] That impression was greatly reinforced by the prime minister's tough response to terrorism during the FLQ crisis of October 1970: Bourassa's wobbling did nothing to build him up into a credible challenger to Trudeau.

With the political tide running his way, Trudeau hoped to end, once and for all, the constitutional conflict that had afflicted Canada for the previous decade. Where external policy was concerned, two occasions presented themselves: the negotiation with Quebec over its place in the ACCT, and the conclusion of the constitutional talks that had begun in 1968. The two items were closely related.

The constitution came first. The action in 1970 and 1971 centred on the control of social policy; external powers, perhaps in default of another francophone conference, were practically absent from public discussion of the constitutional debate. The debate was to culminate at a conference of the prime minister and the ten provincial premiers in Victoria in June 1971. Some observers believed that this conference would finally be able to achieve agreement on a package of patriating the constitution, agreeing on the manner of amending it, establishing some basic human rights, and redistributing some powers and responsibilities in such a manner as to satisfy Quebec without fatally weakening the federal government. These changes were packaged in a document known as the Victoria Charter.

The charter proposed by the federal government contained five articles on the control of foreign policy and responsibility for international affairs. Under both headings, the Canadian government's power was to be exclusive.

The articles on external affairs were as expected: they reflected what the government had already published in two white papers, and it came as no special surprise that the Quebec delegation, to which Morin was adviser, firmly rejected them. Justice Minister John Turner, who was in charge of the federal brief, expressed his disappointment, but in the interest of a larger settlement Ottawa's representatives pressed ahead.[124]

They did not prevail. Bourassa hesitated and temporized, but in the end he would not agree to sign the Victoria Charter. Though it was not at first obvious, the constitutional issue had been put to rest for three years; given the respective positions of the governments of Canada and Quebec, there was no other alternative.

The approach of the francophonie conference, scheduled for October 1971, made it incumbent to negotiate Quebec's participation in francophonie under the old rules and as a continuation of the previous pattern, rather than as part of some novel constitutional regime. François Cloutier, as minister of cultural affairs, headed the Quebec negotiating team. 'On the political level,' he later wrote, 'I reached an agreement fairly easily with Mitchell Sharp, the external affairs minister, and Gérard Pelletier, the secretary of state.' The civil servants were another matter; 'the most finicky' on the Ottawa side, he noted, was Claude Roquet, of External Affairs' francophone team. Roquet would later apply his talents on the other side, after the Parti Québécois came to power.[125]

The Ottawa-Quebec agreement therefore was predictable. Quebec could be a participating government in ACCT, but always subject to keeping Ottawa informed about its activities and after agreeing not to join in any enterprise that Ottawa judged incompatible with its foreign policy. Best of all, from Ottawa's point of view, Quebec was restricted to naming 'a group' within the larger Canadian delegation. It received in return a limited right of veto over Canadian votes that might be cast in areas of provincial jurisdiction.[126]

The ACCT conference was not held exclusively in Ottawa, as External Affairs had originally envisaged, or in Quebec City, as Premier Bourassa wanted. It would start in Ottawa, but after the opening ceremonies it would decamp down the Ottawa River to Montreal, where it would conclude.

Trudeau himself welcomed the ACCT delegates with a speech that proclaimed his faith in a bilingual Canada, in which the French fact occupied more than Quebec. The conference proceeded without incident. ACCT, from being a cause célèbre, had become routine, even banal. For, protocol fights aside, the subjects that concerned ACCT were not those that aroused political passions, or caught headlines in the media.

The 'guerre des drapeaux' was effectively over. It had convulsed Ottawa-Quebec relations for the best part of three years and had helped poison Franco-Canadian diplomacy. Concretely, it left behind an Agence culturelle et technique, to which Canada (with some help from Quebec) contributed 35 per cent of the annual budget: $1.5 million in fiscal 1972–3 and $2.4 million in 1975–6.[127] Aid programs, set in place while Canada was trying to show French-speaking Africa that its affections were more than an irrelevance, continued: they reached $22 million in 1968–9 and $32 million in 1969–70.[128]

Politically, francophonie afforded an outlet inside Canadian foreign policy in which French-Canadian interests and personalities could predominate. In one of the many ironies of the period, Trudeau appointed Paul Gérin-Lajoie, the author of the doctrine that provinces should manage their own external affairs, to be head of the Canadian International Development Agency in 1970. In that capacity he would put as good a face as he could on Ottawa's external-aid policy; he would also see that francophone countries were not neglected. According to Peter Dobell, these developments had a positive impact on the way French Canadians perceived their federal government; so the exercise may in that sense count as beneficial both for the future of Canadian unity and for the fortunes of the Liberal party.[129]

Another event in the fall of 1971 brought some relief. Claude Morin resigned as Quebec's deputy minister of intergovernmental affairs. His departure marked the end of the attempt, launched by Gérin-Lajoie in 1965, to reconcile rigid Quebec nationalism with the Canadian federal system. Difficult in 1965, it had become impossible with the advent of Trudeau. That fact Morin in effect recognized by his resignation.

It is still not clear where Morin's ultimate political affections lay in the years between 1965 and 1971. Working within a federal system, he could claim that he was doing his best to accommodate a fervently nationalist Quebec within a Canadian continuum. Louis Bernard, once Morin's associate deputy minister and since departed to take a position with the Parti Québécois, argued that Morin had been the last federalist inside his department – 'one of Canadian federalism's best defenders.' In future, Bernard wrote, there would be no 'middle way' between the constitutional status quo espoused by Pierre Trudeau and the sovereignty-association preached by René Lévesque.[130]

Morin's Ottawa counterparts had long since decided that accommodation with him was impossible. They believed Morin was simply attempting independence by well-designed, limited, but conscious stages. Each Quebec initiative was therefore treated in terms of the presumptive ultimate goal and must be resisted lest it become a precedent for the next stage. Even in Quebec City Morin was considered a liability – at least as far as the new Bourassa government was concerned. To François Cloutier, the affinity between the higher civil servants of the 1960s and the PQ was plain. The natural desire of the civil service was to expand; if something like federalism or the federal government got in the way, so much the worse. 'Is it a coincidence,' he asked in 1978, 'that so many of the Parti Québécois' top-billed personalities [têtes d'affiche] are former civil servants?'[131]

So Morin departed. There was a brief attempt, in October 1971, to get rid of his department altogether, but it failed.[132] Intergovernmental affairs remained; as Morin wrote to his colleagues on his departure, he was not leaving, merely taking leave of absence.[133] It was considerate of the Bourassa government to keep his ministry in being, pending his return.

There is, however, another irony at work if we consider the organization around which all the controversy had swirled. Quebec had struggled to join ACCT, and France had employed abundant resources and skills to help it do so. But ACCT was itself a marginal organization.[134] Its budgets were not large and its initiatives few. The French government wanted it that way. If, as Daniel Johnson once said, francophonie was as essential to Quebec as oxygen, then francophonie afforded pretty thin air. In the words of Pierre Trudeau, all the Commonwealth had going for it was a common heritage; but francophonie had something that was both more obvious and more nebulous: a common medium of communication.

Among most of its members, however, it was not even that. It remained, as the French had left it, the language of an elite. In Canada, francophonie expressed, ultimately, only the interests of a fraction of an elite.

6

Missing Links:
The Contractual Links
with the European Community
and Japan

Mitchell Sharp was stunned. The telephone call on 15 August 1971 had given the acting prime minister a few hours advance notice that President Richard Nixon was going to announce sweeping unilateral changes in American financial and economic policy. At one stroke, the certitudes that governed Canadian trade and investment policy with its great neighbour were swept away; at the same time, the special relationship, the idea that the United States would never act to harm the interests of its closest ally, was left in tatters. Canadian policy now had to be thought out afresh, and Sharp set his Department of External Affairs to the task at once.

Almost five years later, in July 1976, Canada and the European Community signed a Framework Agreement on Commercial and Economic Cooperation. In October of the same year, Canada and Japan signed a similar pact. For the European Community, the agreement went beyond anything hitherto negotiated with an industrialized nation and marked a step into new areas of international competence; for Canada, the Framework Agreements marked a renewed recognition of the importance of Europe and the Pacific Rim after the quasi-isolationism that had sometimes seemed to characterize foreign policy in the early years of Pierre Trudeau's administration. To a substantial extent, the new direction had been made essential by the Nixon administration's economic measures of August 1971 and, as a result, the Trudeau government had launched itself on yet another search for a counterweight to the enormous power of the United States. And yet, once achieved, the Framework Agreements disappeared into limbo so quickly that it was almost as if a fit of absence of mind had seized their creators.

The results of the defence and foreign policy reviews had demonstrated irrefutably that Canada was half-turning its back on NATO and, to a slightly lesser extent, on Europe. The government declared its new priority to be the development of links with countries in the Western Hemisphere and other regions: 'The predominance of transatlantic ties – with Britain, France and Western Europe generally (and new links with the Common Market) – will be adjusted to reflect a more evenly distributed policy emphasis, which envisages expanding activities in the Pacific basin and Latin America.'[1] The direction was all too clear. Even the ties with Britain and France, despite efforts since 1963 to create links for domestic Canadian purposes with the French-speaking world that could assume an importance in Canada's foreign policy sufficient to offset the historic links with the English-speaking world, were downgraded. De Gaulle's France had meddled overtly in Canadian politics, the Pompidou government made no apparent efforts to alter course, and relations with Paris were distinctly cool. The historic link to Britain had diminished dramatically since John Diefenbaker's political demise in 1963 and the development of a strong Canadian nationalism, evidenced most directly by the instant support won by the new Canadian flag adopted in 1965.[2]

There was, however, some concern about the implications for Canada of Britain's recurring problems with its balance of payments. In mid-1968, for example, the Canadian high commissioner in London sent a telegram to Ottawa headed 'Anglo-Canadian Economic Relations – The End of an Era?' that was as gloomy an assessment of trade relations with Great Britain as had ever been made.[3] The next year, Canadian negotiators forcefully told their British counterparts of their dismay at the 'weakening of [the] trade and economic relationship' and at the number of problems that indicated 'that consideration of Canadian interests appears to have become a distinctly lesser factor in British policymaking.'[4] There was evidence of this turning away when Britain again began to consider reapplying to the Common Market after President de Gaulle's 1968 resignation. One Canadian study made clear that if London was successful in securing entry, 'the British now hold that no attempt would be made by them to seek concessions for Commonwealth countries.' But there was remarkably little serious concern about this possibility, the decline in trade with Britain (from 11 per cent of Canada's total trade in 1964 to 7 per cent in 1968) being so rapid and so marked that Canadian officials thought that trade might *decrease* further if Britain did *not* join the European Economic Community.[5] The British link as a factor in Canadian economic policy was diminishing quickly, and so too was the emotional connection to the Mother Country. Whether it was in or out of the Common Market, in other words, Britain was unlikely to turn Canada's attention to Europe.[6]

At the same time, a key section of the pamphlet on Europe in *Foreign Policy for Canadians* looked first at the military, then at economic and cultural influences exercised by the United States on Canada, and noted that:

All these factors bear upon the nations of Western Europe; Canada faces them in more acute and immediate form. The maintenance of an adequate measure of economic and political independence in the face of American power and influence is a problem Canada shares with the European nations, and in dealing with this problem there is at once an identity of interest and an opportunity for fruitful cooperation. Nevertheless, Canada seeks to strengthen its ties with Europe, not as an anti-American measure but to create a more healthy balance within North America and to reinforce Canadian independence. The United States is Canada's closest friend and ally and will remain so.[7]

The conception of Europe as a potential counterweight to the United States was clearly spelled out there. The one major gap in *Foreign Policy for Canadians,* as we have seen, was that no single pamphlet was devoted to relations with the United States. In October 1972, a few days before the general election, this omission was remedied when Mitchell Sharp published a long paper in *International Perspectives,* the Department of External Affairs' magazine, on 'Canada-U.S. Relations: Options for the Future.'[8] If the United States had figured prominently in the pamphlet on Europe in 1970, so in turn would Europe play its part in the article on Canada-United States relations.

The reason was simple: President Nixon's economic policy statement of 15 August 1971. No one in Ottawa believed the United States was acting harshly to Canada out of inadvertence. The next spring, Nixon visited Ottawa and, spelling out the implications of the Nixon Doctrine, declared the end of the special relationship (see chapter 3).

Within months of the Nixon measures, Canada began to show more interest in Europe and Japan. The Interdepartmental Committee on External Relations, the senior bureaucratic committee in the area, urged a new effort to solidify economic ties with Europe. In September, the Nixon Doctrine was the focus of discussions at the Japan-Canada Ministerial Committee meeting in Toronto,[9] and on 29 September the cabinet considered an External Affairs paper proposing a study of Canada's options. On 4 November the cabinet looked at the first results of that study.[10] The same month, Trudeau defended NATO's virtue in a discussion with President Tito of Yugoslavia.[11] Donald Macdonald, now minister of national defence, told the press in Brussels that Canadian troops in Europe would not be reduced further and would remain for 'most of the present decade, at least.'[12] And Ivan Head was soon indicating to officials in External Affairs that the prime minister was now ready to turn his attention to Europe[13] – none too soon, for at the end of 1971 Trudeau had yet to visit Western Europe. Paradoxically, one aspect of this shift in direction was Mitchell Sharp's paper on 'Canada-U.S. Relations.'

The 'options paper' had been drafted primarily by Klaus Goldschlag, an able External Affairs European specialist. He set out three choices for Canada:

Canada can seek to maintain more or less its present relationship with the United States ... ; Canada can move deliberately toward closer integration with the United States; Canada can pursue a comprehensive long-term strategy to develop and strengthen the Canadian economy and other aspects of its national life and ... reduce the present Canadian vulnerability.[14]

Sharp himself had played a substantial role in conceiving the paper, and he had shepherded it through the Cabinet Committee on External Affairs and National Defence in the face of substantial opposition from the Departments of Finance and Industry, Trade and Commerce.[15] He recalled that the second option drew no support at all from his cabinet colleagues (and the options paper flatly rejected free trade with the United States), but the first option was the choice of the financial and trade departments.[16] The coolness of the critics to Sharp's preferred third option obviously sprang from the paper's implicit turning away from the opulent American market towards the riskier allure of the European Community and Japan. Moreover, by the time Sharp's paper reached the cabinet, the Americans had allowed their August 1971 surtax to lapse; that removed the pressure. There had also been sharp dispute in the cabinet between those ministers, largely French-speaking, who looked to Europe, and those, primarily from the west, who looked to the Pacific Rim countries.[17] The disputes were papered over, however, if not resolved, and Sharp committed his department to the third option. As an External Affairs paper put it in April 1972: 'Option 3 ... if it is to make sense and to be feasible, must be conceived as seeking important but limited relative changes in some dimensions of our relationship with the United States, which continue to involve extensive interdependence.

The main burdens of the strategy initially are likely to be carried by domestic economic measures combined with vigorous efforts to diversify our economic relations, notably with Europe and Japan, and support for international efforts to restore or reconstruct international trading and monetary rules and mechanisms.'[18] Aiming to reduce Canada's vulnerability to American actions, the third option, in other words, had a strong domestic component alongside its push for expanded trade and investment links to Europe and Japan.[19] At the same time, Canadian leaders were quick to add that the turn to Europe was not anti-American. As Sharp said in one speech, Canada was 'not thinking of substituting Europe for the United States as a trading partner. We are North Americans and the United States, of course, remains our most important partner.'[20] The problem now, Sharp said, was to 'remind the European Community that Canadian interests were distinct and separate and not always to be lumped together' with those of the United States.[21]

Sharp knew exactly what he meant by that comment. In April 1971 he had visited Brussels and called for bilateral consultations with the EC, a gesture that met what one of the minister's aides thought was the arrogant assumption that America was in decline and Europe was the hope of the future. This was combined with a near total indifference to Canada and a complete failure to comprehend that Canada did not want to shelter under the U.S. economic umbrella.[22] 'They didn't give us much of a welcome or show much interest,' Reeves Haggan, Sharp's assistant, recalled.[23]

Nonetheless, several months later, Franco Maria Malfatti, the president of the Commission of the European Economic Community, repaid the visit and came to Ottawa.[24] Canada may not have been very important to the EC, but the total trade between Canada and the community was over $2.1 billion in 1971 and that was not to be sneezed at. The Canadians called for 'periodic meetings at the ministerial level' between Canada and the EC, but Malfatti suggested that Canada follow the route already taken by the United States under which the community's commissioner responsible for trade and a Canadian senior official would meet twice a year.[25] That proposal, somewhat grudgingly, was accepted. More pleasing was the decision in mid-1972 by Common Market headquarters to create a Canadian desk 'separate from the United States.' One official in Brussels told the press that 'you may take this as symbolic of our approach to Canada.'[26] The action came as a result of lobbying by the Canadian ambassadors in each of the community members' capitals, as was the call by the community's heads of state in the autumn for the maintenance of a 'constructive dialogue with the United States, Japan and Canada and other industrialized commercial partners.'[27] As Ralf Dahrendorf, the EC commissioner for trade, put it a few months later, the specific mention of Canada was no accident. 'I have always understood this to mean that in our relations with Canada we set up the necessary machinery for consulting bilaterally about whatever problems may result from the enlargement of the Community ... indeed, whatever problems may result from the existence of the Community as such.' 'I think,' Dahrendorf added in words that certainly pleased Ottawa, 'there is agreement between the Canadian government and the European Community that this commitment by the summit has to be realized, has to be translated into a practical arrangement.'[28]

The pace was increasing. In Ottawa, the Senate Committee on Foreign Affairs had begun hearings on Canada's relations with the community. In June 1972, just a half-year before the Six became the Nine, a mission of senior officials from the Departments of Finance, Industry, Trade and Commerce, and External Affairs visited Brussels to propose that Canada and the community explore whether a comprehensive agreement on the most-favoured-nation (MFN) principle could assist in developing relations. As one of the participants put it, 'We imparted a certain amount of urgency to the discussion by reminding the Europeans that some of Canada's preferential trade arrangements with Britain which would soon be terminated, might be usefully discussed between Canada and the Community. For example,' Jeremy Kinsman of External Affairs wrote, 'Canada's assurance that no third country would be granted access to the Canadian market more favourable than that provided Britain might, on a reciprocal MFN basis, be of interest on a Canada-Community level.'[29]

Any idea that a preferential trade agreement might be negotiated between Canada and the EC soon disappeared. In November 1972, as informal semi-annual consultations between the community and Canada began, the Canadian government delivered an aide-memoire to the European Commission exploring the possibility of a general agreement on trade and economic matters. A year later, Sir Christopher Soames, the EC's vice-president for external relations, visited Ottawa.[30] And at the end of 1973, Canada announced that it would name an ambassador to the European Community. This was not yet a special relationship, but progress definitely had been made.

Or had it? The report of the Senate Foreign Affairs Committee, released in the summer of 1973, noted that Canada's share of the European market had actually declined since 1958. In 1960, for example, Canadian exports to the Federal Republic of Germany were 2.1 per cent of Germany's imports; ten years later, Canada's share had dropped to 1.7 per cent. Moreover, the only growth area in Canadian exports to the EC countries was in primary products, only 14 per cent of exports being finished goods. The senators said the government had not provided leadership, but they also lambasted Canadian business for its hesitancy and for falling prey to what it described as the 'natural propensity for the closer and more accessible American market.'[31] Moreover, in Henry Kissinger's self-proclaimed 'Year of Europe,' 1973, there was what one Canadian diplomat saw as 'a regrettable tendency ... to see "trans-atlantic relations" as relations essentially (if not exclusively) between the Nine and the United States.'[32]

Most important, as Michel Dupuy, the assistant undersecretary of state for external affairs, recollected, was that in the fall of 1973 Trudeau was looking for a new foreign-policy direction. What, after all, had he done in five years, Trudeau asked during a long flight from China to Ottawa, except recognize the People's Republic and review Canada's commitment to NATO? Should Canada now not try to establish links with Scandinavia or once-colonial Africa, to operate in the backyard of Europe and in this way make Western Europe appreciate Canadian importance? Dupuy and Ivan Head disagreed. Canada should strike at the heart of Europe, not at its periphery. In this way, Europeans could be made to recognize that Canada was a voice in North America independent of the United States.[33]

Thus when the European Community in November 1973 invited Canada to make its views known on how relations might be defined, there was genuine interest. And on 20 April 1974 Canada presented an aide-memoire to the EC member nations. Ottawa proposed that 'negotiations be initiated with the appropriate Community institution with a view to concluding a trade agreement' that would 'complement rather than supersede existing trade and commercial arrangements between Canada and the Member States and hence would leave intact existing bilateral arrangements.' Such an agreement, the argument ran, would 'effectively underpin the contractual relationship with the Community which is currently based on common adherence to the General Agreement on Tariffs and Trade.' In a discussion draft of the trade agreement, the Canadian government suggested an exchange of MFN treatment on tariff and related charges and the method of levying such duties and charges, and consultations on tariffs and on 'other matters which might contribute to the development and strengthening of economic and commercial relations.' At the same time, Canada proposed agreement on a statement of principles and objectives shared by both parties.[34]

To say that this proposal met a warm reception would be to overstate matters greatly. The Commission of the European Communities, as was noted in a memorandum to the Council of Ministers on 12 September 1974, was dubious for a variety of reasons. 'To proceed to the conclusion of a general Trade Agreement in a strictly bilateral framework with a country of the character of Canada would ... constitute a major innovation on the Community's part,' previous agreements being with less-developed states. Moreover, the Canadian proposals were for 'a conservative rather than a modern instrument, possessed of a certain symbolic value and some capacity for later expansion, but essentially devoid of present substance.' That was a devastating criticism, but the commission was not finished yet, suggesting that an agreement of the kind proposed might weaken GATT's multilateral framework. The commission's preference, as it sought to expand its own role and power in foreign policy and to become less of a political dwarf, was for an agreement that would embrace commercial matters but also provide a framework for economic and commercial cooperation 'extending well beyond the field of classical trade policy.'[35] As one EC official put it, the Canadian proposal squandered 'brilliant theorizing through a maladroit translation into policy.'[36] Unstated was the simple truth that Canada was still regarded in Brussels and elsewhere as an adjunct of the United States and her devotion to the defence of Western Europe had, since the cutbacks announced in 1969, been much in doubt. Moreover, there seemed to be little in such a proposed arrangement for the EC member states as opposed to the too obvious gains for the commission.

The crucial meeting in getting the Canadian proposal for a link with the EC back on track came on 26 September 1974 when John Halstead of the Department of External Affairs, with Michel Dupuy, the co-originator of the idea of the contractual link, flew to New York to address the Political Coordination Committee of the Nine, assembled for their regular meeting each fall to coordinate United Nations policies. Halstead noted that Canada recognized that the negotiation of a trade agreement between Canada and the EC would present 'complications and difficulties' and 'probably take considerable time.' But, he went on, Canada was flexible on the exact form of the trade agreement. The 'very act of negotiating would lead us closer to the determination of the precise form of contractual relationship which would be most appropriate ... What seems to us most important is that both sides, if they are agreed on the importance of our relations, agree that in principle we should seek to establish a contractual basis for our relations.' Halstead then virtually wrote off the Canadian suggestion of a statement of principles and called for 'more formal joint exploration of the possibilities for negotiating a bilateral contractual basis to our relationship.'[37] Helped by the West Germans in particular, he had rescued the Canadian case. 'Even the French,' he remembered, 'said they were prepared to examine the matter.'[38] The EC's Council of Ministers, while it refused to authorize negotiations, duly agreed, somewhat reluctantly, to continue the discussions with Canada.

But the rescue seemed only temporary, as Prime Minister Trudeau discovered when he paid his first official visit to Paris (other than for President Pompidou's funeral) and Brussels from 21–25 October. Trudeau himself, as he told Paul Martin, the high commissioner in London, 'at first ... wasn't very strong on the contractual link policy but gradually he had come to buy it and now was pushing it. It was important to get one's foot inside the door.'[39] But the Canadian press were not cooperating. Correspondents reported that Trudeau and his advisers were 'scrambling' to come up with proposals for a 'headline-grabbing trade accord.' They also told Canadians that one community official had said that any accord would be a 'meaningless piece of political rhetoric' and that the Canadian proposal was 'so vague that officials at EC headquarters here have no idea just what Canada really wants.'[40] In Paris, the French told Trudeau that he was trying to push the EC too far too fast. 'Don't be more European than the Europeans,' one senior elected official said. 'You're ahead of us. You want more than we have reached.'[41]

In a sense that was true. Trudeau told the community officials that 'we want to oblige the Community to define its relations with the rest of the world,' and especially with Canada. Since the EC had signed agreements with other countries, why could it not have one with Canada? 'We are telling the Europeans bilaterally and as a Community,' he said, that 'you may think you are going to be able to take all our raw materials out, but you ain't. We are defining our policies and if you want to get in there, you'd better embark on this process of negotiations.' There was a hint of a threat there in a world faced with rising energy costs after the OPEC embargo, a suggestion that Canada had resources Europe needed now and in the future. But Trudeau also lashed out at the Canadian draft proposals, conceding that the community had found them 'banal' and adding that Canada was being forced 'to put our thinking caps on.' That, as one senior Canadian columnist noted, was 'a crushing rebuke to the ministers and officials responsible.'[42] All that this trip produced was an agreement, as John Halstead later put it, for 'a new negotiating phase ... beginning with exploratory talks for the purpose of defining the form of a possible contractual arrangement.'[43]

That made the 'cloud of vagueness' that constituted the Canadian proposal no clearer,[44] and the confusion persisted. James Callaghan, the British foreign secretary, told an Ottawa press conference in January 1975 that while the British 'regarded ourselves as an interlocutor on Canada's behalf' (in fact London was cool to any expansion of the commission's authority and hence to the Canadian proposal),[45] nonetheless 'we all have to make more precise what it is we have got in mind.'[46] What worried the British (themselves still facing a referendum on whether or not Britain would remain a member of the community) and others in the EC, as the permanent secretary of the Ministry of Trade told the Canadians, were three main concerns: '1) how far the Commission should have the power to speak for the Community as a whole; 2) the extent to which the boundary between the Community and the member states will change in the future; 3) the extent to which there could be disputes in the so-called gray area.'[47] London was fretting, though always with assurances of support for the broad Canadian objective.[48] The EC and Canada were venturing into an uncharted area and the international lawyers were in charge.[49]

Thus, when Trudeau paid a second visit to a number of European capitals in March 1975 (he 'took London by storm!' High Commissioner Paul Martin wrote),[50] there was still no certainty what he or his country wanted, and no guarantee that once confirmed it could be secured. After a conversation with Trudeau just before he left Canada, Jules Léger, now governor general, wrote that 'il cherche sa voie.' The prime minister was following the advice of the Department of External Affairs, 'mais sans être pris au jeu. Il cherche comment il peut produire des rélations meilleures avec l'Europe mais sans encore savoir comment.'[51] In an address in London, nonetheless, Trudeau was somewhat clearer than hitherto in defining what he sought:

We have described our goal as the attainment of a contractual link. Because we do not know – indeed Europe does not know – how far or how fast its experiment in integration will take it ... no overall agreement can be laid in place at this time. But what can be done is to create a mechanism that will provide the means (i.e., the 'link') and the obligation (i.e., 'contractual') to consult and confer, and to do so with materials sufficiently pliable and elastic to permit the mechanism to adapt in future years to accommodate whatever jurisdiction the European Community from time to time assumes.[52]

Trudeau told British Prime Minister Harold Wilson, 'our policy of diversification was not anti-American. It was designed to reduce dependency on the United States by supplementing rather than supplanting relations with that country.' Canada's objective was for a contractual link 'as a basis for dialogue'; he wanted active support from the British government, not just its willingness 'to interpret Canadian policy to the EEC.' As Martin noted, 'Originally our proposal was to concentrate on trade. Now we are looking with the Community at other possibilities for economic cooperation.'[53]

Perhaps Trudeau's trips had achieved something. Although the British refused to be tied down to specific pledges of support,[54] on 3 March Foreign Minister Hans-Dietrich Genscher in Bonn had authorized Trudeau to say that the German government stood behind Canada's bid for a contractual link;[55] Chancellor Schmidt, with whom Trudeau had developed a close and confidential relationship, promised his assistance as far as he could influence developments;[56] and in Rome Premier Moro also offered his country's support. That was progress, even if officials were quick to qualify their leaders' pledges. Another sign of an increasing clarity and urgency in the Canadian position was the appointment of the able Marcel Cadieux as ambassador to the European Communities. A former undersecretary of state for external affairs, ambassador to the United States, and a tough-minded international lawyer, Cadieux was the man to press matters.[57] Thus by May, matters seemed on track. And after a NATO meeting that month at which Canada pledged to increase its commitments to the alliance,[58] Trudeau had discussed the Canadian proposal with the political leaders of all of the EC nations and won statements of support – in varying degrees of warmth – from all but France.[59]

In May 1975, as well, after discussions between Canadian and community officials, discussions that on the European side required endless coordination to secure agreement,[60] the European Commission recommended that the Council of Ministers authorize the beginning of negotiations with Canada for a framework agreement for economic and commercial cooperation. The commission recommended a non-discriminatory agreement to establish cooperation with Canada 'extending beyond the field of classical trade policy and geared to the present state of economic relations ... and their future potential. Thus, future Community-scale cooperation with Canada could complement that of the individual Member States' and provide a framework within which there could be joint ventures, exchanges of information, and the facilitation of contacts.[61]

Again that was progress. But the French government remained distinctly cool to the idea of the community expanding its competence by entering into any such agreement with Canada, and Ottawa feared that Paris would veto negotiations. At the last moment, lobbying by the Canadian ambassador in Paris, Léo Cadieux, and his officials turned the tide. President Giscard d'Estaing, who had himself been pressed hard by Trudeau the previous October, was said to have told his reluctant foreign minister that this was a political question, not simply an economic one, and that he could not vote against Canada.[62] On 25 June 1975, therefore, the Council of Ministers unanimously agreed to empower its experts to prepare a mandate to negotiate a framework agreement with Canada. By late October, Britain and France having dropped their lingering objections to giving the commission the power to negotiate and sign an agreement on behalf of the nine EC members,[63] the commission recommended that negotiations begin.[64]

But nothing was ever simple in the EC. In December the Council of Ministers became stalled over Danish demands for non-discriminatory access to natural resources, a reaction to the Canadian levy on oil exports to the United States which had created a two-price system for Canadian petroleum. Although Denmark imported no oil from Canada, the Danes were clearly worried that British North Sea oil could be priced in the same fashion.[65] In February 1976, after some testy bargaining, the Danes withdrew their complaint, although Canada refused to assure the EC of equal access to Canadian energy resources.[66] The Europeans wanted access to our resources, Allan MacEachen recalled, 'and we resisted that.' They wanted uranium without any political strings or restrictions, he added, but we wanted greater control over our own economic resources.[67] Nonetheless, a satisfactory form of face-saving words having been found, the council duly authorized the opening of negotiations. At last, the lengthy gavotte was drawing to its close.

Once begun, the negotiations proceeded swiftly. Opening statements were exchanged on 11 March and the first round of negotiations opened on 24 March in Brussels, the result being a joint working paper in the form of a draft agreement. Predictably, the resources question was the main difficulty, though there were signs that the EC negotiator wanted to settle.[68] The next round took place on 19 and 20 May and, once a few wording problems had been resolved, produced the Framework Agreement between Canada and the European Communities. As the deputy minister of industry, trade and commerce told his minister, 'In keeping with Canadian Government objectives, no new rights or obligations with respect to access to resources or to markets have been created.'[69] Announcement of success came on 2 June.[70] After some difficulties with France on where the signature of the agreement should occur, it was settled that the locale would be Ottawa on 6 July.[71] With ceremony and speeches, the agreement was duly signed.

The agreement, to come into effect on 1 October 1976 and to remain in force indefinitely subject to termination after five years by either party, gave most-favoured-nation treatment, undertook to promote development and diversification of trade through commercial cooperation, and called for the encouragement and facilitation of broader intercorporate links through joint ventures, increased investment, and exchanges of scientists and information. The parties also established a Joint Co-operation Committee, responsible for promoting and reviewing the various aspects of commercial and economic cooperation.[72] It is also worth noting that the Framework Agreement left intact the competence of EC members to make bilateral arrangements with Canada.[73]

The successful conclusion of the agreement was a triumph for Canadian diplomacy and for Prime Minister Trudeau, whose visits to European leaders had tilted the balance from opposition to support for the Canadian initiative. To persist over four years, to persuade a reluctant and dubious European Community to expand its jurisdiction, and to essay a new direction was a tribute to the skill of the officers of the Department of External Affairs. There can be no doubt of that. Moreover, the EC at last seemed to be aware that Canada existed as an entity separate from the United States.[74]

But what did the agreement itself amount to? It was a foot in the door and an arrangement to consult, to be sure. It was a political symbol, the cornerstone of the Canadian effort to diversify. But what did the Framework Agreement really mean? Very few were certain, including the secretary of state for external affairs, Don Jamieson. At a meeting with Canada's European heads of post in December 1976, Jamieson told his ambassadors that there was scepticism about the link in Canada and in Europe, and he himself had asked, 'What does the contractual link really do?'[75] The minister had stressed that the next twelve to eighteen months were the testing time, the time to advance 'from rhetoric to action.'[76] Most of the ambassadors sat silently through this speech,[77] the only one who spoke strongly about the link being one of its main creators, John Halstead. 'The Community,' Halstead said, 'thought it was worthwhile having a second partner in North America. They wanted Canada to be engaged in the common political and security framework ... The contractual link opened up the way for us to have a greater impact on the Europeans.' Above all, he continued, 'the contractual link did ... offer us a better chance. The problem was one of spreading knowledge and information about each other, of seeking out opportunities.' But Halstead essentially admitted that the link would fail if Canadian business, unused to operating in Europe, refused to try the market there.[78]

That was one of the difficulties. As one German official noted later, it was difficult to fit industry into an agreement. 'You can't force them to take advantage of it.'[79] The European market intimidated many Canadian businessmen and bankers, few of whom had the linguistic ability to move easily among Paris, Amsterdam, and Bonn, and even fewer of whom had the staying power to last through the long process of publicizing their products and slow negotiations. When contracts could be signed with the Europeans, that market always seemed to take second place to sales in the more accessible United States that could be satisfied easily (and in English) by the relatively small Canadian production runs.[80] Then, some businessmen were suspicious of the arrangement, fearing, as Richard Malone wrote in the *Globe and Mail,* that it was 'a springboard for large state trading arrangements and so-called joint (government-private industry) enterprises in selling Canadian goods and resources to Europe through government boards.'[81]

For their part, European businessmen, particularly some in Germany where Canada's hopes for trade expansion with Europe were focused, fretted about the Foreign Investment Review Agency, weak reed that it was. Some worried that monetary policy, the Bank of Canada notwithstanding, was made in Washington. When the United States caught a cold, Canada sneezed – and if that was the case, the Europeans asked, perhaps their investments should be placed in the United States. There were also concerns about Canada's immigration regulations – Would skilled personnel be allowed into Canada to operate a European-controlled factory?[82]

Moreover, businessmen and officials in Europe and Canada had serious concerns about the complementarity of the Canadian economy with Europe's. Was there, as some supporters of the link argued, a natural fit? Or were the two economies competitors? On agricultural products, for example, the EC tariff was effectively shutting Canada out of traditional markets, and the European surpluses were competing with Canadian exports around the world. Even though agriculture's share of Canada's GNP was dropping, there were serious problems here.[83]

There was also the necessity in the new federalism that was taking form in Canada in the 1970s for Ottawa to consult the provinces about the contractual link. The provincial capitals had been kept informed throughout the long process of negotiation and, once the agreement had been signed, arrangements were set in train to give the provinces representation on subcommittees of the Joint Co-operation Committee.[84] But in the light of the Parti Québécois election victory in Quebec in November 1976, the federal government flatly refused to give the provinces a seat at the table during the semi-annual consultations with the EC.[85] The net results of this effort at federal-provincial cooperation were yet another federal-provincial meeting.[86]

If Ottawa had its problems with the provinces, the EC similarly had difficulties with its member states. In 1978 there were suggestions that some EC members wanted to discuss bilateral problems with Canada under the terms of the Framework Agreement. The Canadians resisted these efforts, recognizing in them an attempt to find another forum in which to resolve such problems as duties on shoes and champagne.[87] Inevitably too there were complaints from Canada that the EC nations were not 'doing all they can to put some meat on the contractual link.'[88] In a sense that was inevitable. Full of itself, Europe simply was not very interested in Canada. And Canadians might have expected their sudden affection for Europe to be unrequited. Small powers, as A.E. Ritchie reflected years later, always expect more than they get.[89]

That may have been true, but there were particular Canadian problems behind the failure of the agreement to amount to much. Above all, as one senior Canadian diplomat noted, there was a tendency for Canadian ministers to want a 'quick fix,' to seek, as Jamieson had, results within a year. Ministers failed to realize that a slow educational process was the only way to create a meaningful link.[90] Moreover, the Canadian government did almost nothing to facilitate the implementation of the third option. Aside from Mitchell Sharp, who was a true believer, and Trudeau, who found the idea of the link intellectually convincing, no ministers and almost no senior mandarins in Finance and Industry, Trade and Commerce thought the connection with Europe likely to succeed. Even in External Affairs, officials were far from unanimous in support of the link. The message went out to Canadian business that this policy was not going to work – and no one in Ottawa cared very much if it didn't.[91] There was, Mitchell Sharp recalled, 'no internal restructuring, no political will.'[92]

The story would prove to be much the same with Japan. The astonishing regeneration of the Japanese economy after the Second World War had provided Canada with a growing market for its products, and the first postwar trade agreement with Japan was signed in 1954. But, as with Europe, the Japanese wanted raw materials from Canada, scorning manufactured goods as inferior in quality and workmanship to their own.

Sometimes that complaint was correct; often it was a form of non-tariff barrier that served to keep Canadian products out of Japan.

Still, the Japanese market was large and growing. The trade figures demonstrated that irrefutably. In 1965, Canada secured 2.5 per cent of its imports from Japan and sent it 3.6 per cent of its exports. Five years later, imports were 4.2 per cent, exports 4.8; and in 1975, although imports had dropped to 3.5 per cent in a recession year, their value was $1.2 billion, the same as imports from Britain. Exports in 1975 amounted to 6.4 per cent of Canada's total ($2.1 billion), substantially more than the $1.8 billion sent to the United Kingdom (and sales to Japan by 1984 would be well over twice as large as those to Britain). The Japanese sent Canada their automobiles,[93] communications equipment, and rolling-mill products, as well as a number of products, such as textiles, limited in volume by 'voluntary restraint.'[94] Canada shipped Japan wheat, rapeseed, lumber, ores and coal.[95] Canada was Japan's sixth or seventh most important supplier; Japan was Canada's second-largest commercial partner, next only to the United States, and year by year outstripping the United Kingdom. Moreover, in 1975 the Japanese had responded to a Canadian offer of 'partnership' in joint ventures in processing Canadian raw materials by agreeing to have their officials work with Canadians to 'identify those areas of the Japanese and Canadian economies which held the greatest promise for increased and mutually-beneficial economic cooperation.'[96] That was seen in Ottawa as a breakthrough, and the Japanese had followed up on their undertaking, showing some apparently genuine interest in the CANDU reactor and in Canadian STOL aircraft. Still, the Japanese viewed Canada's demands for a more active relationship as 'an extension of the pressures ... from the United States and the European Communities ... [and] the Japanese response [was] instinctively defensive.'[97]

Politically, relations were friendly but not close. Following a preparatory visit to Japan by Ivan Head, Prime Minister Tanaka had visited Ottawa in 1974.[98] He and Trudeau had agreed, as the diplomats put it, 'to broaden and deepen our relationship,' which had been based largely on economic ties, into one with a significant political and cultural as well as enhanced economic dimension. Canadian ministers and officials had used the regular ministerial meetings, begun in 1961, between the two countries to 'politicize' the relationship. At the seventh meeting in June 1975, for example, discussions on Korea had made the point that Canada had interests in areas of concern to Japan; moreover, as Canadians boasted modestly, they had demonstrated that they were better informed than the Japanese. The secretary of state for external affairs, Allan

MacEachen, had also told Japanese audiences that Canada's third option was not anti-American; indeed, he said, it was 'quite similar to your *Takaku Gaiko* – that is, your own "diplomacy for diversification." '[99] Cooperation had continued in New York and in Tokyo, and the Japanese in 1976 were lending their support to Ottawa's efforts to be included in the five-power Western Summits.[100]

To some substantial extent, the improvement in the political relationship was fostered by the extraordinary Japanese ambassador, Yasuhiko Nara. Almost alone among ambassadors in Ottawa, Nara had hit it off with the prime minister, and Mrs Nara was indefatigable in showing Margaret Trudeau how to make sushi. So relaxed was the familial relationship that Mrs Trudeau breastfed her youngest child in front of the Naras, to the excruciating embarrassment of the Japanese. The relationship between the prime minister and the ambassador, almost as close, helped secure Foreign Minister Miyazawa's and Japan's support for Canada's summit bid and, after the Indian nuclear explosion, to resolve the difficulty created by Canada's ban on uranium exports to Japan.[101] Although pleased with the friendship and appreciative of its potential for resolving problems, Canadian officials sometimes had difficulty finding out what had been decided; diplomats at the embassy in Tokyo were also often startled to be told about pending cabinet shuffles or government decisions by officials at the *Gaimusho* who had had the word from Nara well before the regular Canadian channels delivered it to the outlying posts.[102]

On 26 May 1976 Allan MacEachen proposed to the prime minister that Canada attempt to negotiate a framework agreement with Japan, ideally one that could be signed during Trudeau's scheduled visit to Japan in October. The agreement would be similar to that negotiated with the EC, MacEachen said, but no trade clause would be needed, thanks to the existing Commerce Agreement with Japan.[103] Trudeau agreed, the Japanese were receptive, and on 21 October 1976 Trudeau and Prime Minister Takeo Miki signed the Framework for Economic Cooperation. The two countries agreed to expand their bilateral trade, increase investment, and exchange expertise. A Joint Economic Committee, to be headed by the two countries' foreign ministers, was created to review economic cooperation activities. As Canadian officials noted, the Framework Agreement 'provides a reference point for our respective business communities and signifies the will and the intention of the two governments to promote the development of economic cooperation between them. As a public declaration, it should have an impact on the business communities in both countries.' Nevertheless, 'the major effort will have to come from the private sector.'[104] Bruce Rankin, the ambassador to Japan, frankly commented that the agreement sought 'a better "mix" in our exports – the upgrading of our raw materials and easier access to the Japanese market for our manufactured goods.'[105] Ambassador Nara, who had accompanied Trudeau to Japan, more realistically observed that the agreement was 'not too important.'[106]

Nor did it prove to be. Only 3 per cent of Canadian exports to Japan were finished manufactures. And Canadian business had a fixed view of Japan as a closed market, one with a very tight business-government relationship, and one protected by an array of tariff and non-tariff barriers. The impenetrability of the Japanese language added to the difficulties. On the Japanese side, Canada was perceived as a land of ice, snow, mountains, and the outdoors, not as a technologically sophisticated nation.[107] Moreover, it was much like the United States, a slightly contradictory view, but one nonetheless deeply held. Indeed, whenever quotas were negotiated, Canada, to Canadian annoyance, invariably received one-tenth of that accorded to the United States.[108]

When they looked at Canadian industry at all, the Japanese were not impressed. An industrialists' mission in the fall of 1976 had complained bluntly about the number of strikes, the high wage levels and low productivity, the Foreign Investment Review Agency and federal-provincial jurisdictional disputes, and poor business-government relations.[109] 'Canada sits complacently idle among her natural resources,' the industrialists reported.[110] 'They weren't delicate or subtle,' one Canadian diplomat remembered,[111] and the Japanese were vigorously denounced in the press.

By 1978, although trade had increased dramatically to a two-way total of $5.3 billion, the portion of manufactured goods in exports to Japan remained tiny and the Japanese continued to show little interest in economic cooperation with Canada. Japanese investment in Canada remained small (3 per cent of Japan's foreign investment), and there had been no success, despite efforts that included having Prime Minister Joe Clark raise the subject directly with Prime Minister Ohira at the 1979 Tokyo Summit, in persuading the Japanese to purchase Canadian technology, and especially the CANDU.[112] As with the EC, progress after the Framework Agreement was incremental at best.

Canada's efforts to secure contractual links with the EC and Japan had succeeded – on paper. The effort to diversify Canada's trade, however, had not worked. Why?

Trudeau's principal secretary, Thomas Axworthy, offered his view of what he called 'the sad history of Trudeau's Third Option. Seldom has a policy been more apropos. Instead of hitching our destiny to a declining American hegemony, Trudeau sought to expand our links with Asia and Europe ... The policy failed because of lack of will. The Ottawa mandarinate, especially in Finance, hoped that the policy would go away, and eventually it did ... [Trudeau's] commitment to the Third Option was not equal to the task ... Because his attention was directed elsewhere, the Third Option died a silent death.'[113] Trudeau's gaze, always peripatetic and never fixed for very long on foreign questions, had of necessity been forced to Quebec, the critical problem for his country and his government after René Lévesque's accession to power on a platform of sovereignty-association in November 1976.

Even the architects of the link with the EC seemed to lose interest once the paper was signed. Michel Dupuy ruefully admitted that he thought the job was done after the conclusion of negotiations. The world's weak economic situation made rapid progress impossible and, moreover, the link 'wasn't an initiative for which you would go to the wall.' Dupuy was not surprised when it 'sank quickly into relative oblivion.'[114]

Certainly the Canadian business community showed little surprise – or concern. The corporations had waited for Ottawa to offer incentives to encourage their efforts in Europe and Japan, but there were no tax breaks, no export incentives, and no subsidies to encourage research and development aimed at world markets. In the circumstances, few businessmen seemed interested in trying the EC and Japanese markets when the obstacles of language and culture were so readily apparent and when the payoff, if there was any, was certain to be long-deferred. The inertia of corporate Canada was as impressive as Ottawa's.

Thus, by 1983, all that the Framework Agreement with the Common Market had accomplished in the areas of common research, for example, was an agreement to cooperate on an energy bus that performed on-site analysis of energy efficiency, an agreement into research on radioactive waste disposal methods, and a memorandum of understanding on coordination of research into the treatment of waste water. There was little else – and certainly no vast expansion of trade – that could be directly attributed to the agreement.[115] The United States continued as Canada's major market – and in 1983 the Trudeau government launched its own ill-planned and ill-thought-out effort to negotiate sectoral free trade with the Americans (see chapter 12)[116] – and the contractual links with Europe and Japan were all but dead if not yet buried within a very few years of their signing. The coup de grâce would come in the mid-1980s in the successful negotiation by the Mulroney government of a free-trade arrangement with the United States, an exercise in complete contradiction to the third option. The effort to diversify, the attempt to turn away from the United States, had been put to rest for good. 'The third option, so sensible, so necessary, so obvious, [was] an attempt to secure the triumph of politics over geography,' one academic, who again happened to be one of the present authors, wrote in 1977.[117] Emerson Brown, an American diplomat with long experience of Canadian affairs, put the United States embassy's response to the third option and the contractual link more succinctly still: 'lots of luck, Canada.'[118] As may have been inevitable, geography won out in the end. Here, as elsewhere, Trudeau had created only the illusion of change.

7

The East Is Red:
China and the Soviet Union

After a trip to China in 1960, Pierre Trudeau and his friend Jacques Hébert published a little book in Quebec. Within a few months of his becoming prime minister, Trudeau brought out the volume in English under the title *Two Innocents In China*. The book is a travelogue in the form of a joint diary, interesting but exceptional only because its co-author rose to the top of the greasy pole. But there is one provocative comment in Trudeau's brief introductory note to the English edition: 'If there are any statements in the book which can be used to prove that the authors are agents of the international Communist conspiracy, or alternatively fascist exploiters of the working classes, I am sure that my co-author, Jacques Hébert, who remains a private citizen, will be willing to accept entire responsibility for them.'[1] That flippant comment said much about Trudeau's style. Unfortunately, as his policy to the People's Republic of China (PRC) and the Soviet Union developed, many of his countrymen, and others in the United States, came to the view that Trudeau almost literally was part of the international communist conspiracy.

Like other French Canadians of his generation, Pierre Trudeau was raised on stories told by Roman Catholic missionaries of their struggles in China against the Yellow Peril and for God.[2] Unlike others, however, Trudeau went to China twice before he became prime minister. In 1949, while bumming around the world, he travelled to Canton and to Shanghai, far enough to see the chaos that was Chiang Kai-shek's Kuomingtang in its final moments. On another trip to Asia, Trudeau visited Taiwan. Then, eleven years after his first visit to China, Trudeau was part of a small party of Canadians who visited the People's Republic on a month-long journey. Trudeau observed the latent power of the new China, and he came to understand that Mao Tse-tung's country was fully aware that critical questions of peace, war, disarmament, and nuclear weaponry could not be settled without its participation. It was folly, Trudeau came to believe, to leave a quarter of the human race unrepresented in the United Nations and treated as a pariah by the United States. 'Time is on its side,' Trudeau and Hébert wrote, adding that the idea that Chiang's Republic of China, shrunken to the island of Taiwan, could still be seen by some as the government of China was almost incomprehensible. The United States and its allies were 'well aware' that their Taiwan policy 'is now based only on a question of prestige.'[3]

Trudeau, then parliamentary secretary to the prime minister, went to the United Nations General Assembly in the fall of 1966. Also on the delegation was Donald Macdonald, parliamentary secretary to the secretary of state for external affairs, Paul Martin. Although there had been some indications earlier in the year that Canada was ready to move for the admission of the People's Republic to the UN,[4] and although opinion polls suggested that a majority in Canada favoured China's admission to the UN and recognition of the PRC by Canada,[5] there were countervailing pressures in Ottawa. The United States, protective of Chiang and, as the Vietnam War heated up, still viewing the world struggle through red-coloured lenses, remained adamantly opposed to 'Red China's' admission.[6] There was also some opposition in External Affairs, especially from officers who had served in Vietnam with the International Control Commission and had returned with a hard-line attitude towards Asian Communists.[7] And there might be costs on the Canadian-American front if Ottawa changed its policy. Moreover, as China continued to tear itself apart in the Cultural Revolution and as embassies in Peking came under attack by mobs of Red Guards, a very credible argument could be made against doing anything until the situation there had calmed. Nor was there much to suggest the Chinese wanted to establish diplomatic relations with Canada.[8]

Nonetheless, Trudeau and Macdonald discovered that they thought alike on the need for a new realism towards China, as did Heward Grafftey, a Progressive Conservative MP on the delegation. The two Liberals pushed as hard as they could for change in Canada's position, finding in Martin a cautious ally against the resistance to change (or what political scientists call 'grooved thinking') of some of the senior officials of External Affairs.[9] Trudeau also strenuously pressed Martin to move during the trip to New York.[10] As a result, on 23 November Martin called for the seating of both the PRC and Taiwan in the General Assembly and for Peking (Beijing) to have the Security Council seat.[11] The Americans, 'absolutely dumbfounded ... with this belated and rather scattershot Canadian initiative,' continued their opposition, however, and the attempt to seat China was defeated 58–46.[12] For the first time, however, Canada abstained on the vote. Trudeau and Macdonald had had some impact on the Pearson government's China policy.

Little over a year later, Trudeau was minister of justice and a candidate for the Liberal leadership. Bolstered by the advice of a group of civil servants and friends that he had put together to advise him on the foreign-policy aspects of his portfolio, Trudeau remained firmly of the view that Canada should recognize China. It was something he simply wanted to do. He did not want to be outflanked by the New Democratic Party on this issue and, he recalled, he was vain enough not to want to be the last statesman to move on the China question.[13] He said as much in an address in early March, promising to offer recognition if he became prime minister.[14] After his selection as Liberal leader, the new prime minister retracted not a word of his position. On at least four occasions during the election campaign that followed the Liberal party leadership convention, Trudeau was blunt, most notably in a major speech announcing a review of foreign policy on 29 May:

We shall be looking at our policy in relation to China in the context of a new interest in Pacific affairs generally ... Canada has long advocated a positive approach to Mainland China and its inclusion in the world community. We have an economic interest in trade with China ... and a political interest in preventing tension between China and its neighbours, but especially between China and the United States. Our aim will be to recognize the People's Republic of China Government as soon as possible and to enable that Government to occupy the seat of China in the United Nations, taking into account that there is a separate Government in Taiwan.[15]

A few days later, Trudeau told a press conference in Castlegar, BC, that 'of course recognition is a bilateral street, is it not?' He wanted to establish relations with China, but 'that depends very much on the way Peking reacts.'[16]

The Department of External Affairs was itself moving towards recognizing the PRC. Perhaps comforted by reports from Hong Kong suggesting that China's period of 'diplomacy by mob' was coming to an end and that the control of foreign policy again was in the hands of professional diplomats,[17] External Affairs began to look at China with new interest. On 4 April, just days before the Liberal party had selected Trudeau as leader, department officials had suggested sending an exploratory mission to China. Whether this was genuine interest or simply a desire to be prepared in the event of a Trudeau convention victory remains unclear. The next month, the department's Far Eastern Division had proposed that the review of foreign policy, approved by cabinet a few days earlier, look at the possibilities of broadening contacts with China, the exchange of non-governmental missions, or recognition and the exchange of diplomats. The department had also begun to seek the views of countries such as Britain, Sweden, and France. Later, Marcel Cadieux, the undersecretary, told Mitchell Sharp, Trudeau's new foreign minister, that the China study would examine the possible effect on United States policy of recognition by Canada, the possibility of a chain reaction on other countries that had held back if Canada recognized the PRC, and the security problems that might result if a Chinese embassy located in Ottawa operated as the North American centre for propaganda, espionage, and subversion.[18]

Trudeau's 29 May address delicately raised the possibility of recognizing the PRC while still continuing Canada's recognition of the Nationalist government on Taiwan. No other country had succeeded in doing this, Sharp realized, but, as he told one of his officials, it was not out of the question that Canada could succeed.[19] That, given the strongly held position of Beijing, was a long shot, but it seemed to be one that the Trudeau government was prepared to play. Indeed, on 2 August, Gordon Robertson, the clerk of the Privy Council, and one thought to be especially concerned not to see Taiwan sacrificed for the sake of recognizing China, told Basil Robinson of the Department of External Affairs that 'of all the different parts of the foreign policy review, the one which the Prime Minister seemed most concerned to push ahead with was China.'[20] As Ivan Head, said later, 'In those days, Mr. Trudeau knew exactly what he wanted to do with foreign policy.'[21] With China, too.

The Department of External Affairs' first draft of the review paper on China was completed on 3 July 1968. The initial reaction in the department was cool: Was Canada prepared to sacrifice its economic interests in Taiwan for the sake of recognizing China? If not, Canada might make Beijing angry enough to cut off Canada's wheat sales.[22] That complaint quickly resulted in additions and alterations, and the paper became an omnibus version listing everything and anything, and exploring all the options, before it went to the Prime Minister's Office and to other departments on 12 July. There were potential costs involved in recognition, as some pointed out. Trade specialists, on balance, leaned to the view that the potential gains outweighed the risks. Still, Canada's wheat salesmen, fighting to hold and expand their lucrative sales to China, feared the negative impact of any attempt to make a 'two-China' approach to Beijing. Why queer the pitch with politics?[23] The prime minister had to be aware of the risks.

Another problem was the United States. The Americans were already irritated at Canada's attitude. They were, as the Washington embassy reported on 25 July, unhappier still that Canada now contemplated recognition. Some at the senior levels of the State Department feared that Canadian recognition on Beijing's terms would open the flood-gates and lead to Taiwan's expulsion from the UN. If Canada could avoid those consequences, Washington would not object; if Canada precipitated them, nothing else Ottawa could do would help very much. The view of the American officials, the Washington embassy noted, was that they would be pleased if Canada stuck by the statement that Taiwan was governed by the Republic of China. Then Taiwan might accede to this interpretation and keep its relations with Canada.[24]

If Trudeau himself had already decided to seek the recognition of China, the idea nonetheless had to work its way through the bureaucracy and the cabinet's committees. This was slower than expected, in part because the Cabinet Committee on External Affairs and National Defence had the defence-policy review under consideration, and this was proving very divisive. The committee looked at the China problem initially in mid-September and, by the beginning of 1969, it was ready to consider concrete proposals.

The initial recommendation presented in a memorandum to the ministers was that the Canadian ambassador in Stockholm should approach the PRC embassy there to suggest that talks begin at a convenient time in some Western European capital, in Ottawa, or, if necessary, in Beijing. The American government should be informed of the approach ten days to two weeks before it was made and told that Canada would neither endorse the PRC's claim to Taiwan nor recognize Taiwan as an independent nation. One possibility was to open a trade mission in Taiwan and to permit a similar office in Canada. Most important, the ministers were advised that Canada should resist any attempt by the PRC to secure a public declaration of its sovereignty over Taiwan. That had to be a sticking point. At the same time, Canada should be ready to assure Beijing that it did not intend to maintain formal diplomatic relations with Taiwan. Finally, the memorandum insisted that Canada should not yield to any possible Chinese demand for a prior commitment to vote for their admission to the UN. Mutual recognition had to be unconditional, and this issue was important enough that the talks should be broken off if Peking proved adamant.[25]

The Cabinet Committee finally discussed the memorandum on 27 January, accepting it except for one substantive alteration. Canada would not accept any commitment precluding *eventual* recognition of an independent Taiwan, an important point as it would allow the negotiators to tell the PRC that it was not Canada's intention to recognize Taiwan. Three days later, the full cabinet gave the go-ahead for the approach to be made in Stockholm on 6 February for an appointment on the 8th.[26] Clearly the Canadian government had almost completely abandoned the 'two-Chinas' approach, though the Canadian government still hoped not to abandon Taiwan completely.

As Ottawa told the embassy in Washington, reiterating the government's position, Canada was in no way accepting the PRC's claim to Taiwan by seeking to recognize China; in fact, the object was to continue the best possible non-formal relations with Taiwan, to keep them equal at least to Canada's past relations with the PRC. Nor was Canada cutting off relations with Taiwan because that was a *sine qua non* for Beijing. Recognition of the PRC as the legitimate government of China removed the basis for Ottawa-Taipei relations, but should the Chiang government propose another basis for recognition, Canada would be prepared to consider it. The important point was that Canada no longer accepted that the Taiwan regime had any status as the government of China.[27]

The U.S. government understood the Canadian position, but was not happy with it. A senior State Department officer told A. E. Ritchie, the Canadian ambassador, that his government hoped that Canada would defend its relationship with Taiwan just as long as it could in the negotiating process with the PRC and simultaneously hold to the line at the UN. As he said to Ritchie and Peter Roberts who accompanied him, 'Just don't touch the Security Council. We're friendly as hell, but don't touch the Security Council.' The official's serious, deep concern with the new Canadian policy was all too obvious.[28] President Richard Nixon made similar points to Trudeau when the two met for the first time on Trudeau's visit to Washington the next month. More in sorrow than in anger, Trudeau recalled, Nixon had privately suggested that the timing and tactics of the Canadian move were wrong. It would have been better to have a joint Canadian-American initiative, Nixon said,[29] although no suggestions to that effect appear to have reached Ottawa from any American sources either before or after the Nixon-Trudeau meeting. Other allies were also unhappy with the Canadian move, notably the

Australians, New Zealanders, and South Koreans,[30] and there was opposition too from within the Canadian Chinese community.[31]

Whether the Chinese wanted to negotiate at all was not a matter that had concerned Ottawa. The initial approach on 6 February drew no immediate response, which was not especially surprising. Mitchell Sharp nonetheless told the House of Commons on 10 February that the approach had been made.[32] Finally, on 19 February, the chargé at the PRC embassy in Stockholm called to arrange a meeting two days hence. There was likely some relief in Ottawa – had the PRC not responded, the Trudeau government would have looked foolish indeed.

The negotiations once begun lasted into October 1970, a far longer period than anyone on the Canadian side had anticipated. The PRC's chargé had laid out his government's 'three constant principles' to the Canadian ambassador to Sweden, Arthur Andrew, at the first meeting:

1. A government seeking relations with China must recognize the central People's Government as the sole and lawful government of the Chinese people;

2. A government which wishes to have relations with China must recognize that Taiwan is an inalienable part of Chinese territory and in accordance with this principle must sever all kinds of relationships with the 'Chiang Kai-shek gang';

3. A government seeking relations with China must give support to the restoration of the rightful place and legitimate rights in the United Nations of the PRC and no longer give any backing to so-called representatives of Chiang Kai-shek in any organ of this international body.[33]

The Canadian reaction, quite properly, was that this was a statement of the Chinese position, not preconditions for further discussion.

Nonetheless, there was another delay before the discussions resumed, and the PRC team did not call at the Canadian embassy until 3 April. Then they suggested that the negotiations take place in Stockholm, a venue agreeable to Canada. Each side passed position papers back and forth over the next months, the Canadians stating that they had no intention of pursuing a 'two-China' policy, and the PRC insisting that their principles be accepted. Until that occurred, the Chinese were unwilling to discuss seriously other Canadian areas of interest, such as trade relations, consular questions, and compensation owing for the requisition of Canadian property at the time of the revolution. All the Canadian negotiators would volunteer at this stage was that Canada 'neither challenged nor endorsed' the PRC's position on Taiwan. As Mitchell Sharp told parliament on 21 July, 'We have not asked and do not ask the Government of the PRC to endorse the position of the Government of Canada on our territorial limits as a condition to agreement to establish diplomatic relations.'[34] That was a logical position, but it was not one satisfactory to the Chinese. Nor was Canada's position on PRC representation at the UN acceptable to the Chinese negotiators. Canada had continued to vote for the American position that the admission of the PRC was an 'important question' requiring a two-thirds majority. Ah, yes, replied Margaret Meagher, who had replaced Andrew as ambassador to Sweden and as head of the negotiating team, until Canada and China had agreed to recognize each other the position would remain the same; but once recognition had occurred, then Canada's votes in New York would reflect the new situation.[35] Canada was to be as good as its word in October 1971 when China finally entered the world organization.[36]

By October 1969 the Canadian team, having detected signs of movement on the part of their friendly antagonists on the Taiwan question, had prepared a draft agreed minute that 'noted' the PRC position that Taiwan was an inalienable part of China's territory. Although the talks dragged on much longer as the Cultural Revolution continued to slow decision making in Beijing, that was the ultimate basis on which agreement finally was reached. The Canadian position had changed substantially since Trudeau had first raised the idea of recognition. Initially, the government had hoped to be able to keep relations with Taiwan in a one-China, one-Taiwan policy; then Ottawa had recognized that links with the PRC would 'affect' relations with Taiwan; finally, Ottawa had come to accept that there could be no government-to-government relations with Taiwan if recognition of the PRC was to be secured.[37] People-to-people relations, such as trade, however, could be continued with the Nationalist regime.

The text of the communiqué on recognition, dated 10 October 1970, noted this shift with just enough face-saving to make the exchange of diplomats with the PRC palatable for Ottawa: 'The Chinese Government reaffirms that Taiwan is an inalienable part of the territory of the People's Republic of China. The Canadian Government takes note of this position of the Chinese Government.'[38] That anodyne phrasing allowed Beijing to press its claim to Taiwan as loudly and as often as it chose, but Canada, by simply taking note of that position, did not imply agreement or disagreement with it.

Yao Guang, at this time the director of the Chinese Foreign Ministry's Department of Europe and the Americas and hence the official in charge of the negotiations in Beijing, recalled that the Canadian negotiators had come to understand the PRC's position that Taiwan was an inalienable part of Chinese territory. Once that understanding had been achieved, then the Canadian formula became acceptable to Beijing. Had the United States, with whom the Chiang regime had a military alliance, been on the other side of the table, 'take note of' would not have been accepted by China. But there was no fundamental conflict between Canada and China, Beijing understood the difficulties Canada faced on this issue because of American pressure, and it appreciated Trudeau's courage in seeking recognition. In all the circumstances, Yao Guang said, Mao and Chou En-lai, who had to take the final decision, had decided to accept the Canadian formulation.[39] The same form of words eventually allowed other Western nations to proceed to recognize China.[40]

The reaction in Canada, where the majority of people were glued to the TV screen as the October Crisis dominated the news, was mixed. Liberals and most of the press cheered the news and foreign-policy experts called recognition 'a foreign policy coup rivalling the internationally acclaimed achievements of Lester Pearson.'[41] Progressive Conservative leader Robert Stanfield, however, indicated that he supported recognition of China, but was opposed to the breaking of relations with Taiwan. Former Prime Minister John Diefenbaker, reiterating comments made earlier by the RCMP, complained about the 'deluge of Communist spies who will come in here attached to the Chinese Embassy.'[42] Not to be outdone, Créditiste leader Réal Caouette accused the government of aiding the cause of world revolution, while Tory MP Perry Ryan, whose constituency in Toronto encompassed Chinatown, foresaw a flood of Maoists and their propaganda. Many Chinese Canadians also claimed to be upset at this 'black day in Canadian History.'[43] American official reaction was muted but unhappy, but in Beijing the Chinese hailed the agreement, observing that Trudeau's Canada had successfully resisted the United States' plot to isolate the PRC.[44]

Soon after the announcement, embassies were opened in Ottawa and Beijing. On 13 April the exchange of ambassadors was announced, as China sent Huang Hua, one of its leading diplomatic figures, to Canada. Within months of the Canadian recognition, other countries found the 'take note of' formula their route to recognizing the PRC.[45]

The Canadian recognition of China may have represented a watershed in China's relations with the West. In early April, after secret U.S. – PRC diplomacy underway since 1969, the unyielding hostility between the United States and China began to crack. Ping-pong teams visited the PRC, President Nixon announced that his government would permit trade between the United States and China, Henry Kissinger secretly visited

Beijing, and in July Nixon announced that he himself would go to China. By August the United States had indicated that it now supported Chinese admission to the UN. If Canada had hoped to pave the way for the United States, that had been achieved, though there was apparently no direct connection between the Canadian and American moves nor any Canadian role as an intermediary.[46] If Ottawa had hoped to steal a march on the United States by establishing a firm trade relationship with the PRC, that would now be harder to accomplish. At the very least, however, Nixon's démarche to Beijing meant that right-wing attacks against Prime Minister Trudeau for his government's China policy lost their force.

The American opening to the PRC, however, inevitably took some of the gloss off the Trudeau government's breakthrough achievement, though the Chinese claimed to appreciate Trudeau's decision to act ahead of the Americans.[47] Nor was there any sudden signs of a great boom in commercial relations. Jean-Luc Pepin led a trade mission in June 1971 that won Chinese agreement to 'consider Canada first' as a source of wheat, and a contract for $200 million worth of grain followed in December.[48] There was also a huge Canadian Trade Fair in Beijing in August 1972 that drew a quarter of a million visitors. But after Nixon's 1973 visit and the first U.S. wheat sale to China, the Canadian share of the market began to fall from 100 per cent in 1971 to 65 per cent in 1976 and 41 per cent in 1978.[49] Even so, Canada had a large and continuing trade surplus with China (rising from $123 million in 1970 to $320 million in 1975 and to $1361 million in 1983) that upset Beijing.[50] Yu Zhan, vice foreign minister, 1972–82, and ambassador in Ottawa, 1983–6, said that he had urged Canadian businessmen to invest in China. They could make profits and send them back to Canada. But imports and exports were two legs – with only one leg, no one could go very far or very fast.[51] Such exhortations did little to reverse the trend; neither did the generally low quality of Chinese goods or their packaging. Even the Chinese recognized this problem. The embassy sent its staff into the stores of Ottawa to compare Taiwanese and PRC products; their conclusion was that their exports were equal in quality, but markedly inferior in presentation and packaging to those from Chiang's regime.[52]

The highlight of the immediate post-recognition period was Trudeau's visit to China in October 1973.[53] The Beijing government clearly felt a certain gratitude to the prime minister for his role in pressing recognition forward in the face of domestic and foreign opposition; he was 'an old friend,' a term of high approbation in China. Trudeau had two long and friendly sessions with Chou and a briefer meeting with Mao, and he signed a number of agreements with the PRC government, including a consular understanding, a family reunification agreement, and sports and public-health exchanges.[54] Chou also accompanied Trudeau on some of his trips outside Beijing, as did the just rehabilitated Deng Xiaoping. Most notably, although no preparations had been made by the Chinese, a trade agreement granting each country's goods most-favoured-nation status in the other was hurriedly cobbled together to accommodate the visitors. That, the Chinese said, was possible only when one had the desire.[55] In return, the Canadian government presented the PRC with four Canadian beavers for the Peking zoo.[56]

The only major crisis to trouble the waters of Canada-China relations came in 1976, when Montreal played host to the Summer Olympic Games from 17 July to 1 August. At the end of the 1960s, Canada had pledged to admit any teams 'representing the National Olympic Committees and National Sports Federations recognized' by the International Olympic Committee. A clause had been added to this agreement reserving 'the normal regulations,' whatever they might be.[57] China had reapplied for admission to the IOC in 1975, predictably insisting that Taiwan be expelled. But the IOC temporized, and China was not admitted in time to participate in the games. Although both China and Canada, among others, protested, Taiwan remained and readied its athletes to participate under the label of the 'Republic of China.' The Canadian government position, first advanced to the International Olympic Committee in April 1975, was that no country purporting to represent another nation with which Canada had relations could participate in Montreal. Those presumably were the 'normal regulations.' What they meant, in essence, was that Taiwanese athletes had to perform as representatives of Taiwan, not China, and the government carried through on its position by refusing entry to several Taiwanese athletes in July, a decision in which Prime Minister Trudeau himself took a direct role. To Trudeau, it was the IOC, not Canada, that was mixing sport and politics by allowing Taiwan to participate under a flag that laid claim to territory it did not rule.[58]

Both the IOC and the United States were furious. Taiwan's sympathizers in the United States saw Canada offering aid and comfort to a communist nation, while idealists evidently believed, despite the massive evidence to the contrary, that 'politics' ought not to be allowed to interfere with Olympic sport. The White House gave serious consideration to asking the U.S. Olympic Committee to withdraw American athletes from the Montreal Games, and President Ford wrote privately of his 'regret that political concerns interfered in the conduct of the current Olympiad' and denounced 'narrow political interests.'[59] Perhaps it was because the rejection of Taiwan removed the last 'non-political' fig leaf from the Olympic Games that the matter was taken as seriously as it was. Canada was pilloried on television and in the press,[60] President Ford made his unhappiness public, and Secretary Kissinger declared that he would not attend the games as a result – doubtless relieved to be freed from a pointless duty. Efforts to resolve the matter failed when the Taiwanese rejected an IOC compromise suggestion that they compete under the Olympic banner, and a Canadian suggestion that they use their flag and anthem provided they did not claim to represent China. For a time, some thought the games might be cancelled, and a White House official even suggested that in that event the United States should offer to stage the event – on forty-eight hours notice![61] Taiwan's representatives prevented this mad scheme from being tried when they withdrew in a huff. It had been a curious crisis, but a crisis nonetheless. In London, Canadian High Commissioner Paul Martin wrote in his diary on 13 July that he had received a telephone call from Ivan Head soliciting his advice on the issue: 'the cabinet was in session as we spoke.'[62] The PRC, which had lobbied the prime minister and the Department of External Affairs, was duly grateful for the Canadian stand.[63]

The young Pierre Trudeau who had visited China in 1949 and again in 1960 was also interested in the Soviet Union. In 1951 the World Peace Council and the World Federation of Trade Unions, both communist front organizations, organized an International Economic Conference to meet in Moscow in April 1952. Trudeau, travelling in Europe over the winter of 1951–2, got himself invited to the conference and agreed to write about it and the Soviet Union for Montreal's *Le Devoir* after his return to Canada.

The Korean War was underway,[64] the Cold War was at its frostiest, and very few Canadians, other than Communist party hacks, turned up in Moscow in 1952. In fact, remembered Robert Ford, then an officer on the Canadian embassy staff, there were only three Canadian visitors to the embassy between 1951 and 1954, one of whom was Trudeau. He had apparently become tired of bad hotel food and sought the embassy's western-style meals. 'He liked us and we liked him.'[65] This visit, however, together with the controversy that developed in the Quebec and Franco-Ontarian press over his seven-part series of articles, published under the title 'Je Reviens de Moscou,' did much to create the subsequent image of Trudeau as a crypto-communist. As he himself wrote in the opening lines of his first article, 'for many people, the Soviet Union is hell, and you don't put a foot in it without making a pact with the devil.'

In fact, Trudeau's articles on Russia were by no means a paean of praise. He claimed to have tossed snowballs at a statue of Stalin, found the people 'sickeningly conventional' and blind in their Marxist faith, and noted that the country was developing the way the planners, not the people, wanted with 'flagrant inequality.' But Trudeau also added that he saw no sign of a desire for territorial expansion, and his pieces could fairly be described as sympathetic and only mildly critical.[66] That aroused the ire of some right-wing clergy in Montreal, and Trudeau was roundly, if not soundly, denounced in the clerical press and in Ottawa's Le Droit. The traveller defended himself in the Ottawa newspaper, and L'Action Nationale, a leading nationalist monthly, leapt to his side with André Laurendeau and F.-A. Angers denouncing what they saw as a witch-hunt.[67] This was a minor event, to be sure, but one that fed the demonological interpretations of Trudeau after he rose to power.

By 1968 the Soviet Union had changed since Trudeau's visit in 1952. Stalin was gone, but so was the reformism of Nikita Khruschev. In his place was Leonid Brezhnev, still consolidating his personal power and seeking to keep the increasingly restive satellites in their place. After the 'Czech spring' of 1968 and the brutal Soviet response to it in August, the repressive Brezhnev regime became increasingly stolid, unimaginative, and politically orthodox. Brezhnev appeased the military, which grew fat as the domestic economy stagnated. Though Moscow pursued détente, there were enough inner contradictions, not to say rigidities in its posture to make relations with any Western country uneasy. Canada was no exception. The Trudeau years might have presented an opening for a Soviet regime with some flexibility to forge a creative link with a Western nation; instead, from the Russian perspective, they must seem only years of lost opportunities. In retrospect, the most important event of the period for long-term Soviet-Canadian relations may have been Brezhnev's exiling of Alexander Yakovlev to be ambassador in Canada from 1973 to 1983.

Although Trudeau told Ambassador Ford that he wanted to make the improvement of relations with the USSR a priority,[68] and although he came to office with few fears of Soviet aggression against the West,[69] the invasion of Czechoslovakia got the relationship off to a bad start. Warsaw Pact forces entered the country on 20 August, bringing Dubcek's reforms to an end. The Czechoslovak leaders were arrested. Pierre Trudeau was vacationing in Spain, and the initial Canadian response was offered by Mitchell Sharp. The occupation was 'very disappointing ... a great setback to the growing confidence in Europe and progress toward an East-

West detente.'[70] That was 'incredibly mild,' remembered George Ignatieff, Canada's ambassador at the United Nations,[71] but the next day, after Sharp and Trudeau had talked by telephone, the government issued its official response. The invasion was 'a flagrant breach of the principle of non-intervention' and a 'tragedy for all people who prize human freedom and national independence.'[72] The Soviets paid no attention to either of Sharp's statements; the only Canadian comment that interested them was the approval offered by Canadian Communist leader William Kashtan. At a time when many foreign parties had expressed their opposition to the crushing of Czech reformism, that nod of consent from the utterly insignificant Communist Party of Canada and its inconsequential leader mattered.[73]

At the UN Security Council, Ignatieff organized the Western response, finding support for a resolution condemning Soviet intervention in the 'internal affairs of Czechoslovakia.' When the USSR vetoed that resolution, he introduced another that called on the secretary general to send a representative to Prague to insure the safety of the deposed Czech leader, Alexander Dubcek.[74]

There was little anyone in Canada could do for the Czechs, their struggle for independence aborted for the third time in three decades. Officials in Ottawa attributed the Czech spring to the success of Western efforts at détente, although some had become concerned at the instability generated by Dubcek's efforts to move quickly and far. Ottawa also worried that the moves for easing East-West tension, underway in earnest since the West Germans had made their opening to the East, would be aborted by the Soviet invasion. Officials had their own domestic concern that Soviet efforts to cultivate Canada, part of Moscow's 'selective détente' policy, would similarly cease. The new Russian interest in Canada had led to two huge wheat deals, extensive and expensive USSR participation in Expo 67, and increased trade.[75] Above all, External Affairs appeared convinced that the Czech invasion demonstrated the Soviets' lack of confidence in the vitality of their own system. The crushing of Czechoslovakia showed that the communist system could not adjust to change or withstand the competition of new ideas or pressures from within.[76]

Although Canada supported the NATO allies' agreement to break off social contacts with the Soviets and their Warsaw Pact allies who had participated in the invasion,[77] Trudeau and Sharp clearly believed it was better to have a stable Soviet satellite in Czechoslovakia instead of a destabilized regime.[78] Soon, the government was manoeuvring to determine the best way to handle a ministerial wheat-selling mission to Moscow.[79] By March 1969 the Warsaw Pact countries were calling for a full-scale conference on European security, and, by September, Andrei Gromyko, the USSR's apparently permanent foreign minister, had paid an official visit to Ottawa. (Trudeau gave the Russian a forty-five-minute monologue on global developments and drew Gromyko's response: 'You know, Prime Minister, you don't look at all like your pictures.' In his memoirs, published in 1988, the stolid Gromyko observed that Trudeau had 'great ability and tact,' his 'government would find a way of easing any tensions,' and noted that Trudeau was 'always ready to speak critically' of the United States!)[80] In January 1971 Canada and the Soviets signed an agreement on Cooperation in the Industrial Application of Science and Technology, and six working groups began to meet to discuss exchanges. This agreement was renewed for ten years in 1976. It was business as usual once more.

The prime minister himself had been scheduled to visit the USSR in the autumn of 1970, the first high-level Western visitor since the Czech invasion, but the trip was postponed because of the October Crisis. The visit was then rescheduled for May 1971, and Ottawa had its planning well underway the month before. Subjects for the agenda included the full range of East-West relations and bilateral subjects such as trade, exchanges, and cooperation in northern development. From the Moscow embassy came strong urgings to include 'consular problems' – the reunification of families. If the prime minister only raised such questions orally with the Soviets, Canadian concern might not register strongly enough. Those urgings had their effect, and Trudeau carried a list of names with him to Moscow. Most important was a Soviet draft of a protocol on consultations, an idea that concerned some in Ottawa but that others liked because it could be worked out in the time available and would add an extra dimension to the visit. Trudeau again carried a Canadian revised draft text with him.[81]

He also had the benefit of External Affairs' advice on the general objectives of the USSR's foreign policy and of the tactics employed by its negotiators.[82] In Ottawa, many officials still believed that the Soviets clung to their belief in the inevitable victory of communism and the implacable hostility of capitalism. These tenets, however, were secondary to Moscow's desire to avoid a general war and to keep Eastern Europe quiet, aims which convinced the planners in the East Block that Soviet policy was defensive and inward-looking. That did not mean that the Russians would not negotiate fiercely, however. It was a standard Soviet tactic to open with an extreme position, hoping that any compromise would eventually tilt in their direction. Soviet negotiators, External

Affairs warned, are not inhibited by concepts of fairness when their interests are at stake. Moreover, the USSR negotiators often engaged in tests of endurance or prolonged intransigeance, aiming to wear down their opponents.[83] How much Trudeau paid attention to this is unclear; in all likelihood, the prime minister believed he could get on well with the Soviets.

He did, too. Arriving on 17 May at the head of a large official party and forty accompanying journalists, Trudeau plunged immediately into a round of talks with Soviet leaders Brezhnev and Kosygin. In a two-hour discussion with the impressive Brezhnev,[84] Trudeau asked the general secretary how he envisaged relations between the USSR and the United States. Brezhnev replied that the age of the conquerors was over and that he was a realistic man, one who had seen five American presidents in his time on the Central Committee, not one of whom genuinely wanted to resolve problems. This long monologue, Trudeau recollected, was delivered more in sorrow than in anger and in a despairing way.[85] After some discussion on the good state of Canadian-Soviet relations where Brezhnev saw no 'black clouds,' Trudeau said that if Canada could help in reducing tensions in Europe it was willing to do so. The prime minister referred to his government's gesture of reducing Canadian troops in NATO by 50 per cent, though he added that the larger question was the concern of the superpowers. Trudeau gave away none of the NATO positions.[86]

Trudeau then had extensive talks with Premier Alexei Kosygin, chairman of the Council of Ministers and one Soviet leader whom the Canadians genuinely liked because of his easy manner and rational mind. Trudeau described Kosygin as 'Khruschev without the rough edges, a fatherly man who was a forerunner of Mikhail Gorbachev.' Moreover, Kosygin was ready to discuss issues, so long as the Soviet position wasn't tackled head-on.[87] Kosygin told Trudeau that the 'Canadian move to reduce troops in Europe had been greatly appreciated as an act contributing to the reduction of tension in Europe,' scarcely a surprising comment. For his part, Trudeau rejoined that Canada's phasing-out of its nuclear aircraft in NATO was an example that the Warsaw Pact might follow.

The talks with the premier were quiet and private, and Trudeau easily raised family reunification questions when he produced his list of 291 cases involving 646 persons. His efforts received a generally positive response and, by 1974, 332 of those on the list (and one subsequently submitted by Mitchell Sharp) had been allowed to emigrate to Canada.[88] More formally, they discussed Canadian efforts to control Arctic pollution, which the Soviets claimed to support, but Kosygin had little interest in a Canadian proposal for an international conference on the subject. There were talks on trade, the Soviets seeking economic cooperation in a variety of areas including gas pipelines, atomic power, and pulp and paper mills. The Russian leader, mindful of his country's large (and growing) $93 million trade deficit with Canada in 1970, even tried to sell the Canadians short-range civilian jet aircraft and the Soviet SST. Uppermost on Kosygin's mind, however, was a general agreement on trade and economic cooperation, and Trudeau took away a Soviet draft to consider. A courtesy call on President Podgorny was also made – after which Trudeau climbed aboard a motorcycle in the courtyard and rode around the Kremlin grounds.[89]

The highlight of the visit, however, was the signing of the 'Protocol on Consultations' on 20 May. The protocol aimed to put contacts on a more systematic basis, provided for 'consultation on important international problems of mutual interest and on questions of bilateral relations,' and called for meetings 'whenever the need arises and, in principle, at least once a year.'[90] Trudeau asked Kosygin on 22 May how he envisaged the protocol working. The Russian replied that it would embrace all situations, not only crises, and he added that regular diplomatic consultations were the best way to ensure that the protocol worked. Trudeau indicated that he agreed with this pragmatic approach.[91]

The Soviets, recalled John Halstead, the head of European Division at External Affairs, had played Trudeau correctly, knowing he would be receptive to more dialogue; a protocol served their interest by providing a legal framework that set out relations with nations in a systematic way. The appearances worried the Canadian officials who had struggled with the wording of the protocol to ensure that nothing in it could be construed as prejudicing Canada's alliance links or its basic political orientation.[92] Moreover, the United States, not consulted in advance on the protocol, was upset, seeing this as Canada's first step out of its orbit.[93] So too was the *Winnipeg Free Press*, which called the protocol 'another significant step in the reversal of long-established Canadian policy. ... Will you walk into my parlor? said the calculating spider to the innocent flies. And in walked Messrs. Sharp and Trudeau.'[94]

Cabinet ministers, who learned of the protocol only after it had been signed in Moscow, were also concerned. How, Acting Prime Minister Mitchell Sharp was asked, could Trudeau do such a thing without cabinet discussion? Sharp, described by Transport Minister Donald Jamieson as 'obviously slightly embarrassed,' said the protocol had come up at the last minute. Jamieson added, 'I think it is fair to say that most of us had the impression that even Mitchell himself had not had a great deal of prior notice.' Particularly unhappy was Donald Macdonald, the minister of national defence, who, Jamieson wrote in his diary, said the protocol 'marked a very significant change in policy' and asked that the cabinet minutes record his displeasure.[95]

There was to be even greater displeasure in Canada as the prime minister's words at a press conference in Moscow on 20 May sank in back home. Trudeau pointed out that Canada was a friend and ally of the United States. Then he added: 'Canada has increasingly found it important to diversify its channels of communication because of the overpowering presence of the United States of America and that is reflected in a growing consciousness amongst Canadians of the danger to our national identity from a cultural, economic and perhaps even military point of view.'[96] Trudeau explained that the protocol was 'an important step towards the establishment of the most autonomous foreign policy possible.'[97] It was one thing to say such words about the United States in Canada; in the Soviet Union they had an entirely different ring, not least their echoes in Washington.[98] So too with Trudeau's comparison of Ukrainian nationalists to FLQ separatists in a press conference on 28 May. Both comments produced outraged protests in Canada in the press and in parliament, suggestions that Trudeau was taking Canada on a unilateral course, and predictable fury from columnist Lubor Zink in the *Toronto Telegram* who wrote that 'if Mr. Trudeau were an agent of Moscow he could hardly do any better.'[99] Trudeau may have been confused himself as he struggled to see the Soviet point of view. He responded to a press-conference query suggesting that perhaps he was being used by the Soviets by saying, 'I've been asking myself the same question.'[100] The prime minister also expressed some surprise at 'the tone in which [the Soviet Union] are willing to deal with us as a great power ... To compare [the Canada-USSR protocol] to the protocol signed with France, for instance ... I kept saying no, you know, we're a modest power.'[101]

Trudeau was no agent of Moscow, but his incautious, even foolish, comments had raised fears in Canada and hopes in Moscow that he might be leading Canada in new directions. The best advice to the government after the visit came from Ambassador Ford in Moscow, able, realistic, and with long service in the Soviet Union. The Russians wanted to increase the size of their embassy in Ottawa and the Canadians in Moscow, in turn, hoped to get more space for their embassy. The ambassador agreed that Canada had to bargain with the Soviets but, he added, the tougher Canadians were the more respect they got from the Russians. The difficulty in negotiating, however, was that the USSR always wanted more than Canada, and even the little Canada wanted depended as much on the Treasury Board in Ottawa as it did on the Soviets.[102]

Within six months of the Trudeau visit to the Soviet Union, Premier Kosygin repaid the gesture by coming to Canada. That was almost unprecedented speed in reciprocal formal visits, though the timing resulted primarily from Trudeau's calendar in a pre-election period and from Kosygin's desire to keep Brezhnev from making foreign policy his exclusive province.[103] Whatever the reasons, the visit clearly indicated that the Soviets attached real importance to relations with Trudeau's Canada. Coming as it did after President Nixon had imposed his economic measures on Canada and the world in August 1971, the visit gave the Soviet leader more of an opportunity to make points than might otherwise have been the case.[104]

The visit began disastrously, however, when Kosygin was attacked by a man shouting 'Free Hungary' as he and the prime minister walked on Parliament Hill. Trudeau had altered plans, deciding to walk to the next engagement instead of proceeding by automobile. Although Kosygin was unhurt, there was substantial embarrassment in Ottawa.[105]

There was more when Trudeau spoke at a welcoming dinner and said that 'Canada and Canadians want very much to be able to look to the north, as they have long looked to the south, and see friends in each direction.' Kosygin's reply picked up the same theme: 'We address a program of peace to all people. Therefore Soviet-Canadian collaboration is not directed at anyone. It merely serves ... the cause of international peace. We have no hidden motives.'[106] What bothered some observers was Trudeau's evenhandedness towards the superpowers. 'There is at least an implicit neutralism in all this,' the *Winnipeg Free Press* editorialized, adding that Canada's efforts to plead the special relationship with the United States as it sought to get special treatment under the Nixon financial regime were bound to suffer.[107] Conservative MPs took a similar tack in the House of Commons.[108]

If the visit increased right-wing suspicion of Trudeau, it also had some beneficial results. The Canadians were struck by Kosygin's businesslike approach to bilateral and international problems, although the Soviet premier continued to resist Canada's proposed Arctic conference.[109] On 20 October Canada and the USSR signed a General Exchanges Agreement, for which the Canadian draft text had been given to the Soviets on 27 September, that expanded and regularized scientific, cultural, and academic exchanges between the two countries.[110] The Soviets had also proposed a navigation treaty, arguing that this would encourage 'orderliness.' The Canadians refused, fearing that such an agreement would give the Soviets access to east-coast ports without the necessity of making any concessions to Canada.[111] The official Canadian reaction to the Kosygin visit, whatever the Trudeauvian rhetoric, remained cautious and careful.

Soon the new USSR-Canada relationship began to show uncomfortable similarities to that Trudeau had developed with China. Just as the Canadian recognition of the PRC appeared to pave the way for the United States, so too did Trudeau's new links with the Russians. From Moscow, Ford wrote that *Pravda* talked of a 'period of great events.' Something 'is moving,' he said. 'One can feel it, and the Russians are equally aware of it.'[112] In late 1971 President Nixon announced his intention to go to the USSR in May 1972, an effort to relax tensions despite the strains the Vietnam War still caused. The visit achieved those purposes, led to the signing of SALT I, a product of the Strategic Arms Limitation Talks underway since 1969, added new life to détente, and markedly reduced the Soviet Union's interest in Canada. When Russian-American relations were cool, it seemed clear, the Soviets showed interest in Canada; when relations were good, Canada's relative unimportance to Moscow was evident.[113] The results of the General Exchanges Agreement could only be described as spotty at best, and trade did not boom. The Canadian market had little capacity to absorb shoddy Soviet manufactured goods, especially as neither spare parts nor service were words in the Russian lexicon. And Trudeau himself made no apparent efforts over the next several years to get the relationship back to the heady days of the 'annus mirabilis' of 1971.

There was one exception. In April 1972, for the first time, the best Canadian and Soviet hockey players traded shots in each other's country. Although the Canadians began with over-confidence, the games were a life-and-death struggle that produced an overall Canadian victory only in the last seconds of the final game in Moscow. The Russians displayed a brilliant passing game and fine goal-tending, and one Soviet sportswriter wrote of the games that 'the Canadians made an all-out effort to save their prestige and succeeded, though frequently violating the rules, to win the series. It has become clear to the whole world that the Soviet players are just as good as the famous and really skilled pros.' That was a fair comment. Just as important, a huge and boisterous contingent of 3000 Canadians flew to Moscow for the games there, forcing External Affairs to sit up and take notice.[114]

One Soviet goal for the relationship was to induce Canada to play a major role in supporting a Conference on Security and Cooperation in Europe. The Soviets, officials in Ottawa believed, hoped to achieve an international regime that would be more stable and predictable – stability, in other words, on Soviet terms.[115] Still, the CSCE, for which initial preparatory talks began in Helsinki in November 1972, offered opportunities for the West too, notably an opportunity to press the Soviets on human rights and the free movement of peoples and ideas. When the negotiations began in Geneva in September 1973, Canada was prepared to play and to urge its NATO allies to use the CSCE to enhance détente.[116]

Indeed, the Canadians had a very substantial role in the negotiations, their strong team being led first by Michael Shenstone and then by Thomas Delworth of External Affairs, with close coordination with the department in Ottawa. Trudeau, as John Halstead noted, 'did not follow in detail the negotiations ... It was Sharp who approved the guidelines for those negotiations and he in turn left a large measure of discretion to his officials in carrying them out.'[117]

The Canadian tactic at the CSCE was not to be anti-Soviet but to 'bird dog' the Russians every day and to 'hang tough.' The Canadians' persistent use of such leverage as could be mustered against the Soviets, coordinated with NATO allies and friendly neutrals, more than matched Soviet 'iron bottom' diplomacy on such subjects as family reunification where Canada, along with Denmark, led the Western side. The Canadian goal, tenaciously pursued, was to get ideology out of the human dimension of relations with the USSR, to sweep ideology away and to leave only resolvable facts. The result was that, as one senior diplomat put it, 'the Soviet Union was on the run throughout the talks.'[118] Moreover, when the negotiations had seemingly stalled in 1975 though the shape of agreement was clear, a Canadian initiative brought the Geneva talks to an end and fixed the date for a meeting of heads of government at Helsinki to accept the agreement. The resulting text was wrongly attacked from the right as freezing frontiers in Europe to the Soviet advantage. In fact, loose and shapeless as it was, the Final Act of the CSCE, approved at Helsinki on 1 August 1975, offered a way to secure change, especially in human-rights areas, though more with the Eastern Europeans than with the Soviet Union.[119] The Eastern Europeans could now tell the Russians that they had to do something.[120] The follow-up meetings at Belgrade and Madrid offered Canada, pushed by domestic public opinion, the opportunity to press compliance with the Final Act on the USSR and its allies.[121]

The CSCE was more fruitful in results than the Mutual and Balanced Forced Reduction negotiations that similarly began in 1973 in Vienna. By virtue of its having troops in NATO, Canada was a participant in the MBFR talks that put negotiators from the NATO and Warsaw Pact countries across the table in an effort to secure reductions and limitations in the manpower and armaments of the two alliances. There was some progress, but the pace was glacial; it slackened further as détente began to run into trouble in the mid-1970s.[122] So bad had matters become that a return visit to Moscow by Trudeau kept being delayed. Secretary of State for External Affairs Don Jamieson thought it not domestically cost-effective, and the embassy in Moscow advised that the Soviets would puff up the visit into something it was not meant to be.[123]

Détente had begun to slip away, imperceptibly at first, and then in a fashion obvious to all. Nixon's ouster from power coincided with Brezhnev's illness, and President Ford, who had agreed with Brezhnev to a framework for SALT II in 1974, narrowly lost the American election in 1976 to Jimmy Carter. The Carter administration's emphasis on human rights exposed the USSR's efforts to sweep away its obligations under the CSCE Final Act and heightened the renewal of Cold-War rhetoric, even though the president and general secretary signed the SALT II agreement in June 1979.[124] Nonetheless, the USSR's rapid expansion of its military power, its deployment of new missiles, its use of Cuban surrogates in Angola and Mozambique, and its invasion of Afghanistan at the end of December 1979 increased the damage to détente.

The invasion of Afghanistan infuriated President Carter and completed the destruction of what was left of good Western relations with the USSR. Afghanistan, sandwiched between Pakistan and the USSR, had been slipping into the Soviet orbit for years, and Brezhnev, in a notable misjudgment of his own country's strength and Afghan weakness, determined to make satellite status official by sending in the Red Army. The extent of the error was not apparent at first, and it seemed that the Kabul regime had been safely taken into the fold. But Afghan resistance soon developed, and Carter, outraged at Soviet perfidy, later wrote that 'I was determined to lead the rest of the world in making [Moscow's action] as costly as possible.' The Americans provided money and arms to the Afghan resistance, but ruled out any overt military response; in addition, Carter decided on economic pressure and a symbolic boycott of the Summer Olympics scheduled to be held in Moscow in 1980. The economic measures took the form of an embargo on grain sales to the USSR, and Carter sought the support of other grain-exporting countries.[125]

The Clark government quickly banned Aeroflot flights to Canada and abrogated the Canada-USSR cultural-exchange agreement while External Affairs pressed schemes to restore Afghan neutrality.[126] Clark did not impose a wheat embargo on the Soviets, but he did agree that Canada would not fill wheat orders the Americans had foregone in return for a

U.S. promise not to sell its new-found surplus in traditional Canadian markets such as China. And, although Clark initially indicated a preference to move the Olympic Games to a new venue, the cabinet, on 25 January 1980, under the stress of the federal election campaign, agreed to support Carter's Olympic boycott.[127] Neither boycott won much favour with the Canadian electorate, and grain farmers especially were upset.

Trudeau, returned to power in the February 1980 election, hoped to restore relations with Moscow as quickly as possible. He had serious doubts about Carter's boycott policy ('What has the U.S. done to hurt itself lately?' he asked one senior External Affairs officer),[128] but matters had proceeded too far and the prime minister could only continue Canadian support for the Olympic boycott and maintain the wheat boycott until it was called off by the United States in 1981.

By then, Ronald Reagan had been installed as president of the United States, and the feeble spark of détente had definitely spluttered out. Despite the Liberal leader's personal unhappiness, the Trudeau government again behaved moderately when the Soviets connived at the army's takeover and imposition of martial law in Poland in December 1981.[129] In the circumstances, with East-West relations deteriorating rapidly and with many in the West (including Ottawa) seeing the Soviet empire in the early throes of disintegration, Trudeau arranged for the ambassador to Bonn, the able Klaus Goldschlag, to work with a diplomat nominated by Chancellor Helmut Schmidt in an abortive effort to shape a sensible Western response.[130] Nonetheless, the Canadian role had to be limited in the direct relationship with Moscow. The Protocol of Consultation had 'seldom proven very useful,' the Department of External Affairs said in 1979, though it could on occasion get the Soviets to sit down and talk frankly.[131] That was scarcely sufficient in the new Cold War.

One crucial factor in the relationship was the link that Trudeau and some of his ministers developed with Alexander Yakovlev, the ideological but pragmatic Soviet ambassador to Canada. Sent to Ottawa in 1973 from his post as head of the party's propaganda department because he had called for more effort to integrate Central Asian minorities into Soviet life and because he was convinced the USSR had no business in places like Africa,[132] Yakovlev was a severely wounded veteran of the Second World War, the holder of a doctorate in history from Columbia University, and an able, charming, and shrewd man. Alerted to the presence of this completely untypical Soviet ambassador by Ivan Head, Trudeau had Yakovlev to lunch and came to like him. The prime minister believed in people, not slogans, movements, or labels, and he saw a man he could talk to in the intellectually curious and good-humoured Yakovlev. The two, roughly the same age, regularly covered human rights, East-West relations, disarmament, and other subjects, and Yakovlev invited Trudeau to his residence when important visitors, such as Georgi Arbatov of the USA and Canada Institute, came to town. As Trudeau said, 'I liked caviar so I went.' The prime minister correctly saw Yakovlev as a loyal supporter of the party line, but one who was open-minded when he did not feel obliged to defend the system. 'I think Trudeau saw in Yakovlev the best the Soviet Union had to offer,' Head recalled. As for the ambassador, he might well have agreed with his foreign minister's later comment that Trudeau 'stood head and shoulders above statesmen of other NATO countries who are blinded by their hostility to socialism.'[133]

The prime minister's meetings with the ambassador tended to upset External Affairs, always nervous about conversations where no record was kept. Over time, Trudeau agreed to permit an External Affairs note-taker to attend some of the discussions. How much policy value there was in this relationship is unclear, though it must have been useful to both sides. That may have been especially true after the beginning of 1981 when, according to KGB defector Oleg Gordievsky, Moscow had become persuaded that Reagan's United States was preparing to attack the USSR.[134] As a senior NATO leader, Trudeau ought to have been able to calm the fears. In any case, the Soviets got a 'clear read' on Trudeau, and the prime minister at least came to know Yakovlev well enough to receive an invitation to his home for dinner when he went to Moscow to attend Soviet General Secretary Andropov's funeral – an almost unprecedented gesture.[135]

In May 1983, as his decade-long exile in Ottawa was about to come to its end, Yakovlev arranged a ten-day visit to study Canadian agriculture for Mikhail Gorbachev, then still a little-known member of the Politburo, a former Central Committee secretary for agriculture, and Andropov's choice as secretary of the Central Committee. Gorbachev's host in Canada was the minister of agriculture, the rough-hewn Eugene Whelan, who had visited the USSR in 1981 on a Yakovlev-arranged visit. Visiting farms in Ontario and Alberta on his first trip to North America, Gorbachev was, Whelan wrote, greatly impressed by Canadian agricultural methods and efficiency.[136] Gorbachev must also have been impressed by Yakovlev, with whom he talked extensively during his Canadian trip.[137]

The highlight of the visit was Gorbachev's appearance before a joint meeting of the House of Commons and Senate Committees on External

Affairs and National Defence. This too was a first, the only time a Politburo member had answered questions freely in a Western parliament. Some of the questions were loaded: 'Why do you find it necessary,' Conservative MP Allan Lawrence asked, 'to have so many espionage agents ... here in Ottawa?' But Gorbachev parried them all with confidence and skill, hewing to the party line but admitting faults in the Soviet system.[138] It was an impressive performance, one that presaged the Russian leader's success in dealing with the Western public and press, and none of the MPs laid a glove on him. Trudeau also lunched with Gorbachev because, he said, he knew he was an Andropov protégé. He added that Gorbachev was the first Soviet leader with whom one could have a freewheeling conversation.[139] The visit to Canada had been a success.

Two years later Gorbachev was to achieve the highest position in his country, and he would bring Alexander Yakovlev into the inner circle of the Politburo with him. The long-time Soviet ambassador had left Ottawa in the summer of 1983 as the dean of the diplomatic corps, and when he came to see Head for a farewell lunch, he brought as a gift a lucite-encased medal commemorating the 1980 Moscow Olympics, an event that Canada and most Western nations had boycotted. 'We found we have a few of these left over,' Yakovlev said ruefully.[140]

Trudeau's efforts to open lines to China and the Soviet Union were, at best, a qualified success. The prime minister had broken the log jam of years by recognizing the People's Republic of China in 1970, and that move unquestionably let other countries do the same. Whether the Canadian recognition made the Washington-Beijing reconciliation possible is unclear, though there seems no reason to believe that there was any direct connection. Similarly, Trudeau had tried to put Canadian-Soviet relations on a new plane, signing a Protocol of Consultation and a General Exchange Agreement. For a brief period, as with China, the rhetoric was heady. But the reality proved to be different as both the PRC and the USSR evinced genuine interest in Canada – and in Canadian goods – only so long as the United States turned a cold shoulder. As Ambassador Ford noted of one early burst of Soviet interest in Canadian technology, 'should relations improve with the United States, [the USSR's] interest in Canada would be limited to technology adapted to Arctic conditions.'[141] Once relations with Washington improved, inevitably Canada returned to the second rank.

Worse, Trudeau's own rhetoric was such as to get him into trouble at home. His move to Beijing offended Canadian Chinese and frightened rightwingers who saw floods of spies pouring into Canada. His speeches and press conferences in the Soviet Union were virtually provocations, unnecessary and foolish for the fears they raised. There was a streak of utopian Boy Scout in Trudeau, and in some other practitioners of Canadian foreign policy, that made him grasp at Soviet straws in the hope of finding 'peace' or at least 'compromise.' The same traits appeared to mark Trudeau's persistent refusal to say anything critical of the Soviets, no matter the provocation in Czechoslovakia, Afghanistan, or Poland.[142] Why? Trudeau clearly recognized that the great powers had 'areas of strategic importance,' as he called them, of concern to them. While they did not have rights in international law to decide what went on there, nonetheless different rules had to be applied to their actions in those areas.[143]

If his policies were occasionally less than skilful or sensible, there should be no criticism of the fact that Trudeau had recognized that the frozen hostility of the Cold War had to be broken. China and the Soviet Union could not be ignored or wished away. The prime minister realized this truth and moved. He deserves great credit for his efforts. Through no fault of Canada's, matters worsened in the years after 1975, reaching their nadir in 1983. Trudeau's peace initiative, like his actions early in his administration, was an attempt to break the wall of hostility between East and West.

Part Four

Alarums and Excursions

8

The Clark Interregnum
and Department Reorganization

In the 1979 election Joe Clark led his Progressive Conservative party to power. The victory over Trudeau's Liberals gave Clark only a minority government, but the young prime minister, selected as party leader three years before, stated that he would govern as if he had a majority. Policy was to be bold, not timid; campaign promises were to be carried out, not cynically shelved; and the public service would dance to a new tune, one where the ministers called the tune. With its own perceptions firmly fixed, the Clark government was determined to be different. So it was, briefly.

Clark began his tenure of office by firing Michael Pitfield as clerk of the Privy Council and secretary to the cabinet. Pitfield had not always been admired by his fellow public servants, but he had become positively loathed by the Conservative caucus and had to go if Clark was to appease his followers and demonstrate his determination. To replace him as clerk, Clark chose Marcel Massé, thirty-eight, an able and intelligent deputy secretary in the Privy Council Office and one who had worked successfully for four years in New Brunswick for Progressive Conservative Premier Richard Hatfield as deputy minister of finance and chair of the cabinet secretariat. Massé had developed the idea of policy envelopes in Fredericton after the 1974 provincial election, Pitfield had included the concept in the briefing books prepared for the incoming government, and, although Massé thought that this radical change might be too much for a new and untried government to handle, Clark adopted them.[1] The result was the establishment of a system that theoretically gave ministers in certain areas, social policy and external policy, for example, the responsibility for making the hard choices about policy and programs while taking into account all the implications for budgeting within their envelope – decisions that the full cabinet ordinarily was expected to rubberstamp. Useful as this system was and able as he proved to be, Massé was inevitably just as green as were the ministers. Unfortunately, he was unable to provide the kind of advice that a more experienced secretary to the cabinet could. That had its consequences.

Clark chose Flora MacDonald, the MP for Kingston, Ontario, to be his secretary of state for external affairs. A longtime party official (once fired by John Diefenbaker),[2] MacDonald had been elected in 1972 and had quickly established enormous popularity across the country for her feisty intelligence. Flora, as she was universally known, had run for the leadership in 1976 and had lost to Clark. Her views were Red Tory and, although her political and policy positions were not dissimilar to the prime minister's, Clark was known to be concerned about her popularity which, in truth, far exceeded his own.[3] That, in turn, bothered MacDonald and led to a certain paranoia. Were officials in External Affairs spying on her?[4]

The chief official with whom MacDonald had to deal was her undersecretary, Allan Gotlieb. Gotlieb had had a brilliant career in External Affairs, rising rapidly through the ranks. An adviser to Trudeau both before and after he had become prime minister, Gotlieb had served as deputy minister in the departments of communications and manpower and immigration before becoming undersecretary of state for external affairs in 1977. Cerebral, rumpled in appearance, and an idealistic professional who thought diplomacy was best conducted behind closed doors, Gotlieb did not hit it off with his new minister. The populist Flora had many attitudes towards but little grounding in foreign policy[5] – her shadow portfolio in opposition had been Indian and Northern Affairs and she likely would have admitted that she knew almost nothing of the foreign-policy issues presented to her in two fat volumes of briefing papers[6] – but she, like Clark, was determined that politicians would set the policy direction. The elitist bureaucrats in External Affairs simply got her back up, and they in turn concluded that she was miles beyond her depth – not stupid, but in a job that required different talents from the ones God had given her.[7]

With her usual openness, MacDonald was perfectly frank in setting out the disagreements she developed with Gotlieb. It was only natural, she told the Canadian Political Science Association, that 'advice from public servants would be based on a continuation of existing policy – policy which in large part, had its genesis within the Department.' But a new minister, she said, 'must be able to assess ... where we have been and where we ought to be going.' To that end, MacDonald sought to secure advice from more than one quarter, an attempt to overcome what she described as the senior bureaucrats' 'own methods of gaining approval for the decisions they both needed and especially wanted.' Her personal staff, and most notably Hugh Hanson, her senior political adviser, began to seize a policy role; advice also came from a somewhat formalized group of experts outside the government service. MacDonald also put herself and her staff in contact with desk officers in the department.

What MacDonald had to overcome within her department, she stated, were such 'entrapment devices' as 'unnecessarily numerous crisis corridor decisions' where the senior bureaucrats demanded instant decisions; 'unnecessarily long and numerous memos'; late delivery of submissions to cabinet, 'thus denying me opportunity for a full and realistic appraisal of the presentation I was supposed to be making to my Cabinet colleagues'; and, perhaps most important, 'one-dimensional opinions put forward in memos' which led to the expectation that she would accept the unanimous recommendation of the department. As chair of the Cabinet Committee on Foreign and Defence Policy, moreover, MacDonald maintained that she 'had to be rigorously scrupulous not to allow my departmental interests to prejudice my impartiality as Chairman.' In keeping with her views on ministerial responsibility, she resisted a succession of attempts by the senior bureaucracy to set up a committee of deputy ministers on foreign policy, something that had started in the last years of the Trudeau government. Such a committee, she believed, would cut into ministerial power and also 'usurp or at least conflict with the function of the Cabinet Secretariat in the P.C.O.'[8] It did not matter to the minister that Massé wanted such a committee.[9]

These disputes over process embittered relations with Gotlieb and his senior officials. They were compounded by disagreements on policy questions, such as the way out of Clark's election pledge to move the embassy in Tel Aviv to Jerusalem and the sale of CANDU nuclear reactors to a repressive military regime in Argentina. MacDonald opposed the reactor sale, but Gotlieb, who sympathized with her revulsion of an odious regime, nonetheless believed that Canada had committed itself to a deal. In search of a compromise, the undersecretary advised his minister to withdraw a cabinet memorandum that essentially supported the sale and to replace it with a paper without recommendations. MacDonald agreed, and soon found herself under savage assault in cabinet. Gotlieb took the rap for this, though if any blame had to be affixed for the ultimate loss of the Argentinian contract, it might rest with the minister whose attack on Argentina's human-rights policies at the United

Nations on 25 September 1979 won Canada few friends in Buenos Aires.[10] That she was right in everything she said did not calm her critics at the cabinet table. The result was that MacDonald tried to get her undersecretary fired and, after one particular row, Gotlieb offered to resign. The prime minister, however, preferred his undersecretary's oral briefings to his minister's written ones. And, given his suspicions of MacDonald's popularity and independent power base, he was not entirely unhappy to watch the feuding develop and have Gotlieb as an ally.[11]

External Affairs under MacDonald was not a happy place. The senior officials believed that a cannon was rolling loose on the ship of state, and the minister could barely speak to her officials. That this did not cause Canadian foreign policy to spin out of control may be counted as a fortunate accident.

If Flora MacDonald was a novice in foreign policy, so too was her prime minister. Joe Clark was not a man who had travelled widely, as had Pierre Trudeau, and, although his first trip abroad as leader – to Europe and the United Kingdom in 1976 – had been a success,[12] he had little confidence in his ability to manage foreign policy. His public image in Canada was that of a weak man, but those who knew and worked with him realized he was much better than the image. He had good judgment in the areas he knew, one senior official recalled, but the problem was that in 1979 he did not know very much. Yet he was a quick study, someone who could grasp verbal briefings well and who could then understand and discuss the issues.[13] Clark had been very nervous when he went to the Tokyo Summit soon after he took power, but he came to realize, perhaps to his surprise, that he could at least hold his own with the other leaders of the Group of Seven.[14] At the Commonwealth conference at Lusaka a few weeks later, he seemed noticeably more poised.

Still, Clark remained very unsure of himself on foreign-policy questions, and with good reason. No issue had a more devastating effect on the government than his ill-considered election-campaign pledge, reiterated in the first days of the new administration, to move the Canadian embassy in Israel from Tel Aviv to Jerusalem. That promise, possibly principled but certainly designed to attract Jewish votes to the Progressive Conservative party in a few Toronto constituencies, had not had noticeable electoral success; what it did succeed in doing, however, was in painting the new prime minister as tough in words and desperately weak in action. As the embassy affair moved to its dénouement, Clark's perceived competence in both foreign and domestic policy diminished day by day.

Clark should have been careful in handling this hot potato. Ever since the 1973 Arab-Israeli War, Canadian public opinion, hitherto strongly pro-Israeli, had been swinging to a more balanced position. The Arab oil boycott that followed the war, though widely deplored, nonetheless obliged the Canadian media to examine the Middle East conflict in a more even-handed way. The rise to prominence of the Palestine Liberation Organization assisted this process, too, though the PLO's appalling terrorist actions were condemned.

The one certainty was that Israeli-Palestine questions were political dynamite. The Trudeau government had discovered this in July 1975 when it announced that the fifth United Nations Congress on the Prevention of Crime and the Treatment of Offenders would not be held in Toronto in September as scheduled. The reason, simply put, was that the PLO had been given observer status by the UN General Assembly and was entitled to attend the conference. The possibility of members of a terrorist group attending a conference on crime upset Canadian Jewish groups, who mobilized support and secured strong statements of concern from the Ontario government and Metropolitan Toronto. The Trudeau cabinet caved in to the pressure, overriding advice from the Department of External Affairs and the secretary of state for external affairs, Allan MacEachen, who had been interested both in putting some distance between Canada and Israel and in developing contacts with PLO 'moderates'.[15] As MacEachen put it with uncharacteristic bluntness, this 'was one of the least glorious events in our foreign policy history to have collapsed in the face of internal political pressure.'[16] The media howled at the government. The *Toronto Star,* for example, editorialized on 22 July that the government 'has humiliated Canada ... is abandoning principle, giving into threats and copping out of its responsibility to the world community.' That seemed exactly right, but the next year the government, once burned, twice persistent, hosted the UN Conference on Human Settlements in Vancouver. The Jewish community there was less numerous and well-organized than in Toronto, and a Jewish minister, Barney Danson, was minister of state for urban affairs and the host. Danson travelled widely in the Middle East to line up support, urging the Saudis and others to discuss the issues of housing and not to turn the conference into a vehicle for condemning Israel. He was largely successful, though he recalled that a Pakistani delegate did introduce an anti-Israel resolution. Fortunately, Danson said, the conference centre roof burned down that night, cooling matters![17]

Another major issue concerned the response Canada should offer to the Arab boycott against Israel. After 1973 the Arab nations had extended their boycott to companies that dealt with Israel, and some Canadian companies dealing with the Arab world signed agreements not to deal with Israel. That stirred protest in Canada, notably among the Jewish community which launched a campaign for anti-boycott legislation in May 1975.[18] That month, the prime minister had said in the House of Commons that 'the government is opposed to any such kind of discrimination.'[19] But it took a long and difficult struggle between departments and ministers before the government finally produced a policy. Even then, it was the most moderate of those considered.[20] On 21 October 1976 the secretary of state for external affairs, Don Jamieson, said that the government would deny 'its support or facilities including the support of its trade missions abroad' for all transactions requiring Canadian companies to discriminate against individuals on grounds of race or religion or obliging them to refuse to sell to or buy from any country. Jamieson also said that companies had to report instances where they had been asked to adhere to a boycott.[21] Further regulations were issued in January 1977 by the Department of Industry, Trade and Commerce.[22] But in December Jack Horner, the former Conservative who had crossed the floor and recently become ITC minister, refused requests to publish the names of companies adhering to the Arab boycott, and the cabinet, despite the protests of John Roberts,[23] the member for Toronto St Paul's, a riding with a substantial Jewish population, decided to uphold Horner. All that appeared in 1978 were numerical lists, demonstrating that at least thirty-nine commercial transactions had been reviewed by Ottawa because it was thought they might contravene the anti-boycott regulations. As Roberts observed caustically, ITC's policy was to sell the Arabs as many telephone exchanges as Canada could.[24]

That government action kept the issue at the boil and intensified pressure for tougher action from Jewish organizations. In December 1978 Horner, greatly aided by 'the best deputy minister in Ottawa,' Gordon Osbaldeston, finally introduced legislation to require companies to report boycott requests on pain of a $250-a-day fine. This time the government promised to publish names of companies accepting boycott clauses. That again was a moderate policy, one designed to do the least harm to Canada's developing trade relationship with the Middle East, and Horner recalled that his bill had met some stiff opposition in cabinet. One minister urged that Canada seek 'revenge' on the Arabs for their boycott, an injudicious phrase that led the prime minister 'to zap' the unfortunate.[25] The Canadian Jewish Congress, the major Jewish organization, though not entirely happy with the Horner Bill (or with Horner himself), nonetheless supported the government. The bill died on the order paper when the 1979 election was called.[26]

These contentious events, highly emotional for the Jewish community and equally so for the small but vociferous Canadian Arab community, guaranteed that Israeli Prime Minister Menachem Begin was received with close attention when he came to Canada in November 1978 as a guest of the Canadian government. Begin's main interest in Canada was to get Ottawa to move its embassy to Jerusalem, a suggestion that met with a cool response from Prime Minister Trudeau. Unabashed, the hard-lining Begin then pressed the Canada-Israel Committee (an administrative committee backed by the Canadian Jewish Congress, the Canadian Zionist Federation, and B'nai Brith) towards action.[27] A few days later on 12 November the Israeli prime minister delivered a 'really appalling' speech, as John Roberts characterized it,[28] at Toronto's Beth Tzedec synagogue, calling on Canadian Jews to pressure their government to move its embassy to Jerusalem. This amounted to interference in Canadian domestic politics, and some Jewish groups appeared hesitant to follow Begin's lead. By the turn of the year, however, most of those doubts had been overcome, though some strong Liberal supporters were most uncomfortable.[29]

For the next several months, as Prime Minister Trudeau (who thought that he had treated the Jewish community well since coming to power)[30] developed what one minister recalled as 'a passionate hatred' of Begin[31] and increasing exasperation with those who heeded his call, delegations came to Ottawa where they were warned by officials that 'it would be unwise for the Jewish community to mount a campaign on this issue.'[32] For his part, Deputy Prime Minister Allan MacEachen told John Roberts, by now secretary of state, that he appreciated the emotional nature of the issue for Canada's Jews, Israel, and the Arab states. 'Indeed, for some of the Arab states the status of Jerusalem is the preeminent point of dispute with Israel. For Canada to recognize the Israeli claim now would destroy our own claim to an even-handed policy [and] ... could well involve retaliation against our considerable economic and commercial interests in the Arab world.'[33] MacEachen might have added that Canada had substantial numbers of troops on peacekeeping duty in the Middle East who could be endangered by precipitate action, and that Canada's allies would object to any embassy move that upset the status quo.

That was a good statement of the difficulties involved in this issue into which Joe Clark and the Conservatives blundered so purposefully. The young Tory leader's relations with the Jewish community had got off to a bad start in 1977 when an avowedly anti-Semitic candidate won a Conservative nomination in Quebec. Clark refused to veto the candidate, and matters worsened when, at a meeting with a Jewish delegation at his home in Ottawa in August 1977, his wife Maureen McTeer reportedly said that if the party could tolerate anti-French and anti-feminists, it could also tolerate anti-Semites.[34] In January 1979 Clark made a pre-election trip to Israel where, after almost impaling himself on the bayonets of an honour guard of Canadian peacekeeping troops, he met Begin, who urged him strongly to declare his support there and then for the move of the Canadian embassy. The embassy staff in Tel Aviv counselled caution; so did Clark's advisers, some of whom supported the Begin suggestions but recognized that a statement to that effect in Israel would be a public-relations mistake of substantial magnitude.

By April, however, with the federal election underway and with the Conservatives in a tight race with Trudeau, every seat became crucial to Clark's prospects of forming a government. The Egyptian-Israeli negotiations that culminated at Camp David, where they were skilfully moderated by President Jimmy Carter, had borne fruit, but that did not ease the pressure on Clark to make a statement on the embassy issue. Toronto candidates, especially Ron Atkey of St Paul's, who had prepared a memorandum on the subject for Clark's trip to Israel, and Rob Parker of Eglinton-Lawrence, who had been in Israel during the Clark visit, had large Jewish populations in their constituencies, and Atkey and Parker had been lobbied hard by Jewish groups. Clark had his advisers discuss the question; he himself met two senior officials of the Department of External Affairs who strongly urged caution upon him. So too did a meeting of party campaign officials at the beginning of April which concluded that the embassy issue should not be Conservative policy; but a meeting on 21 April of the party's policy committee had concluded that it should.[35]

On 25 April Clark was to address the Canada-Israel Committee in Toronto, and his campaign team, with Rob Parker also present, met that morning at the Prince Hotel to decide what to do. According to Jim Gillies, a close Clark aide who was there, the key to the decision that emerged was that Eddie Goodman and Hugh Segal, two Jewish campaign advisers who were opposed to announcing support for moving the embassy during the election, arrived at the hotel late. So, Gillies said, the decision was taken for constituency need, no one close to Clark believing that this was an earth-shaking issue.[36] At 2 PM, therefore, Joe Clark told the Canada-Israel Committee that his party, if elected, would move the Canadian embassy in Israel to Jerusalem. This was, as two academics later observed, 'miscalculated deference to the views of a faction of the Canadian Jewish community.'[37]

Clark's announcement, the product, Jeffrey Simpson said, of 'a numbing mixture of unforgivable stupidity and crass politics,'[38] made a small stir during the campaign. Trudeau told an audience at Toronto's Forest Hill Collegiate Institute that the Tory leader was naïve, irresponsible, or stupid. He had, he claimed, told Begin in November 1978, 'don't ask me to get involved in your side if that will mean that the Arabs will break off talks and we'll be involved in another thirty years of war.'[39] Even so, the question did not seem of great importance electorally in Toronto or elsewhere on 22 May. Parker lost and Atkey won, and the swing of votes to Atkey in St Paul's (and away from his Liberal opponent, John Roberts, towards the New Democratic Party candidate)[40] was consistent with that generally in Toronto ridings.

In the interim between his narrow election triumph and taking power on 4 June, Clark apparently received a memorandum in his transition package warning against the consequences of moving the embassy.[41] But he did not take it seriously. On 5 June, as he readied for his first Ottawa press conference as prime minister, Clark met with some of his key advisers, including Gillies and Marcel Massé, just named clerk of the Privy Council, to discuss the points he should make. The prime minister insisted he had to say that his government was different, that it intended to carry out its policy promises, and that the public service must become aware of this change. Gillies suggested that the best issue with which to make this clear was mortgage deductibility, a popular Conservative election plank, and Clark agreed. Apparently, he was urged to stall on the embassy issue.[42] But at the conference the press asked about the move of the embassy, and the prime minister used that issue to make his point:

We certainly intend to do that. Miss MacDonald will be indicating to officials in external affairs that we will be expecting from them recommendations fairly directly as to how it can be accomplished and what other policies will be followed that will be necessary to make that goal realizable ... those questions are now beyond discussion as to their appropriateness and that what we will be seeking from the public service will be indications as to how we accomplish what we have undertaken to do.[43]

The fat was in the fire now. The Department of External Affairs began to warn of the dire consequences to follow, and the relationship between Flora MacDonald and Allan Gotlieb started to disintegrate under the weight of the undersecretary's warnings. Arab ambassadors in Ottawa protested vigorously, and there were threats of economic retaliation from abroad. The Canadian Council of Churches, opposed to any unilateral alteration in the status of Jerusalem, complained. The Department of Agriculture, with sales in jeopardy, was angry, and businessmen, concerned about their sales, began a 'corporate storming' of Ottawa. Six hundred letters eventually poured in,[44] and the Canadian media, largely critical of Clark, focused on the jobs and dollars that would be lost to Arab boycotts.[45] On the morning of 6 June Clark asked for the response so far, and he was promptly told of the firestorm that had begun. That afternoon, the cabinet secretary arranged an impromptu meeting with five industrialists, a meeting the prime minister attended without aides. He emerged two hours later, one observer recalled, white as a sheet and ready to look for a way out.[46] It took some time to find one.

The difficulty was that the new government quickly developed a siege mentality, thanks to this issue. Clark ordered his staff to screen his mail so that letters opposed to his Jerusalem policy would not reach his desk. The Jerusalem question absorbed time needed for other issues and sapped confidence, not least Clark's. And as Clark and the PMO and PCO, along with MacDonald and Gotlieb, looked for some escape, turf fights began. Klaus Goldschlag of External Affairs, Gotlieb, and Massé conceived the idea of sending former Conservative leader Robert Stanfield on a fact-finding mission to the Middle East, their intention being to kill the embassy move, provide a breathing space, and find something prestigious for Stanfield to do. Clark, however, viewed the mission as seeking a way to allow him to move the embassy; and MacDonald, who was unhappy with Clark's position and who heard of the idea of a fact-finding mission only after it had been floated to the PMO, apparently came to believe that the undersecretary and cabinet secretary were conspiring with the prime minister against her. The squabbles continued over the terms of reference for the mission[47] and were resolved only on 23 June when the prime minister emerged from a series of meetings with Arab ambassadors to announce that 'Stanfield of Arabia,' as wags soon dubbed the laconic senior Conservative, would go to the Middle East and report some time in 1980. His task was to 'take into account the views that are put to us before we decide how and under what circumstances to proceed ...' Clark said, 'on the implementation of our policy on Jerusalem in a way that will be compatible with the efforts that are being made to achieve a comprehensive settlement in the Middle East.'[48]

Stanfield toured the area in September and early October, also visiting London where Paul Martin, the high commissioner, steered him to

British officials who 'would caution against going to Jerusalem unless we wanted to lose all influence with the Arabs ... The British,' Martin added, 'are certainly not anxious for us to proceed.'[49] Nor was Stanfield. Although he was not asked to provide an interim report, he had found the Arab nations so unhappy with Canada that he apparently concluded that it was best for the government to cut its losses. On 29 October his interim report was tabled in the House of Commons. Its key paragraph was blunt:

To use effectively whatever influence we may have in the area to encourage moderation and compromise we must retain credibility with both sides as a fair-minded interlocutor. We could not do this if we were to move our embassy to Jerusalem ... I do not think Canada should pursue any course of action which risks making this more difficult or which erodes the credibility of the Camp David accords by creating the impression that they have strengthened the position of one of the parties on a key issue yet to be addressed in the negotiations.

Stanfield also called for Canada to 'broaden contacts' with the Palestine Liberation Organization and to support 'the Palestinians' right to a homeland.'[50] Prime Minister Clark accepted these recommendation, and although there were complaints from Canadian Jews directed at Clark and Stanfield,[51] the issue was finally put behind the government. Clark told a journalist that the damage caused by this issue had left 'a scar that will always be there, although not too large.'[52] The scar it left was a deep one, however, and opposition leader Pierre Trudeau was surely correct when he used the embassy issue to denounce 'the government's incompetence in the matter of foreign affairs.'[53] More important still, the issue, intended to demonstrate to the public service and the country that the prime minister was tough and determined, instead made Clark appear appallingly weak, ill-informed, and ill-advised. Jerusalem had become the Conservative government's wailing wall.

It is also worth noting that the issue left scars on the body politic. Begin's intervention in Canadian politics and the Tories' use of the embassy issue for election fodder embittered many Liberals, and when the Trudeau government returned to power in 1980 it was markedly less sympathetic to the Israelis than Canadian governments had hitherto been. One senior minister recollected that everyone, including Trudeau and his secretary to the cabinet, Michael Pitfield, were 'pro-Arab,' and this same minister described the Quebec caucus as 'anti-Jewish,' except for Marc Lalonde.[54] Trudeau's external affairs minister, Mark MacGuigan, said early in 1982 that 'The legitimate rights and concerns of the Palestinians have to be realized,' and he added that 'the PLO represents an important element of Palestinian opinion.' Pierre DeBané, minister of state (external relations) after the Israelis invaded Lebanon in 1982, stated that the Palestinians were entitled to 'a homeland within a clearly defined territory, the West Bank and the Gaza Strip.'[55] The price paid for transitory advantage by the supporters of moving the embassy had been high indeed.

The impression of flip-flopping incompetence created by the embassy affair was, while tangible, not the whole story of the government's foreign and defence policy. In some areas the Clark administration handled itself well.

There were refugees, most notably the Vietnamese boat people, for example. Canadian refugee policy since the Second World War had been relatively open-handed. During the Trudeau administration, appeals for entry to Canada had come or been anticipated from those fleeing Portuguese Africa, Chile, and Rhodesia. On the Rhodesians, Pierre Trudeau told a press conference in Jamaica that 'I am certainly not panting to have this immigration movement take place ... If they are liberals, white liberals, they should stay and have nothing to fear after Rhodesian independence. If they're ... racist, why shouldn't you [Jamaica] receive them rather than us?'[56] That was pungent and true, though not especially helpful.

After the North Vietnamese conquered South Vietnam and began to 're-educate' the population, tens of thousands fled, often making their escape in small boats and, if they survived pirates, storms, and sharks, ending up in overcrowded refugee camps scattered through Southeast Asia. From 1975 to 1978 Canada took in 9000 refugees from Vietnam, and in December 1978 the Trudeau government agreed to accept 5000 more in the next year.[57] In 1979 the government also established an annual refugee plan, setting out the 'source areas' from which specified numbers of refugees were to be accepted.[58] Immediately it took power, the Clark government overrode the 1979 plan for 10,000 refugees all told by announcing its willingness to accept 12,000 Vietnamese. Then on 18 July MacDonald and Employment and Immigration Minister Ron Atkey announced that Canada was prepared to accept up to 50,000 Indochinese refugees to the end of 1980, the government indicating its willingness to sponsor one refugee for each one receiving private sponsorship.[59] This imaginative scheme was unique in the world, and Canada had committed itself to taking just under one-eighth of the

370,000 Vietnamese in refugee camps. The total refugee intake for 1980 had been planned to be 14,000, but after the MacDonald-Atkey announcement that number was then allocated to non-Vietnamese.[60]

The government's plan for Vietnamese refugees was received with astonishing warmth. Canadians, individually and in groups from churches or communities, queued up to sponsor a refugee. Provincial governments put up substantial sums. Critics such as the National Citizens Coalition, hitherto best known for its opposition to bilingualism, discredited themselves further. By February 1980 Canada had taken in 34,000 Vietnamese refugees, of whom 21,600 had been privately sponsored. So popular did the program prove that the Liberal government, returned to power in the February 1980 election, continued and even expanded upon it by adding an additional 10,000 boat people.[61] This was the most generous program offered by any of the major resettlement countries, and the Clark government deserved the accolades it received. 'Nothing,' MacDonald said later, 'will ever give me greater satisfaction than to have played a major role' in determining the government's refugee program.[62]

The government – and its ambassador in Iran, Kenneth Taylor – also performed well when fanatical mobs of Shiite fundamentalists stormed the local bastion of the Great Satan, the U.S. embassy in Tehran, on 4 November 1979 and took the staff hostage.[63] Five Americans managed to avoid being rounded up with their colleagues and made their way on 10 November to the Taylor's residence; a sixth American arrived there on 22 November. The telegram from Taylor in Tehran informing Ottawa that the Americans were seeking assistance arrived at External Affairs at 1002 hrs GMT on 9 November. The response was virtually instantaneous, the officials, Flora MacDonald, and Joe Clark all agreeing that shelter was to be provided. The reply went back to Tehran at 1826 hrs GMT the same day, most of the intervening eight hours having been spent in deciding where best to hide the escapees.[64] Early in January 1980, under authority of an order in council, Ottawa prepared bogus Canadian passports for them. On 28 January, after consultations between Ottawa and Washington, the Americans made their escape from Iran, and the four remaining Canadians at the embassy prudently departed the same day, leaving the chancery shuttered and barred. On 29 January, in the midst of the federal election campaign, the story broke in Canada, almost certainly leaked to help the government's re-election efforts. Although the Iranian mullahs were understandably unhappy and although some RCMP officers and officials in External Affairs feared that Iranian attempts to assassinate Ambassador Taylor or other Canadian officials might be expected, President Carter and the American people were jubilant.[65] Canada and especially Taylor, who basked in the deserved applause and proved a largely unassuming hero, were lionized in the United States, and the Canadian caper, as it become widely known, eventually led to Taylor's posting as consul-general in New York. Unfortunately for the Clark government, the favourable publicity did not help it in the election. Canadians approved what their government had done, but perhaps, they assumed that any government would have acted in this way and, therefore, no special credit accrued to Clark or MacDonald.

The election also interrupted the review of foreign policy that had been underway when MacDonald become secretary of state for external affairs. The department's Policy Analysis Group, a quasi-think tank with a small staff that had been brought into existence in August 1969 to meet the Trudeau government's emphasis on forecasting and planning,[66] had been charged in the fall of 1977 with the task of preparing a foreign-policy outline for the 1980s.

The Policy Analysis Group had tended to drift uncertainly since its first years. Undersecretaries thought it was a speech-writing bureau or a small pool of firefighters, ready to be rushed to crisis areas.[67] Some members wanted to take advantage of new techniques in political science, and commissioned expensive projects that puzzled, amused, or infuriated the operating bureaux; others were bored and frustrated. The department's inability to use PAG properly was obvious, but that was understandable. Foreign policy for a country such as Canada was bound to be largely reactive, and forecasting techniques were inappropriate to running foreign policy. As Basil Robinson put it, 'How could you tell what de Gaulle would do next year, let alone tomorrow, and pretend to allocate your budget to meet it?'[68] Yet the weakness of PAG was symptomatic of a larger problem – the decline of the 'political' side of Canadian foreign policy.

The Policy Analysis Group, its name soon changed to the Policy Planning Secretariat, now had its opportunity to shine with the preparation of a foreign policy for the 1980s. A first draft was ready by January 1978, just as a new defence white paper, never to see the light of day, was at a similar stage.[69]

'Foreign Policy for Canada in the 1980s,' or FP-80, became the subject of a colloquium held at Touraine near Ottawa on 21–22 September that brought together some of External Affairs' key figures (Gotlieb and Klaus Goldschlag) with a number of outsiders (John Holmes of the Canadian Institute of International Affairs, Ivan Head of the International Development Research Centre), including some from other departments (Gordon Smith of the PCO and Gordon Osbaldeston from Industry, Trade and Commerce). The group's consensus was that Canada faced serious challenges and could no longer take for granted either unity or prosperity. Federal competence had to be maintained, but enhanced cooperation between Ottawa and the provinces was essential if international relations were to be managed successfully. The third option, Mitchell Sharp's conception of 1972, was deemed to be virtually a dead letter. Canada needed counterweights to the United States, of course, but the relationship with Washington now had to be seen more as an asset than a threat. Still, new ways of preserving the Canadian identity had to be devised.

The next stage in the review process, Gotlieb decided, was the preparation of six to eight 'issue papers.'[70] The Policy Planning Secretariat commissioned the papers, largely from officers in the department, and one on 'Foreign Policy, Parliament and the Public' was placed under contract with Peter Dobell of the Parliamentary Centre for Foreign Policy and Foreign Trade.[71] Eight papers were completed, though some arrived only after the 1979 election brought the Conservatives to power. Some in the department expected that the studies were now outmoded, but Flora MacDonald expressed interest in a full-fledged review of foreign policy, an idea confirmed by the Cabinet Committee on Foreign and Defence Policy in August 1979. That decision resulted in the preparation over the next six weeks by the Policy Planning Secretariat of two papers intended to stimulate public discussion and to be considered by a subcommittee of the House of Commons Standing Committee on External Affairs and National Defence and the Senate Foreign Relations Committee.[72] The papers offered *tours d'horizon* in good style, broad and sweeping analyses of the great issues facing the world and the country. But there were few policy prescriptions, most recommendations being of the kind that gave the Commons-Senate subcommittee a full range of choice. For example: 'It will ... be necessary for Canada to assess its contribution to North American defence, the defence of the North Atlantic and of Europe, in the light of the Soviet military build-up, the expectations of our allies and Canada's special assets.'[73] That left the parliamentarians ample room to recommend anything and everything.

The cabinet committee approved both papers, 'Canada in a Changing World, Part I: The Global Framework,' and 'Part II: Canadian Aid Policy,' which were sent for printing. By the kind of mischance that characterized the bad-luck Clark government, finished copies arrived the day the government fell, and their distribution seemed impossible in the circumstances. After the election drove MacDonald onto the opposition benches, the Liberal secretary of state for external affairs, Mark MacGuigan, decided that the 1970 *Foreign Policy for Canadians* remained the government's guide and that the MacDonald review was largely super-fluous. The minister ordered the booklets to be pulped, though he did agree to make their contents public by releasing their text to the House of Commons Committee. Ms MacDonald was duly appreciative.[74]

Flora MacDonald's difficulties with Allan Gotlieb had obviously spoiled her brief tenure as secretary of state for external affairs. That was unfortunate, not least because Gotlieb was one of the most able department officers of his time, an intellectual and a creative mind. But Gotlieb, like many other foreign-service officers, had seen External Affairs bruised and battered during the Trudeau era; the idea that MacDonald would impose her revolution on the department was more than could be borne.

The department in Gotlieb's time as undersecretary was vastly different from the old, tight, elitist group that Trudeau had found when he came to power in 1968. Like the Department of National Defence, unified, civilianized, bilingualized, and governed by managers, External Affairs had been altered out of recognition.

Some of the change in the department was psychological. In the era of Lester Pearson, Hume Wrong, Norman Robertson, and Arnold Heeney, External Affairs was 'the Department,' the repository of all bureaucratic wisdom in Ottawa. Small and exclusive, the External club had almost unchallenged control of access to the levers of power that it wanted to grasp – an important limitation that excluded trade and economics generally. Even in the early 1960s, however, the department represented a paradox. Its numbers were small but the proportion of officers was high, and of senior officers higher still. And though it was strong on the political side, External Affairs was much less so in economics.

Circumstances altered through the 1960s. 'Bureaucratic reactions,' as the ambassador to the United Nations, George Ignatieff, put it, 'have dictated the determination of policy ... [and] led to the present state of affairs where desk officers and divisional chiefs arrive at policy determinations through interminable meetings.'[75] Moreover, for the best and brightest, there were too few challenging jobs available within External Affairs' posts abroad or its divisions at home. Promotion was slow and able officers could end up 'stamping passports.' They could be moved to other departments and given a chance to use their talents to the fullest, an idea that Marcel Cadieux, the undersecretary when Trudeau took power, resented deeply and saw almost as theft.[76] Cadieux was especially protective towards his able francophone officers, a scarce commodity in

Ottawa in the late 1960s.[77] Then, there was clear resentment, not least from Marc Lalonde, Trudeau's closest aide in the PMO, at the diplomatic lifestyle. Even diplomats from an earlier period thought the style extravagant. The limousines, servants, and lavish residences of ambassadors abroad offended Lalonde's deep-rooted puritanism – and that of envious mandarins from other departments in Ottawa who lived a more spartan life.[78]

There was, as a result, some hand-rubbing satisfaction in Ottawa when Prime Minister Trudeau sneered publicly at the department and his government put External Affairs through the hoops in the review process of 1968–70. There were secret smiles when the department underwent a wrenching retrenchment exercise in 1969–70 that saw budgets cut by $7.5 million, seven posts abroad shut down, and compulsory separations of sixty foreign-service officers and 110 support staff.[79] Small though those numbers were, they amounted to 7 per cent of the department's strength.[80] The difficulty for External Affairs was that, unlike others, it had almost all its budget tied up in personnel and their support. In such circumstances, cutbacks hit especially hard. Basil Robinson, undersecretary in 1975 at a time when further budget restraints were mooted, told his minister, 'in External Affairs our major resource is people, more than half of whom serve abroad. Austerity measures fall particularly heavily, therefore, on items which affect the people themselves.'[81]

The government's insistence on bilingualism, confirmed in law with the passage of the Official Languages Act in 1969, also obliged foreign-service officers, including many older, senior ones, to begin the painful task of learning French. Morale in the foreign service plummeted as a result of these successive shocks, so much so that Mitchell Sharp, the secretary of state for external affairs, publicly admitted the problem in 1970.[82] Even a senior PCO officer had his regrets: 'I think the events of the late 1960s were badly handled,' he recalled, 'were traumatic, but were in a sense inevitable.'[83]

There were still more shocks to come. In the fall of 1969 the Task Force on the Consolidation of Personnel and Support Services Abroad had been set up, a product of Michael Pitfield's desire to integrate foreign operations.[84] The deputy secretary (plans) to the cabinet believed in logic and structure, and he wanted power in Ottawa to rest in the hands of the politicians, not the bureaucrats. (Critics maintained, naturally enough, that Pitfield wanted power to rest in *his* hands.) That logic implied a coordinated and consolidated foreign service, and the task force, which reported in March 1970, was to be the vehicle to this end. Led by Sydney Pierce, who had served in senior posts in both the

Departments of External Affairs and Trade and Commerce, the task force had been given a mandate to study the means by which 'the maximum degree of integration consistent with effective achievement of government objectives and efficiency in use of resources' could be accomplished.[85] It had duly recommended the integration of the foreign service and trade divisions, provided that service at least as good as in the past could be provided to the business community. That qualifying thought, inserted into the report by Jake Warren, then the deputy minister of industry, trade and commerce, had saved the Trade Commissioner Service and, as Warren remembered it, temporarily halted the integration 'juggernaut.'[86]

Nonetheless, in June, after study of the Pierce report by an interdepartmental committee, the deputy ministers of external affairs, industry, trade and commerce, manpower and immigration, and the vice-president of the Canadian International Development Agency told their officers of the changes to come in the next eighteen months. First, an Interdepartmental Committee on External Relations (ICER) was to be set up to guide the integration process, with the undersecretary of state for external affairs as chair. In addition, 'country plans' would be prepared to guide the operation of each mission abroad in line with the government's new 'programme planning and budgeting system.' The Personnel Management Committee, a subcommittee of ICER, was created to 'recommend criteria for the selection of heads of mission in the light of the requirements for each mission' and to develop 'common policies in various areas such as recruitment, career development ... [and] evaluation.' At the same time, another task force was to report on how support services for foreign operations could be integrated.[87] For External Affairs, the message was clear: ambassadorships were to be much more open than hitherto to trade commissioners and, as *Foreign Policy for Canadians* had implied, the marketing function of Canadian missions abroad was to become a very high priority. None of that was especially pleasing to the department.

By 1 April 1971 support services abroad had been integrated. In the process, some 1000 employees of other departments and agencies abroad were transferred to External Affairs, along with a budget of approximately $10 million for supporting activities.

If these changes were not enough, the Department of External Affairs undertook its own major reorganization, the first in almost a quarter century. The department was now to have four regional bureaux – for Europe, Africa and the Middle East, Asia and the Pacific, and the Western Hemisphere – as well as a variety of functional bureaux that were, among other things, to coordinate policy with other departments: Economic and Scientific Affairs, Defence and Arms Control, Legal and Consular, United Nations, Public Affairs, and Coordination. There were, in addition, a number of administrative bureaux to run the department's machinery. As Mitchell Sharp told the House of Commons Standing Committee on External Affairs and National Defence, the government was implementing 'integrated and accountable management,' which would produce 'a system of country plans and programmes which provides the flexibility necessary to shape and manage programmes carried out in relatively small packages all over the world. In addition, however, continuous policy formulation and revision is needed, extending far beyond the compass of its country plans and programmes.'[88]

What that meant, beyond the appointment of two additional assistant undersecretaries, was unclear, so much so that the undersecretary felt obliged to write to all missions abroad. 'I can only assure you we are not doing this [country] programming to be stylish or to imitate the Americans,' Ed Ritchie wrote on 26 March 1971. 'We are doing it because it is the best way that we have found to satisfy the various departments (including our own) that their interests are being reflected in the activities of each mission and also to get from the Government the resources required to carry on the priority activities.' Still, Ritchie admitted, for missions that were short-staffed, 'this extra task may seem almost too much to bear.'[89]

If there was a bright spot in the changes that had been forced on the Department of External Affairs, it probably could have been ICER. The interdepartmental committee offered a potential opportunity to coordinate foreign operations, and, although that was not explicitly stated to be its mandate, many hoped that a DEA-directed policy coordination would be the result. The deputies from the other departments naturally had little interest in such coordination, however much Pitfield may have wanted it. True integration of the foreign service could only have been imposed by prime ministerial fiat,[90] and at this stage Trudeau apparently was unwilling to go that far.

As a result, within months of ICER's formation, Al Johnson, secretary of the Treasury Board, was complaining about the time spent in ICER on structures and management to the detriment of discussion on the ways to achieve effective coordination of foreign policy. Johnson recognized that many departments did not inform External Affairs of their activities abroad, most notably in the United States where easy communications fostered cooperation and the exchange of information on a wide range of questions. To achieve coordination, Johnson argued – he spoke to

the already converted in External – the department should offer comments on all cabinet memoranda with international implications.[91] But
as might have been expected, some ministers in the Trudeau government
believed that true integration and effective coordination of policy might
weaken their departmental fiefdoms. In April 1972 the cabinet hedged
its bets, leaving External Affairs to make the best of the situation.[92] The
undersecretary tried. 'Where do we go from here?' he asked in a letter
in May. 'My own answer is that the transitional phase is now firmly
behind us and that the next steps you will need to take will be to bring
about a smoothly functioning common support service for your entire
Mission.'[93]

That was easier said than accomplished. From Geneva, George Ignatieff, the ambassador to the UN offices there, fired off a series of angry
letters to Undersecretary Ritchie. ICER's reports, he said, despite their
'pretentious and repetitive content,' make clear that 'the integration
process appears for various reasons to have ground to a halt.' What
ICER had produced was 'a diffusion of responsibility, both as to policy
formulation and personnel management, and a further focusing on *how*
things should be done, to the detriment of *what* should be done.' What
integration had amounted to, Ignatieff argued, was 'the extinction of
control of policy formulation by the Department: viz., as regards key
issues such as Canada/USA relations and Commonwealth affairs, to the
P.M.'s office and Privy Council.' Ritchie's reply was as blunt: 'Anyone
who thinks that this Department is in the doldrums or is having no effect
on policy simply does not know what is happening.'[94] The weight of
departmental opinion likely would have sided with Ignatieff, however
sadly it did so.

The Cabinet Committee on External Policy and Defence similarly had
little ability to redress the department's growing weakness. For ministers,
control over spending equalled power, and DEA had a relatively tiny
budget at its disposal. Nor did the department generate much legislation,
another test of political potency. Issues tended to reach the committee
only after they had been thrashed out privately by the prime minister and
the secretary of state for external affairs, something especially noticeable
when Allan MacEachen was minister or, later in the Trudeau regime,
after they had been effectively resolved in the Priorities and Planning
Committee of cabinet. In other words, the cabinet committee often had
little impact.[95]

The root of the problem was that External Affairs declined in importance in the Trudeau government. Though the prime minister's interest
in foreign policy could best be described as sporadic, and though strong

ministers like Mitchell Sharp and Allan MacEachen held the portfolio, in fact the department lost the influence it had held since the days of the Great War when Sir Robert Borden consulted Loring Christie on all the details of imperial and foreign policy. Increasingly, the main issues in Canadian foreign policy – the Nixon 'shokku,' the third option, energy – were concerned with trade and economics, and External Affairs, since Ed Ritchie had suffered a stroke and was forced to step down early in 1975, had not had an undersecretary with expertise and power in that era. 'ITC and Finance dominated,' one deputy minister caustically remembered, 'and all DEA did was provide the glassware.' The External people were invited to meetings, he added, because they ran the embassies where the trade commissioners operated, 'but they had little to say. They still thought generalists could operate in a specialized technical era. Their substance on the economic side was nil.'[96]

That was bad enough, but DEA had also lost its dominance in the areas of classical 'foreign policy.' The simple truth was that when Trudeau wanted something done there, he turned not to the department but to Ivan Head, his assistant principal secretary for international relations in the Prime Minister's Office. Head travelled with Trudeau, drafted speeches and replies to questions on international matters, and represented Trudeau abroad on various missions. He also bypassed the undersecretary of state for external affairs; he had little hesitation about ringing up DEA officers directly to discuss issues of concern, and he tended to notify External Affairs, not consult it, about the missions he undertook for Trudeau.[97]

In other words, it soon became all too obvious that the way to reach Trudeau's ear on foreign policy was through Head, not through the Department of External Affairs.[98] That frustrated and enraged most of the senior officials in DEA who viewed Head as 'a vest-pocket Kissinger' and one 'making his own foreign policy.'[99] In 1972, however, Ed Ritchie professed not to be alarmed by Head's role in contributing to 'the extinction of control of policy formulation by the Department.' Those who claimed that were simply wrong, he told one colleague. 'Ivan Head is a very active and able person and has substantial influence with the Prime Minister,' he wrote. But 'with rare exceptions, Ivan's influence (and his travels) have reinforced policies which the Department favoured. I see nothing wrong with such a situation.' The undersecretary added that 'we have had more influence on policy with Ivan there than we would have had if he had not been there.'[100] Those who remembered the battles over the Canadian role in and commitment to NATO might have demurred.

The department wanted to regain its position at the right hand of the prime minister. But that was a slow process, not markedly helped by the secretive MacEachen uncomfortably holding on-record briefings with the press or his appointment of an officer as coordinator between the department and the media.[101] Nor were matters improved after MacEachen left the department in late 1976 to become deputy prime minister, for he kept responsibility for relations with the United States on northern pipeline questions and represented Canada in North-South discussions in 1977. The new secretary of state for external affairs, Don Jamieson, also had to divide his responsibilities with Supply and Services Minister Jean-Pierre Goyer, who advised him on efforts to establish a French-speaking Commonwealth of Nations, or francophonie. This 'ménage à trois' was unwieldy in the extreme.

The situation by the later 1970s demonstrated beyond doubt that DEA had been in the doldrums since the shock of the foreign-policy review. External Affairs could no longer recommend an ambassadorship on its own and was obliged to engage in complicated interdepartmental bargaining over each appointment; the Department of Energy, Mines and Resources, under the aggressive Donald Macdonald as minister, was trying, with some success, to win control of energy foreign policy (see chapter 4); and Maurice Strong at CIDA had carved control of aid out of External Affairs' hide.[102]

The first effective idea on the way to give the Department of External Affairs a more prominent directing role came from Allan Gotlieb, who became undersecretary in 1977. No shrinking violet, Gotlieb was determined to give his old and new department its rightful place, and he came back at the right time, just before Ivan Head left the Prime Minister's Office. Head's departure was virtually a *sine qua non* for Gotlieb, since he was unlikely to have co-existed easily with his operational style. As important, Gotlieb and Michael Pitfield, by now clerk of the Privy Council and secretary to the cabinet, were cautious friends and allies. Pitfield had initially despised External Affairs' elitist pretensions, and he had participated cheerfully in efforts to cut the department down early in the Trudeau years. But this 'Metternich of the public service,' as one deputy minister called him, also sought balance, and by the late 1970s that meant building up DEA once more.[103]

The idea that the Department of External Affairs was a central agency was a first stage in rebuilding its power, and Gotlieb and Pitfield won Trudeau's and the cabinet's approval. Then the undersecretary told the world about the new status of his department when he delivered an important address at the University of Toronto on 15 February 1979. The Privy Council Office, the Treasury Board, and the Finance Department were the traditional central agencies, Gotlieb said, those agencies that provide advice to the government on the broad range of national policies and programs. They approach their work from their unique perspective, but each 'is expected to bring the work of individual departments into harmony with government-wide programs and policies. Each ... has a responsibility to advise not only its own Minister but also, under his authority, the collectivity of Ministers.' And, Gotlieb added, central agencies not only coordinated and consulted, they led. 'The Government considers the Department of External Affairs to be a central agency,' he continued. That meant the revivifying of the Interdepartmental Committee on External Relations, which had begun to 'stagnate somewhat.' The government had 'decided to renew the original goals of integration and operational coherence' and to give ICER an important role in coordinating operations abroad. Gotlieb also announced a reworking of DEA's organization chart, giving the deputy undersecretaries line authority.[104] The aim was to get External Affairs plugged in once more, to ensure that Canadian foreign policy was realistically based on the national interest.

The first stage of the renewed thrust towards integration of the foreign service presaged by Gotlieb's central-agency speech came during the Progressive Conservative government. In July 1979 the Clark government selected Barry Steers, a senior trade commissioner then serving as consul-general in New York, to report on ways to improve the economy and efficiency of foreign operations, to unify the management of posts abroad, and to improve the career prospects of foreign-service personnel. Steers's report, delivered the next month, recommended the integration into External Affairs of the senior officers of the Departments of Industry, Trade and Commerce and of Employment and Immigration. At the operational level, Steers recommended that management control continue to be divided between DEA and ITC, thus preserving the Trade Commissioner Service, much beloved of Canadian businessmen, as a separate operating service. DEA also was to provide all program services to the Canadian International Development Agency, and CIDA's officers could now choose to become full members of the foreign service. The Trudeau government, returned to power after the February 1980 election, quickly announced its approval of Steers's report and put his recommendations into effect.[105] This reorganization apparently took place with the concurrence of the deputies of the involved departments;[106] the incoming secretary of state for external affairs, Mark MacGuigan, was also informed that reorganization was on the way and was not to be resisted.[107]

Another coordinating innovation was the Committee of Deputy Ministers on Foreign and Defence Policy, which began work on 30 May 1980 with the undersecretary of state for external affairs as chair. This mirror committee, so called because its membership paralleled the composition of the Cabinet Committee on External Policy and Defence, had responsibility to review policy and expenditure issues and to ensure that recommendations reaching the cabinet committee were 'sound in substance, correct in form, and consistent with known Government priorities and objectives.'[108] Although that sounded much like the definition of a central agency's role, Gotlieb still had difficulty in enforcing DEA's coordinating role – in a jet and telephone age, departments thought of their opposite number in Washington well before they recalled DEA's overriding powers.[109] Still, there was satisfaction in this mirror committee for DEA and its undersecretary. Flora MacDonald, secretary of state for external affairs in the Clark government, had bitterly resisted any mirror committee during her brief tenure of office; it was for the ministers to make the policy, not the bureaucrats. But MacDonald was gone and Allan Gotlieb remained, victorious.

By the fall of 1980 the process of consolidation had proceeded quickly. There were hard feelings among some in External Affairs, who resented what they saw as the end of the department's elitist traditions and its emphasis on promoting 'peace' as opposed to representing Canada's commercial interests abroad; there were even clandestine meetings in people's homes.[110] So sharp was the feeling in the department, so pronounced the decline in morale that the prime minister in August 1980 created a royal commission to investigate conditions of foreign service.[111] Trudeau's comment to the royal commissioner, Pamela McDougall, that 'traditional concepts of foreign service have diminished relevance in an era of instantaneous, world-wide communications,' while true, did little to persuade External Affairs officials that his years in government had done anything to alter the preconceptions with which the prime minister had come to power.[112]

DEA's unhappiness did not reverse the government's course. As Mac-Guigan told the House of Commons Standing Committee on External Affairs and National Defence, 'the government has decided that the foreign service is a governmental, not a departmental, resource; hence, consolidation.' The new foreign service was to be divided in three parts:

a Personnel Management Committee which was to implement consolidation; an executive group, managed by DEA, from which heads of post and senior appointments were to be drawn; and an operations group, again managed by DEA, except for the Trade Commissioner Service which was to have a separate but coordinated personnel system. Moreover, the foreign service was to be divided into four streams: aid and development; commercial and economic; political and economic; and social affairs (which included immigration and consular affairs). To advance to the executive group, an officer had to have seen service in two streams.[113] The foreign branch of the Canada Employment and Immigration Commission was duly absorbed into External Affairs on 1 April 1981.

If the foreign-service officer cadre had difficulty adjusting to these moves, the Trudeau government was far from finished. The government's economic strategy, laid down in the November 1981 budget, had declared trade to be one of Canada's five priorities. 'The attainment of our goals and the protection of our interests has to rest,' MacGuigan said, 'upon a foundation of domestic well-being. This objective can be secured only through the effective promotion of Canadian trade and commercial interests internationally.'[114]

On 12 January 1982, therefore, the prime minister announced a further restructuring of the Department of External Affairs to give it responsibility for trade policy and promotion as well as the traditional areas of foreign policy and functions relating to immigration. All foreign-service officers from CIDA and the Trade Commissioner Service, along with the trade-policy and trade-promotion sections of the Department of Industry, Trade and Commerce, were to be fully integrated into the Department of External Affairs. Moreover, DEA now had three ministers – the secretary of state for external affairs, the minister of state for international trade, and the minister of state for external relations. It also had three deputies – the undersecretary of state for external affairs, a deputy minister, foreign policy, and a deputy minister, international trade.[115]

This hydra-headed monster had been created by force, that being the only way the objections of External Affairs and the Trade Commissioner Service could be overcome. The chief mover was Michael Pitfield, the secretary to the cabinet who had returned to power with Pierre Trudeau in February 1980. He had become convinced that External Affairs had to be combined with the Trade Commissioner Service to give it the economic and commercial expertise it had lacked since the early 1970s. Pitfield's agent was Gordon Osbaldeston, a former deputy in ITC and a former secretary of the Treasury Board. Osbaldeston had gone to DEA as undersecretary in late 1981 when Gotlieb went to the United States as ambassador. His mandate was to carry through the consolidation.

The key meeting in arranging the shotgun wedding of departments took place over several days at the Donald Gordon Centre at Queen's University. A group of approximately twenty officials from DEA and ITC initially covered the walls with flipcharts of complaints about their opposite departments. Then Osbaldeston told the assembled assistant deputy ministers and deputy ministers that integration was a fait accompli, and allowed them to shout and argue until they saw the logic of it. The generalist DEA officers, who resented Osbaldeston ('wrong side of the tracks, no hankie up his sleeve, a man with dirty fingers'), felt threatened by the emphasis on management and the fact that economics was back. They were, moreover, analytical, introspective, and articulate. The trade commissioners, marketing Canadian goods abroad and hence by definition extroverted doers, operated within a vastly different culture from the DEA officers and felt betrayed by Osbaldeston, one of their own. The commercial policy officials from IT&C had had their own wars against the trade commissioners and with the External Affairs bureaucracy. Yet these trade people had now to depend upon Osbaldeston for protection against the arrogance of the External Affairs officers.[116]

Inevitably, chaos followed the merger. It was incredibly difficult to shoehorn the Trade side into the already overcrowded Pearson Building where External Affairs had operated since 1973. 'A technician without a mission,' or so DEA saw him,[117] Osbaldeston tried to reassure the nervous DEA officers by stating frankly that he would not mess with foreign policy and that he would be invisible for the first year while he handled the reorganization. He prayed that there would be no crisis that would expose the frailty of the new and still ramshackle organization he had created. The Grenada invasion aside, where the response was slow, the crises happily were few and manageable. Sy Taylor handled foreign policy while Robert Johnstone managed the trade side of the hydra.[118]

Then, unexpectedly, Michael Pitfield resigned and went to the Senate. Trudeau named Osbaldeston to be secretary to the cabinet and Marcel Massé, who had spent two years at CIDA, to be undersecretary of state for external affairs. Massé inherited a Department of External Affairs that, while nominally integrated, in fact consisted of two wings. Pitfield and Osbaldeston had always known that completion of the process could not be long delayed, but that task fell to Massé, and the new undersecretary was a more authoritarian manager than his predecessor.[119]

The orders were clear: the new Department of External Affairs was to be made to work with an integrated system of decision-making.[120] The result, announced in June and implemented on 3 September 1983, completed the process of consolidation by concentrating responsibility for all 'geographically formed policies and programs in five geographic branches. The geographic branches were to provide advice to the deputy minister (international trade) on trade and economic matters within their region and to the deputy minister (political affairs) on all other matters.[121] In effect, the trade and foreign-policy wings of External Affairs that Osbaldeston had created were now unified and the department continued to have three ministers and a new mandate to cover all international trade as well as economic and political matters, a process formalized with the passage of the Government Organization Act of 1983.[122]

For Marcel Massé, as for Trudeau and Pitfield, process quite literally was substance, and the proper process was now in place.[123] For the Professional Association of Foreign Service Officers, the trade union in External Affairs, this was much less clear. As PAFSO noted, 'structure alone is not enough. It won't necessarily produce better and more timely advice to Ministers, or deliver more effective programs abroad.'[124] Less calmly, one senior External Affairs officer described Massé as 'a mad organist,' rearranging the pieces and playing so loudly that everyone was deaf at the end. Policy, he said, has quality and process does not.[125] As the vehemence of that comment made clear, the new organization and the man who had implemented it had enemies in the Department of External Affairs.

Like the Department of National Defence, the Department of External Affairs had been pulled, kicking and screaming, into the modern era. The dislocations were severe, the strain enormous. Whether the result improved Canada's capacity to make and operate a foreign policy was much less certain, and it may be that the prime minister and the clerk of the Privy Council had much the same reason for the perpetual reorganization of DEA that they had for turning defence policy on its ear: the old ways had to be shaken up. They were, and the Department of External Affairs could never again be the same elitist group that had steered Canada so confidently through the war and postwar eras.

9

The Trudeau Government
and the Armed Forces

For the Canadian Armed Forces, the Trudeau years were a long, dark night of the spirit. Demoralized, embittered, and frustrated, Canada's unified armed forces struggled to understand a government that treated them as an inescapable nuisance. There was, however, no question of shutting down the Canadian Armed Forces, not even as a subject for academic debate within the cabinet seminar room. There were, however, profound doubts about the purpose of the forces, doubts that went far beyond the roles the politicians periodically assigned to the military.

At its most basic level, the dilemma was this: Canada's armed forces were an anachronism in terms of national defence against an external enemy. The only serious war in which Canada was likely to be engaged would be very brief: a nuclear exchange between the two superpowers in which Canada's conventional forces would probably not have time to participate. Canada itself produced no nuclear weapons – governments since 1945 had wisely brushed aside that expensive course. Instead, Canada was a member of a mutual insurance society, the North Atlantic alliance, to which it had contributed significant resources in the 1950s and 1960s, and it also assisted the United States in the defence of North America. The Cuban missile crisis of 1962, however, had demonstrated to the politicians that Canada's contributions to the Western cause made little difference when the crunch came. In any nuclear crisis, the Americans would find a thousand and one reasons why the Canadian government need not be consulted, their close relations with the Canadian forces notwithstanding.

After 1962, Canadian governments had some difficulty visualizing a function for the military that would be as important, or as useful, as the role Canadian soldiers, sailors, and airmen had played so well in past wars. If eliminating the Canadian forces was excluded as a practical possibility because it would disturb opinion at home and abroad, and if reductions could only go so far, it made political sense to use the armed forces for other purposes.

Some of these purposes were in place by the 1960s. The military had always promoted a limited form of industrial policy to ensure its own supplies, and it had traditionally recruited in areas of low skills and high unemployment. These two functions became more important in the 1970s as the government strove to encourage industry and to fight against regional economic disparities. As obsolescence took its toll of the armed forces' planes, ships, and tanks, the government was willing to consider replacements, but only in the context of spin-offs that might keep employment up, and only within the limits established by the government's other, more important, priorities.

Those limits were severe. Although Ottawa ran a budget surplus until the early 1970s, the armed forces were placed on a strict regimen of $1.8 billion in current dollars. That meant that their budget was steadily contracting as costs rose, in itself a sign of admirable restraint if the government's intention actually was to fight inflation. Unfortunately, the financial policy of the Trudeau government directly contributed to inflation – and to the miseries of the military. Moreover, throughout the 1970s, the government 'connived at an erosion of its own tax base and a further increase in its uncontrollable outlays.'[1]

Fiscal misery was compounded by other factors. The armed forces were still struggling to adjust to unification, begun under Lester Pearson's government. Bilingualism, the *idée fixe* of the Trudeau government, was imposed on them. Perceived weakness in the bureaucracy at National Defence Headquarters invited intervention from the managers at the Privy Council Office – and it came.

Above all, however, there was the suspicion, fast hardening into certainty, that Pierre Trudeau regarded the military as little more than an expensive bargaining chip, to be employed in deals among ministers, in negotiations with Canada's allies, and in transactions between Ottawa and the provinces. These were not unimportant. But as for the defence of Canada, North America, and the West, Trudeau believed that rested in the hands of the Americans and their nuclear deterrent. Should the deterrent fail, what would happen afterwards mattered very little.

Donald Macdonald became minister of national defence on 24 September 1970. For two years he had been president of the Privy Council and government House leader, a post he hated. In his view, the prime minister 'owed me one,' and when Léo Cadieux left the cabinet to become ambassador to France, Macdonald asked for the Defence portfolio. That he was interested in DND must have struck observers as surprising. Macdonald had been a supporter of unification and one of the most vociferous advocates of withdrawal from Canada's European NATO commitments, if not from the alliance entirely. But he was ambitious, young (thirty-eight years old), and DND was a big, expensive portfolio for a hitherto junior minister.

As Macdonald recalled, the prime minister personally gave him his mandate. It was no easy task. His primary tasks were to raise the military's morale and to develop a defence-policy statement. He had to accept the budget freeze and to consider the NATO decision of April 1969 as final – in other words, whatever his personal inclinations, he was not to press for more money or further troop cuts.[2]

The new minister was in office for only two weeks or so when the October Crisis erupted with the kidnapping by Le Front de Libération du Québec first of British Trade Commissioner James Cross and then of Quebec's labour minister, Pierre Laporte. Cross was recovered alive and well in December, but Laporte was murdered by his captors as Ottawa invoked the War Measures Act to deal with an 'apprehended insurrection.' In an atmosphere of public and governmental panic, the armed forces responded quickly and professionally to the government's call. Up to 7500 troops were moved in very quickly for domestic peacekeeping duties,[3] and to assist on the intelligence side which the RCMP and Quebec Provincial Police seemed to be bungling.[4] For the first time since Trudeau came to power in April 1968 the Canadian Armed Forces felt themselves needed and wanted by the Canadian public. Morale briefly skyrocketed among English- and French-speaking servicemen; those who may have had doubts about the forces' Québécois personnel were pleasantly surprised by their complete loyalty.[5] Whether the crisis had any effect on Trudeau's attitude to the military, we cannot say; it certainly produced no increase in the defence budget.

Macdonald's next task was to establish a policy framework for his department. That might be difficult. The prime minister did not care for the department's point of view, or its methods of argumentation. DND projects were held up in cabinet; approvals or disapprovals simply did not issue forth, even on subjects such as Strategic Air Command overflights of Canadian territory. Whether his senior officials were incompetent or merely outmoded, Macdonald clearly needed a new point of departure. For that, in the fall of 1970, he turned to someone new.

Gordon Smith was a recently minted graduate with a PHD from the

Massachusetts Institute of Technology, a 'defence intellectual' in a country where the term was still considered an oxymoron. He had recognized the problem by leaving the Defence Research Board for External Affairs in 1967, and External posted him to NATO headquarters where Macdonald, who had come to know him during a study group on defence, met him again and reinforced an already favourable impression. A deal was soon struck: Smith joined the minister's staff, with an assignment to produce a white paper on defence. By the time the paperwork had been processed and Smith was back in Ottawa, he had a first draft ready for Macdonald's perusal.

Smith's bible was Trudeau's own utterances, especially his April 1969 statement on defence. On 3 April the prime minister, apparently without any DND advice,[6] had defined the armed forces' roles as the protection of sovereignty, the defence of North America, the fulfilment of NATO commitments, and peacekeeping. Although DND and other department planners had difficulty deciding just what the defence of sovereignty meant and devoted substantial time to trying to reach an agreed understanding,[7] Smith had no such difficulty. He worked out a logical Canadian national-interest approach, something that appealed to Macdonald and to the prime minister. And he agreed that there was no direct military threat to Canada in an era of détente. The only danger to this country lay in an unlikely Soviet-American war, and to Smith that possibility, however remote, required Canada to maintain its anti-submarine warfare role and its air-defence role in NORAD as a contribution to the protection of the American nuclear-deterrent force. That danger of nuclear war also implied that the defence of Europe was in the Canadian interest, since any Third World War was likely to arise from East-West confrontation there.

With that conceptual framework in place, Smith worked through the material with Macdonald in an easy, stimulating way. The minister did not share Smith's positive attitude to NATO, but he found himself persuaded by arguments that stressed, not common values and history, but Canadian security interests. Smith then spent substantial time with officials in the PMO and PCO, especially Ivan Head. Once Head was satisfied, Smith concluded, correctly, that Trudeau would be as well. That left only DND itself where Canadian Forces officers tended towards a 'realist' perception of the Soviet military threat and objected to the white paper as, one analyst put it, 'simply an expedient to reduce the already starved defence budget.'[8] The minister was said to have responded to criticism by stating that the draft was final and not to be changed without direct and personal reference to him.[9]

Despite Smith's advance work, Macdonald suffered through a series

of delays in getting cabinet to consider his white paper in the spring of
1971, once even walking out of the cabinet room in anger at yet another
postponement.[10] When, finally, the prime minister allowed the draft to
be discussed, it quickly received approval.[11] Macdonald's white paper –
and his command of it – had impressed all his colleagues. But there was
one incident during the cabinet's discussion that lingered in Transport
Minister Don Jamieson's mind:

> Don Macdonald wanted a very minor revision in his budget, just a few million
> dollars ... most of us saw it as routine, because with such a large budget and
> with the inevitable short-falls in certain types of expenditures etc. by the end
> of the year the odds are that Defence will not have spent all of its allocation ...
> Yet, the P.M. made a big thing out of the fact that this represented a departure
> from the earlier decision to freeze defence spending ... Mitchell Sharp, Ben
> Benson, myself and others argued that the proposed procedure was insignificant.
> The P.M., however, took a lot of persuading on the principle involved and finally
> agreed, only after words were added to the paper, that cosmetically, at least,
> covered the situation.

Jamieson was puzzled by this discussion, speculating that Trudeau was
'inordinately reluctant to change. He may take a long time to reach a
conclusion and to explore all shades of opinion, but, once having moved
(as with the war measures act!) he is tenacious even to the point of
unreasonable stubbornness.'[12] Or, perhaps, Trudeau disliked DND and
the military to such an extent, even after October 1970, that he was
most reluctant to spend a penny more than agreed on the department.
   Released on 24 August 1971, the white paper measured fifty pages. It
charted a course for the future and provided a rationale for the decisions
on defence thus far made by the Trudeau government.
   In the aftermath of the October Crisis, internal security naturally had
a high priority and, the white paper said, Canada had to be able 'to
cope effectively with any future resort to disruption, intimidation and
violence.' Such crises were primarily the responsibility of the civil authorities, but they could rely on 'timely assistance from the Forces.' At the
same time, the white paper looked to the protection of sovereignty
in the Arctic, something that seemed essential in the wake of the SS
Manhattan's 1970 voyage, and to the use of the military on tasks of
'National Development.' That included assistance in natural disasters,
scientific research, communications, and protecting the environment,
especially in the north and on the coasts. However important those tasks
were, their inclusion in a Defence white paper shook fighting soldiers,

sailors, and airmen at first. But soon the military recognized that one way to get equipment in the era of budget freezes was to say that it was necessary for internal security or national development. A helicopter was a helicopter, even if it had to be festooned with lights and loud hailers to win the approval of the Treasury Board!

North American defence received substantial attention. Macdonald's paper announced the retirement of the Bomarc anti-aircraft missiles, installed at such political cost early in the 1960s. But NORAD remained and was due for renewal in 1973, even if the Soviet bomber threat had diminished and even though the resources devoted by the United States to NORAD had similarly declined. 'The policy of the Government at that time with respect to the agreement and the interceptor force posture required will depend on the strategic situation extant.' In the meantime, while continuing to fly CF-101 Voodoo aircraft armed with nuclear weapons ('there is at present no alternative to equipping the CF-101s with nuclear warheads ... Only with such weapons would they have a reasonable prospect of destroying attacking bombers'), the government was not 'prepared to devote substantial sums to new equipment or facilities for use only for active anti-bomber defences.' The white paper, much as Gordon Smith had planned, also resolved a long-standing controversy with the United States, though the final decision was not taken by cabinet until 2 December 1971; SAC bombers could continue to refuel at Goose Bay and to overfly Canada.[13]

In Europe, the policy was to maintain the 5000-man force and, the white paper said, 'the Government has no plans for further reductions.' But the land component was to lose its old Centurion tanks and to have in their place 'a light, tracked, direct-fire-support vehicle' that could be moved by air. Just what those vehicles were to do was never made clear. The air component of the NATO force, three squadrons of CF-104s with two in a nuclear-strike role, was also to be modified. All three squadrons by 1972 would assume a tactical support role. And while continuing to support the Canadian role in anti-submarine warfare, the 'Government believes Canada's maritime forces must be reoriented with the long term objective of providing a more versatile general purpose capability.' How that was to be accomplished in the teeth of a budget freeze remained unspecified.

Finally, peacekeeping also continued as a priority, though cautiously. Canada would accept peacekeeping roles only if the terms of reference for a UN force were realistic; for example, 'a consensus by all parties on the purposes which the operation was intended to serve and the manner in which it was to discharge its responsibilities.'[14] There was no unwillingness to serve, to be sure, but Canada had to be certain there was the prospect of success. By 1971 the UN force in Cyprus had been there for seven years, and the parties had not advanced one inch towards settlement. By 1984, when Trudeau left office, UNFICYP was still on the ground in Cyprus and some Canadian senior NCOs had served seven or eight tours there.

The white paper also pledged to press bilingualism forward and announced that a Management Review Group had been created to examine the organization of the entire Department of National Defence. Its report was expected in the summer of 1972.[15]

Criticism of the white paper was relatively muted. The defence commentator John Gellner called it 'sensible' and noted that 'at long last' participation in common defence efforts had been replaced by 'the concept of the defence of Canada as the main task.'[16] Peyton Lyon believed the emphasis on sovereignty was misplaced, and marvelled at DND's numbers that showed that 48.3 per cent of the defence budget was devoted to 'Canadian Security.'[17] Such a number, of course, was the product of the 1970 committee to define sovereignty and its conclusion, as John Anderson remembered, 'that everything the military did that wasn't directed at a military threat' was protection of sovereignty. 'It's all absolute nonsense,' he admitted cheerfully.[18] There were the predictable attacks from the left (get out of NATO and NORAD) and the right (more guns everywhere), but the general thrust of public response was likely expressed best by Douglas Harkness, John Diefenbaker's minister of national defence: 'The 1971 white paper on defence is more realistic in its approach than was that of 1964. This is particularly apparent in its acceptance of the realities of the Canadian, North American, and world situations and in its statement of the priorities for Canadian defence policy.'[19] That grasp of the realities also gratified the Nixon administration in Washington.[20]

Macdonald's next task was more painful. The white paper called for the establishment of a Management Review Group to study the 'relationships between the military, civil and research organizations of the Department' so as 'to ensure effective planning and control.'[21]

If that was the prescription, what was the diagnosis? It was all too common for Ottawa bureaucrats to argue that DND suffered from administrative and intellectual failure at its heart. Such a disease was far from rare in the federal bureaucracy in the 1970s, and the remedy, the establishment of a systems staff, was already hallowed by American experience in Robert McNamara's Pentagon.[22] But as one student of DND has argued, 'The real dilemma of the government was that they had established defence objectives from which they could not escape but which they did not wish to honour. They attributed their difficulty to many things but mainly to a recalcitrant system of administration in DND and the CF that kept placing the dilemma before their eyes. A main thrust of the White Paper, therefore, was administrative. In particular, Macdonald intended to discipline the management system in order to gain control of the policy options offered to the Minister.'[23]

There was surely some truth in that assessment, but there were other factors present as well. In the first place, as Michael Pitfield remembered, the Department of National Defence was isolated and insignificant with no one who could stand up for defence policy. Only the prime minister, the defence minister, and the external affairs minister had any interest in defence,[24] and Trudeau, quite obviously, was cool to the whole idea and had no respect for the intelligence of the generals – they were drones who carried out the orders of people such as he.[25] Moreover, one general recalled, the military and civilian sides of the department formed two solitudes: all financial authority rested with the deputy minister while the military had the responsibility for operations. In other words, though the forces had the operational responsibility, they had no control of the money necessary to pay for them, and that required clearance through the 'mini-Treasury Board' in the deputy minister's office. 'There was an isolation of the uniformed personnel from the bureaucracy,' he said, 'and the soldiers were not attuned to the realities.'[26] Yet, according to another senior officer, apart from money, the military ran 'untrammelled.' The deputy minister's writ stopped at his office door, his primary influence being his ability to control spending.[27]

Still another factor was that the department had not seemed able to control contracting and procurement effectively. The most flagrant example was the way the costs for a 1966–7 refitting of the HMCS *Bonaventure,* the navy's only aircraft carrier, had soared from $5.7 million to $12.3 million. In September 1969 the government announced that the carrier was to be retired.[28]

Most important of all was the fact that the Defence Council, the senior committee within the department made up of the deputy minister, the chief of the Defence Staff, and the chair of the Defence Research Board, along with other officers as members, seemed to be incapable of producing recommendations, so pronounced was the infighting. The civilians fought with the military, and the Treasury Board, Privy Council Office, and other deputy ministers, naturally enough, preferred to accept the advice of Elgin Armstrong, DND's deputy until 1971, over that of the generals.[29] What Canada needed, Macdonald decided, was a system like that in Britain's integrated civil-military Ministry of Defence, where the career public servants worked well with the military men.[30] For all these reasons, Macdonald decided to move ahead with the MRG study.

In charge was John Pennefather of Montreal, chair of the board of IAC Ltd, who had five members on his group: two businessmen, reporter John Harbron of Thomson Newspapers, one general, and one DND public servant. The MRG, assisted by a substantial staff, produced nine staff papers and a report for the minister. As E.J. Benson, the minister from January to August 1972, told the House of Commons Standing Committee on External Affairs and National Defence:

The principal point is that steps must be taken to overcome the duplication which now results from the parallel structures in the department. I am referring here to the organizations of the Deputy Minister, the Chief of the Defence Staff and the Chairman of the Defence Research Board. The problem is that there are not sufficiently clear lines of authority drawn and consequently responsibility is sometimes less than obvious. The system also tends to produce a layering of responsibility between the military and civilian staffs.

What Mr. Pennefather has recommended is an approach to bring together the department into a single structure with clear lines of authority and responsibility. This makes a great deal of sense.[31]

The MRG reported in the summer of 1972, its recommendations fleshed out in detail.[32]

By that time, however, DND had a new deputy minister in Sylvain Cloutier, who had come from the Treasury Board and the Department of National Revenue in September 1971 at Trudeau's request and with the strong support of Macdonald. Cloutier came from an old civil-service family. He knew bureaucratic politics – some said that he embodied them. He had been brought in quite deliberately to shake up DND's organization or, as one senior PMO official put it later, DND, like External Affairs, had to have its frame of mind changed. Early in 1972 General Jacques Dextraze, a tough fighting leader with exemplary service in the Second World War and Korea and hitherto chief of personnel at Canadian Forces Headquarters, was named chief of the Defence Staff [CDS], though he did not assume office until September after spending six months as special assistant to the chief of the Defence Staff (Reorganization).[33] These two men, Dextraze and Cloutier, were to implement the MRG report in a modified form.[34]

The MRG had proposed that the deputy outrank the CDS. But the basis of the new structure put in place by Cloutier and Dextraze on 2 October 1972 (and altered slightly on 1 February 1973) was the complete equality of the two, although this remained undefined.[35] Their goal was cooperation between the military and civilian heads of the department in a new National Defence Headquarters that numbered some 10,000 military and civilian personnel, but was still a single entity. Dextraze and Cloutier worked together for five years and never disagreed with each other in the myriad of departmental committees and meetings they attended. (In private, it could be a different matter.) Nor did they overstep the parameters laid down in the Pennefather Report: Cloutier was responsible for management and Dextraze for operations. What they did was to integrate activities that had necessarily been parallel under the old structure. Before the MRG, the deputy minister's office was substantial with almost 400 on staff, the number needed so that the civilian staff could assess and approve requests coming from the military. But under the integrated structure such a staff theoretically was unnecessary. The result was that the deputy's personal staff fell to a relative handful, with a single unified staff serving both Cloutier and Dextraze.

To operate the new structure, and to give DND proposals a better chance of acceptance at the Treasury Board, Cloutier named a senior Treasury Board officer as assistant deputy minister for materiel in 1972, and a senior executive from the business world, who accepted a substantial cut in pay to take on the challenge of working in DND, to become financial administrator. He also saw the need, in an attempt to escape the Department of External Affairs' tutelage, for an assistant deputy minister for policy. In future, as when the government was planning for the supervisory Vietnam role in 1972, DND was involved in policy making from the outset.

Nonetheless, there were serious concerns from many senior officers about the new system. Could the armed forces function properly if managers, both civilian and military, had precedence over commanders? The new organization might be more efficient (though some doubted even that), but could it fight?[36] Would the 'civilianization' that Cloutier and Dextraze had imposed get more money for the armed forces? Would it affect the professionalism of the military and weaken further the sense of identity that unification had already shaken so severely?[37]

The new system had its supporters at headquarters in Ottawa, but there were few elsewhere. As early as 1972, before the Cloutier reforms, a DND committee reported that Canadian Forces Headquarters 'has little or no credibility in the field,' and that headquarters was seen as 'an entity unto its own which is incapable of managing itself.'[38] A 1979 study for

Joe Clark's Conservative government condemned the 'influx of civilians into positions of great influence'; altogether these reforms had a 'detrimental effect on operations, due to civilian personnel who work fixed hours, are expensive in overtime, cost less per individual but more per job ... and have a right to strike.' That was bad enough, but the civilians in the department were also permanent staff, unlike the military staff who changed their posts frequently, with the result that 'they tend to provide the continuity and seem to have an undue influence.' The result, Mobile Command said, 'is civilian management, rather than civilian control.'[39]

Economy first, and then organization. Language policy was next. The Canadian forces had always been unilingually English. That characteristic had severely hampered recruiting in two world wars and had helped create the atmosphere in which conscription, one of the most divisive issues in our history, sorely tested governments and the country. Other than the Royal 22e Régiment which had three battalions of largely French-speaking infantry, the forces operated and functioned in English.

Léo Cadieux, the minister of national defence who cracked military unilingualism, was the first French-speaking defence minister in this century. He had assumed the portfolio on 19 September 1967 after serving as associate minister since February 1965. Within ten weeks, he proposed to Prime Minister Pearson that French-speaking units be created and based at Valcartier, Quebec, an idea that had been pressed forward by General Jean Allard, the first chief of the Defence Staff and the first francophone to climb to the top of Canada's military hierarchy.[40] The base north of Quebec City was to house the Van Doos, an artillery regiment, an armoured regiment, and associated combat and support units 'whose cadres,' Cadieux said, 'will be filled with French-speaking personnel.' He also proposed that a francophone air-force squadron equipped with CF-5 aircraft be based at Bagotville, Quebec.[41]

In the difficult atmosphere of late 1967, with Charles de Gaulle's 'Vive le Québec libre' still resonating and with separatism gaining ground, Cadieux's proposals seemed peculiarly ill-timed to some officials close to Pearson. Marc Lalonde in the Prime Minister's Office was blunt: 'We should avoid very carefully the concentration of these French-speaking forces inside Quebec ... We have to think here of the problems that such a concentration would cause in the case of a very serious political upheaval in the Province of Quebec.' He added that 'I don't want to sound unduly pessimistic, but we should avoid providing the Government of Quebec with a ready-made Army at its disposal.'[42] From the

Privy Council Office, Michael Pitfield offered the same advice, calling Cadieux's proposal 'one of the most potentially dangerous decisions that the Federal government could ever take ... I submit that ... unilingual French-Canadian units concentrated in Quebec could – in the circumstances of our times, and with the trends that are likely to become even more powerful in the future – irrevocably lay the groundwork for an exceedingly dangerous situation.'[43]

Nonetheless, Cadieux persisted and got what he asked for. His submission went to cabinet in January 1968, won acceptance in March, and was announced on 2 April, a few days before the Liberal leadership convention put Pierre Trudeau into power. The minister said that although francophones volunteered in rough proportion to their representation in the population, only some 15 per cent of the forces' strength was French-speaking. In other words, French-speaking servicemen and women left the forces at a higher rate than their anglophone compatriots. To overcome this problem, Cadieux said that French Language Units (FLUs) were to be created, within which a francophone could work in French. HMCS *Ottawa,* a destroyer based in Halifax, became the first FLU, a decision immediately denounced by retired Rear Admiral Jeffry Brock as 'sheer, unadulterated lunacy.'[44] The CF-5 squadron (No. 433) to be formed at Bagotville was similarly designated, and 30 per cent of the Canadian Airborne Regiment were to be French-speaking. Cadieux also announced a French-language trades training school for Saint-Jean, Quebec, and the centralization of French-language recruit training there in a program that came to be known as FRANCOTRAIN. As the minister said, 'Now, we're going to have a 22e of the sea and a 22e of the air.'[45]

By 1969, when the Royal Commission on Bilingualism and Biculturalism issued its report covering the Department of National Defence, the 5e Groupement de Combat had come into being. This was Cadieux and Allard's Valcartier-based French-speaking brigade, and the commission hailed its creation as 'the most important development.'[46] Little else about DND's efforts drew praise, the commission concluding that the prevailing assumption in the forces was 'that the English language must be used in all military activities unless there is a specific provision to the contrary.' The equality of the two languages had to be recognized.[47]

There was a long way to go to achieve this equality in the Canadian Armed Forces. One Royal 22e Régiment battalion commander had the task of moving his unit from northern Germany to Lahr after the reduction in the Canadian NATO force in 1969. The Van Doos were French-speaking, of course, but the air force operating the new base was unilingually English and resistant to change – so resistant that when General

Laubman inspected the Van Doos in 1969 he was astounded to discover that the men spoke no English. 'The joke's gone on long enough,' he told the battalion commander. 'Tell your men to speak English to me.' Protests that the men were unable to do so were to no avail. Similarly, the regiment's officers were told not to use French in their mess. Only the sheer weight of numbers forced a change in policy, the Van Doos' Commanding Officer remembered.[48]

When parliament passed the Official Languages Act in 1969, enshrining the concept of bilingualism, the Department of National Defence quickly moved to prepare a 'Bilingual Policy for the Canadian Armed Forces' and an implementation program.[49] In the blizzard of recommendations, one fact stood out: the forces' aim was to have 28 per cent of its strength francophone over a period of several years. The military also insisted that the merit principle had to take precedence over the need for linguistic balance. 'To ignore it would be disastrous to both groups and perhaps even more to the francophone element ... the demands made on any individual of one particular language group must be exactly the same as that of the other language group.' The CDS was told that this principle had to be made clear, 'for too many seem to have a misconception of this.'[50] In the next few years, the merit principle was abused at times as officers needed to command FLUs were pushed upward in rank.

By the next year, however, the emphasis had changed slightly. While the 28 per cent figure remained and while bilingualism was to continue as policy, the prime minister had stated that equal opportunity meant that qualified francophones with little or no knowledge of English had to have the same opportunity as anglophones with limited comprehension of French.[51] The armed forces accepted this stipulation, as they had to, deciding to make provision for 'at least 50% of our Francophones to serve in French language units.' What that meant in overall terms was that with a force strength of 83,000, there should be 59,760 anglophones and 23,240 francophones. Precisely 33,347 service personnel were to serve in English-language units 'manned at the national ratio of 72% Anglophones/28% Francophones,' and 11,620 francophones were to serve in FLUs whose strength, with their anglophone component, was to be 14,525. The plans called for the FLUs to be spread across the country, including ships based in British Columbia, a radar squadron in Beausé-jour, Man., a transport squadron in Trenton, Ont., and a rescue squadron on PEI.[52]

The complications that such linguistic duality could produce were evident, and General Allard, by now retired as CDS, expressed his concern to Donald Macdonald in August 1971. What worried the general was that anglophone officers were being posted to command of FLUs, 'positions that should be reserved for French Canadians.' Moreover, he argued, FLUs were used 'as a language training school for young anglophone officers.' The armoured regiment at Valcartier had twenty young English-speaking officers. 'If we are short of officers, we should adjust the recruiting quotas and our training methods to fill these vacancies by obtaining French Canadian officers.'[53]

That was the difficulty. DND had to struggle to find francophone officers to raise the officer and enlisted ranks to the desired 28/72 ratio. Such a goal was not always supported, even at the top. James Richardson, the minister for four years after November 1972, was extraordinarily cool to bilingualism. One senior francophone official remembered being asked by Richardson what he was working on. 'Bilingualism.' 'It's not a priority,' Richardson replied. 'It's mine,' said the official, who regarded the minister as a 'horse's ass.' Richardson always tried to stall progress on bilingualism, with the result that Trudeau had to be invoked to set him straight.[54]

General Dextraze also had his difficulties with the 'well-meaning' Richardson over bilingualism. 'Do you think you can just bury six million French Canadians? They won't lie down.' Bilingualism cost too much, the minister would reply, and Dextrase, an explosive personality, remembers telling Richardson to 'just speak French' if the cost of bilingualism worried him so much.[55] Richardson duly resigned in October 1976 because of his objections to the Trudeau government's 'B&B' policies.

Did the 'B&B' program work in DND? In 1976–7, for example, 4389 servicemen and women took language training, 2625 of whom were anglophones.[56] And the numbers of francophones in the forces rose substantially. In 1966, 15.8 per cent of armed forces strength was French-speaking; in 1976, 23.18 per cent; in 1982, 26.9 per cent. That was progress, though the percentage of francophone officers in those same years was only 9.4, 18.99, and 21.46, respectively.[57]

Still there were difficulties, not least aboard ship as the navy remained the least sympathetic service in its attitude to bilingualism. The FLU ships were as efficient as others, Admirals Richard Leir and Bobbie Murdoch remembered, but they had to be bilingual because NATO operated in English. That caused problems, though Leir, director-general recruiting and training from 1968 to 1970 and chief of maritime operations from 1973 to 1976, believed that francophone officers had not had a fair chance in the old Royal Canadian Navy and supported the program.[58] Other officers were less happy. Lieutenant-General Allan MacKenzie saw a severe operational impact on the air force because of the necessity to scour units for francophones so FLUs could be manned. Moreover, he maintained, some promotions occurred strictly because of language, and experienced francophones sometimes asked if their promotion was 'part of the charade.'[59] Major-General W.C. Leonard, who had commanded the Canadian forces in Europe, recalled that bilingualism sometimes meant that 'like breasts, we had to have two of everything.' Some French-speakers, he added, counted lines in *The Beaver*, the CFE newspaper, to be sure they got equal space.[60]

All in all, however, the Canadian Armed Forces' experience with bilingualism must be judged a partial success. More francophones than ever before had joined the services and, as they could now operate in their own language a substantial portion of the time, more were staying in the military. Anglophones were trying to become bilingual, though there were no regulations making it a requirement that officers be bilingual and become progressively more so as they rose in rank.[61] As bilingualism was a national goal, the Department of National Defence had to do its part. To its credit it tried to do so and achieved a record of some success.

The Canadian forces struggled through the 1970s to deal with the successive shocks administered by the Trudeau government. Bilingualism, headquarters reorganization, new roles, and no money all hurt morale and force efficiency. But most difficult of all to deal with, at least in the early years of the decade, was unification, the legacy left to the Canadian forces by Paul Hellyer, Lester Pearson's defence minister.

Unification was especially difficult because most senior officers and a very high percentage of junior officers and men actively disliked Hellyer's plan. As General Dextraze said in a letter to the forces when he became CDS in 1972, 'Like most servicemen, I had some initial apprehension about unification.'[62] That was true enough, and Dextraze himself thought that Hellyer simply did not understand the devotion to their regiments or ships felt by navy and army officers and men. But Dextraze was a realist too, and so ultimately were most officers and men. 'What you do,' he said, 'is fight against the idea, lose, and then try to make the new system work.'[63]

That was hard. In Maritime Command, for example, problems existed as the sea and air components of the command merged together, most notably at the junior-officer and senior-enlisted-rank levels.[64] There were difficulties with the training of specialists. 'You couldn't have an army cook on a ship,' Admiral Richard Leir, once director-general training at headquarters, remembered. 'The cook wouldn't be on the team and couldn't handle other roles.' Moreover, he continued, the much-proclaimed reduction in trades specialties that unification was said to have produced was largely bogus. 'In technical areas, one environment's needs were different from the others with the result that the navy had to run unofficial training schools for those specialists emerging from the central schools.' That cost money and took time.[65] So too did the necessity of documenting and presenting equipment and personnel requirements in a unified force. 'In a single service,' one senior officer noted, 'while the documents might be required ... the length and composition would be quite different, i.e. simpler and more to the point ... In other words, in a single service you don't have to teach grandma how to suck eggs.'[66]

Other problems were small but especially frustrating. Military ranks had been made equivalent among the three environments, but slightly different pay and allowances scales existed in some of the ranks. That caused outrage for some. Another example, cited by Léo Cadieux, was the definition of musician: one who could play two instruments and read music. Did that mean that a piper was no musician? Cadieux overcame his heritage to decide that pipers definitely were musicians. Then there were uniforms. No one liked the new green uniforms issued to all three services, especially the navy which feared ridicule from sailors of other nations. Cadieux was willing to allow traditional blue naval uniforms to be worn aboard ship, although DND would not issue them. Nonetheless, he recollected how surprised he was, as ambassador to France, to greet the crew of HMCS *Ottawa* in green uniforms. The whole process was one of trial and error, he remembered.[67]

Still, unification had its successes. The unification of the supply services had reduced the number of depots from fifteen to four, saved money, and resulted in a smaller 'tail to teeth' ratio than in most other countries.[68] At the same time, Canada had a very high ratio of general officers to troops on active service, compared to Britain or France or most other countries, and the proportion had increased by more than a quarter after 1972.[69] Basic training camps had been consolidated, reducing the number from eleven to two, while thirty specialized training schools did the work previously handled by ninety-one. All basic officer training was held at one camp. The number of tri-service committees that had bedevilled DND was reduced, for a time, and National Defence Headquarters had been reduced from 12,000 personnel before unification to 8000. A single capital equipment acquisition process replaced the three that had existed before unification, and there was now one intelligence system, one communications system, one supply system, and one recruiting system.[70] All of this lowered costs, though by how much was difficult to determine in a period characterized by the budget freeze, declining military manpower, and the rapid inflation that hit the country and the Canadian forces in the mid-1970s. As the chief of the Defence Staff and the department's deputy minister noted in 1978, 'DND may have survived both the personnel rundown and the decade of underspending in capital largely because of unification. Without unification, rivalry amongst the three services for diminishing resources might very well have eroded both morale and effectiveness to the point where the Department would have been unable to convince the Government to authorize modest increases in defence spending.'[71] Nonetheless, the doubts about the idea of uniting three services in one persisted in the Canadian forces, and especially in the ranks of the Progressive Conservative party. When Joe Clark led his party to a minority victory in the election of 1979, the opportunity for another look at unification seemed at hand.

Clark's minister of national defence, Allan McKinnon, sixty-two, had served in the army during the war and remained in the forces into the peace. He had retired in 1965 as a major and first won election to the House of Commons seven years later from Victoria. His party's victory had been greeted with almost perceptible sighs of relief from the Canadian forces, but that mood did not last long. The new minister demonstrated very quickly that he was in over his head. McKinnon had difficulty taking a briefing or making decisions; he was evidently whipsawed by his deputy minister, C.R. ('Buzz') Nixon, between his desire to see changes in policy and warnings that changes could produce chaos. He virtually refused to hold meetings with Admiral Robert Falls, the chief of the Defence Staff, and he kept his Parliament Hill office as his prime working space. To some in the Department of National Defence, Major McKinnon seemed to be awed by senior officers and frightened by the bureaucrats.[72]

Although the Conservatives in opposition had promised to increase the defence budget and the size of the forces, McKinnon in his few months in office was unable to achieve anything in those directions.[73] The only area in which he achieved a pre-election goal, in part, was on the question of unification. McKinnon was obviously no admirer of Paul Hellyer's policy, but he was unable to get the department to launch the major review of it that he wanted. As he said later, Nixon and Falls had the attitude, 'Why should we reopen that can of worms? We don't want to stir up that mess.' There were potential supporters of the minister's opposition to unification, notably in the commanders of Maritime, Air, and Mobile Commands, who wanted to increase their influence on policy, and in the reserve forces. Many senior officers saw the Nixon-

Falls position as a patent attempt to preserve NDHQ's dominance over the commanders in the field, but McKinnon apparently could not build an effective coalition of officers in support of his efforts. After what he described as repeated attempts to persuade him to abandon his review, McKinnon and his personal staff acted on their own.[74] On 6 September 1979 the minister created a five-person Task Force on Review of Unification under George Fyffe, a retired businessman, and directed it to report by the end of January next.[75]

The task force's members travelled widely, interviewed service personnel of all ranks, held hearings, and received briefs and briefings beyond count. Perhaps to the members' surprise, unification was by no means universally detested. An analysis of briefs presented to the task force prepared by Dr Albert Legault, one of its members, found that 22.4 per cent opposed unification and 14.5 per cent favoured it, with the rest generally lukewarm in their support or opposition. Individuals were happier than associations, Legault concluded. Still, there seemed little doubt that morale was low,[76] and the task force found 'constant evidence' of 'internal stress and professional concern, frustration, even gloom.' Unification, however, was not entirely to blame. Budgetary problems had contributed enormously to the malaise, and some briefs to the task force made that point very strongly. 'Inflation,' noted Dr J.C. Arnell, previously an assistant deputy minister in National Defence and a special assistant to the deputy minister, 'was probably the main cause of any general decline in the Canadian Armed Forces.'[77]

The task force's report, received six weeks late on 15 March 1980, almost a month after the election that returned the Trudeau Liberals to power, made thirty recommendations, including one calling for a return to distinctive uniforms for the three services and another for changes in the command structure to ensure more 'environmental' – that is, army, navy, and air force – input into decision making. As Fyffe put it in a memorandum, the heads of the three services had to be in Ottawa with a Chiefs of Staff organization that would reduce the civilianization of the Canadian forces. The three services needed 'a voice at the table' to put the 'focus back on operations.'[78] Surprisingly, however, considering its origin, the task force did not recommend the undoing of unification; indeed, it explicitly endorsed the continuation of a single supply system for the forces.[79]

The Liberals' new defence minister was another veteran, Gilles Lamontagne, who set up a three-man Review Group under Major-General Jack Vance on 7 May 1980 to appraise the Fyffe report. Its report, delivered on 31 August, walked carefully in the political minefield of undoing unification but nonetheless accepted twenty-three of the Fyffe recommendations in whole or in part, including the necessity to open the policy process to the environmental commanders. The idea of distinctive uniforms, however, was rejected.[80] That measure had to await the coming to power of another Conservative government in 1984.

The navy had been hardest hit by the whole process of unification, psychologically and in operational efficiency. The Royal Canadian Navy had been very efficient in its anti-submarine role in the 1960s, skilfully using its destroyers, the carrier HMCS *Bonaventure* and its air component, a task that was deemed so complicated that only a naval officer could fill the posts of chief of staff at headquarters in Halifax and Victoria. But there were no new ships, except for four DDH 280 ships, helicopter-equipped destroyers that were too far along the procurement process to be cancelled by the Trudeau government when it came to power.

The prime minister himself was no admirer of the country's anti-submarine role. In cabinet on 20 May 1969, for example, Trudeau had sharply questioned the director-general of operations – maritime, on hand to make a presentation. If, Trudeau said, 'it were assumed that Canadian destroyers could closely identify and track Soviet submarines and if it were assumed that no offensive action would be taken by those Canadian destroyers, then what value would there be in acquiring knowledge of the submarine's location?' Indeed, he went on, what was the value of the present Canadian maritime program? 'Destroyers only become totally effective if they can attack and destroy. If Canadian destroyers attacked in the first instance without warning then the allies would have instigated a nuclear attack. That possibility must be ruled out. If destroyers were attacking submarines, then it must be assumed that a nuclear exchange through ICBMs or bombers had already taken place. At that point it would be difficult to maintain that there was any deterrent value in the destroyer program ... In other words,' Trudeau said in words that must have cast a chill over the navy, 'are destroyers really needed for this type of activity and, in particular, is there a need for 24 destroyers,' the number scheduled for service in 1972–3? The DDH 280s came into use in the early 1970s.[81] For the rest, as might have been predicted given the prime minister's attitude, there was only a Destroyer Extension Life Expectancy Programme [DELEX] designed to squeeze a few more years out of the rusting hulks the navy operated. So bad was the situation that vacuum tubes, absolutely necessary to operate the navy's ancient equipment and no longer produced in the West, had to be purchased in Eastern Europe.

The Defence Structure Review of 1974–5 forced the government to examine the navy's role once more. Some ministers took the view that Canada had no obligation to help keep sea lanes to Europe clear. If Canada was to get new ships, they favoured 'sovereignty' ships, in effect a lightly armed fleet similar to those used by the United States Coast Guard. That meant the effective end of a blue-water navy. Other ministers argued that Canada did have its obligations and that it needed a navy; they wanted conventional naval warships. The decisive argument, tilting the balance to the warships, was cost. Sovereignty vessels were estimated to cost two-thirds the price of naval ships, a small difference given the extra capacity provided.[82] It was a naval victory, one that was confirmed in 1977 when the cabinet authorized DND to proceed with the first stages of a program for the acquisition of six patrol frigates. Contracts were let in 1983 for these ships,[83] three years after the DELEX Project had been accepted. Both programs were an indication that the Macdonald white paper was beginning to be swept aside.

The army too had its problems. The unification of the support services had resulted in 'a significant decline in expertise and capability' for the land forces.[84] There were too few men and there was not enough modern equipment for the tasks to which Mobile Command and the troops in Lahr under NATO were committed. The most pressing need was for a new tank, but the Macdonald white paper had recommended against its purchase. The fact that expensive new armour was eventually secured was the best indication that the priorities of the white paper had been, if not reversed, at least modified substantially.

To acquire new tanks had required a combined operation by Dextraze, Cloutier, and Helmut Schmidt, the West German chancellor. Schmidt had two objects in mind. He sought tangible commitments from his allies to shore up West Germany's security, and he was a tank salesman. When Trudeau and Schmidt first met at the Helsinki Final Act Conference on Security and Cooperation in Europe in the summer of 1975, DND had already begun to consider the need for new armour, though there was scant enthusiasm for the idea elsewhere in the government. Schmidt began to change all that. The chancellor won Trudeau's respect by affirming that he was a social democrat and no militarist, but Germany nonetheless confronted a real security problem. Then Schmidt gave the prime minister a lesson in European security, stressing the necessity of a strong conventional deterrent to which Canada should contribute in the future as in the past. The Bundesrepublik wanted more than one North American partner, Schmidt added.[85]

Trudeau was impressed and, as he was also greatly interested in forging his contractual link with the European Economic Community, he came to accept the re-equipping of the forces – and the need for a new tank – as necessary.[86] He also began to recognize NATO's utility. At the 1975 alliance summit, Trudeau stated that his purpose in attending was 'to state clearly and unequivocally Canada's belief in the concept of collective security, Canada's support for NATO, and Canada's pledge to maintain a NATO force level which is accepted by our allies as being adequate in size and effective in character.'[87] That speech, which sounded very different from the Pierre Trudeau of 1968, was a nail in the white paper's coffin.

But which tank would Canada choose to express its new enthusiasm for NATO? Dextraze would have preferred American tanks, to be as close as possible to the source of supply; but the U.S. army was in the midst of developing a new Main Battle Tank, and there was no time to wait. The new British tank, Dextraze thought, was too heavy, and the best available armoured vehicle was the Germans' Leopard I, which was being brought into service with the Bundeswehr. The CDS arranged a meeting with his West German opposite number, persuaded him that all the Canadian forces needed were 128 Leopards that the Germans could spare from their production schedule, and argued that Trudeau usually opposed any new weaponry but he was in favour of a new tank. That worked.[88]

Meanwhile Sylvain Cloutier, the deputy minister, carried the fight to the Treasury Board and the finance minister, since September 1975 Donald Macdonald. Cloutier had already demonstrated his capacity to get around the freeze, soon after his arrival at DND winning a pay raise for the forces. In 1973 he had won approval for a 7 per cent increase in the defence budget in each year of a five-year period, but double digit inflation (16.5 per cent in 1974–5, 13.4 per cent the next year, and 11.6 per cent the year after) and skyrocketing energy costs meant that DND's funds actually decreased.[89] To make ends meet, the forces' strength was cut to 78,000 in the fall of 1974. So serious had the situation become that General Dextraze, as he later publicly stated, 'advised the Minister that we could not reduce below that assigned level without running a grave risk of being unable to carry out all of our assigned tasks as well as of denuding the Canadian military profession to an unacceptable point.' (The Americans had similar problems. One estimate in 1989 was that 200 divisions were necessary to carry out adequately all of the United States' overseas commitments.) The CDS also stressed that 'any further loss of basic combat capability ... should be in response to basic defence policy objectives and not just current budgetary objectives.'

That fundamental issue led the prime minister to order a review of the Canadian Armed Forces' tasks and the resources necessary to carry them out.[90] This was the Defence Structure Review, conducted by a senior officials' committee chaired by the secretary to the cabinet, which laid down the peacetime structure for the forces. Even so, while the DSR was in process, efforts in May 1975 to get the government to agree to a 1–2 per cent annual increase in defence spending *after inflation* ran into a rough ride in cabinet committee. All that the ministers would accept was a commitment to maintain current funding.[91] The Defence Structure Review, whose results were announced in parliament by James Richardson on 27 November 1975, reaffirmed the four basic defence priorities of 1969, though it reorganized them according to 'combat capability.' In other words, 'hard operational needs,' as Dextraze put it, were now to shape the armed forces.[92] At the same time, the DSR committed the government to increasing the capital expenditures component of the budget in real terms by 12 per cent a year for five years.[93] This was a major victory for Cloutier, whose aim was to have capital expenditures reach 20 per cent of the DND budget. The commitment permitted DND to plan rationally for equipment acquisition. (By 1984–5, equipment acquisition absorbed 24 per cent of DND's net expenditure, or about $2 billion.)[94]

Cloutier, the CDS, and the defence minister, helped substantially by the posting of a high-flying colonel to the Privy Council Office to work on defence questions (something the PCO had asked for so that DND could participate in the policy process),[95] also continued to press Trudeau to agree to a fixed real annual increase in the DND budget. If the budget remained effectively frozen, they had argued, the forces might as well be shut down. NATO added its own pressure on Canada (and all its members), and Trudeau eventually agreed to commit Canada to an annual 3 per cent after inflation increase in 1978.[96] That decision at NATO, Barney Danson recalled, was calculated on the back of an envelope.[97] In fact, after his return to power in 1980, Trudeau did better than the promised 3 per cent – DND expenditures rose from $4.389 billion in 1980 to $6.027 billion in 1982 and to $7.97 billion in 1984.[98]

Cloutier pushed the Leopard acquisition through in 1976, overcoming Finance Minister Macdonald's tight-fisted opposition. A probably apocryphal story has it that Macdonald told Cloutier, 'that's not why we put you there.' To which the deputy he had appointed to DND replied, 'then you should have told me.'[99] For Finance and for the Treasury Board, DND was 'a black hole,' a department with an insatiable appetite;[100] this time, however, DND had won out. The result of these efforts was the purchase for $210 million of eighty-six Leopard I tanks for the 4th Canadian Mechanized Brigade Group with NATO. An additional forty-two Leopards went to Canada so that armoured regiments based there could train with them. In the period before July 1979 when delivery of the Leopards was complete, Canada rented thirty-five tanks from West Germany. The land forces also acquired 491 wheeled armoured vehicles between 1978 and 1982 and 2767 new 2 $^1/_2$ ton trucks between 1981 and 1984. Those programs, unlike the tank acquisition, were examined rather critically by the auditor general in 1984.[101]

Another problem the land forces faced was the commitment to send a combat group to Denmark or Norway. In 1968 Canada had accepted the Canadian Air/Sea Transportable [CAST] role as a low-cost way of showing support to NATO, allocating to it approximately 5000 men based in Canada (eventually the 5e Groupement de Combat) who would be deployed to Denmark or Norway only in the event of a crisis. That suited the Norwegians, who refused to allow foreign troops on their soil. But there were difficulties here. In the first place, Canada did not have the funds available to preposition equipment for the combat group in Norway, even if the Norwegians agreed.[102] Second, there was a problem in getting sufficient sealift capacity to move the unit. Third, every naval wargame study of a move of the CAST brigade demonstrated that the exercise would be a disaster unless virtually all of NATO's North Atlantic resources were deployed to cover the operation; moreover, the same studies showed that Canada needed nuclear depth charges to give the CAST force a chance of reaching Europe.[103]

Finally, the probable locale of operations in Denmark was flat country, an extension of the North German plain, and in November 1975 Defence Minister Richardson told his cabinet colleagues that hostilities there would involve heavy armoured combat for which the CAST combat group was not equipped. Richardson recommended renegotiating the commitment to limit it to Norway, reducing it to 1500 men, or eliminating it altogether. Barney Danson, who took over as minister after Richardson's resignation, shared that concern, as did the CDS; indeed Danson wanted out of the commitment entirely. The government chose the first option, and in April 1977 the CAST commitment was altered to Norway alone.[104] By 1980 Danson had managed to lighten the commitment further, reducing it to the more air transportable Special Service Force of 4000 officers and men. That at least meant that the first Canadian troops to be lost in a major war with the Soviets – for Norway was not thought to be defensible against a major attack – would not be Quebeckers! Not until Perrin Beatty became the Progressive Conservatives defence minister was the commitment to the defence of Norway finally dropped.

The Norway commitment was not the only northern locale for the Canadian forces. In the 1950s the forces had had a substantial presence in the Arctic, employing almost 2500 there. During the 1960s, however, that deployment fell by three-quarters, and all that remained were 200 men at Inuvik, 180 at Alert, and a few handfuls at DEW-line stations.[105] Sovereignty became a Trudeau government defence priority in substantial part because of the SS *Manhattan*'s 1969 voyage in Arctic waters, and the political pressures exerted on the government meant that DND had to give some attention to the north. In fact, however, planning was largely cosmetic in nature, and the Arctic received scant weight in the forces' planning, whatever its apparent priority for the prime minister and in the 1971 white paper.[106] It truly seemed as if the military had decided, as one critic wrote in 1971, that 'sovereignty is a fraud, a patently phony defence priority. There is no physical threat to our sovereignty in the north ... There is simply no justification for using troops in this role that only political weapons, firm leadership, and united public opinion can handle.'[107]

Nonetheless, on 17 April 1970 Brigadier Ramsay Withers, hitherto executive assistant to the CDS, was given the task of commanding a permanent northern headquarters – with a strength of no more than thirty-five officers and men! Withers prepared a 'concept paper' that won immediate approval, designed accommodation that was trucked to Yellowknife, NWT, and the headquarters was effectively operational by the end of the year. The young general had trouble getting resources, and he could not get $1 million dollars to revitalize the Inuit-manned Canadian Rangers.[108] That, at least, seemed to disprove the argument raised in the media that the emphasis on sovereignty in the north was a political sham.[109] Instead, it was a political *and* a military sham, and when Defence Minister Richardson spoke to the Standing Committee on External Affairs and National Defence in May 1973, he completely failed to mention the northern headquarters.[110] Even so, the Canadian forces did conduct more training in the Arctic. That alone demonstrated a regular physical presence there, as did army efforts to build runways and bridges.[111]

For the air force, the Trudeau years were bleak but less so than for the land and sea sections of the Canadian forces. In the first place, the government renewed the NORAD agreement with the United States in 1975, though there seemed to be general agreement that the Soviet bomber threat had diminished.[112] Then the air force got its way when

Air Command, in effect the recreation of the air force, came into being in September 1975, putting approximately 30,000 service personnel under one lieutenant-general. Air Command included Air Defence Group, headquartered at North Bay, Ontario, No. 10 Tactical Air Group, based at Saint-Hubert, Quebec, Maritime Air Group with bases on the east and west coasts, Air Transport Group, and No. 1 Canadian Air Group at Lahr, in the German Federal Republic. From the air force's point of view, the formation of Air Command brought sound standards of training and maintenance into the air elements hitherto controlled by the army and navy.[113]

Most important, the air force had two major procurement programs implemented: one for a long-range patrol aircraft [LRPA] to replace the Argus anti-submarine aircraft and another for a new fighter aircraft to replace the CF-101 Voodoos and CF-5s based in Canada and the CF-104s with NATO.

The LRPA contract, in the works since 1972, was finally settled in 1976. DND originally had hoped to get forty-eight aircraft, but over time the proposal had been whittled down, in part, at least, because the military could not justify its need for so many LRPAs.[114] In the end, the Lockheed Aircraft Corporation bested a Boeing proposal to use 707 aircraft in the LRPA role and won the contract to provide eighteen Aurora aircraft, in effect modified P3C Orions, at a cost of $1.03 billion. As usual, industrial offsets had played an important part in determining the government's choice.[115]

The fighter program was even more important for the air force.[116] The CF-104 aircraft Canadian pilots flew on NATO service were the oldest aircraft in the alliance, requiring forty-five hours in maintenance for every hour of flying time. The CF-101 Voodoos used in NORAD were as old, and budget constraints and maintenance difficulties had reduced the Voodoo complement to thirty-six aircraft by 1975. The need was great, therefore, and the air force exulted when, in March 1977, Defence Minister Danson announced cabinet authorization to begin the process of acquiring some 130 fighter aircraft for $2.3 billion in 1977 dollars.[117] There were six contenders: the Grumman F-14, the McDonnell-Douglas F-15, the single-engine General Dynamics F-16, the twin-engine McDonnell-Douglas-Northrop F-18, the Panavia Tornado, and the Dassault-Breguet Mirage 2000.[118] The air force considered that the F-15 was the hottest aircraft, one that was certain to keep Canada in the 'big leagues,' but its costs were too high and it was eliminated. The chief of the Defence Staff, Admiral Robert Falls, who had succeeded Dextraze in 1977, was said to support the cheaper F-16 – the less spent on the aircraft, the more money that might be available for ships. The F-16 also had a first-rate surveillance capability that was important for NORAD use, but the pilots questioned the morality of sending aircrew over northern Canada in a single-engine aircraft.[119] The F-14 had a superb multiple combat capacity, the ability to take on up to six enemy aircraft at once at a range of 100 miles. That made it ideal for NATO service, but that capacity was unnecessary in Canada. The military logic, therefore, suggested F-14s in Europe and F-16s in Canada.

But logic had relatively little to do with the ultimate choice. DND wanted the best aircraft it could get. External Affairs had international IOUs to pay off. The Ministry of State for Science and Technology hoped to see the greatest possible technology transfer. Industry, Trade and Commerce wanted industrial offsets. Finance wanted the cheapest aircraft. And the PCO and PMO too had their oars in the water, aiming to protect the prime minister from the parochialism of his ministers.[120]

General Dynamics' F-16 seemed a likely choice, in part because the asbestos mines the company owned in Quebec were being nationalized by the provincial government. The company promised to reinvest its billions of dollars in compensation in Canada if its aircraft won the competition. But the F-16 suffered from certain weaknesses. Every cubic inch of the aircraft was already crammed with equipment. For an aircraft intended to last two decades, that made future modifications extremely difficult. There was only a small industrial offset, and, in addition, the technology transfer was limited. General Dynamics also tried to mobilize the Parti Québécois government behind its aircraft, stirring up nationalistic concerns with its claim that the benefits from building the F-16 in Quebec far outweighed the gains that would come from an F-18 program in Ontario.[121] The decision was delayed further by the fall of the Progressive Conservative government – Defence Minister Allan McKinnon was to present his recommendation on 15 December 1979; the Clark administration lost a vote of confidence in parliament the day before.[122] The eventual result, announced on 10 April 1980 by Defence Minister Gilles Lamontagne, saw McDonnell-Douglas' F-18 win out.[123] Its aircraft had room for modifications, and there were industrial offsets that held out the promise of 60,000–70,000 person-years of work over the life of the contract, which lasted until delivery of the final aircraft in September 1988.[124] The air force was satisfied – it had got the best aircraft for the available money.[125] As one participant in the F-18 program noted, this had been one of the few 'positive acquisitions' in the history of Canadian defence procurement.[126] Even so, there were some astonishing increases in the costs for spare parts – an antenna assembly that escalated from an initial cost estimate in 1980–1 of $9 to $2077.29, or a resistor that went from $1.19 to $299.19.[127]

The air force also saw the Trudeau government recognize the new importance of NORAD before its term ended. When the prime minister had come to power in 1968, the anti-ballistic-missile issue was hot, so much so that Trudeau talked on occasion about the pressures on his government. But once the ABM had been shelved, and once the manned bomber threat finally seemed to have diminished, NORAD's importance declined greatly. Forces were reduced, and NORAD's primary responsibilities now seemed to focus on surveillance and warning of ICBM attack. Moreover, the government pressed the reorganization of NORAD's regions so that Canada's airspace was wholly under Canadian control.

By the end of the 1970s, new bomber technology, and especially the development of air-launched and submarine-launched cruise missiles, raised concerns in Washington and Ottawa about the state of the North American warning systems that might, they feared, allow new Soviet bombers and missiles to hit at North America. The result was an American 'Air Defense Master Plan' that became the basis for negotiations with Canada. Trudeau had retired before the ADMP was formally signed by President Reagan and Prime Minister Brian Mulroney at their first summit meeting in Quebec City in 1985, but its groundwork had been laid by his government.[128]

The Trudeau years had been extraordinarily difficult ones for the Canadian forces. Reviews had disrupted training and planning; bilingualism had strained good will within units; managers began to replace leaders; budget freezes and rampant inflation constrained the forces; and the lack of modern equipment helped destroy the regard in which allies had once held the Canadian military. The prime minister had little interest in the armed forces, something that the October Crisis apparently did little to change. Nor was there much support from the opposition parties. Neither the Conservatives nor the New Democrats prepared their own defence policy, and defence questions were scarcely ever raised in parliament. The opposition, in other words, acquiesced in the Trudeau government's policies.[129] That fact alone hurt morale, though it was insignificant compared to the continued opposition directed at DND in the years immediately after 1968. The Canadian forces, like External Affairs, had been shaken up by the Trudeau government – and it is difficult to escape the conclusion that this shaking up was done for its own sake.

10

Helpful Fixations:
Canada and the Third World

In 1968 there were 141 identifiable sovereign states in the world; in 1984 there were 157. In 1968 Canada maintained diplomatic links with 109 countries; in 1984 the number had increased to 140. Many of these were countries that Canadians had never heard of, and certainly could not place on a map; that Canada stationed diplomats on their territory would have come as a surprise, and possibly a shock. Canadians' worlds were limited: the United States, Europe, the Soviet Union, China, Japan, India, Australia, New Zealand, and the Caribbean; these were recognizable. Beyond that, countries faded into continents: South America, Asia, and Africa.

Where Africa was concerned, what little Canadians knew no longer applied. Schoolroom memories of great blotches of green and red on the 'dark continent' were obsolete. The colonial empires they represented were swiftly passing into history. This phenomenon, 'decolonization,' involved Canadians at a distance, but mostly through their media and through an assumed identification with the Europeans departing Africa. Whether it was achieved peacefully or by violence, independence was a caesura in Canadians' consciousness. The connection had been broken, and it was a moot point whether a new one could be, or would be, established in its place.

By the late 1960s, Canadian missions had started to spring up in some of the new countries. Kinshasa, Abidjan, and Dakar on the francophone side, and Lagos, Nairobi, Dar es Salaam, and Lusaka on the anglophone side all hosted Canadian diplomats. They looked after the interests of Canada in Africa – as, in other cities elsewhere, in Asia and South America as well. But how were these interests to be defined?

Not, by and large, in terms of investment. In the palmy days of the

British empire, Canadian money had followed the British flag, to the West Indies, to Africa, and to Asia. Independence for the empire meant that, henceforth, Canadian investments in the ex-colonies had to be dealt with directly by Ottawa: bauxite in Guyana and Jamaica, for example. Yet such holdovers were in the minority, and the category was not noticeably growing.

Canadian investment abroad in the late 1960s *was* growing, but it was concentrated: in 1969, 55 per cent of Canadian investments abroad were in the United States, 12 per cent in the United Kingdom, 9 per cent in Europe, and 5 per cent in Australasia – all, broadly speaking, in the 'First World.' The remaining 19 per cent was represented by 'other North America,' 9.3 per cent, leaving just under 10 per cent for the rest of the world.[1]

By 1984 the picture had altered, but not in the direction of the Third World. A boom in Canadian investment in the United States had pushed that country's proportion of Canadian direct investments abroad ($41.7 billion in 1984) to 72 per cent;[2] direct investment in developing countries was, by contrast, decreasing as a proportion, from 17 per cent in 1980 to 15 per cent in 1984. It did, however, increase somewhat in absolute terms, and when loans and other 'assets' are taken into account, Canadian interests become more substantial. Canadian banks in 1982, for instance, had $22.3 billion in 'assets' in Latin America and the Caribbean.[3]

Nor is the picture substantially different when trade is considered. Taking 0.1 per cent of exports as a benchmark of significant trade, in 1968 Canada had 'significant' exports to thirty-six countries. Using the same criterion for imports, Canada also had 'significant' imports from thirty-six countries. The two lists are not quite the same, the difference in some cases being imports of petroleum and bauxite (Venezuela, Guyana, and Saudi Arabia, for example) and in others the vagaries of state trading systems.[4] By and large, however, Canada's main trading partners were the large countries of the First World, a few countries in the Second World (the so-called socialist bloc), and a very few countries in the Third World: South Africa (whose inclusion in that category is debatable), India, Hong Kong, Taiwan, the Philippines, Argentina, Brazil, and Chile.[5]

In 1984 the tally was not dissimilar. Thirty-eight countries accounted for more than 0.1 per cent of Canada's imports, and thirty-eight took more than 0.1 per cent of Canada's exports. As in 1968, the majority of trading partners were in the First World – to which we might add the Asian success stories of Taiwan, South Korea, and Singapore. Exports flowed to the Second World, but not usually in overwhelming quantity. For example, in that year Canada's trade with Taiwan was three to four times the value of its trade with mainland China. As for the Third World, once again the petroleum-producing states – Venezuela, Indonesia, Iran, Iraq, Mexico – predominate. Setting them aside, there remain India, Thailand, Brazil, Colombia, and South Africa.[6]

These figures can be used for other purposes than to gauge trade. They are a guide to the content of bilateral relations – or, more often, to the lack of content. If Canadian diplomats had to scramble to add 'substance' to the Franco-Canadian relationship, where natural trade flows were not a problem (France lands just under 1 per cent of Canadian trade, year in and year out), how much greater the problem must have been in countries where there were no products appealing to Canadians to buy, and no market in which to sell.

Two radically different conclusions may then be drawn. To some, there was little point in maintaining relations with countries where Canada's economic interests were very slight. And in fact, all too often there was little serious content to bilateral relationships that Canada with some difficulty and expense managed to establish. Yet others could also argue that bilateral relations with many underdeveloped countries were beside the point: the problem of underdevelopment is so vast, so difficult, and so complex that nothing short of a comprehensive and concerted multilateral effort can have any hope of succeeding. The fact that trade is minimal merely reflects the fact that most of the world's wealth is concentrated in the hands of a small fraction of the world's population – a fraction that includes Canada.

Nevertheless, important relationships between Canada and some Third-World countries occurred below the 0.1 per cent trade threshhold, while others that surpassed the magic decimal were not especially significant. In general, however, direct Canadian *material* interests were absent from Canada's relations with most of the countries of the world – roughly three-quarters to four-fifths of them, in fact – with all that that implies for Canada's bilateral relations with these states.

There are other kinds of figures that apply. They were obvious in 1968, and they remained so sixteen years later. India had over 700 million people in 1984, almost double the population of all the West European countries put together. Brazil had nearly six times the population of Canada, and Indonesia seven times. The southern half of the world was notably more populous and poorer than the northern half.

In the long run, these facts would certainly contribute to another crisis; in the short run, they were a reproach; and in the present they helped define the political balance of the world. The foreign-policy elite – defined by political scientists in 1975 as comprising some 300 members –

by and large believed that, as Peyton Lyon put it, 'world peace depends upon narrowing the gap between rich and poor countries.' North-South, they were inclined to believe, rather than East-West, was the proper focus for Canadian policy. At the same time, the elite believed that aid per se was a difficult proposition to sell to Canadians, a view that received a decidedly mixed backing from public-opinion soundings.[7]

Lyon's appraisal was made after seven years of Trudeau; but even in 1968 the problem of poverty in Third-World countries was capturing attention. The means for coping with poverty and for looking at the problem were under debate. Their problems were too large for any single country to solve, and certainly too big for Canada's unaided efforts. Independence, and the growth in membership in international organizations, were providing the poorer nations with a forum for calling attention to themselves, by the sheer weight of their voting numbers. That in itself guaranteed that international fora would be used to examine what ailed the Third World.

Canada's more important contacts with most other countries tended to be multilateral rather than bilateral. With the smaller West European countries, this meant NATO (Denmark, for example, or Portugal). For the poorer African and Asian countries, it was the Commonwealth (Bangladesh or Zambia, for example) or francophonie (for instance, Zaire or Niger). And for all, or almost all, it meant the United Nations.

Canadian relations with the Third World were also less concerned with countries than with governments. Economic relations consisted largely of aid packages. Politicians and diplomats, when they met, could talk about subsistence and the emergencies of the day, or they could concentrate on the long term, in which the underprivileged majority of the Earth's population searched for real power to match its demographic importance. Just how to connect those points, however, baffled Canadians under Trudeau, though in a different way from the bafflement suffered by his predecessors.

Pierre Trudeau had spent time in the Third World. He had passed through Asia as it convulsed in the overthrow of European rule in the years after 1945. He had returned there from time to time, and had spent more time in underdeveloped countries than most of the senior officials in the Department of External Affairs.

Observers might have expected a sentimentalized regard for the Third World from the Canadian prime minister, a desire to spend time and money bringing the underdeveloped world up to the level of the industrialized states. Prime minister St Laurent, when he toured India in 1954, had been shocked and troubled by what he saw; Trudeau, however, was not. He did not expect Indians to live as Canadians did; catastrophes apart, it would be foolish to waste one's time, and theirs, trying to reconcile the incompatible.[8]

But Trudeau was inclined to stretch Canadian perceptions of the external world farther than his predecessors had done. In his first major foreign-policy speech in May 1968 he criticized 'past preoccupation with Asiatic or European affairs.' Using a text written by Ivan Head, the prime minister went on to tell an audience at the University of Calgary, 'never before in history has the disparity between the rich and the poor, the comfortable and the starving, been so extreme.' It was 'an overwhelming challenge,' and, in meeting it, 'the world must be our constituency.' The challenge must be met through development, and, in driving the point home, Trudeau quoted Pope Paul VI: 'The name of peace is development.' Yet development must take new forms. Instead of simply doling out aid, Western countries should seek to establish trade with the Third World. The United Nations, through its two Conferences on Trade and Development (UNCTAD), had already pointed the way.[9] Not coincidentally, the Third World was a majority in the United Nations, and was increasingly using that majority to get its own way. Under the circumstances, some adjustment in attitudes and policy might be indicated. The search for such an accommodation was nothing new in Canadian diplomacy, but it was neither diplomacy nor politics that Trudeau stressed. Instead, he repeated the general message days later in an election speech in Ottawa, calling for measures that would help developing nations to secure 'lasting improvement in their economies.'[10]

It was easier to make that point in 1968 than it would be later. Canada was prosperous and, as important, believed itself to be prosperous. It had been so ever since the Second World War, and in 1968 was enjoying a prolonged boom that had started in 1961. Generosity, even altruistic generosity, might not be unthinkable under the circumstances. The Liberal party was doing well across the country, making local concerns – for example, over textile manufacturing – less urgent as a political matter. In his Ottawa speech Trudeau reminded his audience that 'our paramount interest is to ensure the political survival of Canada as a federal and bilingual sovereign state.'[11] Under that heading, links with distant, unheard-of countries, had proven to have some importance. Events in Africa reinforced his words, when it became evident that the attitudes and actions of distant African governments had acquired significance in the government of Canada's struggle with the government of Quebec.

Paradoxically, the more traditional forms of aid did not lack Trudeau's support during his first decade in office. Canada's aid budget expanded as its defence budget contracted. His cabinet was not unfavourable: it may have contained the highest number of aid supporters of any Canadian government, including Allan MacEachen, after 1974 the second man in the government as well as secretary of state for external affairs. MacEachen, who could afford to spend time on the question of the Third World, or, as it became, the North-South relationship, was transferred to another office just at the point when the government's economic priorities began to tilt towards budgetary restriction and short-term political benefits.

In 1975, when Trudeau and Canada confronted the first stage of the oil crisis that was to have such a heavy and fateful impact on his government's policies, he reiterated in a speech in London his concern that 'we must aim for nothing less than an acceptable distribution of the world's wealth. In doing so,' he added, 'the inequities resulting from the accidental location of valuable geological formations should no more be overlooked than should the present unequal acquisition of technological and managerial skills.' It was a noble ideal, which would prove to be more than the international system could digest, even under the pressure of the oil-price inflation of the 1970s.[12]

In the later 1970s, when large economic problems weighed heavily on Trudeau's government and worries over spending and deficits became a burden, the amount devoted to aid became restricted.[13] Despite some success, aid did not seem to have made a fundamental difference to the situation of the Third World. What years of painstaking programs had done could be undermined in months with the rise of oil prices in the 1970s; the hikes in petroleum costs had a stronger influence on the Third World than all the aid programs from the First World put together.

Nor did Trudeau succeed in establishing a significant amount of trade. His attention was drawn to other things, among them the preservation of national unity. The prime minister came to believe that the preservation of Liberal support in areas where manufactures might be threatened by lowered tariff barriers had a higher priority than boosting economies in the Third World.[14] It is also doubtful whether Trudeau really had the Third World in mind when he urged Canadians to expand their horizons and seek opportunities elsewhere. When he listed some of the countries that had entered his thoughts as 'important partners,' he mentioned Japan, China, and Australia by name, and 'those on the Pacific coast of South America' by region.[15]

The foreign-policy review of the late 1960s gave some thought to

Pacific South American countries and to the problem of increasing Canadian contacts with them and the other countries of Latin America. It was not an area where Canada had concentrated much effort. Ministerial visits were few and information sparse. Embassies and missions were plentiful, however, thirteen in 1968, and they were tapped for ideas. Canadian diplomats in South America thought, briefly, that the millennium had arrived. One member of the government, Gérard Pelletier, was known to take an interest in Latin America. With the advent of 'French power' in Ottawa, surely one traditional object of French-Canadian intellectuals would be achieved: closer contacts with their fellow Latins to the south. As if to signify the change in practice, the government sought the advice of French-Canadian clergy stationed in Latin America as it reviewed its foreign-policy objectives.[16] It was a fair deduction that the government was on the verge of reorienting its gaze from the Atlantic to the Caribbean and the Equator.

This was not wrong, up to a point. Ministers were galvanized for missions to the south. A procession of official Canadians jetted around nine countries in Central and South America on what one termed 'a voyage of discovery' and another 'a new peak.' Others, more sceptical, called it a 'travelling circus,' but only in private.[17] Speeches were made, consciousness rose, and spirits soared. The results are, however, hard to measure, at least in positive terms.[18] Trade remained much as it had been, and oil from Venezuela guaranteed significant figures every year.[19]

While the number of Canadians in transit through Latin America was rising, the number of permanent posts was actually falling. The government decreed the closing of missions in Ecuador, the Dominican Republic, and Uruguay; ironically, for those who had expected great things from the 'Latin' connection, the money saved was rumoured to have gone to pay for new missions in francophone Africa.[20] Even so, some External Affairs officials believed that Canadian embassies in Latin America were still overstaffed, in terms of the business they were actually called upon to transact.[21] The scepticism that Latin America evoked in certain circles was, however, balanced by its prominence in the review: one of the six coloured booklets of *Foreign Policy for Canadians* (1975) had Latin America as its focus.

From time to time Latin America captured attention, not merely inside the government but across the country as well. As regards Brazil, Venezuela, and Mexico, this was because of the pressure of business, and business was expressed largely in terms of oil and tourism. Mexico was the best known Latin American country to Canadians. The closest to Canada, it hosted increasing numbers of Canadian tourists every year.

At the outset of Trudeau's period, Mexico ran a perennial trade deficit with Canada; by 1984, the deficit had reversed, because of oil and increased Canadian imports of Mexican fruits and vegetables.[22]

Mexico was early identified as a focus for Canadian activity in Latin America. A joint ministerial committee was established in 1971, and in the spring of 1973 the Mexican president braved the Canadian climate for a state visit to Ottawa. Trudeau told parliament that 'Mexico is foremost in our thoughts,' and President Echevarria added that, in the past, Mexicans and Canadians had seen too little of one another.[23]

It is true that they saw something more of one another in the years that followed. The joint ministerial committee met again in 1974 to rehearse common interests in trade and finance, and again in 1977. By then Mexican oil had assumed an increased importance in Ottawa's eyes: an energy agreement was actually reached in 1979 that guaranteed a modest amount of Mexican oil to Canadian purchasers (Petro-Canada). The Mexicans for their part promised to give Canada's CANDU reactor serious study.[24]

Mexican President López Portillo visited Ottawa in May 1980 to sign a revised version of the energy pact. He and Trudeau took the opportunity to dismiss the idea, then current, that a 'North American accord' ought to unite the three countries of North America. Although the Mexicans promised to sell Canada 50,000 barrels of oil a day, it soon appeared that the two governments' enthusiasm had outrun Mexico's capacity to supply oil, and Canada's to refine it.[25]

Trudeau returned López's visit in January 1981. Their discussions focused more on multilateral concerns than on bilateral issues, and there is not much doubt that multilateral concerns were of greater concern than strictly Canadian-Mexican matters. The visit was more notable for the criticism it attracted from Canadians freezing at home while their prime minister basked in the tropical sun. Their ministers had already met for the fourth time to discuss trade and energy. The other element in the energy discussions, the CANDU nuclear reactor, languished through the ministerial meeting in 1981, and finally disappeared from the Canadian agenda. Though the Mexicans bought subway cars from Canada, they would not go so far as to purchase a reactor. Their refusal took some time to develop and was only finally revealed under the cover of a financial crisis, in 1982. It was not necessarily disappointing from the Canadian taxpayer's point of view,[26] since Canadian export credits and generous terms of repayment would have been essential.

Canada hoped for trade in other things than reactors, but the spadework done under López went for naught. The fall in oil prices after

1982 – the same crisis that undermined Trudeau's National Energy Policy – also demolished Lopez's grandiose plans for his country's economic and political future. Trade shrank; exports to Canada went down from $715 million in 1981 to $378 million in 1983. It was a notable disappointment, though Canadian trade officials sought comfort by pointing out that Canada's proportion of Mexico's diminished trade actually *rose*. As they argued to a student of the problem, 'if Canada cannot penetrate this market with manufactured goods then the outlook in general is bleak.'[27]

Canada's relations with Mexico under Trudeau can be accounted a modest but episodic success – a result on the political level of Trudeau's and Canada's position in multilateral concerns of mutual interest, and especially the North-South dialogue of the period that guaranteed attention at the highest level in Mexico City. On a more practical level, trade was a function of the oil boom and bust. It was stimulated by Canada's insecurity of oil supply during the oil crisis at the end of the 1970s, and by the development of trade in agricultural products as Mexican farms supplemented supplies from California and Florida. Because Mexico was more or less a democracy, albeit one with absolutely predictable election results, Canadian relations with that country were generally free from ideological pressures from domestic pressure groups.[28]

Canada's largest trading partner in Latin America was Venezuela. Canadians bought $357 million worth of goods from that country in 1968, almost ten times the value of imports from Brazil, and $1.2 billion in 1984; interestingly, that was only twice the amount bought from Brazil that year.[29] Relations with Venezuela turned on oil, which supplied eastern Canada. Because Canada ran a large trade deficit with Venezuela, discussions between the two governments centred on ways and means of increasing Canadian sales.[30] A Canadian-Spanish railway-building consortium doubtless had some effect.[31] As a member of OPEC, the Venezuelan government did not hesitate to raise its oil prices and rejig its petroleum supplies in the late 1970s and early 1980s. Still, Canada's relations with Venezuela, which had a civilian, democratic government throughout this period, were untroubled by domestic opposition.

The same could not be said of many other countries in Latin America, including the two largest, Brazil and Argentina. Brazil was under military rule for Trudeau's entire term of office, while Argentina fluctuated between populist democracy and various forms of military despotism. Brazil, as the largest Latin American country and as the seat of some of Canada's most prominent foreign investments (Canada was the third largest investing country in Brazil, after the United States and Germany), had an obvious importance; but while relations with Brazil were correct, they were not close.[32]

Argentina, because its military were more spectacularly violent, was better reported in the Canadian media, where its various governments attracted considerable attention for their irresponsibility and brutality. Canada's trade with Argentina was not large, but like Mexico it became a target for Canada's reactor salesmen in the late 1960s.[33] Unlike the Mexicans, however, the Argentines bought a CANDU.

To sell a CANDU to the Argentines brought the Canadian government's atomic energy agency, AECL, into partnership with Italimpianti, an Italian engineering firm. Italimpianti established a $5 million budget for the sale, of which AECL contributed half. It was anticipated that what followed would be obscure, and it was. The sale was successful, and Argentina became the first country in South America to acquire a CANDU. AECL, in return, was assisted into a first-class scandal when Canada's auditor general discovered that large sums had vanished into unspecified promotional expenses. Worse, the contract with the Argentines had failed to take into account that country's astounding rate of inflation, with consequent heavy losses for AECL.[34] The scandal drew unwelcome attention to the nature of the Argentine government and when, in 1979, AECL tried to sell a second CANDU to Argentina, it was blocked.

There were other threads of policy involved than simple repugnance for the Argentine government. Canada insisted on stringent safeguards for the end use of nuclear products made with Canadian technology, and the competition were not quite so scrupulous. The Argentine government wanted as few restrictions as possible. In the middle of the negotiations, Flora MacDonald, the secretary of state for external affairs in the Clark government, addressed the United Nations General Assembly; in her speech she condemned human-rights abuses in Argentina. Her speech was warmly received at home but was not highly regarded inside the Argentine government.[35] AECL lost the contract and the loss was considered a heavy blow to the future of Canada's reactor.

The Argentine invasion of the Falkland Islands in 1982 widened the gulf between that country and Canada. Canadians generally supported the British position and approved the British reconquest of the islands in the spring of 1982. The Canadian government invoked economic sanctions against Argentina and offered non-military support to the British. (They did not cancel the contract for the CANDU reactor, which was still under construction.) Trudeau was characteristically outspoken, telling the press on 14 June that Canada was '100 per cent behind the British.' That same day the Argentines on the islands surrendered and shortly thereafter the Argentine military regime fell, rendering moot the question of long-term damage to relations between Canada and Argentina.[36]

Relations with Chile raised many of the same questions that applied to Argentina. Chileans, at least in the twentieth century, had had a more stable and democratic government than their trans-Andean neighbours. In 1970 they exercised their freedom to put in power a leftist coalition headed by an avowed Marxist, Salvador Allende. Many in the Chilean middle class were gravely disturbed. They feared that Allende was planning to impose a dictatorship of the proletariat, and they pointed to extreme acts by some of his followers as positive proof of his intentions. The U.S. government was also markedly nervous at the prospect of a communist government on the South American mainland, and it communicated its jitters to its sympathizers inside Chile.

In September 1973 Allende was overthrown and killed in a military coup, and replaced by army general Augusto Pinochet. The dramatic and bloody coup was well reported in Canada, where public reaction appeared to favour the deposed regime. Because of its remoteness, the issue never became a major focus for public debate in Canada, but that in turn meant that it was of primary interest to a sympathetic minority, a minority increasingly located inside, though not restricted to, Canada's Christian churches.[37]

That minority, which reacted first to the brutality of the Chilean coup and believed that Allende could not have been even the partial author of his own misfortunes, was outraged when the *Toronto Star* published dispatches from Canada's ambassador in Chile that revealed a distinct lack of sympathy with the vanquished leftists. The ambassador, Andrew Ross, argued that 'Chile's military and police have accepted an exceedingly difficult and probably thankless task.' In another dispatch he unsympathetically described the plight of the 'riff-raff of the Latin American left to whom Allende gave asylum' and who now faced a very different atmosphere in Chile. Obviously the dispatches had been leaked, but the government had no success in tracking down the culprit. An embarrassed Mitchell Sharp had to devote some time to defending the ambassador's right to voice his own opinions, in confidence, to his own government.[38]

Chile was one of the most salient occasions on which government opinion, especially in External Affairs, diverged from that of lobby groups on foreign policy. It raises the question why the lobbyists did not wield more influence than they did. The answer is complicated and somewhat uncertain. First, the church lobbyists were not considered to have broad support within their own congregations. It would have been difficult to mobilize even the United Church, the most liberal of Canada's mainstream denominations, on the issue of Chile and to expect its indignation to have electoral impact. Second, as Robert Matthews has noted, 'Ottawa has ... difficulty in understanding the churches, viewing their spokesmen often as "radicals" and "idealists." ' To a government which saw the 'radicals' as a minority enjoying limited support, it was easy to define them as marginal.[39]

The Chilean episode also obliged the government to confront, for the first time, the question of harbouring leftist refugees from Latin America. Some sought refuge directly, in the Canadian embassy in Santiago. This was not an uncommon act in Latin America, but it was considered unusual and generally undesirable elsewhere. The Canadian government did not wish to create precedents for peaceful Ottawa, but under the circumstances it had little choice but to extend protection.

That was only the first step. Other Chileans manifested a desire to come to Canada. Their wish was strongly supported, inside and outside the cabinet, and by mid-December 184 visas had been issued, with another 582 in process.[40] At the same time, relations with the new regime in Chile continued: it was not Canada's business to begin to question the legitimacy of the various regimes that it confronted. The Canadian government did not seem concerned by the fact that the Chilean refugees were on the left; as one student of the phenomenon noted, Canada's response to the refugees was issued by the Department of External Affairs, denoting a high degree of political involvement and calculation in the decision to admit the Chileans.[41] By 1976, some 4000 Chilean refugees had come to Canada.[42]

The Chilean experience, along with an influx of Asians from Commonwealth Africa, may have contributed to the government's revision of the Immigration Act, already underway as the South Americans pounded on Canada's doors. Francophones from Haiti were among the refugees arriving – 1500 of them in 1972–3, with more to come in the early 1980s.[43] The revision helped to create an agitation for better treatment of refugees, particularly leftist ones, and stimulated a lively interest on the left and among humanitarian lobby groups in Canadian policy towards Latin America. The idea that there could be a connection between Canada and the far south of the continent was a novelty; henceforth the government's dealings with Latin America called up an attentive and largely hostile audience at home. Though restricted, it was vocal, and in the early 1980s it would stimulate a more intense Canadian involvement with its southern neighbours.[44]

A green paper on immigration was published outlining concerns in the area, and a parliamentary special committee traversed the country, holding well-publicized and frequently controversial hearings. In November 1976 the government brought in its new Immigration Bill, which proclaimed family reunification and concern for refugees as two of its principal goals. The government did not expect that its bow towards refugees would have large consequences. Refugee movements to Canada up to that time had been strictly controlled and subject to government permission and regulation: Eastern Europeans in the 1940s, Hungarians in the 1950s, Czechs in the 1960s, and East African Indians and Vietnamese in the 1970s were all officially approved, in advance. The few refugees who made it to Canada on their own initiative were rare enough to be newsworthy.

Only in the 1980s did things change. International travel was easier, flights to and from Canada more frequent. Outside Canada, word spread that Canadian laws were easier, Canadian enforcement less rigid and more complex (and expensive). As humanitarian groups, immigration lawyers, and then Canadians in general were to discover, the government had made claiming refugee status in Canada much easier.[45]

The complications of refugee policy were also reflected in the outflow of refugees from Central America, and in particular from Nicaragua and El Salvador, for reasons both political and apolitical: in the one case fleeing from a rebellion against an oppressive left-wing government with its military draft, and in the other from a revolution against a rightist regime supported by the United States. The Nicaraguan government had its friends, however; despite the doubtful policies of the Sandinistas in Managua, it enjoyed considerable support in Canada.[46] This support was motivated by the contrast to its murderous right-wing predecessor government; by comparison with some of the other governments in Central America; and, in some cases, by the antagonism between Washington and the Sandinista regime. It all tended to heighten the level of attention that Canadians paid to Central America. Central America, in Canadian eyes, came to signify human-rights issues.[47] To report on the region, Canadian diplomats survived in the comparative calm of San José, Costa Rica, the only functioning democracy in the area.

After the destruction of the Allende government, there was, for a time, but one leftist government in power in Latin America: Fidel Castro in Cuba. Only two hemispheric powers, Canada and Mexico, had maintained relations with Cuba ever since Castro had come to power in 1959. Castro had visited Canada that same year. Of all Latin American figures he was the most recognizable to Canadians, who had received a forcible reminder of his political identity during the Cuban missile crisis of 1962.

Relations between Castro and the United States government had their ups and downs during the Trudeau years. At times, the two governments seemed on the verge of exchanging embassies. More often, they indulged in recriminations. In one of his more spectacular acts, Castro allowed a horde of refugees to flee his island paradise; he thoughtfully included many of the inhabitants of Cuba's prisons and asylums so as to add to the Americans' burdens. None of this was calculated to enhance Americans' liking or respect for Castro or his policies, especially when, in 1975, the Cuban dictator sent his army to intervene, on behalf of the USSR and the 'socialist bloc,' in Angola.

Canadian relations with the Cubans were different. Because they were different, it was possible to call on Cuban good will in the October Crisis of 1970. Cuba received and housed the FLQ kidnappers of James Cross at Canada's request. Their treatment, however, while adequate, hardly matched their own heroic expectations of their 'revolutionary' status.[48] It did not pass unnoticed that the very large Cuban trade delegation in Montreal, which security officials believed operated as a centre for East bloc espionage in North America, existed largely untroubled by the Canadian government.[49]

When Trudeau toured South America in January 1976, it was only natural that he stop off in Havana on his way home. The visit was in some respects a success. Castro could command his people's attention in a way that more democratic leaders could not, and Trudeau's crowds were good in Havana.[50] Television cameras recorded it all, including a rousing speech that ended with a series of 'vivas.' 'Viva Cuba!' Trudeau shouted. 'Viva Castro!' There was nothing especially unusual about the 'vivas.' Because that was so, Richard Gwyn reported, a conscientious External Affairs official had added them to Trudeau's speech.[51]

The effect at home was not what the prime minister might have desired. Cuban intervention in Angola was in full swing, and it was held that Trudeau's well-publicized presence in Havana undermined the West's disapproval of Castro's action. (No one mentioned that the West's position was purely rhetorical and highly ineffective.) Trudeau reported that he had chosen to go to Havana to talk to Castro about Angola. Castro had agreed to see him, knowing in advance that Canada had taken a strong position condemning Cuba's African adventure. He added, somewhat ambiguously, 'in his own ideological framework he is a man of world stature.'[52]

What was Trudeau seeking from Castro? Certainly he could not realistically have hoped to secure an abatement in Castro's fixed hostility to capitalism and the United States. Yet it was true that communism was not monolithic, and that Castro himself had differed from his Soviet allies on a number of occasions – most often in taking a harder line. That consideration may have justified Ivan Head's remark, at the time, that Cuba represented 'a departure from classical Communism. There is an opportunity to work with these guys in the multilateral field.'[53] It was a forlorn hope: Cuba's main multilateral enterprise for the rest of Trudeau's time in office remained its expeditionary force in Angola; meanwhile its living standards, relative to the rest of the Caribbean, steadily sank.

Consorting with Castro did not help Trudeau's image at home. Yet in terms of anti-American feeling, Castro differed only in degree from the prime minister's other hosts. Cooler heads recognized that Trudeau, in visiting Latin America, had not associated himself with all the opinions that he encountered. He had made a point of reminding his audiences that Canadian relations with the United States remained good. Consciously or not, he was also telling Latin Americans that the Canadian view of the world was different from theirs. That did not preclude cooperation, but it suggested that Canadians were not about to seek a national identity or a foreign policy in solidarity with Latin Americans. There was simply not enough in common for that. And yet Trudeau's actions and speeches also made the point that Canadians were different from Americans. No American leader was likely to visit Castro or to receive the applause of a Cuban crowd, but a Canadian could.[54] Perhaps Cubans, and other Latin Americans, came to share the view that Canada was respectable in its motives and generous in its performance – rather like the Dutch and the Scandinavians, and unlike the United States. It was a useful distinction, and it was reflected elsewhere in Canada's policy.

In Latin America, Canadians were confronting the ruins of someone else's empire; and for better or for worse, they were speaking someone else's language. That consideration did not apply elsewhere. In the Caribbean and in Africa they were confronting the ruins of their own British empire. The dissolution of the colonial empires in Africa and in the Caribbean set the tone, and largely established the priorities, for Canadian relations with these parts of the world during the 1970s and 1980s.

In francophonie, the perpetuation of French influence after the withdrawal of France from its formal empire, Canada's relations were competitive with the former imperial power; but they were also a function of the state of Canada's own relations with France (see chapter 5). The same may be said of Canada's relations with formerly British Africa.

The British, to make a simple point, had created the countries to which they then gave independence. In the Caribbean, the boundaries were simply the shorelines of the various island colonies; and there the British left behind a collection of smallish near-democracies, identifiable and acceptable local elites, and a tradition of civilian rule. Canada had long had investments in the British Caribbean, and, without supplanting the British as a metropolitan power, the Canadian government was ready with aid and, occasionally, influence. Relations between Trudeau and Michael Manley, prime minister of Jamaica in the late 1970s, were close, and Manley occasionally sought his Canadian colleague's advice. But relations with Manley were a double-edged sword; because Manley in the 1970s was believed to be friendly with communist Cuba, it did not help Trudeau's image at home to become known as his confidant.[55]

In Africa, things were less certain. Capitals, boundaries, judiciary, and, most importantly, armies were all shaped by the metropolitan power. British boundary-drawing, for example, created the federal state of Nigeria, with its several mutually suspicious peoples. In 1967 the Ibos in Nigeria's eastern region revolted against the central government in Lagos. They maintained their secession until reconquered by federal forces in January 1970. A comparison with Canada's own situation was not hard to make – and it is not surprising that Canada's federalist-in-chief made the connection.[56] Trudeau blankly refused to recognize or treat with the secessionist state, which called itself Biafra, a position no different from that of the United Nations or the Organization for African Unity.

Had the prime minister stuck to official formulas while striking the requisite attitude of responsible concern, he would not have heard much about Biafra. The rebels did have some Canadian supporters, including former CBC newscaster Stanley Burke. And one of the Lagos government's most effective weapons, an economic blockade, provided Ibo supporters with an effective progaganda weapon. Some went so far as to claim genocide; others were active in a non-governmental aid group known as Canairelief.[57] But one day in August 1968 when Trudeau was interrogated by reporters on Parliament Hill about Biafra, he merely replied, 'Where's Biafra?'

The answer was juridically correct, but politically horrendous, since it implied arrogance, indifference, and ignorance to the television audience.[58] Trudeau managed to offend precisely those liberal and humanitarian segments of opinion whose views he had previously been thought to share. At the same time, he did not manage to convey his understanding of the real situation in Nigeria – a nasty war, but not an extermination campaign.[59] Trudeau kept himself well informed through the Commonwealth secretariat and its Canadian secretary-general, Arnold Smith, who was closely involved with events in Nigeria; and through Ivan Head, his own assistant for foreign affairs.[60] The subsequent appeasement of the various Nigerian minorities has tended to confirm Trudeau's judgment, and not that of his excitable critics. Nevertheless, when Canairelief was unable to meet its debts, the federal government picked up the bill.[61]

The Commonwealth survived Biafra, in part because Trudeau and most other Commonwealth leaders stuck by the Nigerian federal government during the civil war.[62] British overseas settlement had also created the white colonial governments of south and central Africa. South Africa, it is true, had left Britain's formal orbit with its departure from the Commonwealth in 1968, but ties of trade, finance, culture, and language still linked white South Africa with the larger British world, including Canada. Canadians had investments in South Africa, and they traded more with it than with any other African country.[63] They also took a proportionately greater, if generally disapproving, interest in that country.[64] The interest was tied to South Africa's policy of racial segregation and white political and economic dominance, apartheid; it was focused, in the 1960s, through condemnatory resolutions at the United Nations.

Under Trudeau, South Africa became a somewhat larger concern. *Foreign Policy for Canadians* identified social justice in southern Africa as a priority for Canadian policy. As Clarence Redekop has argued,[65] the Canadian pursuit of social justice, involving an end to racialism, was a compromise between an all-out attack on South African apartheid and a tacit acceptance of the status quo, an approach that was harshly condemned by a group of Toronto critics who composed and published a 'black paper' on southern Africa in response to the government's white paper.[66] Under the existing policy, relations were maintained with South Africa and trade continued to flow. South Africa was treated in every way as a normal foreign market: exporters received the usual facilities, including export credits from the government's Export Development Corporation, and investors in South Africa received Canadian tax credits for payments to the South African fisc. Included in the arrangement was South-West Africa (Namibia), which South Africa occupied and governed in defiance of United Nations resolutions on the subject.[67]

Canadian-South African activities of any kind were subject to the attention of anti-South African pressure groups in Canada who vociferously denounced what was termed 'the duplicity' of Canadian policy in southern Africa.[68] The government responded to their concerns in a modest way by asking its agencies, such as Air Canada or Polymer, 'to direct their activities elsewhere.'[69]

The collapse of the Portuguese African empire in 1974–5 added to the pressure on South Africa, while making it possible for the independent African states on its frontier, such as Botswana, to diversify their contacts in black Africa. Rhodesia, fighting a guerrilla war, would be the next to go. That left South Africa itself, well-armed and, in an era of soaring gold prices, prosperous. It was unassailable by any or all of its neighbours, and internal resistance to the government was weak. The Canadian government imposed an arms embargo in 1970, a measure that had little effect since South Africa was well able to supply itself elsewhere. In 1977 the government withdrew from assisting trade to South Africa, and next year it announced a Code of Conduct for Canadian companies operating there, following the example of the United States and the European Community. The code provoked scepticism among the many critics of Canadian policy in South Africa, but short of retaliation against investing firms at home there was nothing more that the Canadian government could do.[70] Some officials explained these moves as personal initiatives on the part of the external affairs minister, Don Jamieson. It was also believed that they would have little concrete effect.[71]

Canada followed up in 1979 by terminating its bilateral trade agreement with South Africa, thereby ending the 'British preference' that South African goods had enjoyed since 1932.[72] That was a step; but imports and exports from and to South Africa continued at a relatively high level.[73] Critics were neither pleased nor satisfied.[74] There was, however, South-West Africa.

South-West Africa was the subject of dissension at the United Nations. It had been a League of Nations mandate before the Second World War and, after the war, the United Nations had demanded jurisdiction. South Africa had refused. As the United Nations acquired a Third-World majority, this group became more exercised, demanding the surrender of South-West Africa or, as it was renamed, Namibia. Using the United Nations as a focus, the Canadian government participated with other Western nations in a prolonged mediation designed to winkle the South Africans out. With the example of a Marxist regime in neighbouring Angola propped up by Cuban troops, the Western countries hoped for a more moderate future for South-West Africa – provided, of course, the South Africans could be persuaded to leave. Though the South Africans listened and talked, the Western gambit for a variety of reasons was fruitless. South-West Africa, it became clear, was part of a larger negotiating package, one that would involve Angola and Cuba as well as South Africa and the West. Thus South Africa, traditionally a bilateral contact, had become a multilateral concern as well as an issue, admittedly a minor one, in Canadian politics.[75]

The same was true of white-ruled Southern Rhodesia, which had unilaterally declared its independence of Great Britain in 1965.[76] Canada had never so much as maintained a consulate in Rhodesia, and the Pearson government refused to recognize the white-settler regime of Ian Smith.[77] Rhodesia was an embarrassment to Great Britain. Its existence contradicted the principle of majority rule that the British had employed to useful effect as they departed the rest of their colonies in Africa, and the African members of the Commonwealth keenly felt the result.[78] Rhodesia had also become a multilateral issue by 1968, ranging the embarrassed and reluctant British government against African states which wanted it to coerce its rebellious colony – an expensive and difficult proposition that held little appeal to the British.[79] The Africans, Asians, and West Indians could not fail to conclude that British reluctance had something to do with the Rhodesians' race and colour.[80]

Rhodesia was pre-eminently a Commonwealth issue, although it had its United Nations aspects too. African wishes, and British unwillingness, helped define every Commonwealth meeting in the late 1960s and early 1970s: they also helped to define Pierre Trudeau's relations with and opinion of the Commonwealth.

The traditional Canadian approach to the Commonwealth was that it was a valuable interracial and interregional bridge. Until recently, Commonwealth members had enjoyed much in common – Great Britain and its empire – and these ties did not die as the British retreated to their tight little island. Pierre Trudeau, however, had scant regard for this Commonwealth history. He was not necessarily anti-British, but he was not seized, as older Canadian leaders had been, by the grandeur of the empire-commonwealth; nor was he greatly impressed by the quality of British leadership.[81] He was reluctant to attend his first Common-wealth conference, the heads of government meeting in London in January 1969, but he went.[82] From his point of view, London was important because of his discovery of the inadequacy of External Affairs' briefings. He liked informal, down-to-earth conversations with other leaders, and he found that, by forming contacts and exploiting friendships based on candour and good will, he could himself serve as a bridge between the several parts of the multiracial Commonwealth.[83] Although the London conference did not lack formality, it had a certain flexibility. Since it could not properly discuss the Nigerian civil war in its regular sessions – that would be an invasion of Nigeria's domestic jurisdiction – it did so over lunch, with the full cooperation of the Nigerian leader, General Gowon.[84] He also began to discern that the Commonwealth permitted such an enterprise, what he later described as 'graduate seminars for heads of government.'[85]

There were three great issues before the Commonwealth leaders. Nigeria was in the second year of fighting its exhausting civil war; there was Rhodesia; and there were the immigration policies of Great Britain and the East African states, all of them being, to some degree, racially determined.[86] Rhodesia proved to be the most volatile subject. As could have been predicted, it pitted Britain and five other states against the majority of twenty-three. Inside what British prime minister Harold Wilson described as the British camp, Canada was the most sympathetic to the African point of view, but that did not prevent Trudeau from interrupting one lengthy African speech with some pointed questions about feasibility and practicality.[87]

Trudeau left London with a positive disposition towards the Commonwealth. That fact was not immediately apparent to the Canadian public, which had seen their prime minister served up to the British tabloids as 'trendy Trudeau,' the womanizer (his dating habits were of special interest to British reporters). He had also experienced the special sanctimony that the British gutter press reserved for their treatment of royalty; when the prime minister slid down a banister after a banquet at Lancaster House, his fate was sealed.[88] Wilson gloated to his cabinet that 'Trudeau had been a flop but Harold was a success.'[89] Nor was respectable opinion at home enthralled with the impression Trudeau had made.[90] In the long term, however, it was less the impression Trudeau made than the impression made on him that counted. In cabinet, Trudeau called the meetings 'of incalculable benefit' and told his colleagues he hoped they could be held every year or so. In the longer term, he mused, the Commonwealth might diminish, but at present it was worthwhile.

Arnold Smith, a Canadian who served as Commonwealth secretary-general in this period, later assessed the value of the Commonwealth in the Rhodesian crisis, which lasted until majority rule was achieved in 1979. Its importance was, he believed, negative. It could not force the British to do something they did not wish, namely, to invade Rhodesia. But it could prevent them from making their peace with Ian Smith and his rebel regime, a factor that eventually and fatally undermined independent Rhodesia.[91] Canada participated in economic sanctions (both UN and Commonwealth) against the Smith government,[92] and, on the larger political issue – independence – encouraged the British to wait and see. The economic sanctions probably accomplished something, but, as was known at the time, they were widely evaded. It was its worsening strategic situation that finally brought the Rhodesian rebels to the bargaining table.[93]

The settler state confronted an increasingly dangerous rebellion, conducted from across its borders with the aid of independent African states. Though it could count on some help from South Africa, that would not prove to be enough, once the Portuguese gave independence to Mozambique. From Canada's point of view, waiting was sufficient for the time being.

By 1977 the rebel regime was visibly weakening; with its demise in prospect, the Trudeau government was willing to assist, possibly with funds, or even, reluctantly, with a temporary peacekeeping role.[94] The Clark government followed what was essentially the same policy in its brief period of office; that span did, however, coincide with a Commonwealth conference in neighbouring Zambia, and with the final disappearance of the Smith regime.[95] The next year, 1980, Rhodesia became Zimbabwe and was admitted to the Commonwealth.[96]

As Rhodesia dominated the 1969 Commonwealth heads-of-government meeting (HGM in the international world of acronyms), South Africa overshadowed the Singapore conference of 1971. It was, again, an imperial hangover: South Africa's defence relations with the British, who had a naval base near Cape Town, and a lucrative British arms supply contract with the South African government. The British government was in 1971 Conservative, headed by Edward Heath; and Heath, though in many respects a man of real ability, was not comfortable in the Commonwealth forum. He was conspicuously not comfortable with Trudeau.[97]

Trudeau was better prepared for Singapore than he had been for London two years earlier. In a throwback to the days of Mackenzie King, he asserted the role of his own office in dealing with other prime ministers.[98] Ivan Head's position as his foreign-policy adviser had developed and expanded, and Trudeau had begun to use him to make and maintain contact with other heads of government. Head, who had served in the Canadian high commission in Malaya ten years earlier, was familiar with the Commonwealth context and moved easily from capital to capital. His movements, and his closeness to the prime minister, were not universally well regarded in External Affairs. One diplomat, asked how Head was received inside the department, replied curtly, 'with deep suspicion.'[99] The line between his functions as the prime minister's adviser and his intervention in diplomatic affairs was a narrow one, but no one denied that Trudeau had the right to cross it if he chose. And Head on his trips around the world in preparation for the Commonwealth conference had already intervened, on Trudeau's behalf, to insure that African leaders would attend. It was in all probability a task that ordinary diplomats could not have accomplished, but that Head could, in his capacity as Trudeau's personal representative.

When Heath visited Ottawa in December 1970, and when he and Trudeau met again over dinner in New Delhi in January 1971, the Africans' objections to British policy received an extensive and, from Canada's perspective, informed ventilation. Canadian officials present at the dinner later described it as a 'no holds barred' exchange, pointing out that afterwards the two men were so drained they could manage nothing more than idle chitchat.[100]

Trudeau, in his public preparation for the conference, talked modestly but optimistically about the Commonwealth. He defended the right of each member state to set its own policies – even Britain, widely condemned for its South African arms transactions.[101] In Singapore, Trudeau shored up relations between Edward Heath and the Africans in private, and in public underlined the importance of avoiding a racial confrontation, and hence a possible race war, over southern Africa.[102] Time and again, it was later reported, the Canadian prime minister had steered discussion away from the trivia of the moment to the longer-term implications of South Africa's policies, and to the question of how racial conflict might be avoided.[103] It was conciliation, but of a specially Trudeauvian kind: he was inviting his colleagues to ask basic questions and, by asking them, to discover a common ground obscured by the passions of the moment. Trudeau was singled out for praise for his conciliatory efforts by the conference host, Lee Kuan Yew of Singapore; but that fact was to some degree overshadowed by press coverage of the Commonwealth's narrow escape from confrontation and implosion.[104]

Also overlooked was another contribution Trudeau made in his reflections on the meeting. He did not, he said, wish to waste time listening to 'set-piece speeches' of the kind that dominated the United Nations and other international organizations. He would far prefer free dialogue, even a seminar format. It was an important departure, for, as participants at Singapore had noted, the plenary sessions had grown too big and too formal to accomplish any kind of meaningful result. Only the private gatherings, for prime ministers and the Commonwealth secretary-general, seemed to be working.[105]

The British left Singapore doubtful whether they would ever return to another Commonwealth meeting. Strong hints were given that the next one ought to be held four or five years in the future – a gap that under the circumstances could well have proved indefinite. But, at Arnold Smith's urging, Trudeau agreed to call one for 1973 in Ottawa.[106] He even made it a part of his 1972 election campaign, and, when he narrowly scraped through, its symbolic importance acquired a direct political character. It was a chance to demonstrate to Canadians that their prime minister counted for something in an international forum. The best way to achieve results was to alter its form.[107]

The first achievement was to secure the Queen's presence. The Commonwealth counted for something in Buckingham Palace, and the Queen let it be known that, if asked, she would attend. Both Trudeau and opposition leader Stanfield agreed that whichever one of them was in power would welcome the Queen.[108] Since Trudeau won, it was Ivan Head who did the preparatory work. Instead of scheduling an agenda according to the taste and perception of the host country, Trudeau sent Head around the world to discover what the leaders themselves wished to talk about.[109] There was a danger that some might not attend, so they were offered a London stopover on their Canadian-financed flights to Ottawa. The most prominent hold-out was Mrs Gandhi of India, who protested that she had too many pressing matters at home to sit through an agenda that would be dominated by British concerns.[110]

Mrs Gandhi misjudged the situation, or at any rate misconceived her excuse. But she was not alone: Edward Heath of Great Britain manifested extreme reluctance to go anywhere after suffering through African criticisms at Singapore. Only the presence of the Queen at the Canadian meetings seems to have moved him, late and reluctantly, to go at all.[111]

The great concern before the 1973 gathering was the bizarre case of Uganda. Uganda had fallen under the control of a military dictator, Idi Amin. Amin in 1972 attracted unfavourable attention when he suddenly decided to expel Asian residents of his country; in the emergency, the Canadian government responded by sending a team of immigration officers to East Africa, and by accepting 7000 Ugandan Asians as refugees. They proved to be hard-working, highly qualified, and extremely successful settlers.[112] Since Canada had no real refugee policy at the time, the immigration officials invented one as they went along.[113]

After expelling the Asians, and damaging the Ugandan economy in the process, Amin proceeded to other tyrannical acts. The Ugandan chief justice was murdered, as well as the vice-chancellor of the local university. It became obvious that no one was safe from Amin's thuggery, and that any pretense of law and order in Uganda was at an end. Amin, meanwhile, broadcast his eccentricities through a pliant world media for whom he was, to say the least, good copy. The increasing chaos in

Uganda, and the very real danger that anyone in that country, foreign or Ugandan, faced, eventually prompted the Canadian government to scale down its aid program and, in 1973, to terminate it altogether. The danger to Canadians living in Uganda was cited as a principal reason.[114]

The British, who Amin criticized most of all, considered seeking to expel Uganda from the Commonwealth. Certainly there was little to be gained by inviting Uganda's barbaric government or its peculiar leader to a heads-of-government meeting, but no other country wanted to expel Uganda from the organization. Amin, in any case, did not attend the Ottawa conference, though he threatened up to the last minute to come. His absence was the greatest contribution he could have made to a gathering that passed off successfully, and that went some way to restoring the Commonwealth's reputation as a bridge between races and between North and South.[115]

It was not only the Commonwealth that was troubled by Amin's reign of terror. Uganda remained a member of the United Nations throughout his dictatorship, and, though human rights were in vogue at the time, the General Assembly found no occasion to chastise Uganda for its internal policies.[116] The Commonwealth at least condemned 'excesses ... so gross as to warrant the world's concern' at its heads of government meeting in 1977. In the end, in 1979, neighbouring Tanzania invaded Uganda and chased Amin from the country; members of the United Nations and the Commonwealth averted their eyes from the invasion.[117]

Trudeau had meanwhile devised a new format for the heads-of-government meeting, which would eventually include Amin's successor, whoever he might be. It was to be heads only, with one adviser. Without an audience, there was no point to speeches; and since there was one common language, English, the other apparatus of an international conference could be dispensed with.[118]

The Commonwealth heads of government did not return to Canada during Trudeau's term of office. Trudeau proved to be a faithful attender at future conferences (Kingston, Jamaica, 1975; London 1977; Melbourne, 1981; New Delhi 1983); since some of the issues remained the same – Uganda and Rhodesia in 1977 and South Africa at all of them – he could invoke increasing experience. Canada's compromising, facilitating role became familiar, ironically enough for someone who had been inclined to doubt the usefulness of being a helpful fixer.[119]

Bridge-building, in the context of the Commonwealth, came naturally to Canada and to Trudeau. In his time in office, the Commonwealth conferences may well have afforded the largest opportunity for helpful fixation. In an age of continuing British retreat from empire, Canada could play a role in easing the transition from colonialism, or in masking those situations where Britain was unwilling, or unable, to employ such power as remained. The exceptions were, of course, Northern Ireland and the Falkland Islands – on Ireland Canada prudently offered no comment. It was an ironically historical role: tidying up the legacy of the past, in an area where Canada's history, British history, and the English language fitted it to be a facilitator – in other words, a fixer.

Were the strictures of the early Trudeau period therefore inaccurate, or misplaced? It proved more difficult than expected not to live up to others' expectations. A positive policy may have been difficult to formulate, but a reactive one was perfectly acceptable and, as it turned out, appropriate. Except for Biafra and Trudeau's Cuban misadventure, the government's performance in its political relations with the Third World attracted mild but favourable attention at home, and some appreciation abroad.

11

The Kindness of Strangers

Philanthropy is an activity that is much admired in the abstract. Generosity, in contrast, is a limited condition, particularly for states. Apart from the first flush of enthusiasm for fire, flood, and earthquake victims, money is an object, and politics an objection. The Trudeau government in its time experienced all the vicissitudes that attach to official humanitarianism; it discovered, possibly not to its surprise, that the roots of altruism grow in strange places.

Canada was a relatively strong aid-giver to the Commonwealth African states, though in no case was it the largest. In Nigeria in 1972, for example, Canada was responsible for not quite 17 per cent of aid from seventeen developed countries. In Ghana the figure was much bigger, 38.38 per cent, but even there the United States, not Canada, was the greatest aid-giver.[1] Even in Tanzania, the home of President Julius Nyerere, Trudeau's principal African colleague, Canadian aid did not predominate: that distinction belonged to socialist Sweden. Sweden's role in the collapsing Tanzanian economy was, accordingly, greater than Canada's. As Robert Matthews has observed, the pattern of Canadian aid, and its failure to dominate anywhere in Africa, lessened its leverage over the governments of any of the recipient countries; perhaps for that reason, perhaps because it is disinclined to interfere, Canada has not put bilateral relations to work in a multilateral context.[2]

The manner in which Canada bestowed aid may have had something to do with this phenomenon. Foreign aid was managed prior to 1968 by a division of the Department of External Affairs. Created in 1960, the External Aid Office oversaw Canada's various aid programs and donations. Its direction had always been a little out of the ordinary, at least for Ottawa, but it was only in 1966 that it acquired a high profile with the appointment of the president of Power Corporation, Maurice Strong, as its head. 'You are going to become one of Canada's most important men,' Paul Martin had once told Strong, and it was not a rhetorical observation. When Strong took over the External Aid Office he also took an 85 per cent cut in salary; with that background, he was not about to be intimidated by the customs and practices of Ottawa's bureaucracy.[3]

Before long, aid was being transformed into 'development' and under-developed countries, the phrase of the 1950s, became 'developing nations.' True enough, they were being assisted, but to 'develop.' In September 1968 the External Aid Office was transformed into the Canadian International Development Agency (CIDA), a crown corporation with its own board and with Strong as its president.[4] In 1970 CIDA's research twin, the International Development Research Centre (IDRC), was created specifically to look at the long term – and from a multilateral perspective that would include representatives of developing countries. Together, CIDA and IDRC represented a merging of the immediate and practical with the philosophical and the future.[5]

CIDA reported to parliament through the secretary of state for internal affairs. It therefore rested with Mitchell Sharp to balance CIDA's view of the world with that in his own department. For Sharp and his successors, the job of making External Affairs and CIDA run in tandem has been compared to 'driving an ill-matched team of horses.'[6] But though CIDA in some respects enjoyed a sense of identity and autonomy, it remained throughout the Trudeau period the responsibility of the external affairs minister.[7]

The creation of CIDA was accompanied by some redefinitions of the purpose and practice of Canada's aid program. 'Direct aid' of the old variety was not 'a satisfactory basis for the relationship between rich and poor nations in the long run.' Instead, 'a much more complex and sophisticated set of arrangements in the fields of trade, investment, education, science and technology' had to be put in place. Their purpose was 'to support and strengthen' the less-developed nations' own efforts at 'self-help.'[8] In recognition of its special mission, and in anticipation of unusual circumstances in the donation of aid, CIDA was granted the privilege of carrying its unspent funds from one fiscal year to the next.[9]

Strong made an immediate and generally favourable impact on the media. He brought in outsiders to advise and consult; he set priorities; and he travelled the world, though with minimal fanfare and protocol. Money was not a problem: parliament had voted more than his agency could spend. His agency, in turn, was the principal, but not the sole, aid dispenser on the Canadian side. Strong had to remind parliamentarians of the need to be cautious with public dollars. Canada was no longer Lady Bountiful dispensing cash and reaping gratitude, but a participant in a serious cooperative enterprise.[10]

Canadian aid was nevertheless dispensed in patterns that were less than novel. It was anticipated that much of Canada's aid would be 'tied aid' – that is, Canadian money for capital goods would as far as possible be spent in Canada, to purchase goods from Canadian suppliers. This led G.K. Helleiner to comment, in 1976, that 'with regard to procurement restrictions ... the Canadian record is a poor one.'[11] It could lead to expensive aid in relation to need.

Nor could Canadian aid be everywhere. Much of it was directed in the 1970s towards the needy countries of francophone Africa, but the older ties with Commonwealth countries were not neglected. Nigeria, for example, received considerable aid at the end of the 1960s, as its civil war wound down. In the 1970s the focus shifted southward and, in particular, to Tanzania, where Nyerere made such an impression on Trudeau.

Nyerere was much respected. His integrity, intelligence, and the modesty of his way of life were a pleasing contrast to the extravagance, follies, and occasional cruelties of some of Africa's leaders. Tanzania was attempting to chart its own course of economic development – 'African socialism – which would develop the country's resources for the many rather than concentrating them, as under capitalism, in the hands of a few. Or so the theory went. It was a respectable theory that appealed to Western idealists of the Fabian kind, and it charted a better way than the coup-ridden regimes elsewhere in Africa.[12] When a House of Commons subcommittee came to report on the subject of aid and development in early 1971, it concluded that 'the most fundamental, durable and important reason for Canada assisting less-developed countries is a concern for "international social justice." ' Its words applied more directly to Tanzania, or at least to Tanzania's leadership, than to most other potential recipients of Canadian aid.[13] In the summer of 1971 Strong's successor as president of CIDA, Paul Gérin-Lajoie, toured east Africa to inspect what Canada was already doing; presumably he also learned something more of what the Tanzanians wanted.[14] Strong had, in the meantime, been stolen by the United Nations to head up its global conference on the environment.

Canadian aid to Tanzania was predicated on Tanzania's own assessment of its needs, and those needs were defined as fundamental. Tanzania needed help to build the infrastructure of its economy and to develop the skills necessary to manage it. The infrastructure, therefore, was where Canadian aid went: to railways, to a waterworks, to hydroelectricity projects, even to a large bakery that was to transform Tanzania's state-produced wheat into bread. Roger Young's study of Canadian aid to Tanzania terms the concentration in this area both 'traditional' and 'well-placed,'[15] but the actual performance of the aid projects left much to be desired, especially under the category of 'self-help.' Canadian help, once given, had to be maintained, and in the same projects. For a variety of reasons, the most obvious being that an aid project might well collapse if Canadian guidance were removed, the Tanzanians did not wish to be without it. The alternative was to admit the failure of a given project – for example, the Tanzanian capital's refurbished waterworks – and allow it to sink into decrepitude.[16]

Clearly there was much to be learned about the techniques of managing aid on the spot. Despite all the studies and inspections, there was also something to be gleaned about the appropriateness of high-technology aid. Trained Tanzanians were in short supply; paradoxically, the funding of certain aid projects imposed intolerable strains on a scarce resource – people. Nor did training programs always help: if some other project acquired a higher priority in the eyes of the receiving government, the trainees would be transferred, or lured, there. There was the risk of unpleasant publicity at home, for an aid project, being tangible, was a proper subject for television journalism. The Tanzanian bakery, for example, produced bread that cost 60 per cent more to bake than its selling price. It did no good to protest that the bakery was what the Tanzanian government had wanted and that CIDA's officials had always had misgivings about it. Instead of a success story, CIDA had financed a cautionary tale. The fact that other aid projects – hydroelectricity, for example – were more successful counted for less than the failure in the eyes of the journalists and the public.[17]

Deficiencies on the spot were only part of CIDA's difficulties. The agency, and the government, had always tried to reinforce the domestic political foundation of aid by tying the provision of funds to the purchase of appropriate Canadian equipment. In the Tanzanian bakery, for example, there was only one possible Canadian supplier, who duly received the contract. The equipment supplied has been criticized as 'grossly overpriced,' compared to similar material manufactured in Germany or Japan; and there has been some speculation as to whether it was properly designed for Tanzanian conditions.[18] But Canadian machinery was part of the political price for aid, a requirement imposed by those who raised and doled out the funds.

CIDA also had to satisfy another branch of government as to how it spent its funds. The auditor general of Canada had adopted the concept of a 'comprehensive audit,' which meant that public auditors were moving out of their traditional restricted scope and into examination of policy decisions by public agencies. It amounted to 'second-guessing,' one of those affected sourly remarked, but it was a type of second-guessing that was beyond the capacity of all but the most narrowly focused parliamentary committee. And so the auditors moved in to fill the vacuum inadvertently created by the politicians.[19]

Gérin-Lajoie's management style – quasi-imperial, in the view of some – did not commend itself to the government's accountants. They harshly criticized CIDA's financial controls in a report to parliament in 1976. CIDA was then subjected to a comprehensive audit, which resulted in a tightening of procedures. Gérin-Lajoie departed and was replaced by a more orthodox figure, Michel Dupuy, a senior diplomat. As one analyst of Canadian aid practices observed: 'Now, like other government departments, CIDA must function within a web of regulations imposed on it by outside departments.'[20]

As a consequence, CIDA found itself subject to the usual 'money-moving' characteristic of financial year-ends; what was not spent was not only lost, but would tell against the agency's ability to justify the next year's appropriation.[21] The new spending requirements not only affected CIDA's ability to commit to large projects, but necessarily helped shape them; sometimes it reduced commitments that the agency had already made, to the dismay of aid recipients obliged to add another element of financial uncertainty to their economic projections.

CIDA was almost literally turned around. Instead of facing outwards, it guarded its rear. Controls and regulations meant increasing staff at the head office. In the division that dealt with bilateral aid, for example, there were 300 personnel at headquarters in 1983 who spent eleven months out of twelve at home, on average, and one month in the field. There were only fifty actually stationed in the field.[22] In the view of the North-South Institute in Ottawa, the distribution of CIDA's staff made it 'particularly difficult for Canadian aid personnel to become fully knowledgeable about particular countries.'[23]

Experience in the mid-1970s conditioned CIDA's corporate culture. Because the real danger lay in political exposure at home, that was where efforts were concentrated; ability to move paper in response to the government's audit requirements became the main criterion for measuring successful job performance. Queried as to job satisfaction in 1982, one CIDA official admitted 'that acquiring country-specific knowledge "is not part of being a good bureaucrat." '[24]

Whether aid could by itself make much of a difference was and remains a subject for heated controversy. Aid packages could not offset large-scale economic fluctuations. If the rise in oil prices after 1973 benefited the energy producers among Third-World countries – Nigeria's trade with Canada, for example, burgeoned during the 1970s – it undermined the economies of many others. Tanzania faced a collapse in its export prices at a time when its energy costs were moving out of control.[25] As a result, Tanzania was forced to restrict imports and to accept the deterioration of its fixed capital; important aspects of its citizens' standard of living suffered accordingly.

Many if not most Third-World countries were inclined to argue in the 1970s that much more was needed – a reversal of the shape of the world economy to break the cycle of 'dependence' that bound their economies to the industrialized West. This topic was much pursued in the United Nations, but bilateral aid does not seem to have been much affected by it.

Bilateral aid was only part of the story. In relation both to South America and to Africa, Canada participated in multilateral aid through development banks or other forms of consortia of aid givers. That aspect of Canadian activity was highly controversial, at least within the government. As the North-South Institute accurately observed, multilateral aid 'has been increasingly denigrated by influence-minded officials who believe Canada should be exerting political leverage through its bilateral program and by a small but active lobby within sections of the business community which has been reluctant to see aid funds disbursed through other than the tied and sheltered bilateral program.'[26]

Little has been said about private investment. In terms of capital, Africa was not highly regarded as a field for Canadian enterprise. The Tanzanian economy, especially after the oil shocks of 1973 and 1979, could hardly pay its own way. The government, having chosen 'African socialism,' was regarded as unreliable if not hostile to Canadian companies. Nyerere's belated attempts to claim the opposite met contradiction even from Trudeau, who at a development conference at Cancún in 1981 'asked the Tanzanian President whether he really thought that the Western nations would invest more in his country, knowing that sooner or later their investments would be jeopardized by government intervention.' After a moment of silence, the United Nations secretary-general wrote, 'suddenly loud laughter broke out, not least from Nyerere himself, and the meeting went on to other matters.'[27]

Trudeau could manage the issue because he had become one of the Commonwealth's most senior leaders. Aid and trade, explored in a Commonwealth context, allowed for a 'Canadian' approach in Africa that might not have worked, by then, in Asia. In Asia, where there was no lingering British presence or remnant of white settlement, the Commonwealth signified less, a portent perhaps for the Commonwealth in Africa once the link between colonial history and contemporary independence is finally broken. Whether the Commonwealth will survive the end of the post-colonial era remains to be seen.

Aid remained a major consideration in assessing Canadian relations with the countries of south Asia. Asia had been Canada's main window on the developing world in the 1950s and early 1960s. There, as later in Africa, aid was a component of a larger policy: in Asia, the Cold War; in Africa, the Cold War and the struggle with France over francophonie.

Canada's longest-standing and most diverse relationship was with India. India was a trading partner of some importance throughout the Trudeau period. Unlike some other Asian countries (Hong Kong or Taiwan, for instance), its importance did not increase very much between 1968 and 1974.[28] India during the Trudeau years was a growing source of immigrants, however – 126,129 between 1968 and 1984; given ethnic conflicts in India and especially among the Sikhs of the Punjab, this fact did not necessarily strengthen the bonds between the governments of India and Canada.[29]

Canada and India were associated in the Commonwealth and through the International Control Commission in Vietnam. The latter link, undertaken with considerable optimism in the 1950s, was productive of more antagonism than comity by 1968. India had in the meantime realigned its foreign-policy priorities away from the United States and the West and towards the Soviet Union. That fact by itself would have influenced its behaviour on the International Control Commission, but the commission was mortally wounded by the failure of a stable government to emerge in South Vietnam by the mid-1960s. It would expire, unmourned, in 1972.[30]

Another feature of 1950s optimism was still very much in place in 1968. In 1954 Canada had begun a program of nuclear aid to India. It had given an experimental reactor, CIRUS, to the Indians, and had followed on with the sale of an early CANDU model in 1962. India had become the principal example abroad of what had also become a strictly Canadian line of reactors: natural-uranium-fuelled, heavy-water-moderated. Platoons of Indian engineers were trained in Canada; Indian designers were anxious to imitate and perpetuate the CANDU line.[31]

There was a significant flaw in the smooth pattern of Indo-Canadian atomic relations. The original gift to India occurred before international safeguards had been negotiated or imposed. Ever since, safeguards had been a lively issue between the Indian and Canadian governments, with the Indians arguing that Canada was principally concerned to apply an unequal and hypocritical standard of conduct to Asians while it was perfectly happy to apply a quite different one with its friends and nuclear allies.

India, its government believed, was the best judge of its strategic situation and needs. Its old associates in the Commonwealth were far away, and unable or unlikely to help in time of need; its new enemies, such as China, were uncomfortably close by. Its relations with one Commonwealth partner, Pakistan, were unfortunately worst of all, a fact that was demonstrated when civil war broke out in 1971 in East Pakistan, the former province of Bengal in old British India. In December 1971 India invaded East Pakistan and defeated the Pakistani military in a short, sharp war. East Pakistan proclaimed its independence as Bangladesh; the western rump of Pakistan left the Commonwealth in January 1972.

During the Pakistani crisis, the Canadian government expressed its grave concern over the situation on the Indian subcontinent. Apart from sending small sums for refugees ($7 million from public and private sources), there was little else it could do.[32] Once a new government in Bangladesh was established, Canada recognized it and approved its admission into the Commonwealth in April 1972.

The new Commonwealth partner was not destined to prosperity. Situated on low-lying lands, subject to periodic floods, overpopulated, badly governed before and after independence from Pakistan, Bangladesh became a permanent aid seeker. During the 1970s it was most often described as a basket case.[33] Although Canada directed a variety of aid (totalling $500 million in the 1970s) to Bangladesh, food aid was necessarily the most urgent and the most important portion of the Canadian aid package. Wheat alone accounted for 58 per cent of the total value of Canadian aid. The aid contributed to the fight against starvation, and it assisted Bangladesh's balance of payments in the face of repeated rises in oil prices.[34]

The war left India militarily predominant on the subcontinent, but still facing an unreconciled enemy in Pakistan. It was not surprising that the government of India continued to give attention to the problem of ensuring its security by less conventional means. The meaning of the Indian victory, the nature of Indian society, and the character of its government under the imperious Indira Gandhi were the subject of intense discussion in Ottawa.

Finally, in 1973, the Department of External Affairs undertook a review of Canadian policy towards the subcontinent. Two main points of view surfaced. The first has been described as 'the sick man of Asia' school: its enthusiasts argued that India was lumbering towards breakdown and collapse. Aid had not made any crucial difference to this fact and it was better to face reality, scale down aid, and refocus Canada's Asian policy towards more successful and less dependent countries such as China. The Indianists naturally differed. India, and the Third World in general, were on the rise. Aid had become a normal part of Western dealings with the developing world – 'a permanent feature of international relations.' Whether the aid under this latter interpretation was to be regarded as blackmail, conscience money, or as reinforcement for other Canadian politics we do not know.[35] Both points of view were soon to receive reinforcement.

In May 1974 the Indian government announced that it had achieved a peaceful nuclear explosion in the Thar desert. The announcement came as a shock, if not a surprise, in Ottawa. There the Trudeau government was in the throes of an election campaign; under the circumstances, it had little option but to announce its disapproval. The prime minister, who had asked for and received assurances from the Indian prime minister that nothing of the kind was contemplated, was especially displeased. Nuclear aid to India was suspended.[36]

Negotiations followed. It was clear that the Indians had derived their nuclear explosive from the Canadian experimental reactor, CIRUS. They nevertheless hoped that matters could be patched up between Canada and India; a cessation of Canada's nuclear aid would be damaging, and possibly disastrous, to India's nuclear program. But nothing was achieved and the suspension of help was made permanent, to the Indians' very considerable and lasting chagrin.[37]

The sequel indicated that Indian technology, even after twenty years of aid, was still sufficiently dependent to be significantly hindered by Canada's action. Yet the refusal of the Indians to give in to Canada's demands for proper safeguards indicated their willingness to live by their own wits if necessary. Over the longer term, we may observe, the Indian nuclear industry was considerably handicapped if not crippled by what had happened, a proposition that in a small way supports the first school of Canadian thought back in 1973.

The Indians were not the only ones concerned. While Canada's nuclear safeguards were strict before 1974, they were much more stringent thereafter, to the annoyance of potential customers for Canadian uranium such as West Germany and Switzerland.[38] As for India, the unique

Canadián relationship, expressed by the CANDU connection, was at an end; in this and other cases Canadian policy would be driven by larger concerns and different perceptions.[39]

Those concerns and perceptions were at the centre of Canada's policies at the United Nations. It was not that the United Nations especially interested the prime minister. He had been there in 1966, as part of the Canadian delegation, and was known to have resisted attempts to speak to the General Assembly. The posturings, the lack of genuine debate, and perhaps the irresponsibility of the international organization were all calculated to cool his enthusiasm. Though the United Nations had its partisans in External Affairs and in the Canadian foreign-policy community, its reputation by the late 1960s was in something of an eclipse in Canada.

That was true elsewhere, of course, but it had a peculiarly Canadian angle. The circumstances of the Six-Day War in 1967 between Israel and the Arabs, and the reckless expulsion of the Canadian contingent of the UN peacekeeping force from Egypt had soured many Canadians on the United Nations and its ability effectively to keep the peace.

The United Nations had become the dwelling place of shattered illusions. It was unable to enforce its own rules, or to collect its dues from delinquent members. Instead, members like Canada contributed extra money to emergency funds to keep the world body staggering onward. Otherwise, diplomats warned, it would lose all credibility because it would abandon the great principle of universality of membership. It lost credibility in any case, but perhaps it was credibility of a lesser sort.

More credibility leaked away when observers contemplated the state of the United Nations' civil service. A system of national appointments was firmly in place; in order to accommodate the Third World the merit principle had been stretched until, by the mid-1970s, it was recognized that competence was not a necessary qualification for well-paid international employment. Under the circumstances, it was fortunate that diligence was not a necessary criterion either.[40]

The secretaries-general of the Trudeau era, U Thant and Kurt Waldheim, were hardly spectacular personalities. U Thant was widely abused for his conduct in the Six-Day War, while Waldheim's reputation declined the closer one got to his office. But even Waldheim by 1981 was deploring the failure of the United Nations to live up to its ideals or to fulfil its function. His particular nostrum, that the UN send its own ambassadors to national capitals, found acceptance in only one such capital: Ottawa.[41]

Waldheim later expressed his gratitude to Trudeau, with whom, he wrote, he had established 'a close relationship over the years.'[42] With allowance made for exaggeration, there is no doubt that Trudeau was anxious to cooperate with Waldheim and the UN, and that he lent his support wherever possible to its efforts. Even after Waldheim's retirement, he lent his name to a so-called Interaction Council that the former secretary-general had created in Vienna. It was by then November 1983, and most of the 'senior statesmen' who made up the council had left active politics; soon Trudeau would too.[43]

The United Nations lacked reputation in the 1970s and 1980s, but it did not entirely lack importance. As an aggregation of states, as nearly universal as circumstances would allow, it reflected not merely the interests of its member states but, to some degree, the actual balance of world opinion. The United States had lost credibility as a model for other countries to follow. Though that did not mean that Americans were not envied by those less rich, there seemed to be insufficient incentive even for Third-World democracies to mimic the pattern of a country whose wealth so far surpassed their own as to pass into the realm of the imponderable.

As much to the point, the Americans lost the Vietnam War. They seemed to be unable to do anything much about the establishment of Marxist regimes in Angola and Mozambique. Even the dispatch of a Cuban expeditionary force to Africa to prop up the Soviet Union's various friends in the region did not provoke any effective response from the Americans. Under the circumstances, it is not surprising that African governments chose not to notice that a second world army was roaming the backwoods of their continent. Instead, African leaders concentrated their fire on the remnants of imperialism, and on issues congenial to the Second World and the Arabs.

The symbol of the Third World's tilt away from the West was the adoption by the United Nations General Assembly in 1975 of a resolution that equated Zionism with racism. Zionism was, of course, the founding ideology of the State of Israel; the condemnation of Zionism, especially in such terms, naturally undermined Israel's moral justification. The Israelis responded with outrage, as did the Americans. On this issue, Canada voted with Israel and the United States, and therefore with the minority in the United Nations. Afterwards, indignation inside Canada closely resembled that in the United States. It found expression in the refusal of the Canadian cabinet to countenance a scheduled United Nations conference in Toronto if it included representatives from the Palestine Liberation Organization, the PLO. MacEachen, then external affairs minister, suffered a defeat in cabinet on the matter; it was a harbinger of the Trudeau government's increasing willingness, in the late 1970s, to follow the tide of domestic opinion and to cultivate political advantage. On the Zionism issue, the Canadian government was being pushed by the UN majority, very much against its own inclination, to draw the line.

Don Jamieson, MacEachen's successor at External Affairs, put the matter bluntly in a speech to the General Assembly in September 1976. Some groups argued that Israel should be deprived of its right to sit in the United Nations. That would be unwise, Jamieson said. The Zionism resolution had 'deeply divided' the UN's membership, and the organization should not seek to perpetuate the division by insisting on the link between Zionism and racism. If it did, Canada would not participate in a forthcoming UN conference on racial discrimination. What Canada would do in the unlikely event that Israel was expelled from the United Nations, Jamieson left unsaid.[44]

The Americans in the late 1970s and 1980s nevertheless 'found Canada's performance in the United Nations disappointing. Daniel Patrick Moynihan, perhaps the most active and intelligent of the American delegates to the United Nations, rated his Canadian colleague, Saul Rae, and the Canadian attitude in New York as the most disappointing he encountered.[45] Perhaps Moynihan expected too much; certainly he believed he had got too little support for his decision to confront the UN majority, when necessary, with a frank description of their character and behaviour. He was determined to do away with, or at least seriously impair, the double standard with which Third-World spokespeople measured Western actions (always found wanting) while exempting themselves from even the mildest scrutiny and criticism.[46] Moynihan and his successors as American representatives denounced the double standard. His initiative distressed friends of the United Nations in the United States, and seems to have caused concern even to Henry Kissinger. Some of the criticism levelled at Moynihan went wide of the mark, but it was possible to set down a philosophical difference about the proper role, and perhaps the proper definition, of diplomacy. If Moynihan and the United States were on one side, Canada as a matter of diplomatic practice was on the other. True to its traditions of quiet diplomacy, Canada would not follow his lead, which old UN hands believed to be ineffective and counter-productive.[47]

Canadian reluctance may have been influenced by the relatively greater success of certain Canadian initiatives in the world body, especially Maurice Strong's global conference on the environment in Stockholm in June 1972. Strong assembled 113 countries under the banner 'Only One Earth.' After eleven days of conference he secured a Declaration on the Human Environment that enunciated, for the first time, principles of international environmental responsibility to which all states were expected to subscribe. They included 'the duty of states not to pollute the environment of other states, the duty not to pollute the sea, the air and outer space beyond the jurisdiction of any state, and the duty to develop the law concerning liability and compensation in respect of such damage.'[48]

Jack Davis, the Canadian minister of the environment, enthusiastically pledged $7.5 million a year from Canada to support a UN environmental agency. Though Canadian officials noted that they had not got everything they wanted – a reference to the duty of coastal states to prevent pollution would have been handy in view of contention with the United States over the Arctic Waters Pollution Prevention Act – they were pleased to see so much progress in so short a time.[49]

It was a sign that Canada's interests did not lie in extending great power conflict to the United Nations, or replacing it with conflict between the West and the Third World. Rather, Canada wanted to obscure and, if possible, sideline such conflicts. It was true that the Third-World delegates in New York often behaved deplorably and recklessly, but they were nonetheless functioning members of the world body and therefore proper targets for Canadian diplomacy. If they needed help during specialized conferences, Canada was happy to provide it. If there was a favour to be done, Canada would at least think about it. In the meantime, Canada would not complain too loudly about breaches of protocol, errors of fact, or even prevarication on the part of other sovereign states. Bread cast on those waters, Canadian diplomats reasoned, might return in strange but beneficial forms.[50]

It was not that the Canadian government was happy about the direction the United Nations was taking. In a period when even the UN's circumspect secretary-general, Kurt Waldheim, was given to lecturing the delegates about the deficiencies of their organization, it would have been difficult for Canadians to take advantage of a case of diplomatic myopia.[51] But, in the words of one undersecretary-general, 'Perhaps its best role is merely to draw off poisons from the international community, to take the world's opprobrium without making overt gestures of its own.'[52]

Unfortunately, the UN majority, the group of seventy-seven Third-World countries, had the bit in its teeth. It wanted to make overt gestures, and it would not stop with Israel. The United Nations Educational,

Scientific and Cultural Organization (UNESCO), which had its own secretariat and secretary-general, set about defining its agenda in terms that
exasperated and frustrated Western delegates. To many if not most of
the Third-World delegates, it seemed that they had been getting a bad
press; it was high time to shoot the messenger. From the point of view
of the Third World, however, or much of it, it was just another case of
colonialism, this time of the intellectual variety, robing them in principles
that could only confirm its dominant position. There could be no reconciliation between the two attitudes.

UNESCO began drafting and defining the responsibilities of the press
in a way that was calculated to please those who wished to muzzle
reporting by Western media. The media, starting in the United States,
reacted sharply, and a public furore followed. It provoked a Canadian
warning to the UNESCO general conference in Nairobi in 1976 that its
proposed media declaration was 'simply ... not acceptable to Canada.'[53]

What UNESCO's majority meant to do was illustrated by the fate of a
report on the Israeli occupation of the West Bank of the Jordan in 1979.
UNESCO expected to hear about wrong-doing and oppression; when
instead it was told that Israel had not done anything especially wrong to
the social and intellectual condition of the occupied territories, the
secretary-general simply suppressed the report and commissioned
another. Since the second investigation produced the proper result, it
was published under UNESCO auspices.[54]

The incongruity of UNESCO's actions did little to attract support in
Canada for the world organization as a whole. Nor did the antics of
the United Nations Human Rights Committee, or its decolonization
committee. Yet the record was not entirely one-sided; when the United
States wished, it could still bring its diplomacy to bear in such a way as
to obviate or defeat hostile resolutions; on such occasions – for example,
the eternal question of Puerto Rico's purported colonial enslavement –
Canada voted with the United States.[55]

The Puerto Rican episode was minor compared to the great issue of
the New International Economic Order, a grandiose term that crept into
public discussion in the mid-1970s although its precursors had been on
the international agenda for quite some time.[56] When Trudeau addressed
the question of the economic imbalance between North and South in
1968, he argued that considerable changes in the policies of the developed countries would have to occur before there was any hope of
reversing the cycle of poverty in the underdeveloped world. This meant,
among other things, that countries like Canada would be obliged to
alter their trade policies to permit freer entry of Third-World goods,

sometimes at the expense of special interests at home. Less loftily put, jobs and protection at home would have to take second place to a preference for products that the Third World could produce to greater advantage.[57]

The argument for justice acquired greater force when coupled with warnings of scarcity. Such warnings were the stock in trade of Aurelio Peccei and his 'Club of Rome,' a group of prominent individuals who publicized the idea that Earth's resources were swiftly becoming exhausted. Such an idea could easily be linked to conservation and ecology, and it is not surprising that it appealed, briefly, to Trudeau. After further exposure to the club and its procedures, however, he concluded that it had few answers to the questions it posed, and that even those questions were of dubious worth.[58]

The position of most of the Third World worsened in the years that followed. There was, of course, a tendency on the part of Canadian opinion to lump all its components together, although, in fact, the Third World consisted of many quite different parts. For one thing, the petro-countries of OPEC were plainly able to alter the terms of trade with the industrialized world greatly to their advantage in the 1970s. For another, the countries of East Asia, especially Singapore, Taiwan, and South Korea (and a bit later Thailand), took a giant step into industrialization and out of underdevelopment in the 1970s. Not all Southeast Asia was so blessed: war-ravaged Indochina and socialist Burma experienced decreasing standards of living while their neighbours flourished. By the end of that decade these successful countries could hardly qualify as underdeveloped, and could only be called developing in the loosest sense. As they produced products to the taste, and pocket-book, of Canadian consumers, these 'newly industrializing countries' (NICs) saw their trade with Canada burgeon, apparently without strong action in their favour by the government of Canada.[59]

This aspect of Third-World economics was perhaps imperfectly understood in the mid-1970s; and perhaps it was easier to put the blame for world poverty on an international economic system, dominated, of course, by the West, than on the internal policies of Third-World governments. Yet seen in this light, the great UN development crusade of the 1970s, embodied in the Sixth Special Session of the United Nations of 1974 and the subsequent Conference on International Economic Cooperation (CIEC) and New International Economic Order exercises, appear in retrospect as a magnificent irrelevance – or what Allan MacEachen has called both 'the high water mark of the North-South Dialogue and ... one of the greatest lost opportunities of the 1970s.'[60]

The oil-price crisis furnished an appropriate opportunity to bring the split into the open. There was danger that the Western countries, scrambling to deal with OPEC, would forget about the other countries affected by the price hikes: as Mitchell Sharp asked at a consumers' conference in Washington in February 1974, 'But where are all those absent countries? Were they not invited?'[61] Would it not be possible to get producers and consumers of all varieties together to discuss their common problems and to move towards common solutions? It would, but there was little to show for it, as MacEachen later reflected. Yet it occupied much time and ink between the early 1970s and the early 1980s, including a large proportion of Trudeau's own efforts.

The Sixth Special Session of the United Nations General Assembly convened in the spring of 1974, in the wake of the oil shocks of the previous fall.[62] It adopted, in May, a Declaration on the Establishment of a New International Economic Order, which immediately became NIEO in international jargon. It was a call for action based on the assertion that the existing economic order, dominated by the developed industrial societies of the First World, was fundamentally inequitable, and that without intervention it would tend to perpetuate itself. That the existing order was not immutable, OPEC had already shown. By acting within their sovereign authority, a group of hitherto disadvantaged countries had reversed the terms of trade and stimulated a huge capital transfer from the North to the South. The UN declaration accordingly bowed in the direction of the absolute sovereign discretion of any state to regulate its own economic affairs, while calling for cooperation among states on the basis of equality and consideration for the worst-off countries. It demanded a just price for raw materials, in relation to their price when made into finished products. And it urged preferential trading relations between the developed and undeveloped worlds. It did not directly mention the oil shock, but it justified it in terms that promised a similar bonanza to other raw-materials producers who could manage to organize themselves effectively in the same way.[63] The conjuncture between OPEC and NIEO was therefore a happy coincidence. They pointed up the apparent vulnerability of the West, and the potential advantage of raw-materials producers in the Third World.[64]

Canadian officials were uneasy with the language and logic of the proposed NIEO. It was true enough that developed countries had paid little attention to the needs and concerns of the less-developed world in their trade negotiations in the 1960s. It was true too that low-cost imports had been discriminated against in the interests of the workforce in developed countries. But the remedy proposed could well be worse than the disease.[65]

External Affairs pointed out that NIEO in its insistence on untrammelled sovereign jurisdiction would license any state to take any action it chose against any company operating on its territory. These could be nationalized, and compensated or not according to the discretion of the host government without reference to precedent or international law.[66] Developed countries were not entitled to protest or to take action on behalf of their investors; at bottom, this was a proposition that Canada could not accept. As for producers' cartels, Canadian analysts argued that they would work against the interest of those Third-World countries that were actually industrializing.[67] OPEC had already rendered the aid and development plans of several developing countries obsolete virtually overnight; such countries instantly became abject clients of those developed countries or international agencies that were willing to lend them money to tide them over the energy crisis.

In any case, raw-materials producers were located outside as well as inside the Third World, making the identification of producer interests with the developing world doubly erroneous. Canada, of course, was a prominent producer and exporter of raw materials. As to trade preference, it would not be possible to exempt one set of suppliers against safeguards designed to protect domestic industry. That, the department reasoned, would be discriminatory, when it was to everyone's advantage to prevent discrimination. And when it was a question of standards at home (sanitary or health standards, for example) it was not in Canada's interest to exempt Third-World producers.[68] MacEachen put it best when he reminded Canadians that 'no government of Canada could alter its economic policies in favour of developing countries unless it were supported by the Canadian electorate: and the Canadian electorate is made up of workers and farmers from Quebec, the Maritimes, the Prairies and other regions.'[69]

These objections tended to underline Canada's standing as a developed trading nation; understandably they clashed with any attempt to redefine Canada's national economic interest or policy to make it match the intentions of the majority in the United Nations.[70] It followed that attempts to redefine Canada as a Third-World country – a raw-material producer with a legacy of colonial oppression – lacked a certain verisimilitude as far as most Canadians were concerned.[71]

Canada's opinion was not, initially, consulted. Nor, as far as the majority in the UN General Assembly was concerned, were the views of more important Western countries. In December 1974 the Assembly adopted a 'Charter of Economic Rights and Duties of States' that parroted the remedies proclaimed by the Sixth Special Session.

Canada was not much noticed in the initial confrontation, or in the subsequent negotiation, between OPEC and the developed world. Sheikh Yamani, Saudi Arabia's oil minister, had a list of significant nations, and Canada was not included. Yamani's list was the basis for the preparatory conferences which led to the CIEC, and Canada, greatly to its government's disgruntlement, was excluded.[72] Yamani was not uniquely at fault; French President Giscard d'Estaing also did his best to omit Canada from his economic summits in 1974 and 1975. Only on American insistence was Canada admitted in 1976.

Canadian views at the time were that the price of oil would continue to rise, and that OPEC would continue united and powerful. North-South confrontation would, in MacEachen's view, be 'detrimental to all,' and 'a genuine energy dialogue respecting the price setting legitimacy of OPEC, some institutional movement towards the NIEO and improved resource transfers to the poorest were desirable, realistic and achievable objectives.' It was these opinions that MacEachen sought to convey when, after the preliminary conferences, Canada was asked to attend the CIEC, and he himself was invited to be its co-chairman.[73] The conference would consist of eight developed entities (G-8, a term that includes the European Community negotiating as one) and nineteen developing countries, or G-19.

The other co-chairman was Manuel Perez Guerrero, a former oil minister in Venezuela. The two men found they could get along as realistic politicians, though MacEachen was struck by the contrast between the First-World luxury inside Perez's hacienda and the Third-World misery found outside his gate. The apparent harmony of objective discovered by the preparatory conference also proved, when the CIEC ministers met in December 1975, to be illusory. The North wanted 'the cooperative management of world energy,' as MacEachen termed it, and the South, 'the reshaping of the world's economic institutions and rules, and an equally dramatic acceleration of resource transfers.' Even these generalizations masked a quagmire of incoherence among the developed, undeveloped, and developing nations present at the conference.[74]

Despite this unpromising background, the first stages of the CIEC managed to hold the participants together. A deadline was set: the end of 1976. G-8 organized itself around and through the International Energy Agency (IEA); G-19's organization was a little more diverse, reflecting the fact that the nineteen developing countries had divergent backgrounds, economies, and interests. There was little enough in common between OPEC and underdeveloped oil-importing countries, and, even within OPEC, for example as between Algeria and Saudi Arabia, there were real differences.[75] It was less a dialogue, MacEachen mused, than a 'trialogue.'

Meeting in specialized commissions, the members could reach some degree of understanding and even transact some business. The most sought-after commission was on energy, reflecting the petroleum-bound origins of the whole process.[76] As Chad Reimer has noted, Canada's objectives included reducing 'the magnitude of the transfers of real wealth from Canadians to oil exporting countries.'[77] Such an object was at one with those of the other developed countries; and it promised little for the future transfer of wealth under that heading or any other, as demanded by the developing countries. But, at the same time, Canada as a raw-material exporting country was not opposed in principle to jacking up the prices of some of its products. The details of the Canadian position had to be fought out among several government departments: on balance, the government was closer to the objectives of its G-8 partners, including a declining price for energy, than it was to the views of the G-19.[78] Yet, on some matters, the Canadian position was that of a maverick within the IEA, especially as the Trudeau government turned its thoughts more and more to energy self-sufficiency rather than to the IEA objective of a pooling of supply and a rational allocation of demand.[79]

OPEC eventually agreed to a more stable pricing arrangement, which naturally gratified Western countries. A United Nations Commission on Trade and Development (UNCTAD) meeting in Nairobi in May 1976 kept up pressure for some kind of commodity marketing arrangement. But by July 1976 not very much had been accomplished, and a meeting of officials in that month ended in disarray.

MacEachen and Perez then met to discuss where the conference could go. The object was important enough to merit further efforts, the differences were not insurmountable, and the alternative, breakdown and confrontation, was frightening. Each co-chairman undertook to persuade his group to compromise. Under discussion were some form of technological cooperation, possibly through an energy institute, and a facility for energy financing. OPEC asserted and maintained a demand for the indexation of oil prices to the prices of commodities the petro-states bought from the developed world; the developed world, for its part, absolutely refused to mortgage its future in that way.[80]

Further contacts in the second half of 1976 proved more fruitful. All parties agreed to put off the day of reckoning from the end of 1976 into

1977, when the new Democratic administration of Jimmy Carter would have had a chance to seize the issues and respond to them.

But what were the issues? MacEachen, thinking as a practical politician, argued that they should be confined to problems where agreement and solution were possible. But the Canadian approach now surpassed the limit of Perez's political pragmatism. Perhaps he knew he could not deliver; the unity of his side was fragile, and could only be maintained by sticking to the letter of their original demands. In any case, he resisted making the active agenda less 'global' and more attainable. The developed countries considered the unity between OPEC and the energy-poor (and therefore really poor) developing countries to be spurious. The spring of 1977 was in fact the autumn of CIEC.

The impasse occurred just as the Canadian cabinet was wrestling with its own list of intractables, and it is noteworthy that it devoted long hours to discovering a way out of the negotiating cul-de-sac. 'Earnest efforts' were made, not just by Canadians but by ministers from other 'leading countries.' But in the end no exit could be found. Although the developed eight were willing to continue the conference indefinitely, Perez, speaking for the developing nineteen, rejected the idea out of hand. They were tired and disappointed, he told MacEachen; it would be best to return the matter to the United Nations General Assembly and to the group of Seventy-Seven who had passed the original resolutions setting out the NIEO.

There was disappointment on both sides. The developed countries felt their concessions during the talks had gone unappreciated. The Americans felt that the Carter administration had not had a fair chance to deal with the problem. MacEachen told the House of Commons on 8 June 1977, after the exercise was finally over, that there had been 'real progress on the main substantial issues at play,' and that he considered it important for Canada to continue to play a role in 'the area of North-South relations in the post-CIEC period.'[81]

North-South issues took a back seat for the rest of the 'Development Decade.' UNCTAD went nowhere, despite elaborate proposals for price stabilization of Third-World staple exports; on such questions Canada stood with its partners in the OECD rather than with the developing countries.[82] A second major escalation in oil prices in 1978-9 attracted global attention to a certain portion of the Third World, and Canadian banks joined a rush to provide facilities, and loans, to Third-World governments – especially in the petro-countries. When in 1980 the North-South Institute came to assess the Trudeau government's performance in foreign aid in comparison with the government's own stated objectives, it found it seriously wanting. Back in 1970 Lester Pearson had set 0.7 per cent of GNP as an appropriate aid target for a rich country. The Canadian government adopted the target and promised to approach it 'by annual increases' between 1975 and 1980. Instead, it turned out that Canada was closer to the target when it began its 'increases' than it was by 1980. It had fallen away, from 0.54 per cent in 1975 to a probable 0.37 per cent in 1981.[83]

The question of development returned to the United Nations in 1980 with its Eleventh Special Session in August and September 1980. Mark MacGuigan as external affairs minister brought hope from Canada, but not very much hope and in a format that was criticized at home for insufficiency.[84] At the June 1980 economic summit in Venice, Trudeau again made mention of North-South issues which had resurfaced in the global conscience because of a report, issued earlier in the year, by a Commission on International Development Issues chaired by former West German chancellor Willy Brandt. It too proposed action, such as bringing the proportion of GNP devoted to aid up to 0.7 per cent by 1985 – the same target Pearson had proposed ten years earlier.[85]

It seemed time for Trudeau to take a hand, as Richard Gwyn proposed in the *Toronto Star* in December 1980. Could he achieve 'some dramatic breakthrough in North-South relations?'[86] The answer was rather mixed. Since he was hosting the Western economic summit in Montebello in July 1981, Trudeau had a chance to put North-South questions firmly on the agenda despite the disinclination of conservatively minded leaders such as President Reagan and Prime Minister Thatcher. In their communiqué, the Western leaders recognized the commonality of some problems, such as oil prices, food production, and population growth; and they recognized as well the usefulness of the forthcoming North-South summit at the luxurious resort of Cancún in Mexico.[87]

Cancún was the preoccupation of its host, Mexican President López Portillo. Ultimately it became a priority for Trudeau as well, who served as co-chairman, replacing Chancellor Kreisky of Austria. As with the CIEC, the conference was representative of the larger and more important countries; unlike the CIEC, it included China and the USSR.

The prospects were not promising. The Carter administration might have been prepared to take the idea of a global redistribution of wealth as a starting point; the Reagan administration was not. Instead, Reagan relied on a variety of the trickle-down theory that characterized his domestic economic policy. If the richer countries promoted a free-market economy, on a world scale, ultimately justice would be rendered to all.[88]

Trudeau exerted himself, but ultimately little came of the conference. And with its demise, the emphasis passed to other topics, if not to newer ones. Though the idea of redistribution lingered on the margins of the international agenda, the decade of development had produced little more than a decade of conferences.

The sixteen years had produced some changes. Canada under Trudeau had probably given more aid than it might otherwise have done. It had channelled research on the fundamentals of aid-giving through the IDRC and the North-South Institute. It had maintained an attitude of engagement with the UN majority, and it had employed as best it could the techniques of diplomacy, with occasionally beneficial results.

Yet as the trade figures showed, the sinews of Canada's relations with the Third World had not changed much or for the better. Trade in 1984 still went pretty much, in volume and in value, where it went in 1968. Put in a larger context, the First World still dominated the world economy. The illusion that the Third World could seriously alter fundamental economic relationships through political confrontations at the United Nations, through UNCTAD or the NIEO, was much battered though not, as yet, entirely discredited.

Nor could Canada's aid givers guard against the unanticipated. The havoc wreaked among petroleum-poor states by the oil-price revolution could not have been seriously predicted; nor could the Soviet determination to expand Russian influence in Asia and Africa have been wholly anticipated. Both were setbacks to Trudeauvian assumptions as to the rational and desirable course of development. Not all such assumptions proved their worth. The attempt to rationalize and plan helped create a top-heavy bureaucracy in Ottawa. And the government's spending habits, as well as a revolution of expectations among the government's auditors, helped lumber Canada's aid program with controls and restrictions that partially negated the bright hopes and freer procedures of the late 1960s.

In the light of circumstance, Canada's relations with the Third World were better conceived, and worse managed, than they deserved to be. The balance is, nevertheless, ever so slightly favourable.

Part Five

Exodus

12

Welcome to the 1980s

The night of 18 February 1980 was dramatic. For the second time in a year, Canadians turned out a government. As the reports flowed in from the Maritimes, Quebec, and then Ontario, Canadians learned that they had elected another majority Liberal government – before the returns from the western provinces were in. That was just as well: the Liberals picked up no seats west of the Manitoba-Saskatchewan border.

The cameras switched to Ottawa's Château Laurier Hotel, where the leader of the opposition was watching the returns. 'Well,' a nonchalant Pierre Trudeau told his television audience, 'welcome to the 1980s.'

It was an experience that many Canadians at the time or later thought they might have been spared. The Liberals' majority was dangerously unbalanced; lacking western MPs, they were forced to stock their cabinet with senators whose political influence at home in Calgary or Vancouver was slight.[1] That political deficit was compounded by the government's growing unpopularity. The 1980s saw the first genuine recession since 1954. Gross national product sank, unemployment rose, and incomes suffered. In short, living standards declined.

The country was confronted by astronomical interest rates, while governments, federal and provincial, struggled with mounting deficits. Quebec attempted to solve its problems by reducing public-service salaries, a move that helped seal the political fate of the PQ government. No government, however, was exempt from the siren call of austerity, and the apparent bankruptcy of government policy in the face of economic adversity was bound to make a negative impression on an electorate bemused by expensive, active, government policies. The Canadian dollar plunged, a boon to Canada's exports but a problem for the government's image as travelling Canadians saw their potential range shrink. The economic shocks of the early 1980s tended to undermine confidence and to upset established assumptions. Even though economic growth resumed after 1982, the electorate was becoming restless.

The cabinet that Trudeau formed to deal with the 1980s looked rather like the old one that had gone out of office in 1979. At his right hand were those who had served him well in the past, and who had masterminded his return to power: Allan J. MacEachen and Marc Lalonde. MacEachen, who was an economist by training, went to Finance; Lalonde, whose intelligence and force of personality commended him to the prime minister, went to Energy. Jean Chrétien, who had risen steadily through the cabinets of the 1970s, was handed Justice and the reform of the constitution.

These appointments, Trudeau's strongest, showed where the government would concentrate its energies. The appointments to the foreign-policy portfolios suggested where it would not. The most surprising appointment, as far as the press was concerned, was Mark MacGuigan, the MP for Windsor Walkerville, and a protégé of Paul Martin. MacGuigan had warmed the back benches ever since 1968; frequently mentioned for appointment to the cabinet, he was as frequently passed over. There were, after all, two other ministers, Herb Gray and Eugene Whelan, from Windsor. He had a considerable background: with two doctorates, he had been a law professor and then a law dean. He was bright and amiable, and known to be ambitious; during the 1970s he had spent his time working in the area of justice and penitentiaries.

That MacGuigan was talented, all agreed. But he was not a heavyweight politician, even in southwestern Ontario, and as a minister he had to contend with the personality, perhaps even the aura, of his deputy, Allan Gotlieb. On international issues, MacGuigan's heart did not beat as one with the prime minister's. MacGuigan knew Americans better than did Trudeau, and he liked them. He had fewer hesitations about the Cold War, or the nature of the Soviet adversary. But unlike Jamieson, who was even more pro-American, MacGuigan had little political weight or public presence.

National Defence got Gilles Lamontagne, the mayor of Quebec City and a former fighter pilot. Lamontagne was liked, but not respected by his troops, who understood that in the firmament of the Trudeau cabinet he was considered a lightweight. When he was later succeeded by Jean-Jacques Blais it was thought to be an improvement, but an improvement in a government that was by then on its last legs.

Industry, Trade and Commerce had more possibilities than National

Defence. It got Herb Gray, the Liberal party's nationalist standard-bearer. Earnest, persistent, and dogged were all adjectives applied to Gray, even by those who were searching to flatter him. But at least Gray's line was clear, and his policies known quantities: nationalism, it seemed, would once more be in flower. The Americans, Canada's most frequent allies in international trade talks, would not be pleased.

Though the government had its points, and was by no means collectively incompetent, it held out little promise beyond its immediate agenda: and that agenda was likely to prove politically and even financially expensive. Trudeau was embarking on a voyage into the unknown with a bare handful of competent officers; if the navigation equipment proved defective, there would be nobody to change the course. And, since they were all crew on the good ship *Liberal Party*, mutiny was unthinkable, given the party's then longstanding tradition of loyalty to the leader. But what if the course were indeed defective, or the captain addled?

There was the possibility, some mused, that Canada was out of step, had fallen behind, that Trudeau's style was becoming tarnished. Perhaps the old liberal (and Liberal) assumptions no longer held the same magic. For as Canadians read their newspapers and gazed at their television sets, they became aware that other countries were trying something different.

Things were very different in the United States. The election of Ronald Reagan to the American presidency in November 1980 was the first sign.[2] A B-movie actor and a latter-day conservative, Reagan became governor of California in the 1960s. His tenure as governor was remembered chiefly as a time of right-wing reaction and student disruption.[3]

Reagan seemed curiously insulated from the advanced issues of the day. His views on ecology were summed up by his press secretary as the campaign plane sailed over western forests: 'Look, killer trees!' Reagan, when he took office, downgraded the Environmental Protection Agency (EPA) and refused to take acid rain seriously.'[4] The EPA did, however, help resolve the Garrison diversion dispute in 1984.[5] Canadians settled in for what liberal opinion leaders and policy makers hoped would be only a four-year siege.[6]

In this Canadians were not unique. What was unique was apparent but generally ignored. Reagan liked Canada. He knew little specifically about the place, but he was aware it was a democratic, English-speaking ally that in its culture and institutions closely resembled the United States; better still it actually bordered on America, relieving that country of immediate concern for its northern border. As a Californian by adoption, Reagan was more concerned about Mexico, where the porous American frontier caused greater worries and where political instability could threaten American security.

Reagan's official announcement on 13 November 1979 of his candidacy for the presidency in 1980 included a proposal for a 'North American Accord' to include the United States, Canada, and Mexico. The idea was not especially novel; proposals for a trilateral deal among the three countries had been circulating for some time. Reagan had barely got this one out of his mouth when Prime Minister Trudeau and Mexican President López Portillo denounced it: such an accord, they proclaimed in May 1980, 'would not serve the best interests of their countries.'[7]

Trudeau and López might have been reacting to what Reagan had not said, for as it stood his North American Accord was hard to oppose. Practically, it meant only two things, neither controversial in terms of international relations: better relations of some kind, either bilaterally or trilaterally, and a condemnation of the Carter administration for its failure to achieve them. If Carter could not manage his own backyard, Reagan implied, how could he hope to lead the Free World? In fact, Reagan's entourage had no idea what the accord was or how to implement it. Inquiries were not reassuring. Shortly after Reagan's victory Douglas Wirthlin, one of his senior political strategists, was confronted by a *New York Times* reporter. 'We haven't heard of the North American accord since [Reagan's announcement], have we?' the reporter asked. 'Who knows?' Wirthlin replied. 'We may again.'[8]

Reagan did in fact make a point of visiting and conferring with the Mexican president between his election and his inauguration. Trudeau, however, demurred. Perhaps he had enough on his plate to keep him busy until after Reagan's inauguration on 20 January 1981. For while Reagan kept his friendly intentions on a level of amiable vagueness, Canadian actions vis-à-vis American interests were almost embarrassingly precise.

The tone was set long before Trudeau and Reagan ever met. On 28 October 1980 Allan MacEachen brought down his first budget as finance minister. Following the common wisdom, it was believed necessary and expedient to introduce major financial reforms in the government's first year; that way, it is (or was) supposed, the electorate and vested interests within it will have got over their shock before the next election rolls around.

Economists tended to like MacEachen's budget: it tried out several advanced ideas that had been circulating, without much hope of adoption, around the Finance Department and in academic seminars. Professional applause was, however, offset by a chorus of condemnation from special-interest groups. The tale of MacEachen's woe is beyond our story, except that it preoccupied his energies, and undermined the government, which was already suffering from an attack of high interest rates.

Those troubles would have been enough for most governments. Simultaneously, however, Trudeau was tackling the constitution, and two of his ministers were in England. To make matters even more complex, the budget proclaimed nothing less than a complete revamping of Canada's energy policies.[9]

Energy was considered to be a strong point for the Liberals. Clark's energy policy had seemed self-contradictory. His waffling over how to privatize Petrocan occurred just as energy prices took a leap upwards; the Liberals capitalized on the electorate's insecurity on energy, especially in Ontario.[10]

The relevant section of the budget was called 'The National Energy Program.' It would be called the National Energy Policy as often as it was labelled 'program,' but it was soon familiar enough to journalists and other interested parties to be called, simply, the NEP. It was introduced with considerable fanfare and to the drumbeat of novelty, despite the fact that it embodied significant elements of continuity with the policies of the 1970s and previous decades.[11] Now was the time, MacEachen told MPs, because 'time is running out.' The government must act now to assure 'security of supply,' an 'opportunity for all Canadians to participate in the energy industry,' and in the interest of 'fairness' in pricing and revenue-sharing.

In pricing, MacEachen proposed a 'blended oil pricing regime which ... should result in a made-in-Canada price which is well below international levels.' The government would encourage Canadian consumers to switch to natural gas, and would assist, if necessary, in the construction of a pipeline from Montreal to the Maritimes. There would be a federal tax on natural gas, though not an export tax, to pay for the government's commitments. There would also be a new 8 per cent tax on net revenue from the production of oil and gas in Canada, effective 1 January 1981. It was not stressed that the 'made-in-Canada' price was expected to rise, slowly, until it approximated world levels.

The effect of the pricing regime and the new taxes was to redistribute income from the production of oil and gas in Canada. According to MacEachen's figures, industry's share would decline from just under 45 per cent to 33 per cent; and the federal government's share would rise from 10 per cent to 24 per cent. The income received by the governments of the producing provinces would decline marginally, from 45 to 43 per cent.

Exploration would be encouraged in the north, under a petroleum incentives program (PIP): it would distribute grants to firms in a direct ratio to Canadian ownership. This was a favourite theme among nationalist opinion. To assist it further, the government proposed a 'back-in' by which it appropriated, both for the future and retroactively, a 25 per cent interest in any oil and gas discovered in the 'Canada Lands,' lands owned by the federal government; these were mainly in the territories. The government also proposed to buy back foreign-owned firms – and without burdening the tax system.[12]

This last proposal impinged directly on international relations, particularly with the United States. The rest of the package was merely bound to stir up trouble with multinational oil companies, which were a major target of the NEP,[13] and with the producing provinces, especially the Conservative government of Alberta.[14] The oil producers tended to be at variance with the rest of the country; indeed, if the views expressed in public-opinion polls are any guide, the oil patch should have known for some time that it was heading for trouble.[15] Perhaps it clung to the hope that disapproval of American investment was a passing phase, or that the investment question was not sufficiently important to merit government attention.[16] Experience was comforting: until October 1980, oil companies dealt primarily with the 'user-friendly' government of Alberta; the federal government was quite a different respondent.[17]

As Americans saw it, the MacEachen budget linked two areas of potential trouble, investment and energy, both of which had been identified as sources of discord. The combination should not have been a surprise, but that did not lessen its unattractiveness. The unpopularity of the oil companies was well known, as was Canadians' mistrust of foreign ownership and manipulation.

It cannot be said that this was an issue to which the prime minister devoted prolonged or profound thought. Trudeau was not, in the fall of 1980, primarily interested in energy or energy policy. He had just won the fight of his life in the Quebec referendum, and he was starting another on the constitution. He understood that some of his lieutenants wanted to shake up the energy sector, to promote Canadian interests, to furnish energy security, and to develop frontier oil and gas. The time was propitious, with oil and gas prices soaring in the aftermath of the Iranian revolution of 1979 and the subsequent war between Iran and Iraq. International oil prices rose abruptly in 1979, from US$20 a barrel in

January to US$26 a barrel (for Libyan oil) in October. It would rise further, to $32 and even $40 a barrel in 1981.[18]

The litany of shortages, scarcity, and non-renewable resources was played again and again in the media. Lucky the country with oil wells and gas fields of its own; unlucky those, like the United States, where profligate demand had beggared domestic supply. Even though energy efficiency had improved since the first oil shock of 1973, consumption was still rising, despite conservation, and by an average of 0.9 per cent a year. It was a circumstance that stood to enrich countries with oil and other forms of energy to sell.[19]

The logic of events suggested that Canada could seize the opportunity to repatriate its energy sector as well as its constitution, expand its energy frontier in the federal territories in the north and offshore, develop high-cost production in the oil sands, and pay for it all with sales of petroleum at world prices. Marc Lalonde, his deputy, Mickey Cohen, and Michael Pitfield and MacEachen all supported the plan. They were close to Trudeau, and all had given signal service in the past. The prime minister would not stand in their way.[20]

It is a moot question how much the Department of External Affairs knew about the National Energy Policy before it was brought to birth. Credible witnesses (most of them, alas, confidential) contradict one another on the subject. The NEP was part of the budget, and therefore subject to more stringent rules of secrecy than ordinary legislation; and External Affairs was not one of the departments normally consulted on budgets. Discussion took place mainly in the cabinet, and away from the usual interdepartmental committees. Mark MacGuigan knew and approved of the program, but he had little hand in shaping its details. It appears more than likely that at the desk level in External there was no information and no preparation for the morning of 29 October, when the American embassy came calling.[21]

The U.S. embassy had much to ask but little to say. The ambassador, Kenneth Curtis, was a former governor of Maine and a crony of Carter's secretary of state, Edmund Muskie. Curtis would be remembered in Ottawa as a pleasant nonentity; in October 1980 he was serving out his time until the virtually inevitable Republican victory, when he would resign. Curtis's staff, under the deputy chief of mission, Richard Smith, outlasted the ambassador and helped set the eventual American response.

What he had to say was not happy. Joe Clark's regime had been essentially friendly, but politically unfortunate.[22] Trudeau, in contrast, gave mixed signals. Sometimes he showed a flair for the unexpected, as in the appointment of Mark MacGuigan to be secretary of state for external affairs.[23] MacGuigan was more at ease with the Americans than Trudeau, and he was more inclined to follow the logic of Canada's established alliance and economic patterns. Like his predecessors in the External Affairs portfolio, he was mainly interested in the political side of policy, and a political crisis like Afghanistan was therefore made to order. So warm was MacGuigan's support for Alexander Haig, Reagan's first secretary of state, that the minister was dubbed 'Al's pal.' The label, needless to say, did not help MacGuigan's prospects in the Liberal party.[24]

High-level relations between the two governments were not frequent during 1980. Secretary Vance visited, on the eve of his resignation from Carter's cabinet. Another American visitor, Senator Claiborne Pell of Rhode Island (as it happened, a former American foreign-service officer), told his Canadian hosts that Carter's fisheries treaty would remain stalled in the Senate as long as Pell had anything to do with it. The only solution, he suggested, would be international arbitration. It was a good suggestion, and it began to find an echo in Canadian speeches on the subject. It was, however, disappointing that Carter had not done better over fish.[25]

Carter's losing battle with re-election was soon over. Some Americans darkly suspected that the NEP had been carefully timed to coincide with the 'lame duck' transition to Reagan, but that was too machiavellian even for Trudeau. In any case, Carter in his last months in office was overwhelmingly preoccupied with getting American hostages back from Iran. Some have suggested that the Carter administration would have understood the Canadian position on energy. But sympathy for goals did not necessarily imply acceptance of the means the Canadians chose to employ.[26]

Certainly the permanent element in the American government, bureaucrats in departments dealing with Canada, did not much like what it saw in the NEP.[27] Canada, they argued, was really a paradox: 'an industrial country with Third-World policies.'[28] The officials would respond, of course, to political direction, but with Reagan taking office it was altogether improbable that that direction would approve what the Trudeau government had done.

The sound and fury in Canada were themselves sufficient to divert Trudeau over the winter. Premier Lougheed of Alberta took to the airwaves to yell defiance at Trudeau and his central Canadian government. It was, as the Alberta attorney general later remarked, 'a major breakdown in inter-regional and intergovernmental relationships' – and in this case allowance does not have to be made for political hyperbole.[29]

Lougheed cut production and withdrew Alberta from a number of joint energy projects; but while his tactics certainly hurt other Canadians, they also hurt his own producers. He had little success with public opinion outside the west; in December 1981, after a year of battle with Alberta and consistent complaints from the United States, 64 per cent of Canadians favoured Canadianization; as Harvie André, the Conservatives' energy critic and an Alberta MP, admitted, 'the NEP is a successful policy. The people like it.'[30] A compromise was indicated, and it had already been reached, in September 1981.[31] Until then, the domestic opposition and the American government were in essential agreement.

Ronald Reagan decided to make Ottawa his first port of foreign call in March 1981, bringing with him the usual large entourage that accompanies American presidents on their social calls.[32] It included the secretary of state, General Alexander Haig. Haig had already signed a note to Canada complaining of the NEP as being 'unnecessarily discriminatory.' It upset the balance between the United States and Canada, he said, and unless the policy were changed, the Americans would have to see how best to redress it. According to Trudeau's press secretary, Patrick Gossage, Haig demanded 'major changes' in the program.[33] Following vigorous representations from the Canadian ambassador to the State Department and the White House, the note was withdrawn at the insistence of Myer Rashish, a Reagan appointment at the State Department.[34] Rashish was believed to have originated the idea of a North American Accord. He wanted a cordial reception in Ottawa, and if withdrawing the note was what it took, it would be done. In a press conference in Ottawa, Haig explained there had been 'an atmospheric or tonal problem' in the note, but the content remained a priority.[35] News of the note duly leaked out.

Rashish came to Ottawa too. His main task was to smooth the way for the next economic summit, scheduled for Ottawa that summer. He also embodied the Reagan administration's considered strategy for Canada: to show that Reagan intended to get along with the Canadians in a civilized way. If that did not work, the withdrawn note could always go back on the table.[36] Because the accord still had some currency, Rashish was a natural choice to be the administration's point man for Canada.[37] When, a few months later, the accord became passé, so did Rashish, but not before he had contributed his bit to the developing controversy over the NEP.

In addition to the State Department contingent, Reagan also brought Secretary of the Treasury Donald Regan, Secretary of Commerce Malcolm Baldridge, and U.S. Trade Representative William Brock; they would have a first chat with their Canadian counterparts about the meaning of the NEP; the Foreign Investment Review Agency (FIRA), a long-standing sore point, was thrown in for good measure.

The Americans mixed motives and policies. The administration disapproved of Canada's explicit policy of favouring its nationals and its promotion of uncompensated government expropriation. This was contrary to OECD policy, even though the Canadian government had reserved its position on national treatment when the policy was adopted in 1976.[38] There was pressure on the U.S. government from multinationals with an American domicile – notably Exxon, parent company of Canada's Imperial Oil (Esso). And there was pressure from congressmen concerned that Canadian companies would use their advantages under the NEP to bid for control of American companies in the United States.[39]

Until the 1980s it was the United States that was the principal foreign investor in most of the capitalist world. There had always been small foreign investment, including Canadian investment, in the United States, but it had attracted little attention. In 1981, foreign investment was a minuscule 0.4 per cent of U.S. GNP; the contrasting Canadian figure was 15 per cent.[40] But the terms of investment were reversing, and 1981 was the year in which more money for investment flowed into the United States than flowed out. The process continued.[41] In the early 1980s a series of Canadian takeovers of American firms were either attempted or occurred. Since this was precisely when Canada was attempting to diminish the American share of the Canadian petroleum industry, it was understandable that the U.S. firms affected should point to a paradox. They found they could do more: they could awaken latent American fears of foreign domination through foreign ownership. Once out in the open, these fears, and their political impact, proved to be remarkably similar to their Canadian cousins. Responding to U.S. political concerns on the issue, the Canadian government urged Canadian banks to amend their lending policies so as to slow the rate of Canadian penetration of the American investment market.[42]

Nervousness about the domestic political consequences of an inflow of foreign investment weighed somewhat with the administration. It was overbalanced by the belief that a substantial outflow of capital from Canada would indicate, graphically, what the true costs of the National Energy Program were.[43]

Most of the foreign investment controversy was in the future when Reagan arrived in Ottawa in March 1981. His advisers came with bags packed with complaints. Fortunately, those complaints had not registered on the president, but he could contrast epithets from an anti-Reagan (and probably also anti-American) crowd of demonstrators on Parliament Hill with civil chats with the prime minister. Trudeau's telegenic appeal for minimal politeness from the demonstrators did Canada no harm on that evening's American television news. And presumably it did no harm when Trudeau took up the idea of the North American Accord and proposed periodic Canadian-American-Mexican summits. Yet Reagan's speech to parliament was notably undistinguished, and its call for harmony and the submergence of differences did nothing to eradicate the differences that existed.[44]

In a broader sense, the meeting accomplished its purpose when it introduced Reagan and his Republican colleagues in government to their Canadian counterparts, and spread before them for the first time the issues they would confront in relations with Canada. As an American participant later observed, 'Ronald Reagan came back from Ottawa in March with a good impression. The anticipation [of the visit] had been a lot worse than the reality.'[45]

To the Canadians the visit was presumably equally instructive. Reagan was poorly prepared on bilateral issues, and discussions were therefore crafted to skirt the president's many areas of ignorance. He came and went with a huge briefing book, but there was no sign that he had read it. 'Our people,' Reagan is reported to have said, will talk about it – later.[46]

Things were not much better when the Canadians and Americans discussed larger matters. 'You should have seen Trudeau's face,' one participant recalled, when in the middle of a discussion on the politics of the Middle East, Reagan launched into an anecdote about two Israeli soldiers on patrol in a jeep; they had been told there was a bounty for each Egyptian prisoner. They fell asleep, and on awakening found they were surrounded by the entire Egyptian army. One turned to the other. 'Wake up,' Reagan delivered the punch line: 'we're rich.' It was not precisely Trudeau's style, though his staff sometimes found their exposure to Reagan's bonhomie a relief.[48] It could, after all, have been worse.[49]

Trudeau, offered the opportunity to comment on Reagan some years later, merely confirmed that to him the American president was different. He opined that 'Reagan has the talent to sense the direction of the crowd and place himself in the front. He has a strong feeling for the movement of affairs. But he's not my kind of politician.'[49] For Trudeau, leadership meant making rather than reflecting opinion on issues where his interest was engaged. On the United States, during this period, it was not.

Haig contributed relatively little to the situation. His connections to the Reaganauts were few, and his relations with the White House were slight. He had problems inside his own department, where a Reagan loyalist from California, Justice William Clark, was deputy secretary. Clark was not well-informed on international affairs, but Haig clutched at him as a conduit to Reagan. That was important in terms of Haig's personal standing, but it was also important for the State Department as a whole, which was not well regarded and in some cases (Canada's being one) was suspected of 'going native,' representing Canadian concerns better than American interests. Clark might, just possibly, be an antidote to these suspicions. As he told Haig, 'I know the Governor's ways.'[50]

The governor and his national security staff no longer had to worry about the destabilization of Quebec or Canada; Trudeau had taken care of that. There was concern that Canada was not pulling its weight in NATO, but it was not clear what could be done about that.[51]

So relations with Canada were left to subordinates at the White House or to the interested agencies. At first Rashish took command, chairing a meeting with the Canadians in early April. Though there was plain speaking at the meeting, representatives of other agencies complained that Rashish had underplayed his hand; all they heard from the Canadians, including Ambassador Towe, was that Canada had not violated any of its international obligations in formulating the National Energy Policy. Among those agencies, the U.S. Departments of the Treasury and of Commerce were especially prominent, and it was those two departments that first produced a list of issues on which the Canadians should be engaged. (Treasury admittedly had its own 'strategic' interests, especially in relation to the Western summits, but these do not seem to have diverted much of its energies or attention where Canada was concerned.) In addition to the NEP, there was patent protection for American drug companies, adversely affected by Canadian legislation, as well as for FIRA, which Trudeau had promised to strengthen during the 1980 election campaign.[52] The back-in provisions attracted the most fire; because they had stimulated adverse criticism in Ottawa, too, the government decided to deflect it without formally conceding a point, and offered an 'ex gratia payment' for its back-in of 25 per cent in existing oil activities in the Canada Lands. There was also an assurance that the government would not discriminate in favour of Canadian companies over American for the tendering of megaprojects.[53]

That was in May. It looked like progress from the Canadian side, but not from the American. Lectures continued all summer, with no substantial movement.[54] Trudeau and Reagan met in Washington in July and at the economic summit in Montebello later in the month. It did Trudeau no good to jibe, in a comment on Reagan's performance, 'Ask Al [Haig]'; the Americans nevertheless persisted in talking the matter out. In the fall they took their complaints about FIRA to GATT, arguing that Canadian practice violated the equal treatment promised under the agreement to all enterprises domiciled in Canada. Reagan himself was oblivious of these complications, telling the press that relations with 'our North American neighbors,' Canada and Mexico, were at their most harmonious level in years.[55]

It was not until a brief meeting in Grand Rapids, Michigan, in September 1981 that any substantial discussion occurred between the president and the prime minister, and their ministers and officials, on the issues of the day. The result, however, was another impasse, each side explaining to the other how important its own position was. Equally, the two men agreed that some solution ought to be possible, and that a cycle of retaliation be avoided; should retaliation occur, it was obvious that it would start on the American side. Relations between Trudeau and Reagan remained polite and even cordial, but lower down, as early as July, some detected a 'heavy atmosphere' among ministers and officials.[56] It would get heavier as the months passed.

There now entered a new actor, uninvolved though not unaffected by earlier events. Reagan had been tardy in appointing an ambassador to Canada; when he finally did, he selected Paul H. Robinson, an energetic Chicago businessman noted for his ability as a fund-raiser for Reagan's presidential campaign. This was taken to mean that Reagan was sending a businessman to 'get tough.' Because Robinson did not back away from scraps, he soon enjoyed a reputation as a diplomatic enforcer, at least in the pages of Liberal organs such as the *Toronto Star*.[57] That he was a right-wing Republican was true enough; that he had a strong political background and an abrasive manner offensive to believers in diplomatic professionalism is also true; but he was not just a Reaganite fire-eater or political hack.

Robinson was in his late fifties; his ancestry (Canadian), his experience, and his predilections dated back to an era of Anglo-Saxon cooperation. He liked Canada, not to mention other English-language countries. He was confident that the United States had a constituency among Canadians; part of his job was to build up that constituency. He wanted, and believed that many Canadians wanted, a larger role for Canada in the common defence: Canada should spend more money. Since spending on social programs was one large reason why money was not going to defence, he pointed it out.[58] But he also wanted the outstanding economic issues to be resolved, and soon came to believe that this was best done slowly, by persuasion rather than power politics.

Robinson was anxious to work on the topics he preferred, but his ambit was limited by the acrimonious disputes under way. He had, therefore, to ensure that nothing worse happened. The NEP issue, Robinson learned, was being considered at a very senior level – in fact, at the level of the cabinet. Discussions with the Canadians, whether ministers or diplomats, had failed; further efforts along those lines would be futile and would possibly generate more ill feeling than was desirable. It was, the ambassador decided, time to try his political connections.

Rather than appeal to Haig, Robinson phoned Clark, the deputy secretary. Clark set up a meeting in front of the president, at which the question of retaliation, pro and con, could be thrashed out. On the minds of those who wanted to retaliate was Canada's prized membership in the 'Summit Seven,' achieved through an American initiative. Summit membership meant that Canada was 'on the varsity,' and must accept the same rules as other OECD members for the treatment of investment and trade.[59]

Immediately at stake was the exclusion of Canada from a high-level trade group set up by the Montebello summit, a blow to Canadian pride and a symbolic warning that Canada was wearing out its welcome as a top-level economic partner; other measures, less symbolically hurtful but with damaging consequences, were being considered.[60] Robinson argued against any such idea. It was inappropriate to get into a public spat with the Canadians; far better, in his view, to have the matter out in private and to rely on the passing of time and the power of persuasion to set matters right. He acted, in other words, in the classic mould of an ambassador attempting to reconcile his home constituency against the success of his mission.

Robinson prevailed, though he may have done so because he crystallized existing arguments against heavy-handed retaliation. Such retaliation could damage Canada, certainly. It might damage other things as well: American economic interests previously unaffected; border communities; even the Reagan administration's international credibility as a responsible actor. 'Anything we've come across so far would hurt us more than them,' a senior official admitted.[61] But were there no consequences?

One possible consequence, 'unheralded' at the time, was an American decision not to follow up on a 1981 'review of North American liberalization options.' Instead, the government concluded, 'the timing was not appropriate for a free trade agreement with Canada.'[62] It was a sensible conclusion, given the political dynamics in Canada and the likely reaction of the Trudeau cabinet. That the Americans decided to file the idea probably owed a great deal to the 'atmospherics' of the NEP.

Less speculative complications were developing. As Canadian investors poured money into the United States (the outflow of equity investment in 1981 alone was $11.4 billion, or 3.5 per cent of Canada's GNP),[63] the Canadian government acquired a more emphatic interest in the equal treatment of its own nationals abroad – with all that implied for the treatment of foreign investors at home. Moreover, Canadian business, including some of the 'Canadianizations' of the early 1980s, required foreign capital too. More intervention in pursuit of nationalist goals could have induced investors to place their money elsewhere.[64] Finally, oil prices had levelled off during 1981, as supply outstripped demand; in January 1982 the 'spot price' of oil passed below the 'official price.' Some OPEC members, the less affluent ones first, were selling their product below the cartel's price and, slowly through 1982, the price went down: to $29, then to $28. It was not a collapse – that would come later – but it was sufficient to undercut one of the assumptions of the NEP.[65]

It was in this not unpromising climate that the Reagan administration decided to try once more. Delegations passed back and forth in September 1981, before and after Trudeau and Reagan met. Myer Rashish took to the podium to denounce Canada in a well-publicized oration. Finally, Haig sent MacGuigan a letter on 9 October to tell him that Donald Regan, the treasury secretary, would be coming to dinner on 13 October.[66]

Regan flew up to Ottawa with an official party to discuss matters with Allan MacEachen, Trudeau's finance minister, his colleagues, and their advisers. The meetings, held in the official guest house at Rideau Gate, did not go well; it remained for years thereafter a benchmark of bitterness and misunderstanding. To the Americans it seemed that no matter what they said, it made no difference. They were even denied, in one participant's recollection, what he called 'the flexibility of listening' by the Canadian side. Regan and company went home incensed; but however incensed they were in this and subsequent meetings, they were constrained by Reagan's decision not to confront the Canadians. The Canadians, for their part, considered themselves not merely confronted but affronted by the Americans' continual pressure, and by their refusal to take Canadian statements at anything like face value.[67]

On the Canadian side, there were a couple of bright signs. Negotiations for the pre-build portion of the Alcan pipeline were successfully consummated, including a U.S. government guarantee in December 1981 securing the participating companies against loss.[68] The governments of Alberta and Canada had finally arranged a slicing up of the oil revenue pie: Trudeau and Lougheed posed for photographers to toast the deal and, with it, the burial of federal-provincial jurisdictional squabbles that could have paralyzed the implementation of the National Energy Policy.[69] With Alberta pacified by sharing the loot from the NEP, Trudeau could go back to battling for the constitution, his main preoccupation in the fall of 1981. The battle for the NEP would continue to be managed by others.

The others meant principally Allan MacEachen. With the government beset by conflicts on all sides, and with a large deficit limiting his room for manoeuvre, MacEachen delivered a pacific budget in November 1981. The NEP, he told the House of Commons, would not expand into other fields; nor would FIRA roam the Canadian landscape unchecked.[70]

The Americans thanked the Canadians kindly, and asked for more. They asked especially about FIRA, but they continued to target those aspects of the NEP that promoted the Canadianization of oil properties. The Canadians, for their part, thought the American demands outrageous, striking at the Canadian government's sovereign ability to manage its economic environment. Officials and ministers dug in, while the Americans proceeded with their complaints about FIRA before a GATT tribunal in Geneva. There, with both sides exasperated, matters rested until the summer of 1982.

The first year of the Reagan administration was fraught with unintended, and frequently ironic, consequences. Reagan was the first president in years to make Canada a priority. His sentiments for Canada were favourable but unfocused, and his style of government left mere details, often very large details, to the actions of others. These others, men like his treasury secretary and his trade representative, strongly believed that Canada was violating accepted practices in its treatment of American investment, both prospectively, in the case of FIRA, and retrospectively, in the case of NEP. The effectiveness of their efforts may be measured by a Gallup Poll in February 1982: in that month only 18 per cent of Canadians affirmed that their country and the Americans were 'drawing closer together', while 49 per cent believed they were 'getting further apart.'[71]

The Canadian government seems to have accepted the notion that Canadians and Americans were 'getting further apart.' It did not spend much time studying the principles that activated the government in Washington – whether Democratic or Republican or even bureaucratic.

State intervention, Trudeau-style, was passé in Washington; so, on the whole, was liberalism. Nationalism, however, was on the upswing.

But that is to anticipate. As of the late winter of 1982, Reagan in a sense held the ring and set limits beyond which American retaliation would not go. Those limits had a foundation in common sense and in the hope that things would get better – as they did.

Things got better because things got worse. The prime rate in Canada touched 19 per cent in 1981; business bankruptcies rose, and gross national product fell $10 billion between 1981 and 1982.[72] (GNP was still below 1981 in 1983.) This was in addition to the outflow of capital to the United States. Current account balances, traditionally negative, rose towards zero in 1980, but fell sharply, to − $6 billion, in 1981. In the trough of the recession, 1982, the current-account balance passed into surplus, but that was because the fall in income, accompanied by record high-interest rates, was so severe as to inhibit imports. Inflation was finally brought down into the 4 per cent range, a slight consolation, and interest rates descended from their historical highs of 1981–2. Economic growth did not resume until the first quarter of 1983, by which time the Trudeau government's popularity, and credibility, had suffered an ultimately fatal setback.[73]

Pierre Trudeau had never been especially attractive to American conservatives; now he was increasingly unpopular with erstwhile liberals in Canada. Confidence in Canada dribbled away along with the money; the recession of 1981–2, and the government's inability to do much except aggravate it, gave many Canadians pause about the appropriateness of their country's go-it-alone policies in energy and trade. The government swung below the opposition in public-opinion polls during 1981; by 1982–3 the government was touching historic lows in its popularity.

Relations with the United States reached their nadir somewhat earlier, in 1981–2; by 1982–3 matters were actually improving. Admittedly they improved from very unpromising beginnings; old personalities had to unlearn the impressions of Reagan's first year in office, and newer ones had to refashion ties that had become dangerously frayed.

Conservatives, American-style, had their own explanations.[74] The *National Review,* a magazine of the respectable but not moderate right, adopted the causes and concerns of Canadian conservatives as their own, and these, predictably enough, had little that was good to say about the Canadian prime minister. Nevertheless it was something of a first when its 25 June 1982 issue featured a vivid portrait of a sinister Trudeau on its cover, coupled with a vitriolic denunciation inside.

The article was by a well-known, right-wing, Canadian news commentator, Lubor Zink. Zink put his audience straight on his first page. 'Like Hitler in *Mein Kampf*,' he wrote, 'Trudeau early in his career put on paper with admirable frankness and clarity everything he believes in, and every tactical twist he has eventually used to bolster his rigid ideology.' Trudeau had 'hijacked' the Liberal party and had used his position as prime minister to espouse détente ('which he promotes on Soviet terms come what may'), cozy up to Castro, and oppose imperialism. Interestingly, Zink denied that Trudeau was anti-American, but since the United States represented imperialism, he would of course work to defeat its purposes.[75]

Reagan read the *National Review*, which gave the magazine pride of place – of a sort – in his administration. While the general opinion of the Reaganites on Trudeau has yet to be rendered, one of them, Treasury Secretary Regan, has told readers of his premature memoir that Trudeau was a socialist or, at best, a social democrat.[76]

Trudeau and Reagan would diverge at the economic summits, where the American president's attendants were determined to extract the maximum amount of credit for their principal in media coverage and analysis. Ideology may in fact have helped them to deal gently with Canada, because officials in Washington, not to mention their political superiors, were convinced that the free market would eventually sort Trudeau out. In the meantime, the Americans tried as best they could to cope with what they saw as Canada's self-deception. 'Dammit, Pierre,' Reagan was quoted as saying, 'how can you object to that?' as the Americans struggled to insert a reference to 'peace and freedom for peoples everywhere' into a summit communiqué.[77] The Americans had sympathy and some support from other members of the Group of Seven; as a result, summit discussions were 'often difficult,' in the words of a Canadian observer.[78]

They became more difficult as Canada's position weakened economically. But, as the Americans expected, economics were having an impact in Ottawa. Reflecting on conversations at the 1981 summit, Trudeau, purportedly influenced by West German Chancellor Schmidt, called for a reappraisal of trade policy. In August 1981 the Planning and Priorities Committee, meeting at Meech Lake, bodied forth a 'decision document.' The key decision was to start a trade-policy review.[79] It started slowly – very slowly, but by the time trade policy had been re-examined and reformulated, the earth had, ever so slightly, begun to shift. It shifted as between Canada and the United States.

The knowledge that Trudeau's government faced mounting economic and political difficulties encouraged some members of Reagan's entourage to speak their minds. 'Your prime minister's a communist,' the spouse of one senior White House crony blurted out to a Canadian embassy wife.[80] It was not necessary to believe that Reagan himself held this opinion, only that those around him saw Trudeau as an alien, conceivably socialist, and possibly hostile force; but they remained divided over what to do about it. Since it was commonly believed that Reagan had no opinions of his own, but held a composite of the views of those around him, the situation was doubly serious. However amiable the Great Communicator might be, what mattered was what others chose to communicate to him.

On one side of the division stood the White House fixers – principally Michael Deaver. 'We got a problem,' a Canadian diplomat was told at a party: 'Your guy and my guy are not getting along.' In fact, 'Your guy really upset my guy; everybody around him is upset.' (The discussion occurred in the wake of the *National Review* article.) 'We shouldn't let this go,' the American continued, 'he likes Canada, you're so important.' But the initiative would have to come from the Canadian side because 'My guy really likes the gestures.'[81]

The word that a gesture would be appreciated was passed to Ottawa. On an appropriate occasion a flattering note from Trudeau arrived in Washington. It was all part of getting along with the Americans, and getting along with them was, of course, part of the job.

It was in this climate that relations between Ottawa and Washington began, slowly, to mend. Bureaucratically, it did not hurt that Ambassador Robinson's contact, William Clark, moved from State to the White House to become national security advisor. There is no evidence that Clark personally held Trudeau in high regard, but he did not obstruct the repair work.

Clark's move was only the first in a series of personnel changes. Alexander Haig resigned as secretary of state in July 1982, citing his frustration with Reagan's entourage – another indication of the importance of the personalities who protected their president. Haig's spectacular departure and his replacement by the quiet and imperturbable George Shultz, a former labor and treasury secretary, had no immediate effect on the issues under dispute between Canada and the United States; but the change of personnel produced a very considerable change in the atmospherics of the relationship. Under the circumstances almost any change would have been for the better, and so it proved.

Shultz's arrival coincided with a cabinet shuffle in Ottawa. Allan MacEachen had tired of Finance, where his efforts to raise Canada's fiscal policy to a higher plane had proved a political disaster. He welcomed a transfer to External Affairs; in External, as it happened, he could consort with his MIT classmate George Shultz. It is not certain that they remembered each other, but the fiction that they did proved a useful peg on which to hang a relationship. In any case, MacEachen was quick off the mark; while he was sometimes maddeningly inscrutable to his subordinates, he had a strong track record as an effective negotiator. He was also senior, and someone in whom the prime minister reposed confidence.

Not that the minister was Shultz's only Canadian contact, or Ottawa his only northern venue. Besides his political career in the 1970s, he was a veteran of the Bechtel Corporation. Thus he knew more people in the Calgary oil patch than many Ottawa politicians did, and his breadth of acquaintance made the secretary feel at ease with at least some Canadians. Prior knowledge of Canada – more than that of any other secretary of state – did not in this case breed hostility or even, as in the previous case of John Foster Dulles, contempt. Shultz knew that some people in his department believed that the NEP was driving oil rigs out of Canada and into the United States. It was not a strange thing to believe: many in the oil patch shared that opinion, oblivious of the fact that they had been leaving for some months prior to the NEP's announcement.

Shultz saw no reason to disturb the departmental consensus that the high international oil prices on which the NEP was predicated might not last, and that in that case the NEP would probably dismantle itself. Reality, if not diplomacy, would eventually return the Canadians to sanity. Patience therefore promised a variety of rewards, most of them pleasing to the United States.

In the meantime, linkages between the United States and Canada were growing, not diminishing. In 1982, the worst year of the recession, Canada imported some $47 billion of goods from the United States, 70.5 per cent of all imports, and exported $58 billion, 68.7 per cent. In 1983 imports rose by $5.5 billion, and exports by over $8 billion, and in 1984 they rose again, rose indeed by a phenomenal amount. In 1984 Canada bought $65.9 billion worth of goods (72 per cent of the total) in the United States, and sold $85 billion (75.8 per cent) there.[82] No other area or country accounted for anything like these sums: they were the kind of figure guaranteed to attract attention, and thought. Statisticians and economists concluded that Canada's own recovery from recession was mostly owing to the resurgence of the American economy. Canada's exports 'reflecting buoyant demand in the United States for motor vehicles, housing and investment goods.'[83]

These matters were not under Shultz's control. The trend was not unfavourable to Canada, and sales were encouraged by a very high American dollar. Although the balance of trade was in Canada's favour (in 1984 $20 billion in 'reconciled data' agreed upon between the two countries), current account favoured the Americans.[84] And although Canadian trade was a considerably smaller percentage of American trade statistics (20 per cent) than of Canadian, Canada was still the Americans' largest trading partner. Given the figures, the economic departments of government were taking an interest.

It was the Canadians who came calling. Trade barriers, the Economic Community Common Agricultural Policy, and a decade's worth of fruit-less policy presented an insurmountable barrier to a renewed concentration on Europe. Although there were voices in External Affairs that argued Canadian insufficiency rather than European obduracy as the prime cause for the failure of the third option, the fact remains that the third option was tacitly buried.

Instead, an official task force worked up a new trade strategy, prosaically labelled *Trade Policy for the 1980s*. When published in August 1983 it attracted considerable comment, especially because it seemed to terminate a number of trade nostrums much prized in the preceding decade. It gave its duty to multilateral trade, currently stalled between GATT rounds with no encouraging signs for the immediate future. The multilateral route was not be abandoned, but in the meantime it was advisable to investigate limited, sectoral free-trade arrangements with the United States. There were positive reasons for doing so, such as the desire to build on the success represented by higher trade figures, but there were negative ones as well. The NEP had run its course, and the negative feelings it had engendered were no longer worth sustaining.

As we have seen, a review of trade policy began as early as the fall of 1981. With a pause to allow for the restructuring of the government's foreign-policy departments, it resumed in April 1982, under the aegis of Ed Lumley, the minister of state for international trade.[85] Once a draft was agreed upon, it was circulated for comment, while outside opinions were sought from businessmen, provincial representatives, labour union officials, and academics.[86] Meanwhile, the economy lurched into its downturn.

Opinions received from the outside by government were not unanimous, but several themes predominated. These were principally a desire to end the isolation of the Canadian economy, with no special access to any larger free-trade area; an acceptance that the United States was crucial to an expansion of Canadian trade; and a realization that American non-tariff barriers posed a threat to an expanding Canadian export sector.[87]

Opinion, however, divided inside government. In External Affairs, Canadian-American relations were being reviewed in the summer of 1982. The External review did not start from the same assumptions as the trade officials', and it did not reach the same conclusions. To the dismay of the economic and trade groups that had been working under Lumley, External's officials plumped once again for the third option, an idea that 'few took serious account of ... outside of External.' But, since the third option was received doctrine inside External, it became necessary to blend the two trends, or to find a way of side-stepping inconvenient pieties.[88]

The trade-policy team decided on an unusual strategy. They would allow a compendium of all points of view to go up to cabinet, and they would publish their own point of view as a government position paper. As Michael Hart, one of the officials involved, later wrote, bureaucrats in Ottawa paid inordinate attention to memoranda to cabinet when those memoranda all too often proved to be ephemeral in their impact. The printed word, rather than a secret, flabby compromise, would be what would count in this instance. 'The process [of creating a cabinet paper] thus became tedious but not important,' he said. Meanwhile, inside the cabinet, ministers watched and waited, and listened to Lumley as he stressed the advantages of Canadian-American trade.[89] Then, once the cabinet paper was out of the way, the government published its trade documents, *Canadian Trade Policy for the 1980s* and *A Review of Canadian Trade Policy*. 'The release of the documents,' Hart concluded, 'marked a triumph of substance over process.'[90] Bilateralism, rather than multilateralism, became the watchword of the day. The third option was quietly and unobtrusively trundled off to the attic.[91]

The United States, for its own reasons, was receptive. The Americans were suffering from a new-found sense of economic vulnerability.[92] Inflation and soaring interest rates had taken their toll. The U.S. trade deficit, large under Carter, was monstrous under Reagan. There was general agreement that trade was a problem, though opinions differed considerably as to the proper remedy. GATT did not seem to be going anywhere fast, especially in its 1982 ministerial meeting, and officials were sceptical of its ability to cope with 'unfair' trading practices that denied national treatment to American business. For the moment, bilateral agreements held promise, and not only to Americans.[93] Canadian officials, reflecting on the failure of the GATT talks, were becoming much more open to an arrangement with the United States.[94]

Economic policy, it must be admitted, did not attract much public notice during 1983–4. There were other issues, and other venues. They showed that on purely political, high-profile matters, relations had not greatly changed.

Reagan's National Security Council took an interest in Canada. That was not unprecedented, though unusual, and may reflect George Shultz's laissez-faire attitudes towards the council and its concerns.[95] The State Department's ability to intervene on Canada's behalf was proportionately weakened, though not discarded. Its diplomats recognized that some events were passing them by, and that the Canadian embassy was reflecting new realities, with its parties and its connections with the White House and Congress. Friends of Canada applauded the stepped-up activity of the Canadian embassy in Washington, and the newly found prominence of the ambassadorial couple, Allan and Sondra Gotlieb. While the Gotliebs were successful, did that also mean that Trudeau carried more weight as a result? Perhaps, but perhaps not too.[96]

The American invasion of Grenada in October 1982 was a sign. The Americans wished to overthrow an obnoxious Marxist regime that had recently fallen under the sway of a murderous soldiery. The former prime minister, Maurice Bishop, was slain on 19 October; at the invitation of Grenada's nervous neighbours in the eastern Caribbean, American troops landed there on 25 October, securing total control within the next two days.

The Canadian government had not been told, either by the eastern Caribbean states or by the Americans. One of the Caribbean leaders later stated that she had lost Trudeau's phone number and a letter would have taken two weeks. More to the point may have been Trudeau's statement that any country could have any government it wished as long as it did not bother its neighbours. The fact that, in this case, the neighbours had decided they were imperilled by the events in Grenada did not seem to cut much ice with the prime minister.[97]

Trudeau's chagrin at not being informed produced a certain amount of scurrying in External Affairs as officials contemplated what could be done in response; eventually, however, cooler heads, among them MacEachen's, prevailed.[98] It had not been a high point of Canadian diplomacy, but it had not done any particular damage, even in Washington.

The Americans had reason to be pleased with another Trudeauvian decision. We have not dealt extensively with the two-track decision and American missile deployment in Europe. The prospect of an accelerating arms race, especially in the low state of East-West relations in 1982–3, stimulated considerable apprehension among peace groups in various Western countries, including Canada. But when Vice President George Bush visited Ottawa in March 1983, and again when Trudeau visited Washington in April, the two countries reaffirmed their devotion to the two-track strategy.[99]

On such issues there was no special, overt difference of opinion between the two countries. Canada accepted the Mutual Assured Destruction doctrine that formed the basis for U.S. strategic thought in the 1970s. Under Trudeau, Canada regularly renewed the NORAD agreement, which represented a declining and increasingly obsolescent response to the Soviet bomber threat.[100] Canada had already signed, in February, a weapons-testing agreement with the United States; it was known that what the Americans wanted to test in particular was their air-launched cruise missile. (The agreement, called CANUSTEP, or Canada-US Test and Evaluation Program, was tabled in the House of Commons on 10 February 1983.)[101] The cruise responded to Soviet technological developments, and it had many attractions, including cheapness.[102] Canada was invaluable for testing it; after all, Canada had large stretches of winter landscape that closely resembled the Siberian tundra. The government defended its decision to sign the testing agreement by describing it as 'consistent' with Canada's support for NATO's two-track policy.[103]

On 13 June the Americans called in their chips and asked Canada to provide facilities for testing the cruise; and on 15 July, after discussion in cabinet, the Canadian government complied. There was a furious reaction from Canadian peace groups, to which Trudeau responded with his customary logical ferocity. So strong, and so strongly reasoned, were Trudeau's comments that Ambassador Gotlieb in Washington pointedly drew them to the attention of administration personalities. As he expected, the attention they got was favourable.[104]

On political issues, however, Trudeau was not taken especially seriously, as the peace mission of 1983–4 would show (see chapter 14). By 1984, the Americans were waiting for the expiry of the Trudeau mandate. 'We put up with Trudeau for so long,' one American official lamented.[105]

The Americans did not have to wait for Trudeau's political demise to find a turning point. The true turning point occurred earlier – in the

1981–2 recession and the collapse of oil prices. The ruin of the National Energy Policy gave satisfaction; bilateral talks with Canada gave hope. After all, as an American trade official argued, the Americans had to talk to somebody. Another Canada-watcher observed, 'If we aren't Canada's friend, it doesn't have any friends.'[106]

The signal was the replacement of Herb Gray by Ed Lumley as minister of industry, trade and commerce in 1982. Gray was virtually persona non grata in Washington; Lumley most definitely was not. In 1983, Lumley, as regional economic expansion minister, and Gerald Regan, as international trade minister, found a proposal for sectoral free trade in their in-basket. Carefully muted, it was the product of the trade-policy review, whose doubtful sponsors had barely consented to include the idea. But it was, at least, an idea, and 'politically sexy' at that. Regan flashed the idea at a press conference, leaving visions of more and better autopacts in the minds of his listeners.[107]

In February 1984 Regan visited Washington and agreed on exploratory talks with the U.S. international trade representative. Various sectors were slated for discussion: steel, agricultural implements, 'informatics' (meaning data processing and certain computer hardware), and subway cars and buses, as procured by government.[108] The two ministers met again in June, and told reporters that they were 'optimistic'; they scheduled another meeting for the fall. That meeting was overtaken by events, and a new Conservative government.[109]

The dazzling vision of sectoral free trade petered out by June 1984, but it was not entirely gone. The initiative opened doors previously closed, and ventilated minds previously fixed on Europe or 'the Pacific Rim,' a mirage that shimmered on the far side of Hawaii for the benefit of westerners. It is not especially difficult to trace the intellectual origins of the later free-trade agreement with the United States to the late Trudeau period; whether that too can be described as a vision or a mirage is for future historians to discover.

13

The Constitution and Other Follies

Relations with Great Britain occupy a peculiar place in the hierarchy of Canadian foreign policy. Unlike Canadian relations with 95 per cent of today's sovereign states, Canada's involvement with the United Kingdom has a history stretching back 500 years – a history of discovery, settlement, empire, and wars. On a symbolic level, Britain bulked large in the Canadian consciousness, so large as to have speeded Canada into two world wars in the twentieth century. The reciprocal was not true, something that bothered Canadians but not Britons. Although the majority of Canadians are no longer of British descent, there was still, in the 1970s and 1980s, a substantial anglophile and monarchical element in the country.[1] As if in recognition of this fact, London was Canada's principal diplomatic post in Europe, and during the Trudeau years its complement of staff was larger than for the embassy in Washington.[2]

The anglophobe element, always present in Canadian life, has tended to lose enthusiasm as the British empire has disappeared. Yet there remains what John Holmes has called an 'Anglo-Canadian neurosis,' and what Nigel Lawson has described in response as 'a purely Canadian neurosis,' having more to do with Canada's search for its own identity in the columns of foreign newspapers.[3]

Canada remains a monarchy, sharing a Queen and a royal family with the United Kingdom itself. There is regular communication between the Canadian governor general, the monarch's representative, and the royal household, even if the sense and the reality of 'sharing' are also uneven or unequal. To the British, the monarch is 'our Queen' and her entanglements in distant lands may be becoming as much a source of confusion as they are a source of pride. Still, when the Canadian prime minister travels to Britain, a visit to one or another of the royal residences can be laid on, to discuss with Elizabeth II the affairs of her Canadian territories.[4]

The contacts continued throughout the Trudeau years. No prolonged thought was given to abolishing the monarchy, although one of Trudeau's senior English-speaking ministers briefly grasped at the idea as a potentially sellable election issue in April 1968. Trudeau himself preserved the forms, observing their letter if not their spirit. Prince Charles once complained to Roy Jenkins that Trudeau placed his collection of autographed photos of the royal family in a desk drawer at home, instead of displaying them in their customary place of honour.[5] In the mid to late 1970s Trudeau and his advisers, in consultation with the governor general and the Queen and their respective counsellors, initiated an alteration in the governor general's letters patent that restricted the duties of the Queen and enhanced those of the governor general. Despite some feeling that the monarchy would ultimately pass away, there the matter rested. The Queen would be available to sign a new Canadian constitution, if one was ever agreed to.

Relations between Canada and the United Kingdom take their cue from their common history as symbolized by a shared monarch. If the monarch can be shared, so can other things: institutions, allegiances, attitudes; put another way, it is not expected that there will be contradiction on important matters between the Queen's British and Canadian advisers.

Fortunately, there are few important matters that can disturb the tranquillity between Great Britain and Canada. By the time Trudeau became prime minister, the British government was well launched on its attempt to join the European Economic Community (EEC). Canada could do little to thwart it, even had it wanted to, but it was inevitable, once Britain joined Europe, for trade with Canada to diminish.

In 1968 Canada sent $1.2 billion in exports to the United Kingdom. The British were our second-largest trading partner, after the Americans (admittedly a long way after) and ahead of the EEC and Japan. By 1975 this was no longer so. Canadian exports to the United States had more than doubled by 1975, but exports to the United Kingdom had risen by less than half (in current rather than constant dollars). Both the EEC and Japan had passed the British. These trends accelerated during the remainder of the Trudeau years. By 1984 Canadian exports to Japan were double those to the United Kingdom, while imports from Japan were more than double those from Britain.[6]

The same decline characterized other contacts between Britain and Canada. The Commonwealth, throughout this period a forum for contacts between the two countries, may be thought of also as a forum for disagreement. 'It must be said,' a future Conservative chancellor of the exchequer wrote in the early 1970s, 'that the British are becoming increasingly sceptical of the value of keeping the Commonwealth in existence; above all if this means keeping it going on Canada's terms.'[7]

In general, British ties to Canada tended to shrink. Some of the remaining links were generational – one Canadian diplomat remarked that his treatment varied according to the age of his interlocutors – or attitudinal; sentiment and tradition played a part in the British perception of Canada, as they did in the Canadian view of Britain. Unfortunately for Canada the generation gap pointed the wrong way. A country that still liked to perceive itself as young and vigorous was, in Britain, most beloved by the older, not the rising generation. But the appropriate generation (over fifty-five) and the appropriate attitudes (Commonwealth and monarchy) were wasting assets at a time when attention centred on 'the British disease' of industrial decline and social disaggregation. The attitude of the trendier part of the younger generation is perhaps best caught by a stray comment in The Times in 1981: Canada, the newspaper's gossip columnist wrote, is 'normally regarded by headline-hungry news editors as one of the most dismally unproductive corners of the earth.' The Times was not alone: sample journalistic comments from London's Fleet Street include 'a great white waste of time,' and 'of all the wet, wooden places, at the end of the earth.'[8] Those who lived by headlines, or relied on them for information, were unlikely to accumulate much of an impression of North America's 'unknown country.'[9]

Still, in the Trudeau period, Canada's sentimental assets in Britain were not completely gone, even if Canada itself was not regarded as a country of interest or importance by the younger generation of British leaders.[10] A flurry of press speculation about 'Trendy Trudeau' when he attended his first Commonwealth conference was little more than a nine days' wonder, and when it was over, he lapsed as a subject of interest.[11] Even the idea that he might be 'anti-British' did not last, though when the decision to halve Canadian forces in Europe was announced the British government took it badly, and said so.[12] That was an issue where British interests were affected, but where Britain itself was not the target of a particular Canadian policy. On the whole the British accepted that Trudeau had little direct interest in them, and few ties to their country. Further down the government hierarchy, the old confidence ebbed away. While the older generation of British diplomats maintained, as best they could, close links with their Canadian counterparts, even they were unsure of the practical benefits. At NATO, for example, there had been regular exchanges of briefings, but by the mid-1970s the British were so uncertain of the quality of the Canadian information and analysis ('so jejune,' according to one source) that they restricted the flow of information to the Canadian delegation. External Affairs complained, but their complaints aroused little enthusiasm.[13]

Harold Wilson, prime minister in 1964–70 and again in 1974–7, had some background in Canadian matters, having dealt with Canadian aid and trade in the late 1940s. But he was regarded as slippery, if clever; he never achieved rapport with his Canadian counterparts. His successors, the Conservative Edward Heath (1970–4) and the Labourite Jim Callaghan (1977–9), were less grounded in Canadian affairs, but Callaghan proved to be sentimentally fond of Canada and Canadians. Whether Heath was capable of sentiment was something that few Canadians ever discovered, but he could be affable, and even entertaining, when circumstance allowed.[14]

There was only one issue of capital interest to Canada on which British opinions and attitudes were essential. The constitution, the British North America Act, was unfinished. The alterations to Canada's sovereign status in the 1920s and 1930s had not resolved the amendment of the act, but, it was assumed, had temporarily left it where it always had been – in the hands of the British parliament. The federal government and the provinces had muddled along since then. On some issues, such as the admission of Newfoundland to Canada in 1949, the federal parliament consulted itself and then asked the British parliament to amend the act; but on other issues, such as the acquisition of old-age pensions as a federal power in 1951, provincial consent was held to be needed, because provincial powers were thereby diminished. Despite repeated attempts, no agreement on the power of amendment in Canada ('patriation') was ever reached. Nor were any significant disagreements exported to the British parliament. For the most part, Canada's political quarrels, even on the constitution, stopped at the water's edge.

Between 1968 and 1971 Trudeau hoped for a harmonious constitutional package, one that would include patriation as its keystone. In the hopeful spring of 1971, prior to the Victoria conference, he had made his dispositions. He sent his cabinet secretary, Gordon Robertson, and his minister of justice, John Turner, to England to tell the British what was intended and to ask what might be expected, but their cause proved to be moot.[15]

Trudeau soon had other issues to worry about: a minority government, the third option, and an oil crisis. He never quite forgot that lurking in the background there was an unfinished item of business – the constitution. The provinces in any case reminded him, offering to exchange the objective of patriation for concessions of federal powers. It accordingly became important to the provinces, or to some of them, to ensure that Trudeau would not proceed with patriation. Trudeau's own desire for a comprehensive deal, one that would include a charter of rights, and his search for a federal-provincial consensus, gave comfort to the assumption that there would be a deal for all, or not at all. But some provinces believed that under certain circumstances the British government could play a political role by refusing to cooperate with any unilateral initiative by Trudeau – or vice versa. Securing British assurances would help to box in the prime minister, and make him readier to concede what they wanted.

The British, for their part, were not anxious to take up the burden of deciding how to respond to a Canadian constitutional initiative, whether provincial or federal in origin. The British government, needless to say, had its own priorities, among which the Canadian constitution did not figure, and in which Canada did not occupy as large a place as it once had done.

That too was generational. The Commonwealth bulked large in the natural order of things to the British high commissioner in Ottawa in the early 1970s. His own career, in the colonies or ex-colonies, reflected a period in which British interests remained significant, strategically and economically, from Suez to Singapore to Sydney. But his establishment in Ottawa was dwindling. It was still rated a 'grade one' post, and its tranquillity and standard of living were considered desirable among British diplomats; but it was reduced in a general austerity drive in the mid-1970s because there was not enough important work to go around, and it was not on the Foreign and Commonwealth Office's priority circulation list for important dispatches.[16]

Despite the exiguous state of Anglo-Canadian relations, London remained a centre of international business and was Canada's largest mission abroad in the 1970s; the high commissionership, with its highly desirable and fashionable house, was much sought after. Two senior professional diplomats, Charles Ritchie and Jake Warren, served there in the early 1970s; Ritchie was a well-known figure in London's literary circles – he had a novel and a play written about him – while Warren, a trade specialist and former deputy minister of industry, trade and commerce, suited Britain's new-found urgency for trade and prosperity.

Warren was succeeded in 1974 by Paul Martin, a former minister of external affairs, Trudeau's leader in the Senate, and Canada's most senior international statesman. Martin's acquaintance with Britain went back to the 1920s, when he had been at Cambridge; in his long and varied curriculum vitae he could even boast that he had known the British prime minister, Harold Wilson, for upwards of thirty years: they had once dossed down together in the same bed while on separate missions to overcrowded Geneva. It would have been surprising had Martin not had the entrée into the British political and diplomatic world; but Martin's experience, acquaintance, energy, and persistence made him a model high commissioner.

Martin found that Wilson's foreign secretary, Jim Callaghan, knew little about Canada; but what little he knew – a vision of forests, lakes, and opportunity – he liked very much. By the time Callaghan succeeded Wilson as prime minister in 1976, Martin had put a Canadian trip on his agenda for September; and Callaghan honoured his commitment. 'It had been an ambition of mine to travel across Canada from coast to coast, inspired by boyhood reading of accounts of the building of the Canadian National Railway and the Canadian Pacific.'

Two things are important about the trip. It was successful, from Callaghan's point of view: he enjoyed himself, consuming en route 'the largest and most tender barbecued steaks I have ever eaten,' and he made a happy impression.[17] The other was an autumn visit Callaghan paid to Quebec City, where he was received by Premier Bourassa. It had become the fashion to shape top-level meetings to provide for privacy and frank interchange, which it was assumed would occur when two leaders found themselves conveniently alone, and so Bourassa had arranged a private lunch with Callaghan. He had, it seemed, something on his mind. He asked the British prime minister if he would promise not to amend the Canadian constitution, or patriate it, unless all the provinces, and especially Quebec, consented.

Callaghan had been briefed to expect something like this and he did not temporize in replying. He would not make the desired promise. The British government's relations were with the Canadian government. As far as Britain was concerned, an address from the Canadian parliament had always been, and would again be, sufficient. What the provinces did at home, inside Canada, was their business. Bourassa goggled at Callaghan and fell silent. The two men found little else to say for the balance of the lunch which, it must be admitted, had amply justified the 'full and frank' format of intimate summit meetings.[18]

Callaghan visited Canada once more, in March 1977. He met Trudeau in Ottawa, and there had a private conversation with him. The details did not become immediately apparent, but when the British prime minister returned to London the Foreign and Commonwealth Office was instructed to review British policy on the patriation of the constitution. Perhaps because the issue was at that stage academic, officials speculated about what would happen if 'the patriation had not been worked out satisfactorily in advance in Canada,' and if the provinces' interests were affected. Paul Martin, when he learned what was afoot, told his diary that the British would do well to drop any idea of interference, and, indeed, 'drop the matter' altogether.[19]

British views proved more helpful than that. Lest there be any doubt, the British high commission in Ottawa arranged for a question to be asked in the British House of Commons. Since it turned out that nobody, either in the Canadian high commission or in Canada, had noticed, they were then obliged to draw attention to it. The meaning was plain. In the minds of senior British officials and politicians, the one correct way to deal with a Canadian constitutional issue was not to 'look behind' a request arriving from Ottawa; if it came from the Canadian government and was certified by a parliamentary resolution, that was sufficient.[20]

It was an answer that might have interested Bourassa, but he was no longer in power. On 15 November 1976 the Parti Québécois defeated the Liberals in a provincial election; just over a week later René Lévesque was premier.

Lévesque had got to be premier by adopting the advice of the former deputy minister of intergovernmental affairs, who had announced his conversion to separatism shortly after quitting the civil service. Claude Morin had read the evidence of the public opinion polls and two provincial elections. It was clear, he told his leader, that Quebeckers would not vote for separatism or independence or even Lévesque's particular nostrum, 'sovereignty-association,' in which Quebec would get the sovereignty and Canada would get the association. But if the PQ ran as a good government party, putting off the question of sovereignty-association until a later referendum, then it had an excellent chance of defeating Bourassa's bumbling Liberals.

So it proved, and as a reward Morin became minister of intergovernmental affairs in the Lévesque government. His aim was to take Quebec to independence, but in the meantime, he promised, the PQ would act like a normal provincial government. Given Morin's definition of 'normal,' his old adversary Trudeau would be in for an interesting time.[21]

For Trudeau it was an unexpected time. Not long before, he had told Canadians that separatism was dead. Now it was alive again, and with it revived the eternal constitutional issue and several other issues besides. This might have been taken as an excessively negative sign, but nothing stimulated Trudeau as much as the prospect of another battle with the separatists. As he told a lunch party in London in May 1977, 'At one time a few months ago he had thought of retiring from the leadership ... [But] there was no thought of his going now.'[22]

Trudeau cranked up the constitutional machinery. He sent a special study team across Canada under the joint leadership of Jean-Luc Pepin, a former minister, and John Robarts, Ontario's retired premier. It was not the best of times to go back to the constitution, but Trudeau would have been remiss had he not tried to find a balance between provincial aspirations and federal powers in an effort to create a counter-attraction to separatism. The provinces were busy quarrelling over the distribution of tax revenues, resources, and offshore jurisdiction; and while there was a trend in public opinion to rally round the beleaguered Ottawa government (reflected in high levels of support for Trudeau and the Liberal party during most of 1977)[23], there was also a trend among intellectuals in both French and English Canada to accept the PQ victory as a definitive sign of the times. A decentralized Canada, with a significantly reduced federal role, was now fashionable.[24]

Trudeau himself was not impervious. He toyed both with constitutional reform and with the idea of a national referendum on separatism, designed to pre-empt Lévesque's plebiscite.[25] But as Don Jamieson told Canadian envoys in Europe a month after the Quebec election, the disposition in the cabinet, while flexible and accommodating on some subjects, was to resist major concessions that would damage Canadian unity.[26]

While awaiting developments, the Canadian government sounded its British counterpart. What would Britain do if and when Canada requested action on the constitution? The question had to be asked, and answered, even though, as Paul Martin later observed, 'There was never any doubt in my time or before as to what the British response would be.' Martin dropped in, chatted to his friends, and arranged dinners, attracting the prime minister, the home secretary, the attorney general, and the lord chancellor; and from his friends he got what he had hoped for. When a request arrived from Canada, Callaghan promised, it would be acted upon.[27]

The request, however, did not come. The federal government drafted a referendum bill, introduced it in the House of Commons in 1978, and allowed it to die on the order paper. Trudeau's latest constitutional enterprise produced what has elsewhere been called 'a badly written and worse conceived potpourri of Senate reform and Supreme Court fiddlings' in the summer of 1978, while his national-unity task force evolved a document that preached regionalism and decentralization as a panacea to Canada's ills. Finally, early in 1979, Trudeau reached another impasse with the provincial premiers. At a February meeting, the federal government offered substantial concessions, hoping in return for patriation and a charter of rights; but the provinces, and in particular Quebec and Saskatchewan, demanded further concessions before such a step could be contemplated.[28] Although some excused the failure of the conference to reach agreement by referring to the approaching expiry of Trudeau's mandate (then five months away), others drew the conclusion that the whole technique of using federal-provincial conferences to get constitutional agreement was wrong. As the *Canadian Annual Review* commented, 'Canadians had become used to the first ministers' publicly airing their differences with little sign of progress.'[29] Trudeau, having gone, as he saw it, so far with no reward, gave up the exercise. Canadians had no immediate chance to discover what other conclusions he had drawn from his experience, because the Liberal government was defeated at the polls in May 1979 and the Trudeau government made way for a minority Conservative administration headed by Joe Clark.

That Trudeau had indeed learned from experience would only become clear the following year.

The re-emergence of separatism as a lively political force had an impact on other countries' perceptions of Canada and on Canadian foreign relations in general. Whether Canada liked it or not, the state of the nation became an item for discussion for travelling Canadians and a point of particular interest to foreigners visiting Canada, whether in a public or private capacity. Was Canada really unstable, as some Europeans had come to believe? Did the PQ victory, Don Jamieson asked, mean that Canada would be 'required to be dependent on the sympathy of foreign governments when it came to issues such as culture and sovereignty?'[30] And would that apply only to culture and sovereignty?[31] How much sympathy would be forthcoming for a remote transatlantic power of no great military capacity? As a German observer remarked, 'Canada was too far away to feel sorry for'; France, for Europeans in the 1970s as for Africans in the 1960s, loomed larger and was closer.[32] The Germans, however, did place an order for Challenger jets at Canadair in Montreal – thereby assisting local prosperity and, presumably, the status quo.

The quickest and most obvious impact of separatism was in France. Public opinion there had become much more attuned to Quebec in the decade since de Gaulle's unexpected intervention. In 1967 there had been astonishment at de Gaulle and sympathy for the Canadian case; there was much less sympathy in 1976.[33]

Fortunately, the French government was not disposed to intervene in quite the same way as its predecessor. The government was, as in 1967, to the political right, but it was not as activist where Quebec was concerned. Perhaps this was the residual effect of six years of Bourassa; perhaps too it reflected a more cautious and impartial estimate of the balance of political forces in Quebec and in Canada. For some French officials, even relatively senior ones, Canadian unity was at least as great a desideratum as the fulfilment of Quebec nationalism.[34]

Nevertheless, Quebec was deemed a positive issue in French politics, and not only on the right. French politicians took a positive attitude to the 'evolution' of Quebec, reserving for the future the question of where that evolution might lead. Claude Morin, back in office, estimated that France would take a favourable, if unspecific, attitude: his hopes were rewarded on the occasion of René Lévesque's official visit to France in November 1977: France, President Valéry Giscard d'Estaing proclaimed at a banquet, would support Quebec no matter what direction the province chose. In his memoirs, Morin alluded to certain 'foreign representatives' who expressed personal sympathy for Quebec's (that is, the PQ's) cause, or who 'informed us that, if sovereignty were achieved, Quebec would immediately be recognized by their country.' It is a fair bet that these representatives (as to whose identity Morin remains coy) included those of France. How many others were involved, and with what authority, awaits further revelations from M. Morin.[35]

The visit to France attracted wide attention in Canada and abroad. Canadians counted the ceremonial coups scored by Lévesque and tried to calculate whether France was in theory, or merely in fact, treating him as the head of a sovereign state. The Canadian ambassador, by now Gérard Pelletier, sought clarifications from the Quai d'Orsay. He was told in December that the French intended 'no change whatsoever' in their relations with Canada. Further, 'The French indicated that they did not intend to intervene in the Canadian problem. It is under this condition that the fraternal relations with Quebec are affirmed.' According to Paul Martin, who saw the relevant reports from Paris, 'Our Ambassador, Pelletier, is of the opinion that the French reply is as favourable as we could have hoped, bearing in mind the political situation in France.' Pelletier recommended that Ottawa accept the French assurances at face value, and hope for the best. Given the ambiguity of the French reply, hope was definitely the requisite commodity.[36]

There was undoubtedly room for the Quebec government to play the 'French card': there were plenty in Paris who would have made even more of a public effort on the province's behalf. But it was judged in

Quebec City that such a ploy would be inopportune and might backfire with public opinion; in any case, Lévesque himself was not thought to be a fervent francophile, and a close collaboration with the 'amis' in Paris might have sat ill with the premier.[37]

It was not, therefore, necessary to appeal to the 'sympathy' of foreign governments to support the federal, or the Quebec, case. Those governments were afforded a breathing space to develop their own attitudes. In the United Kingdom, the bureaucracy in the Foreign and Commonwealth Office was very well disposed to the federal point of view. 'They are aware of our problems, desirous of not adding to them, and well informed of their content and their implications.' So interested were the Foreign Office officials in a happy, non-separatist outcome in Canada that they helped to frustrate the very able efforts of Quebec's agent-general in London, Gilles Loiselle, to forward his government's point of view.[38]

The foreign secretary, David Owen, even asked Paul Martin whether the Canadian government wanted him to see 'what he could do to help us vis-à-vis the French.' In the aftermath of Lévesque's triumphal tour of Paris (and reverential homage to de Gaulle's tomb), the answer for the British, as for the Germans and any other potential well-wishers, was 'to let matters rest.'[39]

That was not the answer conveyed to the Americans. For them, Canada was close at hand, the largest trading partner, the source of oil and electricity; strategically, Canada was the source of the United States's largest remaining supply of predictability, similarity, and stability, all conveniently located along 3000 miles of desensitized border. What affected the structure of Canada also affected its stability; and what detracted from Canadian stability would have a direct and possibly important effect on American security.

The Quebec election occurred during the hiatus between the U.S. presidential election that saw the defeat of President Gerald Ford and his Republican party and the inauguration of his Democratic successor, Governor Jimmy Carter of Georgia. There was no one especially knowledgeable about Canada on the Carter team, and it fell to the incumbents, and to the bureaucrats, to assess the situation in Canada and to determine where advantage lay for the United States. There were two distinct questions in the view of the U.S. embassy in Ottawa. First, was the break-up of Canada to be regarded as a matter of indifference? And second, what should be the American reaction if Quebec tried to establish a relationship with the U.S. government?

To the first question, the answer was strongly negative. Canada was a useful country to have around, another democracy in a world where such countries did not abound. It was doubtful whether substantial economic benefit would accrue to the United States, or to many individual American interests, if Canada split apart. Finally, one federal government ought not to look with indifference on the structural troubles of another, especially one so close, so similar, as Canada's. If Canada had regions, so did the United States, and some of the regions looked much the same.[40]

As to the second question, the Canadians hoped the Americans would be watchful, silent, but cordial. Quebec would, in Ottawa's view, take what it could get, and the federal government wanted to make sure that it got nothing. Ambassador Tom Enders recommended to his government 'that we comport ourselves in such a way as to leave no doubt of any possible support to Quebec.' Enders later recalled that 'these lines of reasoning encountered no dissent within the US government.'[41] Nor would they have met much disagreement outside government, where American businessmen with an interest in Canada and the overlapping foreign policy elite tended to favour a 'strong and united Canada.'[42] Some well-informed Americans, reflecting on possible links between a sovereign Quebec and France, opposed Quebec independence as signifying an increase in French influence on subjects such as NATO.[43]

Presumably these views were brought forward at an interdepartmental meeting in Washington on 13 January 1977, to which Morin alludes. Though the CIA was represented, that fact by itself has no special sinister significance, nor is there any reason to expect that the CIA had any particular handle on the Canadian problem.[44] Though this meeting took place in the dying days of the Ford administration, there is every reason to believe that its conclusions held good for the incoming Carter administration. Carter had been briefed, through his staff, as to what was happening in Canada; his secretary of state, Cyrus Vance, was friendly to Canada and appreciative of Enders's recommendations; only his national security adviser, Zbigniew Brzezinski, was said to be inclined to a contrary view. Ironically, from the federal point of view, Brzezinski had the greatest experience of Canada, particularly Montreal, where his father had been Polish consul-general and where he had spent much of his youth. Probably Brzezinski's view of the Quebec problem, and of the impact of Quebec nationalism, was located more at the level of personal intuition than of actual policy recommendations. Still, intuition is not to be dismissed as an inspiration for decisions, and, had the occasion offered, Brzezinski's sentiments might have had more scope. As it was, the Enders-Vance line, and Carter's own attraction to Canada, prevailed.[45]

Carter's policy towards Canada involved a great deal more than the possibility of Quebec separatism; that this was so was part of the strength of the Canadian position in Washington. He invited Trudeau to visit very early in his term and provided the forum of a speech to Congress. Trudeau rose to the occasion, as he had to an earlier oration before an audience of New York businessmen, and the effect was to reassure opinion both in the United States and at home as to the stability and prospects of the Canadian government in its battle with separatism.

Interestingly, Ambassador Enders assessed Trudeau's own reaction to Americans as cautious and uncertain; Trudeau knew few Americans, and in any case in his relations with the United States 'he did not want to appear to be "demandeur." ' Enders's communications with the prime minister on the subject of Quebec were conducted at arm's length, either through the cabinet secretary, Michael Pitfield, or through private intermediaries who included, in the months after November 1976, Paul Desmarais of Power Corp. and Ian Sinclair, the president of the Canadian Pacific Railway.[46]

Equally important, Trudeau and Carter met privately; inevitably, Carter asked the Canadian prime minister what he thought of his prospects. Trudeau replied, simply, that the federal government and Canada were in a real jam, and that the crisis over separatism would last for some time. In the end, however, Trudeau was confident that his country would surmount the challenge of the Parti Québécois; using an American analogy, he suggested that Canada would emerge strengthened from the ordeal, just as the United States had been strengthened in the aftermath of its civil war.[47]

Carter was said to be pleased by Trudeau's candour and by the friendly and informal discussions that had occurred. The 'vibes,' it was reported, had been extremely good.[48] Perhaps because he had been reassured on the prospects for Canada, Carter could turn his attention to crises elsewhere; while he and Trudeau discussed and cultivated multilateral concerns in later meetings, the Quebec problem did not resurface as a major concern. Instead, Vice-President Mondale, who haled from the border state of Minnesota and who had taken something of an interest in Canada's energy policy after the energy shocks of 1972–4, carried the Canadian ball in the administration. Mondale, who had an extremely close working relationship with the Canadian ambassador, Peter Towe, was also inclined to favour Ottawa over Quebec.[49]

Carter did not completely refrain from public comment on Canada's constitutional troubles. It was an internal Canadian affair, he told the press, but, he added, 'if I were the one to make the decision a confederation would be my preference.' Carter's comment maintained just the right mix of friendliness and ignorance: Canada has never been 'a confederation,' though the events leading to the founding of the country in the 1860s bear that title. As for Mondale, he told Canadians in 1979 during a visit to Ottawa that naturally Americans hoped their country would remain united; but he quickly added that Canadians and Quebeckers would settle that matter for themselves.[50]

Lévesque's adventures in the United States were not as happy as Trudeau's – an ironic fact, because Lévesque, who had served as a reporter with the U.S. army during the war, was said to prefer Americans to English Canadians; perhaps, one may speculate, he even preferred them to the French.[51] Lévesque chose to make his first public pitch for foreign sympathy in the United States – in New York City, before the Economic Club, on 25 January 1977. Lévesque, as was natural, was trying to reassure his audience. Quebec, he told them, was merely engaging in the same kind of righteous activity as the Americans themselves 200 years before, when they had their revolution; and to demonstrate that this was so he served up a potted history of the province that explained Quebec in the nationalist terms that his voters at home found so familiar and reassuring.[52] To be fair, it was not Lévesque himself who had written the speech but Claude Morin, Jacques Parizeau, his finance minister, and Louis Bernard; and Lévesque knew, even as he was delivering his text, that he had, as the *Baltimore Sun* put it, 'laid an egg.'[53]

Lévesque's supporters charged that his dismal performance had been contrived by hostile English Canadians; certainly, English Canadians in the audience did not forward his cause.[54] But Lévesque had done most of it himself, to himself, and what he had not caused resulted logically from the Americans' concerns with their own self-interest.

Contacts between the Quebec government and the American administration were therefore minimal during the period 1976–80. The Americans discouraged the idea of a permanent Quebec mission in Washington; instead, the Quebeckers worked out of New York. Morin nevertheless operated a considerable low-key publicity enterprise in the United States, working through foreign-policy study groups, such as the Council on Foreign Relations, and through academic grants and study programs.[55]

Conceding that the Americans might have good reason to suspect a political party that proclaimed neutralism as part of its stock in trade, Morin arranged, ultimately, for the PQ to drop its foreign-policy stance: instead, after 1979, the PQ told the world that its basic foreign-policy orientation would be just the same as Canada's and that an independent Quebec would wish to join both NATO and NORAD.[56] That one notable point of difference between the Quebec nationalist view of the world and the putative, stultified, Anglo-Saxon Canadian viewpoint had just been eliminated was not stressed; perhaps it later helped to account for the fact, cited by René Lévesque, that an increasing number of Quebeckers believed that Ottawa rather than Quebec City should handle foreign affairs.[57]

For the rest, the Lévesque government engaged in an apparently endless series of escapades designed to prove that Quebec should have, and did have, a role to play in foreign affairs. The various episodes do not merit repetition here: essentially, Morin was forwarding the policy enunciated years before by Gérin-Lajoie that Quebec should have control over the external aspects of its internal powers. Thereby it would prove, at least to Lévesque's supporters, that it had developed the capacity to take over Ottawa's residual duties when the moment came. To Ottawa's partisans, of course, the history of Quebec's external involvements in the 1970s showed that provinces should have no role at all in the conduct of foreign policy of any description.[58]

Foreign relations did not play very much of a role in the eventual Quebec referendum on sovereignty-association, held on 20 May 1980. There were analogies to events and institutions abroad, and there was considerable foreign interest in what was happening. There was, however, remarkably little official foreign involvement, even by way of speeches; both the pro-sovereignty 'yes' forces and the federalist 'no' coalition wanted it that way.

But the fact that there was a referendum, and that Lévesque, Morin, and the 'yes' forces lost, 60–40, would have a profound effect on Canadian foreign policy. Nowhere would that effect be more visible than in the forthcoming struggle over the constitution: for it was not forgotten, especially in Ottawa, that Pierre Trudeau had promised a 'renewed federalism.' What that would mean only became apparent in September 1980.

The political history of Canada in the 1980s was shaped by two events. In the first, the short-lived Conservative government of Joe Clark was defeated, initially in the House of Commons and then at the polls in February 1980. The Trudeau Liberals were returned with an overall majority in the House, Clark resigned, and Trudeau formed a government on 3 March. Unluckily for the new government, its support was concentrated in the east and centre of Canada; west of Ontario the Liberals elected only two MPs, and west of Winnipeg none at all. The

Liberals, however, won 67 per cent of the vote, and 73 out of 74 seats, in the province of Quebec.

The second event was the referendum in Quebec in May. The Lévesque government had submitted the principal element of its platform to the voters and had been defeated. It had no mandate to proceed with sovereignty-association: as far as the constitution was concerned, it had no mandate to do anything at all. On the contrary, the initiative on the constitution had passed to the federalist camp, and, in short, to Trudeau.

Trudeau's views on the constitution were well known. Patriation and a charter of rights were important to him; so was the unity of the country. Less known, or less fathomable, were the conclusions he and his entourage had drawn after the failed constitutional negotiations of 1968–71 and 1978–9. On the second occasion in particular Trudeau had offered to alter the balance of power between the federal government and the provinces, but the provinces had merely asked for more.

With little to show in the constitutional field, despite all the effort expended on the subject, Trudeau had even less to boast of in other areas. Two majority governments in 1968 and 1974 and one minority government in 1972 had been exhausted in housekeeping tasks; Trudeau's ministers were determined not to do the same with their fourth mandate.

At first the pattern seemed very familiar. The federal government proposed a new kick at the constitutional can. The minister of justice, Jean Chrétien, jetted from provincial capital to capital. Committees were formed and drafts circulated. First ministers assembled in Ottawa in September 1980 and failed utterly to reach agreement. Canadians had seen it all before.

Unbeknownst to most Canadians, Trudeau had decided to do something different this time. He put it to his caucus that a crisis of opportunity had come: Would they take the risk? They would. 'Allons-y Cadillac,' an exuberant Quebec MP urged his colleagues: broadly, 'Let's go in style.' And so in a country more notable for pragmatism than for principle, a group of apparently sane and presumably sober politicians did a most un-Canadian thing: they put their principles ahead of their practice. It was the Cadillac option they chose even though they had no idea whether the Cadillac was a limousine or a hearse.

The Cadillac, ultimately, would be going to London. Only Trudeau could send it there, but it was up to the British to say what they would do with it. At a very early stage, not quite a month after the Quebec referendum and before Chrétien's summertime rambles indicated what to expect from the provinces, Trudeau took up the subject of a constitutional package with the British.

More precisely, he talked to Margaret Thatcher, the British prime minister. Thatcher was not a stranger to Canadian affairs. Since becoming Conservative party leader, she had visited Canada and had met various Canadians in London. One of them, in May 1977, was Premier Peter Lougheed of Alberta; in discussion with him, Thatcher gave evidence of what Paul Martin called 'interest and study' on the topic of the Canadian constitution. To Thatcher, at least at that time, the Canadian arrangements indicated an 'already de-centralized country,' which did not prevent Lougheed from hinting that he would like to make it a little more so.[59] As opposition leader Thatcher had also visited Canada, though her tour was by some lights less than successful.[60] Canada was not a subject that need preoccupy a political leader in Britain, and when she defeated James Callaghan and the Labour party in April 1979 it was, she knew, because of the force of her beliefs and personality, highlighted by the dismal record of her predecessor in combatting Britain's industrial unrest and economic decline.

Neither Canada nor the Commonwealth occupied much of Thatcher's attention. With Britain in the Common Market she was obliged to be mindful of Europe, and she perforce had to give thought to the United States, her country's major ally. But knowledge of foreign affairs was not her strong suit, or that of her advisers, whom Harold Macmillan, one of her Tory predecessors, dismissed as 'a rather suburban lot.'[61] Her foreign secretary, Lord Carrington, might have been an exception to the rule, but, as an astute observer wrote, 'he was easily bored by less pressing issues' than Europe or the United States, 'including the North-South debate [and] most of the Commonwealth.'[62]

The Thatcher cabinet was, in fact, a rather mixed bag, a combination of the right and left wings of Tory politics. Thatcher's ability to make them combine into an effective unit of government was, at first, quite unclear. A Canadian assessment of Thatcher's political skills dating from March 1981 noted that on a budget measure that year, 'forty of her own MPs either voted against her or abstained.' Of her early supporters, only one, St John Stevas, was in the cabinet; he was leader of the House, in charge of parliamentary business and scheduling.[63] It was a key position, but also an exposed one, where satisfactory performance for 'she who must be obeyed' was crucial – though in the early days ministers did not yet know how crucial. She did not lack an agenda of her own, and there was no doubt that much had to be done; the instrument to hand was the parliamentary timetable, which in Britain was always very tightly packed.

It would be to parliament that a Canadian constitutional revision must go. Thatcher cannot have been overjoyed when in June 1980 Trudeau personally raised the possibility that he would be sending a constitutional package to her for passage. He could give her few details (even in Ottawa the details had not jelled), beyond warning that it would likely be disapproved of if not actually opposed by some of the provinces. It seems clear that Thatcher responded briskly and favourably to what she had been told. She would make the Canadian legislation a government measure, and she would put the whips on it. Whether she promised a three-line whip, the highest degree of enforced conformity she could exact from her MPs, is another matter; so is whether she could enforce such a promise. But she promised *something*.[64]

Reassured, Trudeau began to plan for an event in which it would not be necessary to secure the unanimous consent of Canada's provinces to a constitutional amendment. This was a momentous change in federal tactics and strategy. Until 1980, the requirement for unanimity among the provinces meant that Trudeau was negotiating from weakness. But the requirement was, as the federal Justice Department argued, a convention rather than a legal necessity. It was not that constitutional conventions lacked force, but they did not, in all circumstances, have the force of law. The decision to ignore convention was a political one, just as conventions had been developed as political expedients. In the last resort, Trudeau's legal advisers speculated, if a convention demonstrably did not work, it could be abandoned; after all, the justification of a convention was that it made matters easier and more certain. But no one could call the convention that governed the constitutional discussions workable; quite the contrary.[65]

Unilateral action could take many forms. Trudeau himself favoured a national referendum to break the logjam, while his advisers suggested a reference to the Supreme Court on the role of constitutional conventions.[66] In the end, following the break-up of the 1 September ministers' conference, the government decided to deal with the problem by embodying its unilateral solution in legislation, which it would present to the people in a national telecast by the prime minister on 2 October and then introduce into the House of Commons. Trudeau proposed to enact patriation, a charter of rights, and an amending formula. He would not surrender any powers to the provinces in return. He would not, by that token, get much provincial support, and, as it happened, he was certain of the support of only two provincial governments, Ontario and New Brunswick.

As a matter of courtesy, the secretary of state for external affairs, Mark

MacGuigan, notified Lord Carrington what was afoot while the two attended the September session of the United Nations in New York. Carrington was not pleased. The inclusion of a charter of rights, he told MacGuigan, would complicate matters and would almost certainly prove unhelpful in securing swift passage of a Canadian constitutional bill. Nevertheless, help had been promised, and help would be afforded; it would be most improper, Carrington told his Canadian counterpart, for his government or parliament not to do exactly as the Canadians wished.[67]

The Canadian news was even less welcome in London. But when MacGuigan and John Roberts, the science minister, carried Trudeau's package to Thatcher in early October, they reported that she did not wince.[68] The British would accept the Canadian package whatever its contents. They did not like the contents, and they knew, if they looked at their own reports from the high commission in Ottawa, that Sir John Ford, the high commissioner, considered Trudeau's actions bad business.[69] A charter of rights might be unwelcome, as well as philosophically unpalatable to believers in the tradition of an unwritten constitution, but it would be dealt with as a part of government business. Nicholas Ridley, the junior minister at the Foreign Office and the man who would pilot the Canadian bill through the House of Commons (Lord Carrington, of course, being exiled by birth to the Lords), repeated Thatcher's assurances.[70] MacGuigan told them that the Canadian government hoped that the amendments would be ready to come into force by Canada Day, 1 July 1981. For that, it would be necessary to get the Canadian amendments into British hands by the end of January. To top it off, MacGuigan saw the leaders of the opposition Labour and Liberal parties, and was assured that they would cooperate.[71]

It remained for Trudeau to get his confection officially to London. If the British were to swallow it, it must be in due form, an address from the Canadian parliament. That address had to pass the Canadian parliament, and Joe Clark and the opposition Conservatives did not propose to make it easy for Trudeau. The provinces opposing the deal (at first six and then eight, better known as the Gang of Eight) began a series of court challenges. Time dragged, and as the fall became winter, it was clear that Trudeau's constitutional package was in trouble.

The lapse of time allowed the opposition to muster its resources, and these proved to be considerable. In London, most of the provinces had agents-general, a practice that dated back before Confederation. Some were mossbacks, enjoying a desirable perk; but some, such as the Quebec representative, Gilles Loiselle, had been living for the day when their talents could finally be put to the test. The agents-general had connections and linkages independent of the Canadian high commission; they knew friendly British MPs, peers, and journalists, and they were now afforded the resources to cultivate them. It may even be said that in the country of the legendary Fleet Street journalist, Lunchtime O'Booze, there was ample inclination to accept cultivation; by the same token, allegiances were won and lost in the crook of an elbow. Mere attendance at Quebec House did not necessarily imply a devotion to provincial autonomy, yet the opportunity was undeniably present. When the Commons Select Committee on Foreign Affairs decided to place the Canadian constitution on its agenda, as it did early in November, it was obvious that Trudeau must do more than rely on the ordinary assurances of what had been until then an apparently friendly government.[72]

The Thatcher cabinet was notoriously leaky; its political position was not strong, and Canada was an easy issue for rebellious Tories to break ranks on. With Canada on its agenda it was not surprising that the cabinet developed a few extra pinholes, or that Canadian secrets began to appear in the newspapers. In late October it occurred to St John Stevas that he should simplify matters. He informed his Canadian counterpart, Yvon Pinard, that even if the Canadians obligingly got rid of their Charter of Rights, he could not promise delivery of the constitution until the spring of 1982. If the Charter of Rights stayed in – something he plainly considered a legislative folly – then it might take until August 1982. Astounded, Pinard asked why the British were prepared to look into a matter which pertained solely to Canada, only to be told that 'if the package were to include a Bill of Rights "then it becomes our problem." '[73]

It was already clear to Ridley that Stevas might be part of the problem rather than part of its solution; there was reportedly 'a testy exchange' in cabinet between the two ministers as Ridley struggled to get the Canadian business back on track and to keep his colleagues committed to it. Other ministers, with more urgent concerns of their own, simply wished the whole business would go away.[74]

The Canadian high commissioner, Jean Wadds, did what she could. Wadds was a veteran Conservative politician from eastern Ontario who had been sent to London by the Clark government. Trudeau had not wished to dislodge her, and his decision to keep her in London proved wise. She was loyal, indefatigable, and possessed of the necessary social skills to join enthusiastically in the 'dinner party war.' But Wadds could not do it all alone. The high commission's staffing arrangements had not contemplated that Canada would be the centre of a lively British political debate; there were not enough personnel nor, possibly, quite the right personalities to manage the constitutional business. The task was the more difficult because of the propensity of ministers and other politicians to drop in to lend a hand and, incidentally, to sample some of the persuasions being employed; the only consolation was that the provincial agents-general had the same problem. Not all ministers proved useless or counter-productive, but some were not helpful. Nor were the free-loaders all politicians.[75]

That there was a larger problem was signalled by a call from James Callaghan, who was still well disposed to Canada and struggling to keep his Labour party in line, though he was not actively interested in the Canadian proposals. At the end of October, Callaghan phoned Wadds to tell her that there had been some slippage, not among the Labour leadership but among the backbenchers. He was worried particularly by the Charter of Rights, by Indian rights, and by federal-provincial relationships, all of which could, he warned, find their champions. He did not need to add that each and every champion could introduce limitless amendments in the House of Commons and tie up government business for some considerable time. That prospect did not necessarily trouble the Labour party, but it was enough to give the government nightmares. As of December 1980 the Canadian government was definitely losing the popularity battle in London, and losing it to its own dissident provinces.[76]

The government decided to dispatch a member of its constitutional team to London, and the choice fell, probably inevitably, on Reeves Haggan. Haggan had once worked in External Affairs in Mitchell Sharp's office; before that he had been a CBC executive, while later in the 1970s he had served in the solicitor general's department. Pitfield plucked him out of that ministry, a boneyard for most of those who served there, and brought him back to the Privy Council Office. Rumpled and raspy, Haggan served up good Scotch and good humour in equal portions: they were useful adjuncts to doses of good advice. With the assistance of Dan Gagnier, a regular foreign-service officer, Haggan started to make his way around London.[77]

Haggan's appointment put the federal government in business as far as lobbying the British was concerned, though it was too late to help much with the foreign-affairs committee – a damaging circumstance. Relations with the Thatcher government were conducted on two levels. On the surface, the British stuck to their prime minister's original promise to Trudeau, repeated to MacGuigan in October 1980. They would, according to that scenario, proceed as and when the Canadians wished.

But it was equally obvious that large parts of the British government, on the political and the bureaucratic levels, were very unhappy at the prospect. Thatcher herself was known to be unhappy, believing that she had been sold a bill of goods by Trudeau back in June 1980; by not mentioning a charter or bill of rights, she seems to have thought, Trudeau had presumed on the British government's good faith.[78]

The British foreign-affairs committee, which was beyond Thatcher's ability or perhaps desire to manage ('the only effective element of Parliament,' according to a perceptive observer), reported unfavourably on Canada's new constitutional demands; it had listened attentively to a parade of witnesses and briefs, most of which were hostile to Trudeau's initiative. Some of the British experts heard by the committee were already in the service of the Quebec government; and some of those experts, familiar to external-affairs lawyers through international law conferences, provoked scorn and derision when their testimony was scanned in Ottawa. Unfortunately it was also without effective contradiction where the committee was concerned, since Ottawa took the position that as a sovereign government it would not appear as a witness before a foreign legislative tribunal; and it also took the position that it would not pay consultants to do its work for it. When the committee reported in January 1981, it concluded that the British ought not to proceed with the Canadian measure unless substantial prior agreement of the provinces was secured.[79]

The British government told Trudeau and his colleagues that the postponement would be welcome; according to Francis Pym, who visited Ottawa in December, it was reluctant to proceed without more show of provincial acquiescence. If it did, then defeat in the House of Commons or House of Lords was a real possibility. On the positive side, Pym was tipped to succeed Stevas as Thatcher's House leader; in the words of the Canadian high commission in London, Ottawa 'should welcome [his] removal. It does away with a House leader who was opposed certainly to the timing of the patriation proposals and probably also in part to its [sic] substance.'[80] Bad news from the government side was accompanied by bad news from the opposition; while the Labour leadership remained solid on the question of the constitutional amendments, opposition backbenchers were definitely getting out of hand.

If the Supreme Court ruled clearly in the government's favour, then Thatcher's justification for piloting the Canadian amendments through her own parliament would be unassailable. Though the various agents-general and other Canadian pressure groups (particularly native) remained active, their efforts were matched if not checked by the high commission's own work through the winter and spring of 1981. Most of them were kept within the bounds of politeness; the exceptions, an emotional speech by Richard Hatfield and a frantic denunciation of Trudeau by the publisher of the *Globe and Mail,* Roy Megarry, remained just that. Trudeau, Megarry argued, was not speaking for Canada: he was touting the ideas of 'the Ottawa-Toronto axis,' which was animated because it was 'afraid of losing its hegemony.'[81]

Mischief-making was not confined to the British side of the Atlantic or to Canadians. The British high commission, under its chief Sir John Ford, was conducting its own guerrilla campaign against Trudeau. Megarry, in his speech on 3 February 1981, told his audience that Trudeau did not have Thatcher's 'assurance that his unilateral constitutional proposals will receive her support, including a three line whip.' On the contrary, Megarry proclaimed, 'the *Globe and Mail* has access to high British government sources who deny that he has this assurance.'[82]

Ford was extremely active. He advised his government that Trudeau's proposals were wrong and dangerous. He let the Canadian government know that the British had serious misgivings about the constitutional schedule. He lobbied provinces and MPs likely to be favourable to Trudeau's propositions, and in one case hopped a plane for Toronto to tell an Ontario minister of London's disapproval, as expressed by Pym. Most of Ford's interlocutors took his involvement with the requisite grain of salt, even though as a diplomat he was skating very close to the line that divides proper advocacy from interference in another country's political affairs. Perhaps Ford's fervour detracted from the message he had to convey – that realistically the British parliament was a most uncertain instrument and that the Canadian government had misjudged Thatcher's ability to command it on this issue.[83]

Finally, one night in February 1981, Ford literally skated over the line, at the governor general's skating party. Seated by chance next to an NDP member of parliament (the NDP was supporting the Trudeau package), Ford took the opportunity to tell him that the new constitution had not the slightest chance of being passed by the British parliament. How did he know? Because, he told his astonished listener, 'I'm the British high commissioner.'[84]

The news reached Mark MacGuigan the next day, and then NDP leader Ed Broadbent. Broadbent called a press conference, so Ford riposted with his own interpretation of events. According to two generally perceptive observers, 'he succeeded in making the affair look as idiotic as it was'; they do not add that Ford was the chief contributor to what they correctly identify as its salient characteristic.[85]

The next day the undersecretary of state for external affairs, Allan Gotlieb, was on his way to London to chat with his British opposite number. In London Gotlieb was asked to grant a decent interval, after which Ford would be returning to London. Days later, Ford's retirement was announced; he would be succeeded by the British ambassador to Lisbon, Lord Moran, who was described in *The Times* as being of 'above average intelligence for a career foreign service officer.'[86]

Within the British diplomatic service Ford had not been regarded as a high flyer; his government was not willing to go to bat for him even when news of the imbroglio was leaked to the press, a sign that he had left himself dangerously overexposed. A crisis over the conduct of a British diplomat was not desired, perhaps in part because the service was in any case under fire for the quality of some of its appointments.[87]

Whatever the justification for Ford's removal, the gating of another country's envoy is seldom a sign of a healthy relationship. That this was the case is indicated by a paper prepared by Michael Kirby inside the Prime Minister's Office on 5 March. Kirby advised that the situation in London remained uncertain. Some observers, especially New Brunswick's premier, Richard Hatfield, thought the federal government was not doing enough in London. But Haggan, from London, argued that 'while many backbenchers are opposed in theory to being asked to amend the BNA Act before sending it back to Canada, they will nevertheless pass it when the vote is called because they realize both the enormous consequences in terms of damaging U.K.-Canadian relations if the measure is defeated and the virtual impossibility of amending the measure.'[88] That was, perhaps, excessively optimistic. There is evidence that some Canadian officials were considering ways and means of bringing pressure to bear on Thatcher should she seek to delay the constitutional package; the means ranged from soliciting support for the Canadian government among the Commonwealth and from friends like Helmut Schmidt to discretionary measures against British economic interests in Canada. It should be stressed that these measures were merely considered and not adopted: they were in their nature implausible and of very doubtful utility.[89] Fortunately they were overtaken by events.

As long as the federal government could hope for favourable decisions from the courts in Manitoba, Quebec, and Newfoundland, its persuasive powers might suffice in London; but if one or two ruled against, then something more would be required. Trudeau had already decided that even in case of one unfavourable decision he would have to refer the matter to the Supreme Court of Canada; and the unfavourable decision came at the end of March in Newfoundland. (Manitoba and Quebec courts were both favourable to the federal government.) Spurred on by the Newfoundland decision, and relying on a promise from the chief justice that the Supreme Court would get down to the business in April, Trudeau made the reference.[90]

The British government breathed a sigh of relief. Its officials had already been inclined to ask Trudeau to delay for a Supreme Court reference, and now he had to do it.[91] The House leader, Pym, had told Jean Chrétien only a few days before that he considered piloting the Canadian measure 'the most difficult thing I have ever done,' and described his mood as 'extremely apprehensive.' Pym promised speedy action, if the Canadians still desired it: the introduction of a bill before the end of April. But he would rather not have to do it, and, as it turned out, circumstances changed.[92]

The Trudeau government hoped that the Supreme Court would act quickly, and indeed it held its hearings as promised, in April. But then spring passed into summer, and summer into fall, before its decision was announced. It had at least the assurance that the Thatcher government would indeed do as it was asked, and there were signs that cooperation among officials and politicians from both sides was by September 1981 much improved over what it had been the previous winter. Lord Moran made a good impression on the prime minister at their first interview in June. Two weeks later, on 26 June, Trudeau followed up with Thatcher in person at a meeting at 10 Downing Street. Delays in Canada made it possible for Trudeau to be more relaxed and grateful than might otherwise have been the case; and Thatcher could be cautiously forthcoming about the timetabling when and if the Canadian matter arrived in England.[93]

The Supreme Court judgment was long delayed. When it came, on 28 September, it did practically what the Justice Department had predicted in the summer of 1980. A convention did exist that required substantial provincial consent to constitutional amendments that affected provincial rights and powers. Yet Trudeau's action was also justified in law. Regardless of the practices that had grown up since the 1930s, restated in a federal government white paper of 1965, the power to make representations to the British parliament had never formally been surrendered. What Trudeau proposed to do was within the plenitude of power of the federal parliament: a power does not disappear merely because it has not often been used.

The legal effect of the Supreme Court decision was that Trudeau could now proceed. Jean Chrétien immediately proclaimed victory. But in the public eye the victory was closer to a draw. Had the Supreme Court ruled in the federal government's favour both as to the conventionality and the legality of Trudeau's actions, then he would, indeed, have scored a famous triumph. Since it had not, the significance of the Supreme Court's ruling became once again a matter for debate.

In Canada and in London the provincial governments opposing Trudeau prepared for the final battle. When Trudeau and Thatcher met at the summit conference at Montebello, Quebec, in July, the British promised to make the constitution a first item of business at their next parliamentary session, starting on 4 November – always providing the Canadians were able to deliver the measure in time. Since the constitutional amendments had already passed the Canadian parliament and the Supreme Court had pronounced, there was only one stage left, at Westminister. The Gang of Eight ordered its letterhead, took out advertisements, and mobilized its supporters. The federal government followed their manoeuvres with some interest, for while the provinces and the press had their (frequent) sources of information inside the federal government, federal partisans were known to exist inside some provincial establishments.[94]

When the Supreme Court decision came down at the end of September, Trudeau and Thatcher were both heading towards Melbourne, Australia, for a Commonwealth conference. Time was by then pressing, since the British throne speech was in its final drafting stages. Before meeting Thatcher, Trudeau told reporters that when she got the Canadian proposal, 'I would simply expect her to pass it.'[95] Thatcher made clear, when the two met on 5 October, that passage was not what she could promise; she could and would bring the Canadian proposal forward. What her backbenchers would do with it was another matter entirely.[96]

Again, just as in the spring, what could have been an unpleasant outcome was overtaken by events. In mid-October Trudeau and the dissident premiers agreed that they would once again try to reach agreement, some kind of compromise, on the constitution. On 5 November they did, all but Lévesque. When the Canadian proposal, altered but still recognizable, reached Westminster, it would be with the support of nine provinces, not two; isolated, and lacking a strong mandate of its own, the Quebec government could only fulminate. It would not be able by itself to prevent passage in Britain.

Nor could the various native groups do much to hold back the constitution. Some legal manoeuvring in the winter of 1981–2 held up legislation, as did procedures in parliamentary debate. Trudeau pressed once again for action, but in the end the Canadians were assured that Pym knew best. The British House of Commons passed the Canada Bill on 8 March 1982, and the bill was given royal assent on 29 March. On 17 April the Queen signed the new constitution in a rainstorm on Parliament Hill, as Trudeau, his ministers, and officials proudly looked on.

The last of Canada's internal-external problems was over, and the British connection had survived, or so it must have seemed. Trudeau had succeeded in patriating the British North America Act: it became the Canada Bill and then the Constitution Act. In doing so he relied on the principle that a constitution must, finally, be workable; ironically, in seeking a Canadian solution – in affirming that Canada was a unified, workable, modern state – he was obliged to invoke a vestige of Canada's colonial past. The inducements for the British were that they would never have to do it again, and that they could count on Canada as an ally. And it must be admitted that had there been any chance of repetition, the British themselves might have been induced, unilaterally, to cut their ties with the only one of their former colonies that still had the power to rearrange the mother country's own political agenda.

14

The Last Hurrah

As Pierre Trudeau passed the fifteenth anniversary of his assumption of power in 1983, the war of words between East and West was fierce. The USSR had expanded its military power in the 1960s and 1970s. Now it was the Americans' turn. Under Ronald Reagan, a true believer in the evils of Soviet communism and expansionism, the United States was in the midst of a massive expansion of its military power. The Soviets, increasingly concerned about what they perceived as the increased American military threat to their country, took a variety of defensive precautions. The situation in no way eased when the USSR's geriatric leadership, stable for so long, at last began to pass from the scene. First Brezhnev died and was succeeded by the KGB chief, Yuri Andropov. Then Andropov too took sick and died. His successor, Konstantin Chernenko, was a feeble, wheezing stopgap. The rest of the Politburo became preoccupied with the wait for him to expire. Meanwhile, the Soviet war in Afghanistan continued to rage. The discussions between the two blocs at the Mutual and Balanced Force Reduction (MBFR) talks and at the START (Strategic Arms Reduction Talks) and INF (Intermediate Range Nuclear Forces) negotiations were going nowhere.[1] In Western Europe, as the time neared for the installation of the Pershing missiles agreed to under the two-track decision, peace groups stepped up their huge protests in the streets – financed by Soviet money, those on the right maintained. At home, the Canadian government had agreed after acrimonious debates in cabinet to allow the Americans to test cruise missiles over Canadian territory.[2] Against his every instinct, Trudeau had supported cruise testing, knowing that his willingness to do so might win him some credit with Ronald Reagan that could have its effect on other issues. At the very least, the anger at the decision in Canada would let him tell the American leader that he had done his bit for Western defence and had the scars to prove it.[3] It was not the best of times in the Cold War.

Soon the tense international situation worsened further and the possibility of a real war began to seem more threatening. On 30 August 1983 Soviet interceptors shot down an off-course Korean Airlines Boeing 747 airliner near Sakhalin Island with huge loss of life. Ten Canadians had been on the flight. In Ottawa, the government responded to the Soviet shoot-first-and-ask-questions-later policy by strongly condemning the attack ('nothing short of murder,' Gérard Pelletier, ambassador to the United Nations, called it on 2 September,[4] and by joining Washington on 5 September in sanctions against Aeroflot, the Russian airline, and other measures. The outrage in Canada and throughout the Western countries over this tragedy was pronounced, and the attack was everywhere painted as the deliberate response of a paranoid regime. The Russians compounded their difficulties by saying nothing and, when they did finally speak, by implying that the KAL aircraft was on a spying mission. So strong was the American response that Grigory Romanov, the party boss in Leningrad and soon a contender for the position of general secretary, told a meeting: 'Comrades, the international situation at present is white hot, thoroughly white hot.'[5]

Trudeau was aware of the increasing tension, of course, but though the shooting down of the aircraft appalled him, his own response was much calmer than that of the Americans. On 25 September and 1 October the prime minister told Liberal party audiences that the destruction of KAL 007 had been an 'accident,' a word that stirred some outrage of its own in parliament on 4 October. Trudeau countered by saying that 'I do not believe that the people in the Kremlin deliberately murdered or killed some 200 or 300 passengers ... I do not believe that. I believe it was a tragic accident, an accident of war.'[6] Some time later, Trudeau acknowledged to the American reporter Seymour Hersh, who was preparing a book on the KAL tragedy, that he had based his statements on secret communications intelligence that the U.S. National Security Agency had shared with Canada's Communications Security Establishment. 'It was obvious to me very early in the game,' Trudeau said, 'that the Reagan people were trying to create another bone of contention with the Soviets when they didn't have a leg to stand on.' He added that 'the Americans knew that it was an accident and the Soviets knew that the plane was not sent by the Americans. The two superpowers were talking past each other.'[7]

The superpowers *were* talking past each other and had been since

President Reagan came to office in January 1981. As much as anything else, that fact deeply troubled the prime minister. He had spoken out on the dangers of war in his address on nuclear 'suffocation' to the United Nations Special Session on Disarmament in June 1978 and again at UNSSOD II in 1982.[8] Trudeau had also caused a stir in the United States with his convocation address at Notre Dame University on 16 May 1982, where he had first raised the idea that the superpowers had a special responsibility for the prevention of war and insisted that arms control, however difficult, had to be seriously tackled.[9] That speech, his first to suggest that Canada was edging towards 'equidistance' between the superpowers, was a product of Trudeau's progressive disillusionment with NATO and the summit meetings, and his fears that the political leaders were losing control of the arms race and East-West relations generally. The Americans, said one senior official at the embassy in Washington, 'hated' Trudeau's rhetoric that Canada was good, a peace-maker, and morally equidistant from the 'naughty boys' with nuclear weapons.[10]

There was still more antagonism generated at the Williamsburg Summit at the end of May 1983. His 'heart on the side of the peaceniks,' Trudeau had deliberately pressed Reagan and Prime Minister Margaret Thatcher, so much so that Thatcher accused him of giving comfort to the Soviets. A Canadian effort to have the summit accept a statement on peace and security met a similarly hostile response, notably from the Americans (who found Trudeau's harping 'tiresome'), though the leaders did approve a mundane text.[11] Trudeau had also talked with Dr Helen Caldicott, the Australian crusader against nuclear weapons, and lunched with Robert McNamara, John F. Kennedy's and Lyndon Johnson's defense secretary and an advocate for change in nuclear policies. How much influence they had was uncertain. Most important, Trudeau realized that he had only a short time left in power and, as he recalled later, he did not intend to spend all his time on economics now that the constitution had been patriated. As he said to some of his officials, 'it is irresponsible for me to wait until I'm out of power to do something,' a comment provoked by watching leaders like former German Chancellor Willi Brandt and U.S. Secretary of Defense Robert McNamara speak out on the need for peace now that they were out of office. Even before the KAL disaster, Trudeau had begun convening meetings of officials and friends to discuss ways of easing the Cold War of words between Moscow and Washington. Now, after the disaster, it was suddenly urgent to act. The prime minister wanted 'to lower tensions, to civilize the dialogue, to get out of the Cold War era.'[12]

Trudeau took his first step towards his peace initiative on 21 September when he presided over a meeting of his external affairs and defence ministers along with some of the key officials from their departments and the Privy Council Office and Prime Minister's Office.[13] Trudeau had put his hands on his head, one official recalled, and rocked back and forth in his chair saying we had to do something. But what? There was no clear idea where the prime minister wanted to go, just the barebones of a general direction to be discussed at a meeting at Meech Lake in two weeks time.[14] Nor was there overwhelming enthusiasm for the idea of a Canadian peace initiative that the External Affairs officials present knew was doomed to fail. One senior official even had the temerity to argue that the public reaction was sure to see the effort as politically motivated, and so much so that bad press in Canada would imperil all efforts abroad. Exasperated, Trudeau snapped that the bureaucrat should leave political considerations to the politicians.[15]

Obviously, Trudeau 'couldn't be stopped despite the best efforts of External Affairs and others. [He] was going to do what he believed in.'[16] Later cabinet discussions were much the same. As John Roberts remembered, 'You can't say, "No, Prime Minister, you shouldn't undertake a mission to save the world!" '[17] The 21 September meeting set up a steering committee of nine officials and directed the creation of a working group. Only one official, Louis Delvoie, the director-general of the International Security and Arms Control Bureau in External Affairs, served on all three committees.[18]

The Working Group, headed by the very able Delvoie, was the critical body, the source of the ideas. Robert Fowler, Trudeau's PCO adviser on foreign and defence policy, was determined that the bureaucracy would not take over this prime-ministerial initiative and turn it into another bland exercise. Both he and Trudeau were insistent that ideas come forward in raw form, not blended out of existence by the bureaucracy. Fowler, in other words, was the man to whom the officials were responsible, not the Department of External Affairs, which was being bypassed yet again. The Working Group met for the first time on Friday, 23 September, at 10 AM, the beginning of an exhilarating but exhausting period of 'soggy pizza and warm coke,' as one participant remembered it.[19]

Delvoie told the group that the prime minister was concerned about the risks of war, and the Trudeau initiative was intended to cover the next three months. There would be consultation with Canada's allies, dialogue with the United States, and a public dimension to the effort as well. Why three months? one member asked. Because Trudeau did not want anyone to see his efforts as a pre-election gambit. Moreover, the group learned that Trudeau had made a major commitment of time to the preparation of the initiative – one hour a day. (In fact, the Working Group had even greater access than that to Trudeau.) The group also heard that the Steering Committee was to meet on 28 September, five days hence, and their ideas had to be ready for that gathering. The public announcement of the initiative was to come in the form of a speech at a conference on 'Strategies for Peace and Security in the Nuclear Age' at the University of Guelph on 27 October. That address, one official said, had to be 'more than just pretentious.' It had to 'set the universe of discourse for the next five months.'[20]

Before the 'universe of discourse' could be set, the peace initiative's proposals had to be put in place. They took shape in marathon Working Group sessions that did not conclude until the early morning hours of 28 September. Some ideas were spontaneously generated as the group brainstormed and argued. Others had been under consideration and were trotted out for the blue-covered book of proposals that the group prepared for the Steering Committee. Each of the twenty-six proposals followed a specific format – background, evaluation, 'upside' and 'down-side,' negotiability – and each covered four or five pages in the blue book. Among the proposals were a five-power conference on nuclear-arms control, a ban on the testing and deployment of high-altitude weapons, a comprehensive nuclear-test ban, a joint NATO-Warsaw Pact consultative process, and suggestions on ways to eliminate or ameliorate the presence of Cuban troops in Angola. The last three, thought contro-versial and likely to upset the great powers, were deemed non-starters. In the end, six proposals were recommended.[21]

The Steering Group looked at the proposals in the book, now labelled 'Proposals on East-West Relations and International Security' and dated 1 October, and, after revisions had been incorporated, passed them on to Trudeau and his ministerial-official group, including some of Canada's senior ambassadors abroad, for the meeting at Meech Lake on 7 October. With the blue book was a draft of the prime minister's Guelph speech. At Meech Lake, the participants, with Trudeau clearly making the final decisions, tried to decide which options they preferred, and they settled on five: a conference of the five nuclear powers; beefing up the non-proliferation treaty; turning the Stockholm Conference on Security and Cooperation in Europe into a foreign ministers' meeting; accelerating the pace of MBFR negotiations; and a ban on high-altitude anti-satellite weapons. Trudeau, who participated extensively and substantively, liked what he had been given, liked the way it had been done, and especially liked the way he was dealing with a small group and not the entire – and faceless – Department of External Affairs.

Moreover, Trudeau agreed that his initiative should initially be aimed at the leaders and only secondarily at the people.[22] That meant a substantial program of travel before the year end, first to Western Europe, then to Asia (where he had to attend the Commonwealth conference in New Delhi in any case), and then to Moscow and Washington. The prime minister examined his calendar to ensure that these travels could be fitted in, decided they could, and issued the order to 'go.' Trudeau also said that while an election was likely in the spring or fall of 1984, the government could go on another year if necessary. 'We have to act as if we are eternal,' he said, 'taking action now if we believe we are right.'[23]

Clearly Trudeau believed he was right. Perhaps that explained why there were no consultations with the United States or NATO, only letters to NATO leaders, before the initiative was launched on 27 October. No one doubted, after the response to Trudeau's Notre Dame speech and his performance at Williamsburg, that the Reagan administration (just then sending the army and the Marines into Grenada) and the NATO hawks in Brussels would be unhappy; at the same time, most of the officials involved in the initiative seemed to think that American approval was not a necessary condition. Some, in fact, believed that the initiative would have been doomed if Trudeau had been seen as a stalking horse for the United States, although others feared American wrath if Trudeau was seen to be playing intermediary. Moreover, it was a truism that Canadian-Soviet relations improved when U.S.-USSR relations were bad, and that might help get the Russians to listen to what Trudeau had to say. (Trudeau exchanged letters with General Secretary Andropov in early November.)[24] After all, he was a NATO head of government and the longest-serving Western leader; these qualifications, as well as his personal standing, gave him far more clout than a Canadian leader could usually muster. On balance, the initiative had only a slim chance of success – it seemed a bit much to try to do in two weeks, one official remembered, what Trudeau had failed to do in the previous fifteen years – but the world situation was such that the chance had to be seized.[25]

The Guelph speech, preceded by guidance telegrams sent to Canadian posts abroad, launched the peace initiative. Trudeau himself had spent time working over the drafts in a tough-minded way – he was preparing his legacy for history, one senior PCO officer believed.[26] Standing before a phalanx of Canadian flags, the prime minister sketched the 'intellectual climate of acrimony and uncertainty' that troubled East-West relations, and he referred to the 'ominous rhythm of crisis.' Then, pointing to the shared responsibility of Washington and Moscow and to their 'lack at the present time ... [of] a political vision of a world wherein their nations can live in peace,' he said it was essential 'to create a stable environment of increased security for both East and West ... essential to Western purposes ... to maintain in our policies elements of communication, negotiation, and transparency about our own intentions – plus a measure of incentive for the Soviet Union first to clarify, and then to modify, its own objectives toward the West.' Trudeau indicated his support for NATO's two-track strategy of deploying 275 medium-range Pershing missiles in Europe along with a simultaneous willingness to negotiate with the Soviets to reduce nuclear weapons. To those two tracks, however, he proposed to add a 'third rail' of 'high-level political energy to speed the course of agreement – a third rail through which might run the current of our broader political purposes, including our determination not to be intimidated.' The prime minister proposed a strategy of confidence-building that could re-establish high-level dialogue between the Soviets and the Americans, and he said that in his forthcoming consultations with foreign leaders he hoped to explore ways to stabilize East-West relations, to draw the superpowers away from their concentration on military strength, to persuade the five nuclear powers towards negotiations, to arrest nuclear proliferation, and to improve European security by raising the nuclear threshold.[27] It was an impressive statement, heartfelt, and certain, with its renewed theme of equidistance, to stir controversy, not least in the United States.

The Western Europeans were first on the travel agenda, however. Paris, The Hague, Brussels, Rome, the Vatican, Bonn, and London – the stays were short, the conversations slightly tepid, the press coverage in Europe insipid.[28] The French did not dismiss the idea of a five-power conference out of hand, and Chancellor Kohl in Bonn was said to be supportive, as was the opposition party, the SPD. Privately, however, senior officials of the Bonn government, themselves trying desperately to get the Reagan administration to be more reasonable, said Trudeau's activities 'were not seen as being particularly helpful.'[29] Perhaps that was because Trudeau, though fully committed to the idea of his initiative, had come very late to the arcane and changing subject matter of nuclear disarmament and was often uncomfortable with the all-important details.[30] Some of that must have showed in his discussions with leaders who were more conversant with the minutiae.

Though the auguries were not hopeful, Trudeau nonetheless claimed to be pleased. As he remembered later, he had not intended to visit

London on his trip because he had seen Thatcher, and clashed sharply with her, on a late September visit she had paid to Canada. But near the end of the European swing, an annoyed message reached Trudeau from Thatcher, asking why he did not intend to come to London. To Trudeau, that proved that his judgment on the worth of his initiative, even if the United States was cool, was correct: Thatcher wanted to see him because he was mobilizing support.[31]

After his return to Canada, Trudeau on 13 November delivered another address on the world situation in Montreal (unfortunately to a Liberal party gathering, a circumstance that inevitably cast a partisan pall over the peace initiative), wrote again to NATO heads of government, and then it was on to New Delhi's Commonwealth meetings. Commonwealth support was useful, but it was far more important to have the support of the People's Republic of China, one of the five nuclear powers, for the initiative.

Geoffrey Pearson and Gary Smith of External Affairs had preceded the prime minister's Asian trip with trips to Beijing and Moscow between 21 and 27 November to explain Trudeau's intentions. Gromyko had been interested in the Canadian ideas, but he was completely unwilling to guarantee that the prime minister would be able to see General Secretary Andropov. Only later did the world learn that Andropov was so near death that he could literally see no one. That hurt the initiative's progress as Trudeau's intent had been to visit Washington after Moscow, ideally so that he could tell Reagan that the Soviets were interested in his points. Now that was impossible. In Beijing, Pearson saw a senior political director of the Foreign Ministry and learned that it was highly possible a visit could be scheduled to take place at the time of the Commonwealth meetings.[32]

The Commonwealth conference endorsed Trudeau's 'efforts to restore active political contact among all the nuclear powers' but could not agree on the strengthening of the Non-Proliferation Treaty, a rather small return for years of Canadian foreign aid. But the highlight of the Asian trip occurred on 23 November when word came from Beijing: Trudeau could come. As Richard and Sandra Gwyn observed in a long and able *Saturday Night* article, 'In that instant Trudeau's peace initiative sprang to life. It ceased to be, at best, a noble but futile gesture ... and became substantive, an exercise worth taking seriously.'[33] Perhaps, but little that the Chinese leaders said lent much support to Trudeau's initiative. To Chairman Deng Xiaoping and Premier Zhao Ziyang, the Americans and the Soviets were the main dangers to world peace: they had the most nuclear weapons and only they could start war. The comparative weakness of the other nuclear powers, Britain, France, and China, was obvious, so much so that the Chinese leaders believed a conference of the five nuclear states unrealistic and liable to create confusion by diverting attention from the two superpowers. The Chinese position, presented by Deng in a non-stop oration that Trudeau was unable to interrupt and that continued for at least an hour, was that Trudeau's five-power conference could not work. Far better, Zhao added, to have more countries present.[34]

The prime minister returned to Ottawa on 5 December, and three days later the NATO Council agreed to send foreign ministers to the Stockholm meeting in mid-January. That was the first – the only – one of Trudeau's proposals to meet success. The initiative's original timetable soon suffered a derailment when Andropov's grave illness postponed a Moscow trip. Georgi Arbatov, the head of Moscow's Institute on the United States and Canada and a key adviser to the Politburo, said that he had spoken to Andropov about the Trudeau initiative (and Arbatov had seen Trudeau on the Tokyo stopover of his Asian trip), but nothing could be done because of 'the leadership situation.'[35] Thus it was Washington and Ronald Reagan on 15 December, a meeting without much in the way of Christmas cheer for Trudeau.

The American public and administration were in a particularly jingoistic mood in late 1983. The Grenada invasion, botched though it was in its military implementation, had been trumpeted as a sign of a new resurgence of pride in the military, patriotism, and the old American virtues. The propaganda tomtoms were beating furiously to hail the virtues of the Strategic Defense Initiative (popularly known as 'Star Wars'), announced by President Reagan (without consultation with his allies or even with the State Department) in a TV address in March 1983, as a way to protect America completely from nuclear attack. While few took SDI seriously in the West, the Soviets had been greatly alarmed.[36] In Washington, the president continued to ride high in the opinion polls, many of his advisers remained true believers in the necessity to grapple with the communists, and Trudeau, a proponent of Canadian equidistance, inevitably was seen as suspiciously soft on the Soviets. A Pentagon official recalled that when he heard of the initiative, his response was, 'Oh, God, Trudeau's at it again.' But why worry, he added, if Trudeau had no influence on other people? An officer of the National Security Council noted that 'there was no predilection here to alter [Trudeau's] lack of influence.'[37] And Lawrence Eagleburger, the third-ranking official of the Department of State, told a private dinner party a week before Trudeau arrived in Washington that the Canadian's peace efforts resembled nothing so much as those of a leftist high on pot.[38] Eagleburger was thought to be one of the more 'pro-Canadian' officials in the State Department, which made that slap all the more stinging – and outrageous.

In these unpropitious circumstances, how Trudeau presented his case to Reagan was obviously critical. Some of his advisers insisted that the prime minister say precisely the same things he had said to other leaders. But the ambassador to Washington, Allan Gotlieb, urged Trudeau to appeal directly and personally to Reagan on the high ground. The prime minister agreed and handled himself well. Realizing that he was approaching from the margin, he took the softest of soft lines. As the Gwyns reconstructed it, Trudeau had said: 'Mr. President, your intentions are good and I agree with them wholly. You are a man of peace. You want peace through strength. Because of your policies, the U.S. has regained its strength and self-confidence. But, Mr. President, your message is not getting through. The people think you want strength for its own sake, and that you are ready to accept the risks of war. That must change, Mr. President. You must communicate what you truly believe in.'[39] At least one American present felt offended by this approach, even if Reagan was not. Trudeau, he remembered, 'took a condescending view of the President as a simpleton in international affairs.' Instead, 'that hour was a tutorial for Trudeau on superpower politics. We never heard much more about the initiative.'[40]

Reagan emerged from the White House after the meeting to wish Trudeau 'Godspeed,' a phrase that struck many Canadians as dismissive and patronizing and as an indication of Canada's – and Trudeau's – influence. The Canadian was important enough to be treated politely, but his message was not. Still, for whatever reason, the president's militant rhetoric toned down slightly in the weeks that followed, and Trudeau and other Canadians clung to that as a positive result of the prime minister's visit. Even some Canadian officials in Washington who thought the initiative nothing other than 'a form of local madness to which Canadians are prone' believed that Trudeau had cooled the president's perfervid expressions of anti-communism.[41] To no one's surprise, however, very few American officials appeared to agree.[42]

The Trudeau initiative paused for a month over the Christmas holiday and into the new year. In the middle of January, the prime minister met UN Secretary-General Pérez de Cuellar to urge him to convene a meeting of the five nuclear powers, a request that met no action. Later in the month, with Andropov still ill and unable to receive visitors, Trudeau took his show on the road once more, this time to Eastern Europe.

Perhaps the satellites, known to be troubled by Soviet missile deployment on their territory and by the slow pace of negotiation between Moscow and Washington, might have more freedom to act if the Soviet leadership was incapacitated, or so Trudeau was said to feel. As one official working on the initiative put it, 'If there was no one home in the USSR, then you went to the satellites.'[43] That at least was the motivation behind the visits to Czechoslovakia, East Germany, and Romania, the first two of which were sites for Soviet SS-20 intermediate-range missiles. The Czechs called the initiative 'useful and correct,' but denounced the Americans for deploying cruise missiles in Europe. The East Germans, pleased that Trudeau was the first NATO leader to visit East Berlin, pledged their support. President Ceausescu of Romania, the most independent-minded of satellite leaders, hailed Trudeau's efforts for peace, even though the prime minister generally hewed close to the NATO line in his seven hours of conversations with the Bucharest leader.[44]

After his return to Ottawa, Trudeau wrapped up the peace initiative – and declared victory – in a speech in the House on 9 February. In this speech, the prime minister suggested 'ten principles of a common bond between East and West,' a new decalogue that had been put together by Ivan Head,[45] then the president of the International Development Research Centre:

1. Both sides agree that a nuclear war cannot be won.
2. Both sides agree that a nuclear war must never be fought.
3. Both sides wish to be free of the risk of accidental war or of surprise attack.
4. Both sides recognize the dangers inherent in destabilizing weapons.
5. Both sides understand the need for improved techniques of crisis management.
6. Both sides are conscious of the awesome consequences of being the first to use force against the other.
7. Both sides have an interest in increasing security while reducing the cost.
8. Both sides have an interest in avoiding the spread of nuclear weapons to other countries ...
9. Both sides have come to a guarded recognition of each other's legitimate security interests.
10. Both sides realize that their security strategies cannot be based on the assumed political or economic collapse of the other side.

To state that the superpowers accepted those principles stretched the truth. Many Americans close to Reagan, for example, thought of the

Strategic Defense Initiative as a policy that could force the Soviet Union to economic ruination as it sought to compete with the United States. And few could argue that SDI was not destabilizing.

The prime minister reiterated that his goal had remained the one he had announced in October at Guelph: to change the trend line of crisis. There had been, he believed, some small successes in Reagan's cooled rhetoric, in the Soviet return to the MBFR talks, in the meeting between Shultz and Gromyko at Stockholm. In any case, Trudeau concluded on the highest note possible by saying that 'Canada and Canadians ... saw the crisis; that we did act; that we took risks; that we were loyal to our friends and open with our adversaries; that we lived up to our ideals; and that we have done what we could to lift the shadow of war.'[46] The prime minister's initiative was endorsed by opposition leader Brian Mulroney and NDP leader Ed Broadbent, striking testimony to the popular support Trudeau's efforts had received in Canada.[47]

Though apparently concluded, the initiative had one last gasp remaining. Within days of Trudeau's address to parliament, Soviet leader Andropov finally expired and Trudeau jetted to Moscow for the funeral and, with luck, a meeting with Konstantin Chernenko, the new general secretary and a man whose health was little better than Andropov's had been. Trudeau got his thirty-five minutes, and used them to tell Chernenko that there was now a window of opportunity for accommodation between East and West. The dour Gromyko, present at the talks, responded bleakly that the West had to put something in the window if relations were to improve.[48] Although the prime minister emerged from the meeting to claim that the initiative had received another jolt of political energy, there was room for doubt. Chernenko, desperately ill, could take only the most cautious steps in the direction of détente. And Robert Ford, long-time ambassador in Moscow, delivered a damning assessment two years later. Trudeau's 'peace initiative was a total absurdity,' Ford told the Globe and Mail, 'and the Russians just laughed at it.' Trudeau had no leverage in Washington and 'no corresponding clout in Moscow ... he had no credit in the banks of either place.'[49]

The prime minister had one final crack at his allies when he attended the summit meeting in London in his last days in office and helped secure a communiqué that called for 'security and the lowest possible level of forces.' Trudeau had a shouting match with Reagan, telling the president 'you have to do more' to promote détente. That led the usually unflappable (or comatose) president to pound the table and shout, 'Damn it, Pierre, what the hell can I do to get those guys back to the table!' The source for that story, Patrick Gossage noted sourly, was 'a well-detailed U.S. briefing.'[50]

Perhaps Ford's was the proper assessment of the whole of Trudeau's failed crusade or 'world walkabout,' as some sneered at it.[51] Somehow, although he had been in power for sixteen years and a participant in NATO, Commonwealth, and summit meetings, Trudeau seemed not to understand how great power relations worked. Convinced of his intellectual powers and in no way immune from vanity, Trudeau naïvely continued to believe in the power of words and ideas, to believe that reason could dislodge the strenuous pursuit of self-interest by great powers, and to believe in his own star. He was and remained an adventurer in ideas, certain that he could persuade other leaders to join him in personal involvement in altering the nuclear threat. But for all his brilliance, he could not grasp why the Soviets and Americans were unwilling to take any risks for peace. Nor could he understand the American and Russian disinclination to allow smaller states to get in their way. In addition, as a believer in equidistance and a respecter of the superpowers' spheres of influence, Trudeau suffered from what his critics saw as an apparent unwillingness or inability to distinguish between the superpowers. Andropov's Russia was infinitely worse than the United States, even Reagan's United States, but Trudeau often seemed unable to make the distinction.

As important, Canada simply did not have the standing and power to make such an ambitious effort. Canada was a small country, despite its citizens' puffed-up view of its power and influence. If Canadian foreign policy had had influence in the past, and it had, that was because of the unusual global situation that had followed the Second World War, not because of any fundamental shift in power. In other words, once the ravages of war had been repaired, Canada sank back to its normal place in the centre of the third rank. Only a near-Great Power could have had a chance of success in a peace initiative in the 1980s – and only if the preparations and plans had been carefully prepared well in advance.

That was not true of the Trudeau initiative. Inevitably, given Trudeau's sporadic interest in foreign policy, his unilateral initiative had been hurriedly cobbled together. Some of its ideas, notably the five-power meeting, were non-starters – 'one of the worst ideas in arms control produced in modern times,' one senior Canadian ambassador called it. And no effort had been made to build support for the initiative through patient low-level diplomatic discussions. Without that, success was virtually impossible.[52] The result was that at times Trudeau seemed to be flying around the world, desperately trying to be received by national leaders. If he got in the door, he was listened to politely enough, but his message, satirized by one Canadian official as 'let's love one another,' left glazed eyes. On balance, this official concluded, the effect had been to diminish Trudeau – and his nation.[53]

Still, Trudeau had been right to try, and not only because the Canadian public overwhelmingly supported his efforts (and realistically expected little to come of them). The world was in crisis, and Soviet-American relations were so bad that war seemed to be a possibility. Someone had to speak out, and Trudeau took the risk. Whether or not the prime minister could claim the credit, the upward spiral of tension did ease. Leaders like Kohl in West Germany and Craxi in Italy began to press their allies towards accommodation, Thatcher in Britain eased off on her hard line, and Reagan became less interested in painting the Soviet Union as an 'evil empire' than in beginning to talk to it. Trudeau had taken the risks, and he deserved some of the credit.[54]

There was a definite irony here, however, most notably for those who seek consistency in their leaders' deeds and thinking. Trudeau at the end of his career had clearly resumed his assault on the entrenched positions of the Cold War, an effort he had earlier abandoned after his cuts in the Canadian NATO contingent in 1969. Moreover, he had turned himself into a helpful fixer. The prime minister who in 1968 had attacked Lester Pearson's style and role was, by 1983–4, trying to don the Pearsonian mantle – and probably with less success than the original. Pearson certainly would have realized that preparation and careful lower-level negotiation were essential first stages to any peace initiative. Mike Pearson had his vanity and his desire to shine on the world stage, to be sure, but he also knew the strengths, weaknesses, and potential of middle-power diplomacy. Despite sixteen years in office, Trudeau still did not recognize the limitations that living precariously in a superpowers' world placed on his country.

Conclusion

In an essay on Pierre Trudeau's impact on Canadian foreign policy written in 1978, Carleton University political scientist Harald von Riekhoff noted that there was no dramatic episode in Trudeau's career that linked his name with a specific doctrine or crisis. 'The terms isolationism, when referring to Mackenzie King's interwar foreign policy, or internationalism, when describing Pearson's approach to international relations during the postwar period, capture the essence of their respective foreign policy orientations. No single label,' he suggested, 'can encapsulate Trudeau's more amorphous foreign policy.'[1] Von Riekhoff is surely correct, even though Trudeau remained at the helm for another six years after the publication of his article and launched his peace initiative at the end of his final term.

How then can we characterize Trudeau's role in foreign policy? There can be no room for doubt that international questions took second place to domestic matters for Trudeau. The question of Quebec, the patriation of the constitution, and the entrenchment of the Charter of Rights were at the beginning and at the end of his long term in office far more important to him than relations with Canada's friends or foes abroad. As von Riekhoff noted, again correctly, foreign policy was 'a residual function of his over-all political activity and hardly the one which will determine his place in history.'[2]

Still, Trudeau was in power for sixteen years, and he outlasted almost every world leader who was in office when he became prime minister in 1968. Nixon, de Gaulle, Brezhnev – all had passed from the scene before Trudeau stepped down in 1984. His extraordinary name recognition around the world and his political longevity conveyed some clout, as did his capacity to learn and to apply his intelligence to the problems the world faced. Trudeau's role in the Commonwealth and in North-South negotiations, in both of which he had the high regard of the non-white world for his sincerity and activism, also gave him influence. Even the North Atlantic Treaty nations, initially so sceptical of Trudeau for his unilateral cuts in the Canadian forces at the beginning of his term, had by the end of his years in power come to appreciate the Canadian's support for NATO and his willingness to begin to bolster Canada's contributions to the alliance again. Nonetheless, there was widespread doubt, if not alarm, at his peace initiative of 1983–4.

And yet, when the whole Trudeau record in foreign policy is examined, the inescapable and overwhelming reaction is wonderment at the on-and-off nature of his interest, the lack of follow-through, the peripatetic nature of his concerns. If one word is required to characterize his interest in foreign affairs, in fact, *sporadic* is the one that leaps to mind. No one could use that word to describe his single-minded obsession with Quebec or the constitution or the Charter of Rights; but sporadic is the best word to characterize his foreign policy.

Trudeau began his time in power with a major review of foreign and defence policy. These reviews amounted to a frontal assault on the structures created by the Cold War; and they shook the Departments of National Defence and External Affairs to their core. He came to office mistrustful of NATO and not a little ignorant of the arguments for and against the alliance.[3] Then, with the tacit acquiescence of politicians from other parties and much of the Canadian political elite, he halved the Canadian contribution to NATO. The unhappy armed forces saw their priorities revised to give far greater stress to the defence of Canadian sovereignty. The Macdonald white paper enshrined the new defence orientation in seemingly immutable terms. Only a few years later, however, Canada purchased Leopard tanks for the NATO force, and Trudeau's government soon allocated substantial additional sums for the purchase of more capital equipment for the forces.

By the late 1970s, it seems clear, the prime minister had come to an appreciation of the value of the North Atlantic alliance to Canada and to the maintenance of peace. To his surprise, he learned that leaders such as Helmut Schmidt, good social democrat that he was, believed in the necessity for substantial military forces in Western Europe. That had its impact on Trudeau. When the Liberals left office in 1984, therefore, though the country's defence forces were not in good shape, the Mulroney government's efforts to improve matters clearly built on the work that had begun in the second half of the Trudeau government's life. Where else had the new frigates, the new fighter aircraft, and other modern equipment come from? In other words, in the area of defence, one in which Trudeau had no burning interest either when he took office or left it, his policy on balance tended, weakly to be sure, towards the reinforcement of the status quo. The prime minister's sporadic desire for change ran into reality – the pressures of the United States and Canada's alliance partners, as well as the Canadian people's desire for their country to be seen to be doing its part – and produced no ultimate result, though it did cause enormous upset in the Canadian forces.

The same story was evident in virtually every aspect of foreign policy. The prime minister arrived on the scene in 1968 insisting on a full-scale review of foreign policy. The net effect, beyond shattering morale in the Department of External Affairs and producing a six-pack of multi-coloured booklets, was minimal. China was recognized at last, there was an emphasis on Canada-first (that produced some useful advances in protecting Canadian sovereignty in Arctic waters and at the long Law of the Sea negotiations), and greater stress was put on trade. There was a direct link between that latter emphasis and the contractual links Trudeau's government negotiated with great skill with the European Community and Japan. But again, those links, once accomplished, were frittered away as Trudeau's interests waned or shifted. The contractual links were hamstrung by the bureaucracy in Finance and Trade and never pressed. It was as if the achievement of the links, not their fulfilment, was all that mattered.

Trudeau did press for greater emphasis on the development of the Third World. His government increased its contributions to foreign aid in dollar terms, though never to the promised level of 1 per cent of the Canadian gross national product. He played a useful role in chairing the mini-summit at Cancún, Mexico, in 1981, and Allan MacEachen was a powerful influence for change in the mid-1970s. Nonetheless, it was probably quixotic to expect the rich nations of the North to do much to help the starving countries of the South. Certainly nothing much resulted, and Trudeau seemed to acquiesce in the failure.

His successes in realizing nuclear disarmament were no more substantial. Trudeau had called for the 'suffocation' of the arms race in a major address at the United Nations in 1978, and he had repeated the call in New York in 1982. But until his peace initiative, launched in the last days of his administration, he had done little more. The initiative, naïvely heartfelt and gallant as it was, had almost no chance of success, so hasty was it in conception, so ill-prepared the ground, so opposed the Americans, British, and others. And even here, Trudeau's support for the testing of American cruise missiles over Canadian territory in the summer of 1983 removed in advance much of the lustre earned by the initiative. The prime minister had hoped to win some credit with his allies, but his decision served only to illuminate the sporadic nature of Trudeau's involvement with nuclear-disarmament questions.

Nor was Trudeau any more consistent in his dealings with the Soviet Union. His initial trip to the Soviet Union and his incautious speeches there clearly led the Soviets to think that they could begin to change the Canadian government's longstanding alliance policies, a position that might fairly be surmised from the alacrity with which Premier Kosygin returned Trudeau's visit. The Soviet assessment was almost certainly a misjudgment, though an understandable one. Some Canadians, and more than a few senior people in American administrations, came to believe then and later that the prime minister, if not a communist himself, had at least been motivated by anti-Americanism or gulled by Soviet propaganda. Trudeau did use the new closer relationship with Moscow to get a variety of agreements that had some utility. And then? Nothing. It was his turn to visit the Soviet Union after Kosygin's visit to Canada, and Trudeau failed to go. His government allowed the regular and crisis meetings called for under the Protocol on Consultations to become pro forma.

Trudeau's flirtation with the USSR produced virtually nothing for Canada, although it may have helped to moderate his government's reaction to a number of aggressive Soviet actions during his period in office. The invasion of Czechoslovakia in 1968, the Afghanistan invasion a decade later, the crushing of Solidarity in Poland, and the shooting down of the Korean airliner in 1983 drew from Trudeau only the mildest of public rebukes. Those actions took place in the Soviet sphere of influence (or, as Trudeau prefers to put it, 'the area of strategic importance to the USSR'),[4] and Trudeau was evidently willing to leave the Russians a free hand in the task of controlling their part of the globe. To the prime minister, the KAL disaster was obviously the product of an error of judgment, not of the innate malevolence of the Soviet state. The Russians, in other words, were a political problem to be dealt with, not a moral one.[5] Trudeau was likely as appalled by the Reagan administration's dangerous willingness to exploit the tragedy for the purposes of the new Cold War as he was by the KAL shooting itself. There was great good sense here, although Trudeau never managed to convey his view clearly to the Canadian people, let alone to the Americans and others. Trudeau was at least consistent in his position on spheres of influence. His reaction to American actions in their sphere was no less mild. His government was unforthcoming in its support for the Sandinista government in

Nicaragua, for example, and only moderately more so in its attitude to Castro's Cuba, however much fellow-feeling Trudeau may have had for the Cuban leader. Trudeau realized that Canada's geographic position gave the United States the right to be concerned about Canada, certainly an area of strategic importance to the Americans. But that was only the right to be concerned, not the right under international law to decide questions.[6]

Trudeau's overall attitude to the United States, however, can only be seen as inconsistent. His relations with Nixon and Reagan were cool, with Ford and Carter pleasant. But there was no consistent thread that ran through the 1968–84 years. Trudeau could express gratitude for President Nixon's recognition that Canada was different from the United States, or shock over the August 1971 measures. But his policy was almost always reactive. The contractual links with Europe and Japan took shape in response to the Nixon 'shokku' of 1971 and *might* have worked had they been pressed; as we have seen, they were not. The National Energy Policy in Trudeau's last term was forceful and direct – and a slap in Washington's face that, in retrospect, achieved little other than to anger the U.S administration. The Foreign Investment Review Agency had the same effect, as did the peace initiative. The aims were always worthy, but the execution was often half-hearted, the policies sometimes badly conceived.

What seems evident in retrospect is that Trudeau's foreign policy, unlike his policy on constitutional questions and to Quebec, was made up of a mishmash of ideas and attitudes.[7] There was idealism, so evident in the North-South area. There was goodwill, demonstrated in the peace initiative and in Trudeau's recognition of China and his feelers towards the USSR. There were also occasional traces of *realpolitik,* most notably in the hardheaded role Canada played in the Conference on Security and Cooperation in Europe. Indeed, the CSCE position emerged full-blown from within the Department of External Affairs and never was of direct interest to Trudeau. That may explain its nature. But consistency was never present in Canadian policy during the Trudeau era – except on national unity. How could it be when Trudeau came to power scorning the 'helpful-fixer' attitude that had characterized the golden age of Canadian diplomacy, and left office on the heels of a crusade for world peace that embodied the helpful-fixer concept writ large?

How much of this inconsistency was the prime minister's doing? We have to conclude that most of the blame lies at his door. Yes, the era of unusual postwar influence that Canada had enjoyed was over by 1968. Yes, the great men who had shaped Canadian policy in the golden age were dead or in retirement by the time Trudeau came on the scene. Yes, the constellation of powers after 1968 had little room for a well-meaning smaller state like Canada. Those things were true, and they undoubtedly constrained Canadian policy in Trudeau's time in office.

Still, Trudeau set out from his arrival in power to shake up the elitists in the East Block, a process that he continued in various ways throughout the whole of his term. The department was repeatedly reorganized, its policies subject to endless review, and an unhealthy inwardness replaced the old confidence. That was Trudeau's doing. So too was the use the prime minister made of Ivan Head, his extraordinarily able foreign-policy aide, and the Privy Council Office as new foci for the making of foreign policy. And so too was the inconsistency with which Trudeau dealt with the areas where he chose to take a personal interest: China, the USSR, the contractual links, North-South, and nuclear disarmament. There was nothing wrong in a prime minister having deep concerns, nothing at all. But although Trudeau's interest in North-South questions, for example, undoubtedly energized Canadian diplomacy for a time, the lack of consistent focus tended to leave ministers and diplomats frustrated and unhappy.

Perhaps it really was, as one very thoughtful senior official of the Department of External Affairs put it, that Trudeau was never a serious thinker, only an adventurer in ideas with great articulation and little commitment. He understood the world as few Canadians did, but he was vain, convinced that he knew more than the experts in the External Affairs bureaucracy. To this official, Trudeau had no commitments in the area of foreign policy other than his own amusement, whims that changed from year to year with little connection one to the next. Moreover, the prime minister recognized that much of his domestic political appeal lay in his staying relevant and trendy. That explained his sporadicity, his fear of becoming grey and dull like the other politicians.[8]

Certainly, there is substantial evidence for this interpretation in the on-and-off nature of Trudeau's interest in foreign policy. Certainly, everything in the man's career before and since 1968 suggests the adventurer seeking challenges to test himself. Certainly, 'Trendy Trudeau' was a political factor of much weight, and there can be no doubt of the man's overweening vanity and arrogance. But to charge lack of commitment may be unfair.

That, at least, is the view of another senior official who worked closely with Trudeau. To this bureaucrat, the prime minister both in his domestic and foreign policies was a man driven primarily by the desire to help individuals flourish in freedom. At home, this could be seen in such things as his wish to spread bilingualism across Canada and to entrench the Charter of Rights. Abroad, he and his country did not have the chips to play that Henry Kissinger did, for example. The prime minister, therefore, had to be 'a niche player,' one who would and could move only when he saw the opportunity to help people. That, in this observer's view, explained 'his bleeding-heart side,' his interest in the Commonwealth and the Third World. The disadvantaged nations looked admiringly to Trudeau for the right reasons: he really did care for and understand them. His desire to help individuals flourish was the driving force in Trudeau's foreign policy, and this policy, admittedly opportunistic but people-centred, simply could not be consistent. For the prime minister, a consistent Canadian policy was essentially unrealizable, and any attempt to create consistency for its own sake was bound to end up in posturing, certain to waste countless hours in sterile debate. Abstract debate without a practical result was, to Trudeau, always a waste of time. This explained the peace initiative as something Trudeau simply had to do, despite the best efforts of External Affairs to rein him in. As an individual, he could not give up power without trying to increase the safety of mankind. He acted for himself, to be sure, but for the best of reasons.[9] In other words, there was a coherence to it all, even if Trudeau was almost the only one who could see it.

The truth about Trudeau's foreign policy likely lies somewhere in between these two disparate views. Trudeau was an adventurer in foreign policy as in other areas, but he did have that one unshakeable belief that everyone in the Third World, just as much as in the First, had the right to develop in peace and freedom. That was no ignoble creed, and if his overall policy lacked consistency and sometimes commitment, his belief in this principle does much to redeem his failures elsewhere.

Whatever else he was, Trudeau never became grey and dull. At the outset of his long career, he attracted the world's notice because of his pirouettes, not his policies. But as he learned how to play the few chips he had with increasing confidence, Trudeau began to attract attention for his ideas. They were good ideas, too, the right ideas in a world menaced by nuclear war, the fossilized Cold War, and the increasing disparities between rich and poor.

Notes

ABBREVIATIONS

CAR   *Canadian Annual Review of Public Affairs*
CYB   *Canada Yearbook*
DEA   Department of External Affairs
DHist Directorate of History, Department of National Defence
DND   Department of National Defence
NA   National Archives of Canada
PCO   Privy Council Office
SCEAND House of Commons Standing Committee on External Affairs and
       National Defence
USNA   United States National Archives, Washington
USSEA Undersecretary of state for external affairs

CHAPTER 1: *Trudeau Takes Over*

1 Peter Newman, *The Distemper of Our Times: Canadian Politics in Transition,
  1963–68* (Toronto 1968), 207–8
2 Ibid., 199, and confidential interview. Newman places Cadieux with 'secondary
  ministers ... who become footnotes to history.'
3 Mitchell Sharp interview, 8 Dec. 1987; H.B. Robinson interviews, 5, 11 Aug.
  1987; J.F. Anderson interview, 7 Aug. 1987; NA, Peter Stursberg Papers, Léo
  Cadieux interview, 12 Sept. 1978; confidential interview
4 Published in translation as *Two Innocents in Red China* (Toronto 1968)
5 'Pearson où l'abdication de l'esprit,' *Cité Libre,* avril 1963, 7
6 Cited in Peter Dobell, *Canada's Search for New Roles* (Toronto 1972), 19
7 John Sawatsky, *The Insiders: Government, Business and the Lobbyists* (Toronto
  1987), 31
8 Bruce Thordarson, *Trudeau and Foreign Policy* (Toronto 1971), 71. See also
  Marilyn Eustace, *Canada's Commitment to Europe: The European Force
  1964–71* (Kingston 1979).

9 Confidential interview
10 Anderson interview
11 J.L. Granatstein, *Canada 1957–1967: The Years of Uncertainty and Innovation* (Toronto 1986), 218ff
12 Robinson interviews
13 Michael Howard, 'Peace: The Vital Factors,' *Encounter,* May 1984, 18
14 For example, see Stephen Clarkson, ed., *An Independent Foreign Policy for Canada?* (Toronto 1968). One of the authors was a participant in this volume and in the protest against the policies of the day.
15 Confidential interview. See Mitchell Sharp's comment, 'NATO: Reviewed, Revised and Renewed,' *Bout de Papier* 6 (1988):27.
16 Walter Gordon Papers, Toronto, NATO Meetings June 1967 file, Gordon to Cadieux, 30 June 1967
17 The Department of National Defence was contemplating reductions in the NATO contingent. See documents in DHist, Office of the Chief of the Defence Staff Records, Programmes General files, vol. 3.
18 The papers were 'Canada and NATO,' nd, and 'Canada and North American Air Defence,' 29 June 1967, both in Gordon Papers, NATO Meetings June 1967 file. Gordon's note is dated 27 June 1967.
19 Ibid., Agenda, Cabinet Committee on External Affairs and Defence, 11 Sept. 1967, and Gordon's pen notes; letter, H.B. Robinson to authors, 21 Aug. 1987
20 Robinson interview, 5 Aug. 1987; confidential interview
21 Arnold Heeney, *The Thing's That Are Caesar's: The Memoirs of a Canadian Public Servant* (Toronto 1972), 182ff
22 Confidential source
23 Geoffrey Murray interview, 15 May 1979; Geoffrey Pearson interview, 8 June 1979
24 Geoffrey Murray, 'In Search of Foreign Policy,' *Bout de Papier* 2 (Dec. 1984):1
25 Confidential source
26 Confidential interview
27 Ramsay Cook interview, 7 Aug. 1987
28 CBC TV interview, 1 Jan. 1969, quoted in Basil Robinson Papers, Ottawa, 'Prime Minister's Comments on Foreign Policy and Matters Related to It,' Oct. 1969
29 Confidential source. Trudeau was said to have been influenced in his views by a memo, received during the leadership campaign, by David Golden, a former deputy minister of defence production and the Department of Industry. Golden called for a phased withdrawal from NATO, maintenance of the status quo in North America, and reduced emphasis on peacekeeping. Ibid.
30 Paul Hellyer Papers, Toronto, Cabinet notes, 15 May 1968
31 Cited in Robinson Papers, Annex A to Agenda, Interdepartmental Meeting on Defence and Foreign Policy Review, 14 June 1968
32 Sharp interview, 8 Dec. 1987
33 Hellyer Papers, Cabinet notes, 15 May 1968
34 DEA Records, file 20-1-2-STAFEUR-8, Memo for prime minister, 27 May 1968

35 Murray, 'Search,' 1, alludes delicately to his authorship.
36 Office of the Prime Minister, Press release, 29 May 1968
37 Confidential interview
38 Robinson Papers, Annex A to Agenda, 14 June 1968
39 Office of Chief of the Defence Staff Records, Programmes General files, vol. 4, M. Cadieux to E.B. Armstrong, 30 May 1968, and reply, 3 June 1968
40 Confidential interview
41 Office of Chief of the Defence Staff Records, Programmes General files, vol. 4, 'Outline,' 30 May 1968
42 DEA Records, file 20-1-2-STAFEUR-8, Robinson to Collins, 17 June 1968. There had been two previous major studies of European relations: 'Eurocan: A Policy-Planning Paper on Relations Between Canada and Europe,' 10 Nov. 1965; and 'Canada's Stake in Europe,' 30 May 1967, by the Departmental Study Group on Europe.
43 Letter, H.B. Robinson to authors, 21 Aug. 1987. See on STAFEUR, Robert A.D. Ford, *Our Man in Moscow* (Toronto 1989), 115.
44 Robinson Papers, Annex A to Agenda
45 Donald Macdonald interview, 5 April 1968
46 Hellyer Papers, Diary, 12 July 1968; NA, Marcel Cadieux Papers, vol. 4, Diary memorandum, 11 juil. 1968
47 PCO, Cabinet minutes, 19 July 1968; Hellyer Papers, Cabinet notes, 19 July 1968
48 Cadieux Papers, vol. 4, Diary memorandum, 19 juil. 1968
49 Office of Chief of the Defence Staff Records, Programmes General files, vol. 4, Memo, VCDS to CDS, 1 Aug. 1968
50 Cadieux Papers, vol. 4, Diary memorandum, 13 août 1968; PCO, Cabinet minutes, 19 July 1968
51 Cadieux Papers, vol. 4, Diary memorandum, 29 oct. 1968
52 Marcel Cadieux, *The Canadian Diplomat* (Toronto 1963), 90
53 Confidential interview
54 Douglas Ross, *In the Interests of Peace: Canada and Vietnam, 1954–73* (Toronto 1984), 18, 204
55 Confidential interview
56 'Eulogy on Marcel Cadieux,' 24 March 1982, Canadian Institute of International Affairs obituary file
57 PCO, Cabinet minutes, 30 Aug. 1968; Cadieux Papers, vol. 4, 'Compte-rendu d'un entretien ... 30 septembre 1968'
58 Robinson Papers, Memorandum for the minister, 9 Nov. 1968. Trudeau had said similar things to a Queen's University, Kingston, Ont., audience the day before. Cited in Robinson Papers, 'Prime Minister's Comments on Foreign Policy and on Matters Related to It'
59 Cadieux Papers, vol. 4, Diary memorandum, 10 déc. 1968
60 DHist, file 112.11.003(D3), 'The Prime Minister's Remarks at the December 9th Meeting'

61 Cadieux Papers, vol. 4, Diary memorandum, 10 déc. 1968
62 Robinson Papers, F.R. Sharp to minister, 20 Dec. 1968
63 Cadieux Papers, Diary memorandum, 10 déc. 1968
64 Copy in ibid.
65 David Stewart-Patterson, *Post Mortem* (Toronto 1987), 144, assesses Kierans's attitudes at this period.
66 Richard Gwyn interview, 12 March 1989; Jamie Swift, *Odd Man Out: The Life and Times of Eric Kierans* (Vancouver 1988), 207. Defence minister Cadieux felt obliged to respond on 27 January 1969 in an address to the Ottawa Rotary Club. See *CAR 1969,* 227.
67 Robinson Papers, Memorandum, Sharp to prime minister, 13 Feb. 1969
68 DEA Records, file 20-1-2-STAFEUR-8, Sharp memo to cabinet, 28 Feb. 1969
69 Robinson Papers, Memorandum, Sharp to prime minister, 25 March 1969. The House Committee's recommendations, released on 26 March 1969, called for the maintenance of the status quo – at least until the NATO force's equipment had to be replaced. *CAR 1969,* 231–2. Sharp felt that academics had not made a great contribution to the process. 'When asked to accept a retainer to contribute,' he told cabinet on 29 March 1969, 'academics were opposed; when it was suggested that academics be given access to secret documents they were opposed; then when officials prepared short position papers they were very critical saying the government had made up its mind without academic contributions.' PCO, Cabinet minutes
70 One of the authors attended a meeting at the Park Plaza Hotel, Toronto, on Sunday, 16 March 1969. See also *CAR 1969, 231.*
71 Robert A.D. Ford interview, 15–16 Oct. 1987
72 Anderson interview
73 Ford interview
74 One part of the STAFEUR process was a country-by-country study. That on West Germany noted that the NATO troops were seen as 'valuable both in military and political terms. Indeed, were it not for the presence of these forces ... Canada would have far less importance in German eyes and their interest in our views and proposals would be correspondingly less.' Bank of Canada Archives, Bank of Canada Records, file 4E-270, Nov. 1968
75 DEA Records, file 20-1-2-STAFEUR-8, 'Canadian Policy Review on Europe,' 14 March 1969
76 Hellyer Papers, Diary, 7 March 1969
77 Confidential interview
78 Ford interview
79 The term 'Non-Group' may have originated in Washington where a group of Vietnam doves from the State and Defense departments held frequent 'non-meetings.' See Walter Isaacson and Evan Thomas, *The Wise Men* (New York 1986), 684.
80 Based on interviews with Ford, Anderson, and a confidential interview; and on

Robinson Papers, M. Cadieux to minister, 20 April 1969. See also Thordarson, *Trudeau,* 158.

81 Head's views were also strikingly similar to those advanced in a spring 1968 study by Lt.-Col. Leonard Johnson of the Directorate of Strategic and Force Planning at National Defence Headquarters. See his *A General for Peace* (Toronto 1987), 73ff. Trudeau told cabinet on 29 March 1969 that the Head paper 'should not be regarded as a reflection of his own views.' This was apparently a result of the angry telephone conversation with Sharp and Cadieux the day before. PCO, Cabinet minutes

82 Stursberg Papers, Sharp interview, 31 Aug. 1978. Sharp said the same thing publicly in an interview in *Bout de Papier* 3 (fall 1985):22.

83 Based on Albert Legault, 'La nouvelle politique de défense du Canada,' *Le Devoir,* 25 nov. 1969; Swift, *Odd Man,* 207–8; on interviews with participants and officials as cited above; and on PCO, Cabinet minutes, 29–30 March 1969

84 Hellyer Papers, Diary, 29–30 March 1969

85 Based on PCO, Cabinet minutes, 29–30 March 1969; Paul Martin interview, 10–11 Feb. 1987, Gérard Pelletier interview, 14 Aug. 1987, Paul Hellyer interview, 6 Nov. 1987, and Hellyer Papers, Diary, 29 March 1969. Cadieux, in the Stursberg Paper interviews, counted Trudeau among those favouring withdrawal. Sharp, in ibid., was uncertain where Trudeau stood. See also Sharp, 'NATO,' 28.

86 Hellyer Papers, Diary, 30 March 1969; Robinson interview; Stursberg Papers, Sharp interview, 31 Aug. 1978, and Léo Cadieux interview, 12 September 1978

87 Confidential interview

88 PCO, Cabinet minutes, 1 April 1969; Hellyer Papers, Diary, 1 April 1969

89 Robinson interview, 11 Aug. 1987

90 Léo Cadieux interview, 9 Dec. 1987

91 PCO, Cabinet minutes, 3 April 1969; confidential interview

92 Ibid.

93 Toronto *Globe and Mail,* 4 April 1969

94 Pierre Siraud interview, 12 Oct. 1987

95 Robinson Papers, telegram, E. Ritchie, Washington, to Ottawa, 3 April 1969; ibid., telegram, Washington to Ottawa, 5 April 1969; Ambassador W. Behrends interview, 7 Dec. 1987; Sharp interview, 8 Dec. 1987. We are indebted to Professor Wilhelm Bleek for drawing the Brandt visit to our attention.

96 As this was a period in which Britain was substantially reducing its military commitments around the globe, there was a certain Canadian resentment at Healey's carping. See on UK policy, John Baylis, *Anglo-American Defence Relations, 1939–84* (London 1984), 164ff.

97 Sharp, 'NATO,' 29. Cf PCO, Cabinet minutes, 17 April 1969.

98 DEA, Statements and Speeches, No. 69/8
99 Confidential interview
100 Anderson interview
101 Robinson Papers, Memorandum, Cadieux to minister, 20 April 1969
102 Hellyer Papers, Diary, 23 April 1969
103 Confidential interview; Robertson interview
104 Confidential source
105 DHist, General Jean Allard Papers, 84/126, dossier 105, Gen. M. Dare to CDS, 7 Aug. 1969
106 Stursberg Papers, Cadieux interview
107 Cited in Thordarson, *Trudeau*, 141
108 Confidential interview
109 *CAR 1969*, 239
110 Hellyer interview, 6 Nov. 1987
111 Allard Papers, 84/126, dossier 105, Preliminary report, Project 'Bronze Nimbus,' 31 July 1969
112 Ibid., dossier 105, Dare to CDS, 7 Aug. 1969
113 Ibid., dossier 45, Ross Campbell to Allard, 23 Sept. 1969
114 Gerald Porter, *In Retreat: The Armed Forces in the Trudeau Years* (Ottawa, nd), 157
115 Gen. W.C. Leonard interview, 15 June 1989
116 *Globe and Mail,* 20 Sept. 1969. See also Alex Nickerson, 'Canada in the NATO Framework,' Halifax *Chronicle-Herald,* 1 May 1971.
117 Trinity College Archives, George Ignatieff Papers, MSS 144, box 2, Head to Ignatieff, 12 Sept. 1969
118 DEA press release, 24 Jan. 1969; Cadieux Papers, Diary memoranda, 17 nov. and 5 déc. 1968
119 Documents on DEA Records, file 20-1-2-1970
120 Although Ignatieff produced his report, one that circulated publicly, he was clearly unimpressed with the process. In his memoirs he complained about 'mind-numbing futility ... Interminable hours ... the lowest common denominator among divergent points of view.' *The Making of a Peacemonger* (Toronto 1985), 245
121 Robinson Papers, Memorandum, 25 March 1969
122 DEA Records, file 20-1-2-1970, nd
123 Ignatieff Papers, MSS 144, box 6, W.H. Barton to Ignatieff, 9 Sept. 1969; Robinson Papers, M. Crowe to Robinson, 10 June 1969
124 Ibid., Cadieux note on Robinson memo, 27 June 1969
125 DEA Records, file 20-1-2-1970, Murray to Langley, 11 Sept. 1969
126 Robinson Papers, Memorandum for minister, 6 Oct. 1969
127 Office of Chief of the Defence Staff Records, Foreign Policy in the 70s file, 'Consolidation of Operations Abroad,' 29 Dec. 1969
128 Mitchell Sharp before SCEAND, 24 March 1970, 10ff

129 Ibid.; DEA Records, file 20-1-2-1970, Halstead to Brown and Mathieu, 18 Nov. 1969, and enclosures

130 Confidential interview

131 DEA Records, file 20-1-2-1970, Memo, K.J. Burbridge to Murray, 5 Jan. 1970

132 Office of Chief of the Defence Staff Records, Foreign Policy in the 70s file, Gen. F.R. Sharp to Cadieux, Jan. 1970

133 Robinson interview, 5 Aug. 1987; confidential interview

134 DEA Records, file 20-1-2-1970, M.N. Bow to USSEA, 4 March 1970

135 Ibid., Murray to USSEA, 12 March 1970

136 Confidential interview

137 DEA Records, file 20-1-2-1970, Murray to Cadieux, 28 May 1970

138 Ibid., Halstead to PDM, 26 March 1970

139 Ibid., Murray to Cadieux, 28 May 1970

140 *Foreign Policy for Canadians* (Ottawa 1970), 'Foreign Policy for Canadians' pamphlet, 8–9, 32

141 Ignatieff Papers, MSS 144, box 2, Ignatieff to J.W. Holmes, 10 Feb. 1970

142 *Pravda* attacked Canada's 'military, imperialistic' policy, and a protest was made to the Soviet ambassador in Ottawa on 10 July 1970. DEA Records, file 20-1-2-1970, Head to Trudeau, 9 July 1970

143 *Foreign Policy for Canadians*, 'Pacific' pamphlet, 24

144 DEA Records, file 20-1-2-1970, 'Report of the Latin American Task Force,' Nov. 1969; ibid., Bridle to Murray, 30 Oct. 1969

145 On response to *Foreign Policy for Canadians* see *inter alia*, Murray, 'Search'; 'Comments on the White Paper,' *Behind the Headlines* 29 (Aug. 1970); *CAR 1970*, 313ff.

146 Marked copy of the report in NA, Lester Pearson Papers, N 5, vol. 13, Canadian Foreign Policy file; typed comments are in ibid., vol. 31.

147 'Report on Foreign Policy for Canadians,' nd. We are indebted to Geoffrey Pearson for allowing us to see this paper.

148 Related to the authors by Geoffrey Pearson, 6 Aug. 1987

CHAPTER 2: *A Curious Absence*

1 Robert Endicott Osgood testifying before SCEAND, 24 Feb. 1971, 14:8. We are grateful to Robert Prince, a graduate student at the University of Toronto, for drawing the reference to our attention.

2 One fascinating study of political media at the time was called *The Shouting Signpainters*. The title is extraordinarily appropriate for the many proponents of open-mouth diplomacy.

3 See Robert Bothwell, Ian Drummond, and John English, *Canada since 1945: Power, Politics and Provincialism*, 2nd ed. (Toronto 1989), 312.

4 See Ronald Manzer, *Canada: A Socio-Political Report* (Toronto 1975), 172-5.

5 Canadian Institute of Public Opinion, *The Gallup Report*, 18 May, 12 Oct. 1968

6 Consider the extraordinary play by Michel Tremblay, *St Carmen of the Main,*
   in which a Quebec cowgirl singer travels to the American south to improve
   her technique.
7 See *CYB 1976–7,* 217; *Historical Statistics of Canada* 2nd ed. (Ottawa 1983),
   A 411.
8 Larry Martin, Vancouver, BC, quoted in Kim Willenson et al., *The Bad War: An
   Oral History of the Vietnam War* (New York 1987), 259
9 See Roger N. Williams, *The New Exiles: American War Resisters in Canada* (New
   York 1971).
10 Gallup Poll, *Toronto Star,* 7 Aug. 1989, A9
11 Canadians can find some amusement, and some comfort, from the recent American bestseller, Martin and Susan Tolchin, *Buying into America: How Foreign
   Money Is Changing the Face of Our Nation* (New York 1989). The alarmist tone,
   breathless prose, and the consequent horror stories described therein would
   have been music to Walter Gordon's ears.
12 One useful book on the subject is Michel Crozier, *The Trouble with America:
   Why the System Is Breaking Down* (Berkeley, CA 1984), in which the author
   compares his experience in postwar, prosperous, and untroubled America with
   what he found thirty years later.
13 The Gallup Poll during 1968 showed a steady decline in Canadian approval of
   the U.S. government and its principal personality, Lyndon Johnson – until
   Johnson chose not to seek another term.
14 Poll results quoted in Martin Goldfarb and Thomas Axworthy, *Marching to a
   Different Drummer: An Essay on the Liberals and Conservatives in Convention*
   (Toronto 1988), 84–5. More Liberals than Conservatives tended to believe that
   Soviet communism was no longer a threat, but not many more. The pattern is
   constant for each of the questions cited.
15 Very few embodied all three tendencies!
16 Ian Lumsden, ed., *Close the 49th Parallel: The Americanization of Canada*
   (Toronto 1970). Other titles of the period include *The New Romans,* featuring
   a bespectacled, pot-bellied American in centurion's costume on the cover; *Gordon to Watkins to You,* denoting the eternal quality of the nationalist ideas of
   Walter Gordon, as interpreted by Mel Watkins; or *Silent Surrender,* a book on
   the handing over of the Canadian economy to all-powerful American multinational companies.
17 Ian Lumsden, 'American Imperialism and Canadian Intellectuals,' in Lumsden,
   ed., *Close,* 322
18 See on this point Myrna Kostash, *Long Way from Home: The Story of the Sixties
   Generation in Canada* (Toronto 1980), chap. 3. One ironic consequence of the
   inflow of American radical ideas (and sometimes American radicals) was the
   supersession of Canadian radical issues by American ones. Ibid., 67–8
19 House of Commons, *Debates,* 1 May 1970, 6496. We are indebted to Robert
   Prince for this reference.

20 See Bothwell, Drummond, and English, *Canada since 1945*, chap. 27.

21 See Charles Ritchie, *Storm Signals: More Undiplomatic Diaries, 1962–1971* (Toronto 1983), 77–84.

22 Annette Baker Fox, *The Politics of Attraction: Four Middle Powers and the United States* (New York 1977), 209

23 Per capita income for Americans in 1968 was U.S. $3421; for Canadians, Cdn $2675.

24 See above, note 19.

25 These were of course few. There were some in the State Department and the Treasury, a small number of economists scattered in universities from Massa-chusetts to Michigan, and the odd political scientist. In the age of globalism, American scholars preferred to study something else. As Samuel Huntington of Harvard is said to have observed, Canada was on a par with South Dakota as a field of interest.

26 See Stanley Tupper and Douglas L. Bailey, *One Continent: Two Voices* (Toronto 1967), 17: 'The truth of truisms should not be dismissed. No two neighbors ever shared a more compatible cultural heritage; no two neighbors ever shared a longer unfortified boundary; no two neighbors ever shared so many years of relative peace and harmony. All this we have heard endlessly before.'

27 The Maine congressman Stanley Tupper may have had a special interest, since he was related to a Canadian prime minister of the 1890s.

28 SCEAND, 24 Feb. 1971, 14:6. We are once again indebted to Robert Prince's excellent research.

29 This point is discussed in Robert W. Tucker, 'The American Outlook: Change and Continuity,' in Robert E. Osgood, ed., *Retreat from Empire? The First Nixon Administration* (Baltimore 1973).

30 Robert E. Osgood, 'The Nixon Doctrine and Strategy,' in ibid., 9

31 Quoted in Lawrence Martin, *The Presidents and the Prime Ministers: Washington and Ottawa Face to Face: The Myth of Bilateral Bliss 1867–1982* (Toronto 1982), 238

32 USNA, Richard Nixon Papers, WHCF, EX CO28/1/CO-14, Kissinger to Butterfield, 20 March 1969

33 Ibid., WHCF CO28 2, box CO-14, Kissinger to Nixon, 24 March 1968 [sic]. The professor in question, W.Y. Elliott, was described as 'an active Republican.'

34 Confidential source

35 NA, Don Jamieson Papers, vol. 329, file H1-2, briefing note, 'The President and the USA Political Scene,' 7 April 1972; Trudeau quoted in B.W. Powe, *The Solitary Outlaw: Trudeau, Lewis, Gould, Canetti, McLuhan* (Toronto 1987), 128

36 Martin, *Presidents and Prime Ministers*, 239

37 Confidential source

38 Quoted in Martin, *Presidents and Prime Ministers*, 253

39 Emerson Brown interview, Washington, 11 Jan. 1988

40 Confidential interview
41 NA, Jules Léger Papers, vol. 29, 'Notes personnelles – rencontre avec le Premier Ministre (17 oct/75)'
42 Daniel Patrick Moynihan with Suzanne Weaver, *A Dangerous Place* (Boston 1978), 51
43 Martin, *Presidents and Prime Ministers,* 239
44 Léger Papers, vol. 29, 'Notes personnelles – rencontre avec le Premier Ministre (17 oct/75)'
45 *Historical Statistics of Canada,* G 216
46 See the revealing discussion in Michael Bliss, *Northern Enterprise: Five Centuries of Canadian Business* (Toronto 1987), 566–8.
47 The 'nationalist' position was closely associated with the Gordon wing of the Liberal party, and, in a socialist variant, with the Waffle movement in the New Democratic Party. Mitchell Sharp represented those who did not see the immediate necessity for Gordon and his economic remedies, but Sharp would not have rejected the term 'nationalist' as describing his position.
48 Confidential source. Auto trade data from I. Gonnidis, 'The Canadian Motor Vehicle Assembly Industry' (PHD thesis, Queen's University, 1978), 124
49 Robert Duemling interview, Washington, DC, Jan. 1988
50 Quoted in Martin, *Presidents and Prime Ministers,* 241
51 Ivan Head interview, Ottawa, 6 Aug. 1987
52 Ibid., Toronto, 31 Aug. 1987
53 USNA, White House Tapes, US vs Mitchell et al., exhibit 16, 22 March 1973
54 Henry Kissinger, *The White House Years* (New York 1979), 383
55 PCO, Cabinet minutes, 30 March 1969; Bruce Hutchison, *The Unfinished Country: To Canada with Love and Some Misgivings* (Toronto 1985), 90
56 The text of Trudeau's remarks is in Roger Frank Swanson, ed., *Canadian-American Summit Diplomacy, 1923–1973* (Toronto 1975), 274–85.
57 See Martin, *Presidents and Prime Ministers,* 241; Solange Chaput-Rolland, in 'Canada–U.S. Relations: Options for the Future: 2, Canadian Reaction,' *Behind the Headlines* 32(2) (April 1973): 1–2, recalled Trudeau's 'whimsical remark,' delivered 'smilingly.'
58 McGeorge Bundy, *Danger and Survival: Choices about the Bomb in the First Fifty Years* (New York 1988), 149
59 On force levels and the bombing see Guenter Lewy, *America in Vietnam* (New York 1978), 147, 410–1.
60 The year started with a poll in which U.S. entrance into Vietnam was declared a mistake by a majority of Canadians (5 Feb.), and ended with a survey in which 'most question[ed] US ability to handle world problems.' Canadian Institute of Public Opinion, Gallup Surveys
61 Kissinger, *White House Years,* 1446–7
62 Lewy, *America in Vietnam,* 414–17; we are inclined to agree with Douglas Ross, *In the Interests of Peace: Canada and Vietnam 1954–73* (Toronto 1984), when he concludes that the American air raids were not 'terror bombing.'
63 The usual clerical opposition to the war made itself known, from the heads of

both the Anglican and United churches. See *CAR 1972* (Toronto 1974), 319–20. One Canadian diplomat quipped, just before Christmas, that peace was 'at arm's length' rather than 'at hand.' Confidential source

64 Confidential interview
65 Willis Armstrong interview, Washington, 13 Nov. 1988
66 Kissinger, *White House Years*, 1442
67 On this point see Ross, *In the Interests of Peace*, 329–30.
68 Confidential source
69 Ross, *In the Interests of Peace*, 330–1
70 On Canada and the ICC see Paul Bridle, 'Canada and the International Control Commissions in Indochina, 1954–1972,' *Behind the Headlines* 32(4) (Oct. 1973).
71 Confidential source; Ross, *In the Interests of Peace*, 335–6
72 Confidential source
73 Ibid.
74 Ross, *In the Interests of Peace*, 337
75 The Canadians presented the U.S. government with six conditions by the end of November. They were (1) that all belligerents be bound by the agreement establishing the ICCS, and that all of them formally invite Canada to join; (2) that there be a continuing political authority to which the ICCS should report; (3) failing (1) and (2), Canada's participation would lapse; (4) that the ICCS be enabled to move freely throughout South Vietnam; (5) that Canada not sign the protocol, which it had not helped to negotiate, but merely signify acceptance of its obligations; and (6) that arrangements for the ICCS be workable.
76 Confidential source
77 Ibid.
78 Ross, *In the Interests of Peace*, 346–7
79 Ibid., 348
80 Confidential interview
81 Confidential source
82 Ibid.
83 Quoted in Ross, *In the Interests of Peace*, 357
84 See the summary of testimony in ibid., 358–9
85 This bizarre offer was made to Marcel Cadieux at a Washington reception on 15 March. Confidential source.
86 Confidential source
87 Ross, *In the Interests of Peace*, 362
88 Ibid., 365
89 Ibid., 366–7
90 Confidential source. The reference to the happy state of Canadian-American relations was made by the late Bill Casey, then assistant secretary of state for economic affairs.
91 Quoted in Ross, *In the Interests of Peace*, 366. Kissinger did not think the event worth mentioning in his memoirs, *Years of Upheaval* (New York 1982).
92 Ibid., 366–7

93 The charge was first made in Frank Snepp, *Decent Interval* (New York 1978); it is analysed in Victor Levant, *Quiet Complicity* (Toronto 1986), 252.

CHAPTER 3: *The Amiable Beast*

1 Richard Nixon, 'The Challenge of Peace,' USIS press release
2 USNA, Richard Nixon Papers, WHSF, Staff member files, H.R. Haldeman chronological files, box 197, Memo from Haldeman to Ray Price and Bill Safire, 30 Aug. 1971
3 Ibid., Action Paper: Heads of Government to be Briefed, 15 Aug. 1971
4 Douglas Fisher column, *Toronto Telegram,* 17 Aug. 1971
5 *Financial Times* [of Canada], 2 Aug. 1971
6 According to Emerson Brown, then economic counsellor at the American embassy, the last meeting was a fiasco. 'Almost the whole damned [Canadian] cabinet was there; our side included two lame ducks and not one of our people had looked at his briefing book before he got on the plane.' Brown concluded, 'We realized that this was a losing game.' The next meeting was for the Americans to host; it mysteriously failed to happen. Brown interview, Washington, Jan. 1988
7 Canadian Institute of Public Opinion, *The Gallup Report,* 28 March 1970: 'Public Feels US Domination Is Increasing.' The public in this case represented 50 per cent of Canadians, 54 per cent of westerners, and 57 per cent of Ontarians.
8 Gary Hufbauer and Andrew Samet, 'Investment Relations between Canada and the United States,' in Willis C. Armstrong, Louise Armstrong, and Francis O. Wilcox, *Canada and the United States: Dependence and Divergence* (Cambridge, Mass. 1982), 114
9 *The Gallup Report,* 28 Nov. 1970: 'Enough US capital here, claim 6 in 10 Canadians.'
10 Ibid., 14 Oct. 1970: ' "Buy Back Canada" say most – despite lower standards of life.' The point is important to bear in mind, because opinion in the 1980s held that Ontario and western Canada were at odds, and had always been so, on issues of trade and investment. The polls indicate that this was not the case.
11 The contradictions in government attitudes were not apparent to all. See Jim Laxer, 'Canadian Manufacturing and US Trade Policy,' in Robert Laxer, ed., *(Canada) Ltd., The Political Economy of Dependency* (Toronto 1973), 140, in which the author refers to 'the continentalist Liberal government.'
12 *The Gallup Report,* 23 Jan. 1971: 'Canadian Development Corporation to be very important say 8-in-10.'
13 Edward F. Wonder, 'US-Canada Energy Relations,' in Armstrong et al., *Canada and the United States,* 88
14 See *Canadian Forum* 51 (Dec. 1971): in bright red letters on a glossy black cover the magazine proclaimed: 'A Citizen's Guide to the Herb Gray Report: Domestic Control of the National Economic Environment.'

15 Confidential source
16 Ibid.
17 Henry Kissinger, *The White House Years* (New York 1979), 957
18 Julius Katz interview, White Plains, New York, 23 Feb. 1983
19 Ibid. Figures are derived from the *Bank of Canada Review,* and are cited in Sperry Lea, 'A Historical Perspective,' in Robert M. Stern, Philip H. Tresize, and John Whalley, eds., *Perspectives on a U.S.–Canadian Free Trade Agreement* (Ottawa and Washington 1987), 25.
20 Katz interview
21 A.E. Ritchie interview, Ottawa, 15 March 1988; confidential interview. Our source continued: 'Here I told him [a Canadian official] and he didn't believe me.'
22 Quoted in Peter C. Dobell, *Canada in World Affairs, 1971–1973* (Toronto 1985), 15
23 Reeves Haggan interview, Ottawa, 4 Feb. 1988
24 Maurice Western, 'Divergent Approaches in Ottawa,' *Winnipeg Free Press,* 17 Aug. 1971; David Crane, 'Ottawa to Ask for Exemption from New US Tax,' *Toronto Daily Star,* 17 Aug. 1971
25 A.F. Gill interview, Toronto, 12 Feb. 1989
26 W.A. Wilson, 'Canada Pins Hope on Logic,' *Montreal Star,* 17 Aug. 1971
27 Confidential interview
28 Confidential source. Immediate press accounts were superficial.
29 Text of Trudeau's televised statement in *Ottawa Citizen,* 21 Aug. 1971
30 *Globe and Mail,* 3 Sept. 1971
31 NA, Don Jamieson Papers, vol. 328, Sitrep file, J.M. Davey, program secretary, PMO, to ministers, 10 Sept. 1971 (Sitrep 2)
32 *Ottawa Citizen,* 17 Sept. 1971
33 Jamieson Papers, vol. 328, Sitrep 1, 'Employment Support Bill and U.S. Countervail,' nd, but early September 1971; confidential source; Dobell, *World Affairs,* 19–20
34 Clair Balfour, 'US Doesn't Care about Canada: PM,' *Globe and Mail,* 24 Sept. 1971
35 Dobell, *World Affairs,* 21
36 Walter Gordon, while deploring the American actions, suggested that protectionism was not the proper response. *Toronto Daily Star,* 21 Aug. 1971
37 See Ian Lumsden, ed., *Close the 49th Parallel: The Americanization of Canada* (Toronto 1970), for the nationalism of the period; on the other side see Robert Fulford, *Crisis at the Victory Burlesk* (Toronto 1968). Daniel Boorstin is said to have told Trudeau, on the occasion of a visit to Washington, that when a country did something one did not like, its actions were often pejoratively described as nationalistic. The embassy official was Peter Towe, talking to Peter Flanigan. USNA, Nixon Papers, WHCF, CO28, EX, Flanigan to Alexander Haig, 3 Dec. 1971

38 Trudeau's remark to this effect first appeared in an interview with Barbara Frum, quoted in the *Globe and Mail* on 24 September. Quoted in Dobell, *World Affairs*, 22

39 Ibid., 26

40 Ibid., 25; Ivan confidential interview

41 John Kirton and Robert Bothwell, 'A Proud and Powerful Country: American Attitudes towards Canada,' *Queen's Quarterly* 92 (Spring 1985): 119

42 Nixon Papers, WHSF, SMOF; USNA, H.R. Haldeman Papers, box 44: Haldeman yellow notepad, 6 Dec. 1971

43 Ibid.

44 See Laxer, 'Manufacturing and US Trade Policy,' 144, for an expression of this attitude.

45 See Stephen Ambrose, *Nixon: The Education of a President* (New York 1987), 111–14, on Nixon's sense of tactics and strategy.

46 Head interview, 31 Aug. 1987

47 Transcript of press conference, Washington, 7 Dec. 1971, in Roger F. Swanson, *Canadian-American Summit Diplomacy 1923–1973: Selected Speeches and Documents* (Toronto 1975), 285–93

48 See Kirton and Bothwell, 'Proud and Powerful Country,' 119

49 Dobell, *World Affairs*, 27–9; Head interview, 31 Aug. 1987

50 Nixon Papers, WHCF, CO 28, 11 July, 7 Jan. 1970

51 One of the authors enjoyed a conversation at the time with an American staffer – a Republican – who complained bitterly of the sceptical attitude of other embassy employees towards their president.

52 Jamieson Papers, vol. 329, file H1-2, 'Visit to Canada of President Nixon: Canadian Identity and Independence, and Foreign Policy Reviews by Canada and the United States,' 5 April 1972

53 See the description of the arrival in Lawrence Martin, *The Presidents and the Prime Ministers: Washington and Ottawa Face to Face* (Toronto 1982), 249; John Holmes, *Life with Uncle: the Canadian-American Relationship* (Toronto 1981), 4, called it 'one of the best speeches an American political leader has ever made about Canada.'

54 Text of the speech is in Swanson, *Canadian-American Summit Diplomacy*, 298–302; see also Martin, *Presidents and Prime Ministers*, 250–2. The preparation of the speech is in Nixon Papers, WHSF, SMOF, Haldeman chronological files, April 1972, Haldeman to Ray Price and Henry Kissinger, 4 April 1972, 'Some additional guidance for the speech to the Canadian Parliament.'

55 Some of the presidential staff tried to get out of going to Ottawa at all, and had to be ordered north by Haldeman. Nixon Papers, WHCF, TR, EXTR 31, Dwight Chapin to Haldeman, 10 April 1972, with note by Haldeman: 'You are in charge of the trip[s] and you damn well better be on them.'

56 Head interview, 31 Aug. 1987

57 *The Gallup Report*, 11 June, 19 July 1975

58 This provision entered into force on 22 September 1976. See Hyman Solomon, 'Border-TV Issue Surfaces Again,' *Financial Post*, 16 May 1981.

59 Holmes, *Life with Uncle*, 66

60 Lyon testimony quoted in Standing Senate Committee on Foreign Affairs, *Canada–United States Relations*, vol. 1 (Ottawa 1975), 9

61 Confidential source

62 On this point see William Hyland, *Mortal Rivals: Superpower Relations from Nixon to Reagan* (New York 1987), especially chap. 10.

63 See Seyom Brown's perceptive critique of Kissinger's statesmanship: *The Crises of Power: An Interpretation of United States Foreign Policy during the Kissinger Years* (New York 1979), especially 111–29.

64 Confidential interview

65 Confidential source

66 Confidential interview

CHAPTER 4: *Freezing in the Dark*

1 The senior men in the government showed a high propensity to depart: first the minister of finance, John Turner, then Bud Drury and Mitchell Sharp, and later Pépin and Marchand.

2 See Christina McCall-Newman, *Grits: An Intimate Portrait of the Liberal Party* (Toronto 1982), 214, 217.

3 Gen. Brent Scowcroft interview, 11 Jan. 1988

4 Leonard Waverman, 'The Reluctant Bride: Canadian and American Energy Relations,' in Edward Erickson and Leonard Waverman, eds., *The Energy Question: An International Failure of Policy*, vol. 2: *North America* (Toronto 1974), 222

5 See J.G. Debanne, 'Oil and Canadian Policy,' in ibid., 130.

6 Julius Katz interview, White Plains, NY, 23 Feb. 1983

7 See the excellent study by Richard Vietor, *Energy Policy in America since 1945: A Study of Business-Government Relations* (New York 1984), chap. 6.

8 Confidential source

9 On this general subject see Robert Sherrill, *The Oil Follies of 1970–1980: How the Petroleum Industry Stole the Show (and much more besides)* (New York 1983).

10 See *Historical Statistics of Canada*, 2nd ed. (Ottawa 1983), series Q59-63. The same derivation of statistics obtained in the United States: Sherrill, *Oil Follies*, 126. Proven reserves equalled 8168.9 million barrels in 1967, 8381.6 million in 1968, and 8619.8 in 1969. The reserves had risen every single year since 1947.

11 See John N. McDougall, 'The National Energy Board and Multinational Corporations: The Politics of Pipe Lines and Natural Gas Exports, 1960–1971' (PHD thesis, University of Alberta, 1975), 201–4.

12 NA, Donald Jamieson Papers, Jamieson diary, 21 Sept. 1970

13 Ibid.

14 Ibid.; James F. Keeley, 'Constraints on Canadian International Economic Policy' (PHD thesis, Stanford University, 1980), 443

15 Vietor, *Energy Policy,* 195–9

16 See Don Munton and John Kirton, 'The *Manhattan* Voyages and Their Aftermath,' in Franklyn Griffiths, ed., *Politics of the Northwest Passage* (Kingston and Montreal 1987), 67–97.

17 *CAR 1970,* 184–5

18 See Donald J. Slimman, 'The Parting of the Waves: Canada-United States Differences on the Law of the Sea,' *Behind the Headlines* 33(6) (April 1975).

19 Ibid., 185–6

20 The analogy to 'precious bodily fluids' in *Dr Strangelove* is irresistible.

21 Slimman, 'The Parting of the Waves,' 12

22 These divergences are examined in Ann L. Holick, 'Canadian-American Relations: Law of the Sea,' in A.B. Fox, A.O. Hero, and J.S. Nye, eds., *Canada and the United States: Transnational and Transgovernmental Relations* (New York 1976), 169–72.

23 Confidential interview

24 *Globe and Mail,* 25 Aug. 1973

25 Munton and Kirton, 'The *Manhattan* Voyages,' 93–6

26 *CAR 1970,* 353

27 François Bregha, *Bob Blair's Pipeline: The Business and Politics of Northern Energy Development Projects* (Toronto 1979), 18, points out that circumstances dictated that oil be pumped first from the Alaska Prudhoe Bay field; only later would natural gas be pumped.

28 Keeley, 'Constraints,' 445

29 Bregha, *Bob Blair's Pipeline,* 22, argues that the United States was trying to pressure Canada into a continental energy agreement. If so, they were under some illusion as to the time available.

30 Sherrill, *Oil Follies,* 73–4

31 Jamieson Papers, Jamieson diary, 21 Sept. 1970

32 But see, for example, the comment by a Toronto Liberal MP, Barney Danson, that Greene's discounting of Canadian nationalist opposition 'shook me and it shook a lot of people.' *Maclean's,* Feb. 1970, 1–2

33 Quoted in Keeley, 'Constraints,' 449

34 The NEB report is summarized in *CAR 1969* (Toronto 1970), 348.

35 Bregha, *Bob Blair's Pipeline,* 24

36 Keeley, 'Constraints,' 449, 451

37 See David DeWitt and John Kirton, *Canada as a Principal Power* (Toronto 1983), 299.

38 USNA, Nixon Papers, WHCF, CO28-EX, fg6-11-1, Whitaker, John, Peter Flanigan, Memorandum for the files, 24 Feb. 1971

39 The American proposals, and the Canadian response, are summarized in two documents: Nixon Papers, WHCF, CO28-EX, memorandum of a telephone conversation between Peter Flanigan, Jules Katz, and Jim Loken on the American

side, and Ed Ritchie, Jack Austin, and Robert Howland on the Canadian, 3 Dec. 1971; and Flanigan to Haig, 7 Dec. 1971.

40 Ibid., CO28-EX, Flanigan memorandum to the files, 3 March 1971, reflecting a discussion with Peter Towe of the embassy and Jack Austin, deputy minister of energy, mines and resources

41 Vietor, *Energy Policy,* 200–1; Pierre Terzian, OPEC: *The Inside Story* (London 1985), chap. six

42 Vietor, *Energy Policy,* 205–6, notes that in 1973 most Americans attributed the energy shortage to a conspiracy among the multinationals.

43 Confidential source

44 Bregha, *Bob Blair's Pipeline,* 28–9

45 As Bregha observes, ibid., 29, U.S. officials were genuinely doubtful of Canada's ability to deliver on its pipeline promises. See also Sherrill, *Oil Follies,* 154–8.

46 Confidential source

47 Sherrill, *Oil Follies,* 158–60

48 Keeley, 'Constraints,' 459

49 Ibid., 458–61

50 Ibid., 462–3

51 See, for example, James Laxer, *The Energy Poker Game: The Politics of the Continental Resources Deal* (Toronto 1970).

52 Annemarie Jacomy-Millette, 'David et Goliath: l'équilibre fragile des relations énergétiques canado-américaines à l'aube de la création de Petro-Canada,' *Revue des Etudes internationales* 13(4) (déc. 1982):644, citing Larry Pratt

53 *CAR 1973,* 322

54 Confidential source

55 Terzian, OPEC, omits Canada from his lists of unfriendly and friendly states; perhaps no one noticed.

56 See McCall-Newman, *Grits,* 217.

57 *CAR 1973,* 255–6

58 Peter C. Dobell, *Canada in World Affairs, 1971–1973* (Toronto 1985), 205

59 Keeley, 'Constraints,' 468

60 DeWitt and Kirton, *Canada as a Principal Power,* 303–4

61 Ibid., 305–6: Quebec was negotiating with Iran for a deep-water oil terminal on the St Lawrence, the Maritime premiers were concerting policy with the New England governors, and British Columbia was consulting its own interests.

62 G. Bruce Doern and Glen Toner, *The Politics of Energy: The Development and Implementation of the* NEP (Toronto 1985), 138–9

63 Ibid., 483. We should observe that the chairman of the commission was one of those principally responsible for the 'superb' expedient. The figures on the oil export tax are from Waverman, 'Reluctant Bride,' 221.

64 *CAR 1973,* 321: the United States was taking 1.2 million barrels a day in 1973, 60 per cent of Canadian production.

65 Ibid., 483

66 The argument was proposed by H.S. Houthakker; Waverman termed it 'non-

sense,' pointing out that the Americans were paying no more for Canadian oil than they would be paying for petroleum procured elsewhere and suggesting that the Canadian policy might actually have slowed the rate of price increases below what private firms would have charged.

67 Julius Katz, whom readers will remember as one of the saviours of the Autopact in 1971, was one of this group.

68 Donald Macdonald interview, Toronto, 2 Nov. 1979

69 See Stephen Clarkson's analysis in his *Canada and the Reagan Challenge: Crisis and Adjustment, 1981–1985*, 2nd ed. (Toronto 1985), 296–7.

70 Bregha, *Bob Blair's Pipeline*, 26

71 Ibid., 36, 39

72 We apologize for the term, but it was the cliché of the day. There were also representatives from the State and Interior departments present on the American side; Simon's principal backer at this point was George Shultz, by then secretary of the treasury.

73 Macdonald interview, 2 Nov. 1979

74 Keeley, 'Constraints,' 476–8

75 *CAR 1974*, 300

76 Macdonald interview, 2 Nov. 1979: Henry Jackson, John Stennis, and Warren Magnuson were examples; *CAR 1974*, 300

77 *CAR 1974*, 300–1

78 *CAR 1974*, 286; Steven A. Schneider, *The Oil Price Revolution* (Baltimore 1983), 336–9, reviews the IEA's modest record.

79 On Lougheed's background and connections see John Richards and Larry Pratt, *Prairie Capitalism: Power and Influence in the New West* (Toronto 1979), 153–5, 162–70.

80 Canada's status received some apparent recognition when the State Department raised the head of its Canadian desk, Rufus Smith, to the rank of deputy assistant undersecretary. Smith was a Canadian specialist and he had fought hard for the post; but when he left the department he was not replaced by another Canadianist. The job's responsibilities were expanded to other countries and the new DAS, Richard Vine, was expected to be both realistic and tough. But realism could, and did, often mean that Canadian and American interests could be made to coincide.

81 *CAR 1974*, 298–9

82 For the termination of this interminable issue see *CAR 1975* (Toronto 1976), 19–22.

83 This had been a suggestion of the U.S. ambassador William Porter in a speech. On the new 'continentalism' see John Kirton and Robert Bothwell, 'Proud and Powerful Country,' *Queen's Quarterly* 92(1) (spring 1985).

84 Paul Daniel and Richard Shaffner, 'Lessons from Bilateral Trade in Energy Resources,' in Carl Beigie and Alfred Hero, eds., *Natural Resources in US-Canadian Relations*, vol. I (Boulder, Colorado 1980), 310–1

85 Gerald Ford Library, WHCF, TN3, box 3, Congressman Les Aspin (D-Wis.) to Ford, 29 July 1975

86 *CAR 1974*, 401–2. Berger was an unusual choice in one sense: he had been a federal NDP MP as well as leader of the NDP in British Columbia. His appointment was popular with the NDP, however, at a time when the Liberals depended on NDP votes to stay in power in a minority parliament.

87 The information on Trudeau's preparation for his meeting with Ford is derived from a confidential source close to the discussions.

88 There is a shrewd sketch of MacEachen in Richard Gwyn, *The Northern Magus: Pierre Trudeau and Canadians* (Toronto 1980), 146–8.

89 Confidential source

90 Ford Library, WHCF, subject files, FG 31, 2, 3, Dec. 1974

91 Confidential source

92 Ibid.

93 See Roger Frank Swanson, 'The Ford Interlude and the U.S.–Canadian relationship.' *American Review of Canadian Studies* 8 (spring 1978): 3–17.

94 Allan MacEachen interview, Ottawa, 14 March 1988

95 Jamieson Papers, vol. 354, Gerry Stoner, deputy minister of IT&C, to Jamieson, 3 Oct. 1975, commenting on a draft report to cabinet

96 It was believed that the Garrison project would contaminate the Red River basin with organisms from the Mississippi-Missouri system. *CAR 1976*, 308–9

97 Jamieson Papers, vol. 354, Stoner to Jamieson, 3 Oct. 1975, commenting on a draft report to cabinet

98 Ibid., vol. 351, Stoner to Jamieson, 17 Nov. 1975

99 Ibid.

100 See Kirton and Bothwell, 'Proud and Powerful Country,' 123

101 Ford Library, Ron Nessen Papers, 1974–7, box 122, file Canada, 'Canadian Participation in the Summit,' 4 Nov. 1975

102 Quoted in Lawrence Martin, *The Presidents and the Prime Ministers: Washington and Ottawa Face to Face* (Toronto 1982), 259

103 Robert Bothwell, Ian Drummond and John English, *Canada since 1945*, 424–5; *Canada Year Book, 1976–77* (Ottawa 1977), 414–15, 1023. It is true that Canada's rise in the consumer price index of 10.8 per cent lagged behind the United Kingdom's 24.3 per cent.

104 Canadian-American Committee, *A Time of Difficult Transitions: Canada-US Relations in 1976* (Montreal 1976), 44

105 Statistics Canada, *Perspectives III* (Ottawa 1980), 299

106 T.A. Keenleyside, L. LeDuc, and J.A. Murray, 'Public Opinion and Canada-United States Economic Relations,' *Behind the Headlines* 35 (4)(1976): 17

107 Scowcroft interview

108 Martin, *Presidents and Prime Ministers*, 258–9

109 On Kissinger in 1975–6 see Seyom Brown, *Crises of Power*, 144–6.

110 Scowcroft interview; Ford Library, Council of Economic Advisers Records, Alan Greenspan files, box 39, Greenspan and Scowcroft to Ford, 25 June 1976;

Allan Gotlieb, 'Canada and the Economic Summits: Power and Responsibility,' Bissell Paper Number One, University of Toronto Centre for International Studies, Dec. 1987, 4

111 Bregha, *Bob Blair's Pipeline*, 101–2, citing the work of John Helliwell, an economist at University of British Columbia. Helliwell's view was, according to a contemporary economic summary, 'not widely shared by others' who submitted briefs along with Helliwell's to the NEB: *Time of Difficult Transitions*, 43n.

112 *CAR 1975*, 248–9

113 Judy Steed, 'A Not-So-Diplomatic Ambassador,' *Globe and Mail*, 21 May 1982

114 Ibid.; quoted in Martin, *Presidents and Prime Ministers*, 260

115 Moynihan, *A Dangerous Place*, 121, quoted in William Shawcross, *Sideshow: Kissinger, Nixon and the Destruction of Cambodia* (New York 1979), 268

116 Ibid., 322; Barry Rubin, *Secrets of State: The State Department & the Struggle over US Foreign Policy* (New York 1985), 207

117 Confidential interview; Scowcroft described Enders as 'strong aggressive, exuded confidence.' Shawcross, *Sideshow*, 269

118 *CAR 1976*, 302–3

119 The Canadian minister had served as chairman of the CIEC, the Conference on International Economic Co-operation.

120 Jamieson Papers, vol. 325, 'Summary of Discussion: SSEA's Visit to Washington, August 17–18, 1976'

121 This information is derived from an MA paper by Jim Davidson at the University of Toronto, spring 1989. A similar view was expressed by Patrick Gossage.

122 Davidson paper. The correspondent was Andrew Malcolm.

123 Davey's view, in ibid.

124 On Carter's attitudes see Robert C. Gray, 'The United States and the Soviet Union,' in R.C. Gray and Stanley J. Michalak, eds., *American Foreign Policy since Détente* (New York 1984), 5–6, and Michael Charlton, *From Deterrence to Defense: The Inside Story of Strategic Policy* (Cambridge, Mass. 1987), 70–2; confidential interview.

125 Zbigniew Brzezinski, *Power and Principle: Memoirs of the National Security Advisor 1977–1981* (New York 1983), 5

126 There is a useful summary of Carter's attitudes in Lawrence S. Kaplan, *NATO and the United States: The Enduring Alliance* (Boston 1988), 146–7.

127 NA, E. Goldenberg Papers, vol. 7, file Minister's Visit, briefing notes, nd but probably 1977–8

128 Ibid.

129 Ibid.

130 William R. Young, ed., *Paul Martin: The London Diaries, 1975–1979* (Ottawa 1988), 217–18

131 We are again indebted to Jim Davidson's study of American press coverage of Canada. As he notes, the *Wall Street Journal*, the *New York Times*, and the *Washington Post* gave the 'Canadian' side of the separation debate generally favourable coverage.

132 Young, ed., *Paul Martin*, 221–2, entry for 22 Feb. 1977
133 Trudeau in fact followed the president of Mexico in Washington; Lopez Portillo on this and subsequent occasions failed to make a good impression: Brzezinski, *Power and Principle*, 26–7.
134 Confidential interview
135 Robert Hunter interview, Washington, 15 Nov. 1988
136 Ibid.
137 Confidential interview
138 Thomas Enders interview, New York, 13 May 1988
139 Ibid.
140 Confidential interview
141 McCall-Newman, *Grits*, 355, 358. On Jamieson's political record see Keith Davey, *The Rainmaker: A Passion for Politics* (Toronto 1986), 32, 218.
142 Confidential interview
143 Gwyn, *Northern Magus*, 304
144 Steven A. Schneider, *The Oil Price Revolution* (Baltimore 1983), 329–30
145 Canadian-American Committee, *Bilateral Relations in an Uncertain World Context: Canada-US Relations in 1978* (Montreal 1978), 72
146 Such a study was in fact underway: Schneider, *Oil Price Revolution*, 342–3; Bregha, *Bob Blair's Pipeline*, 122–3.
147 *CAR 1977*, 341–2
148 Bregha, *Bob Blair's Pipeline*, 142–3
149 Quoted in ibid., 129
150 Ibid., 146–7
151 Ibid., 147–8, is highly critical of the government's negotiating stance.
152 Ibid., 153–6, gives a chronology of the negotiations. American negotiators were reported 'angered' by Carter's 'interference.'
153 Canadian-American Committee, *Bilateral Relations*, 72–3
154 The results of the negotiation are covered in detail in Bregha, *Bob Blair's Pipeline*, 156–62.
155 It is, of course, possible that other students have simply accepted Bregha's conclusions: Doern and Toner, *Politics of Energy*, accept his conclusions while citing him as principal source.
156 Daniel and Shaffner, 'Lessons from Bilateral Trade,' 323
157 *CAR 1979*, 149–50
158 *CYB 1988*, 11–16
159 Bregha, *Bob Blair's Pipeline*, 150–1
160 *CYB 1988*, tables 11.5 and 11.7; *CYB 1976–77*, 687
161 Clyde Sanger, *Ordering the Oceans: The Making of the Law of the Sea* (Toronto 1987), 62–7
162 Laurent Legault, 'A Line for All Uses: The Gulf of Maine Boundary Revisited,' *International Journal* 40(3) (summer 1985): 463
163 R.M. Logan, *Canada, the United States, and the Third Law of the Sea Conference* (Montreal 1974), 34–5; *CAR 1977*, 252

164 Charles Doran, *Forgotten Partnership: U.S.-Canada Relations Today* (Baltimore 1984), 199–200
165 *CAR 1978*, 259–62
166 *CAR 1977*, 252–3; *CAR 1979*, 197–9
167 Doran, *Forgotten Partnership*, 201
168 Legault, 'A Line for All Uses,' 473–7
169 Edward F. Wonder, 'US-Canada Energy Relations,' in Willis Armstrong, Louise Armstrong, and Edward Wilcox, *Canada and the United States: Dependence and Divergence* (Cambridge, Mass. 1982), 99

CHAPTER 5: *One Country or Two?*

1 Jean Lacouture, *De Gaulle*, vol. 3 (Paris 1986), 520–1. For de Gaulle in 1964 see Escott Reid, *Radical Mandarin* (Toronto 1989), 363.
2 For the rest, PCO, Cabinet minutes, 25 July 1967. This account may seem at variance with those that identify Marchand and Pierre Elliott Trudeau, minister of justice, as 'hard-liners'; but the cabinet minutes do not indicate any particularly 'hard' statement by Trudeau, and they do not support such a label for Marchand.
3 *CAR 1968*, 78
4 On the clash of ideologies in French Canada see Ramsay Cook, *Canada, Quebec, and the Uses of Nationalism* (Toronto 1986), chap. 2.
5 Claude Morin, *L'art de l'impossible: La diplomatie québécoise depuis 1960* (Montréal 1987), 28–32; Dale Thomson, *Jean Lesage and the Quiet Revolution* (Toronto 1984), 435–7
6 The origins of the délégation générale are described in Dale Thomson, *Vive le Québec libre* (Toronto 1988), 95–100.
7 On Lesage, Johnson, and de Gaulle see Christopher Malone, 'La politique québécoise en matière de relations internationales: Changement et continuité, 1960–72' (PHD thesis, Université d'Ottawa, 1975), 3–30.
8 See, for example, the capsule description of Quebec's history in Maurice Couve de Murville, *Une politique étrangère, 1958–1969* (Paris 1971), 451–2.
9 One who did was the foreign-affairs editor of *Le Monde*, Claude Julien: in his book, *Canada: Europe's Last Chance* (Toronto 1968), published in France in 1965, he argued that a united Canada stood the best chance of escaping absorption into the United States. He found the English-French debate in Canada 'sterile because it ignores the international dimension.'
10 As Thomson points out, there was a substantial difference in interpretation between de Gaulle and Lesage as to the meaning of Franco-Quebec contacts. *Vive le Québec libre*, 99–100
11 A partial record of the cabinet minutes of 4 and 11 May 1965, at which Pearson reported on negotiations with Lesage, has been released. Although the public portion indicates that Pearson stood 'firm on the principles involved,' we cannot be certain what was said in the ensuing discussion. See ibid., 157.

12 Ibid., 144–50

13 Quoted in Ron Graham, *One-Eyed Kings: Promise & Illusion in Canadian Politics* (Toronto 1986), 66; see also Jean Chrétien, *Straight from the Heart* (Toronto 1985), 151.

14 NA, Jules Léger Papers, vol. 1, file 1, Cadieux, 'Conversation with Mr Daniel Johnson in Montreal on January 9, 1968,' 10 Jan. 1968

15 *CAR 1968*, 223–4

16 See Donald Peacock, *Journey to Power: The Story of a Canadian Election* (Toronto 1968), 197–214

17 *CAR 1968*, 82

18 Jean Lacouture, *De Gaulle: Le souverain, 1959–1970* (Paris 1986), 531

19 Gérard Bergeron, *Du Duplessisme à Trudeau et Bourassa, 1956–1971* (Montreal 1971), 437–68

20 Pierre Godin, *Daniel Johnson: 1964–1968: La difficile recherche de l'égalité* (Montreal 1980), 266–71

21 According to Thomson, *Vive le Québec libre*, 103–4, Lesage had also given French investment a high priority, with little result.

22 Pierre de Menthon, *Je témoigne: Québec 1967* (Chili 1973; Paris 1979), 17; Morin, *L'art de l'impossible*, 37–8; see also the analysis by Stephen Clarkson and Christina McCall, 'De Gaulle's gaffe 20 years ago was a pivotal point for Canada,' *Globe and Mail*, 24 July 1987.

23 Godin, *Johnson*, tome 2, 312

24 As Anne and Pierre Rouanet note in their book, *Les trois derniers chagrins du général de Gaulle* (Paris 1980), 197, 'en cet été 1967 secoué par l'affaire du Québec, c'est de Gaulle qui est détenteur du pouvoir confié par la nation, et non point Giscard et Pompidou,' both of whom had grave reservations about de Gaulle's Quebec policy.

25 On 2 November 1977, during a state visit by Lévesque to France, a number of dispatches from the French embassy in Ottawa were made public, among them one dated 29 July 1967 explaining that Pearson's own reasonable and pacific disposition was not reflected in his response to de Gaulle's 24 July speech. Nevertheless, the dispatch added, there was a 'deep wound' that must somehow be healed. Pearson's wounded feelings, de Gaulle responded, were not 'the question. The question is that the French people of Canada must have full self-determination.' See Pierre-Louis Mallen, *Vivre le Québec libre* (Paris 1978), 242–3.

26 De Menthon, *Je témoigne*, 24–6

27 Quoted in Mallen, *Vivre*, 321–2. Paul Martin, in his autobiography *A Very Public Life*, II: *So Many Worlds* (Toronto 1985), 603–4, states that he had heard that Leduc had discredited himself with de Gaulle as early as July 1967 by criticizing his city-hall escapade; by April 1968 he was, therefore, just serving out his term.

28 Mallen, *Vivre*, 321–2

29 See Christopher Beatty, Jacques Désy, Stephen Longstaff, *Bureaucratic Careers:*

Anglophones and Francophones in the Canadian Public Service (Ottawa 1972), 559–62.

30 Robert A.D. Ford Interview, La Poivrière, 15–16 Oct. 1987

31 Beatty, Désy, and Longstaff, *Bureaucratic Careers,* 13

32 Gilles Lalande, *The Department of External Affairs and Biculturalism* (Ottawa 1969), 27–9; T.A. Keenleyside, 'Career Attitudes of Canadian Foreign Service Officers,' *Canadian Public Administration* 19(2) (summer 1975): 211n

33 Confidential interview; A.E. Gotlieb, 'Eulogy on Marcel Cadieux,' 24 March 1982, CIIA obituary file

34 Martin, *Very Public Life,* 379

35 Gotlieb, 'Eulogy'; Paul Tremblay, 'Funeral Eulogy for Marcel Cadieux,' CIIA obituary file; Morin, *L'art de l'impossible,* 45–6

36 See Martin, *Very Public Life,* 577–8, for Cadieux's first unhappy meeting with Morin in 1964. The information on Cadieux's relations is from a confidential interview.

37 Martin, *Very Public Life,* 599–600

38 Léger Papers, vol. 4, DEA, Western European Division, 'Les relations franco-canadiennes, 1964–1969,' 2 juin 1971, passim

39 Maurice Copithorne interview, Vancouver, 23 Sept. 1987; confidential interviews

40 Confidential interview

41 Léger Papers, vol. 4, file 'France,' DEA, West European Division, 'Relations franco-canadiennes, 1964–1969,' 2 juin 1971, 32

42 Confidential interview

43 Ibid.

44 Trinity College Archives, George Ignatieff Papers, contain a memorandum by Cadieux that sketches out a model foreign service officer; Cadieux makes it clear that no dilettantes need apply.

45 Confidential interview

46 The Gabonese president of the day was known to be a 'vieil ami de la France'; French companies were interested in Gabon's minerals, and, in any case, the French suspected his would-be supplanter to be pro-American. Pierre Biarnès, *Les Français en Afrique noire de Richelieu à Mitterrand* (Paris 1987), 367–8

47 Alain Peyrefitte, *The Trouble with France* (New York 1981), 289

48 Interview with Gérard Pelletier, Ottawa, 14 Aug. 1987; Marc Lalonde interview

49 J.-M. Léger, *La francophonie: Grand dessein, grande ambiguïté* (Paris 1987), 37, 50. Léger dates the term 'francophonie' to 1880.

50 Morin, *L'art de l'impossible,* 114–15

51 Léger Papers, vol. 4, file 'France,' DEA, West European Division, 'Les relations franco-canadiennes, 1964–1969,' 2 juin 1971, 15

52 Morin, *L'art de l'impossible,* 115–17

53 Confidential interview

54 Ibid.; John P. Schlegel, *The Deceptive Ash: Bilingualism and Canadian Policy in Africa, 1957–1971* (Washington, DC 1978), 250–1; NA, Paul Martin Papers, vol.

15, 'Colloque de l'IDEF à Lômé et voyage de M. P.E. Trudeau en Afrique francophone,' nd but probably 1968

55 Morin, *L'art de l'impossible*, 130–1; the French government had, as one of its officials later admitted, already 'advised Gabon and other countries that they could have direct relations with Quebec in matters of education.' *CAR 1969*, 201

56 Morin, *L'art de l'impossible*, 125

57 Confidential interview

58 NA, Lionel Chevrier Papers, vol. 42: Paul Martin, 'Aid Mission to Francophone Africa,' 24 Jan. 1968, urged that the mission depart soon, to which Pearson responded, 'Yes – but he will have to be briefed now on the relationship between federal aid and the recognition of the Federal position in Canada.' See also P. Appavoo, 'The Small State as Donor: Canadian and Swedish Development Aid Policies, 1960–1976' (PHD thesis, University of Toronto, 1989), 164.

59 The Gabonese response is quoted in Morin, *L'art de l'impossible*, 132–3. There was, from the federal point of view, some useful publicity. The Liberal opposition in Quebec ridiculed the Johnson government's 'gaboniaiseries,' and evidently made some impression on public opinion; their opportunism is solemnly denounced in ibid., 134. On Chevrier's mission see Schlegel, *Deceptive Ash,* 265; Chevrier Papers, vol. 42, Marcel Cadieux à Maurice Strong, 6 fèv. 1968, encl. 'Mission de coopération économique en Afrique française.'

60 Morin, *L'art de l'impossible*, 134–9

61 Léger Papers, vol. 4, DEA, Western European Division, 'Les relations franco-canadiennes, 1964–1969,' 35–35A

62 The account of the evening's events by Pierre-Louis Mallen, the pro-separatist reporter from the French state radio and television network, mentions Trudeau's 'audace provocatrice mais physiquement courageuse.' *Vivre,* 323

63 Pierre Siraud interview, Paris, 12 Oct. 1987

64 A good example is the conversation between Cadieux, Jurgensen, and Leduc in Ottawa on 4 April 1968. Léger Papers, vol. 4, file 'France,' DEA, Western Europe Division, 'Les relations franco-canadiennes, 1964–1969,' 33–4.

65 Morin, *L'art de l'impossible*, 114

66 See *CAR 1968*, 229–31; Marshall Crowe interview, 14 March 1988; T.S. Axworthy, ' "To Stand Not So High Perhaps But Always Alone": The Foreign Policy of Pierre Elliott Trudeau,' in Axworthy, ed., *Towards a Just Society* (Toronto 1990).

67 NA, Marcel Cadieux Papers, vol. 4, Cadieux memorandum, 26 Sept. 1968

68 Morin, *L'art de l'impossible*, 89–90

69 Cadieux Papers, vol. 4, memorandum of 29 Oct. 1968; Pierre O'Neill et Jacques Benjamin, *Les mandarins du pouvoir: L'exercice du pouvoir au Québec de Jean Lesage à René Lévesque* (Montreal 1978), 81–2, make the point that Bertrand was concerned about the loyalty of the prime ministerial staff, and that Chouinard's appointment responded to that concern.

70 Léger Papers, vol. 4, file VI, Department of External Affairs, GEO, 'Les relations franco-canadiennes, 1964–1969,' 2 June 1971, quoting an External Affairs dispatch of 4 Oct. 1968

71 See Montreal *Gazette,* 19 Feb. 1969, for a discussion of these individuals; on Jurgensen see Morin, *Art de l'impossible,* 119, and Thomson, *Vive le Québec libre,* 158–9.

72 Michel Tétu, in his *La francophonie: Histoire, problématique, perspectives* (Montreal 1987), 59–60, quite properly draws attention to this article.

73 Ibid., 80

74 Ibid., 195; New France was, of course, Quebec's colonial name under Louis xv.

75 See Schlegel, *Deceptive Ash,* 264–5; Martin, *Very Public Life,* 664; Morin, *L'art de l'impossible,* 146, in which the French consul-general in Quebec confesses that France's relations with the Congo (soon to become Zaire) are not all they could be.

76 Morin, *L'art de impossible,* 148–53

77 See Léger Papers, vol. 15, file 1, for a lengthy anonymous essay prepared in External Affairs in February 1974, entitled 'Conférence des ministres de l'éducation nationale des états d'expression française d'Afrique et de Madagascar.'

78 Ironically, the French did manage to adjust the Kinshasa conference documents to show that Ottawa was present only as an observer, an assertion that was obviously false. On Biafra, Ottawa, and de Gaulle see Schlegel, *Deceptive Ash,* 161, citing Mitchell Sharp's testimony to a parliamentary committee.

79 Martin, *Very Public Life,* 665, is more optimistic about his interview than others at the time. We have also used DEA records.

80 See Robert Bourgi, *Le général de Gaulle et l'Afrique noire, 1940–1969* (Paris 1980), 429: 'Il était inévitable ... que les bénéficiaires de la politique culturelle française allaient se faire en grande partie instruments de l'influence de la France dans ces nouvelles Républiques.'

81 See Keith Spicer, *A Samaritan State? External Aid in Canada's Foreign Policy* (Toronto 1966), 56–61.

82 Ibid., 60; Léger, *La francophonie,* 75–81

83 Gérard Pelletier interview, Ottawa, 14 Aug. 1987

84 DEA file 20-1-2-3, External Aid Office Quarterly Letter (unclassified), July 1968

85 Spicer, *Samaritan State?* 251; Morin, *L'art de l'impossible,* 183, notes that Diori wanted money for a road, to be called 'route de l'Unité.'

86 Canadian diplomats also believed that the counsellor sent to Niamey from the Quai was a well-known enthusiast for an independent Quebec. Confidential source

87 Morin, *L'art de l'impossible,* 184. There is some evidence that Bourges was not the only French emissary to bring French pressure to bear on Diori: according to information received from a third country, the ubiquitous Rossillon asked Diori not to exchange the friendship of France for the financial support of Canada. Confidential source

88 Confidential source

89 Ibid.

90 Ibid.

91 Martin, *A Very Public Life,* 665

92 Confidential source

93 PCO, Cabinet minutes, 27 Feb. 1969. Also, confidential source. A number of African countries were also opposed to a hasty convening of the conference; Belgium, Luxembourg, and Switzerland had decided, as of December, not to be represented.

94 The 'entente Trudeau-Bertrand' is reproduced in Morin, *L'art de l'impossible,* 188; see also *CAR 1969,* 197–8.

95 Léger, *La francophonie,* 105–6, renders Pelletier's remark as 'Madame, vous chantez mieux que vous ne criez.' Our source is another, albeit anonymous, participant. An enquiry immediately started to discover who had brought Julien: the *Toronto Star,* 18 Feb. 1969, pointed its finger at Rossillon.

96 *CAR 1969,* 197–8; PCO, cabinet minutes, 27 Feb. 1969.

97 Léger, *La francophonie,* 107–8

98 See Donald Baker, 'Quebec on French Minds.' *Queen's Quarterly* 85 (summer 1978):249–64.

99 See, for example, Pompidou's press conference reported in the *Ottawa Citizen,* 24 Sept. 1971; Siraud interview, 12 Oct. 1987.

100 Bank of Canada Archives, file 4E-260, ambassade, Paris, à DEA, 2 April 1971

101 The title of Mallen's book, *Vivre le Québec libre,* gives a fair idea of his point of view. On this point see Thomson, *Vive le Québec libre,* 104, 158–9.

102 See Schlegel, *Deceptive Ash,* 286–7.

103 Léger, *La francophonie,* 109–16, recounts his voyages, mentioning that he spent longer, and more pleasant, hours in Quebec than he did in Ottawa. His travels were assisted, not to say enhanced, he tells us, by the friendship and confidence of French emissaries around the world. Canadian reactions are derived from a confidential source.

104 NA, Arnold Smith Papers, vol. 5, diary, 'Report on Visit to Commonwealth Secretariat of M. Jean-Marc Léger of "La Francophonie," ' 28 Nov. 1969

105 Ibid.

106 Morin, *L'art de l'impossible,* 197, 207–8

107 *CAR 1970,* 233–4; Morin, *L'art de l'impossible,* 210–11

108 Morin, *L'art de l'impossible,* 217–18

109 Claude Morin notes the federal reliance on Bertrand and argues that it assumed too much. Ibid., 170.

110 Confidential interviews

111 Pelletier interview; confidential source

112 Cameroun's support for Canada is according to confidential sources; Morin, *L'art de l'impossible,* 220, places Cameroun in the other camp.

113 Léger, *La francophonie,* 117–19

114 Morin, *L'art de l'impossible,* 229

115 Schlegel, *Deceptive Ash,* 297–8. It was one of the supreme ironies of this unusual conference that the nationalist-separatist Léger was suspected of being a stalking horse for the Canadians.

116 Smith Papers, vol. 105, diary, Jan.–April 1970, 'Second Francophone Conference: Niamey 1970'

117 Confidential interview

118 Smith Papers, vol. 105, diary, Jan.–April 1970, 'Second francophone conference: Niamey 1970,' 3 April 1970

119 Léger's appointment, according to journalists on the spot, was opposed by the French because of the too great independence he had shown in his draft statutes and in his budgetary proposals: CAR 1970, 323–4. Léger himself makes no reference to conflicts with the French, although his lack of enthusiasm for the arrangements of the ACCT is most evident: La francophonie, 120–1. We have also used a confidential interview.

120 Or so at least one of the authors heard him say at a function in Boston in the fall of 1969.

121 Quotations are from a Social Research Inc. survey, with comments from a senior Liberal. Quoted in Graham Fraser, PQ: René Lévesque and the Parti Québécois in Power (Toronto 1984), 51–2

122 François Cloutier, one of Bourassa's ministers, suggests that an 'unconditional federalist' leading the Quebec Liberal party in 1970 would have had to govern against the inclination of 'a majority of ministers and members,' against the higher civil service, and even against the tendency established by the Quiet Revolution of the 1960s. Cloutier, L'enjeu: Mémoires politiques, 1970–1976 (Montreal 1978), 59

123 See Joseph Wearing, The L-Shaped Party: The Liberal Party of Canada, 1958–1980 (Toronto 1981), 108, and George Radwanski, Trudeau (Toronto 1978), 337.

124 Morin, L'art de l'impossible, 232–4; CAR 1971, 56, 59

125 Cloutier, L'enjeu, 69

126 Schlegel, Deceptive Ash, 300–1; Morin, L'art de l'impossible, 235–40

127 Michel de Goumois, 'Le Canada et la francophonie,' Etudes Internationales 5 (2) (juin 1974), 355–66

128 CIDA Annual Report, 1970–1, 73

129 Peter Dobell, Canada in World Affairs, XII: 1971–73 (Toronto 1985), 217–22

130 Louis Bernard, 'Le départ de Claude Morin ou l'échec de la 3e voie,' Le Devoir, 10 sept. 1971

131 Cloutier, L'enjeu, 66

132 Le Devoir, 'Une proposition suspecte,' 21 Oct. 1971

133 Morin, L'art de l'impossible, 257

134 Ibid., 253

CHAPTER 6: *Missing Links*

1 Foreign Policy for Canadians (Ottawa 1970), 'Foreign Policy for Canadians' pamphlet, 39. An assessment of the 'Pacific' pamphlet is T.A. Keenleyside, 'Canada and the Pacific: Perils of a Policy Paper,' Journal of Canadian Studies 7 (May 1973): 31ff.

2 See J.L. Granatstein, Canada 1957–67 (Toronto 1986), 60–1, 201ff.

3 Bank of Canada Archives, Bank of Canada Records, file 5B-140, London to External, 21 June 1968

4 Ibid., file 5D-450, telegram, External to London, 19 Nov. 1969

5 Ibid., file 50-450, 'British Application to Join E.E.C.,' Canada-U.K. Continuing Committee paper, 23–24 Oct. 1969. See generally F.S. Northedge, 'British Foreign Policy in a Community Context,' in K.J. Twitchett, ed., *Europe and the World: The External Relations of the Common Market* (London 1976), 183ff.

6 See, for example, Charles Lynch's column in *Ottawa Citizen,* 5 March 1971.

7 *Foreign Policy for Canadians,* 'Europe,' 14

8 Autumn 1972

9 DEA Communiqué, 14 Sept. 1971

10 Michel Dupuy interview, 18 Jan. 1988

11 Toronto *Globe and Mail,* 5 Nov. 1971

12 *Montreal Star,* 9 Dec. 1971

13 John Halstead interview, 9 Dec. 1987

14 Sharp, 'Options,' 1

15 J.H. Warren, deputy minister in trade and commerce until 1971, was scornful of the third option: he had been through 'that nonsense' before with the 15 per cent trade diversion of 1957. Interview, 8 Dec. 1987

16 Mitchell Sharp interview, 8 Dec. 1987; Halstead interview

17 Confidential interview

18 DEA Records, file 20-USA-9-Nixon, 'Canadian Identity and Independence,' 5 April 1972

19 For academic comment see articles in *International Perspectives* (Jan.–Feb. 1973), 3ff.

20 DEA, Statements and Speeches, no. 73/29, 2 Nov. 1973

21 Mitchell Sharp, 'Canada and Europe,' in Nils Orvik, ed., *Canada and the European Community* (Kingston, nd), 9.

22 A few years earlier French journalist Claude Julien had published *Le Canada, dernière chance de l'Europe* (Paris 1965), which argued that the United States would always be stronger than Europe and that Canada was a necessary counterweight. He suggested too that Europe could help Canada avoid assimilation. The book made substantial impact in Canada but little in Europe.

23 Reeves Haggan interview, 4 Feb. 1988

24 DEA Communiqué no. 62, 9 Sept. 1971

25 *Globe and Mail,* 15 Jan. 1972

26 *Ottawa Journal,* 25 July 1972

27 *Globe and Mail,* 23 Oct. 1972

28 *Toronto Star,* 8 Jan. 1973

29 Jeremy Kinsman, 'Pursuing the Realistic Goal of Closer Canada-EEC Links,' *International Perspectives* (Jan. – Feb. 1973), 26

30 See the conference report, 'Canada and the European Community,' *Behind the Headlines* 32 (Feb. 1974), for Soames's address and other papers.

31 'Canadian Relations with the European Community,' Report of the Standing Senate Committee on Foreign Affairs (July 1973), 20ff

32 John Halstead's 'Official Communication to the Political Coordination Committee of the Nine,' 26 Sept. 1974, tabled in the House of Commons, 5 Nov. 1974. Halstead was not identified in parliament as the official delivering the speech.

33 Dupuy interview

34 Aide-Memoire, 20 April 1974, and Discussion Draft of 'Trade Agreement Between Canada and the European Communities,' nd. Both documents were tabled in the House of Commons on 5 November 1974. Paul Martin observed in his diary that the question of Canada's relations with the EC never went to the cabinet. NA, Paul Martin Papers, Diary, 1 Jan. 1975

35 Doc. SEC (74)3372, 12 Sept. 1974, printed in A.J. Easson, ed., *Canada and the European Communities: Selected Materials* (Kingston 1979), 86ff. An official of the Wirtschaftsministerium, Bonn, said that 'We at meetings tried to impress on our Canadian visitors that their request was beneath Canada's dignity ... the substance was so slight. But the political interest of Canada was powerful.' Confidential interview

36 Quoted in Ulrich Strempel, 'Towards Complex Interdependence: Canada and the European Community, 1959–80' (PHD thesis, University of Alberta, 1982), 207

37 'Official Communication,' 26 Sept. 1974; Halstead interview

38 Halstead interview

39 Martin Papers, Diary, 14 March 1975

40 *Financial Post*, 12 Oct. 1974, as printed in Easson, ed., *Canada and the European Communities*, 95

41 Dupuy interview

42 Based on *Vancouver Sun*, 25, 28 Oct. 1974; *Globe and Mail*, 26 Oct. 1974, and Trudeau's report on the trip in the House of Commons *Debates*, 28 Oct. 1974, 783ff

43 'Restoring Relations with France and Opening New Doors to Europe,' *International Perspectives* (Jan. – Feb. 1975)

44 Terry Empson interview, London, 7 Oct. 1987. Empson had served at the British high commission in Ottawa.

45 Martin Papers, Diary, 12 March 1975. 'It was clear that from what Prime Minister Wilson and Jim Callaghan said, in my judgment if not in that of Prime Minister Trudeau, the British are more interested in having a Declaration ... instead of a contractual document.' Martin later noted that Trudeau had rejected the declaration idea. 'What he wanted was some guarantee, some compulsion that there would be consultation.' Ibid., 24 March 1975

46 Ibid., vol. 396, Wilson file, Transcript of Press Conference, 29 Jan. 1975

47 Ibid., vol. 383, Minutes of Canada/UK Continuing Committee, Ottawa, 15–16 Oct. 1975

48 Ibid., Diary, 16 Oct. 1975

49 The best Canadian account of the legalities is Charles Pentland, 'Linkage Politics: Canada's Contract and the Development of the European Community's External Relations.' *International Journal* 32 (spring 1977): 207ff.

50 Martin Papers, vol. 397, High Commissioner's diary file, Martin to J.P. O'Callaghan, 25 March 1975

51 NA, Jules Léger Papers, vol. 42, Premier Ministre recontres 1976 #1, Notes à la suite de rencontre du 21 février 1975

52 DEA, Statements and Speeches, no. 75/6, Address, 13 March 1975. John Halstead noted that the text of this speech did not include any references of substance to the contractual link until he prepared a major rewrite in Rome a few days before the scheduled address. This new draft was rejected but some of its message got through. Interview, 20–23 Feb. 1988

53 Martin Papers, Diary, 12 March 1975. A more detailed account of the talks is in ibid., vol. 391, telegram, London to External, 14 March 1975

54 Ibid., Diary, 13 March 1975

55 After reading the Auswartiges Amt files, German officials concluded that this reorientation in Canadian policy had been welcomed, but their predecessors saw the contractual link as an 'intellectual exercise,' there being serious impediments to real change in Canada's relations with Europe. Even if Canadian trade with the FRG were doubled, for example, it would only amount to 2 per cent of German trade. Interview with Dr Schneppen and Dr von Lutkowitz, Canadian desk, Auswartiges Amt, Bonn, 19 Oct. 1987. Some Bonn officials, however, saw the proposed contractual link as a backward step. Hitherto a strong supporter of multilateralism, Canada was receding into nationalism. Confidential interview

56 DEA Records, file 20-CDA-9-Trudeau-Eur, G.G. Crean to Trudeau, 6 March 1975

57 For Cadieux's reports see Léger Papers, vol. 17, 20, 27 Oct. 1975.

58 Some ministers thought this was deliberately done to increase support for the contractual link. Barney Danson interview, 10 Nov. 1987. See also Robert Boardman, 'European Responses to Canada's Third Option Policy,' in M. Fleming, ed., *Proceedings of Workshop on EC and EC-Canada Relations,* Ottawa, 11–13 Dec. 1978 (European Politics Group, 1979), 135–6, and Peter Dobell, *Canada in World Affairs,* XII: *1971–73* (Toronto 1985), 140–1. For details on the commitments see Larry Stewart, ed., *Canadian Defence Policy: Selected Documents, 1964–1981* (Kingston 1982), 46ff.

59 There were twenty-four pages of arrangements, agreements, commissions, or visits as a result of Trudeau's trips. DEA Records, file 20-CDA-9-Trudeau-Eur, 'Suites des Visites du Premier Ministre en Europe,' nd [June 1975]

60 Confidential interview

61 House of Commons, *Debates,* 26 May 1975, 6088–9; Information Memo, E.C. Commission, May 1975, printed in Easson, ed., *Canada and the European Communities,* 148–9

62 Léo Cadieux interview, 9 Dec. 1987. The French ambassador in Canada at the time, M. Viot, confirmed that Paris acquiesced because the link was a political necessity for Ottawa. Interview, 13 Oct. 1987. Paul Martin speculated that

'access to our natural resources could be foremost among the [French] reasons.' Martin Papers, Diary, 21 July 1975

63 For an assessment of the situation on 8 October 1975 see the Canadian briefing paper for the Canada-UK Continuing Committee, 'Canada-European Community Relations: The Contractual Link,' in Martin Papers, vol. 383.

64 There was substantial Canadian lobbying behind this development. Ibid., Diary, 20 Oct. 1975

65 Cited in Easson, ed., *Canada and the European Communities*, 173

66 Ibid., 181

67 Allan MacEachen interview, 14 March 1988

68 NA, Donald Jamieson Papers, vol. 351, External Policy and Defence Committee file, O.G.S[toner] to minister, 14 April 1976

69 Ibid., O.G.S[toner] to minister, 21 June 1976

70 DEA Communiqué, no. 55, 2 June 1976

71 DEA Records, file 35-20-EEC-3-1, Cadieux to Ottawa, 8 June 1976; DEA Communiqué no. 68, 30 June 1976

72 'Accord-Cadre de Cooperation Commerciale et Economique entre le Canada et les Communautés Europeenes,' 6 July 1976; DEA Communiqué, no. 70, 6 July 1976

73 Robert Boardman et al., *The Canada-European Communities Framework Agreement: A Canadian Perspective* (Saskatoon 1984), 15

74 See *Le Monde*, 31 Jan. 1978, as quoted in Strempel, 'Complex Interdependence,' 174.

75 Martin Papers, Diary, 13 Dec. 1976

76 This stress on fast results was made public. See *Globe and Mail*, 8 Dec. 1976.

77 Jamieson nonetheless wrote his ambassadors to note how 'struck' he had been by the 'unanimity of views expressed' and their 'deep sense of commitment' towards the Framework Agreement. Martin Papers, vol. 373, Jamieson file, Jamieson to Martin, 14 Dec. 1976. This was persiflage. Jamieson himself was lukewarm, and he and Halstead had a bitter exchange on the subject at the Heads of Post meeting. Halstead interview, 20–23 Feb. 1988

78 Based on Martin Papers, vol. 388, Marcel Cadieux to USSEA, 15 Dec. 1976, and ibid., Diary, 13 Dec. 1976

79 Confidential interview

80 Ibid.

81 16 July 1976. Martin, a friend of Malone's, disagreed sharply. See Martin Papers, vol. 374, Malone file, Martin to Malone, 22 July 1974 [not sent].

82 Confidential interviews; Erich Straetling interview, 20 Oct. 1987

83 Donald S. Macdonald interview, 5 April 1988. Between 1968 and 1987, agricultural production dropped from 4.3 to 3.0 per cent of the GNP; the primary sector of the economy as a whole fell from 16.9 to 9.8 per cent. See André Downs, 'Canada-Québec 1968–88: Une Perspective Economique,' a paper presented to the Italian Association of Canadian Studies, Sestri Levante, Feb. 1989.

84 DEA Records, file 35-3-1-EEC, Robinson memo for minister, 24 Nov. 1976, and attached memo, 24 Nov. 1976

85 Boardman et al., *Framework Agreement,* 23

86 DEA Records, file 35-3-1-EEC, 'Federal-Provincial Meeting,' 14 March 1977 and attachments

87 Ibid., Memo, 8 March 1978

88 Martin Papers, vol. 401, Outgoing Correspondence, Martin to M. Beaudoin, 27 July 1978

89 A.E. Ritchie interview, 15 March 1988

90 Confidential interview

91 Confidential interviews

92 Sharp interview, 8 Dec. 1987

93 See K.S. Courtis and Paul Summerville, 'Canada-Japan Relations: The Case of the Automotive Industry," *Area Studies Tsukuba* 4 (1986): 251ff.

94 Frank Langdon, 'Problems of Canada-Japan Economic Diplomacy in the 1960s and 1970s: The Third Option,' in Keith Hay, ed., *Canadian Perspectives on Economic Relations with Japan* (Montreal 1980), 75ff

95 *CYB 1976–77,* 873, 911, 915. See also the Standing Senate Committee on Foreign Affairs, *Report on Canadian Relations with the Countries of the Pacific Region* (Ottawa, March 1972), 13ff; Lorne Kavic, 'Canada-Japan Relations,' *International Journal* 26 (summer 1971): 567ff.

96 Jamieson Papers, vol. 358, External Affairs Briefing Book, 'Canada/Japan Relations,' 1976; Langdon, 'Problems,' 79

97 Tadayuki Okuma, 'Passive Japan – Active Canada,' *International Journal* 33 (spring 1978): 443–4

98 Stephen Heeney, 'Common Goal of Expansion Unites Canada and Japan,' *International Perspectives* (Jan. – Feb. 1975): 18

99 Speech by the secretary of state for external affairs to the Japanese Press Club, 25 June 1975. Cf PCO, Cabinet Minutes, 24 April 1969

100 Jamieson Papers, vol. 358, External Affairs Briefing Book, 'Canada-Japan Relations,' 1976

101 Yasuhiko Nara interview, 20 May 1987; Frank Langdon, *The Politics of Canadian-Japanese Economic Relations 1952–83* (Vancouver 1983), chap. 6

102 Confidential interview

103 Jamieson Papers, vol. 358, External Affairs Briefing Book, 'Visit of PM to Japan'

104 Ibid., vol. 326, Briefing Book, Scenario for 21 October 1976

105 DEA, Statements and Speeches, no. 77/2, Address in Toronto, 10 March 1977

106 Nara interview. Klaus Pringsheim, *Neighbours across the Pacific* (Oakville 1983), 183, called the Framework Agreement 'basically a public relations document.'

107 Jamieson Papers, vol. 326, Briefing Book, Scenario

108 Based on interviews with Nara; with Michiaki Suma, 12 May 1987; and with Kiyohisa Mikanagi, 12 May 1987

109 Jamieson Papers, vol. 377, Tokyo Summit file, Tokyo Summit Bilateral Discus-

sions, 28–29 June 1979, book, 'Overview of Canada/Japan Bilateral Relations.' Michiaki Suma, ambassador in Ottawa after 1979, noted that one joint Japanese-Canadian venture, a plant producing TV sets, had productivity half that in Japan. Suma, *From the Country of the Maple Leaf* (Tokyo 1982), chap. 26. We are indebted to Ambassador Suma for a copy of the book and to Ken Yoshida, late of the Canadian embassy in Tokyo, for an abridged translation.

110 Quoted in Michael Donnelly, 'Growing Disharmony in Canadian-Japanese Trade,' *International Journal* 36 (autumn 1981): 884

111 Confidential interview

112 Jamieson Papers, vol. 377, Tokyo Summit file, 'Tokyo Summit ... Bilateral Discussions,' 28–29 June 1979

113 'A Singular Voice: The Foreign Policy of Pierre Elliott Trudeau,' in C. David Crenna, *Lifting the Shadow of War* (Edmonton 1987), xv. Michel Dupuy said that the 'technical departments' thought the link was an attempt to make something out of nothing. Interview. This argument is developed fully in Margaret Royal, 'Canadian-American Relations: The Last Option' (PHD thesis, Queen's University, 1984).

114 Dupuy interview.

115 DEA Records, file 35-3-1-EEC, J. Gignac to Sir J. Scott-Hopkins, 22 March 1983, and enclosure

116 See DEA, *Canadian Trade Policy for the 1980s* (Ottawa 1983). A PCO official recalled that DEA produced a draft of this document that was trashed by Ambassador Gotlieb. The result, a pastiche of compromises, went to cabinet where, the paper not meeting the political requirements of the moment, conclusions were grafted on, 'free-floating with respect to the rest of the document.' Confidential interview

117 Robert Bothwell, ' "The Canadian Connection": Canada and Europe,' in N. Hillmer and Garth Stevenson, eds., *Foremost Nation: Canadian Foreign Policy and a Changing World* (Toronto 1977), 35

118 Emerson Brown interview, 11 Jan. 1988

CHAPTER 7: *The East Is Red*

1 Preface (Toronto 1968), np

2 For a useful account of Quebec attitudes to China in the period of Trudeau's youth see Alain Larocque, 'Losing "Our" Chinese: The St Enfance Movement,' Working Paper no. 49, University of Toronto – York University Joint Centre for Asia Pacific Studies, 1987. See also Alvyn Austin, *Saving China: Canadian Missionaries in the Middle Kingdom 1888–1959* (Toronto 1986).

3 Trudeau and Hébert, *Innocents,* 151

4 See *CAR 1966,* 204–5. For an assessment of Canadian policy towards China in 1965 see John Holmes, 'Canada and China: The Dilemmas of a Middle Power,' in A.M. Halpern, ed., *Policies Toward China: Views from Six Continents* (New York 1965), 103ff.

5 See Paul Evans and Daphne Taras, 'Canadian Public Opinion on Relations with China ...' Working Paper no. 33, University of Toronto – York University Joint Centre on Modern East Asia, 1985, 8, 12, 16. The same authors measure public opinion in their article in D. Taras, ed., *Parliament and Canadian Foreign Policy* (Toronto 1985), 66ff.

6 See Norman St Amour, 'A Colossus and a Conundrum: The United States as a Factor in Sino-Canadian Relations, 1963–66,' paper presented at the Canada-China Relations Conference, Montebello, Que., 1985; and Paul Evans, 'Cognitive Variables and Foreign Policy Analysis: "Solving" the Recognition Problem, 1949–68,' ibid.

7 Confidential interview

8 DEA Records, file 20-China-14, Hong Kong to Ottawa, 1 June 1967

9 For one account of the Canadian position on recognition by a Sinophile participant see Chester Ronning, *A Memoir of China in Revolution* (New York 1974), chap. 12.

10 Donald Macdonald interview, 5 April 1988; Paul Martin interview, 10 Feb. 1987; confidential interview; Heward Grafftey, 'The Perennial UN Debate,' *Montreal Star,* 16 Aug. 1971; Don Page, 'Admission to the U.N.: Canadian Perspectives and Initiatives,' a paper presented to the Canada-China Relations Conference, Montebello, Que., 1985, 43–4

11 Canadian Mission to the United Nations, Press Release no. 74, 23, Nov. 1966

12 St Amour, 'Colossus,' 43ff; confidential interview

13 B. Frolic-Paul Evans conversation with Pierre Trudeau, 27 Jan. 1987; Evans, 'Cognitive Variables,' 29

14 John Harbron, 'Canada Recognizes China: The Trudeau Round 1968–1973,' *Behind the Headlines* 33 (Oct. 1974): 2

15 Office of the Prime Minister, Press release, 29 May 1968

16 H.B. Robinson Papers, 'Prime Minister's Comments on Foreign Policy and on Matters Related to it,' prepared by GSM[urray], Oct. 1969

17 DEA Records, file 20-China-14, Hong Kong to Ottawa, 4 Dec. 1967

18 Ibid., file 20-1-2-China-1, Memo to USSEA, 4 April 1968; Memo, 23 May 1968; telegram, USSEA to Stockholm, 23 May 1968; Memo, USSEA to SSEA, 6 June 1968. On U.S. attitudes see Evans's valuable discussion, 'Cognitive Variables,' esp. 32ff.

19 DEA Records, file 20-1-2-China-1, A.S. McGill to Far Eastern Division, 10 June 1968

20 Robinson Papers, Robinson to R. Collins, 2 Aug. 1968

21 Quoted in Harbron, 'Trudeau Round,' 2.

22 Confidential source. On wheat sales see Karen Minden, 'Politics and Business: The Canada-China Wheat Trade, 1960–84,' a paper presented at the Canada-China Relations Conference, Montebello, Que., 1985.

23 Confidential source and confidential interview

24 Confidential source

25 Ibid.

26 B. Michael Frolic, 'The Recognition of China, 1968–71: A Preliminary Sketch,' paper prepared for the Canada-China Relations Conference, Montebello, Que., 1985, 14–15
27 Confidential source. There were a number of complexities in the international law involved in de-recognizing the Nationalist Chinese. See Arthur Andrew, ' "A Reasonable Period of Time": Canada's De-recognition of Nationalist China,' a paper presented at the Canada-China Relations Conference, Montebello, Que., 1985.
28 Peter Roberts interview, 5 Feb. 1988; confidential source
29 Based on conversation between Trudeau and Frolic-Evans, 27 Jan. 1987
30 Confidential source
31 See Janet Lum, 'Recognition and the Toronto Chinese Community,' a paper presented at the Canada-China Relations Conference, Montebello, Que., 1985.
32 House of Commons, *Debates,* 10 Feb. 1969, 5307, 5321–2
33 Frolic, 'Recognition,' 19. See also PCO, Cabinet minutes, 20 Feb. 1969
34 House of Commons, *Debates,* 21 July 1969, 11383–4. Trudeau recollected that he was the author of this neat phrasing. Frolic-Evans conversation
35 Confidential source
36 See Canadian Delegation to the United Nations, Press Release no. 5, Statement made by Yvon Beaulne, permanent representative, 18 Oct. 1971; NA, Donald Jamieson Papers, Diary, 10 Sept. 1970; ibid., vol. 329, file H1-5, 'Representation of China in the United Nations,' 14 Oct. 1971; *Globe and Mail,* 27 Oct. 1971; and Peter Dobell, *Canada in World Affairs,* XII: *1971–73* (Toronto 1985), 163–5.
37 Confidential source
38 House of Commons, *Debates,* 13 Oct. 1970, 49. See Maureen Molot, 'Canada's Relations with China Since 1968,' in N. Hillmer and Garth Stevenson, eds., *Foremost Nation: Canadian Foreign Policy and a Changing World* (Toronto 1977), 230ff.
39 Yao Guang interview, 25 May 1987. Yao Guang was ambassador in Ottawa, 1972–3, and vice foreign minister, 1982–6, among other postings.
40 Including Italy, Chile, and Belgium. See the list of countries recognizing the People's Republic of China (PRC) in S.S. Kim, *China, the United Nations and World Order* (Princeton 1979), Appendix A.
41 B. Michael Frolic, 'Canada's Relations with China 1970–86,' unpublished paper, 1987, 5. Frolic interviewed over thirty officials and experts.
42 Quoted in Frolic, 'Recognition,' 60–1. There were in fact spy cases emanating from the PRC embassy in 1975 and 1977.
43 *CAR 1970,* 330–1; Lum, 'Toronto Chinese,' 1
44 Minden, 'Wheat,' 23
45 For example, see Montreal *Gazette,* 7 Jan. 1971.
46 Frolic-Evans conversation with Trudeau; Yao Guang interview
47 Ibid.
48 DEA Records, file 20-USA-9-Nixon, Memo, 4 April 1972

49 Minden, 'Wheat,' 26–7, 31
50 See Frolic, 'Relations,' 16.
51 Yu Zhan interview, 27 May 1987. In 1981 Secretary of State for External Affairs Mark McGuigan announced that Canada would start a Canadian International Development Agency program in China which, by 1984, had expended $7.6 million. See Jack Maybee, 'The China Program of the Canadian International Development Agency,' paper presented at the Canada-China Relations Conference, Montebello, Que., 1985.
52 Wang chu-liang interview, 26 May 1987. Wang was counsellor at the embassy in Ottawa, 1973–8.
53 Canadian objectives for the visit are in DEA Records, file 20-Cda-9-Trudeau-PRC, Draft Objectives, 27 Aug. 1973. The best account of the visit and its results is Frolic, 'Relations,' 10ff.
54 See Margaret Trudeau's account of her role on public-health discussions in *Beyond Reason* (New York 1979), 150.
55 Yu Zhan interview. See also excerpts from Trudeau speeches in *International Perspectives* (Jan.–Feb. 1974), 10–11, and confidential interview.
56 See S.A. Freifeld, 'Just Right for the VIP Who Has Everything,' *Bout de Papier* 5 (2) 1985: 12ff.
57 *CAR 1976,* 330
58 Frolic-Evans conversation with Trudeau
59 Gerald Ford Library, David Gergen Papers, box 7, Olympics file, Memo and draft replies to question, 19 July 1976; ibid., Ford Papers, WHCF, RE14, Ford to F.D. Miller, 9 Sept. 1976, and Ford to Lord Killanin, 15 Oct. 1976
60 Russ McKinney interview
61 Ford Papers, WHCF, RE14, Memo, Mike Duval to Dick Cheney, 10 July 1976
62 W.R. Young, ed., *Paul Martin: The London Diaries 1975–79* (Ottawa 1988), 158
63 Wang chu-liang interview. This section is based on *CAR 1976,* 329ff, and Frolic, 'Relations,' 66ff.
64 *Cité Libre,* Trudeau's journal, commented frostily on the Korean War (May 1951) and on Canada's policy of blindly following the United States. For example, 'Fidèle à une tradition qui remonte à la rebellion du Nord-Ouest et à la guerre des Boers, le Canada est toujours pret à défendre le fort contre le faible,' 9.
65 Robert A.D. Ford interview, 15, 16 Oct. 1987; Robert A.D. Ford, *Our Man in Moscow* (Toronto 1989), 113
66 *Le Devoir,* 14–21 Juin 1952. See also David Somerville, *Trudeau Revealed* (Richmond Hill, Ont. 1978), chap. 5.
67 The first attack appeared in *Nos Cours,* 15 Nov. 1952. *Le Droit* joined the fray, 1 Dec. 1952, and Trudeau replied there, 18 Dec. 1952, his article opening 'Je suis opposé au communisme.' The Laurendeau-Angers articles appeared in *L'Action Nationale* 41 (Jan. 1953): 37ff and 78ff.
68 Ford interview; Ford, *Our Man,* 113–14

69 Bruce Thordarson, *Trudeau and Foreign Policy* (Toronto 1972), 67
70 *CAR 1968*, 241
71 George Ignatieff, *The Making of a Peacemonger* (Toronto 1985), 234
72 *CAR 1968*, 241
73 Confidential interview
74 Ignatieff, *Peacemonger,* 231ff
75 DEA Records, file 20-1-1-1, telegram, Ottawa to NATO Delegation, 10 Sept. 1968; ibid., 20-1-2-STAFEUR-8, 'Canadian Relations with the Soviet Union – The Future of Detente,' 23 Sept. 1968
76 Ibid., file 20-1-1-1, 'East-West Relations in the Aftermath of Czechoslovakia,' 12 Dec. 1968
77 Ibid., Ottawa to Moscow, 30 Jan. 1969. Cf PCO, Cabinet Minutes, 30 Aug. 1968.
78 William Hooper interview, 21 April 1988
79 DEA Records, file 20-1-1-1, Moscow to Ottawa, 31 Jan. 1969; ibid., External to NATO Delegation, 6 Feb. 1969
80 Confidential interview; Andrei Gromyko, *Memories* (London 1988), 227–8
81 DEA Records, file 20-CDA-9-Trudeau-Eur, Turner to Head, 21 April 1971; Ford to External, 22, 24 April 1971; External to Moscow, 3 May 1971; A.E. Ritchie interview, 15 March 1988
82 Trinity College Archives, George Ignatieff Papers, MSS 144, vol. 7, Moscow Visit file, telegram, Moscow to Ottawa, 22 May 1971. Trudeau's wife, Margaret, also had advice from the department's officers on the spouses of Soviet leaders, most of whom came from not-far-distant peasant backgrounds, were interested in trying to appear elegant without much success, and were at heart kindly disposed. DEA Records, file 20-CDA-9-Trudeau-Eur, Ford to External, 27 April 1971. Her difficulties in the USSR arose not from the wives but from men who plied her with food, saying, 'We like our women *big*.' Trudeau, *Beyond Reason,* 106
83 DEA Records, file 20-CDA-9-Trudeau-Eur, A.E. Ritchie to Ivan Head, 14 May 1971
84 Ritchie interview
85 Conversation with Pierre Trudeau, 30 June 1988
86 DEA Records, file 20-CDA-9-Trudeau-Eur, Ford to External, 21 May 1971; Ritchie interview. To the USSR, Canada itself was not a country of great concern, except for the impact of its actions on NATO and the United States. In view of this significance, the Canadian action in reducing its NATO force 'was seen as contributing to larger objectives concerning the Atlantic Alliance.' L.E. Sarty, ' "A Handshake Across the Pole": Canadian-Soviet Relations During the Era of Detente,' a paper presented at the Canada-Soviet Relations Conference, Elora, Ont., Sept. 1987, 8
87 Ignatieff Papers, MSS 144, vol. 7, Moscow visit file, telegram, Moscow to Ottawa, 22 May 1971
88 Ritchie interview; Trudeau conversation; Barney Danson interview, 10 Nov.

1987; H.F. Heald, 'Scanning the Broad Implications of Sharp's trip to Soviet Union,' *International Perspectives* (Jan. – Feb. 1974): 17

89 Danson interview; Heald, 'Implications,' 17

90 DEA Records, file 20-CDA-9-Trudeau-Eur, Ford to External, 20, 23, 24 May 1971. For an account of Canada-Soviet trade relations see Ian Drummond, 'Canadian-Soviet Trade and Competition from the Revolution to 1986,' paper presented at the Canada-Soviet Relations Conference, Elora, Ont., Sept. 1987. For useful tables see A. Balawyder, ed., *Canadian-Soviet Relations 1939–80* (Oakville, Ont. 1981), 141ff.

91 Ford, *Our Man*, 118. The text is in *External Affairs* (June 1971), 228–9.

92 John Halstead interview, 20–23 Feb. 1988; Murray Goldblatt, 'Canadian-Soviet Bilateral Ties,' *International Perspectives* (Jan. – Feb. 1972), 21

93 Ford interview

94 *Winnipeg Free Press*, 21 May 1971

95 Jamieson Papers, Diary, nd [June 1971], 37–8. Barney Danson, Trudeau's parliamentary secretary and in the USSR on this trip, remembered the surprise with which he learned of the Protocol. Interview

96 *CAR 1971*, 259

97 Quoted in *Montreal Star*, 30 Oct. 1971

98 Ford, *Our Man*, 136. Ford notes that when President Nixon visited Moscow in May 1972, the statement of 'Basic Principles' he signed with Kosygin went so far beyond the Canada-USSR agreement that if Canada had signed such an agreement, 'it would have evoked a sharp outcry in Washington,' 271.

99 See *Toronto Telegram*, 31 May 1971; *Canadian Commentator* 15 (June 1971): 3; *Ottawa Journal*, 25 May 1971; *Winnipeg Free Press*, 2 June 1971; House of Commons, *Debates*, 28 May 1971, 6185ff. See also Zink's book *Trudeaucracy* (Toronto 1972), 78ff. For an academic response see J. Petryshyn, 'The "Ethnic Question" in Canadian-Soviet Relations: The Case of the Ukrainian-Canadians,' paper presented at the Canada-Soviet Relations Conference, Elora, Ont., Sept. 1987, 29.

100 Christina Newman, 'Our Heroes on the Russian Front,' *Maclean's* (Aug. 1971), 31

101 Press Conference, 28 May 1971, cited in Thordarson, *Trudeau*, 68–9. The Soviets put substantial emphasis on the Protocol. See Sarty, 'Canadian-Soviet Relations,' 15ff. For a Soviet view see the quote from Sergei Molochkov of the USA and Canada Institute in W. McGrath, 'Canada in the Soviet Mirror, 1964–1974,' in J.L. Black and Norman Hillmer, eds., *Nearly Neighbours: Canada and the Soviet Union: From Cold War to Detente and Beyond* (Kingston 1989), 94.

102 DEA Records, file 20-CDA-9-Trudeau-Eur, Ford to External, 14 June 1971. By 1976, External Affairs noted that the size of the Soviet 'community' in Canada had grown to 188 from 140 two years before; of that number, sixty-four were accredited as diplomats in Ottawa. Jamieson Papers, vol. 325, 'Bilateral Discussions: Scenario,' for visit 14–17 July 1976. On 9 February 1978 Ottawa expelled

eleven Soviet nationals for engaging in 'inadmissable activities.' More followed in 1980. House of Commons, *Debates,* 9 Feb. 1978, 2697ff

103 Ford interview, 15–16 Oct. 1987; Jamieson Papers, vol. 329, file H1-5, 'Soviet Leadership,' 29 Sept. 1971

104 Briefing books on the Kosygin visit are in Jamieson Papers, vol. 329, file H1-2.

105 Paul Martin, *A Very Public Life,* II: *So Many Worlds* (Toronto 1985), 672–3; *Globe and Mail,* 19 Oct. 1971; *Montreal Star,* 19 Oct. 1971

106 *External Affairs,* Nov. 1971, 406; *Globe and Mail,* 23 Oct. 1971

107 *Winnipeg Free Press,* 21 Oct. 1971

108 House of Commons, *Debates,* 21 Oct. 1971, 8881–4

109 DEA Records, file 20-USA-9-Nixon, Trudeau to Nixon, 2 Nov. 1971; NA, Martin Papers, vol. 358, Kosygin file, 'Notes on Informal Discussions between Chairman Kosygin and Paul Martin,' nd

110 Jamieson Papers, vol. 329, file H1-5, 'General Exchanges Agreement,' 5 Oct. 1971. John Halstead negotiated the agreement. See his paper, 'The Place of Europe in Trudeau's Foreign Policy,' Augsburg Universitat, FRG, Feb. 1988, 16.

111 Confidential source

112 Jamieson Papers, vol. 329, file H1-5, 'Soviet Foreign Policy,' 27 Sept. 1971

113 A point made by Sarty, 'Canadian-Soviet Relations,' 19

114 See McGrath, 'Soviet Mirror,' 96, and Anne Hillmer, 'Sport in Diplomacy,' *Bout de Papier* 5 (2) 1985: 25–6.

115 DEA Records, file 20-USA-9-Nixon, 'Canadian-Soviet Relations: Evolution and Implications,' 6 April 1972

116 Ibid., file 20-1-1-1, External to NATO Delegation, 18 Nov. 1974

117 Halstead, 'Place of Europe,' 16

118 Confidential interview. Peyton Lyon has argued that Canada played a 'Cold Warrior' role at the CSCE. See his letter in *Bout de Papier* 6 (1988): 6, and his article in Robert Spencer, ed., *Canada and the Conference on Security and Cooperation in Europe* (Toronto 1984), 110ff.

119 Trudeau took advantage of the Helsinki Summit to settle a Soviet-Canadian North Atlantic fishing dispute. He walked over to Brezhnev's seat, put his case, and the general secretary picked up the telephone, made a call, and it was all but done. Ivan Head negotiated the terms with Viktor Sukhedrov, the Soviet interpreter at major meetings and a Foreign Ministry Canadian specialist; it was, Head said, 'the hardest time I ever had,' in part because the Russians kept asking, 'How can you control captains at sea?' Conversation with Trudeau; conversation with Ivan Head, 30 June 1988

120 Confidential interviews; John Halstead interview, 20–23 Feb. 1988. See also Spencer, ed., *Canada,* and G.G. Crean, 'European Security – The CSCE Final Act ...' *Behind the Headlines* 35 (1976).

121 Documents on DEA Records, file 20-1-1-1

122 A useful summary of MBFR is John Toogood, 'Conventional Arms Control Negotiations in Europe,' Background Paper, Canadian Institute for International Peace and Security, April 1986.

123 DEA Records, file 20-CDA-9-Trudeau-Eur, 'Possible Visit by Prime Minister to Soviet Union,' 8 Aug. 1977; Ford to Gotlieb, 9 May 1977

124 A Canadian assessment of the situation in early 1978 is in ibid., file 20-1-1-1, 'Alliance Study on East-West Relations,' prepared by Ambassador Ford for NATO.

125 Jimmy Carter, *Keeping Faith: Memoirs of a President* (New York 1982), 472–7. Robert Ford, the Canadian ambassador in the USSR at the time, suggests in his memoirs that he proposed an Olympic boycott to the U.S. ambassador the day after the Afghan invasion. Ford, *Our Man*, 320

126 DEA Records, file 20-1-1-1, Moscow to External, 28 Jan. 1980; Delworth to USSEA, 21 March 1980; confidential interview

127 Jeffrey Simpson, *Discipline of Power: The Conservative Interlude and the Liberal Restoration* (Toronto 1980), 330ff

128 Confidential interview

129 Ibid.; DEA Records, file 20-1-1-1, 'The Prospects for East-West Relations in the Light of the Afghan and Polish Situations,' 26 Nov. 1980, by Ambassador Ford

130 Ibid., Memo for prime minister, 5 Feb. 1982; confidential interview

131 Jamieson Papers, vol. 377, 'Brief for Meeting with Mr. Gromyko,' 1979

132 Yakovlev would say, 'there's no proletariat in Africa,' and add that he was not a Marxist but an Engels man. William Hooper interview, 21 April 1988

133 Bill Keller, 'Moscow's Other Mastermind,' *New York Times Magazine,* 19 Feb. 1989, 42; Gromyko, *Memories,* 228

134 John Newhouse, 'Annals of Diplomacy,' *The New Yorker* (2 Jan. 1989), 39; Michael MccGwire, *Military Objectives in Soviet Foreign Policy* (Washington 1987), 296ff

135 Based on a conversation with Trudeau; Peter Roberts interview, 5 Feb. 1988; Georgi Arbatov interview, 25 Feb. 1988; confidential interview; *Toronto Star,* 22 April 1968

136 Eugene Whelan, *Whelan* (Toronto 1986), 255ff

137 Keller, 'Mastermind,' 31

138 SCEAND, 17 May 1983, 7ff. Earlier Georgi Arbatov, director of the Institute of U.S. and Canadian Studies, had appeared before the committee. Ibid., 23 Feb. 1982

139 Conversation with Trudeau. Gorbachev had been picked as a possible successor by Robert A.D. Ford as early as 1979. DEA Records, file 20-1-1-1, Paris to External, 6 Dec. 1982

140 Keller, 'Mastermind,' 42

141 Ford, *Our Man*, 106

142 A point made by J.A. McCordick, 11 April 1988

143 Conversation with Trudeau

CHAPTER 8: *The Clark Interregnum*

1 Confidential interview

2 MacDonald told the story of meeting the old Chief on the day she was appointed

secretary of state for external affairs. 'This is a very exciting day, Mr Diefenbaker,' she said. The reply: 'They should never have made you Foreign Minister –
it's all wrong – all wrong.' Flora MacDonald, 'Ministers, Civil Servants, and
Parliamentary Democracy,' *Dalhousie Review* 60 (summer 1980): 239

3 Confidential interview; David Cox, 'Leadership Change and Innovation in Canadian Foreign Policy: The 1979 Progressive Conservative Government,' *International Journal* 37 (autumn 1982): 560

4 Confidential interview

5 Her views were likely somewhat different from those discovered by an opinion
survey published by External Affairs in August 1979: *Perspectives on World
Affairs and Foreign Policy Issues,* 36. Canadians' major priorities were protection
of oceans and resources, negotiation of trade treaties, peacekeeping, arms
control, and NATO. The Commonwealth, aid, and the promotion of human
rights, all subjects of concern to the minister, were well down the list.

6 Copies of MacDonald's briefing books are in NA, Donald Jamieson Papers, vol.
377.

7 Confidential interviews

8 MacDonald, 'Ministers, Civil Servants,' passim

9 Confidential interview

10 Ibid.; Warner Troyer, *200 Days: Joe Clark in Power* (Toronto 1980), 112ff; *CAR
1971,* 251ff, discounts MacDonald's role.

11 Confidential interview; Jeffrey Simpson, *Discipline of Power: The Conservative
Interlude and the Liberal Restoration* (Toronto 1980), 132

12 NA, Paul Martin Papers, documents on vol. 385, and Diary, 19 Sept. 1976 and
following

13 Confidential interview

14 Simpson, *Discipline,* 182ff. Tokyo Summit briefing books are in Jamieson Papers,
vol. 377.

15 Confidential interviews

16 Allan MacEachen interview, 14 March 1988

17 Barney Danson interview, 10 Nov. 1987

18 See Howard Stanislawski, 'Canadian Corporations and their Middle East Interests,' in David Taras and David Goldberg, eds., *The Domestic Battleground:
Canada and the Arab-Israeli Conflict* (Montreal 1989), 68ff. All the articles in
this collection are useful. See also David Taras, 'Canada and the Arab-Israeli
Conflict: A Study of the Yom Kippur War and the Domestic Political Environment' (PHD thesis, University of Toronto, 1983). Taras's chapter title conveys
the mood: 'From Passivity to Politics: Canadian Jewry and the Yom Kippur
War.'

19 House of Commons, *Debates,* 8 May 1975, 5583

20 The struggle is detailed in Jamieson Papers, vol. 351, Boycott file. See especially
Memo to minister, 20 May 1976; Stoner to minister, 28 June 1976; Robinson
to minister, 4 Oct. 1976; External Affairs memo, 5 Oct. 1976, which detail the
efforts to produce an acceptable policy.

21 House of Commons, *Debates,* 21 Oct. 1976, 302ff

22 *CAR 1977,* 270–1

23 Jamieson Papers, vol. 351, Boycott file, Memo, Roberts to Jim Coutts, 17 April 1978

24 John Roberts interview, 3 Dec. 1987

25 Jack Horner interview, 28 Sept. 1987

26 Jamieson Papers, vol. 351, External Affairs general file, Jacques Roy memoranda for file, 31 Oct. and 28 Nov. 1978. See David Taras and Daphne Gottlieb Taras, 'The Canadian Media, Domestic Interest Groups and Middle East Reporting,' *International Journal* 42 (summer 1987): 543ff.

27 On the Canada-Israel Committee see Taras, 'Canada,' 187ff.

28 Roberts interview

29 See Howard Adelman, 'Clark and the Canadian Embassy in Israel,' *Middle East Focus* (March 1980): 13.

30 Roberts recalled that Trudeau would rhyme off the appointments Jews had received – chief justice, cabinet ministers, deputy ministers – for which there had been scant thanks. Interview

31 Confidential interview

32 Jamieson Papers, vol. 351, External Affairs general file, Jacques Roy to prime minister, 29 Nov. 1978

33 Ibid., MacEachen to Roberts, 26 Jan. 1979

34 Adelman, 'Embassy,' 6

35 Confidential interview; Adelman, 'Embassy,' 9, 14–15; G. Takach, 'Clark and the Jerusalem Embassy Affair: Initiative and Constraint in Canadian Foreign Policy' (MA thesis, Carleton University, 1980), 37ff.

36 Jim Gillies interview, 2 March 1988

37 John Kirton and Blair Dimock, 'Domestic Access to Government in the Canadian Foreign Policy Process 1968–82,' *International Journal* 39 (winter 1983–4), 78. See also E.A. Goodman, *Life of the Party: The Memoirs of Eddie Goodman* (Toronto 1988), 216–17.

38 Simpson, *Discipline,* 146

39 Takach, 'Clark,' 73

40 Roberts recalled that, while he had opposed the idea of the embassy move, he did not express that belief to his constituents. He 'probably' tried to play down the issue. Interview, 3 Dec. 1987

41 Takach, 'Clark,' 45; Simpson, *Discipline,* 153

42 Gillies interview; confidential interview

43 Quoted in Simpson, *Discipline,* 154

44 Takach, 'Clark,' 79

45 See Taras and Taras, 'Media,' 548ff.

46 Confidential interview

47 Confidential interviews; Takach, 'Clark,' 84ff. Simpson, *Discipline,* 155, attributes the idea of Stanfield to MacDonald.

48 *CAR 1979,* 232

49 Martin Papers, Diary, 12, 15 Oct. 1979
50 *CAR 1979,* 233–4
51 Adelman, 'Embassy,' 17–18
52 Troyer, *200 Days,* 68
53 House of Commons, *Debates,* 29 Oct. 1979, 695
54 Confidential interview
55 D. Dewitt and J. Kirton, 'Canada and Mideast Realities,' *International Perspectives* (Jan.–Feb. 1984): 19–20. See also articles by Peyton Lyon and Paul Noble in ibid. (Sept.–Oct. 1982) and (Sept.–Oct. 1983), respectively.
56 Trudeau quoted on DEA Records, file 47-CDA-1, Carter memo, 17 March 1976
57 Ibid., documents on file 47-1-1
58 Ibid., D.S. McPhail to Hartling, 11 Feb. 1980
59 DEA, Statements and Speeches no. 79/12, Address by Flora MacDonald to UN Conference on Refugees, 20 July 1979
60 DEA Records, file 47-1-1, McPhail to Hartling, 11 Feb. 1980
61 Ibid., J.R. McLachlan to Dr D.C. Wilson, 7 April 1980
62 MacDonald, 'Ministers, Civil Servants,' 241
63 A shrewd and perceptive early evaluation of the Iranian revolution is Michael Shenstone's memorandum of 9 March 1979, 'After Iran – A Sense of Uncertainty,' in Jamieson Papers, vol. 351, External Affairs general file. See also Roger Lucy, 'Letters from the Iranian Revolution,' *Bout de Papier* 6 (4) (1986): 31ff, which details the evacuation of Canadian civilians from Iran early in 1979.
64 Confidential interview; confidential source
65 Confidential interview. See inter alia, 'Kenneth Taylor's Press Conference After Escape of "the Six" from Iran,' *International Perspectives* (Jan.–Feb. 1980): 5ff; Jean Pelletier and Claude Adams, *The Canadian Caper* (Markham, Ont. 1981).
66 DEA Records, file 20-1-2-1980, Roy to Goldschlag, 31 Oct. 1977; Policy Planning Secretariat to Gotlieb, 6, 13 Jan. 1978; Trinity College Archives, University of Toronto, George Ignatieff Papers, MSS 144, box 6, Ignatieff to W.H. Barton, 8 Aug. 1969, and reply, 9 Sept. 1969. See also D. Madar and D. Stairs, 'Alone on Killers' Row: The Policy Analysis Group and the Department of External Affairs,' *International Journal* 32 (autumn 1977): 727ff; G.A.H. Pearson, 'Order Out of Chaos? Some Reflections on Foreign Policy Planning in Canada,' ibid., 764, and Don Page, 'Some Thoughts on Policy Planning in External Affairs,' *Bout de Papier* 6 (4) (1986): 16.
67 H.B. Robinson interview, 5 Aug. 1987; G.A.H. Pearson interview, 30 Aug. 1988; Page, 'Some Thoughts,' 17
68 Robinson interview
69 DEA Records, file 20-1-2-1980, Roy to Goldschlag, 31 Oct. 1977; Policy Planning Secretariat to Gotlieb, 6, 13 Jan. 1978
70 Ibid., Touraine Foreign Policy Colloquium minutes, 21–22 Sept. 1978; 'Foreign Policy for the 1980s: Substance and Process,' notes for Committee of Deputy Ministers on Foreign Policy, 27 Oct. 1978; Jamieson Papers, vol. 377, 'Current

Issues in Canadian Foreign Policy,' 4 June 1979, vol. II, K1, 'Planning for the Future: Canadian Foreign Policy in the 1980s'

71 DEA Records, file 20-1-2-1980, Policy Planning Secretariat to USSEA, 14 Dec. 1978; V.G.T[urner], to Taylor, 15 July 1980; confidential interview

72 Confidential interview; SCEAND, MacDonald testimony, 25 Oct. 1979, 13–15; NA, Jules Léger Papers, vol. 3, file 3, 'Canada in a Changing World,' 18 Oct. 1979; Cox, 'Leadership,' 370ff

73 Léger Papers, 'Canada in a Changing World,' 35

74 DEA Records, file 20-1-2-1980, V.G.T[urner]. to Sullivan, 31 July 1980; confidential interview; Flora MacDonald in House of Commons, Debates, 21 April 1980, 215–16; SCEAND, Appendix EAND-5, 10 June 1980

75 Ignatieff Papers, MSS 144, box 6, Ignatieff to Mitchell Sharp, 11 Nov. 1969

76 Confidential interview

77 Ibid.

78 Christina McCall-Newman, Grits: An Intimate Portrait of the Liberal Party (Toronto 1982), 215

79 SCEAND, App. J, 24 March 1970, 47; Cf Globe and Mail, 17 July 1970

80 SCEAND, 7 April 1970, 15

81 H.B. Robinson Papers, Memo to Allan MacEachen, 28 Aug. 1975

82 Globe and Mail, 16 March 1970. Some serving and retired officers looked to the arrival of Edgar Ritchie as undersecretary to 'change the air' and 'relieve many tensions.' Ignatieff Papers, MSS 144, box 2, Ignatieff to J.W. Holmes, 28 Jan., 10 Feb. 1970, and reply, 4 Feb. 1970

83 Confidential interview

84 Ibid. See Colin Campbell, Governments under Stress (Toronto 1983), chap. 4.

85 A.S. McGill, 'A Study of the Role of the Department of External Affairs in the Government of Canada' (mimeo, DEA 1976), II, 18

86 J.H. Warren interview, 8 Dec. 1987

87 'Integration of the Government's External Operations,' External Affairs (Oct. 1970): 354–5. See also A.E. Ritchie's testimony to SCEAND, 5 May 1971, 5ff; Arthur Andrew, 'The Diplomat and the Manager,' International Journal 30 (winter 1974–5): 50ff; and W.M. Dobell, 'Interdepartmental Management in External Affairs,' Canadian Public Administration 21 (spring 1978): 88ff.

88 SCEAND, App. T, 5 May 1971, 31. For detail on the bureaux see DEA Reference Paper no. 69, 'The Department of External Affairs,' July 1973.

89 Ignatieff Papers, MSS 144, box 6, E.A. Ritchie printed letter, 26 March 1971

90 Robinson interview; confidential interview

91 Confidential source

92 Ibid.

93 Confidential interview; Ignatieff Papers, MSS 239, box 2, Ritchie printed letter, 19 May 1972

94 Ibid., MSS 144, box 6, Ignatieff to Ritchie, 30 May 1972, and reply, 6 June 1972

95 John Roberts interview, 3 Dec. 1987

96 Confidential interview
97 Ibid. Generally see John Kirton, 'Foreign Policy Decision-making in the Trudeau Government: Promise and Performance,' *International Journal* 33 (spring 1978): 289ff.
98 *Calgary Herald,* 28 April 1976
99 Confidential interview
100 Ignatieff Papers, MSS 144, box 6, Ritchie to Ignatieff, 6 June 1972
101 See Geoffrey Stevens in *Globe and Mail,* 1 May 1976.
102 Confidential interview. Ritchie argued that consultation on ambassadorships 'has proven to be a considerable protection against the nomination of "duds" by particular departments.' Ignatieff Papers, MSS 144, box 6, Ritchie to Ignatieff, 6 June 1972
103 Confidential interview
104 DEA, Statements and Speeches, no. 79/11, 15 Feb. 1979. Note that Colin Campbell and George Szablowski, *The Super-Bureaucrats: Structure and Behaviour in Central Agencies* (Toronto 1979), does not even mention DEA in its index!
105 See Office of the Prime Minister, Press release, 21 March 1980; DEA, Background Paper on Foreign Service Consolidation, 12 March 1980; and SCEAND, 28 Oct. 1980, 5–6.
106 Confidential interviews
107 Ibid.
108 App. EAND-26 to SCEAND, 9 April 1981, 10
109 Confidential interview
110 Ibid. For academic grumbling see Cranford Pratt, 'Canadian Foreign Policy: Bias to Business,' *International Perspectives* (Nov.–Dec. 1982), 3ff.
111 Office of the Prime Minister, Press release, 28 Aug. 1980; *Report of the Royal Commission on Conditions of Foreign Service* (Ottawa 1980); SCEAND, 4, 5, 6, 20 May 1982
112 Quoted in James Eayrs, 'Canada's Department of External Affairs,' a paper prepared for the Royal Commission on Conditions of Foreign Service
113 SCEAND, 28 Oct. 1980, 2–3
114 Ibid., 24 March 1982, 7
115 Gordon Osbaldeston, 'Reorganizing Canada's Department of External Affairs,' *International Journal* 37 (summer 1982): 453ff; DEA, *Annual Report 1982–3*
116 Confidential interviews
117 Ibid.
118 Ibid.
119 Ibid.
120 Ibid.
121 DEA, *Annual Report 1983–84,* vii
122 House of Commons, *Debates,* 22 June 1983, 26697ff
123 Confidential interview
124 'Reorganized Again,' *Bout de Papier* 3 (3) (Sept. 1983): 1
125 Confidential interview

CHAPTER 9: *The Trudeau Government and the Armed Forces*

1 See Robert Bothwell, Ian Drummond, and John English, *Canada since 1945*, 2nd ed. (Toronto 1989), 351–5. Uncontrollable outlays included payments to persons and provinces and debt service.

2 Donald Macdonald interview, 5 April 1988. Macdonald soon discovered that the freeze put constraints on DND's ability to operate. See DHist, 80/225, f 45, Notes for an Address by Hon. D.S. Macdonald, 28 April 1971.

3 SCEAND, 18 Feb. 1971, 9–10

4 General James Tedlie interview, 5 March 1988

5 Assessments of the military role include Brian Cuthbertson, *Canadian Military Independence in the Age of the Superpowers* (Toronto 1977), chap. 8; Dan Loomis, *Not Much Glory: Quelling the F.L.Q.* (Toronto 1984); and J. Dendy, 'The Canadian Armed Forces and the "October Crisis" of 1970: A Historian's Perspective,' paper presented to XIVth International Military History Colloquium, Montreal, Aug. 1988.

6 Douglas Bland, *The Administration of Defence Policy in Canada, 1947 to 1985* (Kingston 1987), 58

7 See DHist, Office of Chief of the Defence Staff Records, Canadian Defence Policy Rationale, E.B. Armstrong to J.F. Anderson, 23 July 1970; J.C. Arnell and J. Anderson, 'Program Management in the Department of National Defence,' *Canadian Defence Quarterly* (autumn 1971): 31–3; J.F. Anderson interview, 7 Aug. 1987.

8 Douglas Bland, 'Controlling the Defence Policy Process in Canada: White Papers on Defence and Bureaucratic Politics in the Department of National Defence,' *Defence Analysis* (spring 1989)

9 Bland, *Administration*, 59

10 NA, Donald Jamieson Papers, Diary, nd [June 1971?]

11 Macdonald interview; confidential interview

12 Jamieson Papers, Diary, 11 Dec. 1971, recounting events in late July

13 Confidential source

14 E.J. Benson, Macdonald's successor, told SCEAND on 3 March 1972, 9–10, that 'Canada will not quickly forget that it was asked at short notice by the host country to withdraw from the United Nations Emergency Force.'

15 *Defence in the 70s: White Paper on Defence* (Ottawa 1971)

16 *Commentator* 15 (Sept. 1971): 16; *Globe and Mail,* 28 Aug. 1971. See also Colin Gray, 'Defence in the Seventies: A White Paper for all Seasons,' *Canadian Defence Quarterly* 1 (spring 1972): 30ff.

17 *Commentator* 15 (May 1971): 8–9

18 Anderson interview

19 In 'Defence in the 70s: Comments on the White Paper,' *Behind the Headlines* 30 (Oct. 1971): 12–13

20 Confidential source

21 *Defence in the 70s,* 42–3

22 NA, DND Records, vol. 18189, category VII, book 1, Major D.L. Bland submission to Task Force on Review of Unification of the Canadian Forces, 1979
23 Bland, *Administration*, 61
24 Confidential interview
25 Ibid.
26 Ibid.
27 Admiral D.A. Collins interview, 24 Sept. 1987
28 *CAR 1969*, 267–8. Admiral Richard Leir noted that the air force had pressed for this, arguing that naval air was unnecessary in a unified force. Interview, 24 Sept. 1987
29 General J.A. Dextraze interview, 12 April 1988
30 Confidential interview
31 SCEAND, 3 March 1972, 10. See also *Canadian Forces Bulletin* 7 (March 1972).
32 DHist, 84/32, f 1, *Report to the Minister of National Defence on the Management of Defence in Canada*, July 1972
33 Confidential interview
34 An accessible chart of the MRG proposal is in Bland, *Administration*, 74. See also DHist, Jean Pariseau Papers, file NDHQ s1/85 Study Report, 'The Impact of Integration, Unification and Restructuring on the Functions and Structure of National Defence Headquarters,' 31 July 1985.
35 See the mid-1972 letter from Cloutier, Dextraze, and General Sharp, as printed in 'Impact'; Colonel P.D. Manson, 'The Restructuring of National Defence Headquarters – 1972–3,' *Canadian Defence Quarterly* 3 (winter 1973–4): 11. For a critique see Colonels J.E. Neelin and L.M. Pederson, 'The Administrative Structure of the Canadian Armed Forces: Over-Centralized, Overly Staff-Ridden,' *Canadian Defence Quarterly* 4 (autumn 1974): 33ff.
36 For an assessment of the state of the forces see John Hasek, *The Disarming of Canada* (Toronto 1987).
37 These points were made in DND Records, vol. 18190, category VII, book 5, Paul Hellyer submission to task force, 29 Nov. 1979.
38 DHist, 80/225, f 31, 'Conditions of Service Study on Chain of Command Presented to Conditions of Service Steering Committee,' 16 June 1972
39 Ibid., f 49, pt I, Mobile Command Brief to Unification Task Force, Annex D, 26 Oct. 1979. A more positive view is in ibid., 78/165, 'Integration/Unification: Ten Years Later,' 27 Jan. 1978, a paper signed by the chief of the defence staff and the deputy minister.
40 See Jean Pariseau and Serge Bernier, *Les Canadiens français et le bilinguisme dans les Forces armées canadiennes*, tome 1 (Ottawa 1987), chap. 8, and Armand Letellier, *DND Language Reform: Staffing the Bilingualism Programs 1967–77* (Ottawa 1987), 6ff.
41 NA, L.B. Pearson Papers, N 4, vol. 32, file 043.6 Pers. and Conf., Cadieux to prime minister, 27 Nov. 1967
42 Ibid., Lalonde to prime minister, 5 Dec. 1967
43 Ibid., Pitfield to prime minister, 1 March 1968

44 *Toronto Star,* 13 April 1968
45 *CAR 1968,* 281. See J.V. Allard, *Mémoires du Général Jean V. Allard* (Boucher-ville, Que. 1985), chap 14, and Letellier, *DND Language Reform* chap. 6, which details infighting behind the Cadieux announcement.
46 *Report of the Royal Commission on Bilingualism and Biculturalism,* vol. 3 (Ottawa 1969), 301
47 Ibid., 329
48 General François Richard interview, 8 Oct. 1987
49 Pariseau Papers, 'Policy on Bilingualism for the Canadian Armed Forces October 1969,' Annex D to CDS Minutes 20/69, 12 Nov. 1969; ibid., Summary of Memorandum from CP to CDSAC, 27 Oct. 1970
50 Ibid., Presentation to CDS for Consideration and Approval at CDS Advisory Committee, 28 Oct. 1970
51 House of Commons, *Debates,* 23 June 1970, 8487ff
52 Pariseau Papers, Briefing to CDSAC by DGOM on Plan and Goals to Increase Biculturalism in the Canadian Armed Forces, Annex B to Summary Record of CDSAC 19/71 Meeting, 17 Nov. 1971. See also Letellier, *DND Language Reform,* chap 9.
53 DHist, General J.V. Allard Papers, 84/126, dossier 45, Allard to Macdonald, 30 Aug. 1971
54 Confidential interview. See also Letellier, *DND Language Reform,* chap. 13ff.
55 Dextraze interview
56 SCEAND, Appendix EAND-12 to minutes, 15 Nov. 1977
57 DHist, Réal Boissonnault Papers, 84/331, vol. 105, 'Officers Participation in CF'
58 Admiral Leir interview; Admiral Bobbie Murdoch interview, 25 Sept. 1987
59 General Allan MacKenzie interview, 28 Sept. 1987
60 General W.C. Leonard interview, 15 June 1989
61 Max Yalden interview, 5 Aug. 1988
62 Dextraze, 'From the Chief of the Defence Staff to all Members of the Canadian Forces,' Nov. 1972
63 Dextraze interview
64 MacKenzie interview
65 Leir interview
66 DND Records, vol. 18183, file 1150-9, General P.A. Neatby to chair, Unification Task Force, 17 Sept. 1979
67 Léo Cadieux interview, 9 Dec. 1987
68 Collins interview
69 *Globe and Mail,* 8 April 1988
70 DND Records, vol. 18188, category V, pt 10, General D.G. Loomis, 'Canadian Forces Unification in Retrospect,' 1977
71 'Integration/Unification: Ten Years Later,' 16
72 Confidential interview
73 See his testimony to SCEAND, 27 Nov. 1979, 4ff.
74 'How Bureaucrats Beat McKinnon,' Montreal *Gazette,* 27 Dec. 1980

75 On senior officers' attitudes to the task force see Bland, *Administration,* 122.
76 DND Records, vol. 18189, category VI, pt 3, 'Content Analysis of Public Briefs'
77 Ibid., vol. 18190, category VII, book 5, Arnell submission
78 Ibid., vol. 18188, category V, file 1g, Fyffe to members, 1 Feb. 1980
79 See Pariseau Papers, file NDHQ S1/85, 'The Impact of Integration,' 136ff. For Fyffe's comments on the outcome see SCEAND, 2 Dec. 1980, 1ff.
80 Pariseau Papers, 84/331, vol. 5b, 'Results of the Review Group on the Report of the Task Force on Unification,' 31 Aug. 1980; Bland, *Administration,* 122–3
81 PCO, Cabinet minutes, 20 May 1969. On the DDH280 program see S.M. Davis, 'Naval Procurement, 1950 to 1965,' and J.W. Arsenault, 'The DDH280 Program: A Case Study of Governmental Expenditure Decision-Making,' in D. Haglund, ed., *Canada's Defence Industrial Base* (Kingston 1988).
82 Confidential interview
83 A useful analysis of the navy's condition in 1983 is 'Canada's Maritime Defence,' Report of the Subcommittee on National Defence of the Senate Standing Committee on Foreign Affairs, May 1983.
84 DHist, 'Integration/Unification,' 23–4
85 McGeorge Bundy, *Danger and Survival* (New York 1988), 567, on Schmidt's mistrustful attitude
86 Colonel H.G. Summers, Jr, 'A Bankrupt Military Strategy,' *Atlantic,* June 1989, 40
87 DEA, Statements and Speeches, 75/19. See R.B. Byers, 'Defence and Foreign Policy in the 1970s: The Demise of the Trudeau Doctrine,' *International Journal* 33 (spring 1978): 312ff.
88 Dextraze interview
89 See DHist, 80/225, f 4, L.E. Davies, 'Department of National Defence Funding Problems 1964 to 1979,' 7 May 1979; Dan Middlemiss, 'The Pitfalls of Formula Funding,' *Canadian Defence Quarterly* 12 (winter 1982–3): 24ff.
90 Dextraze address to Conference of Defence Associations, 16 Jan. 1976, printed in L.R. Stewart, ed., *Defence Policy: Selected Documents 1964–81* (Kingston 1982), 53ff.
91 NA, Eddie Goldenberg Papers, vol. 30, External Policy and Defence file, MacLean to Osbaldeston, 8 May 1975, Osbaldeston to Chrétien, 9 May 1975, and MacLean to Osbaldeston, 12 May 1975
92 D.W. Middlemiss and J. Sokolsky, *Canadian Defence Decisions and Determinants* (Toronto 1989), 39
93 House of Commons, *Debates,* 27 Nov. 1975, 9205ff; C.J. Marshall, 'Canada's Forces Take Stock in Defence Structure Review,' *International Perspectives* (Jan.–Feb. 1976): 26ff
94 *Report of the Auditor General of Canada to the House of Commons Fiscal Year Ended 31 March 1984* (Ottawa 1984), 12
95 Confidential interview
96 Despite this success, by 1978–9 the defence share of the budget was only 10.9

per cent. Jamieson Papers, vol. 359, Main Estimates, chart. In 1980 constant dollars, defence received $5.3 billion in 1970, $5.2 billion in 1975, $5.7 billion in 1980, and $7.2 billion in 1984. Table 1, *NATO Review* (Dec. 1987). The 3 per cent increase of 1977 saved DND from the worst of Trudeau's budget-slashing exercise, costing it only $300 million. See Richard Gwyn, *Northern Magus* (Toronto 1980), 325–7; Barney Danson interview, 10 Nov. 1987.

97 Danson interview
98 Data in D.W. Middlemiss, 'Economic Considerations in the Development of the Canadian Navy since 1945,' in W.A.B. Douglas, ed., *RCN in Transition 1910–1985* (Vancouver 1988), 257
99 Confidential interview
100 Ibid.
101 *Report of Auditor General,* 12ff.
102 In 1979 Norway agreed that Canada could pre-position supplies for one company of infantry for thirty days. DHist, 80/587, P.T. Alward, 'Defence Review – Summer 1980,' Aug. 1980
103 Leir interview
104 Jamieson Papers, vol. 359, NATO file, Danson to Trudeau, 25 Nov. 1977; Joseph Jockel, 'Canada's Other Commitment: The Defence of Norway,' *International Perspectives* (Jan.–Feb. 1980); Danson interview; confidential interview
105 Morris Zaslow, *The Northward Expansion of Canada 1914–67* (Toronto 1988), 354. On the navy's non-role in the Arctic see Harriet Critchley, 'Canadian Naval Responsibilities in the Arctic,' in Douglas, ed. *RCN,* 280ff.
106 See, eg, Office of Chief of the Defence Staff Records, Programmes General, vol. 6, 'Canadian Armed Forces Program: Proposed Activities or Sub-activities,' 28 April 1970.
107 J.L. Granatstein, comment on 'Defence in the 70s,' *Behind the Headlines* (Oct. 1971): 11–12
108 Confidential interview
109 See Robert Cameron in Toronto *Telegram,* 8 April 1970.
110 SCEAND, 22 May 1973, 37ff
111 As late as 1984 the auditor general reported that 'Canadian comprehensive exercises to test Canadian defence objectives ... are not imposed regularly ... The only large scale exercises ... are NATO exercises, and these are not designed specifically for Canadian purposes.' *Report,* 12–19
112 See Defence Minister Richardson before SCEAND, 27 Feb. 1975, 11. See also Colin Gray, 'Canada and NORAD: A Study in Strategy,' *Behind the Headlines* 31 (June 1972), which argues that renewal of NORAD had ceased to matter.
113 MacKenzie interview. For the rationale for the creation of the command see SCEAND, 27 May 1975, 15ff.
114 Confidential interview
115 Jamieson Papers, vol. 354, Cabinet Briefing file, Memo for minister, 17 Nov. 1975

116 The best account is Frank Boyd, Jr, 'The Politics of Canadian Defence Procurement: The New Fighter Aircraft Decision,' in Haglund, *Canada's Defence Industrial Base,* 137ff.
117 Cost in 1988 dollars was $4.94 billion. *Toronto Star,* 30 Sept. 1987
118 See Captain M.D. McKay, 'The Fighter Debate: Past Lessons – Present Options,' *Canadian Defence Quarterly* 7 (autumn 1977): 24ff.
119 MacKenzie interview
120 Confidential interview
121 Boyd, 'Politics,' 147–8
122 See 'How Bureaucrats Beat McKinnon.'
123 Brigadier-General P.D. Manson, 'The CF-18 Hornet: Canada's New Fighter Aircraft,' *Canadian Defence Quarterly* 10 (summer 1980): 14ff.
124 See *CAR 1980,* 218ff. On offsets see *Toronto Star,* 30 Sept. 1987.
125 Confidential interview; MacKenzie interview; Danson interview; Jack Horner interview, 28 Sept. 1987
126 Cited in Boyd, 'Politics,' 149
127 *Report of the Auditor General,* 12–24ff
128 Middlemiss and Sokolsky, *Canadian Defence,* 41. On air-defence generally see John Anderson, 'Canada and the Modernization of North American Air Defense,' in D.G. Haglund and J.J. Sokolsky, *The U.S.-Canada Security Relationship* (Boulder, Col. 1989), 167ff.
129 R.B. Byers, 'Canada and Maritime Defence: Past Problems, Future Challenges,' in Douglas, ed., *RCN,* 320

CHAPTER 10: *Canada and the Third World*

1 Statistics Canada, *Canada's International Investment Position, 1926 to 1967* (Ottawa 1971), 68–71
2 Statistics Canada, *Canada's International Investment Position, 1981–84* (Ottawa 1986), 14; this figure was up from 53 per cent in 1977.
3 Ibid.; Edgar J. Dosman, 'Hemispheric Relations in the 1980s: A Perspective from Canada,' *Journal of Canadian Studies* 19(1) (Winter 1984–5): 47
4 Figures are from *CYB 1973,* 759–61.
5 This point is also made in Roger Ehrhardt, 'Canada's Response to the Call for a New International Economic Order' (MA thesis, University of Alberta, 1977), 52.
6 Figures from *CYB 1988,* 21-36-41
7 Peyton Lyon, 'North-South Summitry,' *Policy Options* 2 (May–June 1981): 8
8 Confidential interview
9 PMO press release, 29 May 1968
10 Text of the speech is in C. David Crenna, ed., *Pierre Elliott Trudeau: Lifting the Shadow of War* (Edmonton 1987), 7.
11 Ibid., 7–8

12 DEA, Statements and Speeches 75/6, speeech by Trudeau at the Mansion House, 13 March 1975
13 See the discussion in Lyon, 'North-South Summitry.'
14 See Glenn P. Jenkins, *Costs and Consequences of the New Protectionism: The Case of Canada's Clothing Sector* (Ottawa 1980).
15 Quoted in Peter Dobell, *Canada's Search for New Roles: Foreign Policy in the Trudeau Era* (London and Toronto 1972), 103
16 André Donneur, 'La pénétration économique en Amérique latine,' *Etudes internationales* 14(1) (mars 1983): 83
17 Quoted in J.C.M. Ogelsby, 'Canada and Latin America,' in P.V. Lyon and Tareq Ismael, eds., *Canada and the Third World* (Toronto 1976), 181–2; Dobell, *Canada's Search for New Roles*, 115–16
18 DEA press release, 24 Jan. 1969, with accompanying preliminary report of the ministerial mission to Latin America. Discussions included the topics of the United Nations, Rhodesia, and the possibility that Canada might join the Organization of American States (OAS).
19 *CYB 1975*, 729–32
20 Dobell, *Canada's Search for New Roles*, 116
21 Confidential interview
22 *CYB 1975*, 729–32; *CYB 1988*, 21-36-41
23 *CAR 1973*, 268
24 *CAR 1979*, 212–13
25 *CAR 1980*, 199–200
26 *CAR 1981*, 302; *CAR 1982*, 174
27 Dosman, 'Hemispheric Relations,' 48
28 See Ogelsby, 'Canada and Latin America,' 188–90, for a discussion of non-governmental organizations with an interest in Latin America.
29 There has been a declining trend in imports from Venezuela, which fell in 1986 to a mere $516 million. Figures are taken from *CYB 1988* 21–38.
30 A Trudeau visit in 1976 concentrated on this issue. *CAR 1976*, 322.
31 *CAR 1977*, 266
32 The fate of Brazilian Traction, later Brascan, Canada's largest investment in Brazil, is summarized in Duncan McDowall, *The Light: Brazilian Traction, Light and Power Limited* (Toronto 1988), 394–9. On later developments see Donneur, 'Pénétration économique,' 97.
33 Robert Bothwell, *Nucleus: The History of Atomic Energy of Canada Limited* (Toronto 1988), 390
34 Ibid., 436
35 *CAR 1979*, 252–3
36 *CAR 1982*, 172–3
37 The position of churches in and on foreign policy is thoughtfully considered in Robert O. Matthews, 'The Churches and Foreign Policy,' *International Perspectives* (Jan.–Feb. 1983): 18–21.

38 *CAR 1973,* 270–1
39 Matthews, 'The Churches and Foreign Policy,' 21
40 Ibid., 271–2
41 Gerald Dirks, *Canada's Refugee Policy: Indifference or Opportunism?* (Montreal and London 1977), 247
42 *CAR 1976,* 325
43 Donneur, 'Pénétration économique,' 88
44 On this point see John Foster, 'The Cauldron: A Report on Latin America,' *This Magazine* 14(6) (dec. 1980): 8–14; see also External Affairs, *Statements and Speeches,* statement to the SCEAND by Allan MacEachen on his return from a trip to Colombia and Central America, 10 May 1984; see also the 'Response to the Inter Church Committee on Human Rights in Latin America Brief of October 1983, Canadian Policy on Central America,' prepared by the Caribbean and Central American Relations Division of DEA, March 1984.
45 Amazingly, the Immigration Act did not rate a mention in either the 1976 or 1977 *CAR.* See also *CYB 1976–77,* 1980; Charlotte Gray, 'Refugee Run-Around,' *Saturday Night* (Jan. 1989): 11–13, notes that in 1976 immigration officials warned the Liberal government that their act's provisions 'were open to abuse, since they were too cumbersome.'
46 The Inter Church Committee brief of November 1983 urged the Canadian government to single out Nicaragua for specially favourable treatment as a 'core country' recipient of Canadian aid.
47 See Dosman, 'Hemispheric Relations in the 1980s,' 44.
48 Dobell, *Canada's Search for New Roles,* 118–19
49 *CAR 1972,* 303–4
50 Richard Gwyn, *Northern Magus: Pierre Trudeau and Canadians* (Toronto 1980), 307
51 Ibid., 303n
52 Thirteen years later Trudeau's Cuban tour was still being remembered, and denounced, in Canada. Peter Foster, 'Forever Fidel,' *Saturday Night* (Jan. 1989): 14–16
53 Quoted in ibid., 14
54 *CAR 1976,* 324; George Radwanski, *Trudeau* (Toronto 1979), 185
55 See Dosman, 'Hemispheric Relations in the 1980s,' 45–6, on Canada's Caribbean connection.
56 On this point see C.P. Onwumere, 'At Arm's Length: Canada's Relations with West Africa' (MA thesis, McMaster University, 1978), 61–75. Arnold Smith noted that as early as February 1968, 'key officials' in the Department of External Affairs were drawing parallels between Biafra and Quebec. Arnold Smith with Clyde Sanger, *Stitches in Time: The Commonwealth in World Politics* (Toronto 1981), 90
57 *CAR 1969,* 253–7
58 Anthony Westell, *Paradox: Trudeau as Prime Minister* (Scarborough 1972), 197–8

59 Smith, *Stitches in Time,* 100–1, recalls that Trudeau had him present his own view of the situation in Biafra to Canadian MPs in October 1968: charges of genocide, Smith testified, were 'entirely unfounded.' The Nigerians had previously done the same, and Sharp reported 'no evidence of genocide' to his colleagues. PCO, Cabinet minutes, 10 Oct. 1968

60 Confidential interview

61 Westell, *Paradox,* 199: the government paid $1 million; two days after it made the grant, the civil war finally ended.

62 Tanzania recognized Biafra.

63 *CYB 1973* gives the trade figures for 1968–71. For the period 1968–70, South Africa accounted for more than half of Canada's exports to Africa. In 1971 imports from Nigeria, an oil-producing state, surpassed those from South Africa for the first time. See also Brian Tennyson, 'Canada-South Africa Economic Relations,' *South Africa International* (Jan. 1981): 147–59.

64 See Brian Tennyson, *Canadian Relations with South Africa* (Washington 1982). Not all Canadians disapproved of South Africa; the proportion of those approving varies according to one's view as to whether Canada is an inherently racist, or blindly profit-seeking, society.

65 Clarence Redekop, 'Commerce over Conscience: The Trudeau Government and South Africa, 1968–84,' *Journal of Canadian Studies* 19(4) (winter 1984–5): 84–5

66 The text of the black paper may be found in SCEAND, 1 June 1971.

67 Ibid., 86

68 See Toronto Committee for the Liberation of Southern Africa (TCLSAC), 'Liberals and Liberation,' in *This Magazine* 9 (2) (May–June 1975): 21–5.

69 Peter C. Dobell, *Canada in World Affairs, 1971–1973* (Toronto 1985), 200

70 Redekop, 'Commerce over Conscience,' 95

71 Tennyson, 'Canada-South Africa Economic Relations,' 153

72 Linda Freeman, 'Canada and Africa in the 1970s,' *International Journal* 35 (4) (autumn 1980): 813; Tennyson, 'Canada-South Africa Economic Relations,' 151

73 *CYB 1988,* 21–37, 21–39: figures for 1982–4

74 Freeman, 'Canada and Africa,' 819–20

75 See Paul Martin, *A Very Public Life,* vol. 2: *So Many Worlds* (Toronto 1985), 530–1.

76 This had an acronym, UDI, for Unilateral Declaration of Independence.

77 Canada had been consulted at an earlier stage of Rhodesia's existence. J.D.B. Miller, *Survey of Commonwealth Affairs: Problems of Expansion and Attrition, 1953–1969* (London 1974), 184

78 The idea was expressed in an acronym, NIBMAR: No Independence Before Majority Rule.

79 Martin, *Public Life,* 531

80 Miller, *Survey,* 206

81 Smith, *Stitches in Time.* 285

82 Confidential interview
83 Peter Boehm, 'Canada and the Modern Commonwealth: The Approaches of Lester Pearson and Pierre Trudeau,' *Bulletin of Canadian Studies* 3 (Jan. 1979): 28
84 Ivan Head interview, 6 Aug. 1987
85 Smith, *Stitches in Time,* 285–6
86 Miller, *Survey,* 238
87 Ibid., 239; Boehm, 'Canada and the Modern Commonwealth,' 27; confidential source
88 Smith, *Stitches in Time,* 285
89 Richard Crossman, *The Diaries of a Cabinet Minister,* vol. 3 (London 1977), 326
90 See, for example, the critical appraisal in *CAR 1971,* 267.
91 PCO, Cabinet minutes, 21 Jan. 1969; Smith, *Stitches in Time,* 53
92 Margaret Doxey, 'Economic Sanctions: Past Lessons and the Case of Rhodesia,' *Behind the Headlines* 27 (Jan. 1968)
93 Margaret Doxey, 'Human Rights and Canadian Foreign Policy,' *Behind the Headlines* 37 (June 1979): 14
94 William Young, ed., *Paul Martin: The London Diaries, 1974–1979* (Ottawa 1988), 208–9
95 Canada sent observers, but no soldiers, to the election that ratified the black majority government of Robert Mugabe. Smith, *Stitches in Time,* 241
96 *CAR 1979,* 225–7
97 Young, ed., *Paul Martin: London Diaries,* 82, 94, comments on Heath's inflexible personality.
98 Head interview
99 W.A. Wilson, 'Behind Trudeau's Singapore Triumph,' *Montreal Star,* 30 Jan. 1971
100 Ibid.
101 The British Conservative government had announced the day after its election victory in 1970 that it was resuming arms shipments to South Africa.
102 *CAR 1971,* 269
103 Wilson, 'Behind Trudeau's Singapore Triumph'
104 Ibid.
105 Smith, *Stitches in Time,* 292–3
106 Ibid., 272
107 Quoted in Boehm, 'Canada and the Modern Commonwealth,' 28, 30
108 Smith, *Stitches in Time,* 273
109 Head interview
110 Confidential interview
111 Smith, *Stitches in Time,* 273
112 Ibid., 257; Dirks, *Canada's Refugee Policy,* 238–44
113 Canada was criticized for taking the cream of the crop of the Asians, but it is also true that it selected from the bottom of the heap, accepting 400 or 500

who could not even meet the medical requirements for immigration. Confidential interview
114 Dobell, CIWA, 203–4
115 Amin did send his foreign minister with instructions to read out a diatribe against the British. The minister, in fear of his life should he fail in his mission, was permitted to do so. See *CAR 1973*, 263.
116 Thomas N. Franck, *Nation against Nation* (New York 1985), 185
117 Ibid., 229; Smith, *Stitches in Time*, 260–1
118 Head interview
119 On Trudeau in the 1977 conference see Young, ed., *Paul Martin: London Diaries*, 264, 267.

CHAPTER 11: *The Kindness of Strangers*

1 Robert O. Matthews, 'Canada's Relations with Africa,' *International Journal* 30 (3) (summer 1975): 559, table 2
2 Ibid., 559–60
3 Alan Phillips, 'Mister Clean is a Canadian,' *Maclean's,* Nov. 1971, 50, 52; Sally Lindsay, 'Global Pollution II: Cleanup Man Maurice Strong,' *Saturday Review,* 7 Aug. 1971, 43–4, 47
4 A brief history of CIDA may be found in Paul Gérin-Lajoie, 'CIDA in a Changing Government Organization,' *Canadian Public Administration* 15 (1) (spring 1972): 46–58; see also P.J. Appavoo, 'The Small State as Donor' (PHD thesis, University of Toronto, 1989), 160ff.
6 Quoted in Kim Richard Nossal, *The Politics of Canadian Foreign Policy* (Scarborough, Ont. 1985), 107
7 Ibid., 110
8 Quoted in *CAR 1968*, 274
9 Roger Ehrhardt, *Canadian Development Assistance to Bangladesh* (Ottawa 1983), 110
10 *CAR 1969*, 258–9
11 G.K. Helleiner, 'Canada and the New International Economic Order,' *Canadian Public Policy* 2 (3) (summer 1976): 456
12 Roger Young, *Canadian Development Assistance to Tanzania* (Ottawa 1983), 5–11. African socialism, Tanzanian style, was proclaimed in the 'Arusha declaration' of 1967 and implemented through 'ujamaa,' which in practice seems to have meant villagization. Villagization, in turn, meant the concentration of the rural population in settlements determined by the central government.
13 Quoted in Peter C. Dobell, *Canada in World Affairs, 1971–1973* (Toronto 1985), 330
14 Ibid., 338
15 Young, *Canadian Development Assistance to Tanzania*, 104
16 Ibid., 53–5, 107

17 Ibid., 75–7. The bakery was featured on both CBC and CTV news programs during 1979.
18 Ibid., 76, citing a United Nations study of the project
19 For an example of a mid-1970s audit see Bothwell, *Nucleus,* chap. 12.
20 Ehrhardt, *Canadian Development Assistance to Bangladesh,* 110
21 Ibid., 112
22 Ibid., 116
23 North-South Institute, *North-South Relations/1980–85: Priorities for Canadian Policy* (Ottawa 1980), 64
24 Ibid., 117
25 Young, *Canadian Development Assistance to Tanzania,* 18–19
26 North-South Institute, *North-South Relations/1980–85,* 66–7
27 Kurt Waldheim, *In the Eye of the Storm* (London 1985), 124
28 *CYB 1988,* 21–38, 21–40
29 *CYB 1972, 1975, 1977, 1979, 1981, 1985.* See also Barrie Morrison, 'Canada and South Asia,' in P.V. Lyon and Tareq Ismael, eds., *Canada and the Third World* (Toronto 1976), 49.
30 See the discussion in Douglas Ross, *In the Interests of Peace* (Toronto 1984), 252–3.
31 These developments are described in Bothwell, *Nucleus,* 350–71.
32 Dobell, *World Affairs,* 178–9
33 Ehrhardt, *Canadian Development Assistance to Bangladesh,* 4–20
34 Ibid., 80ff
35 Morrison, 'Canada and South Asia,' 43
36 Bothwell, *Nucleus,* 428–9
37 David Hart, *Nuclear Power in India: A Comparative Analysis* (London 1983), 56–9
38 The flavour of the nuclear industry's incredulity at the government's action is best caught in W. MacOwam, 'The Nuclear Industry and the NPT: A Canadian View,' in David DeWitt, ed., *Nuclear Non-Proliferation and Global Security* (London 1987), 145–6; for an Indian point of view see Ashok Kapur, 'The Future of the NPT: A View from the Indian Sub-continent,' ibid., 201, in which he writes, inter alia, of 'the tendency (and hypocrisy) of vertical proliferators and the crypto-nuclear states (such as Canada).'
39 Morrison accuses the Department of External Affairs of intellectual inadequacy and policy incoherence in its dealings with India. Fragmentation of responsibility for external relations was in his mind a major problem. 'Canada and South Asia,' 54–5
40 See Arkady N. Shevchenko, *Breaking with Moscow* (New York 1985), 131–2, 220–9. Shevchenko, a UN undersecretary who defected from the USSR, was especially critical about the role and function of Soviet employees.
41 Thomas M. Franck, *Nation against Nation: What Happened to the UN Dream and What the US Can Do About It* (New York 1985), 131–3
42 Waldheim, *In the Eye of the Storm,* 190

43 Ibid., 237
44 *Statements and Speeches*, 76/24, Jamieson at the UN, 29 Sept. 1976
45 Daniel P. Moynihan, *A Dangerous Place* (New York 1978)
46 Franck, *Nation against Nation*, 224ff
47 George Davidson interview, New York City, May 1988
48 Quoted in Dobell, *World Affairs*, 247
49 Ibid., 248–9
50 Confidential interview
51 Franck, *Nation against Nation*, 131–3
52 Shevchenko, *Breaking with Moscow*, 223
53 DEA, press release, 5 Nov. 1976
54 Franck, *Nation against Nation*, 237
55 Ibid., 199–200
56 Foremost among these was the United Nations Conference on Trade and Development (UNCTAD). Meeting first in 1964, UNCTAD was one of the earliest theatres for economic confrontation between the developing world and the industrialized West. See J. King Gordon, 'The New International Economic Order,' *Behind the Headlines* 34 (5) (1976).
57 Trudeau's Calgary speech in 1968 had taken up this point.
58 See the brief discussion in Gordon, 'The New International Economic Order,' 13–14; confidential interview.
59 This change is reflected in their trade statistics with Canada. See *CYB 1988*, 21-37-8. One interesting comparison is that imports from the non-communist parts of China, Hong Kong, and Taiwan dwarfed imports from the People's Republic in 1984 by roughly $2.1 billion to $0.3 billion.
60 Allan MacEachen, 'Opportunity Missed: The Conference on International Economic Cooperation,' mimeo, nd [1987]
61 Quoted in ibid., 4
62 As Mitchell Sharp put it to the House of Commons in March 1974, in 1972 aid to developing countries approximated roughly twice their annual oil-import bill; in 1974 it would be approximately half that bill: 'Oil and the Less-developed Countries,' in A. Blanchette, *Canadian Foreign Policy 1966–1976: Selected Speeches and Documents* (Toronto 1980), 251.
63 These are of course only a few of its points, but they are the main ones as far as Canada was concerned. United Nations General Assembly, sixth special session, agenda item 7, A/RES/3201 (S-VI), 9 May 1974
64 A point made by MacEachen in his 'Opportunity Missed,' 3.
65 External Affairs Library, DEA, 'New Economic Order: Selected Documents' (Ottawa, May 1975); Aid and Development Division, 'Development and International Cooperation: The New International Economic Order,' 30 Sept. 1974
66 As Allan Gotlieb and C.M. Dalfen put in a paper in 1972, under Trudeau, 'Canadian representatives have worked keenly for the adoption of stringent rules of international law in areas of national interest to Canada.' Gotlieb and Dalfen, 'National Jurisdiction and International Responsibility: New Canadian

Apporoaches to International Law,' Oct. 1972, mimeo. The problem was to get developing nations, in their own self-interest, to support such rules.

67 Korea and Singapore, and possibly India and Mexico were cited.

68 This is what MacEachen, who succeeded Sharp as minister in August 1974, meant by Canada's 'serious reservations' to the NIEO; 'Opportunity Missed,' 5. See also Roger Ehrhardt, 'Canada's Response to the Call for a New International Economic Order' (MA thesis, University of Alberta, 1977), 34–5, where the pro-NIEO rhetoric of Canadian ministers is contrasted with Canada's hesitations and reservations.

69 Quoted in Ehrhardt, 'Canada's Response,' 62

70 A point recognized by Ehrhardt. Ibid., 43

71 See Ivan Head, *Le Monde*, 2 Sept. 1974, and criticism of it in Robert Bothwell, Ian Drummond, and John English, *Canada since 1945*, 1st ed. (Toronto 1981), 376.

72 MacEachen, 'Opportunity Missed,' 5

73 Ibid., 6

74 Ibid., 8

75 On this and other points we are most grateful to Chad T. Reimer for allowing us to use his graduate essay for York University, 'Canada and the Conference on International Economic Cooperation (CIEC): The International and Domestic Dialogue on Energy.'

76 Ibid.

77 MacEachen statement to SCEAND, 6 Nov. 1975, quoted in ibid., 14

78 Ibid., 23–4, citing the high-pricing inclinations of the Department of Energy, Mines and Resources, which saw rising prices as a ticket to the development of Canada's northern oil and gas.

79 Ibid., 28–9

80 Ibid., 39

81 This narrative closely follows MacEachen's account, ibid., 7–20.

82 North-South Institute, *North-South Relations/1980–85*, 34–5

83 See ibid., 53–73.

84 *CAR 1980*, 204–5

85 Ibid., 211–12

86 Quoted in ibid., 215

87 *CAR 1981*, 322–3

88 Ibid., 331–2

CHAPTER 12: *Welcome to the 1980s*

1 Compare Alan Fotheringham, *Malice in Blunderland, or How the Grits Stole Christmas* (Toronto 1982), 65–7, for an acerbic description of Trudeau's western representation.

2 An example of mild foreboding is Gerald Wright, 'Canada and the Reagan

administration,' *International Journal* 36 (1) (winter 1980–1):228–36, which prophesied 'an imperfect fit' between Trudeau's policies and Reagan's.

3 More to the point, Reagan came into office in California as an agent of right-wing change against an entrenched liberal establishment; in that sense his agenda would closely resemble that of Canadian conservatives in the 1980s. Garry Wills, *Reagan's America: Innocents at Home* (New York 1987), 299

4 Don Munton, 'Reagan, Canada and the Common Environment,' *International Perspectives* (May – June 1982):3–6; see also Charles Doran, *Forgotten Partnership: US-Canada Relations Today* (Baltimore 1984), 204–5. Doran takes a relatively optimistic view of the controversy's prospects; but prospects are still mixed.

5 *CAR 1984*, 154–5

6 Polls showed that as many Canadians thought relations with the United States under Reagan would worsen (28 per cent) as thought they would improve (27 per cent): Munton, 'Reagan, Canada and the Common Environment,' 3. As Munton observed, this was a notable contrast with Canadian anticipations of Carter, when twice as many believed relations would improve (50 per cent) as thought they would deteriorate (25 per cent).

7 See *CAR 1980*, 198–9.

8 See Jonathan Moore, ed., *The Campaign for President: 1980 in Retrospect* (Cambridge, Mass. 1981), 10. See also Laurence I. Barrett, *Gambling with History: Reagan in the White House* (New York 1984), 206.

9 House of Commons, *Debates*, 28 Oct. 1980, 4186–90

10 See Mary Joy Aitken, 'National Energy Program: A Case Study of State Energy Policy' (MA thesis, University of Alberta, 1983), 86.

11 Ibid., chap. 3

12 Bruce Doern and Glen Toner, *The Politics of Energy: The Development and Implementation of the NEP* (Toronto 1985), 50–1

13 See the perceptive discussion in Doran, *Forgotten Partnership*, 212–13.

14 Annemarie Jacomy-Millette, 'David et Goliath: L'équilibre fragile des relations énergetiques canado-américaines à l'aube de la création de Petro-Canada,' *Revue des Etudes internationales* 13 (4) (Déc. 1982):645

15 See the Gallup polls quoted in Mildred Schwartz, *The Environment for Policy-Making in Canada and the United States* (Montreal 1981), 124–5. The key poll asked Canadians whether they would accept 'a big reduction in our standard of living' to 'buy back a majority control ... of US companies in Canada.' In 1975, 58 per cent said yes, in 1977, 41 per cent, and in 1978, 52 per cent.

16 See the trend line in P.V. Lyon and Brian Tomlin, *Canada as an International Actor* (Toronto 1979), 104. Negative feelings on American investment peaked in 1973, and declined thereafter.

17 Doran, *Forgotten Partnership*, 219

18 P. Terzian, *OPEC: The Inside Story* (London 1985), 291

19 Eric Hirst, 'Energy Conservation,' in *McGraw-Hill Encyclopedia of Energy*, 2nd ed. (New York 1981), 3

20 Doern and Toner, *Politics of Energy*, 37–9, make the point that Peter Foster's analysis of the bureaucratic origins of the NEP is too simplistic. See Foster, *The Sorcerer's Apprentices: Canada's Super-Bureaucrats and the Energy Mess* (Toronto 1982), 56–63, 127–51.

21 Foster, *Sorcerer's Apprentices*, 159–60, claims that External Affairs was 'livid' at the inadequate consultation it had received. Russ McKinney, then the assistant undersecretary for economic affairs, recalled very firmly that DEA had not been consulted. McKinney interview, Ottawa, 12 April 1988

22 Jimmy Carter, *Keeping Faith: Memoirs of a President* (New York 1982), 472–7

23 MacGuigan was forty-nine years old in 1980. He had taken over Martin's old riding when the latter was appointed to the Senate in 1968, and had warmed the Liberal back benches through three intervening elections until the 1980 election precipitated him into the ministry.

24 Confidential interview

25 Ibid.

26 Doern and Toner, *Politics of Energy*, 34–5; see also Edward Wonder, 'The US Government Response to the Canadian National Energy Program,' *Canadian Public Policy* 8 (supplement 1982):480–97, especially 485.

27 Wonder, 'US Government Response'

28 Confidential interview

29 See Neil Crawford, 'Canada's Energy Dilemma: The Viewpoint of the Government of Alberta,' in Carl Fry, ed., *Energy Development in Canada: The Political, Economic and Continental Dimensions* (Provo, Utah 1981), 133–55.

30 Gallup Poll results and André quoted in Doern and Toner, *Politics of Energy*, 107–8

31 *CAR 1980*, 328–9; see also Kenneth Norrie, 'Canada's National Energy Program – A Call for Perspective,' in Fry, ed., *Energy Development*.

32 The choice of Canada was personal to Reagan; he was the first American president since Kennedy to make his initial visit to Canada. Confidential interview

33 Patrick Gossage, *Close to the Charisma: My Years between the Press and Pierre Elliott Trudeau* (Toronto 1986), 226–7

34 Haig's note was not the first; Richard Smith, the chargé in Ottawa, had sent one two weeks before: S. Clarkson, *Canada and the Reagan Challenge: Crisis and Adjustment*, 2nd ed. (Toronto 1985), 29. David Crane, *Controlling Interest: The Canadian Gas and Oil Stakes* (Toronto 1982), 25, called the U.S. note 'extraordinary' but 'unsurprising.' See Wonder, 'US Government Response,' 485, for activity in Washington.

35 Ibid.

36 Confidential interview

37 Later he would not get the chance. After a stormy interlude in the State Department, where he was 'barely on speaking terms' with Haig, Rashish departed

government service. Barry Rubin, *Secrets of State: The State Department and the Struggle over U.S. Foreign Policy* (New York 1985), 207–8

38 Wonder, 'US Government Response,' 484
39 Doern and Toner, *Politics of Energy*, 107; Wonder, 'US Government Response,' 487
40 Alan M. Rugman, *Outward Bound: Canadian Direct Investment in the United States* (Toronto 1987), 8
41 Ibid., 6–7
42 Doern and Toner, *Politics of Energy*, 111
43 Ibid., 503
44 Joseph Jockel, 'The Canada-United States Relationship after the Third Round: The Emergence of Semi-institutionalized Management,' *International Journal* 40 (4) (autumn 1985):695–6
45 Confidential interview
46 Ibid.
47 Ibid.; L. Martin, *Presidents and Prime Ministers* (Toronto 1982), 281, refers obliquely to this discussion
48 Jockel, 'Canada-United States Relationship,' 695
49 Quoted in B. Powe, *The Solitary Outlaw* (Toronto 1987), 128–9
50 Quoted in Alexander Haig, *Caveat: Realism, Reagan and Foreign Policy* (New York 1984), 66
51 Haig's memoirs show that Canada surfaced while he was considering such questions as the U.S. grain embargo, the Anglo-Argentinian war, and a European-Soviet gas pipeline: *Caveat*, 111–12, 280, 304. On Haig and Canadian troops, confidential interview
52 Clarkson, *Canada and the Reagan Challenge*, 30; on FIRA see James M. Spence, 'FIRA: A Decade of Evolution,' in James M. Spence and W.P. Rosenfeld, eds., *Foreign Investment Review Law in Canada* (Toronto 1984), 317.
53 Clarkson, *Canada and the Reagan Challenge*, 31
54 Confidential interview
55 Ibid., 33; observations on Reagan at the summit from confidential interviews; Wonder, 'US Government Response,' 481
56 *CAR 1981*, 273–4, 276; confidential interview
57 The heavily publicized departure of the U.S. embassy chef – because, some said, he would not cook hamburgers – helped set the tone for Robinson's press coverage. See Andrew Malcolm, *The Canadians* (Markham, Ont. 1985), 181–2.
58 Martin, *Presidents and Prime Ministers*, 283–4, lists Robinson's gaffes, real and presumed
59 Doran, *Forgotten Partnership*, 234
60 Confidential interview; Clarkson, *Canada and the Reagan Challenge*, 35
61 Quoted in Clarkson, *Canada and the Reagan Challenge*, 37, from an interview in *Fortune*
62 Gary C. Hufbauer and Abdrew J. Samet, 'US Response to Canadian Initiatives

for Sectoral Trade Liberalization, 1983–84,' in D. Stairs and G.R. Winham, eds., *The Politics of Canada's Economic Relationship with the United States* (Toronto 1985), 205 n29

63 R.G.M. Sultan, 'Canada's Recent Experience in the Repatriation of American Capital,' *Canadian Public Policy* 8 (supplement 1982):501

64 Doran, *Forgotten Partnership,* 236–7

65 Terzian, OPEC, 293, 311

66 Ibid., 39

67 Ibid., 40

68 Doran, *Forgotten Partnership,* 246–8

69 Nigel D. Bankes, Constance D. Hunt, and J. Owen Saunders, 'Energy and Natural Resources: The Canadian Constitutional Framework,' in Mark Krasnick, ed., *Case Studies in the Division of Powers* (Toronto 1986), especially 82–7

70 Ibid., 41–2

71 Canadian Institute of Public Opinion, *The Gallup Report,* 24 Feb. 1982

72 Figures from table 1.14, Gross domestic product by industry at factor cost in 1981 prices, *Canadian Economic Observer: Historical Statistical Supplement, 1987* (Ottawa 1988), 25

73 Economic figures from *CYB 1988,* 23–2, 23–3

74 Even Robert Sherrill, whose work was heavily critical of U.S. oil companies, took a jaundiced view of the workings of the NEP. *Oil Follies* (New York 1983), 480–1

75 Lubor J. Zink, 'The Unpenetrated Problem of Pierre Trudeau,' *National Review,* 25 June 1982, 751–6. Years before, Zink had published some of his newspaper columns in a small book, *Trudeaucracy* (Toronto 1972), that rehearsed many of the same themes.

76 Donald Regan, *For the Record* (New York 1988), 258–9

77 Ibid.

78 As Allan Gotlieb later put it ('Canada and the Economic Summits,' unpublished lecture, University of Toronto, 1987, 5), 'Canada tended to be the odd man out in the emerging consensus on how the domestic economy functioned best. Discussions at the Summits were often difficult. Canada found that the other Summit members saw it clearly as a developed industrialized nation. Accordingly, they saw some of Canada's more interventionist and restrictive policies as a legacy of its self-perception as a weaker, or in the broadest sense, a developing nation.'

79 Confidential interview

80 Ibid.

81 Ibid.

82 Figures are in *CYB 1988,* 21–8.

83 Ibid., 23–2

84 Ibid., 21–9

85 See M.M. Hart, 'Reviewing Canada's Trade Policies: Canada-United States Sec-

toral Free Trade: Two Essays on the Government's Trade Policy Review,' *Institute for Research on Public Policy* (April 1984):7–8.

86 Ibid., 9–11
87 See A.R. Moroz and K.J. Back, 'Prospects for a Canada-United States Bilateral Free Trade Agreement: The Other Side of the Fence,' *International Journal* 36 (4) (autumn 1981), which outlines the Canadian sectoral preference, as opposed to across-the-board reductions.
88 Ibid., 14–5
89 Ibid., 18
90 Ibid.
91 *CAR 1983,* 146–7
92 Carl Beigie and James K. Stewart, 'New Pressures, Old Constraints: Canada-United States Relations in the 1980s,' *Behind the Headlines* 40 (6) (1983):4
93 Hufbauer and Samet, 'United States Responses to Canadian Initiatives,' 182
94 Confidential interview
95 Rubin, *Secrets of State,* 212
96 Gossage, *Close to the Charisma,* 250–1
97 See House of Commons, *Debates,* 27 Oct. 1983, 28380ff, for Trudeau's view of consultation before the invasion, and SCEAND, 22 Nov. 1983, 100:7–10, for MacEachen's comments.
98 Confidential interview
99 *CAR 1983,* 150–1
100 See David Cox, 'Trends in Continental Defence: A Canadian Perspective,' *CIIPS Occasional Papers* 2 (Ottawa 1986).
101 David Cox, 'The Cruise Testing Agreement,' *International Perspectives* (July – Aug. 1983):3–5
102 Cruises were estimated to cost $2 million each: Charles Morris, *Iron Destinies, Lost Opportunities: The Arms Race between the US and the USSR, 1945–1987* (New York 1988), 339–40.
103 SCEAND, 15 March 1983, 83:29
104 Confidential interview
105 Ibid.
106 Ron Graham, 'The View from Washington,' *Saturday Night,* April 1984, 55
107 Confidential interview
108 *CAR 1984,* 138–9; SCEAND, 22 March 1984, 4:5–6
109 *CAR 1984,* 139

CHAPTER 13: *The Constitution and Other Follies*

1 When, in 1977, Canadians were asked whether they preferred their country to remain a monarchy or to become a republic, 59 per cent plumped for the monarchy – up from 50 per cent in 1968. Canadian Institute of Public Opinion, *The Gallup Report,* 5 Nov. 1977. While anglophones were 74 per cent in favour

of the monarchy, and 17 per cent against, francophones were 49 per cent against and 31 per cent in favour.

2 The Foreign Office and the Department of External Affairs handle their bilateral business through small national desks; by the mid-1970s, informed observers considered the most important part of Anglo-Canadian diplomatic contacts to be multilateral rather than bilateral. Terry Empson interview, 7 Oct. 1987

3 John Holmes, 'The Anglo-Canadian Neurosis,' in his *The Better Part of Valour: Essays on Canadian Diplomacy* (Toronto 1970), 103–12

4 One such occasion occurred in February 1979, when Trudeau flew to England to tell the Queen of his nomination of Ed Schreyer to be governor general of Canada. That day, Allan MacEachen, the deputy prime minister, presided over a regular meeting of the cabinet. At a certain point in the proceedings, the story goes, MacEachen told his colleagues that the prime minister would have finished lunch with Her Majesty, and would have given her the name of the individual he proposed for governor general. MacEachen then paused, and stared down at the table. 'Well, aren't you going to tell us who it is?' MacEachen looked up, picked up a card, turned it over and read: 'Edward Schreyer.' He put the card down, and resumed his silent contemplation. The same voice interrupted: 'Is this a joke?'

5 A revelation Jenkins made in his memoirs. *Globe and Mail,* 21 Feb. 1989

6 Statistics Canada, *Historical Statistics of Canada,* 2nd ed. (Ottawa 1983); *CYB 1988*

7 Nigel Lawson, 'Public Images and Perceptions,' in Peter Lyon, ed., *Britain and Canada: Survey of a Changing Relationship* (London 1976), 180

8 Quoted in Richard Gwyn, *The 49th Paradox: Canada in North America* (Toronto 1985), 186; *The Times,* Alan Hamilton, 'London Diary,' 12 Feb. 1981

9 Confidential interview; Charles Ritchie, *Storm Signals: More Undiplomatic Diaries, 1962–71* (Toronto 1983), 99, diary entry for 22 Jan. 1968

10 Of the older generation, Harold Macmillan, prime minister from 1957 to 1963, had actually lived in Canada for a time in the 1920s. Lord Beaverbrook, the enfant terrible of British politics and publishing, was of course Canadian, and sentimentally attached to his birthplace.

11 Lawson, 'Public Images and Perceptions,' 178, notes that twice the proportion of Britons wishing to emigrate in 1971 preferred Australia to Canada.

12 Ritchie, *Storm Signals,* 114, entry for 30 Aug. 1968

13 Confidential interview

14 Ritchie, *Storm Signals,* 146, entry for 31 Jan. 1971

15 Confidential source

16 Confidential interview; Terry Empson interview

17 James Callaghan, *Time and Chance* (London 1987), 421

18 Confidential interview

19 William Young, ed., *Paul Martin: The London Diaries, 1975–1979* (Ottawa 1988), 232, entry for 21 March 1977

20 Ibid.

21 Nevertheless, normal and cordial contacts persisted. When Gilles Loiselle became Quebec's agent-general in London in 1977, he made a point of informing the high commissioner that he would behave normally and appropriately. Some time later difficulties arose concerning the proper role of the high commission in arranging visits to the Foreign Office by PQ ministers. NA, Paul Martin Papers, Diary, 7, 20, and 27 Sept. 1977

22 Ibid., 11 May 1977

23 In July 1977, for example, Liberal voting intentions were expressed by 51 per cent of those polled, compared to 27 per cent for the Conservatives. Ibid., 20 July 1977

24 See Robert Bothwell, Ian Drummond, and John English, *Canada since 1945,* 1st ed. (Toronto 1981), 398.

25 Martin Papers, Diary, 22 Nov. 1977

26 Ibid., vol. 388, 'Heads of Post Meeting, Brussels, December 10/11, 1976'

27 Paul Martin interview

28 Bothwell, Drummond, and English, *Canada since 1945,* 398; *CAR 1979,* 88–90

29 The *Globe and Mail,* which was in a prolonged anti-Trudeau, decentralizing phase, was particularly forward with the expiry-of-mandate argument. *CAR 1979,* 89

30 Martin Papers, vol. 388, notes on Heads of Post meeting, Brussels, 10–11 Dec. 1976

31 As Tom Enders put it, during the period after November 1976 the Canadian government became less active in creating barriers to cross-border exchanges. Interview, New York City, 13 May 1988

32 Karl Kaiser interview, Bonn, 20 Oct. 1987

33 Donald Baker, 'Quebec on French Minds,' *Queen's Quarterly* 85 (spring 1978):249–64

34 On the ambassadorial level, relations had been improving for some time. Léo Cadieux interview, Ottawa, 9 Dec. 1987; Jacques Viot interview, Paris, 13 Oct. 1987; Martin Papers, Diary, 16 Dec. 1977, citing the views of J.-V. Sauvagnargues, the French ambassador in London

35 Claude Morin, *L'art de l'impossible: La diplomatie québécoise depuis 1960* (Montreal 1987), 263, 265

36 Martin Papers, Diary, 7 Dec. 1977. The external affairs minister, Jamieson, grumbled that he would at least like to cancel the exclusive French use of the term 'champagne,' then a lively issue because of its generic use by Ontario wineries.

37 Morin, *L'art de l'impossible,* 262–3; Martin Papers, Diary, 26 Nov. 1976

38 Martin Papers, vol. 401, Martin aux Affaires Extérieures, 27 Nov. 1978

39 Martin Papers, Diary, 6 Dec. 1977

40 Enders interview

41 Ibid.

42 The quotation is attributed to the U.S. State Department in 1983, but it would have applied with equal force seven years earlier. Alfred O. Hero and Louis

Balthazar, *Contemporary Quebec and the United States, 1960–1985* (Latham, Md 1988), 30

43 Ibid., 31

44 Morin, *L'art de l'impossible,* 259

45 Enders interview. Morin points to one of Brzezinski's television interviews in which the national security adviser sounded his different note. *L'art de l'impossible,* 265

46 Enders interview

47 Confidential source

48 Ibid.

49 Confidential interviews

50 *CAR 1977,* 244; Morin, *L'art de l'impossible,* 264. Morin claims that he warned the U.S. consul in Quebec City that a stronger pro-Canadian statement from the vice-president would provoke other third-country responses on the subject of Canada and Quebec; presumably he was referring to France

51 René Lévesque, *Memoirs* (Toronto 1986), 84, 122–3

52 Many besides Lévesque share the nationalist perspective of history: see, for example, Hero and Balthazar, *Contemporary Quebec and the United States,* chaps 3 and 4, in which the views of non-nationalist Quebeckers are ignored or treated as self-evidently unrepresentative.

53 Graham Fraser, *René Lévesque and the Parti Québécois in Power* (Toronto 1984), 88–9

54 Hero and Balthazar, *Contemporary Quebec and the United States,* 16–23, identify the Anglo-Canadian filter as a particular problem in overall American understanding of Quebec.

55 Morin, *L'art de l'impossible,* 275

56 Ibid., 278–83

57 Lévesque, *Memoirs,* 31

58 Ibid., 285–314

59 Martin Papers, Diary, 31 May 1977

60 Confidential interview

61 Quoted in Anthony Sampson, *The Changing Anatomy of Britain* (London 1982), 44

62 Ibid., 238

63 Ibid., 45: 'It was soon clear that Thatcher's cabinet was more disloyal and leaky than any Tory cabinet since the war.' Though matters would change later, it was this cabinet that had to consider the Canadian constitution. On Thatcher's 1981 political troubles, see NA, Eddie Goldenberg Papers, vol. 16, file Memos to PM, Kirby, 'Report on Mr. Chrétien's London Trip,' 27 March 1981. See Hugo Young, *The Iron Lady* (New York 1989), 138–9.

64 Confidential source; Sir John Ford interview by Paul Litt, 23 Feb. 1989. In the interview Ford made plain that Trudeau had not specifically raised a charter of rights, a point on which Canadian sources seem to agree.

65 Goldenberg Papers, vol. 16, file PM, Michael Kirby to Trudeau, 26 Aug. 1980,

enclosed memoranda by B.L. Strayer, 13 Aug. 1980, and Roger Tassé, 15 Aug. 1980

66 Ibid., handwritten minute by Trudeau, nd

67 There were no twentieth-century precedents for the alteration of any constitutional amendments by the British government or parliament without Canadian consent. The British parliament had several times passed amendments, such as the admission of Newfoundland, for which there was provincial opposition and by which provincial privileges were affected. Carrington's reaction is derived from a confidential source.

68 Sir John Ford disputes this interpretation. Ford interview

69 Robert Sheppard and Michael Valpy, *The National Deal: The Fight for a Canadian Constitution* (Toronto 1982), 206–7

70 Confidential interview

71 Goldenberg Papers, vol. 16, Yvon Pinard to prime minister, 27 Oct. 1980

72 Reeves Haggan interview, Ottawa, 4 Feb. 1988; on parliamentary committees see Young, *The Iron Lady*, 209–10.

73 Goldenberg Papers, vol. 16, Pinard to prime minister, 27 Oct. 1980

74 Sheppard and Valpy, *National Deal*, 209

75 Haggan interview; confidential interview

76 Confidential source

77 Haggan, born in Ulster, had also been a British barrister before coming to Canada. Haggan interview; Sheppard and Valpy, *National Deal*, 216–17

78 Confidential interview and source

79 Sheppard and Valpy, *National Deal*, 211

80 Ibid., 211–12; the high commission dispatch is at 212n.

81 The speech was, to put it mildly, illogical, but its lack of logical consistency was surpassed by its venomous tone. 'Mr. Trudeau has accomplished nothing of any significance during his 12 years of office,' Megarry told the Royal Commonwealth Society. 'On the contrary, separatism in Quebec reached its peak during his reign.' The last quotations come from a question-and-answer session after the speech.

82 Megarry's speech appears in official records.

83 Tom Wells interview, Toronto, 23 Nov. 1987

84 Sheppard and Valpy, *National Deal*, 123

85 Ibid., 123

86 See *The Times*, 12 Feb. 1981, 'Britain recalls its high commissioner in Canada.' His successor, according to *The Times'* gossip column of the same date, was to be Lord Moran. Moran was described as 'considerably more discreet than his father,' who had written 'a splendidly indiscreet memoir' in the 1950s.

87 Some of the information is derived from confidential interviews. In the happy phrase of Anthony Sampson, 'the uprooted career of a British diplomat sets him apart with that combination of grandeur and insecurity which can often generate pomposity'; *Changing Anatomy of Britain*, 234. Many of the diplomats serving in Ottawa did not meet this bill, but some did.

88 Goldenberg Papers, vol. 16, Kirby to prime minister, 'Elements of a London strategy,' 5 March 1981

89 Confidential source

90 *CAR 1981* (Toronto 1984), 39

91 The 5 March 1981 Kirby memorandum noted that the Foreign and Commonwealth Office officials dealing with Canada very much preferred such a tactic. Goldenberg Papers, vol. 16

92 Ibid., vol. 16, file Memos to PM, Kirby, 'Report on Mr. Chrétien's London Trip,' 27 March 1981

93 Confidential source; on the Trudeau-Thatcher meeting, confidential interview

94 Confidential source

95 John Hay, 'Bora Laskin's Fateful Legacy,' *Maclean's*, 12 Oct. 1981, 28

96 Sheppard and Valpy, *National Deal*, 254–5

CHAPTER 14: *The Last Hurrah*

1 Michael MccGwire, *Military Objectives in Soviet Foreign Policy* (Washington 1987), 300. On the nuclear negotiations see Strobe Talbott, *Deadly Gambits: The Reagan Administration and the Stalemate in Nuclear Arms Control* (New York 1984).

2 John Roberts interview, 3 Dec. 1987

3 Confidential interview

4 *CAR 1983*, 167

5 John Newhouse, 'Annals of Diplomacy,' *The New Yorker*, 2 Jan. 1989, 39

6 House of Commons, *Debates*, 4 Oct. 1983, 27720

7 Seymour M. Hersh, *'The Target Is Destroyed': What Really Happened to Flight 007 and What America Knew About It* (New York 1986), 245. This interpretation of the files was generally accepted by a senior External Affairs officer who read them. Confidential interview

8 See DEA, Statements and Speeches No 82/10, 'Technological Momentum the Fuel that Feeds the Nuclear Arms Race,' 18 June 1982.

9 Prime Minister's Office, Transcript of Remarks, 16 May 1982

10 Confidential interview. See David Cox, 'Trudeau's Foreign Policy Speeches,' *International Perspectives* (Nov.–Dec. 1982): 7ff.

11 See Patrick Gossage, *Close to the Charisma: My Years Between the Press and Pierre Elliott Trudeau* (Toronto 1986), 253.

12 Pierre Trudeau conversation, 30 June 1988; confidential interviews

13 Those present included MacEachen and Blais, the two ministers concerned, Gordon Osbaldeston, secretary to the cabinet, Tom Axworthy of the PMO, Robert Fowler of the PCO, and Marcel Massé, de Montigny Marchand, Louis Delvoie, and Gary Smith of External Affairs.

14 Confidential interviews

15 Ibid.

16 Ibid.

17 Roberts interview
18 The Steering Committee included Osbaldeston, Massé, Delvoie, Daniel Dewar, John Anderson, the chief of the Defence Staff, Fowler, de Montigny Marchand, and Michael Shenstone. The Working Group was Delvoie, Gary Smith, Peter Hancock, Arthur Mathewson, General M. Archdeacon, Captain John Toogood, Ken Calder, Jim Mitchell, and Jim Harlick. Patrick Gossage joined the Working Group some time after it had begun. For the relations between the Working Group and the Steering Committee see H. Von Riekhoff and John Sigler, 'The Trudeau Peace Initiative: The Politics of Reversing the Arms Race,' in B. Tomlin and M. Molot, eds., *Canada among Nations, 1984: A Time of Transition* (Toronto 1985), 57.
19 Confidential interviews
20 Ibid.
21 See Michael Pearson, et al., ' "The World is entitled to ask questions": The Trudeau Peace Initiative Reconsidered,' *International Journal* 41 (winter 1985–6): 144; R.B. Byers, 'Trudeau's Peace Initiative,' in D. Leyton-Brown and M. Slack, *The Canadian Strategic Review 1984* (Toronto 1985), 152.
22 Trudeau conversation
23 Confidential interview. Participants in the initiative acquit Trudeau of political motives in launching the peace effort, although some acknowledge that ministers and PMO officials were aware of the political value the initiative could have. One official, in fact, remembers Allan MacEachen offering him either an Order of Canada or a Senate seat if the polls went up another five points. 'Why not both?' the official replied. To which MacEachen said 'Sure, providing the polls justify it.' Ibid. John Roberts recalled that the initiative had the political effect of 'pre-empting the Cruise' missile decision. Interview
24 Geoffrey Pearson, 'Trudeau Peace Initiative Reflections,' *International Perspectives* (March–April 1985): 3ff
25 Confidential interviews
26 Ibid.
27 DEA, Statements and Speeches, No. 83/18, 'Reflections on Peace and Security,' 27 Oct. 1983
28 David Halton interview, 12 Nov. 1987
29 Egon Bahr interview, 22 Oct. 1987; confidential interview. The German reaction was summed up as 'positive but skeptical' by the Canada desk at the Auswärtiges Amt. Interview with Drs von Lukowitz and Schnappen, 19 Oct. 1987
30 Confidential source
31 Trudeau conversation
32 Geoffrey Pearson interview, 30 Aug. 1988
33 Richard and Sandra Gwyn, 'The Politics of Peace,' *Saturday Night,* May 1984, 20
34 Yu Zhan interview, 27 May 1987; Pearson interview
35 Georgi Arbatov interview, 25 Feb. 1988
36 Newhouse, 'Annals,' 47ff

37 Confidential interviews
38 Gossage, *Charisma,* 260
39 Gwyn and Gwyn, 'Peace,' 29; Gossage, *Charisma,* 257ff. Confirmed by confidential interviews
40 Confidential interview
41 Trudeau conversation; Pearson interview; confidential interviews
42 None of our U.S. confidential interviewees shared the Canadian view. MccGwire, *Military Objectives,* 300, notes that Reagan 'in pursuit of reelection ... agreed to adopt a more conciliatory approach.'
43 Confidential interview
44 Ibid. Romania was in economic crisis with food and electricity shortages in 1984 (and after) and a leadership that heaped praise on itself. The current joke in Bucharest asked why Romanians were like penguins. The answer: because they live in the cold, eat no meat, and clap all the time.
45 Trudeau conversation
46 House of Commons, *Debates,* 9 Feb. 1984, 1213 ff. The DEA assessment of the results of the initiative was guarded but positive. DEA Records, file 20-1-1-1, Ottawa to all posts, 29 Feb. 1984. Trudeau subsequently wrote to Reagan and Chernenko to urge their endorsement of his decalogue. Ibid., file 28-6-1 Trudeau Peace Mission, Trudeau to Reagan, 28 May 1984; Chernenko to Trudeau, 6 June 1984
47 House of Commons, *Debates,* 9 Feb. 1984, 1216ff. See Byers, 'Trudeau's Peace Initiative,' 158, which indicates that a quarter of those surveyed had a higher opinion of Trudeau after the initiative, and Von Riekhoff and Sigler, 'Peace Initiative,' 60–1.
48 DEA Records, file 28-6-1 Trudeau Peace Mission, Trudeau to Callaghan, 23 March 1984
49 *Globe and Mail,* 26 Sept. 1986. Trudeau corresponded on his initiative with Reagan, Chernenko, Mme Gandhi, and Premier Zhao until a few days before he left power. DEA Records, documents on file 28-6-1 Trudeau Peace Mission
50 Gossage, *Charisma,* 263; *CAR 1980,* 185; See also Don Jamieson, *No Place for Fools: The Political Memoirs of Don Jamieson,* vol. I (St John's 1989), 9ff.
51 Cited in Tom Keating and Larry Pratt, *Canada, NATO and the Bomb* (Edmonton 1988), 41
52 See Adam Bromke and Kim Nossal, 'Trudeau Rides the "Third Rail," ' *International Perspectives* (May–June 1984): 3ff.
53 Confidential interview
54 Based on confidential interviews. See John Kirton, 'Trudeau and the Diplomacy of Peace,' *International Perspectives* (July–Aug. 1984): 3ff.

CONCLUSION

1 Harald von Riekhoff, 'The Impact of Prime Minister Trudeau on Foreign Policy,' *International Journal* 33 (spring 1978): 285–6

2 Ibid., 267
3 Pierre Trudeau conversation, 30 June 1988
4 Ibid.
5 Confidential interview
6 Trudeau conversation
7 See Robert Held, 'Canadian Foreign Policy: An Outsider's View,' *International Journal* 33 (spring 1978): 454.
8 Confidential interview
9 Ibid.

Bibliography of Primary Sources

MANUSCRIPT SOURCES

Bank of Canada Archives, Ottawa
Bank Records
Louis Rasminsky Papers*

Jimmy Carter Presidential Library, Atlanta, Georgia
White House Central Files

Department of External Affairs, Ottawa
Department Records*

Directorate of History, Department of National Defence, Ottawa
General J.V. Allard Papers
Réal Boissonnault Papers*
Departmental Records
Office of the Chief of the Defence Staff Records
Jean Pariseau Papers*

Gerald Ford Library, Ann Arbor, Michigan
Arthur Burns Papers
Council of Economic Advisors Records
David Gergen Papers
Ron Nessen Papers
Edward Savage Papers
White House Central Files

* Closed or partly closed records

National Archives of Canada, Ottawa
Marcel Cadieux Papers*
Department of National Defence Records
Lionel Chevrier Papers
Eddie Goldenberg Papers*
Arnold Heeney Papers
Paul Hellyer Papers*
Donald Jamieson Papers*
Jules Léger Papers*
Paul Martin Diaries and Papers*
Lester Pearson Papers*
Arnold Smith Papers*
Peter Stursberg Papers

Private Collections
Eddie Goldenberg Papers (Ottawa)*
Walter Gordon Papers (Toronto)*
Paul Hellyer Papers (Toronto)*
H. Basil Robinson Papers (Ottawa)*

Privy Council Office, Ottawa
Cabinet Minutes*

Trinity College Archives, University of Toronto
George Ignatieff Papers

United States National Archives and Records Service, Alexandria, Va
Richard M. Nixon Papers
  President's Personal File
  White House Confidential Files
  White House Confidential Files, Staff Member and Office Files
  White House Special Files
  White House Tapes
Council on International Economic Policy Records

INTERVIEWS AND CONVERSATIONS

Hon. Anthony Abbott, London, 6 October 1987
J.F. Anderson, Ottawa, 7 August 1987
Georgi Arbatov, Moscow, 25 February 1988
Willis Armstrong, Washington, 25 June 1986; 13 November 1988
Egon Bahr, Bonn, 22 October 1987

* Closed or partly closed records

William Barton, Ottawa, 22 April 1988
Wolfgang Behrends, Ottawa, 7 December 1987
Lord Brimelow, London, 13 April 1987
Emerson Brown, Washington, 11 January 1988
Gen. G.G. Brown, Calgary, 22 September 1987
Hon. Léo Cadieux, Ottawa, 9 December 1987
Marcel Cadieux, Ottawa, 15 May 1979
Pierre Carraud, Paris, 13 October 1987
Dr Karl Carstens, Bonn, 22 October 1987
Adm. D.A. Collins, Victoria, 24 September 1987
Dr Ramsay Cook, Ottawa, 7 August 1987
Maurice Copithorne, Vancouver, 23 September 1987
Marshall Crowe, Ottawa, 14 March 1988
Hon. Barney Danson, Toronto, 10 November 1987
George Davidson, New York City, 13 May 1988
Hon. Jack Davis, Vancouver, 25 September 1987
Gen. J.A. Dextraze, Ottawa, 12 April 1988
Robert Duemling, Washington, 12 January 1988
Michel Dupuy, Ottawa, 18 January 1988
Terry Empson, London, 7 October 1987
Thomas Enders, New York City, 13 May 1988
Sir John Ford, Florida, 23 February 1989
Robert A.D. Ford, La Poivrière, France, 15–16 October 1987
A.F. Gill, Toronto, 12 February 1989
James Gillies, Toronto, 2 March 1988
Carl Goldenberg, Montreal, 30 November 1987
Edward Goldenberg, Ottawa, 29 August 1988
Richard Gwyn, Toronto, 12 March 1989
Reeves Haggan, 4 February 1988
John Halstead, Ottawa, 9 December 1987; Grainau, Augsburg, FRG, 20–23 February
    1988
David Halton interview, Toronto, 12 November 1987
A.F. Hart, Ottawa, 21 April 1988
Hon. Richard Hatfield, Fredericton, 11 July 1989
Ivan Head, Ottawa, 6 August, 18 November 1987; Toronto, 31 August 1987
Hon. Paul Hellyer, Toronto, 6 November 1987
William Hooper, Ottawa, 21 April 1988
Hon. Jack Horner, Winnipeg, 28 September 1987
Robert Hunter, Washington, 15 November 1988
Tadashi Ikeda, Tokyo, 11 May 1987
Karl Kaiser, Bonn, 20 October 1987
Julius Katz, White Plains, NY, 23 February 1983
Hon. Otto Lang, Winnipeg, 13 June 1988
Gen. W.C. Leonard, Oakville, Ont., 15 June 1989

François Leduc, Paris, 12 October 1987
Gen. Bruce Legge, Toronto, 23 November 1987
Adm. Richard Leir, Victoria, 24 September 1987
J.H.A. Luns, Brussels, 9 October 1987
J.A. McCordick, Ottawa, 11 April 1988
Hon. D.S. Macdonald, Toronto, 2 November 1979, 20 May 1987, 5 April 1988
Hon. Allan MacEachen, Ottawa, 14 March 1988
Gen. Allan MacKenzie, Winnipeg, 28 September 1987
Russ McKinney, Ottawa, 12 April 1988
Adm. M.A. Martin, Victoria, 24 September 1987
Hon. Paul Martin, Windsor, 10–11 February 1987
Dr Peter Meekison, Edmonton, 21 September 1987
Kiyohisa Mikanagi, Tokyo, 12 May 1987
Robert Morris, Washington, 27 June 1986
Adm. Robert Murdoch, Victoria, 25 September 1987
Geoffrey Murray, Ottawa, 15 May 1979
Yasuhiko Nara, Tokyo, 20 May 1987
Edward Nef, Washington, 12 January 1988
G.A.H. Pearson, Ottawa, 10 January 1979, 30 August 1988
Hon. Gérard Pelletier, Ottawa, 14 August 1987
Hon. J.W. Pickersgill, Ottawa
Richard Post, Washington, 13 January 1988
Lord Pym, London, 9 February 1989
Myer Rashish, Washington, July 1986
A.E. Ritchie, Ottawa, 15 March 1988
Hon. John Roberts, Toronto, 3 December 1987
Peter Roberts, Ottawa, 5 February 1988
R.G. Robertson, Ottawa, 19 January 1988
H. Basil Robinson, Ottawa, 5, 11 August 1987
H. Paul Robinson, Chicago, 30 June 1985
Gen. Brent Scowcroft, Washington, 11 January 1988
Hon. Mitchell Sharp, Ottawa, 8 December 1987
Thomas Shoyama, Victoria, 24 September 1987
Pierre Siraud, Paris, 12 October 1987
Arnold Smith, Ottawa, 15 March, 12 April 1988
Rufus Smith, Washington, 14 January 1988
Erich Straetling, Bonn, 20 October 1987
Michiaki Suma, Tokyo, 12 May 1987
Gen. James Tedlie, Victoria, 5 March 1988
Peter Towe, Ottawa, 9 December 1987
Rt-Hon. Pierre E. Trudeau, Montreal, 30 June 1988
Jacques Viot, Paris, 13 October 1987
Drs von Lukowitz and Schnappen, Bonn, 19 October 1987
Wang chu-liang, Beijing, 26 May 1987

J.H. Warren, Ottawa, 8 December 1987
Thomas Wells, Toronto, 23 November 1987
Yao Guang, Beijing, 25 May 1987
Yu Zhan, Beijing, 27 May 1987

Off-record interviews, not listed by name, numbered 86.
Note: The majority of interviews were conducted by Bothwell and Granatstein
together; some were conducted individually. Interviews in China were, with one
exception, done by Granatstein with Professor Bernie Frolic. Some on- and off-
record interviews in Washington were conducted by Bothwell and Professor John
Kirton. Professor Ian Drummond and Paul Litt each conducted an interview on our
behalf, and Barbara Treviranus did a number of interviews for us in East Africa.
We have also had access to the transcript of a conversation on Canada's China
policy between the Rt-Hon. P.E. Trudeau and Professors Frolic and Paul Evans
and to a memorandum of a conversation between Professor Wilhelm Bleek and
Willy Brandt. We are grateful to these colleagues for their assistance.

Index

United States: relations with xiii, 6, 13, 52; civil disturbances in 17, 40, 73–4; and withdrawal of troops from Europe 27–8, 51; in foreign-policy review 32, 160; public opinion and 40, 41, 63, 80, 92–3; Canadian influence in 43–4; American views of Canada 44, 93; foreign policy of 45–7; special relationship with Canada 48–9, 65–7, 73–5, 95; investment in Canada 49; Nixon shok-ku 61ff; joint cabinet committees 62; economic relations with Canada 75; energy policy of 78, 79, 80–2; oil quotas 82; energy shortages 84, 98, 101; and Quebec separatism 98–9; and fisheries dispute 105–7; and third option 160, 161–2, 176–7; and China 182–3; Olympic boycotts 188–9, 199–200; and Canadian-Soviet relations 194; Iranian embassy crisis 219–20; cruise missiles 260, 334, 363–4; and Chile 271; and Cuba 273–4; foreign aid 286; and India 292; and UN 297, 299; and NEP 317–27, 330, 382; bureaucracy 318, 322; trade with 330–1; trade negotiations 331–3; trade deficit 332; and Quebec question 346–50
Uruguay 267
U Thant 295

Valcartier 244, 245
Vance, Cyrus 97, 318, 347

Vance, Jack 251–2
Venezuela 78, 79, 263, 267, 269
Victoria Charter 154
Vietnam War 7, 17, 52–5, 71, 72, 74, 179, 292, 296; draft dodgers 40–1; DEA opinion of 53, 179; ICCS and 55–60; Canadian investment in 162; refugees 218–19

Wadds, Jean 355–6
wage and price controls 92
Wahn, Ian 63
Waldheim, Kurt 295–6, 298
War Measures Act 236
Warren, Jake 99, 224, 340
Whelan, Eugene 201, 312
Wilson, Harold 167, 280, 339, 341
Winnipeg Free Press 194, 195
Winters, Robert 113
Wirthlin, Douglas 314
Withers, Ramsay 257

Yakovlev, Alexander 200–1, 202
Yalden, Max 11n
Yamani, Ahmed Zaki 303
Yao Guang 185
Young, Robert 289
youth culture 40

Zaire 137, 264
Zambia 264, 281
Zhao Ziyang 370
Zink, Lubor J. 195, 328
Zionism 296–7

Cartoon Credits

The cartoons in the book are reprinted with permission from the **Toronto Star Syndicate**: Trudeau's diplomatic form; Gérard Pelletier on safari; Northern sovereignty; Diplomatic recognition; Frankly yes; Trudeau visits Nixon; 'We're not anti-Arab or anti-Israel, but we are anti-American'; Donald Macdonald; Between friends; Harold Wilson; Fireside chat; Claude Morin; Clark, Trudeau, and Broadbent; Rescue from Iran; The peace initiative; Canada's political options; **Isaac Bickerstaff**: Allan MacEachen; **Donato/Toronto Sun**: Joe Clark; Détente; **Edd Uluschak**: So what's the fuss?